SOCIOLOGY

SOCIOLOGY

DONALD LIGHT, JR.

SUZANNE KELLER

BOTH OF PRINCETON UNIVERSITY

Alfred A. Knopf New York

THIS IS A BORZOI BOOK PUBLISHED BY ALFRED A. KNOPF, INC.

First Edition
987
Copyright © 1975 by Alfred A. Knopf, Inc.

Library of Congress Cataloging in Publication Data

Light, Donald, 1942–
    Sociology.

    Includes bibliographies and indexes.
    1.   Sociology.   2.   United States—Social conditions.
I.   Keller, Suzanne Infeld, 1927–   joint author.
II.   Title.
HM51.L52   301   74-23939
ISBN 0-394-31822-6

Manufactured in the United States of America

Typographic Design by Susan Postow Phillips

ACKNOWLEDGMENTS

Table 2:1   Permission granted by George Gallup.

Table 3:1   Adapted from Leonard Goodwin, DO THE POOR WANT TO WORK? A SOCIAL-PSYCHOLOGICAL STUDY OF WORKING ORIENTATIONS. © 1972 by the Brookings Institution, Washington, D. C.

Table 5:2   From W. Dennis, J. GERONTOLOGY 21:2 (1966).

Table 6:2   From Leonard L. Baird, Mary Jo Clark and Rodney T. Hartnett, THE GRADUATES. Copyright © 1973 by Educational Testing Service. All rights reserved. Adapted and reproduced by permission.

Table 7:1   Copyright © 1962, the Free Press.

Table 8:3   Copyright © 1973 by The Brookings Institution, Washington, D. C.

Table 8:4   Copyright © 1966 by the Free Press, a Division of Macmillan Publishing Co., Inc.

Table 9:1   From William Brink and Louis Harris, THE NEGRO REVOLUTION IN AMERICA. Copyright © 1963 by Newsweek, Inc. Reprinted by the permission of Simon and Schuster.

Table 9:2   Copyright © 1969 by the American Psychological Association. Reprinted by permission.

Table 9:3 and Table 9:4   Morris Rosenberg and Roberta G. Simmons, "Black and White Self-Esteem: The Urban School Child," ROSE MONOGRAPH SERIES, 1971, two tables on p. 34.

Table 9:6   Reprinted by permission of the publisher, the Survey Research Center of the Institute for Social Research of the University of Michigan.

Table 13:4   Evelyn M. Kitagawa and Philip M. Hauser, DIFFERENTIAL MORTALITY IN THE UNITED STATES: A STUDY IN SOCIOECONOMIC EPIDEMIOLOGY (Cambridge, Mass.: Harvard University Press, 1973) Table 8.1.

Table 17:1   Charles Y. Glock and Rodney Stark, RELIGION AND SOCIETY IN TENSION, © 1967 by Rand McNally and Company, Chicago, Table 5-1, p. 91. Reprinted by permission of Rand McNally College Publishing Company.

Table 18:1   Table 1-1 from THE COMING OF POST-INDUSTRIAL SOCIETY, by Daniel Bell, © 1973 by Daniel Bell, Published by Basic Books, Inc., New York.

Figures 6:2 and 14:1   Copyright by JDR 3rd Fund for Edna McConnell Clark Foundation, Carnegie Corporation of New York, Hazen Foundation, Andrew W. Mellon Foundation.

Figure 13:2   Reprinted with the permission of The Population Council.

Figure 13:4 and 16:1   Copyright © 1974 by The New York Times Company. Reprinted by permission.

Figure 16:3   Copyright © 1970 Children's Television Workshop.

Figure 17:1   Copyright 1973 by the American Association for the Advancement of Science.

Figure 18:3   The Annals of the American Academy of Political and Social Science, Volume 242, November, 1945.

Figure 18:4   THE LIMITS OF GROWTH: *A Report for THE CLUB OF ROME'S Project on the Predicament of Mankind,* by Donella H. Meadows, Dennis L. Meadows, Jørgen Randers, William W. Behrens III. A Potomac Associates book published by Universe Books, New York, 1972. Graphics by Potomac Associates.

Excerpts from INVITATION TO SOCIOLOGY by Peter L. Berger. Copyright © 1963 by Peter L. Berger. Reprinted by permission of Doubleday and Company, Inc.

Excerpts from TALLY'S CORNER by Elliot Liebow. Copyright © 1967 by Little, Brown and Co.

Excerpt from THE AGE OF ANXIETY by W.H. Auden. Copyright © 1948 by Random House.

Excerpt from BLUE COLLAR MARRIAGE by Mirra Komarovsky. Copyright © 1967 · by Vintage.

Excerpt from Letters to the Editor of May 16, 1963; excerpt from "School Integration Resisted in Cities of North" by William E. Farrell of May 13, 1974. © 1963/1974 by the New York Times Company. Reprinted by permission.

Excerpt from THE PANIC BROADCAST by Howard Koch. Copyright © 1940 by Hadley Cantril, © renewed 1967 by Howard Koch, by permission of Little, Brown and Co.

Excerpt from THE SELLING OF THE PRESIDENT 1968 by Joe McGinness. Copyright © 1969 by Joemac Inc. Reprinted by permission of Trident Press, a division of Simon and Schuster, Inc.

RA:LB

PREFACE

In studying sociology, you will learn far more than new facts, because sociology is also a way of analyzing world events and human behavior. If our textbook and your instructor are successful, you will learn to think about American society as well as other societies in novel and interesting ways.

We began this book by deciding that four characteristics are essential for a good sociology text. First, it must be *interesting*. Too often, students get more satisfaction from turning textbook pages than from reading them. Our goal has been to make each chapter a pleasure rather than a chore. Second, we wanted our book to be *up-to-date* and wide-ranging in its subject matter. We have presented current research as well as classic theories, hopefully in ways that will interest and enlighten introductory students. Third, since sociology is the study of social life, we wanted to show students how sociological concepts can be *applied to real life*. Every chapter, therefore, uses contemporary issues and events to illustrate concepts and theories. Fourth, we thought that an introductory text should be *unbiased,* exposing students to a variety of sociological thinking.

To fulfill these goals in a book of this size required a team effort. A number of people helped us decide what material to include, assisted us with research, and provided its readable style. We are particularly indebted to Ann Levine, a writer of extraordinary talent and sensitivity. We received excellent assistance from Stephanie Wald and Karen Reixach, who helped us research and organize several chapters. Above all, our editor, Roberta Bauer Meyer deserves our gratitude and admiration for advising us on the selection of materials, for her exceptionally fine editing of the book, and for coordinating the entire project.

We would also like to thank Charles Page, Clifton Bryant, Robert Werhlin, Joseph Curran, Jr., Harold Blau, Dean R. Hoge, Jane Menken, and Robert Althauser for reviewing chapters of the manuscript and for suggesting valuable improvements. Finally, we wish to thank Barry Fetterolf who first encouraged us to undertake this project.

All of these people helped us to achieve the goals we set. If we fell short, the responsibility, of course, is ours.

DL, Jr.
SK
Princeton, N.J.

CONTENTS

BOXES

SOCIOLOGY

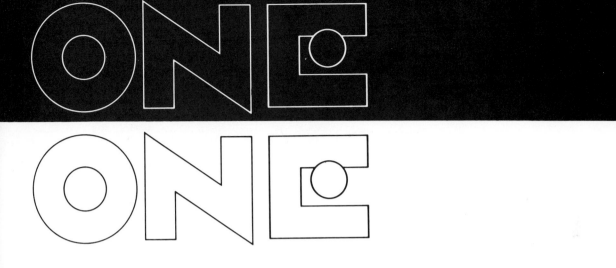

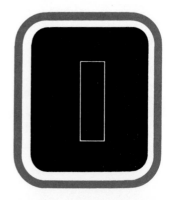

When we look at the world sociologically, we see it from a very special perspective. Sociology invites us to step back from our cramped personal visions in order to view with greater clarity and objectivity the forces that shape and control our individual lives. Like all scientific pursuits sociology attempts to understand the nature of things—to locate what exists in the social universe and to explain how it works. The particular "things" that sociology explores are the patterns and regularities of behavior which people exhibit as they go about the daily business of living.

Sociologists are concerned less with individual idiosyncracies and unique events than with predictable patterns and regular occurrences. Thus, a sociologist would be more interested in the effects of marijuana on teen-age dating behavior than in the number of joints a particular teen-ager smokes a month. A sociologist would be more interested in discovering the facts about best-selling novels (how they come to be published, how they are cir-

THE
SOCIOLOGICAL
EYE

culated and publicized, and why they are read by some groups and not by others) than in discussing the merits and flaws of a particular best-seller. A sociologist would be more interested in discovering the similarities among families that produce schizophrenic children than in learning the particular case history of a particular family in order to arrive at a treatment for a particular child.

There is nothing mysterious or cold-blooded about the sociological perspective. It is just one more way of dividing up the social universe in order to make sense and meaning out of the numberless forces that shape our individual destinies. It complements the perspectives and angles of vision we already have at our command. In this first chapter, we will discuss how the sociological perspective is used and the meaning of social facts. We will also consider the main theoretical orientations in sociology, the origins of sociology, and its uses in contemporary society.

USING
THE SOCIOLOGICAL
PERSPECTIVE

Before starting a new course, students may know who is teaching it and what other students have said about the instructor and the subject. During the first class they will be interested in learning who else is in the class, what the professor looks and sounds like, what is on the reading list, how many papers are required, and whether and when exams are given. Throughout the course, students will assess the lecturer's knowledge, personality, and skill as an instructor. In short, a student's evaluation of a class is based on a *personal* reaction to a particular professor and subject.

A sociologist looking at the same college classroom would analyze it somewhat differently, focusing on social relationships, rather than on individual behavior or the specific course content. Some of the things a sociologist might focus on would be power relations, rules of conduct, and class characteristics.

There is an unequal distribution of power in the classroom: the teacher has control over the topics of conversation and directs the flow of class discussion by determining who will talk when. The teacher also has the ultimate power to determine grades. There are many social supports for this unequal distribution of power. The instructor gets paid for being in the classroom, while the students must pay. The teacher stands at the front of the group and can fully observe each of the students, while the students line up in rows and can only make direct contact with a limited number of other students. The in-

A sociologist looking at this classroom would study social relationships rather than individual behavior. (Lynn McLaren/Rapho Guillumette)

structor has access to each student's work and thereby has the full power of comparison and judgment, while each student sees only his or her own work.

Teachers have a variety of institutional supports at their command: they can delay returning reserve books to the library without paying a fine; they can examine each student's academic record; and they can have any student physically expelled from the classroom. All of these factors contribute to a teacher's power. On the other hand, the teacher's power is not absolute. If the students refuse to come to class, refuse to pay attention in class, refuse to do the work, or complain to the administration about the quality of teaching, the teacher's power will be curtailed. These power relations in the classroom operate without regard to any particular student or any particular teacher. The classroom has a sociological power structure all its own, which can be analyzed in its own right without consideration for individual habits, histories, personality traits, or desires.

The sociologist will also analyze the rules of conduct in a classroom. These are the unspoken rules and expectations that everyone more or less follows. For example, people rarely rip off their clothes during class time; everyone shows up pretty much on time; the teacher talks about the intended course material and not about his or her hobbies or sports interests; people take turns when they speak and do not speak all at once; everyone (except perhaps the teacher) sits down during the class time; the class period has a designated beginning and ending which are observed. These rules, again, belong to the accepted order of things in the classroom and can be discussed without any reference whatsoever to particular students or particular teachers.

As a unit the class has characteristics of its own, which are not properties of any individual in the class. For example, the class meets in a certain room; is of a certain size; has a specific average age of students; has a specific number of men and women in it; has a specific number of science majors, upper and lower classmen; and so on. Each of these characteristics belongs to the *class* as a whole; they are not the characteristics of each individual in that class.

All of these observations about the college classroom are sociological observations. They concern patterns and regularities that will occur regardless of the individuals who occupy that classroom. The sociological perspective clearly differs from other perspectives one might use to observe a classroom. An architect, for example, might pay attention to the size of the space, the comfort of the furniture, the arrangement of the desks in relation to the space, the quality of the acoustics. A doctor might look at the physical condition of class members, including skin tone, eye brightness, manifestations of fever or disability. And a painter or photographer might notice the quality of the light in the room and how it affects shadows and contours, the variety of poses assumed by class members, the differences in anatomy, the colors of students' clothing.

Whenever we attempt to make sense of the world around us we must make choices about what details we will attend to in constructing our meanings. The *sociological perspective* trains us to pay attention to those details that are regular and patterned, details that are not unique to a particular situation or to particular people in those situations.

Social Facts

For those of us brought up to believe in our individual worth and uniqueness it is sometimes difficult, if not infuriating, to hear ourselves talked about as if our individual histories, biographies, and feelings were of no consequence at all. Since all of us feel ourselves to be unique and special, we may resent being chucked into categories for the convenience of a sociologist. But the truth of the matter is we all use categories and abstractions all the time. How often have you used or heard the terms "the older generation," "hippies," "dope addicts," "feminists," "blacks," "jocks," "wasps"? These are all categories of people who have something in common, but who as individuals have a great deal that is unique. And yet, the terms are useful for explaining and giving meaning to the things in the world which we try to understand.

Despite our resistances to categorization, there are certain things about human social life that simply cannot be explained by reference to individual feelings or behavior. Emile Durkheim, a pioneering French sociologist of the nineteenth century, pinned down this truth when he posited the existence of something called a *social fact*, which is an entity in its own right, different from the elements (or individuals) of which it is composed (Durkheim, 1938). Durkheim compared the uniqueness of the social fact to the uniqueness of the human body: although the human body is made up of cells, there would be no way of discovering the properties or capacities of the human body by examining only its separate cells. In short, the whole is greater than the sum of its parts. "It is very certain that there are in the living cell only molecules of crude matter. But these molecules are in contact with one another, and this association is the cause of the new phenomena which characterize life, the very germ of which cannot possibly be found in any of the separate elements" (Durkheim, 1938).

The same part-whole relationship is true for individuals and social facts. There are properties of social life that simply cannot be explained by reference to the activities, sen-

sibilities, or characteristics of any individual. We need only look at our own lives to realize how inescapable this conclusion is. For example, consider a few social facts that make modern urban life less than pleasant—crime rates and bureaucratic red tape.

Crime Rates When we walk down a big city street late at night most of us are, to say the least, wary. Is this wariness purely a psychological trait of ours? Can we explain it by exploring our childhood experiences? Not likely. Our wariness stems from the social fact of crime rates. We know that, statistically, street crimes occur most often at night in urban areas. Our private fears as we hasten down the street are attributable not to psychological quirks but to social facts. Even the crime rates themselves, although composed of the sum of individual acts, are social realities that surpass the activities of any one criminal. If we compare the rates of crime in different localities at different hours of the day, we find that crime rates are highest in urban areas at night. Thus, our fear as we walk down a deserted city street after dark is not prompted by our knowledge of individual criminals nor by our own psychological obsessions, but rather by our knowledge of a social fact—a crime rate—which surpasses both us as individuals and criminals as individuals.

Red Tape When we find ourselves entangled with large bureaucratic organizations, such as government agencies, and we encounter the frustrations of "red tape run-around," are those frustrations attributable to our own inabilities to get things done quickly? Are they the fault of the receptionists and secretaries who shuttle us around with triplicate forms? The frustrations are, of course, the fault of neither. Large organizations require complicated record-keeping procedures, ordered hierarchies, and separate departments simply by virtue of their size. The unpleasantness of bureaucratic procedures can be explained only by a social fact—the size of the organization. Since it is true that the larger an organization the more division of labor there will be, the more clear-cut the hierarchy will be, and the more divisions and departments there will be (Blau and Meyer, 1971), we can understand our private experiences of frustration only in terms of a nonpersonal reality. The size of an organization is a property of that organization and not of any of the individuals involved in it, and therefore we must look to a social reality to explain a very individual experience. These two examples suggest that Durkheim was right: "Society is not a mere sum of individuals. Rather, the system formed by their association represents a specific reality which has its own characteristics" (Durkheim, 1938).

But the existence of social facts that have characteristics and properties of their own is not the only reason for adopting the sociological perspective. There is another even more compelling reason. Every experience that a human being undergoes, no matter how private it may seem, is somehow touched and shaped by social forces that are not of that person's making. While this statement may seem exaggerated and overly dramatic, by examining a few of our most private experiences we can see just how important social conditions are in determining the course of our inner lives.

Being Sick Surely, it would seem, being sick is an entirely private experience. When we are lying in bed with fever, aches, and pains, absorbed in our own personal miseries, how can there be any social forces at work on us? There can be and there are. In the first place, how do we know that what we are feeling is sickness? In some societies fever, aches, and pain are symptoms of visitations from spirits. The individual plagued with these discomforts is not treated as a sick person but as a person "possessed." In our society, however, we treat these symptoms as manifestations of treatable diseases. When we experience these symptoms we have learned from our culture to call ourselves sick. There are some maladies which may be just as uncomfortable as flu symptoms—such as a pulled muscle, a broken finger, a poison ivy rash—but we do not call them sicknesses. Thus the very definition of what is "sick" is something we have learned from our social world; it is not a property of the physical discomfort itself.

The society we live in also has a set of widely understood rules about how we behave when we are sick. For certain illnesses we are entitled to malinger in bed, free from all obligations that might sap our strength. For others, we are expected to continue our daily round of activities. Thus, if your sociology lecturer did not show up for a scheduled class one day and sent word that he or she was absent because of a painful stubbed toe or an infected hangnail, class members would be rightfully indignant at the lecturer's irresponsibility ("rightfully" because we have all learned that these are not debilitating illnesses). On the other hand, if the lecturer showed up for class despite a raging fever and headache, he or she would have been responsible beyond the call of duty, that is, beyond the expectations of our society about sickness behavior (Jaco, 1972).

Rules about behavior during illness govern not only how much activity the sick person is excused from, but also how the sick person is to conduct his or her recovery. In our society a sick person who is not terminally ill has an obligation to behave in a way that will lead to full recovery. He or she is expected to follow medical instructions concerning medication,

Whether sick people are treated by medical doctors or by other kinds of healers is a matter of social custom. Among the Huichole Indians of Mexico, shamans are the accepted curers. (Kal Muller/Woodfin Camp & Associates)

rest, exercise, and interaction with others. An individual who does not follow these instructions, and thereby prolongs the illness, is termed "a malingerer," "an attention seeker," "a self-destructive person," or a downright "burden." When we are sick we take on a very specific role, that of a "sick person," and thereby incur a set of obligations and rights that have been carefully defined for us by our society's "sickness rules."

The sickness rules also tell us who is qualified to heal us. In American society we are expected to be healed by a qualified medical doctor. We do not go to medicine men, to witch doctors, to spiritual exorcists, or to mediums for cures (as is done in other societies) but we go to a man or woman who has had a certain amount of certified education and training and who the society says is qualified to perform healing practices.

Thus, being sick is far from a purely private experience. While, again, there is a great deal of room within the confines of the sick role for individual performances, the general outline of the role is *socially* and not individually defined.

Suicide One final example, involving the seemingly most private act of all, should convince us that no crevice of our inner lives is unaffected by social forces. From studies of rates of suicide among different groups in the population and among populations in different nations, it has been discovered that certain social factors influence an individual's chances for self-destruction (Durkheim, 1951). The details of Durkheim's study of suicide are described in chapter 2, but for the present we need only note that suicide rates are higher for single people than for married people, higher during periods of economic inflation or depression than during periods of economic stability, higher among urbanites than rural citizens. In fact, certain social conditions that have nothing to do with the individuals who are the subjects of their results operate to create "suicide currents" within a population, and these currents "are just as real and just as much external to the individual as are the physical and biological forces that produce death by disease" (Barnes, 1948, p. 510). Thus even those lonely moments of self-obliteration may have their roots in the larger context of the social order.

If, then, we recognize that individual experiences can only be understood with reference to larger social forces, how are we to go about understanding those forces? How, in short, are we to *do* sociology?

THE DEVELOPMENT OF SOCIOLOGY

The history of doing sociology in a systematic, recognizable manner is a very short one. Although attempts to develop patterned social codes to enhance the social order date back to 2000 B.C., it was not until the end of the eighteenth century that social philosophy (philosophical *ideas* about how the world does or might run) gave way to social science (systematic *studies* of how the world does, in fact, run). The roots of the scientific approach to the study of society were established early in the seventeenth century with the arrival of the Age of Reason, when men like Bacon and

Descartes argued that observation, experimentation, and reason must replace philosophy, religion, and moral musings. But it was not until the French philosopher Henri de Saint-Simon (1760–1825) imagined a "political science" that the discipline as we now know it achieved a recognizable form (Saint-Simon, 1964). When Saint-Simon's student and colleague Auguste Comte changed the name of the new approach to *sociology*, the sociological enterprise was officially underway.

Comte theorized that human intellectual development was an evolutionary process based on scientific progress. He believed that positivism—the use of experimentation and observation—was crucial for encouraging and continuing the natural process of progress. If human beings were to create a more satisfying social world, they would have to encourage the natural process of progress toward that goal through the exercise of scientific discipline (Comte, 1915).

Once sociology had been given an official baptism by Saint-Simon and Comte, the science of society became a tool for those who were wrestling with the vast social problems that were arising everywhere in Europe as a result of the changes brought by the Industrial Revolution. Social thinkers all over Europe began turning to sociology or to the sociological perspective for solutions to the misery and confusion left in the wake of urbanization, industrialization, and bureaucratization. But the solutions these thinkers arrived at were not always the same or even compatible.

Herbert Spencer, for instance, an Englishman who wrote in the late nineteenth century and was extremely influential in his time in both Europe and America, believed that society developed through natural processes. It was he (and not Darwin) who coined the phrase "survival of the fittest." By this he meant that through natural selection societies would work out the optimum social arrangements. Spencer believed, for example, that national governments should not make legislation concerning social progress because such legislation would interfere with the natural order of societal development. Thus, such public policies as public education, public health care, and work laws should not be undertaken by social legislation because those who were fittest would be able to fend for themselves. Furthermore, to interfere with their successes would be to interfere with the progress of natural societal growth. For Spencer, what *was* in the universe was synonymous with what *ought* to be (Spencer, 1898).

This view was vehemently opposed by Karl Marx, who believed that revolution and not evolution was the key to Europe's ills. Marx felt that differentiation in society comes about not through natural selection of the fittest but through the consolidation of groups of people who have similar economic interests and experiences. The structure of society, for Marx, was based on economic foundations: people's relationship to the means of production determines their position in the society, and this position fully influences values, attitudes, and behavior. Since the different groups, or classes, had different economic interests, they would, inevitably, be antagonists. For Marx, the only means by which the economically oppressed classes could convince the economically advantaged classes to relinquish some of their supremacy was through revolution. After the revolution, it would be possible to create a classless society in which everyone labored according to ability and everyone received according to need. Thus Marx believed that social change would come about by planned social action (Marx, 1955, 1967). This, of course, is a very different view from Spencer's, which suggested that if you leave the world alone it will eventually cure its own ills.

Although both these theorists believed that they were describing the world as it really was, neither of them drew upon strictly scientific methods to document their observations convincingly. What was needed now were innovative research techniques that would be suitable to the scientific study of society. The first major step toward this needed innovation was taken by Emile Durkheim (see chapter 2 for details of his study on suicide). He collected international statistics on the incidence and preconditions of suicide and organized these statistics in such a way that they empirically documented his theories about social organization.

Durkheim's empirical approach, the giant step between social philosophy and social science, has been pursued particularly vigorously by American sociologists. As in Europe, American sociology first focused on the formidable social problems of the day, including crime and poverty, social disorder and deviance. But early in its development, American sociology began to adopt the scientific perspective, placing heavy emphasis on observation and scientific measurement. However, the total acceptance of the scientific approach has always been tempered by the realization, first fully elaborated by Max Weber, that human beings are not inanimate objects that can be manipulated and studied like rocks, minerals, or cells. Human beings have feelings, thoughts, consciousness, attitudes, and values which are best reckoned with and accounted for by empathy, or *Verstehen*, as Weber called it (1964). The scientific study of human beings must include elements of insight and empathy if it is to stay true to the actual conditions of human life.

Today, sociology reflects the change from social philosophy to social science (tempered with insight and empathy), and "schools" of sociology have come to emphasize one or the other of the approaches put forth by the founders of the field.

THEORETICAL ORIENTATIONS

The first and most crucial step in the exploration of any unknown phenomenon is the formulation of questions about that phenomenon. The questions we ask strongly influence the explanations we arrive at. An old joke about a pessimist and an optimist perfectly illustrates this axiom of scientific pursuit. The pessimist, pointing to a glass with some water will say, "That glass is half empty." The optimist will answer, "No, it's not; it's half full." Although both pessimist and optimist have observed the same phenomenon, their explanations of what they saw differ because they are concerned with different questions. So it is when sociologists try to explain human social behavior. Depending on how they formulate their questions, they often come up with different explanations for the same phenomena. The different types of questions that a sociologist is likely to ask reflect his or her theoretical orientation. In sociology, as in all scientific disciplines, there are several different theoretical orientations, each of which has its ardent admirers and detractors. In America the most prevalent theoretical orientation is the structural-functional approach.

Structural-Functionalism

Sociologists with a *structural-functional* approach study the way each part of a society contributes to the functioning of the society as a whole. Social balance is emphasized. Since sociologists with the structural-functional orientation view society as a system of interrelated parts, they are mainly interested in the contributions or "purposes" these parts serve for on-going social life. For example, in trying to explain why all human societies have a family system, the structural-functionalists will ask: What function (need) does the family system fulfill for the larger society? The answers to this question will all highlight the contributions that family systems make to the on-going life of societies. For example, families ensure that someone will be responsible for the care of dependent infants. Or take the case of political machines, which continue to flourish in American cities despite periodic condemnations by important members of American society (Merton, 1968). Structural-functionalists would say that these machines serve positive (though unrecognized) functions for some members of society. For example, they provide a political voice for new immigrants and minority groups.

By looking at the social world through a structural-functionalist perspective, sociologists often develop convincing explanations for the existence of social phenomena that would otherwise be puzzling or incomprehensible. For example, one of the most influential functionalists, Kingsley Davis, once asked these questions: "What is there about the nature of human society that causes it to give rise to, and maintain [prostitution] while at the same time it condemns the practice? What functions does prostitution serve that are not served by other institutions in the society?" (Davis, 1937). As a result of this line of questioning, Davis came up with some innovative and convincing answers. For example:

1. Prostitution provides a sexual outlet for those who cannot at the moment find permanent or stable partners (for example, traveling salesmen, sailors, businessmen at conventions).
2. Prostitution provides a sexual outlet for those who do not have the energy or will to pursue more elaborate forms of courtship.

3. Prostitution provides a source of sexual satisfaction during times when more stable relationships are temporarily out of kilter (for example, during separation, divorce, widowerhood).

4. Prostitution provides an outlet for sexual perversions that cannot be expressed in long-term enduring relationships, helping to preserve those relationships.

5. Prostitution provides partners for those men who are, for whatever reason, unable to compete in the ordinary sexual marketplace (for example, the disfigured, handicapped, impotent).

While Davis's analysis makes sense, it provides only a limited explanation for the existence of prostitution, and this limitation is imposed by the very questions he asks in the beginning: "What functions does prostitution serve that are not served by other institutions in the society?" (Note that Davis is viewing society from the male perspective alone.) There are more questions to ask about prostitution, but they would probably come out of a different theoretical orientation.

Conflict Orientation

One of the orientations standing in opposition to the functional approach focuses on conflict and opposition rather than on social balance. This approach has several contemporary proponents, whose objections to the functionalists are echoed in the statement: "[In functionalism] there is much concern with social order and norms, little with social discord and power, opposition and oppression. The functional orientation introduces a conservative bias into sociological analysis . . . in the specific sense that it directs attention to system maintenance and stability and diverts attention from conflict and change" (Blau, 1972).

A sociologist with the *conflict* approach would ask questions about who benefits and who is systematically deprived by certain social patterns. They would ask about the overall conditions of society that even allow certain phenomena to be functional at all. For example, a sociologist with a conflict orientation would ask these questions about prostitution:

1. If prostitution has arisen and flourished to accommodate the restless male, why has it not also arisen to accommodate the restless female?

2. What are the costs of prostitution to society? These include the costs of creating an out-caste group, the prostitutes themselves, and the costs for men, in hypocrisy, deception, and *self*-deception.

3. What are the contradictions in the laws of society that create legal institutions (monogamous marriage) and at the same time condone the violation of these institutions?

4. How can changes in the practice of prostitution be brought about?

These questions will clearly give rise to different answers about the nature of prostitution—its causes and consequences—than resulted from the functionalist approach. While neither approach is "right" or "wrong," each provides a distinctive explanation for the same social phenomenon, and sociologists of one orientation must be aware of the questions that might arise from a different perspective.

Symbolic Interaction

A third and increasingly popular orientation to studying social phenomena is the *symbolic interactionist* approach. Sociologists who follow this perspective focus their attention not on large social structures and institutions, but on the day-to-day communication that occurs when people interact in face-to-face situations. The emphasis is on the meaning of social life as it is interpreted by individuals going about their daily business. Regarding prostitution, an interactionist would want to know not so much why it exists or why it generally is practiced by women, but *how* people actually go about contracting for sexual services. The interactionist would ask questions like these:

1. What kinds of interactions take place between purchaser and purchased?
2. How are the signals arranged between a prostitute and her "john" so that each knows the other as a potential temporary partner.
3. What do the prostitute and her customer make of their interaction; what meaning does it have for each?
4. How are the rules of the interaction established, and what are the codes of understood behavior?

These types of questions would tell us more about the process of prostitution and its meaning for the participants than about its consequences for the larger social system.

Using any one of these perspectives we would come to understand something about the ubiquitous social phenomenon, prostitution, but we would learn different things from each orientation. In doing or studying sociology we must always remain aware of the underlying orientation so that we will be alert to the questions that have not been asked and to the biases of those that have been.

THE USES OF SOCIOLOGY

Whatever a sociologist's orientation, his or her task will always be the same: to understand and interpret events and patterns that transcend particular individuals, particular cultures, and particular historical moments. Unlike the psychologist, who is concerned with specific individuals in specific situations, the sociologist tries to uncover basic truths about human social behavior in general. "Know thyself" becomes, for the sociologist, "Know thy social being." But what good does it do to know the social being? Have sociologists simply devised a new vocabulary for personal introspection? Not really.

Sociological concepts and findings have been adopted for many purposes beyond self-revelation. For example, historians have begun to focus on issues like the daily workings of family life—just how many people actually did live together under one roof and who was in charge? Questions are now being asked about the prestige of specific historical occupations—was it considered better in a certain period and place to be a shipbuilder or a tradesman? Historians have recently begun to use sociological techniques in their research, and their findings will give us better information about the quality as well as the chronology of the historical past.

Political scientists, too, have incorporated the sociological perspective. They have begun to focus on such sociological issues as: How do different people acquire political views? What is the relationship between political attitudes of parents and children? How does the process of formal education contribute to political opinions? These are sociological questions which, until the last few decades, have been overlooked by most political scientists.

But sociology has been useful not only in enriching its fellow disciplines, it has also had its own unique impact on public programs and policy. For example, sociologists and psychologists have informed us of the effects of public school segregation for both white and black children over the past several years (Coleman, 1966; Mosteller and Moynihan,

1972; Averch, 1972). The findings of sociological studies have been applied to such thorny problems as how to provide better health care for low-income families (Rainwater, 1968; Dreitzel, 1971), and how to demobilize soldiers without provoking anger and resentment in those left behind (Shils, 1961).

Sociology has also been useful in exploding unexamined popular myths. For example, it is the work of sociologists that has led to the realization that most of the people who are incarcerated in state mental hospitals are not psychotic or dangerous (Scheff, 1966). On the basis of this work the laws permitting involuntary commitment to mental hospitals have been made stricter, and civil rights are gradually being restored to mental patients. The mental hospital was also the site of the remarkable finding by sociologists that when mental patients become psychotic on the ward, they are sometimes responding not so much to inner erratic impulses as to tension generated by the staff when it is in conflict over patient care (Stanton and Schwartz, 1954).

Recently, in response to the increasing interest in a negative income tax (which would provide extra income to those who earn less than a certain minimum), sociologists studied the ways in which poor people spend additional income. They demonstrated with hard evidence that poor people, like people everywhere, spend the money to free themselves from menial tasks and to provide their children with niceties (Mathematica, 1974). If and when Congress does consider a proposal for a negative income tax, sociologists will be ready with data on how such extra income would be spent, allaying the fears of cautious Congresspersons that the poor will "squander" the extra funds.

One of the newest, and perhaps most ambitious, undertakings of sociologists concerned with applied rather than theoretical work has been the attempt to develop *social indicators*. Every January the Council of Economic Advisors issues detailed reports on the nation's economy, as measured by statistics on growth, employment, inflation, and the gross national product. But until quite recently there has been no parallel attempt to monitor the *quality* of life in this country. As Harvard professor Raymond Bauer told a Senate subcommittee on social planning in 1971, "While we could reduce hunger, we do not know just who is hungry. While we could reduce crime, our knowledge of even how many crimes of what type are committed is highly imperfect. While we could improve the quality of life, we do not know what our citizens value in their lives" (Bauer, in Melville, 1973, p. 13).

In the last five to ten years sociologists, along with other social scientists, have begun to develop a system of social indicators comparable to our existing system of economic indicators. These social indicators are designed to measure such seeming intangibles as aspirations and satisfactions in health, work, friendship, family, marriage, and community. Other quality-of-life issues that are being studied and measured include prejudice, political alienation, changing roles (particularly for women), and fear of crime. (We will discuss social indicators in greater depth in chapter 19.)

The goal of all these studies is to develop a set of social indicators that will give policy-makers a sense of what it is like to live in America during a certain year or period. If the quality of life at any particular moment can be accurately assessed and compared with the quality at another time, policy-makers will have a factual and realistic foundation on which to base their decisions about social programs. The social-indicators movement is one of the first large-scale attempts to put sociological knowledge to practical work. As the public begins to gain more confidence in sociological approaches and methods, surely there will be others. In the next chapter, we discuss several of the methods sociologists use in doing research.

summary

Sociology invites us to stand back from our personal visions in order to view with greater clarity and objectivity the forces that shape and control our lives. It attempts to understand the social nature of things—in particular, the patterns and regularities of behavior that people exhibit as they go about their daily lives. The *sociological perspective* focuses on those details that are regular and patterned, details not unique to a particular situation or to particular people in that situation.

A compelling reason for using the sociological perspective is that human experience—no matter how private and individual it may seem—is touched and shaped by social forces that are not individually made or controlled. Being sick or committing suicide are two seemingly private experiences that, when viewed sociologically, turn out to be affected by social forces.

The sociological perspective is not a rigid, singular way of looking at society; there are several different theoretical orientations. The most prevalent orientation in America is the *structural-functional* approach. The emphasis is on society and the interrelationships of its components, rather than on groups or individuals as such. Structural-functionalists try to discover the social function something serves in society. They often develop convincing explanations for the existence of phenomena that would otherwise be puzzling or incomprehensible. *Conflict orientation* focuses on conflict and opposition rather than on positive functions. The proponents of this approach feel that the structural-functionalists introduce a conservative bias into sociological analysis by directing attention toward maintaining the system as it is and away from conflict and change. A third and increasingly popular orientation is loosely labeled *interactionist.* Attention is focused on day-to-day communication that takes place when people interact face-to-face. The emphasis is on the meaning of social life as it is interpreted by individuals going about their daily business, rather than on large social structures and institutions. Each of these orientations influences the results of a sociological inquiry in a different way. The type of questions that a sociologist asks reflects his or her theoretical orientation, and the questions are often reflected in the answers.

No matter what his or her orientation, the task of every sociologist is always to understand and interpret events and patterns that transcend particular individuals, cultures, and historical moments. The sociologist tries to uncover basic truths about human social behavior. Sociological concepts and findings have been adopted for many purposes. The study of history has been affected: it has begun to use sociological techniques to explore everyday life in the past. Political science, too, has been influenced; it now explores such issues as: How do different people acquire political values? What is the relationship between the political attitudes of parents and those of their children?

Sociology has also had its own unique impact on public programs and policy. The findings of sociological studies have been applied to such diverse issues as school segregation, and how to provide better health care for low-income families. One of the newest undertakings of sociologists concerned with applied rather than theoretical work is the attempt to develop *social indicators*, which measure the quality of such seeming intangibles as aspirations and satisfactions in health, work, friendship, marriage, family, and community. If the quality of life at any particular moment can be accurately assessed and compared with the quality of life at another time, policy-makers will have a factual and realistic basis on which to reach their decisions about social programs.

glossary

conflict orientation   a theoretical perspective that emphasizes conflict, opposition, and change within a society.

social indicators   measures of the quality of life, including such seeming intangibles as aspirations and satisfactions in health, work, friendship, marriage, family, and community.

sociological perspective   a way of observing social life that focuses on regular and patterned details, aspects that are not unique to a particular situation or to individuals in that situation.

structural-functionalism   a theoretical perspective that emphasizes the way each part of a society contributes to the functioning of the society as a whole. A structural-functionalist tries to discover the social function something serves in society.

symbolic interactionist orientation   a theoretical perspective that focuses on the day-to-day communication that takes place when people interact in face-to-face situations, rather than on the large social structures and institutions.

references

Harvey Averech, et al., *How Effective Is Schooling*? Princeton, N.J.: Princeton University Press, 1972.

Harvey Elmer Barnes, *An Introductory History of Sociology*, Chicago: University of Chicago Press, 1948.

Peter Blau, "Dialectical Sociology: Comments," *Sociological Inquiry* (Spring 1972): 17–22.

——— and Marshall W. Meyer, *Bureaucracy in Modern Society*, New York: Random House, 1971.

James Coleman, et al., *Equality of Educational Opportunity*, Washington, D.C.: U.S. Government Printing Office, 1972.

Auguste Comte, *The Positive Philosophy*, trans. and ed., Harriet Martineau, London: Bell, 1915.

Kingsley Davis, *Human Society*, New York: Macmillan, 1937.

———, "The Sociology of Prostitution," *American Sociological Review*, vol. 2, 1937: 744–755.

Hans Peter Dreitzel, ed., *The Social Organization of Health*, New York: Macmillan, 1971.

Emile Durkheim, *The Rules of Sociological Method*, Chicago: University of Chicago Press, 1938.

———, *Suicide* (1897), trans. J. A. Spaulding and G. Simpson, New York: Free Press, 1951.

Eliot Freidson, *Profession of Medicine: A Study of the Sociology of Applied Knowledge*, New York: Dodd, Mead, 1970.

E. Gartly Jaco, ed., *Patients, Physicians, and Illness*, 2nd ed., New York: Free Press, 1967.

Karl Marx, *Capital*, ed., Friedrich Engels, New York: International, 1967.

——— and Friedrich Engels, *The Communist Manifesto*, ed., Samuel H. Beer, New York: Appleton, 1955.

Mathematica and the Institute for Research on Poverty, "Final Report of the New Jersey Graduated Work Incentive Experiment," Princeton, N.J. and Madison, Wis., unpublished report, June 1974.

Keith Melville, "A Measure of Contentment," *The Sciences* (December 1973): 12–15.

Robert K. Merton, *Social Theory and Social Structure*, New York: Free Press, 1968.

F. Mosteller and Daniel P. Moynihan, eds., *On Equality of Educational Opportunity*, New York: Vintage, 1972.

Talcott Parsons, *The Social System*, New York: Free Press, 1951.

Lee Rainwater, "The Lower Class: Health, Illness, and Medical Institutions," in Irving Deutscher and E. Thompson, *Among the Poor*, New York: Basic Books, 1968.

Henri de Saint-Simon, *Social Organization: The Science of Man*, trans. and ed., Felix Markham, New York: Harper & Row, 1964.

Thomas J. Scheff, *Being Mentally Ill*, Chicago: Aldine, 1966.

Edward Shills, "The Calling of Sociology," in Talcott Parsons, et al., eds., *Society*, New York: Free Press, 1961.

Herbert Spencer, *The Principles of Sociology*, New York: Appleton, 1898.

Alfred H. Stanton and Morris S. Schwartz, *The Mental Hospital*, New York: Basic Books, 1954.

Max Weber, *The Theory of Social and Economic Organization*, trans., A. N. Henderson and Talcott Parsons, New York: Free Press, 1964.

for further study

The Sociological Perspective. As a basic orientation to sociology, we can recommend two small books written for the beginning student: Peter Berger's popular *Invitation to Sociology* (Garden City, N.Y.: Doubleday, 1963) and Alex Inkeles' *What Is Sociology?* (Englewood Cliffs, N.J.: Prentice-Hall, 1964). Many students will be interested in *The Humanities as Sociology*, edited by Marcello Truzzi (Columbus, Ohio: Merrill, 1973). A whimsical and interesting approach to social life is represented in a book edited by Marcello Truzzi, *Sociology and Everyday Life* (Englewood Cliffs, N.J.: Prentice-Hall, 1968). One of the finest books by a sociologist who saw social life largely in terms of power and conflict is *The Sociological Imagination*, by C. Wright Mills (New York: Oxford, 1967). One sociologist has recently criticized the social sciences for their pretensions and deceptions: Stanislav Andreski, *Social Sciences as Sorcery* (New York: St. Martin's Press, 1972).

Theoretical Orientations. A useful book for exploring the major theories that characterize sociology today is *Sociological Theory* (New York: Macmillan, 1969). The editors, Lewis Coser and Bernard Rosenberg, have selected some of the most important writings by major sociologists on the character of social life. Another good collection is edited by Marcello Truzzi, *Sociology: The Classic Statements* (New York: Random House, 1971).

The Uses of Sociology. Irving L. Horowitz, ed., *The Use and Abuse of Social Science* (New Brunswick, N.J.: Transaction, 1971), discusses the ethical problems of sociological research. Examples of sociology as a tool of social reform are found in Gary Marx's book, *Muckraking Sociology: Research as Social Criticism* (New Brunswick, N.J.: Transaction, 1972). Arthur Shostak's *Sociology in Action* (Homewood, Ill.: Dorsey, 1966) discusses the practical uses of sociology.

(While you and i·have lips and voices which
are for kissing and to sing with
who cares if some oneeyed son of a bitch
invents an instrument to measure Spring with?[1]

[1] From "voices to voices, lip to lip" by E. E. Cummings, copyright 1926
by Horace Liveright; renewed, 1954, by E. E. Cummings. Reprinted from
his volume *Complete Poems 1913–1962* by permission of Harcourt Brace
Jovanovich, Inc.

SCIENCE AND METHODS IN SOCIOLOGY

e. e. cummings is right, of course: people don't need a scientific instrument to know when spring or love has arrived. In everyday life our senses, intuition, and common sense are important but narrow means of understanding. They are particularly limited as tools for understanding social forces and large social patterns, because any individual's perspective is incomplete and usually biased. The sociological eye *does* need the assistance of scientific instruments.

This chapter describes a key instrument of science—the scientific method—and its application to the study of society. It also explores some of the basic questions that confront all sociologists. Is sociology a science? How do sociologists work? Is it ethical to experiment with people? We begin this chapter with the most fundamental question: What is science?

THE NATURE OF SCIENCE

Essentially, science is a *method* for collecting and explaining facts. Scientists confine their investigations to phenomena that can be observed and measured, and to statements about the relationships among phenomena that can be verified by independent observers. Empirical proof is the basis of all science. Researchers are expected to approach their work in a detached way and to report their findings accurately. Other scientists then retest these findings to make sure they contain no false statements. In the words of one of the characters in C. P. Snow's novel *The Search*, "Now if false statements are to be allowed, if they are not to be discouraged by every means we have, science will lose its one virtue, truth. The only ethical principle which has made science possible is that the truth shall be told at all times" (p. 281). Scientists seek the truth and attempt to eliminate, or at least minimize, personal bias and error by applying the scientific method to their research.

French sociologist Emile Durkheim, whose research on the causes of suicide was one of the first scientific studies of social behavior. (The Bettmann Archive)

The Scientific Method: Emile Durkheim's Study of Suicide

The publication of Emile Durkheim's *Suicide* in 1897 marked the beginning of a revolution in thinking about social behavior. In Durkheim's time suicide was explained as an individual act caused by either mental illness or inherited suicidal tendencies, or as the effect of climate on reasoning. If these really *were* the causes, then why did suicide rates vary from period to period? If suicide is caused by forces within individuals, why should more people kill themselves in one country than in another? Durkheim decided to find out why by conducting one of the first scientific studies of social behavior.

He began by checking existing theories against the facts. A preliminary review of official records revealed that suicide rates were highest in countries that had the lowest rates of mental illness, suggesting that insanity alone did not explain suicide. And while more women than men were confined to mental asylums, more men than women committed suicide. This observation suggested that suicide is not related to heredity for if it were, men and women would be affected equally.[2] Nor did the facts support the climatic theories of suicide. All that remained was the fact that suicide rates varied from one social group to another. Durkheim concluded, "We have shown in fact that for each social group there is a specific tendency to suicide explained neither by the organic-psychic construction of the individuals nor the nature of the physical environment. Consequently, by elimination, it must necessarily depend upon social causes and be itself a collective phenomenon . . ." (1951, p. 145).

At this point Durkheim had done nothing more than formulate a proposition: suicide has some relationship to social causes. A philosopher might stop here, having shown by the logical process of elimination that suicide is related to social causes. But logical deduction is not enough; scientists demand empirical proof. The first step toward obtaining such proof is to translate the problem into terms that can be tested.

Defining the Problem Defining terms and concepts in a precise way is often more difficult than it would seem. For example, what is suicide? If a person dies because he or she miscalculates danger or fails to take necessary precautions, is that suicide? Examining the different implications of this word, Durkheim concluded that the term *suicide* refers to "all cases of death resulting directly or indirectly from a positive or negative act of the victim himself, which he knows will produce this result" (p. 44).[3] Durkheim decided to use official records for his study,

even though he realized that many suicides went unreported.

The next problem was to define *social causes* in some concrete way. When scientists study abstract concepts such as prejudice, religiosity, or economic stability, for example, they must define these ideas in terms of variables that can be measured. This is called an *operational definition*. For purposes of study the scientist may define religious beliefs in terms of membership in religious organizations; economic stability in terms of fluctuations on the stock market. In *Suicide*, Durkheim decided to use statistics on religious affiliation, marital status, military involvement, and economic and political stability as measures of the social causes of suicide.

Durkheim hypothesized that suicide rates would vary: for Catholics, Protestants, and Jews; for married and unmarried people; for soldiers and civilians; in times of economic and political stability and unrest. An *hypothesis* is a statement about the relationship between two or more variables, phrased in such a way that it can be proved *or disproved* empirically. For example, the statement, "God exists," is simply an assertion; it can be neither proved nor disproved. The statement, "People who attend church regularly believe in God," can be tested (by interviewing people who attend church and people who do not), and is therefore an hypothesis. A *variable* is some fact or condition that is subject to change. In Durkheim's study religious affiliation, marital status, and so on were the independent variables, the factors thought to affect the suicide rate; the suicide rate was the dependent variable, the factor expected to change in relation to the independent variables.

In any scientific study the *independent variable* is a quality or factor that influences the dependent variable. The *dependent variable*

---

[2] Both of these conclusions are questionable. Criteria for mental illness vary from culture to culture, and the number of people confined in asylums does not necessarily reflect the number of people who are depressed or disturbed. Moreover, the question of whether suicidal tendencies are inherited is still unanswered.

[3] By positive acts Durkheim meant such things as shooting oneself or jumping off a bridge. Negative acts include failing to take medicine or not getting out of the path of a moving vehicle.

is a quality or factor that is affected by one or more independent variables.

Collecting and Interpreting Data Once his terms were defined and his hypotheses formulated, Durkheim had to decide how to collect data that would prove or disprove the hypotheses. This involved selecting the group or groups to be studied, evaluating various sources of information, and deciding how to measure the variables. Depending on the problem being investigated, a researcher might design an experiment, conduct interviews, spend time observing the way people interact in certain settings, or examine records. (A researcher may actually use several of these data-collection methods.) Durkheim chose to use official records on suicide from a number of European nations.

Examining these records, he found that more Protestants than Catholics, and more Catholics than Jews committed suicide. Suicide rates varied inversely with marital status (single people committed suicide most often, married people with children least often), and soldiers were more prone to suicide than civilians. Durkheim also discovered that suicide rates rose during periods of sharp economic reversals (inflations or depressions), but fell during periods of political instability. These findings had to be interpreted. Why, for example, do suicide rates vary with religious affiliation?

The answer was not obvious. Certainly religious beliefs did not explain the variations Durkheim found. The Catholic church teaches that suicide is a sin, while Jewish doctrine is vague on the subject. Yet Jews had the lowest suicide rates. Durkheim resolved this paradox by looking beyond specific religious beliefs to the *social impact* of different faiths. Protestantism emphasizes skepticism and individualism; Catholicism and Judaism stress tradition and authority while at the same time demanding that a person become involved in the religious community. Similarly, married people (particularly parents) are involved with other people in a way that single people are not. Durkheim reasoned that the stronger the social groups to which people belong, the more they depend on these groups and the more likely they are to take other people into account when making decisions. People who have few ties to their community are more likely to take their own lives than people who are deeply involved with their families and religious groups.

Forming a Theory Building on this interpretation of the available data on suicide, Durkheim formulated a general theory about the individual's relationship to society. In everyday conversation we use the word theory to distinguish abstract ideas from fact: we say, "That may be true in theory, but not in fact." In science, a *theory* is an explanation of something. Durkheim's theory may be summarized as follows: Society is not simply a collection of people; it has an existence of its own and exercises a determining influence on the way people think and act. In other words, the individual is a product of the groups to which he or she belongs.

The function of theory in science is to summarize and order information in a meaningful way, to suggest new ways of looking at phenomena, and to stimulate new research. The test of a theory is whether or not it can predict what will happen, given certain conditions.

Critical Assessment Like other communities, the scientific community is governed by certain values and norms, which in turn distinguish it from most other communities. These norms include making results available to everyone and analyzing each other's work according to preestablished impersonal criteria. The norms of science have been applied to Durkheim's work on suicide. Some soci-

Even suicide, which seems like the most solitary act of all, has social causes. (UPI)

ologists have questioned his data by asking whether official records are an accurate measure of suicide rates. Not only do people cover up suicides, but they may do so in systematic ways that would distort the patterns that Durkheim analyzed. For example, records revealed that Protestants had a higher suicide rate than Catholics. But what if Catholics simply concealed more suicides than Protestants did?

Still other researchers have built on Durkheim's work, either replicating the study in another place and time or extending his ideas to other forms of social life. For example, some sociologists have asked whether a lack of social involvement is related to other forms of deviant behavior, such as crime.

The value of a scientific study lies partly in the information the researcher collects and partly in the new investigations it stimulates. The accuracy of scientific findings is assessed by testing their validity and reliability. *Validity* is the degree to which a scientific study measures what it attempts to measure. *Reliability* is the degree to which a study yields the same results when repeated by the original researcher or by other scientists.

SCIENCE AND SOCIOLOGY

[T]here can never be, and has never been, "disinterested" research in the social field, as there can be in the natural sciences. Valuations are, in fact, determining our work even if we manage to be unaware of it. And this is true, however much the researcher is subjectively convinced that he is simply observing and recording the facts. (Myrdal, 1973, p. 9)

The question of whether sociology is a science comparable to physics, biology, and astronomy has never been completely resolved. Auguste Comte, the French philosopher and founder of positivism, believed that all aspects of social life could be measured, analyzed, and explained with the tools of natural science. He also believed that sociologists would ultimately be able to solve social ills, just as medical scientists have learned to cure many physiological ills. In contrast, Max Weber, the German sociologist and political economist, emphasized the *subjective* elements of social behavior. He argued that empathy and insight are as valuable to the sociologist as hard facts are; that to understand social phenomena, the researcher must "get inside" them.

This debate continues today, with some sociologists emphasizing the need to replace insight with hard facts and others arguing that sociology can not and should not imitate the natural sciences because they are fundamentally different. Quite simply, people are not atoms. They do not always march obediently through experiments: they change their minds, they talk back, they elude precise quantitative analysis—sometimes deliberately. Nor do social variables remain constant over time and place. The law of gravity and the composition of water are the same in America and Europe, the same today as they were yesterday. But no two families are exactly alike, and even ideas about what the family *should be* vary enormously from one culture to another, from one generation to the next. In the words of economist Gunnar Myrdal:

The really important difference between [social scientists] and our natural science colleagues is that we never reach down to constants—like the speed of light or sound in a particular medium, or the specific weights of atoms or molecules. We have nothing corresponding to the universally valid measurements of energy, voltage, ampere, etc. The regularities we find do not have the firm general validity of "laws of nature." (1973)

Perhaps most significant, the sociologist's relationship to his or her subject is quite different from the astronomer's relationship to the stars or the physicist's relationship to energy. Objectivity is a major problem for all social scientists. As Herbert Spencer wrote nearly a hundred years ago:

To cut himself off in thought from all his relationships of race, and country, and citizenship—to get rid of all those interests, prejudices, likings, superstitions, generated in him by the life of his own society and his own time—to look on all the changes societies have undergone and are undergoing, without reference to nationality, or creed, or personal welfare; is what the average man cannot do at all, and what the exceptional man can do very imperfectly. (1877, p. 74)

Does this mean that sociology is merely masquerading as a science, or does it mean that sociologists should confine themselves to collecting hard facts, to conducting surveys, and to other forms of information-getting in which personal bias can be minimized? Not necessarily. It means, first, that it is essential for sociologists to recognize their biases and assumptions and to state them explicitly, and second, that they should combine the quantitative (or hard) and qualitative (or soft) approaches to the study of social behavior. Durkheim's study of suicide illustrates this last point. By collecting data he was able to prove that suicide rates varied with religious affiliation, marital status, military involvement, and economic and political stability. But it was *insight* that enabled Durkheim to perceive the underlying variable—the degree of involvement in social groups. The uniqueness of social behavior enables sociologists to contribute to the natural sciences by examining the social forces that influence physicists, biologists, and astronomers (see, for example, Kuhn, 1970).

The Methods of Sociology

Having described how Durkheim used scientific methods to analyze suicide rates, we now examine the specific procedures and techniques that sociologists use to study social behavior. They include both objective and subjective measures.

Survey Research *Surveys* composed of questionnaires, interviews, or a combination of the two, enable sociologists to gather information about large numbers of people. Surveys may be used to make predictions about how people will behave (for example, election polls), to test hypotheses, and to measure public opinion.

The validity of a survey depends on the care with which the researcher constructs interviews or questionnaires and on the selection of a representative sample. Theoretically, a sociologist who is interested in the attitudes of American college students toward politics or sex or any other issue could hire an army of interviewers to contact every student in the country. However, the cost and time involved in such a venture would be prohibitive. For these very practical reasons, sociologists generally question only a sample of the population. In this context, *population* refers to all the people with the characteristics the researcher wants to study—all American college students, for example. A *sample* is a limited number of people selected from the population.

There are several ways to choose a sample, and the method used depends on what the researcher is studying. One form is the *random sample*. In effect, the researcher puts the names of all people in the population in a barrel, blindfolds himself, and picks as many names as he needs, leaving the selection to chance. The more sophisticated and more usual technique is to assign each person in the population a number and to pick a sample from a table of random numbers, which is designed so that there is no pattern reading across, down, or diagonally. With a random sample each person in the population has an equal chance of being selected; researcher bias is eliminated.

Most people think a big sample is more accurate than a smaller one, but this is not

---

SURVEYING PUBLIC OPINION

The questions given below have been selected from a public opinion survey conducted by the National Opinion Research Center. NORC is a general research institute designed to measure public opinion, to conduct surveys for government agencies and nonprofit organizations, and to train graduate students.

1. Think of how your life is going now. Do you want it to *continue in much the same way as it's going now*; do you wish you could *change some parts of it*; or do you wish you could *change many parts of it*?

   _____ Continue much the same way
   _____ Change some parts
   _____ Change many parts

2. In Chicago recently a family had to decide between letting its newborn baby die, or have an operation that would leave the baby blind for life. Which course would you have chosen?

   _____ Let die
   _____ Operate
   _____ Don't know

3. Do you think it will be best for the future of this country if we take an active part in world affairs, or if we stay out of world affairs?

   _____ Active part
   _____ Stay out
   _____ Don't know

4. Suppose there is a revolution in one of the countries of South America, and it looks as though a Communist government will take over. Do you think the United States should or should not send in American troops to prevent this?

   _____ Should send American troops
   _____ Should not send American troops
   _____ Don't know

SOURCE: Survey Research Service, NORC, University of Chicago, SRS–857; June 1965.

necessarily true. Not size, but polling a true cross section of the population being studied is the key to accuracy. A famous example of this was the attempt to predict the winner of the 1936 presidential election. A popular magazine, *Literary Digest*, sent post card ballots to 10 million people chosen from telephone directories and auto registration lists. The *Digest* predicted, on the basis of 2 million returns, that Landon would beat Roosevelt by a landslide. Meanwhile, a young man named George Gallup sampled 312,551 people and correctly predicted that FDR would win. The editors of the *Literary Digest* were stunned by

Surveys enable sociologists to collect information about large numbers of people, but accuracy depends on unambiguous questions and truthful answers. (Wayne Miller/ Magnum)

the election results. How could their giant survey have been so wrong? The key to accuracy was not the *number* of people polled, but their characteristics. During the depression, only middle- and upper-class people could afford telephones and automobiles, and a disproportionate number of middle- and upper-class people were Republicans. As it turned out, the less well-off, who voted heavily for Democrat Franklin Roosevelt, decided the election (Labovitz and Hagedorn, 1971, p. 33; Hennessy, 1970, pp. 79–81). The *Literary Digest* had incorrectly assumed that the more people they contacted, the better their chances of accurately predicting the election.

Gallup's success was not a matter of luck—he had polled a scientific cross section that accurately represented the proportion of Republicans and Democrats in the *entire* population of voters. Selecting a sample that accurately reflects the proportion of different groups in the population being studied is called *stratified random sampling*.

The accuracy of a survey also depends on the way questions are worded. A survey will be meaningless if respondents do not understand the questions, if they do not answer truthfully, and if their answers can be interpreted in different ways. With mailed questionnaires, it is difficult to judge whether or not respondents take the survey seriously, and the information collected may be only a superficial measure of actual beliefs, habits, and preferences.

There is also a danger of middle-class bias. It is generally easier to elicit responses from middle-class respondents than from welfare clients, who have reason to be suspicious of official-looking papers and of strangers who ask questions. Moreover, in face-to-face interviews, people tend to give the socially acceptable answer. For example, Richard Carter found that when he asked Bowery bums if they were married, a surprising number said no. However, when he asked instead, "Where is your wife?" many more gave truthful answers, without stopping to think about the implications of desertion (Carter, in Hennessy, 1970, p. 110).

In addition, researchers face the problem of translating responses into statistics. If a pollster asks a hundred different people what they think of an administration, he or she may get a hundred different answers. How, then, can the results be presented? Because of this problem, researchers use structured questions wherever possible—that is, questions that can be answered yes or no, true or false; multiple-choice questions; and rating questions, where a respondent indicates the extent to which he or she agrees or disagrees with a statement on a scale of one to five.

Experiments Sociologists conduct experiments when they want to study cause-and-effect relationships. In simplest terms, sociological *experiments* consist of exposing subjects to a specially designed situation and systematically recording their reactions. The advantage of experiments over other methods is that they allow the researcher to study the impact of only one or two variables, which is hard to do in real-life situations.

For example, Philip Zimbardo wanted to study the impact of prison life on guards and inmates. He might have studied actual prisoners and guards in their natural setting, but he would have had to follow prison rules, and his findings would have been complicated by such variables as differences in individual background. Instead, he ran an experiment using student volunteers (Zimbardo, 1972). By using people who were neither guards nor prisoners, Zimbardo was able to study the effects of social roles on behavior. In actual prisons he would not have been able to separate the actors from their roles as easily.

Zimbardo began by constructing a prison

To study the impact of prison life on guards and inmates, Philip Zimbardo designed an experiment using volunteer prisoners and guards. This picture shows a "superintendent" and inmates. (Philip Zimbardo)

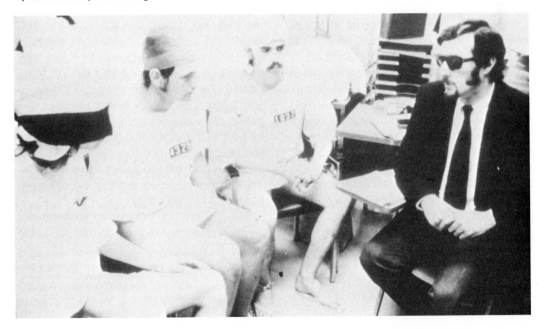

in the basement of the psychology building at Stanford University. A group of twenty-four normal college students ("normal" according to accepted psychological tests) were divided into two subgroups—half were guards, half were prisoners. The two groups were matched for socioeconomic background, education, and race. One night, without warning, the prisoners were collected in a simulated arrest. All were given uniforms and numbers and confined in the basement jail. The guards were dressed appropriately and instructed on their responsibility for maintaining order. Two days after the experiment began, rumors of a prisoner rebellion began to spread. The "guards" reacted with surprising brutality, to which the "prisoners" submitted with little resistance. This brief experiment dramatized how even ordinary students could succumb to prison roles in just a few days. Zimbardo concluded that the institutional structure of prisons has much more to do with how real guards and prisoners behave than do their personalities. (We will discuss some of the ethical problems raised by this experiment later in the chapter.)

Stanley Milgram's experiments on obedience were equally controversial (1965; 1973). Milgram recruited subjects by placing ads in a local paper, calling for volunteers for an experiment on learning. Over a period of several years, over a thousand people from all walks of life participated. When a subject arrived at the lab, he or she was introduced to two other people. One, dressed in a lab coat, was the experimenter; the other, dressed in street clothes, was supposed to be a second volunteer. In reality, however, this second person was part of the experimental team. Milgram explained that he was conducting a test of the effects of punishment on learning, and asked the subject to play the role of "teacher." The second person, or "student," was strapped to a chair and wired with elec-

trodes. The "teacher" was given a seat at an impressive-looking shock machine and was told to ask the "student" a series of questions and to administer increasing doses of electric shock for each wrong answer. The shock board was labeled from 15 volts (SLIGHT SHOCK) to 450 volts (DANGER—SEVERE SHOCK).

As the experiment proceeded, the "student" gave a number of wrong answers. He began to complain when the shocks reached 175 volts, and by 285 volts was emitting what Milgram describes as agonized screams. Eventually, the "student" demanded to be released. Nearly all of the "teachers" became troubled when the "student" complained, and turned to the experimenter for advice. They were told to continue. In reality, the shock machine was a fake and the "students" were acting, but the "teachers" did not know this. Nevertheless, two-thirds of the subjects continued to press the shock button, right up to 450 volts.

The chief drawback with experiments is that a laboratory is one step removed from real life, and the setting itself may influence the way people behave. For example, Milgram's subjects may have obeyed the experimenter because they believed he was a doctor and, presumably, doctors do not harm people.[4] For this reason, researchers may run two tests with two matched groups. One group, the *experimental group*, actually undergoes the experiment. The other, the *control group*, is brought to the lab and exposed to everything *but* the independent variable. The experimenter then compares the responses of the two groups.

Still, the question of whether observations made in a laboratory apply to real-life situa-

---

[4] Milgram tested this contingency by performing a second series of experiments in an unimpressive office building that was identified as a commercial research organization; the results were much the same.

tions remains. Some researchers avoid this problem by conducting experiments in the field. One of the most famous field experiments in sociology was conducted by Elton Mayo at Western Electric Company's Hawthorne plant in Chicago (Roethlisberger and Dickson, 1939). Mayo wanted to learn how variations in lighting, coffee breaks, pay plans (salary vs. piece rate), and the like affected worker output in a factory. The management felt sure that employees would work harder if they were paid in proportion to what they produced; they also thought that coffee breaks would improve morale. To their dismay, however, Mayo and his colleagues found that *every* change they made increased output. Employees worked faster when management increased coffee breaks as well as when they *decreased* them. Mayo concluded that it wasn't lighting or coffee breaks or even salary incentives that raised productivity, but rather the attention the employees were getting. The positive impact that an experiment has just because the researchers are giving people extra attention is known as the *Hawthorne effect*. Sociologists may try to eliminate the Hawthorne effect by using hidden tape recorders and other "unobtrusive measures" (Webb, et al., 1966), but there is some question as to whether it is ethical to experiment on people without their knowledge.

Participant Observation   One of the oldest yet most controversial research methods in sociology is *participant observation*. Participant observers deliberately involve themselves in the activity, group, or community they are investigating in order to gain an insider's view. William Foote Whyte (1955), for example, moved into a low-income, Italian-American community that was uncharted territory in the late 1940s. Before Whyte's study, street corner residents were known to the outside world primarily as clients of social

workers, as defendants in criminal trials, or simply as the masses (p. xvii). Whyte met Doc, the leader of the Norton gang, through a social worker. Doc then introduced him to the other residents, and for eighteen months Whyte shot pool, played cards, bowled, dated, "chewed the fat," and most important, watched his subjects. In time he became a fixture on the street corner, a trusted friend who was able to learn how these people conducted their daily lives. Like Herbert Gans, author of a similar study (*The Urban Villagers*, 1962), Whyte "tried to describe the way of life of [these] people as they might describe it themselves if they were sociologists" (p. x). This is the primary goal of participant observation: to obtain intimate, firsthand knowledge of a way of life. In effect, the investigator uses himself as a research instrument. He knows how the people he is studying feel because he feels the same way. Other studies in this genre include Festinger's report on a doomsday group (*When Prophecy Fails*, 1956); Becker's investigation of medical students (*Boys in White*, 1961), and his studies of dance musicians and marijuana smokers (*The Outsiders*, 1963).

Participant observation requires exceptional self-discipline. The first problem for field workers is gaining access to the group he or she wants to study and establishing rapport with its members.[5] If researchers reveal their intentions, they risk putting their subjects on guard; if they conceal their motives, they must live with pretense and duplicity for the duration of the study. Participant observers must develop techniques for recording their observations faithfully and systematically without influencing the way people act. They must become involved in the group life with-

---

[5] Gans never was able to win the confidence of the young, single men who frequented West End bars; Whyte's success depended largely on his informant and collaborator, Doc.

out letting their own emotions blind them.

An important advantage of participant observation is that it is extremely flexible. Whyte found, for example, that "as I sat and listened, I learned the answers to questions that I would not even have had the sense to ask" (p. 303). Skilled field workers observe behavior in its natural setting; they can see behind individuals' public selves and discern the relationships between what people say and what they do. However, even good participant-observational studies have problems. The observations of the researcher may or may not reflect the group as a whole. There is always some danger that the field worker will rely on information gained from the more articulate and outgoing members of the group; that he or she will misinterpret the significance of certain events. Moreover, in participant observation the sample is necessarily small.

For these reasons, observational studies are generally used to uncover relationships that can then be tested more systematically. But despite the limitations of participant studies, many of the classics of sociology rest on observational research that uncovered significant aspects of social life. For example, Whyte found that low-income neighborhoods are highly structured communities—not the chaotic places they appear to be to outsiders; Gans argued that residents of Boston's West End were not "frustrated seekers after middle-class values" (p. x), but had a culture of their own. Both of these findings were radical ideas in their time.

A *case study* is an intensive observational study, supplemented by formal interviews, surveys, data gathered from official records, and whatever other information may seem relevant. The researcher attempts to learn everything there is to know about a particular group, community, or incident. Examples are the Lynds' profiles of Middletown, U.S.A.

(1929; 1937); Clifford Shaw's life history of a juvenile delinquent (1966), and Hadley Cantril's anatomy of a lynching in Leeville, Texas (1963).

The Time Variable   An important variable in much of sociological research is *time*. People and institutions often change more slowly than can be easily observed. Sociologists solve this problem in two ways. One is the *cross-sectional study*, which simultaneously looks at different groups of people at different stages of change. For example, a survey may sample the political opinions of adolescents, parents, and grandparents in order to see how aging affects political ideology. This is a quick and economical method, but it has its dangers. It assumes, for example, that the adolescents it samples today will become like their parents in twenty years and like their grandparents in forty years, when in fact young people today may not adopt their parents' attitudes twenty years from now; they may think very differently.

The second solution, a *longitudinal study*, is a more accurate research tool because it follows the same people over a number of years. No assumptions about people becoming like other people are necessary. In one well-known longitudinal study, T. M. Newcomb analyzed the effect of Bennington College on students' political attitudes. Newcomb questioned the same group of graduates over twenty years, and found that, years after they had left college, Bennington alumni were still unusually liberal for people of their socioeconomic class (1943; 1963). One problem with longitudinal studies is that they are expensive and slow. We are often so eager for quick results that they are rare in American sociology, though more common in Europe.

Sometimes the problem is not slow change but change so rapid that an event is over before we can begin to study it. Then the sociologist has no choice but to do an *ex post facto study*. In such studies, variables that could not be measured while an event was happening, can be controlled statistically after the fact. The numerous government studies of civil disorders, initiated after the riots of the late 1960s, are ex post facto studies.

Interpreting Data

Politicians, advertisers, and journalists are so fond of quoting statistics that it sometimes seems as if they believe there is magic in numbers. Many people take statistics as gospel: "You can't argue with the facts," they say. Others believe you can use numbers to prove or disprove almost anything, and automatically stop listening when they hear the phrase, "Statistics indicate . . ." The truth lies somewhere in between these two points of view.

The data a researcher collects in a survey, experiment, or observational study does not speak for itself. Data must be classified, and trends and relationships identified for a study to be meaningful. For example, knowing the age of every American is useless, but knowing what percent of the population is under twenty-five, between twenty-six and forty, forty-one and sixty-four, sixty-five and over is extremely valuable. The most common and useful methods of classifying statistics are explained in the accompanying boxes.

CLASSIFYING DATA: MEAN, MEDIAN, AND MODE

Frequently researchers summarize data on a given population by calculating central tendencies, or averages. There are three ways to do this:

The *mode* is the figure that occurs most often in the data. For example, a researcher studies seven families and finds that their yearly incomes are:

$ 3,000	$11,000
$ 3,000	$15,000
$ 7,500	$90,000
$ 9,000	

The modal income in this group of families is $3,000 a year. The mode does not give any indication of the range in data, and it is only useful when a researcher wants to show which statistic appears most often.

The *mean* is what we call the average in everyday conversation. To calculate the mean you simply divide the sum of all the figures by the number of items. The mean or average income for the families above is $19,786 ($138,500÷7). Researchers frequently calculate the mean because it includes and reflects all the available data. However, as the example here illustrates, the mean can be misleading: The fact that one of the families in this group has an income of $90,000 a year obscures the fact that six of the seven families have incomes of less than $19,786 a year. The mean is most useful when the range of figures is narrow.

The *median* is the number that falls in the middle of a series of figures, in this case $9,000 a year. The median is useful because it does not allow extremes (here $3,000 and $90,000) to hide the central tendency. Frequently, researchers calculate both the mode and the median in order to present an accurate impression of their findings.

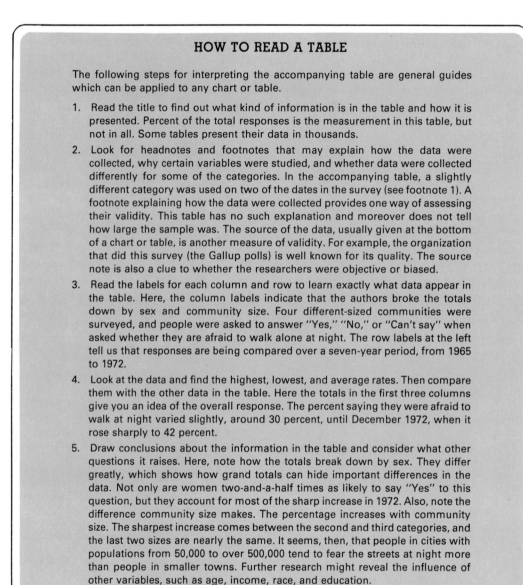

HOW TO READ A TABLE

The following steps for interpreting the accompanying table are general guides which can be applied to any chart or table.

1. Read the title to find out what kind of information is in the table and how it is presented. Percent of the total responses is the measurement in this table, but not in all. Some tables present their data in thousands.

2. Look for headnotes and footnotes that may explain how the data were collected, why certain variables were studied, and whether data were collected differently for some of the categories. In the accompanying table, a slightly different category was used on two of the dates in the survey (see footnote 1). A footnote explaining how the data were collected provides one way of assessing their validity. This table has no such explanation and moreover does not tell how large the sample was. The source of the data, usually given at the bottom of a chart or table, is another measure of validity. For example, the organization that did this survey (the Gallup polls) is well known for its quality. The source note is also a clue to whether the researchers were objective or biased.

3. Read the labels for each column and row to learn exactly what data appear in the table. Here, the column labels indicate that the authors broke the totals down by sex and community size. Four different-sized communities were surveyed, and people were asked to answer "Yes," "No," or "Can't say" when asked whether they are afraid to walk alone at night. The row labels at the left tell us that responses are being compared over a seven-year period, from 1965 to 1972.

4. Look at the data and find the highest, lowest, and average rates. Then compare them with the other data in the table. Here the totals in the first three columns give you an idea of the overall response. The percent saying they were afraid to walk at night varied slightly, around 30 percent, until December 1972, when it rose sharply to 42 percent.

5. Draw conclusions about the information in the table and consider what other questions it raises. Here, note how the totals break down by sex. They differ greatly, which shows how grand totals can hide important differences in the data. Not only are women two-and-a-half times as likely to say "Yes" to this question, but they account for most of the sharp increase in 1972. Also, note the difference community size makes. The percentage increases with community size. The sharpest increase comes between the second and third categories, and the last two sizes are nearly the same. It seems, then, that people in cities with populations from 50,000 to over 500,000 tend to fear the streets at night more than people in smaller towns. Further research might reveal the influence of other variables, such as age, income, race, and education.

Once a researcher has organized his or her findings, a decision must be made about what the facts mean. A few simple examples illustrate the hazards of interpreting data. Suppose a researcher who is interested in the relationship between literacy rates and income collects data on Spain, Israel, and Ku-wait. He or she discovers that per capita income is highest in Kuwait, where literacy rates are lowest, and concludes that the less literate people are, the more money they earn. This researcher has made the common error of relying on grand averages, which often conceal significant patterns. For al-

table 2:1 PERSONS AFRAID TO WALK ALONE AT NIGHT: 1965–1972

By Sex and Community Size (by percent)

	TOTAL			SEX MALE			FEMALE			COMMUNITY SIZE (POPULATION) UNDER 2,500			2,500 TO 49,999			50,000 TO 499,999			500,000 AND OVER		
YEAR (MONTH)	YES	NO	CAN'T SAY	YES	NO	CAN'T SAY	YES	NO	CAN'T SAY	YES	NO	CAN'T SAY	YES	NO	CAN'T SAY	YES	NO	CAN'T SAY	YES	NO	CAN'T SAY
1965 (April)[1]	34	63	3	17	80	3	49	47	4	21	77	2	29	67	4	41	54	5	48	49	3
1967 (August)[1]	31	67	2	16	82	2	44	53	3	21	78	1	22	77	1	38	57	5	40	57	3
1968 (September)	35	62	3	19	79	2	50	47	3	24	74	2	33	65	2	42	53	5	41	56	3
1972 (December)	42	57	1	22	77	1	61	39	—	28	71	1	40	59	1	51	49	—	48	51	1

– Represents zero.
[1]The category "Don't Know" was used instead of "Can't Say."
SOURCE: American Institute of Public Opinion, Princeton, N.J.

though Kuwait is a rich *nation*, the vast majority of its *people* are extremely poor. If the researcher had examined literacy rates for different *income groups* in each country instead of literacy rates for entire nations, he or she would have discovered that there is a direct relationship between literacy and income.

Data on crime and deviance are notoriously misleading. Statistics on mental illness, drug use, and homosexuality are nothing more than a count of the people who happen to come to the attention of police, social workers, and other public officials. These data do not include drug users who escape detection, or those people who are wealthy enough to afford private treatment for mental illness. Most people assume that crime is a lower-class phenomenon, whereas in fact white-collar (or middle-class) crimes, such as fraud and embezzlement, account for far greater dollar losses than do muggings and burglaries. Similarly, most people believe the crime rate has risen sharply in the last decade. While the crime rate may indeed have risen, some of this increase is due simply to improved methods of reporting and recording crimes—how much, it is difficult to say. In short, the way in which researchers interpret and analyze their data is as important as the care they take in collecting it.

THE POLITICS OF SOCIOLOGY:VALUES, ETHICS, AND USES

Sociology is founded on the belief that it is possible to apply the scientific method to the study of social behavior. Yet if sociology has proven anything in its brief history, it is that people are cultural animals, and that separating them from their social moorings is impossible. Thus sociologists find themselves in the awkward position of striving for objectivity on the one hand and recognizing the importance of subjectivity on the other. Can this dilemma be resolved?

Value-free Sociology: A Myth or a Reality?

For generations sociologists have labored under the eleventh commandment, "Thou shalt not commit a value judgment." Every textbook, every lecturer stresses this point. But what do they mean? Do they mean that sociologists should not express opinions about issues that lie outside their sphere of competence? Should they be indifferent to the moral implications of their work? Should they never speak out on the probable consequences of public policy? Should they never attempt to correct popular beliefs, such as the idea that certain races or ethnic groups are inferior? Should they never express values in their role as teachers?

In Alvin Gouldner's view, sociologists must stop pretending that their field can or should be value-free. Sociologists, like everyone else, are products of their times, and they cannot divorce themselves from their values and beliefs. In choosing an area for study, in deciding how to research a particular question, the sociologist inevitably makes certain assumptions about what is significant. For sociologists to deny their predispositions and biases, writes Gouldner, is absurd.

If truth is a vital thing, as Weber is reputed to have said on his deathbed, then it must be all the truth we have to give, as best we know it, being painfully aware that even as we offer it we may be engaging in unwitting concealment rather than revelation. If we would teach students how science is made, really made rather than as publicly reported, we cannot fail to expose them to the whole scientist by whom it is made, with all his gifts and blindnesses, with all his methods and his *values* as well. (1962, p. 212)

Gouldner agrees with Gunnar Myrdal (1969) that sociologists can counteract bias only by explicitly stating their theoretical assumptions and values.

Howard S. Becker carries this argument a step further. He contends that sociologists always take sides, not only because they have the sympathies and likes and dislikes of all people, but because investigating one point of view requires them to temporarily disregard another (1967). For example, the researcher who talks to inmates after a prison riot will arrive at one picture of the incident; the researcher who talks to guards and wardens will obviously come to another. Which is correct? For the sociologist both are true, both relevant. Even interviewing both guards and inmates does not solve the problem, because the researcher will still analyze the data according to her or his theoretical orientation (see chapter 1). Social realities are always complex; there is always more than one side to a story. Only by including these different perspectives can sociologists gradually approach all the facts. Becker acknowledges that this is a long-term solution.

What do we do in the meantime? . . . We take sides as our personal and political commitments dictate, use our theoretical and technical resources to avoid the distortions that we might introduce into our work, limit our conclusions carefully, recognize the hierarchy of credibility for what it is, and field as best we can the accusations and doubts that will surely be our fate. (1967, p. 247)

Becker cautions, however, that in giving some rein to their sympathies sociologists must resist the desire to suppress unpleasant findings and the temptation to disregard what they do not like seeing.

Professional Ethics

The debate over objectivity in sociology spills over into a number of complex ethical questions. Sociology is not a self-supporting enterprise. Like most researchers, sociologists depend on grants from public and private institutions for financial support. While these organizations do not dictate what researchers should find in their studies, they do exercise indirect control over the choice of topics by funding research in some areas but not in others. Intentionally or not a discipline may adjust its priorities to those funding agencies.

Often there is a fine line between obtaining funds from an agency and working *for* the government or private interest groups. This is why Project Camelot, for example, became so controversial. The project was conceived in the Special Operations Research Organization (SORO) of the army. Its purpose, as described in a recruiting letter, was to devise procedures for "assessing the potential for internal war within national societies" and to "make it possible to predict and influence politically significant aspects of social change in the developing nations of the world" (Horowitz, 1965, p. 4). In other words, the army wanted to learn what circumstances sparked revolutions in underdeveloped nations, and what the governments of these nations could do to prevent them—hence the name "Camelot," which in the director's mind connoted "a stable society with peace and justice for all."

The army backed its interest with an allocation of $6 million and successfully recruited some of the most respected social scientists in this country. Enthusiasm was high; participants believed Project Camelot would be an opportunity to influence government policy directly and to "educate" the army. As far as they could tell, military officials had no intention of interfering with their work.

The project was abruptly terminated when Chilean officials protested to the State Department, and the Chilean press began to publish stories about academic spies. Neither the State Department nor the Senate was willing to jeopardize friendly relations with Latin American nations for the sake of gathering data, and there was some question as to the army's true motives.

Although Project Camelot never got off the ground, it did raise numerous questions during its brief history. Is it ethical for social scientists to work for the military? Many American sociologists thought not. But Project Camelot was an opportunity to study political order and disorder in depth. Would the project have become so controversial if it had been launched with private funds? After all, there is nothing to prevent military strategists from using (or misusing) research conducted with private money.

Equally problematic are questions about sociologists' responsibilities toward the people they study. Does a researcher have the right to deceive people about his or her intentions, to risk exposing and hurting them in the name of scientific inquiry? Milgram, for example, recruited subjects for his experiment by lying to them. It is difficult to estimate the impact participation had on the subjects: one man told Milgram his wife had said, "You can call yourself Eichmann" (1973). Zimbardo's techniques have also been questioned. The "prisoners" had not been told that they would actually be arrested, and they did not know where they were being taken. During the experiment, three became so hysterical or depressed that they were released after two days, and the entire study was canceled after six days, although it was originally planned to run six weeks.

George Ritzer (1972) suggests that we ask the following questions in evaluating research:

1. Did the researcher harm the subjects he or she studied?
2. Did the researcher affect the subject's behavior and thereby invalidate his or her conclusions?

To which we add,

3. Could the researcher have obtained the

same data without deceiving people and injuring their self-esteem?

The question of whether sociologists should actively participate in the political arena also involves ethical issues. Many believe sociologists should remain neutral; that taking a stand would contaminate the discipline. But as Robert Lynd suggested in *Knowledge For What?*:

Somebody is going to interpret what the situation [the facts] means. . . . When the social scientist, after intensive study of a problem, avoids extrapolating his data into the realm of wide meaning, however tentatively stated, he invites others presumably more biased than himself—e.g., the National Association of Manufacturers, the American Federation of Labor, the advertising man, the American Legion and so on—to thrust upon the culture their interpretations. (1939, pp. 185–86)

In short, Lynd and many other sociologists argue that social scientists should suggest social policies because if they don't, others, with their own special interests at heart, will.

---

summary

Science is a method for collecting and explaining facts, based on the following procedures: (1) defining the problem to be studied and forming an hypothesis; (2) planning the kind of data to be collected; (3) collecting the data; (4) interpreting the data; (5) forming a theory or explanation.

Emile Durkheim was a pioneer in applying the scientific method of collecting and explaining facts to the study of social behavior. Durkheim did not believe that mental illness, heredity, or climate explained variations in suicide rates. He hypothesized that suicide was related to social causes, which he defined operationally in terms of religious affiliation, marital status, military involvement, and economic and political stability. Examining official records, he found that suicide rates did indeed vary along these dimensions. Through a combination of statistical analysis and insight, he reached the conclusion that suicide rates vary in relation to the strength of social group ties (to families, religious organizations, etc.). Building on this observation Durkheim theorized that society has a determining influence on the way people think and act.

Sociologists can not put human beings under a microscope or weigh social behavior in imitation of physical scientists. Sociologists deal with meanings as well as facts, with change as well as constants, and they must count themselves as variables in any research they do. This does not mean that sociology is not a science, but rather that studying social behavior effectively, requires the use of both quantitative and qualitative data.

Sociologists collect their data in three basic ways: through *survey research, laboratory experiments*, and *field studies*, including *participant observation*. A *survey* is a collection of facts, figures, and/or opinions. The validity of a survey depends on the care with which the researchers construct their questions and on the selection of a representative sample. In *random samples*, every member of the population being studied has an equal chance of being selected. *Stratified random samples* re-create the proportions of significant groups in a population.

In an *experiment* researchers can control the variables they are studying, but their very presence may influence the results. Participant observers deliberately involve themselves in the activity, group, or community they are investigating in order to gain an insider's view.

Despite methodological precautions against error and bias, sociologists find themselves in the awkward position of striving for objectivity on the one hand, while recognizing the importance of subjectivity on the other. Can sociology be value-free? This may be an unrealistic goal since sociologists are as culture-bound as all people; they inevitably take sides. Rather than pretend to absolute objectivity, sociologists must make their values and assumptions clear. Should sociologists work for the government? Is it ethical for sociologists to conceal their true objectives from the people they study? Would it contaminate the field if sociologists used their expertise to influence politicians and other decision-makers? All sociologists must face these questions.

glossary

control group In an experiment, the subjects who are not exposed to the independent variable, giving the experimenter a basis for comparison with subjects who are.

cross-sectional research A quick way to study long-term changes by studying people in different phases of change all at the same point in time. This research method can be misleading.

dependent variable A quality or factor that the researcher believes is affected by one or more independent variables.

experiment A research method that exposes subjects to a specially designed situation. By systematically recording subjects' reactions, the researcher can assess the effects of several different variables.

experimental group In an experiment the subjects who are exposed to the independent variables and observed for changes in behavior.

ex post facto research A way in which variables that could not be measured at the time of an event can be analyzed after the fact.

hypothesis A proposition about how two or more variables are related to each other.

independent variable A quality or factor that the researcher believes to affect one or more dependent variables.

longitudinal research Studies designed to measure change over time.

mean A statistical average calculated by dividing the sum of a series of figures by the number of items in the series.

median The number that falls in the middle of a series of figures.

mode The figure that occurs most often in a group of data.

participant observation A method in which researchers join and participate in the groups they plan to study in an effort to gain intimate firsthand knowledge of a way of life.

population In a research study, all the people an investigator wants to learn about.

random sample A sample that gives every member of the population being studied an equal chance of being selected. In this way experimenter bias is eliminated.

reliability The degree to which a study yields the same results when repeated by the original researcher or by other scientists.

sample A limited number of people selected from the population being studied.

social indicators Statistics that provide a measure of the quality of life in a society.

stratified random sample A sample that reflects the proportions of different groups in the population being studied.

survey A set of questions administered to groups of people in order to learn how they think, feel, or act. Good surveys use random samples and pretested questions to ensure high reliability and validity.

theory A comprehensive explanation of apparent relationships or underlying principles of certain observed phenomena.

validity The degree to which a scientific study measures what it attempts to measure.

variable An attitude, behavior pattern, or condition that is subject to change.

references

Stanislav Andreski, *Social Sciences as Sorcery*, New York: St. Martin, 1973.

Solomon E. Asch, "Opinions and social pressure," *Scientific American*, vol. 193 (Nov. 1950): 408.

Bernard Barber, *Science and Social Order*, New York: Collier, 1962.

Raymond A. Bauer, *Social Indicators*, Cambridge, Mass.: MIT Press, 1966.

Howard S. Becker, *The Outsiders*, New York: Free Press, 1963.

———, "Whose side are we on?" *Journal of Social Problems*, vol. 14, no. 3 (Winter 1967): 239–47.

——— et al., *Boys in White: Student Culture in Medical School*, New York: Brown, 1961.

Hadley Cantril, *The Psychology of Social Movements*, New York: Wiley, 1963.

Emile Durkheim, *Suicide: A Study in Sociology* (1897), trans. by John A. Spaulding and G. Simpson, New York: Free Press, 1951.

Amitai Etzioni, "Policy Research," *American Sociologist*, vol. 16 (1971): 8–12.

James Fennessey, "Some probabilities and possibilities in related research," *Social Science Research*, vol. 1, no. 4 (December 1972): 359–83.

L. A. Festinger, Henry Riecken, and Stanley Schacter, *When Prophecy Fails*, Minneapolis: University of Minnesota Press, 1956.

Herbert J. Gans, *The Urban Villagers*, New York: Free Press, 1962.

William J. Goode and Paul K. Hatte, *Methods in Social Research*, New York: McGraw-Hill, 1952.

Alvin W. Gouldner, "Anti-minotaur, the myth of a value-free sociology," *Journal of Social Problems*, vol. 9, no. 3 (1962): 199–213.

Bernard Hennessey, *Public Opinion*, 2nd ed., Belmont, Calif.: Wadsworth, 1970.

Irving Louis Horowitz, "The Life and Death of Project Camelot," *Transaction*, vol. 3 (November–December 1965): 3–7.

Thomas Ford Hoult, *Dictionary of Modern Sociology*, Totowa, N. J.: Littlefield, Adams, 1969.

Thomas S. Kuhn, *The Structure of Scientific Revolutions*, 2nd ed., Chicago: University of Chicago Press, 1970.

Sanford Labovitz and Robert Hagedorn, *Introduction to Social Research*, New York: McGraw-Hill, 1971.

Robert S. Lynd, *Knowledge for What?* Princeton: Princeton University Press, 1939.

———, *Middletown in Transition: A Study in Cultural Conflicts*, New York: Harcourt Brace Jovanovich, 1937.

———and Helen M. Lynd, *Middletown*, New York: Harcourt Brace Jovanovich, 1929.

Keith Melvill, "A measure of contentment," *The Sciences* (December 1973): 12–15.

Robert K. Merton, *Social Theory and Social Structure*, New York: Free Press, 1957.

William Michelson, "The reconciliation of 'subjective' and 'objective' data on physical environment in the community," 68th Annual Meeting of ASA, August 27–30, 1973.

Stanley Milgram, "Some conditions of obedience and disobedience to authority," *Human Relations*, vol. 18 (1965): 57–76.

———, *Obedience to Authority: An Experimental View*, New York: Harper & Row, 1973.

Kewal Motwani, *A Critique of Empiricism in Sociology*, New York: Allied, 1967.

Gunnar Myrdal, "How scientific are the social sciences?" *Bulletin of Atomic Scientists* (January 1973).

———, *Objectivity in Social Research*, New York: Pantheon, 1969.

T. M. Newcomb, *Personality and Social Change*, New York: Holt, Rinehart and Winston, 1943.

———, "Persistence and regression of changed attitudes: long-range studies," *Journal of Social Issues*, vol. 19 (1963): 3–14.

George Ritzer, *Issues, Debates and Controversies; An Introduction to Sociology*, Boston: Allyn & Bacon, 1972.

F. J. Roethlisberger and William Dickson, *Management and the Worker*, Cambridge, Mass.: Harvard University Press, 1939.

Clifford R. Shaw, *Jack-Roller: A Delinquent Boy's Own Story*, Chicago: University of Chicago Press, 1966.

Julian L. Simon, *Basic Research Methods in Social Science*, New York: Random House, 1969.

Gideon Sjoberg, ed., *Ethics, Politics, and Social Research*, Cambridge, Mass.: Schenkman, 1967.

C. P. Snow, *The Search*, New York: Scribner, 1958.

Herbert Spencer, *The Study of Society*, New York: Appleton, 1877.

Samuel A. Stouffer, *Communities, Conformity and Civil Liberties*, New York: Doubleday, 1955.

Eugene Webb et al., *Unobtrusive Measures: Nonreactive Research in the Social Sciences*, Chicago: Rand McNally, 1966.

William Foote Whyte, *Street Corner Society: The Social Structure of an Italian Slum*, rev. ed., Chicago: University of Chicago Press, 1955.

Philip G. Zimbardo, "Pathology of imprisonment," *Society*, vol. 9 (April 1972): 4–8.

for further study

Understanding Science. Although most beginning students will not want to pursue the details of different methods, some may be interested in the basic questions of how we know that something is true, and how we go about explaining the way things are. Abraham Kaplan, in *The Conduct of Inquiry* (San Francisco: Chandler, 1964), explores these fundamental problems of science in a clear and intelligent way. One serious alternative to the usual approach to these questions is to be found in *Discovery of Grounded Theory: Strategies for Qualitative Research* (Chicago: Aldine, 1967), by Barney Glaser and Anselm Strauss, two sociologists who use mainly participant observation for their research.

Participant-Observation Studies. Since all of us are to one degree or another participant observers of social life, it is informative to read what advice serious practitioners of that method have to offer. In *Tally's Corner* (Boston: Little, Brown, 1967), Elliot Liebow discusses his experiences as a participant observer in an urban ghetto. Another good participant observer is Howard Becker, and Part I of his book, *Sociological Work* (Chicago: Aldine, 1970), is devoted to case studies, life histories, and field methods. An excellent set of essays by several distinguished field workers can be found in Part V of *Institutions and the Person: Essays Presented to Everett G. Hughes*, edited by Howard Becker et al. (Chicago: Aldine, 1968).

Ethics in Sociology. The uses and abuses of sociology are not only interesting in themselves but are becoming increasingly important as the social sciences gain influence in shaping social policy. One of the clearest and most thoughtful books on this subject is by Robert Lynd, with the appropriate title, *Knowledge for What?* (Princeton, N.J.: Princeton University Press, 1969). An actual case of the abuse of sociological research is described by Irving Louis Horowitz in *The Rise and Fall of Project Camelot: Studies in the Relationship Between Social Science and Practical Politics* (Boston: MIT Press, 1967). Since Project Camelot, a number of essays have been written on the "sociology of sociology," that is, on how sociological research is influenced by public policy, on the internal structure of the sociological community, and on the values of the investigators. These have been collected in *The Sociology of Sociology*, edited by Larry T. Reynolds and Janice Reynolds (New York: McKay, 1970). A good book in which sociologists describe how they have applied sociology to various problems is *Sociology in Action*, edited by Arthur Shostak (Homewood, Ill.: Dorsey, 1966).

"Imagine a sociology class in a Southern college where almost all
the students are white Southerners. Imagine a lecture on the subject of the racial system of the South. The lecturer is talking here of
matters that have been familiar to his students from the time of
their infancy. . . . They are quite bored as a result. It seems to them
that he is only using more pretentious words to describe what they
already know. Thus he may use the word 'caste,' one commonly
used now by American sociologists to describe the Southern racial
system. But in explaining the term he shifts to traditional Hindu
society, to make it clearer. He then goes on to analyze the magical
beliefs inherent in caste tabus, . . . the economic interests concealed within the system, the ways in which religious beliefs relate
to the tabus, the effects of the caste system upon the industrial
development of the society and vice versa—all in India" (Berger,
1963, p. 22).

As the professor returns to his original subject, race relations in the
South, students begin to straighten up in their chairs. Suddenly,
the world they live in comes alive; the countless gestures and
nuances they have always taken for granted have a new meaning.
This is our goal here.

   People are creatures of habit. Every day of our lives we get up
and head for the bathroom to wash up; choose clothes appropriate
to the weather and occasion; gulp coffee; make our way to class or
work, all without giving much thought to what we are doing or
why. How often do people break into a line at the supermarket or
turn on a transistor radio in a museum? How often do students get
up in class and tell a professor he doesn't know what he is talking
about (no matter how regularly they express that opinion among

THE STRUCTURE OF SOCIETY

themselves)? Rarely. We know, without thinking about it, how to act in different settings, such as classrooms or sports events or funerals; how to deal with store clerks, doctors, panhandlers, and others we may never know personally; what to expect in school or on the job. In fact, most daily activities are so familiar, so routine and mundane, that it takes a good jolt—such as the comparison of India with the American South—to bring them into focus.

Social structure refers to the stable patterns of collective rules, roles, and activities in a society or in one of its parts. One way to explain this concept is to focus on a familiar example—the university. Every year seniors depart and a new class of freshmen enters; some faculty members are replaced; new classes are added to the curriculum; the administration agrees to include student representatives in its planning sessions; curfews are abolished; and tuition rises. Yet despite changes in personnel and policy, some things about the university remain unchanged. Faculty members still design their courses, assign work to students, and evaluate their progress. The ways in which individual faculty members and students perform their roles vary, but the *general patterns* are much the same and fit together into an overall structure that we call a university. Although the structure itself remains invisible, it silently shapes our actions. Thus, analyzing the form and influence of social structure gives sociology its distinctive power in understanding human affairs.

In this chapter we will examine the levels of social structure; the elements of social structure, including norms, status, and roles; the impact of social structure on our everyday lives; and the social institutions that have formed around the basic needs of our own society. We begin in Washington, D.C., on Tally's corner.

LEVELS OF SOCIAL STRUCTURE

A pickup truck drives slowly down the street. The truck stops as it comes abreast of a man sitting on a cast-iron porch and the white driver calls out, asking if the man wants a day's work. The man shakes his head and the truck moves on up the block, stopping again whenever idling men come within calling distance of the driver. At the Carry-out corner, five men debate the question briefly and shake their heads no to the truck. The truck turns the corner and repeats the same performance up the next street. In the distance, one can see one man, then another, climb into the back of the truck and sit down. In starts and stops, the truck finally disappears.

What is it we have witnessed here? A labor scavenger rebuffed by his would–be prey? Lazy, irresponsible men turning down an honest day's work for an honest day's pay? . . .

Let us look again at the driver of the truck. He has been able to recruit only two or three men from each twenty or fifty he contacts. To him, it is clear that the others simply do not choose to work. Singly or in groups, belly-empty or belly-full, sullen or gregarious, drunk or sober, they confirm what he has read, heard and knows from his own experience; these men wouldn't take a job if it were handed to them on a platter. (Liebow, 1967, pp. 29–30)

Why are these men hanging around on streetcorners? And why are many others like them hanging around corners in urban ghettos across the country?

Sociologists answer these questions in two ways. One way is by examining the *micro-level* of social structure, that is, the pattern of personal interactions that characterize every-day life. This would mean investigating interpersonal relationships on the streetcorner to learn how these men see themselves and relate to others in face-to-face situations; how they balance their values and aspirations with their experiences.

The second approach is to focus on the *macro-level* of social structure, that is, the large social patterns that shape an entire society. These patterns are beyond any one person's control, yet they play a powerful role in shaping our lives. For example, the hierarchy of jobs and rewards, national patterns of prejudice and discrimination, the expectations that each sex has for the other are macro forces, which strongly influence the lives not only of streetcorner men but of all of us.

The Micro-level

From all appearances the truck driver is correct. But appearances can be misleading, as Elliot Liebow demonstrates in *Tally's Corner* (1967).[1] In fact, most of the men who refused the driver's offer already have jobs. Sweets, for example, works nights in office buildings, hotels, and other public places, "cleaning up middle-class trash"; Tally, a laborer, has the day off because bad weather stopped construction where he was working. Irregular hours and irregular jobs such as these are the rule in the ghetto. Other men on the street refused work because they were disabled. (Accidents occur more often on construction sites and in factories where unskilled laborers work than they do in offices.) Some of the men are drawing nearly as much and in some cases more money from unemployment compensation than they could earn

---

[1]   Elliot Liebow spent over a year as a participant observer on the streets of a ghetto in Washington, D.C., only blocks from the Capitol. During this time he came to know the two dozen or so men who frequented a neighborhood carry-out shop that was a popular social center.

table 3:1 WORK ORIENTATIONS OF WELFARE AND NONWELFARE FATHERS[1]

ORIENTATIONS	WELFARE FATHERS		URBAN, WORKING FATHERS	
	BLACK	WHITE	BLACK	WHITE
1. Life aspirations	3.61	3.63	3.71	3.66
2. Work ethic	3.40	3.36	3.53	3.41
3. Lack of confidence in ability to succeed	2.76	2.55	3.22	2.44
4. Acceptability of welfare	2.40	2.21	1.97	1.61
5. Work beyond need for money	2.97	3.04	3.26	3.09
6. Train to improve earning ability if poor	3.74	3.58	3.60	3.63
Number of respondents	81	163	500	175

[1]Items were rated on four-point scales. The higher the rating, the stronger the orientation.

SOURCE: Adapted from Leonard Goodwin, *Do the Poor Want to Work?* (Washington, D.C.: The Brookings Institution), 1972, p. 73.

A recent survey of welfare and working fathers, both black and white, found no significant differences in life aspirations, the desire to work, and several other orientations listed in table 3:1. The orientations were rated on a four-point scale, with (4) being the highest possible rating. It is clear that fathers on welfare as well as those who work have a strong desire to work, to improve themselves, and to earn more than a minimal income. At the same time, they are not very confident that they will succeed (orientation 3). The one notable difference concerns the orientation toward welfare; those who are on it are more inclined to accept it than those whose taxes pay for it.

as laborers. A few are working quite hard at illegal activities—"buying and selling sex, liquor, narcotics, stolen goods, or anything else that turns up" (p. 33). And Tonk is on the corner because he is afraid that if he goes to work his wife will disgrace him by taking the opportunity to be unfaithful.

Actually, only a handful of the men lingering on the street fit the truck driver's image: Arthur has no intention of looking for a job; Leroy is playing pinball instead of reporting to work; Sea Cat quit a job last week without giving notice; and Richard drank away his entire paycheck on the weekend. Why aren't these men out working or looking for work? Many people think the poor don't want to work, that somehow they have escaped the work ethic. (See table 3:1 for the results of a study that disputes this view.)

The streetcorner man, many believe, lives from moment to moment, indulging his whims "with no thought for the costs, the consequences, the future" (p. 64). Working regularly, saving, accepting responsibility for a wife and children, planning for the future are alien to him. He doesn't care about being respectable; in fact, he makes fun of those who are. He lives in a world of gambling, liquor and drugs, fancy cars and clothes (when he can get them), "fancy women," fast talk, and fast money. Liebow rejects this characterization entirely. He argues that to understand these men's attitudes and why they hold the kinds of jobs they do or why they fail to look for work, we have to look beyond the streetcorner to the macro-level of social structure.

The Macro-level

Moving back from the close-up view, Liebow analyzes the position of Tally and his neighbors in the American economic and class system, and shows that this position shapes not only their jobs, but also their feelings about themselves. First, Liebow calls attention to the kinds of jobs that are available to these men—unskilled laborer, janitor, dishwasher, elevator operator, bus*boy*, delivery *boy*. Not one of these occupations pays enough to enable a man to support a family. Not one has any future. "The busboy or dishwasher who works hard becomes, simply, a hard-working busboy or dishwasher. Neither hard work nor perseverance can con-

ceivably carry the janitor to a sit-down job in the office building he cleans up. . . . [T]he job . . . is a dead end" (p. 63). Perhaps more important, none of these jobs offers any kind of prestige or status.

Neither the streetcorner man who performs these jobs nor the society which requires him to perform them assesses the job as one "worth doing and worth doing well." Both employee and employer are contemptuous of the job. The employee shows his contempt by his reluctance to accept it or to keep it, the employer by paying less than is required to support a family. Nor does the low-wage job offer prestige, respect, interesting work, opportunity for learning or advancement, or any other compensation. (p. 58)

Social forces, not laziness, explain why these men and many others spend their days on urban streetcorners. The hierarchy of jobs and rewards and national patterns of racial discrimination are two such forces. (Leo Stashin/Rapho Guillumette)

There are several reasons why Tally and the other men Liebow observed find themselves in unstable and unrewarding jobs. Most obviously, they lack the education or training that would qualify them for better jobs. More subtly, they lack the contacts in the business world that middle-class people establish in the process of growing up. Also, they are black, which may explain all the rest.

Tally, like many of his contemporaries, was raised in the South some forty years ago, when schools were segregated and local boards of education did not consider educating blacks very important.[2] Recent studies indicate that conditions for blacks in big cities as well as in rural southern districts have not changed as much as one might expect. For example, Owen (1972) found that expenditures per pupil in terms of teachers' salaries are significantly higher in predominantly white, middle-class schools than they are in predominantly black, inner-city schools. Typi-

---

[2] A 1973 Department of Labor report cited "rural origins with poor educational opportunity; migration to the city or elsewhere; [and] lack of skills and training" as the major factors keeping some Americans poor. Joe A. Miller and Louis A. Ferman, "Welfare Careers and Low Wage Employment," A Report Prepared for the Manpower Administration, U.S. Department of Labor, December 1973.

IN THE NEWS

Unanticipated Consequences: "A Health Problem on the Reservation"

In our discussion of poverty and unemployment among a group of black men, we uncovered one of the most basic principles of sociology—that the society in which we live affects our lives in ways that we may not always be aware of. Knowing the social structure clarifies these unanticipated consequences. Racial discrimination, for example, boomerangs back at society by contributing to the welfare rolls. Similarly, an action that has been carefully planned to effect a change in one institution or segment of society may have a totally unanticipated consequence in another, as the following excerpt suggests.

WHITESBURG, Ky.—The elimination of the military draft is considered one of the good things of the Nixon years. But it has also meant the end of a fairly regular flow of draft detesting young medical students seeking to do their time in the Public Health Service.

This has hit the Indian Health Service's 51 Indian hospitals and 77 health centers hard. These critical facilities had been staffed to a large extent by medical personnel seeking to avoid the draft. This means that to a large extent these facilities are now facing difficulties in being staffed at all.

"We don't do anything really spectacular or medically unique," one overworked Indian Health Service doctor said in South Dakota. "What would be monumental is the mess if these services were cut."

Though by no intentional act of policy, this is precisely what is happening now. Even as health statistics continue to point to continuing unnecessary Indian health tragedies, the hospitals that are the base for whatever medical services do exist on reservations are facing an imminent shortage of personnel. . . . In 1969, for example, over 3,000 medical students sought Public Health Service jobs, with many specifying reservation work as a first or second choice. In 1973, the number of applicants had plummeted to under 500.

SOURCE: Phil Primack, "A Health Problem on the Reservation," *The New York Times*, January 7, 1974.

cally, teaching posts in ghetto schools are considered hardship assignments; seniority brings transfers out. Thus inner-city schools lose their most experienced and often most talented teachers. "The schools in the ghetto have lost faith in the ability of their students to learn, and the ghetto has lost faith in the ability of the schools to lead," wrote black psychologist Kenneth Clark (1965). Martin Deutsch (1960) found that teachers in urban schools spend as much as 80 percent of their time in the classroom coping with nonacademic problems and trying to maintain control. In the meantime the demand for higher education in the job market grows.

In addition, American society is structured in such a way that blacks and other minorities are seldom able to obtain training as apprentices in the lucrative trade unions. As recently as 1968, the Justice Department was prosecuting sixteen trade unions and one building trades council of the AFL-CIO for racial discrimination (Hill, 1969, p. 201). Racial prejudice, manifest in many ways, set distinct boundaries around the opportunities available to Tally and his friends.

In summary, attempting to explain poverty and unemployment by analyzing only the micro-level of social structure—the way a group of men conduct their lives on a day-to-day basis—does not give us a complete picture. The larger aspects of social structure—including the educational system, the hierarchy of jobs and rewards, and racial discrimination—must all be taken into account.

ELEMENTS OF SOCIAL STRUCTURE: NORMS, STATUS, AND ROLES

Our discussion so far has focused on the levels of social structure, on the way social forces affect our lives. In this section we will take a closer look at the elements of social structure through which society shapes our attitudes and actions—*norms*, *status*, and *roles*.

Norms

In *Games People Play* (1964), Eric Berne describes the greeting ritual of the American:

"Hi!" (Hello, good morning.)
"Hi!" (Hello, good morning.)
"Warm enough forya?" (How are you?)
"Sure is. Looks like rain, though." (Fine. How are you?)
"Well, take cara yourself." (Okay.)
"I'll be seeing you."
"So long."
"So long." (p. 37)

This brief exchange is conspicuously lacking in content. If you were to measure the success of this conversation in terms of information conveyed, you would have to give it a flat zero. Nevertheless, both people leave the scene feeling quite satisfied. They have said no more and no less than the situation (a meeting of co-workers, neighbors, or acquaintances) required. Each behaved quite properly,[3] in accord with accepted social norms.

Norms are the guidelines people follow in their relations with one another; they are shared standards of desirable behavior. Norms not only indicate what people should or should not do in a given situation, but they also enable them to anticipate how others will interpret and respond to their words and actions. Norms vary from society to society, from group to group within societies, and from situation to situation. Behavior which in one society is the height of propriety in another may be disgraceful. For example:

---

[3]　Berne calls this type of ritual exchange *stroking*.

Among the Ila-speaking peoples of Africa, girls are given houses of their own at harvest time where they may play at being man and wife with boys of their choice. It is said that among these people virginity does not exist beyond the age of ten. [In contrast] among the Tepoztlan Indians of Mexico, from the time of a girl's first menstruation, her life becomes "crabbed, cribbed, confined." No boy is to be spoken to or encouraged in the least way. To do so would be to court disgrace, to show oneself to be crazy or mad. (Ember and Ember, 1973, p. 318)

In this country a generation ago, virginity was highly prized; today, in marked contrast, vir-

The hand-shake is not a "natural" greeting, but is a social norm in most Western societies. In traditional Japan, bowing is the customary way of exchanging hellos. (Right, Philip Teuscher. Bottom, René Burri/Magnum)

gins of twenty-two or twenty-three probably try to hide their inexperience, and may even wonder about there being something wrong with themselves.

Some norms are situational, that is, they apply to specific categories of people in specific circumstances. We consider it appropriate for a person to pray to God in church, or to speak to people who have long since "gone to the other side" during a séance (even if we think the séance is phony). But a person who addresses God or invokes spirits during a dinner party or in a subway train will probably be considered insane. (See Goffman, 1959, pp. 75–79 on occult involvement.)

Norms also vary in intensity, that is, some are more important to people than others. The days when people stare at men who wear their hair long are over. Nobody bothers very much if students lie about having been sick when they hand in papers late, or if a woman violates custom by retaining her maiden name after she is married. But other norms (called mores) are held more intensely. Incest taboos, for example, are nearly universal. The degree to which norms are enforced—through social pressure or legal action—depends on both the intensity of the norm and on the number of people who consider it important. The fact that the penalty for rape in some states is the death sentence tells a great deal about the intensity of norms concerning sexual relations, womanhood, and male aggression. The more serious the crime, the more intense the norm (or norms) behind it. (We discuss the questions of deviance and social control in depth in chapter 12.)

Social norms even govern our emotions and perceptions. For example, people are *supposed* to feel sad and act depressed when a member of their family dies. The jury in Camus's novel *The Stranger* condemns Meursalt to death primarily because he went to a movie (even worse, a comedy) on the day his mother died—certain proof that he was "inhuman" (Henry, 1965, p. 15). Similarly, people are supposed to pay attention to some things but not to others. For example, we consider it bad taste to gawk at a couple who are quarreling bitterly or to eavesdrop on an intimate conversation (particularly if the conversation is about the eavesdropper).[4] We expect a male doctor to ignore the beauty of a female patient who disrobes in his office, but we would consider it odd for him to do so under other circumstances.[5]

What is so interesting about social norms is how most people follow them automatically; alternatives never occur to them. This is particularly true of unspoken norms that seem self-evident, such as answering a person who addresses you. People conform because it seems right; because to violate norms would damage their self-image (or "hurt their conscience"); because they want approval and fear ridicule, ostracism, and in some cases, punishment. As a result, social relations are relatively predictable and orderly—at least on the surface.

Status and Roles

A *status* is a position in the social structure that determines where a person fits in the community and how he or she should relate to other people. Status may be ascribed or achieved. An *ascribed status* is one that is assigned to a person at birth or at different stages in the life cycle—for example, being male or female, a Mexican-American, a Ken-

---

[4] This is one reason why the public was shocked to learn President Nixon was taping conversations without informing others that he was doing so.

[5] Erving Goffman coined the phrase *rules of irrelevance* to describe this type of selective inattention, when people pretend not to see or hear.

nedy, a teenager, a senior citizen. Each of these characteristics (sex, ethnic background, age) influences how a person is expected to act and how he or she will be treated. For example, to be born a Rockefeller guarantees a high social position; to be born poor and black still guarantees obstacles and restrictions. An *achieved status* is a position a person attains through personal effort. Physician, politician, artist, teacher, the town drunk, or the Boston Strangler—each of these is an achieved status. (Once a person attains a deviant status, he may be marked for life. We will discuss this problem in chapter 12.)

One of a person's ascribed or achieved statuses may largely determine his or her social identity. This may be an occupation that demands most of a person's time and energy (such as the presidency), or it may be position of particular symbolic significance. For example, impressionist Jean Renoir was not just a man who happened to earn a living by painting; he *was* an artist. When Renoir was so crippled by arthritis that he could no longer use his hands, he had brushes strapped to his wrists so that he could continue with his life's work. For children in our society, age and sex are most salient: they identify themselves as five- or seven-year-olds, as boys or girls. These are important facts they know about themselves. For adults, occupation is usually most significant. However, race, sex, or age may come first; for example, Kenneth Clark is a *black* psychologist, Bella Abzug is the *female* Representative from New York, and Eubie Blake is a ninety-year-old pianist.

Statuses have considerable impact on how people act, and on how others act toward them. Every status carries with it a socially prescribed *role*—that is, expected behavior patterns, obligations, and privileges. From the age of five, for example, American children begin to learn the role behaviors that are associated with their status as students. Raising hands, doing homework, studying for tests are all aspects of the role that students are expected to perform.

One status may carry several roles. For example, a medical student fills one role in relation to his or her teachers and others in relation to fellow students, nurses, and patients. Similarly, an actor or actress fills different roles with other actors, the director, stagehands, the audience, the press. The complex of roles that accrues to a single status is a *role set* (Merton, 1968, pp. 422–23).

Of course, there is a great deal more room for role interpretation in real life than there is in the theater. No two people who occupy the same status perform their roles identically. Individuals differ in what they believe is expected of them. For example, one professor perceives her role to be that of challenging students, making them doubt and question established theories; another sees his role as dispensing knowledge. Whether or not individuals live up to their roles is still another question. A father who perceives his role as being a pal to his children may actually relate to them in a formal and rather distant way; a president who perceives his role as upholding the Constitution may actually violate that document in his day-to-day decisions.

Although in the beginning, playing a new social role may involve acting and pretense, people tend to *become* what they play at being:

One feels more ardent by kissing, more humble by kneeling and more angry by shaking one's fist. That is, the kiss not only expresses ardor but manufactures it. Roles carry with them both certain actions and emotions and attitudes that belong to these actions. The professor putting on an act that pretends to wisdom comes to feel wise. The preacher finds himself believing what he preaches. The soldier discovers martial stirrings in his breast as he puts on his uniform. In each case, while the emotion or attitude may have been present before the role was taken on, the latter inevitably strengthens what was there before. In many instances there is every reason to suppose that nothing at all anteceded the playing of the role in the actor's consciousness, in other words, one becomes wise by being appointed a professor, believing by engaging in activities that presuppose belief, and ready for battle by marching in formation. (Berger, 1963, p, 96)

Roles, then, transform both the action and the actor.

Role Strain and Role Conflict "People generally want to do what they are supposed to do" (Goode, 1969, p. 485), but it isn't always easy or even possible. Sometimes people experience difficulty in meeting the demands of a role. *Role strain* may occur when conflicting demands are built into a role. For example, one part of a foreman's role is to maintain good relations with the people working under him. At the same time, he is expected to act as a representative of management, enforcing decisions from above. Often these two demands are in direct conflict.

Role strain also occurs when people cannot meet the demands of their role. Liebow found, for example, that most street-corner men had married early, with high hopes of becoming good husbands and fathers. But most failed, financially at first, then emotionally. "Where the father lives with his own children, his occasional touch or other tender gesture is dwarfed by his unmet obligations. No matter how much he does, it is not enough" (p. 87).

Role conflict describes situations where fulfillment of one role automatically results in the violation of another. The classic example is the black policeman. As a black man he knows the system is weighted against black people; as a policeman, however, he acts as an agent of that very same system.[6] Soldiers may experience intense role conflict. Young men who have been brought up to feel that killing is wrong are expected to fire guns and drop bombs. Many try to resolve this conflict by not using their weapons. Writing after World War II, S. L. A. Marshall estimated that even when being fired upon, only 25 percent of the soldiers fired back (1947, p. 50).

THE IMPACT OF SOCIAL STRUCTURE: PRISONERS OF SOCIETY?

Having said that norms structure emotions and perception as well as overt behavior, that people tend to become what they play at being, and that role strain and conflict create intense personal anguish, we run head on into the question of whether people are prisoners of society. Are we mere puppets, blindly following society's rules, obediently acting out our parts? To deny the impact of norms, statuses, and roles on our attitudes and behavior would be foolish. At the same time, however, people *feel* that they are free, that they make decisions, that they are the authors of their lives. Is this feeling of self-determination a delusion? Sociologists would agree that to some extent it is. People tend to lose their awareness of the impact of social pressure (if they were ever conscious of it at all). There is much debate within

---

[6] Peter L. Berger notes that one response to role conflict is increased zealousness. "The theologian who doubts his faith will pray more and increase his church attendance, the businessman beset by qualms about his rat-race activities starts going to the office on Sundays too, and the terrorist who suffers from nightmares volunteers for nocturnal executions" (1963, p. 97).

sociology as to how free we really are. In this section we present that debate.

Society in People: The Structuralist Position

Peter L. Berger has few, if any qualms about unmasking our most cherished beliefs, including our ideas about love.

In Western countries, and especially in America, it is assumed that men and women marry because they are in love. There is a broadly based popular mythology about the character of love as a violent, irresistible emotion that strikes where it will, a mystery that is the goal of most young people and often of the not-so-young as well. As soon as one investigates, however, which people actually marry each other, one finds that the lightning-shaft of Cupid seems to be guided rather strongly within very definite channels of class, income, education, racial and religious background. (1963, p. 35)

Berger goes on to describe the courtship ritual as a couple proceeds from movie dates to meeting the family, from holding hands to "what they originally planned to save for afterwards," from planning evenings to planning a future, and to the decisive scene in the car, under the moon, when one or the other proposes. He writes, "Neither of them has invented this game or any part of it. They have only decided that it is with each other, rather than with other possible partners, that they will play it." While there is room for innovation and improvisation, "too much ad-libbing is likely to risk the success of the whole operation" (p. 86).

Is Berger just being cynical? No, he is expressing a view shared by many students of human behavior. One of America's great social theorists, Robert K. Merton, has explained how people acquire the attitudes of society and come to think of them as their own (1938). In Merton's view, conforming and nonconforming behavior alike are the result of social pressure. Individuals construct a self-image by comparing themselves to members of groups to which they belong, groups with which they want to be affiliated, and those from which they want to disassociate themselves. (We will discuss Merton's concept of *reference groups* further in chapter 7.) In the process, individuals assimilate norms and values that direct their behavior. For example, in the 1950s and 1960s American society taught that it is right and legitimate—perhaps even mandatory—to seek love and marriage by courting a member of the opposite sex in prescribed ways. The feelings of free choice, of spontaneity and passion that accompany the chase only indicate the extent to which these goals and means have been internalized.

Society . . . is not only something "out there," . . . but it is also something "in here," part of our innermost being. . . . Society not only controls our movements, but shapes our identity, our thoughts and our emotions. The structures of society become the structures of our own consciousness. (Berger, 1963, p. 121)

It seems then that we are not only prisoners of society, we are prisoners who busily mend and strengthen the walls of our jail.

Innovation and Improvisation: The Symbolic Interactionist Position

The idea that people act out the roles society prescribes, unthinking and unreflecting, strikes many sociologists as an exaggeration. In attempting to describe and fix the patterns of everyday life, there is a danger of slipping into the notion that the patterns create the behavior, rather than vice versa. This is roughly equivalent to saying the game plays the person. Moreover, critics of the structuralist view argue that it underplays the ambiguity in face-to-face encounters. Only on stage is the outcome of two people meeting predetermined.

Symbolic interactionists stress the situational character of social behavior. They argue that people do not interact according to a blueprint of social instructions. Instead, they constantly evaluate each other's behavior and react accordingly (Blumer, 1966). Social interaction is seen by the symbolic interactionists to be a very delicate and complex process. Even the statement "I love you" may evoke several reactions.

If a man says "I love you," to a woman, she may wonder whether he means it, whether he loves her only, how much he loves her, whether he will love her next week or next year, or whether this love only means that he wants her to love him. She may even wonder whether his love includes respect and care, or whether his love is merely physical. "I love you" is surely an ambiguous message. The woman may come to the conclusion that his idea of love is not hers and therefore the kind of love he has to give would not make her happy. So in spite of his caresses and in spite of the fact that she enjoys the man, the woman . . . breaks off. . . . Everything depends on who says what to whom and how he says it, and human beings scan each others' utterances to see what lies behind the words. (Henry, 1965, p. 191)

W. I. Thomas also pointed to the subjective quality of reality in his famous statement, "If men define situations as real they are real in their consequences" (1928, p. 572). Thomas meant that reality, like beauty, lies in the eye of the beholder. By itself, a symbol or a gesture—for example, hitting one's hands together—is meaningless. It becomes significant only when people invest it with meaning—in this case, applause. When two people meet they bring their own meanings, their own definition of the situation. Social order exists to the extent that people approach one another with similar understandings and expectations and share a common definition of the situation.

Discovering the Rules: Ethnomethodology

Some sociologists have become interested in uncovering the implicit understandings and expectations that guide social behavior. *Ethnomethodology* refers to the study of the rules that underlie ordinary, everyday activities. (*Ethnos* is Greek for people; *meth* is a way of doing things.)

One ethnomethodologist, Harold Garfinkel, has devised a technique for uncovering these rules. His method is to discover the rules by *breaking* them (1967). For example, Garfinkel asked some of his students to pretend to be strangers on their next visit to their families. For fifteen minutes to an hour, the students maintained the polite distance of guests—speaking only when spoken to, using formal modes of address (Mr. Jones instead of Dad), avoiding personal exchanges. Two of the forty-nine families thought the students were joking; one ignored the student's behavior; the remainder were upset and annoyed. "Family members demanded explanations: What's the matter? What's gotten into you? Did you get fired? Are you sick? What are you being so superior about? Why are you mad? Are you out of your mind or just being stupid?" (pp. 47–48). In one way or another, the students' families tried to restore normal relations.

In other experiments, Garfinkel's students "made trouble" by attempting to bargain for items in a store (something Americans generally do not do); by breaking the rules in a game of tic-tac-toe (erasing the opponent's first move); and by closing in during a conversation so that they were nose-to-nose with the unsuspecting subject. Each of these violations of the rules of interaction produced confusion and often anxiety (in the students as well as in the "victim") and anger.

Garfinkel and the symbolic interactionists, then, do not deny that there are patterns in the way people relate to one another. Rather, they emphasize the point that "the established patterns of group life do not carry on *by themselves*" (Blumer, in Wallace, 1969, p. 237, italics added). Patterns exist because people bring similar meanings to situations, because they repeat behavior that has "worked" in the past, because it is generally easier to live within norms than to violate them. Social guidelines and habits free people from the impossible task of reviewing alternatives and making decisions every minute of their lives. The micro, interpersonal structure of society emerges from this process of defining situations, interpreting the acts of other people, and adjusting one's own behavior accordingly.

"The Presentation of Self" For sociologist Erving Goffman, many of our daily activities can be explained as the self-conscious effort to manage (that is, control) the impression we make on others. In part to keep up appearances and save face, in part to get what we want from situations. Examples of this abound. College athletes wear practice shirts with their team number to class and social gatherings; girls living in dormitories often wait to answer the phone until they've been paged several times, so that everyone within earshot knows they received a call (Waller, in Goffman, 1959, p. 4). Practically no one answers the phone on the first ring—it would appear overanxious. At the beginning of a semester students generally try to impress

professors with how bright they are. After exams, during the grading period, they may try to appear harried, even sick to evoke sympathy. In short, the way people act in public has an "on-stage" quality to it.

In the beginning of a romance, when man and woman are both a little unsure of how the other person perceives them, impressions become very important. In the following passage from Sylvia Plath's *The Bell Jar* (1971), Esther Greenwood, a shy studious freshman, receives her first kiss from Buddy Willard. Ecstatic, she strives to appear nonchalant.

I stood pretending to admire the lights behind the chemistry lab while Buddy got a good footing on the rough soil. While he kissed me I kept my eyes open and tried to memorize the spacing of the house lights so I would never forget them.

Finally, Buddy stepped back . . . "Wow, it makes me feel terrific to kiss you."

I modestly didn't say anything.

"I guess you go out with a lot of boys," Buddy said then.

"Well, I guess I do." I thought I must have gone out with a different boy every week for a year.

"Well, I have to study a lot."

"So do I," I put in hastily. "I have to keep my scholarship after all."

"Still, I think I could manage to see you every third weekend."

"That's nice," I was almost fainting and dying to get back to college and tell everybody. (pp. 67–68)

In most cases, the person or persons one tries to impress—the audience—will act as if the performance were real. There is an unspoken pact: you support my act and I will support yours. Violations, by actor or audience, lead to hostility and ostracism. Occasionally a person will work to create a negative or antisocial, eccentric impression. More often, however, people strive to live up to socially accepted ideals of behavior.

THE PATTERNS OF SOCIAL RELATIONSHIPS

Although most people think a lot about their relations with other people, few are aware of the structural regularities that underlie social interaction. Yet the same patterns emerge again and again. In the following pages, we will discuss four basic patterns of social relationships, common to individuals as well as to whole societies: *exchange*, *cooperation*, *competition*, and *conflict*.

Exchange

Gratitude is like mercantile credit. The latter is the mainstay of business; and we repay our debts, not because it is right that we should discharge them, but in order more easily to borrow again. (La Rochefoucauld, *The Maxims*)

When a person or a group assists another for the express purpose of obtaining some material or emotional reward—and both parties understand this—they are engaged in an exchange, not in exploitation. *Social exchange* is based on the principle of reciprocity; that people should both help and not injure people who have helped them. By extension, giving a gift or performing a service creates an obligation on the part of the recipient—one that may be repaid in kind, or simply with gratitude. As George Simmel wrote, "Often the subtlest as well as the firmest bonds among [people] develop from this feeling" (in Nisbet, 1970, p. 65).

Exchange is the most basic form of social interaction,

Social exchange can be observed everywhere once we are sensitized . . . to it, not only in market relations but also in friendship and even in love . . . as well as in many social relations between these extremes in intimacy. Neighbors exchange favors; children, toys; colleagues, assistance; acquaintances, courtesies; politicians, concessions; discussants, ideas; housewives, recipes. (Blau, 1964, p, 88)

These reciprocal transactions serve the important function of binding individuals and groups together with on-going networks of mutual obligations and gratitude.

Of course, social exchange is not always equal; love or respect may be one-sided. If one group in a society controls most of that society's resources, it may exercise unlimited power. Similarly, a person who extends assistance to someone who cannot reciprocate (but who does not refuse aid) places himself or herself in a superior position (Blau, in Nisbet, 1970, p. 66). But equal or unequal, exchange creates social bonds—between king and peasant, man and wife, the Senator from Maine and the Senator from Texas, officer and enlisted man, nation and nation. These links are crucial for the simple reason that many (if not most) of the things people need and value are scarce. And perhaps even more importantly, many are beyond the reach of individual effort.

Cooperation and Competition

Cooperation is one of several solutions to the problem of scarcity: people who recognize a common objective join forces to achieve their goal and share in the rewards. This is well illustrated by the net hunting once practiced by the Ik and neighboring East African tribes. As many as a hundred people would move out onto the plains together. Some would set up a wide arc of nets attached to poles. From an advance position, women and small children would begin beating the grass to force the game toward the

trap. Men and boys would wait with spears and bows and arrows—some within the net arc, some behind to catch the animals that escaped. Each member of the hunt shared equally in the day's catch (Turnbull, 1972, pp. 24–25). Net hunts were a tradition among the Ik; they had hunted this way for as long as anyone could remember.

The men and women in this Ghana village work together to bring in fishing nets which they have put into the Atlantic Ocean. Their catch will be used to feed their own families, and any extra fish will be sold on the beach. They work together because the nets are too heavy for one or two people to operate alone. A community effort is required for success. (Peter Buckley)

Nisbet distinguishes this kind of *traditional cooperation*, which carries the weight of custom, from directed, contractual, and spontaneous cooperation. By *directed cooperation* he means the kind of joint activity people in authority force on those beneath them (1970, pp. 68–69). For example, an officer commands enlisted men to take a hill; a teacher insists that children share the baseball diamond; the federal government directs American citizens to pay taxes. Deutsch (1949) directed cooperation when he divided a class of psychology students into five-member teams for a six-week course in problem-solving. He informed half the teams that individual grades would depend on what the *team* accomplished as a whole. Members of the other team were graded for individual achievement, the more common practice in American education. Deutsch found that students were more productive when they cooperated than when they competed with one another—at least on the tasks he assigned. But to generalize from this to the idea that cooperation is better than competition would be simplistic. We return to the question later in the chapter in the section on conflict.

Contractual cooperation is a limited, preplanned agreement to join forces in specific ways, for a specific period of time, to achieve specific goals. Unlike traditional cooperation, which is woven into a group's entire way of life, contractual cooperation is strictly utilitarian. According to exchange theorists, *all* cooperation is implicitly contractual, because the underlying question is, "What am I getting out of this? What am I giving?"

Of course, "the oldest, most natural, and widespread" form of cooperation is neither directed nor preplanned: it arises *spontaneously* when a situation seems to call for joint action. For example, during the northeast power blackout of 1965, New Yorkers helped to direct traffic; storeowners by and large resisted the temptation to raise the price of candles to meet the demand; and hotels opened their lobbies to stranded commuters.

This is not to say that crises always inspire cooperation. During the 1960s, for example, the Ik were forced off their game-rich plains (which were designated national parks and reserves) into the arid mountains above. Threatened with starvation they became extremely individualistic. No one shared food anymore; children were left to forage on their own; people literally took food from the mouths of the old and the sick. In his somewhat controversial analysis of "the sociology of survival" among the Ik, Colin Turnbull suggests that cooperation, brotherhood, and even love can only exist where people enjoy at least a minimal standard of living. Whether or not this is true, spontaneous cooperation does depend on the norms of reciprocity, on the capacity to imagine oneself in another's role, and on communication (a shared definition of the situation) (Nisbet, 1970, p. 67).

Competition, two or more parties striving individually for an objective that only one can achieve, is a second solution to the problem of scarcity. In competition only one person or group wins; only one person can be elected president; only one team can win the World Series; in our society a man may marry only one woman at a time.

On the surface competition appears to be the opposite of cooperation, but this is not really the case. Competition rests on a foundation of cooperation: rivals seek to *out*do, not *un*do, one another. In other words, competition, like cooperation, has its rules and limits. For example, oil companies compete for buyers by advertising how many services they provide at local stations. But, with rare exceptions, they avoid so-called price wars; when one company raises prices, the others do so also. Only when environmentalist groups began to exercise pressure did the oil and auto companies begin to run ads about their concern for ecology—and, again, they acted together. In other words, they compete only within narrow, well-defined limits.

Conflict

The difference between competition and conflict is the difference between a prize fight and a brawl. *Conflict* develops when two parties conclude (rightly or wrongly) that the only way to obtain a contested goal is to thwart, overpower, injure, eliminate, or otherwise neutralize the opposition. Conflict is unlimited: destroying the enemy becomes both the means and the end. The attempt to injure may be physical, as in wars, or symbolic, as when combatants wage a war of threats and insults (Turner, 1969, p. 823).

Common sense suggests that conflict is inherently disruptive and should be avoided at almost any cost. A logical assumption to be sure, but sociologically inaccurate. In fact, one of the primary functions of conflict is the stimulation of *cooperation* within opposing groups (Simmel, 1955). Struggles with outsiders invariably bring insiders closer together. As Georg Simmel notes, France owes its unity to the wars with England; Spain, to its battles against Moorish invaders; this country, originally to the War of Independence (p. 101). Similarly, students begin to think and act as a group when the administration suddenly raises tuition; families tend to draw together when one member is attacked.

Conflict may also define problems and revitalize norms and values that have fallen into disuse. For example, in the early 1950s relatively few white Americans were conscious of the extent to which blacks were being denied even the most basic civil rights: "[T]he shock of recognition, the jolt of conscience, occurred only when the Negroes, through by-

and-large nonviolent action in the South and through increasingly violent demonstrations in the North, brought the problem forcibly to the attention of white public opinion and the white power structure" (Coser, 1967, p. 86). Similarly, the shooting of student protestors at Kent State and Jackson State in 1970 exposed the more sinister implications of an all-out drive for law and order. Yes, a great many people saw student demonstrators as unwashed, ungrateful, un-American riffraff and supported politicians who said as much, but shooting and killing unarmed young people was another matter.

On a more personal level, conflict may revitalize relationships. "It has been said . . . that intimate relations, such as love and friendship, need occasional quarrels in order to be reminded of the happiness by the contrast with the discord they suffered; or in order to interrupt the closeness of the relationship—which, after all, has something coercive and enclosing for the individual—by an alienation which removes this pressure" (Simmel, 1955, pp. 110–11).

Conflict may also act as a catalyst for needed social change. After the race riots of the late 1960s both the McCone Commission appointed in California and the Kerner Commission appointed by President Johnson described the riots as more or less justified expressions of black outrage, and went on to recommend a "reordering of priorities" in America. In this sense, conflict can serve as a safety valve, bringing issues to the surface before they explode on a massive scale.

How are conflicts ended? When one party defeats the other; when one concedes; when both calculate that the costs of continued antagonism exceed the possible benefits of success and agree to a compromise; or when a sudden change in circumstances gives the two parties reason to forget their differences and join ranks. Surrender is always based on

Social conflict may expose previously unrecognized social patterns. For many people, the shooting of students at Kent State revealed the sinister implications of an all-out drive for law and order. (John Paul Filo)

the assumption that the victors will discontinue their attacks (Turner, 1969, p. 823). The Biafrans, for example, did not surrender for so long, even though they were threatened with extinction, because they did not believe the federal government of Nigeria would (or could) stop its troops from killing them.

Achieving a compromise is even more complex. By definition, conflicts involve irreconcilable goals and/or groups. As Ralph Turner writes, "agreement on [the] issues does not erase the injury that each has done to the other in the course of the conflict"

(p. 823). In essence, compromise depends on the willingness of each antagonist to act as if "the other did not fully mean what he said, that his threats were not really meant to be carried out, and that his insults did not express his most enduring feelings and views" (p. 824). There is an element of irrationality in compromise and accommodation, "something like a denial of what existed a moment before" (Simmel, 1955, p. 117). Soon after World War II, for example, the people we had been killing—the Germans and the Japanese—became our close allies.

Surrender or compromise will be unnecessary, if, by chance or design, irreconcilable parties suddenly find they have an enemy or a problem in common. Muzafer Sherif (1958) demonstrated this in a famous experiment at a summer camp for boys. He divided the campers into two teams, and by setting up competitions where only the winning team got prizes, by tricking one team into thinking the other had spoiled its food, and by other means, Sherif created an extremely volatile situation. (In fact, he and his colleagues found it difficult to prevent as real a war as ten-year-olds are capable of waging!) However, when the camp's water supply was cut off and when a group of boys from another camp were brought in for a day of sports, the teams forgot how much they hated each other and joined forces. Thus larger goals may turn enemies into collaborators, who then direct their energies against a new enemy.

SOCIAL INSTITUTIONS

Much of social life and social controversy centers around certain basic needs that confront all societies: (1) organizing activities so that people obtain the goods and services they need to live, while the society maintains a balanced relationship with the environment; (2) protecting people from external threats, such as military invasions, and from internal threats, such as crime; (3) replacing people who die or migrate; (4) transmitting norms and values to new members (children and immigrants); and (5) motivating people to fulfill their roles, to support the norms and values that define the meaning and purpose of life in a society. To some extent, solving these problems is a prerequisite for survival—survival of the people who make up a society and of their way of life.

Sociologists use the term *institution* to describe the relatively stable, widely accepted clusters of norms and values that develop around basic needs of a society. An example is the family, which is the center of a complex web of shoulds and should nots, ranging from the proper ways to feel and express sexual desire to norms defining responsibility for old people. The family is one solution to the problems of regulating sexual activity, replenishing the population, assigning responsibility for children and initiating them into the ways of a society, defining relationships between people in a community (the kinship system), and settling economic questions (such as inheritance). Religion and law sanctify and protect the family. It is one of the natural facts of life that people take for granted. To be sure, not everyone in our society grows up in the traditional nuclear family (a mother, a father, and their children all living together), and not everyone grows up wanting to marry and have children of their own. Still, the traditional idea of a family carries considerable moral weight. We saw in the discussion of *Tally's Corner*, for example, that fathers may desert their families because they cannot fulfill the traditional role of provider, and that relations between fathers and children are often tense for just this reason. Young and old couples living together without getting married, women demanding freedom from the home, easy divorce, easy sex, abortion, and the like would not be so controversial if the family were not a major social institution.

Institutions such as the family, religion, and political, educational, and economic systems channel human experience and activity in much the same way that instincts channel animal behavior (Berger, 1963, p. 87). They are the basic social structures, the ideas and customs around which life in a society is organized. (We will examine these institutions in later chapters.)

summary

Social structure refers to the pattern of collective rules, roles, and activities in a society. There are several ways to examine social structure. One way is to study the *micro-level* of social structure, the pattern of personal interactions that characterize everyday life. Another way is to look at the *macro-level* of social structure, the large social patterns that shape an entire society. In our examination of *Tally's Corner,* we concluded that while studying the micro-level of streetcorner society showed us how Tally and his friends related to each other and how they viewed themselves and their positions in life, it did not really explain their poverty and unemployment. For that kind of analysis and understanding, the larger aspects of social structure—including the educational system, the hierarchy of jobs and rewards, and racial discrimination—must all be taken into account.

Norms, status, and *roles* are the translation of social structure onto the personal level. *Norms* are the guidelines people follow in their relations with one another. They govern our emotions and perceptions and make social relations relatively predictable and orderly. A *status* is a position in the social structure that determines where a person fits in the community and how he or she should relate to other people. A status may be *ascribed* (assigned at birth or at different stages in the life cycle), or *achieved* (attained through personal effort). Status affects an individual's actions and how others act toward him or her because of the roles that each status carries. Social *roles* are the expected behavior patterns, obligations, and privileges that are associated with a status. *Role strain* may occur when conflicting demands are built into one role. *Role conflict* may occur when meeting the demands of one role automatically results in the violation of another.

The existence of roles, norms, and status raises the question of how free people actually are in a society. Robert Merton, expressing the *structuralist* point of view, insists that people's actions are largely the result of social pressure. We construct a self-image by comparing ourselves to members of groups to which we belong, groups with which we want to be affiliated, and to those from which we want to disassociate ourselves. *Symbolic interactionists* stress the situational character of social behavior, and view social interaction as a delicate process in which people constantly evaluate each other's behavior and react accordingly. Social order exists to the extent that people approach one another with similar understandings and expectations and share a common definition of the situation.

Symbolic interactionists focus on the way people behave in the ordinary course of everyday life, and try to discover the shared pattern of expectations that guide social behavior. One way to do this is through *ethnomethodology*: the study of the rules that underlie ordinary, everyday activities. Ethnomethodologist Harold Garfinkel tries to uncover these rules by breaking them and observing how people react when the behavior patterns they have come to take for granted are disrupted. For sociologist Erving Goffman, many of our daily activities can be explained as the self-conscious effort to manage (that is, control) the impressions we make on others.

Relationships between individuals, groups, and whole societies follow four basic patterns: exchange, cooperation, competition, and conflict. *Exchange* occurs when a person, group, or society assists another for the express purpose of obtaining some material or emotional reward. Another basic social relationship is *cooperation*, where those who recognize a common objective join forces to achieve their goal and share rewards. *Competition* describes a relationship in which two or more parties strive individually for an objective only one can achieve. Competition has rules and limits; parties seek to *out*do, not *un*do, one another. *Conflict*, however, is unlimited, and results when two parties conclude that the only way to obtain a contested goal is to somehow neutralize the opposition. Conflict may prove destructive, but it may also increase cohesion within a group, revitalize norms, or provoke needed change. Enemies may even become collaborators when they encounter a common threat.

Much social life and social controversy centers around certain basic needs that confront all societies—organizing activities for the acquisition of vital goods and services; protecting the members of the society from external and internal threats; replacing lost population; and motivating members of the society to fulfill their roles and support the society's norms and values. *Institutions* are the clusters of norms and values that form around the basic needs of a society. Institutions such as the family, religion, and political, educational, and economic systems are the basic social structures around which life in a society is organized.

glossary

achieved status A social position that a person attains through personal effort.

ascribed status A social position that is assigned to a person at birth or at different stages in the life cycle.

competition A social relationship in which two or more parties strive individually for an objective that only one can achieve.

conflict A social relationship in which two parties conclude that the only way to obtain a contested goal is to thwart, overpower, injure, eliminate, or otherwise neutralize the opposition.

contractual cooperation A limited preplanned agreement to join forces in specific ways, for a specific period of time in order to achieve specific goals.

cooperation A social relationship in which people recognize a common objective and join forces to achieve their goal and share in the rewards.

directed cooperation The kind of joint activity people in authority impose on those beneath them.

ethnomethodology The study of the rules that underlie everyday behavior.

exchange A social relationship in which a person or a group assists another for the express purpose of obtaining some material or symbolic reward.

institution The relatively stable, widely accepted cluster of norms and values that develop around the basic needs of a society.

macro-level of social structure The large social patterns that shape an entire society, including the hierarchy of jobs and rewards, patterns of prejudice and discrimination, and the educational system.

micro-level of social structure The pattern of personal interactions that defines everyday life.

mores Norms that are held very intensely, such as incest taboos.

norms The guidelines that people follow in their relations with one another; shared standards of desirable behavior.

role Expected behavior patterns, obligations, and privileges that are attached to a particular status.

role conflict Situations where fulfillment of one role automatically results in the violation of another.

role set The complex of roles that accrues to a single status.

role strain Personal difficulties that result when inconsistencies are built into a role.

social structure The pattern of collective rules, roles, and activities in a society.

status A position in the social structure that determines where a person fits in the community and how he or she is expected to act.

references

D. F. Aberle et al., "The functional prerequisites of a society," *Ethics*, vol. 80 (July 1949–July 1950): 100–111.

Peter L. Berger, *Invitation to Sociology*, New York: Doubleday, 1963.

Eric Berne, *Games People Play*, New York: Grove Press, 1964.

Peter Blau, *Exchange and Power in Social Life*, New York: Wiley, 1964.

Herbert Blumer, "Sociological implications of the thought of George Herbert Mead," *American Journal of Sociology*, vol. 17 (March 1966): 534–48. (Also in Wallace, 1969.)

Kenneth Clark, *Dark Ghetto: Dilemmas of Social Power*, New York: Harper & Row, 1965.

Lewis A. Coser, *The Functions of Social Conflict*, Glencoe, Ill: Free Press, 1956.

————, *Continuities in the Study of Social Conflict*, New York: Free Press, 1967.

Martin P. Deutsch, "Minority Group and Class Status as Related to Social and Personality Factors in Scholastic Achievement," *Society for Applied Anthropology*, Monograph no. 2, 1960.

Morton Deutsch, "An Experimental Study of the Effects of Cooperation and Competition upon Group Process," *Human Relations*, vol. 2 (1949): 199–231. (Also in Jones and Gerard, 1967.)

Carol R. Ember and Melvin Ember, *Anthropology*, New York: Appleton, 1973.

Amitai Etzioni, *The Active Society*, New York: Free Press, 1968.

Harold Garfinkel, *Studies in Ethnomethodology*, Englewood Cliffs, N.J.: Prentice-Hall, 1967.

Erving Goffman, *Presentation of the Self in Everyday Life*, New York: Doubleday, 1959.

————, *Behavior in Public Places*, New York: Free Press, 1964.

William J. Goode, "A theory of role strain," *American Sociological Review*, vol. 11 (1969): 483–96.

Jules Henry, *Pathways to Madness*, New York: Random House, 1965.

Herbert Hill, "Black Labor in the American Economy," in Patricia Romero, ed., *In Black America*, Philadelphia: United Publishing Corporation, 1969.

Christopher Jencks et al., *Inequality: A Reassessment of the Effect of Family and Schooling in America*, New York: Basic Books, 1972.

Edward E. Jones and Harold B. Gerard, *Foundations of Social Psychology*, New York: Wiley, 1967.

Elliot Liebow, *Tally's Corner: A Study of Negro Streetcorner Men*, Boston: Little, Brown, 1967.

S. L. A. Marshall, *Men Against Fire*, New York: Morrow, 1947.

Robert Merton, "Social structure and anomie," *American Sociological Review*, vol. 3 (1938): 672–82. (Also in Wallace, 1969.)

————, *Social Theory and Social Structure*, New York: Free Press, 1957.

Joe A. Miller and Louis Ferman, "Welfare Careers and Low Wage Employment," A Report Prepared for the Manpower Administration, U.S. Department of Labor, December 1973.

Robert A. Nisbet, *The Social Bond*, New York: Knopf, 1970.

John D. Owen, "The distribution of educational resources in large American cities," *Journal of Human Resources,* vol. 7 (1972): 26–38.

Sylvia Plath, *The Bell Jar,* New York: Harper & Row, 1971.

Muzafer Sherif, "Superordinate goals in the reduction of intergroup conflict," *American Journal of Sociology*, vol. 63 (1958): 349–56.

Georg Simmel, *Conflict and the Web of Group Affiliations*, New York: Free Press, 1955.

William I. Thomas and Dorothy Swaine Thomas, *The Child in America*, New York: Knopf, 1928.

Colin M. Turnbull, *The Mountain People*, New York: Simon & Schuster, 1972.

Ralph H. Turner, "The public perception of protest," *American Sociological Review*, vol. 34 (1969): 815–30.

Walter A. Wallace, ed., *Sociological Theory: An Introduction*, Chicago: Aldine, 1969.

Willard Waller, "The Rating and Dating Complex," *American Sociological Review,* vol. 2 (1937): 730.

for further study

The Micro-structure. Sociologists have done considerable work on the microstructure of social life, and since this level of analysis involves people directly interacting with each other, the perspective of the authors tends to be symbolic interaction. One of the greatest modern observers of micro-structure is Erving Goffman. See his books, *The Presentation of Self in Everyday Life* (Garden City, N.Y.: Doubleday, 1959) and *Behavior in Public Places* (New York:

Free Press, 1963). Another book discussing social interaction is *Defining the Situation* by Peter McHugh (Indianapolis: Bobbs-Merrill, 1968). Finally, two collections of essays on micro-structure are *Sociology and Everyday Life*, edited by Marcello Truzzi (Englewood Cliffs, N.J.: Prentice-Hall, 1968), and *People and Places: Sociology of the Familiar*, edited by Arnold Birenbaum and Edward Sagarin (New York: Praeger, 1973).

The Macro-structure. On the macro-level, social scientists have identified several different types of societies, and some think that the comparative analysis of whole societies is the only way to develop powerful concepts in sociology. Research in one country, they argue, is bound to mistake particular features for general patterns. Gerhard Lenski has recently analyzed differences between societies ranging from hunting and gathering groups to industrial social structures in *Human Societies* (New York: McGraw-Hill, 1970). Another analysis of macro-structures is Robert Marsh's *Comparative Sociology* (New York: Harcourt Brace Jovanovich, 1967).

Social Structure and Individual Behavior. Good studies of social life in one aspect or another provide excellent material for seeing what the social structure is and how it affects the people being studied. In this chapter we made this kind of analysis using *Tally's Corner*. Another good report for this kind of analysis is *The Police and the Public* by Albert J. Riess (New Haven: Yale University Press, 1971). Finally, *Lawyer's Ethics* by Jerome Carlin (New York: Russell Sage Foundation, 1966) unravels the social structure behind what most people think of as a personal matter—ethical behavior.

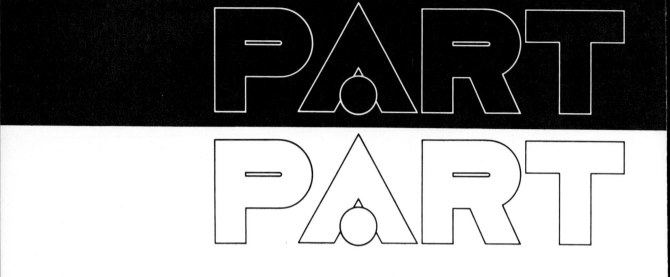

"That's Patty Baby and that's the girl with the dancing feet and that's Freddy Cannon there on the Dick Mickie Show in the night time ooohbah scuba-doo how are you boo-boo. Next we'll be Swinging on a Star and ssshhhwwoooo and sliding on a moonbeam. Waaaaaaa how about that . . . one of the goodest guys with you . . . this is lovable kissable D. M. in the P.M. at 22 minutes past nine o'clock there, aahrightie, we're gonna have a Hitline, all you have to do is call WAlnut 5-1151, WAlnut 5-1151, tell them what number it is on the Hitline" (McLuhan, 1964, p. 81). For most people, the word *culture* conjures up visions of people who attend the opera and ballet regularly, prefer Shakespeare to best sellers, have a taste for fine wine and food, and know their way around the capitals of Europe. It is a discriminating word, applied to discriminating people. Dick Mickie would hardly qualify.

For social scientists the tastes of the few yield only a clue to culture. Social scientists use the word *culture* to describe all of a people's shared customs, beliefs, values, and artifacts, including

CULTURE

everything from the Top Forty, car fads, and methods of housekeeping to science and art. In the words of anthropologist Ralph Linton, culture "refers to the total way of life of any society, not simply to those parts of this way which the society regards as higher or more desirable. . . . It follows that for the social scientist there are no uncultured societies or even individuals. Every society has a culture, no matter how simple this culture may be, and every human being is cultured, in the sense of participating in some culture or other" (1947, p. 30). The disc jockey, yelling and growling and moaning half coherently, is, from this perspective, as cultured as anyone else.

In this chapter we will focus on the seen and unseen elements of culture and consider reasons for the almost infinite variety of cultural expressions. We will also discuss the ways in which culture works for and against people, with particular attention to American culture.

THE ELEMENTS OF CULTURE

Much of what is known about culture comes from anthropological field studies of people whose ways are quite different from our own. In the field, anthropologists confront a dazzling array of unfamiliar objects and customs. They observe the way people design their villages and build their homes; they study their arts, the tools they make and how they use them. They analyze the family structure, economic transactions, and political organization. They listen to the villagers' tales, and watch children at play. Where possible they attend religious and other ceremonies. Gradually they begin to understand how the people think, what they expect from one another, and what they value.

One lesson of anthropology is that a people's material culture, the things they produce (*artifacts*), reflects the nonmaterial elements of their culture (their *norms, values,* and *beliefs*). It is no accident, for example, that the Oglala Sioux traditionally arrange their camp in a circle.

The Oglala believe the circle to be sacred because the great spirit caused everything in nature to be round except stone. Stone is the implement of destruction. The sun and the sky, the earth and the moon are round like a shield, though the sky is deep like a bowl. Everything that breathes is round like the stem of the plant. Since the great spirit has caused everything to be round mankind should look upon the circle as sacred, for it is the symbol of all things in nature except stone. It is also the symbol of the circle that makes the edge of the world and therefore of the four winds that travel there. Consequently it is also the symbol of the year. The day, the night, and the moon go in a circle above the sky. Therefore the circle is a symbol of these divisions of time and hence the symbol of all time.

For these reasons the Oglala make their *tipis* circular, their camp-circle circular, and sit in a circle at ceremonies. (Walker, in Dundes, 1968, p. 304)

Similarly, in modern America the automobile reflects a whole complex of core values: freedom, physical and social mobility, individuality *and* "keeping up with the Joneses," prosperity, and the supremacy of technology. Most teenagers look forward to becoming sixteen because they will be able to drive. (How the gasoline shortage will affect this aspect of American culture is an intriguing question.)

Norms, values, beliefs, art, and technology all play a part in that complex we call culture. The study of culture is the study of the meanings people attach to the things they do and the things they make. These meanings are stored in such symbols as the circle of the Oglala, the cross of Christians, the automobile, the flag, the handshake, and even the kiss.

Symbols

A *symbol* is an object, gesture, sound, color, or design that represents something *other than itself*. For example, a circle is really nothing more than a closed curve, all points of which are at an equal distance from a point at the center. But for the Oglala Sioux, the circle represents all that they know and feel and believe about the universe. Symbols are arbitrary—they do not necessarily look, sound, or otherwise resemble what they stand for. In some cultures black is the color of mourning; in others, white or red suggests grief. These colors, like all symbols, derive their meanings from tradition and consensus, not from any inherent qualities. Symbols are collective creations—people in a society must agree on their meanings if they are to be understood. A gold band worn on the third finger of someone's left hand tells us that he or she is married *only* because in our culture it is a commonly recognized symbol for marriage. Of course, even though a wedding band is commonly understood to mean the wearer is married, the way the wearer and each of us interprets that condition has become quite flexible. For some, it means a lifelong partnership and absolute fidelity; for others, a greater measure of sexual and emotional freedom may be implied. Symbolic interactionists (see chapter 3) argue that the heart of social life is the sharing, conflict, and manipulation of symbols.

Much human behavior and nearly all human communication is symbolic. You may recall how witness after witness at the Senate hearings on Watergate told of the inner certainty that any order coming from the White House was legal and in the national interest; of the awe they said they felt in the presence of "the leader of the free world," "the most powerful man on earth." The presidency,

Symbols are arbitrary. The V-sign for example may mean victory or peace, depending on who uses it and where. (UPI)

they claimed, overwhelmed them. And Lyndon Johnson, the story goes, used to become enraged when he had invited antiwar spokesmen to the White House, talked with them, and as far as he could tell reached an understanding, only to find the very same people renewing their attack the next day. Why? Because they had not dared in his presence to disagree with The President.

Because symbols are arbitrary, they are highly flexible: the meaning of words and gestures can and does change. For example, the two fingers held in a V, once a very rude gesture, came to stand for victory when Churchill used it (palm forward) during World War II. In the 1960s antiwar activists revived the gesture as a symbol for peace, and this in turn became a standard greeting among members of the counterculture. (Although it seems to have died from overexposure, the V gesture will probably reappear with some new meaning in the future.)

Language

A *language* is a system of verbal and, in many cases, written symbols, with rules for putting them together. It is impossible to overestimate the importance of language in the development, elaboration, and transmission of culture. Language enables people to store meanings and experiences and to pass this heritage on to new generations. Through words, we are able to learn from the experiences of others and from events at which we were not present. In addition, language enables us to transcend the here-and-now, preserving the past and imagining the future; to communicate with others and formulate complex plans; to integrate different kinds of experiences; and to develop abstract ideas.

The study of different languages has yielded numerous insights into culture. For example, the number of words available to describe an object, event, or concept in a language indicates how important it is to a people. Arabs, for example, have hundreds of words to describe camels and camel trappings, and almost as many to describe different kinds of horses. Eskimos have not one, but many words for snow. Water, a precious commodity in the arid Southwest, has numerous names in the Hopi language, as do yams in the Trobriand Islands (located north of New Guinea), where they are a staple. Similarly, Americans distinguish between sedans, station wagons, fastbacks, sports cars, convertibles, and compacts, suggesting the importance of automobiles in our culture. These words sensitize the individual Arab or Eskimo or Hopi or American to subtle variations that a person from a different culture might not even notice.

Language and Reality: The Sapir-Whorf Hypothesis Cross-cultural studies led Edward Sapir and his student Benjamin Lee Whorf to theorize that language doesn't simply reflect culture, it actually *shapes* our thoughts and directs our interpretation of the world.

[L]anguage is not merely a reproducing instrument for voicing ideas but rather is itself the shaper of ideas, the program and guide for the individual's mental activity, for his analysis of impressions, for his synthesis of his mental stock in trade. . . . We dissect nature along lines laid down by our native languages. The categories and types that we isolate from the world of phenomena we do not find there because they stare every observer in the face; on the contrary, the world is presented in a kaleidoscopic flux of impressions which has to be organized by our minds—and this means largely by the linguistic systems in our minds. (Whorf, in Carroll, 1956, pp. 212–13)

Whorf based this theory on his comparison of the way Hopi Indians and English-speaking people think and speak about time. There are no tenses in the Hopi language, as there are in English, and no nouns for times, days, or years. As a result, the Hopi tend to think in terms of continuous movement, of becoming. In contrast, the English language provides numerous ways of marking or counting time, as if hours and days were things or objects. The necessity to choose one of several tenses makes English-speaking people acutely conscious of time and of time passing. English-speaking people think in terms of linear progressions.

In our own culture, the line is so basic, that we take it for granted, as given in reality. . . . The line is found or presupposed in most of our scientific work. Our statistical facts are presented lineally as a *graph* or reduced to a normal *curve*. And all of us, I think, would be lost without our *diagrams*. We *trace* a historical development; we *follow the course* of history and evolution, *down* to the present and *up from* the ape. . . . And we . . . follow a *line* of thought, a *course* of action or the *direction* of an argument . . . we *bridge* a gap in the conversation, or speak of the *span* of life or of teaching a *course,* or lament our *interrupted career.* (Lee in Dundes, 1968, pp. 334–35)

Such a linear conception of reality is alien to people in the Trobriand Islands. Dorothy Lee offers this approximation of how a Trobriand Islander would describe the planting of a coconut:

THE POWER OF LANGUAGE

Does the generic use of the word *man* to denote human beings, male and female, perpetuate sexism? Writers use Man, with a capital M, when they want to sound grand, dignified, elegant. We speak of the average person as "the *man* in the street," and without thinking about it, link *he* to such high-prestige occupations as doctor and vice-president while using *she* with secretary and nurse. Men roar, bellow, and growl, whereas women squeal, shriek, and purr. Textbooks for young children paint a valiant picture of *man's* accomplishments; more often than not women are treated as luggage: "the pioneers crossed the Plains with their wives, children and belongings" (Farb, 1973, pp. 141–44).

Joseph W. Schneider and Sally H. Hacker's study (1973) of the effects of the generic usage of *man* is particularly relevant here because they have focused on sociology textbooks. Over three hundred students in introductory sociology courses were asked to select photographs from newspapers and magazines to help illustrate topics in a proposed text. Students were given one of two lists. One of the lists included Society, Urban Life, Political Behavior, Industrial Life, and Economic Behavior; the other substituted Social Man, Urban Man, Political Man, etc. Schneider and Hacker wanted to know if there would be any difference in the pictures students submitted for these topics.

The results? Approximately 64 percent of the pictures illustrating titles with the word *man* showed men only, compared to 50 percent of the pictures submitted for Society, Urban Life, and other sexless titles. Where women did appear, they were usually on the periphery of action (for example, sitting in an audience)—except in pictures for the topics labeled the Family, Population, and Social Man (which students apparently interpreted as Sociable Man). There were only a handful of women in the pictures for Crime and Delinquency. The researchers concluded that the generic use of man *does* perpetuate stereotyped images of men running the world.

SOURCE: Peter Farb, *Word Play*, New York: Knopf, 1973. Joseph W. Schneider and Sally H. Hacker, "Sex-Role Imagery and Use of the Generic 'Man' in Introductory Texts: A Case in the Sociology of Sociology," *The American Sociologist*, vol. 8 (1973): 12–18.

Thou-approach-there coconut thou-bring-here-we-plant-coconut thou-go thou-plant our coconut. This-here it emerge sprout. We-push-away this we-push-away this-other coconut-husk-fiber together sprout it-sit together root. (Lee in Dundes, 1968, p. 336)

To an English-speaking person, accustomed to thinking of events as having beginnings, middles, and ends, such an account is confusing. But to a Trobriand Islander, whose only connecting word is one meaning *jump,* the description is very realistic and clear. Trobrianders do not think about beginnings and ends; the present is all. They do not see pleasurable sensual experiences as having a climax, but as an aggregate of good sensations. When talking about the pleasures of sex, Trobrianders attach no particular significance to orgasm. At Trobriand feasts the dessert is not saved for the end but eaten along with the other dishes in a meal. Pregnancy is welcomed, not as a time of waiting, but as a beautiful thing in itself. The essence of Trobriand culture is the celebration of life as a state of being. Their language, which does not permit them to arrange events in a linear or chronological way, shapes that reality.

Silent Communication Anthropologist Edward T. Hall has extended Sapir and Whorf's theories about the role language plays in shaping thought to the study of *silent communication.* In his books *The Silent Language* (1959) and *The Hidden Dimension* (1966), Hall cites numerous examples of cultural differences in perception of time and space and sensory experience. For example, in public places Americans act as if they were alone. If an American is in a position to overhear a private conversation, he or she pretends to be deaf (often feigning involvement in a newspaper). Germans, in contrast, would never think of carrying on a private conversation in a public place; they wait until

they are behind closed doors (1966, chaps. 11 and 12). When Arabs talk they like to be right up close to the other person; Americans tend to maintain a social distance of a foot or more, except for very intimate exchanges. Hall concludes that people from different cultures not only speak different languages, they inhabit different sensory worlds, and their experience of life can, as a result, vary considerably.

Values and Norms

The Tangu, who live in a remote part of New Guinea, play a game called *taketak,* which in many ways resembles bowling. The game is played with a top that has been fashioned from a dried fruit and with two groups of coconut stakes that are driven into the ground (more or less like bowling pins). The players divide into two teams. Members of the first team take turns throwing the top into the batch of stakes; every stake the top hits is removed. Then the second team steps to the line and tosses the top into their batch of stakes. The object of the game, surprisingly, is not to knock over as many stakes as possible. Rather, the game continues until both teams have removed the *same* number of stakes. Winning is completely irrelevant (Burridge, 1957, pp. 88–89).

In a sense games are practice for "real life"; they reflect the values of the culture in which they are played. *Values* are the criteria people use in assessing their daily lives, arranging their priorities, measuring their pleasures and pains, choosing between alternative courses of action. The Tangu value equivalence: the idea of one individual or group winning and another losing bothers them, for they believe winning generates ill-will. In fact, when Europeans brought soccer to the Tangu, they altered the rules so that the object of the game was for two teams to score the same number of goals. Sometimes their soccer games went on for days! American games, in contrast, are highly competitive; there are *always* winners and losers. Many rule books include provisions for overtime and "sudden death" to prevent ties, which leave Americans dissatisfied. World Series, Superbowls, championships in basketball and hockey, Olympic Gold Medals are front page news in this country. In the words of the late football coach Vince Lombardi, "Winning isn't everything, it's the only thing."

Norms, the rules that guide behavior in everyday situations, are derived from values, but norms and values can conflict, as we indicated in chapter 3. You may recall a news item that appeared in American newspapers in December 1972, describing the discovery of survivors of a plane crash 12,000 feet in the Andes. The crash had occurred on October 13; sixteen of the passengers (a rugby team and their supporters) managed to survive for sixty-nine days in near-zero temperatures. The story made headlines because, to stay alive, the survivors had eaten parts of their dead companions. Officials, speaking for the group, stressed how valiantly the survivors had tried to save the lives of the injured people and how they had held religious services regularly. The survivors' explanations are quite interesting, for they reveal how important it is to people to justify their actions, to resolve conflicts in norms and values (here, the positive value of survival vs. the taboo against cannibalism). Some of the survivors compared their action to a heart transplant, using parts of a dead person's body to save another person's life. Others equated their act with the sacrament of communion. In the words of one religious survivor, "If we would have died, it would have been suicide, which is condemned by the Roman Catholic faith" (Read, 1974).

Similar conflicts in norms and values are bound to occur as we gain the ability to alter genes. The ability to modify unborn children's genes so that they grow up taller or darker or even smarter than their parents lies in the not very distant future. Already scientists have made genetic copies of carrots and frogs. This is done by cloning, a process that creates a duplicate organism from a single cell. What is there to prevent people from seeking immortality through one or more facsimiles of themselves? And if artificial wombs are perfected, will parents decide to reject their offspring on delivery if the child does not live up to their expectations? Tampering with life may go against our cultural grain, but self-improvement, on the other hand, is very strongly favored. The conflict between the two could create serious dilemmas.

These questions bring us to a crucial point about the elements of culture. A people's technology, art, language, norms, and values are closely intertwined. Culture influences all areas of life. The things people take for granted as right and good and as valuable and possible, the way they respond emotionally and intellectually to their lives ultimately depends on the culture in which they live.

UNITY IN DIVERSITY

What is more basic, more "natural" than love between a man and woman? Eskimo men offer their wives to guests and friends as a gesture of hospitality; both husband and wife feel extremely offended if the guest declines (Ruesch, 1951, pp. 87–88). The Banaro of New Guinea believe it would be disastrous for a woman to conceive her first child by her husband and not by one of her father's close friends, as is their custom.

The real father is a close friend of the bride's father. . . . Nevertheless the first born child inherits the name and possessions of the husband. An American would deem such a custom immoral, but the Banaro tribesmen would be equally shocked to discover that the first born child of an American couple is the offspring of the husband. (Haring, 1949, p. 33)

The Yanomamö of northern Brazil, whom anthropologist Napoleon A. Chagnon (1968) named "the fierce people," encourage what we would consider extreme disrespect. Small boys are applauded for striking their mothers and fathers in the face. Yanomamö parents would laugh at our efforts to curb aggression in children, much as they laughed at Chagnon's naïveté when he first came to live with them.

The variations among cultures are startling, yet all peoples have customs and beliefs about marriage, the bearing and raising of children, sex, and hospitality—to name just a few of the universals anthropologists have discovered in their cross-cultural explorations. But the *details* of cultures do indeed vary: in this country, not so many years ago, when a girl was serious about a boy and he about her, she wore his fraternity pin over her heart; in the Fiji Islands, girls put hibiscus flowers behind their ears when they are in love. The specific gestures are different but the impulse to symbolize feelings, to dress courtship in ceremonies, is the same. How do we explain this unity in diversity?

Cultural Universals

Cultural universals are all of the behavior patterns and institutions that have been found in all known cultures. Anthropologist George Peter Murdock identified over sixty cultural universals, including a system of social status, marriage, body adornments, dancing, myths and legends, cooking, incest taboos, inheritance rules, puberty customs, and religious rituals (Murdock, 1945, p. 124).

The universals of culture may derive from the fact that all societies must perform the same essential functions if they are to survive—including organization, motivation, communication, protection, the socialization of new members, and the replacement of those who die. In meeting these prerequisites for group life, people inevitably design similar—though not identical—patterns for living. As Clyde Kluckhohn wrote, "All cultures constitute somewhat distinct answers to essentially the same questions posed by human biology and by the generalities of the human situation" (1962, p. 317).

The way in which a people articulate cultural universals depends in large part on their physical and social environment—that is, on the climate in which they live, the materials they have at hand, and the peoples with whom they establish contact. For example, the wheel has long been considered one of humankind's greatest inventions, and anthropologists were baffled for a long time by the fact that the great civilizations of South America never discovered it. Then researchers uncovered a number of toys with wheels. Apparently the Aztecs and their neighbors did know about wheels; they simply didn't find them useful in their mountainous environment.

Adaptation, Relativity, and Ethnocentrism

Taken out of context, almost any custom will seem bizarre, perhaps cruel, or just plain ridiculous. To understand why the Yanomamö encourage aggressive behavior in their sons, for example, you have to try to see things through their eyes. The Yanomamö live in a state of chronic warfare; they spend much of their time planning for and defending against raids with neighboring tribes. If Yanomamö parents did *not* encourage aggression in a boy, he would be ill equipped for life in their society. Socializing boys to be aggressive is *adaptive* for the Yanomamö because it enhances their capacity for survival. "In general, culture is . . . adaptive because it often provides people with a means of adjusting to the physiological needs of their own bodies, to their physical-geographical environment and to their social environments as well" (Ember and Ember, 1973, p. 30).

In many tropical societies, there are strong taboos against a mother having sexual intercourse with a man until her child is at least two years old. As a Hausa woman explains,

A mother should not go to her husband while she has a child she is sucking . . . if she only sleeps with her husband and does not become pregnant, it will not hurt her child, it will not spoil her milk. But if another child enters in, her milk will make the first one ill. (Smith, in Whiting, 1969, p. 518)

Undoubtedly, people would smirk at a woman who nursed a two-year-old child in our society and abstained from having sex with her husband. Why do Hausa women behave in a way that seems so overprotective and overindulgent to us? In tropical climates protein is scarce. If a mother were to nurse more than one child at a time, or if she were to wean a child before it reached the age of two, the youngster would be prone to *kwashiorkor*, an often fatal disease resulting from protein deficiency. Thus, long postpartum sex taboos are adaptive. In a tropical environment a postpartum sex taboo and a long period of breast-feeding solve a serious problem (Whiting, in Goodenough, 1969, pp. 511–24).

No custom is good or bad, right or wrong in itself; each one must be examined in light of the culture as a whole and evaluated in terms of how it works in the context of the entire culture. Anthropologists and sociologists call this *cultural relativity*. Although this way of thinking about culture may seem self-evident today, it is a lesson that anthropologists and the missionaries who often preceded them to remote areas learned the hard way, by observing the effects their best intentions had on peoples whose way of life was quite different from their own. In an article on the pitfalls of trying to "uplift" peoples whose ways seem backward and inefficient, Don Adams quotes an old Oriental story:

Once upon a time there was a great flood, and involved in this flood were two creatures, a monkey and a fish. The monkey, being agile and experienced, was lucky enough to scramble up a tree and escape the raging waters. As he looked down from his safe perch, he saw the poor fish struggling against the swift current. With the very best intentions, he reached down and lifted the fish from the water. The result was inevitable. (1960, p. 22)

Enthnocentrism is the tendency to see one's own way of life, including behaviors, beliefs, values, and norms as the only right way of living. Robin Fox points out that "any human group is ever ready to consign another recognizably different human group to the other side of the boundary. It is not enough to possess culture to be fully human, you have to possess *our* culture" (1970, p. 31).

Accounts of the first European contacts with Africa are a study in enthnocentrism. The Greeks and Romans were acquainted with the Egyptians and the Carthaginians, the Libyans and the Ethiopians, but not until the fifteenth century did Europeans venture south of the Sahara. The letters and journals of fifteenth- and sixteenth-century explorers, merchants, and missionaries were popular reading in their day, and no wonder. Their tales overflowed with lurid descriptions of cannibalism, incest, and "unbridled lust."

Spreading our own customs around the world is a form of ethnocentrism. Here, a United States military Santa Claus delivers Christmas gifts to Yapese children. (Dorreen Labby)

Deep in the interior of the dark continent father "knew" daughter, sexuality ran rampant, people feasted on their friends and relatives (as well as their enemies). Religion, law, and government, reported the Europeans, were unknown. Any evidence of the great Sonniki dynasty in Ghana, founded in the second century A.D. (to name just one of the empires that flourished in African history) was overlooked. The following description is typical:

The majority of them . . . are entirely savage and display the nature of the wild beast . . . and are as far removed as possible from human kindness to one another; and speaking as they do with a shrill voice and cultivating none of the practices of civilized life as these are found among the rest of mankind, they present a striking contrast when considered in light of our own customs. (quoted by George, in Dundes, 1968, p. 25)

These accounts tell us a great deal more about what Europeans thought of human nature, left unfettered, than they do about African culture. Surveying the literature on Africans in the fifteenth and sixteenth centuries, Katherine George found only one favorable report, written by a Dutch visitor to South Africa.

I am astonished that . . . those half-truths that are spread about our [sic] Africans should have reached even your ears. I found this people . . . living in harmony with nature's law, hospitable to every race of men, open, dependable, lovers of truth and justice, not utterly unacquainted with the worship of some God, endowed . . . with a rare nimbleness of mother wit, and having minds receptive of instruction. . . . [I]t is through the faults of our own countrymen . . . that the natives have been changed for the worse. . . . From us they have learned . . . misdeeds unknown to them before, and, among other crimes of deepest die, the accursed lust for gold. (quoted by George, in Dundes, 1968, p. 32)

The history of race relations in this country suggests how far this observer was ahead of his times.

As conscious as Americans are of the shame of slavery, most have forgotten (or never knew about) the history of Oriental-Americans. In the mid-nineteenth century, Samuel Gompers, president of the American Federation of Labor and American Manhood Against Asiatic Coolieism, became famous for his attacks on Orientals. Why did he oppose "coolie" labor? Not because the Orientals, brought here to work on the railroads, threatened to take jobs away from Americans, but because—as everyone "knew"—Orientals are congenitally immoral. "The Yellow Man found it natural to lie, cheat and murder and 99 out of every 100 Chinese are gamblers," wrote Gompers. He went on to describe in intimate detail how the Chinese enticed little white boys and girls into their opium dens, where they remained, "condemned to spend their days in the back of laundry rooms, yielding up their virgin bodies to their maniacal yellow captors." Visions of the Mongolian hordes rising up to conquer the world lurked throughout the American West. In fact, Gompers was so successful that in 1902 Congress extended the Chinese Exclusion Act to quiet widespread fear of the "yellow peril." Although political motivation was substituted for racial epithets in the 1960s, the war in Southeast Asia was closely linked to ethnocentrism.

Cultural Integration

A people's customs, beliefs, values, and technology are *interdependent*. Changes in one area invariably affect other areas, sometimes throwing the entire system off balance. For example, missionaries succeeded in converting large numbers of Madagascans to Christianity. The result? Theft, which was practically unknown in the pre-Christian days, became commonplace; people stopped caring for their homes and villages. The reason? "The fear of hell and the police are a poor substitute for the fear of ancestral ghosts who know everything and punished the evil doer with sickness on earth and exclusion from the ancestral village in the hereafter" (Linton, 1947, p. 357).

Similarly, the introduction of steel virtually destroyed the highly integrated Stone Age culture of aboriginal societies in Australia. To the Europeans who brought them, steel axes were clearly an improvement over stone implements. But to the aborigines the ax was more than a tool: relations between families and tribes were based on the ceremonial exchange of cherished stonework (Arensberg and Niehoff, 1964, p. 50).

Cultural integration refers to the degree of internal consistency in a culture. In a well-integrated culture, there are few contradictions between the way people think and the way they act; established traditions enable them to make efficient use of the environment and to carry on the daily business of living with minimal inner conflicts. The Yapese, for example, once ruled the thousands of Caroline Islands that stretch across the western Pacific. Huge stone fish traps in the lagoons and a system of fresh water irrigation for taro patches (the Yap staple) enabled the island of Yap itself to support some 40,000 people in the nineteenth century. Women tended the gardens while the men fished. Men had special houses for their ceremonies and parties; women isolated themselves during menses and childbirth. The Yapese were divided into two classes, landowning chiefs and landless servants. Every family and every individual was ranked according to the property he owned.

Only a few old people on Yap remember this past. Yap was claimed by Spain in 1886, sold to Germany in 1899, captured by Japan during World War I, and lost to the United States in World War II. Today it is part of the American Trust Territory of the Pacific Islands, under mandate from the United Nations. The Yapese resisted Western ways for centuries and a visitor today may still see women in grass skirts and men in elaborate loin clothes. Nevertheless, Yap culture has given way to "a new set of material wants, needs, and satisfactions and a new set of social relations" (Labby, 1973, p. 35).

Motorboats have replaced outriggers, and the lagoons are polluted; villages in the interior have been abandoned along with yam and taro patches. The people depend on expensive imported food (paid for largely with income from scrap metal salvaged from the wrecked military equipment of World War II). The land-based hierarchy of social status has given way to a job-based hierarchy that centers on American employers. Old people, who disapprove of American ways, nevertheless encourage the young to seek jobs and education in the city of Colonia; but they feel cut off. Those young people who adhere to traditions do so only to please their grandparents. High rates of juvenile delinquency and drunkenness testify to the difficulty new generations are having in coping with the loss of old values, in finding new patterns of authority, and in maintaining a sense of identity in the midst of cultural confusion and change.

What do the Yapese tell us about culture? Does their example indicate that a well-integrated culture is good and that a poorly integrated one is bad? Not necessarily. In *The Study of Man* (1947), Linton notes that a highly integrated culture, where religious, economic, and family life are all of one piece, is extremely vulnerable. The Comanche were able to adjust to the ways of the white conquerors more easily than other Indian tribes precisely because their traditions were comparatively weak (pp. 364–65). Linton writes, "Cultures, like personalities, are perfectly capable of including conflicting elements and logical inconsistencies" (p. 358). We needn't go very far to illustrate this point, for American culture is truly a study in paradox.

AMERICAN CULTURE

Attempting to write the definitive profile of American culture is attempting the impossible. This country is unquestionably one of the most heterogeneous nations on earth. For every pattern one identifies, there will be myriad exceptions and contradictions. In addition, one of the dominant themes in our culture is change; it is Americans who have spread the gospel of progress around the world. Almost anything we say today will seem outdated next year. Nevertheless, certain basic orientations emerge, and certain forces of the past can be identified that are still active today. The portrait that follows describes these basic patterns. While it cannot possibly describe all the details, it does highlight the variations and contradictions in American culture.[1]

Basic American Values

We begin with the sacred triad American children learn in first grade: freedom, equality, and democracy. Polls indicate that Americans are far more likely than people of other nationalities to mention freedom and "our system of government" when asked what they are proud of in their country, and that the majority believe this *is* the land of opportunity (Williams, 1970, pp. 491, 478).

By freedom, Americans generally mean freedom *from* external controls, and freedom *to do* something in a manner they see fit (to pursue happiness, success, and so on). But the emphasis is on noninterference. There is a tendency "to think in terms of rights rather than duties, a suspicion of established (especially personal) authority, a distrust of central government, a deep aversion to acceptance of obvious coercive restraint . . ." (Williams, 1970, p. 480). This aversion can be seen in President Eisenhower's warnings about the military-industrial complex, in George Wallace's successful campaigns, in the vilification of the Establishment in the 1960s, in the generation gap and the concomitant rebellion against the constraints of traditional marriage. Indeed, the American system of checks and balances is based on a strong fear of tyranny. Whether the founding fathers feared the tyranny of one of their peers acting like a king, or the tyranny of the landless mobs beneath them is debatable. On the personal level, freedom means autonomy and voluntary isolation: each person or couple takes care of themselves.

[1] Many of the ideas here are drawn from Robin Williams, *American Society* (1970), chapter 11, "Values in American Society."

The cluster of values that center around the ideal of equality in American culture is very complex. On one level, equality connotes a belief in the inalienable rights of all, in the inherent dignity of all people. The celebration of the average person runs deep in America: people say, "I'm just an average, run-of-the-mill guy," with a hint of pride. A strong tradition of humanitarianism (for example, helping people recuperate from natural disasters), a tendency toward generosity, gregariousness, and informality are linked to the belief in equality. People think of this country as a haven for the downtrodden, and enjoy seeing the underdog triumph. On the other hand, Americans have never interpreted the word equality to mean equality of condition: the idea of leveling, of equal distribution of wealth, arouses a fear of governmental control. Rather, Americans take equality to mean that every individual has (or should have) an equally good position at the starting gate. The fact that some horses start the race lame has, until recently, been ignored.

Racism, which surely is as American as apple pie, is problematic for just this reason. Americans in general are highly ethnocentric—both in the sense of seeing the United States as "bigger and better," and in clinging to their "own kind" within the country. At the same time, however, Americans go to considerable lengths to deny prejudice and discrimination. (We hasten to add "without regard for race, creed, color, national origin," and most recently, "sex," to every statement. In the want ads, companies now print "equal opportunity employer" in bold type.) This conflict between equality and discrimination is but one of the contradictions built into American culture (see Myrdal, 1944).

The word *democracy* is conspicuously missing from the Constitution; nevertheless, this document symbolizes democracy to most Americans and to people throughout the world. The protection of individual rights (principally from government infringements) and of private property, rule by law (as distinguished from personal rule), and faith in the electorate are all part of the democratic creed. Every school child is taught to respect Patrick Henry's plea for liberty or death, and each July Fourth evokes new speeches celebrating the freedoms guaranteed by the Constitution.

Yet, the results of a national survey indicate that many Americans favor curbs on some of the basic tenets of the Bill of Rights (see the accompanying box).

Another survey found that six out of ten young Americans believe that this society is democratic in name only, with most of the power residing in special interest groups (Yankelovich, 1973). Nevertheless, the word

---

HOW MUCH DO WE VALUE FREEDOM?

The majority of Americans seem willing to restrict some of the basic freedoms constitutionally guaranteed by the Bill of Rights. Specifically, about three-fourths (76 percent) of the 1,136 people interviewed in the nationwide CBS News telephone survey [March 10–12, 1970] believe extremist groups should not be permitted to organize *demonstrations* against the government, even if there appeared to be no clear danger of violence. Moreover, . . . over one-half of the people (54 percent) would not give everyone the right to *criticize* the government, if the criticism were thought to be damaging to our national interest; and, a comparable number (55 percent) feel newspapers, radio, and television should not be permitted to *report* some stories considered by the government to be harmful to our national interests (wartime censorship was excluded in the question).

Two additional freedoms that people would restrict involve "double jeopardy" and "preventive detention." In the case of the former, nearly three out of every five adults (58 percent) feel that if a person is found innocent of a serious crime, but new evidence is uncovered after the trial, he should be *tried again*. In the case of the latter, three out of every five adults (58 percent) also feel that if a person is suspected of a serious crime, the police should be allowed to *hold* him in jail until they can get enough evidence to charge him with the crime. [Note the date of this poll, 1970, following the turbulence of the sixties and Richard Nixon's presidential campaign of 1968, which was conducted on a platform of "law and order."]

On the other hand, other constitutional guarantees involving the judicial process appear to be so deeply embedded in our way of life that Americans emphatically uphold them. In particular, four out of five people (82 percent) feel that guilt or innocence in a criminal case should be decided by a *jury*, not by the judge alone; three out of four (75 percent) believe that the government should never be allowed to hold a *secret trial*; and two out of three (66 percent) feel that the police should not be allowed to enter someone's home without a *search warrant* even if they suspect that drugs, guns, or other criminal evidence is hidden there.

Less strongly, but nonetheless acceptable to most people, are the rights of defendants in criminal cases to avoid self-incrimination and to confront witnesses against them. In both cases, more than one-half of the people (54 percent) feel that the individual should have the right to *refuse to answer* questions if he feels his answers may be used against him, and that the prosecution should never be allowed to keep the *identity of witnesses* secret during a trial.

SOURCE: Robert Chandler, *Public Opinion: Changing Attitudes on Contemporary Political and Social Issues*, New York: Bowker, 1972, pp. 5–6.

democracy still carries sacred overtones in this country.

Put together, this triad—freedom, equality, and democracy—leads to two very different brands of patriotism. On the one hand, there are those who, believing this country has been good to them, define all criticism and protest as un-American (by which they mean treasonous). This American-first-ism, with its emphasis on rituals and symbols (the sacred flag), its inquisitions (the McCarthy hearings, for example), and its unquestioning loyalty, approaches the level of a religion. On the other side, there are those who see unquestioning loyalty as antithetical to freedom and democracy, and count criticism and protest among the citizen's moral obligations. For example, the most militant critics of the war in Southeast Asia—those who refused the draft, left the country, renounced their citizenship—defended their actions by pointing to violations, which they maintain were committed by the American government, of the principles of freedom, democracy, self-government, and humanitarianism. The American government had lost legitimacy in their eyes, but their allegiance to American ideals motivated their behavior.

"The business of America is business," said Calvin Coolidge, and indeed, Americans value success the way other people value holiness, family, or military prowess. Success is our primary measure of self-worth.

The comparatively striking feature of American culture is its tendency to identify standards of personal excellence with competitive occupational achievement. . . . The value attached to achievement does not comprehend the person as a whole but only his accomplishments, emphasizing the objective results of his activity. Because of the preoccupation with business, the most conspicuous achievements have been centered in business enterprise. (Williams, 1970, pp. 454–55)

Such expressions as "business is business," and the persistence of organized crime and the relative toleration of white-collar crime indicate the extent to which Americans suspend other values in their admiration of people scrambling for success. In addition to its practical significance, wealth has symbolic significance in this country, for it is one of the only measures of personal merit.

The rugged individualism of American culture finds its fullest expression in occupational competition. We still enjoy rags-to-riches stories; the idea that anyone who works hard and takes advantage of his opportunities can make it to the top dies hard. The problem is, of course, that in reality there is not much room at the top. This is the darker side of the American dream. The myth that any boy who tries can grow up to be president implies that there is something *wrong* with those who do not.[2] Success and failure are personalized to an enormous degree in American culture; the individual who does not rise above his origins has only himself to blame. To be sure, many Americans are content with their work and their standard of living, but many others are haunted by a sense of personal inadequacy. Success in the land of unlimited opportunity is as elusive as the carrot on the stick dangling one foot beyond the proverbial donkey's nose. "The competitive life is a lonely one, and its satisfactions are very short-lived, for each race leads only to a new one" (Slater, 1970, p. 6).

Closely related to the achievement syndrome is the belief that work is a good thing in and of itself.[3] Contemporary Americans have inherited their respect for purposeful activity from the Puritans, who endowed hard work and frugality with religious overtones and believed worldly success was a sign of grace.

---

[2] We refer to boys here purposely. For girls, the American dream has been to marry the man at the top.

[3] Again, we must qualify this by saying that no one places much value on menial jobs, such as street cleaning or house cleaning.

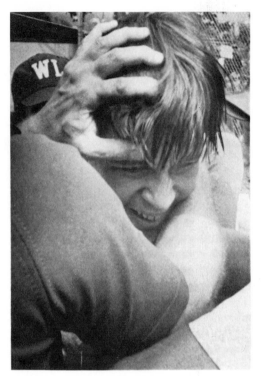 

Winning and losing characterize much of American life. From an early age, children prepare for the rigorous competition of adulthood. (UPI)

According to a poll conducted in 1964, 80 percent of laborers said they would continue working even if they were able to maintain their current standard of living without a job (Williams, 1970, p. 461). During the 1960s student protests, hippie attire, sexual freedom, and the call for new life-styles led many people to conclude that American youth were abandoning traditional values and social norms, including the work ethic. But the results of a nationwide survey of attitudes and values among American youth, conducted by Daniel Yankelovich in 1973, present a less clear-cut picture. The accompanying box reveals the way college youth feel about the work ethic. (Throughout this book, we will

return to this survey to discover the way young people feel about life in American society, and in chapter 19 we will summarize the new values of American youth.)

A practical people, Americans value innovation and efficiency—which has often meant "single-minded attainment of a goal or accomplishment of a task, with minimal attention to attendant costs, injuries, or disruptions outside the narrow zone of immediate attention" (Williams, 1970, p. 466). The pollution of our air and water in the name of progress testifies to this. However, it would be foolish to ignore the positive effects of pragmatism in medicine, for example. Americans have made dramatic advances in extending the science of curing.

The cult of progress is closely intertwined with the idea that science can and eventually will overcome all natural and man-made difficulties—an extraordinarily optimistic position, if you stop to think about it. The idea that some natural, social, and psychological phenomena are beyond rational comprehension, that some things happen for no reason at all, disturbs most Americans. Witness, for example, the numerous task-force reports commissioned by the federal government, or the heavy reliance of the Kennedy and Johnson administrations on experts during the war in Southeast Asia. Even when Pentagon calculations were proving highly inaccurate, no one apparently raised the possibility that political behavior cannot always be measured and qualified.

We said earlier that values are the criteria people use in assessing their daily lives and in choosing between alternative courses of action. It is likely, then, that the conflicts between social conscience and competitiveness, equality and racism, the myth of opportunity and the realities of stratification—to name just a few—all contribute to a restless undercurrent in American culture.

**COLLEGE YOUTH
AND THE WORK ETHIC**

79 percent believe that commitment to a meaningful career is "very important," *but* 30 percent would welcome less emphasis on working hard.

85 percent agree that business is entitled to make a profit, *but* 94 percent feel the business community puts profits too far ahead of social responsibility, and 54 percent believe business should be overhauled or eliminated.

67 percent maintain that "private property is sacred" and 62 percent say that "competition encourages excellence," *but* less than half (44 percent) agree that "hard work will always pay off."

SOURCE: Yankelovich Youth Study ©1973 by the JDR, 3rd Fund.

Subcultures

Another reason for the inconsistencies and exceptions in American culture is that this country includes a wide range of subcultures. When a group's perspective and life-style are significantly different from other people's in their culture, and when they define themselves as different, we say they belong to a *subculture*. Members of a subculture share a set of norms, attitudes, and values that give them a distinct identity within the dominant culture. Subcultures may develop in occupational groups, ethnic or religious groups, socioeconomic groups, or age groups. Adolescents, for example, build a private world out of their peculiar position as not-quite-adults and no-longer-children; medical students share common experiences, goals, and problems, and hence a common viewpoint. Subcultures grow among people who are isolated together from the conventional world—isolated physically (adolescents in school, inmates in prison, soldiers on a base, or poor people in a ghetto), or isolated by what they do and think, by their world of meanings.

Jazz musicians are a perfect example of the subculture. Although often called *the* American art form, jazz has never gained the respect or popularity in this country that it has enjoyed in Europe. Blues, Dixieland, ragtime, and other schools of jazz were once considered just "whorehouse music," something nice people looked down on (Mezzrow and Wolfe, 1972, p. 51). Pianist Eubie Blake, for example, tells how his mother threw him out of the house when he was about six because she heard him playing *that* music. Even today, beyond a relatively small cult of admirers, jazz is usually linked to rock and other pop music, as opposed to so-called serious music—a custom that spurred trumpet player Dizzy Gillespie's comment, "What do they think we're doing up there, kidding?"

Jazz musicians, part of a unique American subculture, prefer to "play what they feel" rather than catering to commercial interests. (UPI)

Howard S. Becker, a sociologist who doubled as a dance-hall pianist when he was in college, studied the jazz world in the late 1940s and published his observations in *The Outsiders* (1963, chaps. 5 and 6). With few exceptions, the people Becker met had become musicians against the wishes of their families—jazz not being an altogether respectable profession in the estimation of most people. Although many of the musi-cians had married, their hours (usually 9 P.M. to 3 or 4 A.M.), frequent traveling, generally low pay, and chronic job instability (except for the very few at the top) made family life problematic. As a subculture, jazz musicians contribute to the variety in American culture. Typically, this group places little emphasis on the American dream of wealth and suburban success, but they are very tolerant of in-dividual differences. Jazz players think of their music as art—an attitude the public generally does not share. But it is this public who, by their patronage, control the musi-cian's livelihood. Jazzmen inevitably find themselves forced to choose between "playing what they feel" and thereby earning the respect of their peers (but little "bread") and "playing what the people want to hear" and perhaps losing their own self-respect.

In reaction to this uncomfortable dilemma, musicians practice what Becker calls "self-segregation." They tend to be suspicious of and often hostile toward the music-consuming public and toward the conventional world in general. At the same time, they are inclined to be extremely tolerant of their own. It is a rule among jazz musicians, for example, never to criticize a fellow player's music or life-style, whatever you think of it. Eccentricity, flouting convention, a devil-may-care approach are highly valued among players, whom Becker found to be self-styled outsiders.

People who engage in activities that are unusually demanding, isolating, unconventional, rebellious, or highly specialized often invent a language of their own—a jargon or argot. Jazz musicians are no exception:

I'm standing under the Tree of Hope, pushing my gauge. The vipers come up, one by one.

First Cat: Hey there Poppa Mezz, is you anywhere?
Me: Man, I'm down with it, stickin' like a honky.
First Cat: Lay a trey on me, ole man.
Me: Got to do it, slot. (*Pointing to a man . . .*) Gun the snatcher on your left raise—the head mixer laid a bundle his ways, he's posin' back like crime sure pays.
First cat: Father grabs him. I ain't payin' him no rabbit. Jim, this jive you got is a gasser. I'm goin' up to my dommy and dig that new mess Pops laid down for Okeh. I hear he rifled back on Zakly. Pick you up at The Track when the kitchen mechanics romp.

Translation:

I'm standing under the Tree of Hope, selling my marijuana. The customers come up one by one.

First Cat: Hello Mezz, have you got any marijuana?

Me: Plenty, old man, my pockets are full as a factory hand's on payday.
First Cat: Let me have three cigarettes (fifty cents' worth).
Me: I sure will, slotmouth [a private interracial joke]. Look at the detective on your left—the head bartender slipped him some hush money, and he's swaggering around as if crime *does* pay.
First cat: I hope he croaks [dies], I'm not paying him even a tiny bit of mind. [Literally, "father grabs him" suggests that the Lord ought to snatch the man and haul him away; and when you "don't pay a man no rabbit," you're not paying him any more attention than you would a rabbit's butt as it disappears hurriedly over the fence.] Friend, this marijuana of yours is terrific. I'm going home and listen to the new record Louis Armstrong made for the Okeh company. I hear he did some wonderful playing and singing on the number *Exactly Like You*. See you at the Savoy ballroom in Harlem on Thursday. [That is, the maid's night off when all the domestic workers will be dancing there.] (Mezzrow[4] and Wolfe, 1972, pp. 187, 316)

In-words and usages, as the passage above suggests, serve multiple purposes: they pin down ideas that are only vague in everyday language; describe events and experiences for which no word exists; promote in-group solidarity; and keep outsiders out. As Becker points out, hip talk expresses new meanings, conceals meanings, and makes the speakers feel separate from other groups. For example, there is no dictionary synonym for "square," a word Becker found jazz musicians used to describe most, if not all, non-musicians. The word connotes ignorance, intolerance, conventionality, and a general lack of enlightenment. Other words in the jazz-

---

[4] Mezz Mezzrow, a white jazz musician from Chicago, carried on a lifelong love affair with black music and life-styles. He was, in the words of his coauthor, a "Negrophile." When Mezzrow was dealing marijuana in Harlem, he earned a reputation for having the best grass around. The word *mezz* came to stand for the very tops; the word *mezzroll*, for a fat, well-packed joint.

man's lingo—"gig," "bread," "gauge"—do have everyday equivalents—a job, money, marijuana—but they do not have that special quality of in-words that enhances a musician's feelings of being special and different. And, as Harold Finestone writes, the earthy colorful terms of hip talk convey "an attitude of subtle ridicule towards the dignity and conventionality in the common usage" (1957, p. 4).[5] The jazz world, with its own view of reality and its private jargon, is but one of the subcultures that flourishes on American soil, giving our culture its complex and heterogeneous flavor.

CULTURE AGAINST PEOPLE

After all that we have said in this chapter, the phrase "culture against people" would seem to be a contradiction in terms. How can

---

[5] Interestingly, much hip talk has found its way into mainstream slang; most Americans know what "square" and "bread" mean. Other hip words, however, have remained in-words—for example, "ofay," which means white and comes from pig-latin for "foe." Some have taken on new meanings: musicians formerly used the word "hippie" to describe people who thought they were hip, but weren't.

Old people, once useful and respected in traditional Japanese culture, are being forgotten in the new technological society. (Fred Ward/Black Star)

culture be against the people who create it, who live in and by it? In Jules Henry's view, people have been so preoccupied with finding ways to feed and protect themselves, "inner needs have scarcely been considered. . . . [This orientation] toward survival, to the exclusion of other considerations, has made society a grim place to live in, and for the most part human society has been a place where, though [people have] survived physi-cally [they have] died emotionally" (1965, pp. 11–12).

Sigmund Freud, too, believed that discontent was built into the human condition, that the conflict between the individual and society would never be completely resolved. He questioned the possibility of people ever finding satisfaction. Freud argued that by nature, people are egocentric, irrational, antisocial: without coercion, we would never

---

IN THE NEWS

Fight Pollution and Feed the World: Use Manure

Pollution and food shortages, two of the severest problems facing people throughout the world, may be eased considerably by a new use for an old product—manure. Cattle waste, recycled to produce animal feed, has been hailed as "an agricultural milestone that could substantially reduce a growing world protein shortage, transform the beef raising industry, virtually eliminate animal feed lot pollution and lower meat prices."

Cattle in feed lots produce some 600 million tons of manure a year, but hardly anyone has wanted manure since synthetic fertilizers became popular.

Researchers for the United States Department of Agriculture estimate that the protein extracted only from this feed-lot manure would equal the protein contained in this country's total yearly soybean crop.

The soybean is the leading source of plant protein and the United States grows 75 percent of the world's supply. It is the chief protein source in animal feed in this country and in human food in poor countries.

Even partly replacing soybean meal with manure-derived feed in farm animal diets would greatly increase the amount of soybean protein left over for people. And as soybean prices rise, it may become uneconomical to use them for animal feed.

For the food industry, which Ralph Nader has called one of the most polluting in the country (because of animal wastes), this new use for manure solves two problems at once. The recycling process, developed by an economist and a nutritionist "converts the manure to protein feed simply, cheaply and without pollution." Not only can cattle raisers rid their feed lots of polluting manure, they can also purchase its protein-rich by-product at a considerable savings over the cost of traditional feed. The one snag in the process is "image." Will cattle-raisers and consumers accept recycled manure as a protein-source for their steaks and chops? A traditional value—waste not, want not—may be called upon to increase public acceptance of the new product, but with a new twist—waste yes, want not.

SOURCE: James P. Sterba, "Cattle Fed From Own Waste to Cut Protein Shortage," *The New York Times* (September 9, 1973), pp. 1 and 40.

consent to the "instinctual sacrifices" that are necessary in any social order (1961, pp. 6–7). However, he believed that overcivilization—the complete subjection of the self to social demands—was destructive. People can become neurotic when they give up too many of their desires and impulses.

The question today seems to be whether the conflict between individuals and society isn't "escalating," whether in our expansiveness we haven't created a cultural monster that will ultimately destroy love, quietness, and fun. Mental illness and crime flourish in big cities, and it is difficult to forget how thirty-eight people sat silently by as a woman was stabbed to death in New York in 1964. Social and physical mobility have cut people off from the families and communities that once gave them a sense of who they were. The pace of technological change continues to accelerate. Increasingly we live by the rhythms of machines, whose pace and timing bear little relation to human rhythms. In W. H. Auden's words:

> . . . this stupid world where
> Gadgets are gods and we go on talking,
> Many about much, but remain alone,
> Alive but alone, belonging—where?
> Unattached as tumbleweed.[6]

Yet, if people have the ability to create cultural problems, they also have the ability to solve them. Our values, of course, will affect how and if we choose to seek solutions. In the remaining chapters, we will consider many of the problems in American society, as well as some possible solutions.

---

[6] From W. H. Auden, *The Age of Anxiety* (New York: Random House, 1948), p. 44.

---

summary

Culture describes all of a people's shared customs, beliefs, values, and artifacts. The study of culture is the study of the meanings people attach to the things they do and the things they make. These meanings can be found in studying the various elements of a culture: material goods as well as symbols, norms, and values.

A *symbol* is an object, gesture, sound, color, or design that represents something other than itself. Much human behavior, and nearly all human communication, is symbolic. Symbols only have significance in a culture if their meaning is commonly agreed upon.

Studying the language of a people can yield many insights into their culture. For example, if there are a number of words available to describe an object, event, or concept, this is a clue to its importance in the culture. Language can also tell us about a people's view of reality. Sapir and Whorf have theorized that language doesn't simply reflect culture, it actually *shapes* our thoughts and directs our interpretation of the world. They compared the way time is denoted in the Hopi language and in English and found that there are no tenses in the Hopi language. The Hopi speak and think of time in terms of continuous movement, whereas English, with its numerous tenses, makes people acutely conscious of time and of time passing. Edward Hall extended the Sapir-Whorf hypothesis to the study of *silent communication* and concluded that people from different cultures not only speak different languages, they also inhabit different sensory worlds. For example, in social conversations Americans tend to maintain a distance of a foot or more, while Arabs like to be right up close to the person they are talking to.

Values are the criteria people use in assessing their daily lives, arranging their priorities, measuring their pleasures and pains, and choosing between alternative courses of action. One way of examining values is to study the games that people in a society play, for the games reflect the values of the culture in which they are played. *Norms*, the rules that guide behavior in everyday situations, are derived from values, and vary from culture to culture. Norms and values can conflict, as shown in the experience of survivors of an Andes plane crash who resorted to cannibalism in order to stay alive.

Although the details of culture vary from society to society, anthropologists have identified many *cultural universals*—behavior patterns and institutions that are found in all cultures. Cultural universals exist because all societies must fulfill the same basic needs to survive. But the way these universal patterns are articulated depends on the society's physical and social environment. Culture is adaptive—it provides people with a means of adjusting to the physiological needs of their own bodies and to their physical, geographical, and social environments.

When social scientists study culture, they evaluate customs and beliefs not on individual moral grounds, but in light of the culture as a whole and in terms of how they work in the context of the entire culture. This way of thinking about culture is called *cultural relativity*. In contrast, *ethnocentrism* is the tendency to see one's own ideas, beliefs, and practices as being the only civilized way of living. *Cultural integration* refers to the degree of internal consistency in a culture. A people's customs, beliefs, values, and technology are interdependent, and changes in one area invariably affect other areas.

American culture is riddled with inconsistencies and exceptions even in terms of the basic values we hold. Our core values of freedom, equality, and democracy contain contradictions that can lead to much confusion and disquiet. The disparities between social conscience and competitiveness, equality and racism, the myth of opportunity and the realities of economic and social stratification all contribute to a restless undercurrent in American society. One reason for the variations in American culture is the wide range of *subcultures*—groups whose perspective and life-style are significantly different from the cultural mainstream, and who define themselves as different. Members of a subculture share a set of norms, attitudes, and values that give them a distinctive identity. Members of a subculture may also share a language of their own—a *jargon*. This *jargon* pins down ideas that are only vague in everyday language; it may describe events and experiences for which no words exist in the conventional language; it promotes in-group solidarity; and it keeps outsiders out.

Culture, as Americans seem to be finding out, can also work against people. Mental illness and crime flourish in big cities, social and physical mobility have separated people from the strong community ties they once had. Yet if people have the ability to create destructive cultural elements, they also have the ability to create constructive elements.

glossary

artifacts The elements of a people's material culture.

cultural integration The degree of internal consistency within a culture.

cultural relativity The doctrine of examining a custom in light of the culture as a whole and of evaluating it in terms of how it works in context, not in terms of right or wrong.

cultural universals The behavior patterns and institutions that have been found in every known culture.

culture All of a people's shared customs, beliefs, values, and artifacts.

ethnocentrism The tendency to see one's own way of life, including behavior, beliefs, values, and norms, as the only "right" way of living.

jargon The specialized language of a subculture.

norms Rules that guide behavior in everyday situations. Norms vary from culture to culture.

subculture A group whose perspective and lifestyle are significantly different from those of other groups or individuals in their culture, and who define themselves as different.

symbol Anything that represents something other than itself, including objects, gestures, colors, designs or words.

values The criteria people use in assessing their daily lives, arranging their priorities, measuring their pleasures and pains, and choosing between alternative courses of action.

references

Don Adams, "The Monkey and the Fish: Cultural pitfalls of an educational advisor," *International Development Review*, vol. 2 (1960): 22–24.

Conrad M. Arensberg and Arthur H. Niehoff, *Introducing Social Change*, Chicago: Aldine, 1964.

W. H. Auden, *The Age of Anxiety*, New York: Random House, 1948.

Howard S. Becker, *The Outsiders: Studies in the Sociology of Deviance*, New York: Free Press, 1963.

Kenelm O. L. Burridge, "A Tangu Game," *Man*, vol. 57 (1957): 88–89.

John B. Carroll, *Language, Thought, and Reality: Selected Writings of Benjamin Lee Whorf*, Cambridge, Mass.: MIT Press, 1956.

Napoleon A. Chagnon, *Yanomamö: The Fierce People*, New York: Holt, Rinehart and Winston, 1968.

Alan Dundes, *Every Man His Way: Readings in Cultural Anthropology*, Englewood Cliffs, N.J.: Prentice-Hall, 1968.

Carol R. Ember and Melvin Ember, *Anthropology*, New York: Appleton, 1973.

Peter Farb, *Word Play*, New York: Knopf, 1973.

Harold Finestone, "Cats, Kicks, and Color," *Social Problems*, vol 5, no. 1 (1957): 3–13.

Robin Fox, "The Cultural Animal," *Encounters,* vol. 35 (July 1970): 31–42.

Sigmund Freud, *Civilization and Its Discontents*, New York: Norton, 1961.

Katherine George, "The Civilized West Looks at Primitive Africa: 1400–1800, A Study in Ethnocentrism," *Isis*, vol. 49 (1958): 62–72. (Also in Dundes, 1968.)

Mary Ellen Goodman, *The Individual and Culture*, Homewood, Ill.: Dorsey Press, 1967.

Edward T. Hall, *The Silent Language*, Garden City, N.Y.: Doubleday, 1959.

———, *The Hidden Dimension*, Garden City, N.Y.: Doubleday, 1966.

Douglas Haring, ed., *Personal Character and Cultural Milieu*, rev. ed., Syracuse, N.Y.: Syracuse University Press, 1949.

Jules Henry, *Culture Against Man*, New York: Vintage, 1965.

Clyde Kluckhohn, "Universal Categories of Culture," in Sol Tax, ed., *Anthropology Today: Selections*, Chicago: University of Chicago Press, 1962.

David Labby, "Old Glory and the New," *Natural History* (June–July 1973): 26–37.

Dorothy Lee, "Codification of Reality: Lineal and Nonlineal," *Psychosomatic Medicine*, vol. 12 (1950): 89–97.

Ralph Linton, *The Study of Man*, New York: Appleton, 1947.

Marshall McLuhan, *Understanding Media: The Extensions of Man*, New York: Signet, 1964.

Mezz Mezzrow and Bernard Wolfe, *Really the Blues*, New York: Random House, 1972.

George Peter Murdock, "The Common Denominator of Cultures," in Ralph Linton, ed., *The Science of Man in World Crisis*, New York: Columbia University Press, 1945.

Gunnar Myrdal, *An American Dilemma*, New York: Harper & Row, 1944.

Piers Paul Reed, *Alive: The Story of the Andes Survivors*, Boston: Lippincott, 1974.

Hans Ruesch, *Top of the World*, New York: Harper & Row, 1951.

Joseph W. Schneider and Sally H. Hacker, "Sex-Role Imagery and Use of the Generic 'Man' in

Introductory Texts: A Case in the Sociology of Sociology," *The American Sociologist*, vol. 8, (1973): 12–18.

Philip Slater, *The Pursuit of Loneliness: American Culture at the Breaking Point*, Boston: Beacon Press, 1970.

James Walker in Alan Dundes, *Every Man His Way: Readings in Cultural Anthropology*, Englewood Cliffs, N.J.: Prentice-Hall, 1968.

J. W. M. Whiting, "Effects of Climate on Certain Cultural Practices," in W. H. Goodenough, ed., *Explorations in Cultural Anthropology*, New York: McGraw-Hill, 1969.

Robin Williams, *American Society*, 3rd ed., New York: Knopf, 1970.

Daniel Yankelovich, *Yankelovich Youth Study*, copyright © 1973 by the JDR, 3rd Fund.

for further study

American Culture. A "land of immigrants," the United States has considerable cultural diversity. One major attempt by a sociologist to encompass this diversity is Robin Williams's book, *American Society*, 3rd ed., (New York: Knopf, 1970). A landmark in the study of American society is Max Lerner's *America as a Civilization* (New York: Simon & Schuster, 1957). Lerner's well-written text is particularly good at showing the interdependence of institutions in America. A more opinionated but still very interesting book on American culture is *The Americanization of the Unconscious* by John Seeley (New York: Science House, 1967). Another sociologist, Philip Slater, has written powerfully about the pathologies of American culture in *The Pursuit of Loneliness* (Boston: Beacon Press, 1970). Finally the drive to achieve is at the center of American life, and Richard Huber analyzes its influence on American history in *The American Idea of Success* (New York: McGraw-Hill, 1971).

Subcultures. This country is filled with subcultures that are fascinating to explore. David Maurer, for example, describes the world of pickpockets and their trade through firsthand interviews in *Whiz Mob* (New Haven: College and University Press, 1964). Laud Humphreys reports on life among some kinds of homosexuals in *Tearoom Trade* (Chicago: Aldine, 1970). Juvenile delinquents have been studied by sociologists more than almost any subgroup. One of the best studies of the delinquent subculture was the first: *The Jack-Roller* written by Clifford Shaw appeared in 1930 (Chicago: University of Chicago Press, 1966). Another fine book on a subculture is *The Professional Thief* (by a professional thief), interpreted by Edwin H. Sutherland in 1937 (Chicago: University of Chicago Press, 1972).

Cultural Conflict. Important features of two societies or subcultures are brought out by cultural conflict. In the United States, Indians have been fighting the ways of white men ever since the Europeans arrived. The following books, written by Indians, describe their conflicts with Europeans. *Custer Died for Your Sins*, by Vine Deloria, Jr. (New York: Macmillan, 1969), provides an overview of Indian-white conflicts. More specific works include: Hal Borland, *When the Legends Die* (New York: Bantam, 1972); Barbara Bonham, *The Battle of Wounded Knee* (Chicago: Reilly & Lee, 1970); Oliver LaFarge, *Laughing Boy* (New York: New American Library, 1971); Leo W. Simmons, ed., *Sun Chief* (New Haven: Yale University Press, 1963).

Infants come into this world with a helplessness that is unequaled in the animal kingdom. No other creature is quite so dependent. Babies may grow up to be da Vincis or Einsteins—but first they must be *taught* to sit up, to walk, to feed themselves, to talk, to know where danger lies, to live among people who expect certain kinds of behavior from them. In short, children must *learn* to be human.

The process of acquiring the physical, mental, and social skills that a person needs to survive and to become both an individual and a member of society is called *socialization*. It is this initiation into culture that makes social life possible.

"Without this process of molding, which we call socialization, the society could not perpetuate itself beyond a single generation and culture could not exist. Nor could the individual become a person;

SOCIALIZATION

for without the ever-repeated renewal of culture within him [or her] there could be no human mentality, no human personality. Both the person and society are alike dependent on this unique process of psychic amalgamation whereby the sentiments and ideas of the culture are somehow joined to the capabilities and needs of the organism." (Davis, 1948–49, p. 195)

We will begin our discussion by considering the interaction of biology and culture in human development. Then we will discuss the way in which self-image is affected by socialization—how the growing child learns to think of himself or herself. Next, we will focus on the people and institutions that socialize the child. Before concluding this chapter we will also look at the process of socialization during adulthood.

BIOLOGY, CULTURE, AND SOCIALIZATION

Ideas about the origins of human nature are a story in themselves. Once the nineteenth century overcame its initial shock at the idea that people and apes shared some distant ancestors, it accepted Darwin with all the devotion of true believers. Humans, after all, are animals. Then, like other animals, people reasoned, they must be born with instincts, or innate predispositions toward certain kinds of behavior. The herding instinct was used to explain the fact that people everywhere lived in societies; the maternal instinct explained mothering; the acquisitive instinct, the pursuit of private property; the aggressive instinct, war; and so on. A similar kind of reasoning was used to explain individual differences. Why did one person become a thief, one a saint? Because the first, it was held, inherited criminal tendencies (just as he or she inherited brown eyes and a crooked nose), while the second inherited holiness. The notion that human behavior is biologically determined dominated nineteenth-century thought.

Then, near the end of the century, a Russian physiologist named Ivan Pavlov upset the entire scheme by calling attention to the fact that much behavior, even among lower animals, is *learned*. A hungry dog salivates instinctively when it sees food, but Pavlov showed that a dog could learn to associate the ringing of a bell with food and to salivate whenever it heard the bell, whether or not it saw food. With this experiment, Pavlov cast a shadow of doubt over the instinct theory of human behavior. In time the idea that the infant is a *tabula rasa* (a blank slate) and that people are *products* of their environment gained a considerable following. Nowhere is

this position better stated than in psychologist John B. Watson's manifesto:

Give me a dozen healthy infants, well-formed, and my own specific world to bring them up in and I'll guarantee to take any one at random and train him to become any type of specialist I might select—a doctor, lawyer, artist, merchant chief, yes even a beggerman and thief, regardless of his talents, penchants, tendencies, abilities, vocations, and the race of his ancestors. (1924, p. 104)

Today, the vast majority of social scientists reject both biological *and* environmental determinism (Clausen, 1967). Neither heredity nor environment (learning) *alone* can explain the behavior patterns that distinguish one person from another, and the members of one society from those of another. The key to individuality is socialization, where biology and culture meet.

Biological and Cultural Interaction

Socialization begins with the people who care for an infant, attending to the child's many needs. Dependency is one of our biological givens. Newborn children are totally incapable of providing for themselves: they must be fed and sheltered from the environment. But food and shelter are not enough: infants also need to be handled and loved.

Psychologist Harry F. Harlow demonstrated the need for body contact in his famous experiments with rhesus monkeys. Harlow took infant monkeys away from their mothers and raised them in isolation. Each was given two wire "mothers," one equipped with a bottle, one covered with soft terry cloth. Surprisingly, the young monkeys became attached to the cloth "mothers" rather than to the "mothers" with bottles. Clinging to something soft meant more to them than food. Most significant, however, was the fact that *none* of the animals raised in isolation developed normally. When given the chance to associate with others of their species, all were frightened and hostile (Harlow and Zimmerman, 1959).

For obvious reasons, no similar experiments have been performed with human infants. However, we do know of at least one child who was raised in near-total isolation. Anna was the illegitimate child of a farmer's daughter. After trying to place the child in a foster home or institution, Anna's mother brought her home as a last resort. No one in the family was very proud of the new member; in fact, her grandfather refused even to acknowledge her existence. To avoid his violent disapproval, the mother put Anna in an attic room, where she remained for nearly six years. Except for feeding the child just enough to keep her alive, the mother ignored her. When social workers discovered Anna, she could not sit up or walk, much less talk. In fact, she was so apathetic, so uncommunicative, they assumed she was deaf, mentally retarded, or possibly both. However, the progress Anna made once she was placed in a special school indicated that she was capable of coordinating her body, communicating, and learning. With help, she began to talk and eventually learned to care for herself, to walk and run, and to play with other children. What Anna proved in the four-and-a-half years between the time she was discovered and her premature death was that practically none of the behavior we associate with human beings arises spontaneously (Davis, 1948, pp. 204–205). Without attention, infants do not develop normally, either physically, mentally, or emotionally.[1]

Although we know, from the case of Anna and from studies of children in foster homes, that socialization should begin with mutual trust between parent and child, every society has ideas about the right and wrong ways to satisfy an infant's basic needs. There are as many ways of holding, feeding, clothing, and training children as there are cultures. Moreover, each parent interprets child-rearing norms in his or her own way—in part because of the kind of person he or she is, in part because of the kind of infant the child is.

This brings us to another point about biological givens—each human being comes into the world with a unique genetic make-up. In large part, morphology (size and shape), facial features, and rate of physical and sexual development are genetically determined.[2] Differences in temperament are also apparent at birth; some infants like to be handled and cuddled, some kick and scream whenever they are picked up. These characteristics influence socialization in several ways.

Size and strength will limit the activities a person chooses and the roles for which he or she is recruited. A frail person cannot realistically expect to participate successfully in activities that demand strength—for example, rowing against stiff currents or playing professional football. In addition, most, but not all, people still distinguish between male and female activities.[3] More subtly, disposition, appearance, and rate of development affect the way parents and others respond to a child. If the community into which a boy is born values aggressive men, a male infant who energetically explores his surroundings

---

[1] Studies of institutionalized children support this conclusion. Even with the best physical care—good food, regular changes and baths, clean sheets, bright and airy nurseries—infants who are not handled and played with develop slowly, if at all. Mortality rates in orphanages are alarmingly high (Spitz, 1951; Bowlby, 1973).

[2] To date, studies of the relative influence of heredity and environment on intelligence are inconclusive. For a look at the controversy surrounding this topic, see *Harvard Educational Review*, vol. 39 (1969). We will discuss this question more fully in chapter 9.

[3] Sex roles will be discussed in depth in chapter 6.

and struggles vigorously, resisting any sort of constraint, will please his parents: "He's a 'go-getter,' they will proudly conclude. A placid baby boy, on the other hand, will cause his parents to wonder: Will he be able to keep up with the others? Similarly, if a community expects young people to assume adult responsibilities at the age of twelve or thirteen, the child who matures slowly will be considered a misfit. A girl whose family and peers consider her exceptionally pretty has different experiences than a girl who is considered homely.

The point is that all communities project *meaning* onto any number of physical characteristics. People respond differently to bright and slow, homely and attractive, frail and robust children, and their expectations subtly shape a child's self-image. In the next section we focus on these influences to show how the child develops a sense of self and a feeling for his or her place in a community.

THE SELF AND SOCIALIZATION

In the course of growing older, people develop a kind of amnesia about their early years. Perhaps a few incidents stand out, like being taken to a strange place full of strange children and suddenly realizing your mother intends to leave you there. But how many people actually remember being put on a toilet and having no idea what it was for, or banging a spoon on a highchair table, or lying in a crib watching a toy circle overhead and feeling pleasant gurgles inside?

One reason why these early memories fade is that infants are fundamentally different from the people they become as they grow.

As adults it is almost impossible for us to recall being speechless, uncoordinated, and unselfconscious. For the first month or two of life, babies do not distinguish between their own bodies and actions and the people and objects around them. Nor do they feel happy and sad, proud and ashamed. Infants cry spontaneously when they are wet or hungry or cold. Only gradually do they realize that they are making these sounds, that they can turn crying on and off, that turning it on brings someone running, and much later, that crying is "baby stuff." The emotions and thoughts and sense of identity that adults take as givens emerge, step by step, during the process of socialization. The analyses of socialization that we examine in this section all focus on interaction—on the dialogue between children and the people around them, and on how this dialogue shapes the sense of self.

Charles Horton Cooley: The Looking-Glass Self

Charles Horton Cooley (1864–1929) won a permanent place in the annals of sociology with his insights into the ways in which people establish and maintain a sense of personal identity. Adults take the words "I" and "me" for granted; we experience ourselves as distinct persons, separate from all others. But can there be an "I" without a corresponding "they"? Cooley thought not. The "self," he believed, is a social product that emerges as the child interacts with other people. He used the image of a looking-glass to explain how others influence the way we see ourselves:

Each to each a looking-glass
Reflects the other that doth pass.

By this, Cooley meant that we gain a feeling about ourselves by imagining what others

THE SELF AND SOCIALIZATION

think about the way we look and behave. For Cooley, the self has three main elements: our imagination of the way we appear to others; our perception of the way others see that appearance; and the way we feel about those judgments.

In Cooley's view, a person's self-image and self-esteem depend heavily on the feedback he or she receives as a child, a student, a worker, a parent, and so on. Without the social mirror, there can be no sense of self.

George Herbert Mead: Taking the Role of the Other

Taking his cue from Cooley, George Herbert Mead (1863–1931) traced the development of self-awareness back to the interaction between mother and child.[4] At a very early age children begin to realize that they depend on other people (usually their mothers) to keep them comfortable, and that their behavior influences the way these important people act toward them. Infants learn that crying brings food, smiles bring cuddling, and so on. Gradually, as they explore different ways of arousing desired feelings and responses in others, their vocabulary of significant gestures and sounds expands.[5] As children learn to understand other people's attitudes, they gain some control over what happens to themselves.

By the time children begin to walk and talk, they have already acquired strong impressions about the world around them—impressions they work out in play. Children at ages two, three, and four spend much of their time in the world of make-believe. For hours on end they play at being mothers and fathers, mailmen and doctors—often embarrassing adults with the accuracy of their imitations. Mead called this form of play "taking the role of the other." In effect, the child becomes one of the people who figure importantly in his or her social world, whom Mead called *significant others*. Exploring various roles firsthand, children learn how different activities look from the perspectives of parents, brothers and sisters, and others. One minute the child is a father demanding his dinner; the next, a mother saying she is too busy to cook. By so doing, children learn to look at themselves through the eyes of other people. Children at this age seem especially fond of playing mothers fussing at babies who have wet themselves, and at lecturing other children on their behavior.

In time the characters children pretend to be become part of their internal landscape. They learn to imagine how people will respond to them without actually having to act out the situation. Thus a five- or six-year-old will stop with his hand halfway to the cookie jar and say to himself, "No, you will spoil your appetite." Thinking, as Mead conceives it, is an internal conversation between the self and others who have become part of the self. The individual becomes aware of himself or herself, Mead wrote, "not directly or immediately . . . [but] only by taking the attitudes of other individuals toward himself within a social environment or context of experience and behavior in which he and they are involved" (p. 138).

Gradually, as children move out from their family into the world of other children and adults, they begin to develop a generalized impression of what people expect from them and of where they fit in the overall scheme of things—what Mead called the *generalized other*. At the age of eight or nine, children

---

[4] This discussion is based on George Herbert Mead's *Mind, Self and Society*, Part 3, Chicago: University of Chicago Press, 1934.

[5] Symbolic interactionism, which we discussed in chapter 3, has its roots in Mead's theory.

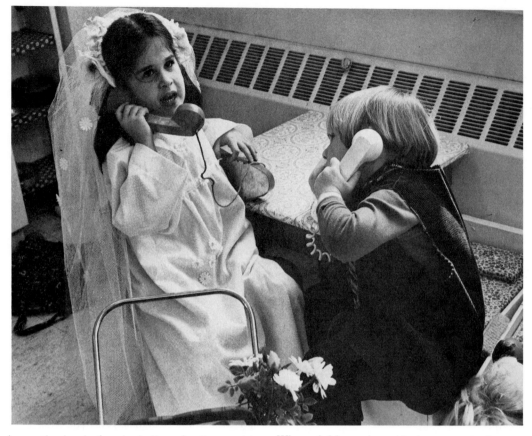

When children play at being parents, they are "taking the role of the other." Not only are they having fun, but they are learning to see how different activities look from their parents' perspective. (Alice Kandell/Rapho Guillumette)

leave the land of make-believe for the world of games. They learn to play for real. Mead explained this transition by calling attention to the complexity of organized games. To play baseball a child must understand the rules of the game—anticipate what will happen if the batter slugs a ball into right field—and adjust his or her own behavior accordingly. Similarly, to "play the game of life," that is, to participate in the social world of the community, children must be able to understand their position in terms of the community as a whole. The values and attitudes of the community become an integral part of the child's personality.

Mead was among the first to conceive of psychology in social terms. He believed the self was composed of two parts: the active, spontaneous, idiosyncratic self, which he called the "I," and the social self (the internalized social expectations and demands), which he called the "me." Without these two parts, Mead reasoned, we would not be able to reflect on our own behavior and develop a sense of inner continuity, or identity. "The self is something which has a development; it is not initially there, at birth, but arises in the process of social experience and activity, that is, develops in the given individual as a result of his relations to [the social] process and to other individuals within that process" (p. 135).

Sigmund Freud: The Psychoanalytic View

No discussion of socialization would be complete without some mention of Cooley and Mead's famous contemporary, Sigmund Freud (1856–1939). Although the number of orthodox Freudians in psychology today is relatively small, Freud's work did represent a turning point in our conceptualization of human behavior and personality. Americans, especially, seem fond of invoking the doctor's name as well as ideas rightly and wrongly associated with him. (We often speak of Freudian slips, Freudian symbols, and so on.) Freud did not enjoy this popularity in his lifetime.

Freud shocked—perhaps outraged is more accurate—the Victorian world with his first papers on infant sexuality. These papers were based on Freud's impression that many of the female patients he was treating had been seduced by their fathers in early childhood.[6] In his writings, Freud attacked the common belief that infants and children are asexual. Instead, he described the family circle as a hotbed of passions and the scene of guilt-ridden father/daughter, mother/son romances. No sooner were these ideas published, however, than Freud realized that he was wrong: his patients had *imagined*—not experienced—seduction, but the effect on their inner lives was much the same. This

realization led to Freud's unprecedented exploration of the unconscious mind, surely one of the most significant discoveries of the last century.

Throughout his life Freud's primary concern was to establish a science of the mind that compared with the physical sciences. He assumed that every aspect of human behavior could be explained rationally, in terms of cause and effect. This would even apply to seemingly accidental slips of the tongue and to the most bizarre dreams and hallucinations. His clinical work led him to conclude that childhood experiences have a determining effect on personality.

Freud's description of socialization begins with amoral, egocentric, aggressive, pleasure-seeking infants. In the first years of life all of the energies of children are directed toward oral gratification (sucking and eating), the pleasurable release of tension in defecation, and the joys of masturbation. Freud used the word *id* to describe not only sexual and aggressive urges, which he believed were inborn biological givens, but all bodily pleasure. Society—by way of parents—interferes with children's pleasure-seeking:

"Good evening, Harry Chadwick. This is your id." (Drawing by W. Miller; © 1969 The New Yorker Magazine, Inc.)

---

[6] Most of Freud's female patients were suffering from hysterical symptoms, such as paralysis without physical cause. Common in Freud's day, hysterical disorders are very rare today (a fact suggesting that psychological problems enjoy vogues and have some sociological basis).

their demands for food are met only at certain times; they are forced to control their bowels; and they are punished for masturbating. As children struggle to accommodate to these and other social demands, there begins to develop what Freud called the *ego*. The ego is the rational part of the self that interprets information obtained through the senses and finds realistic ways of satisfying biological cravings. However, the pleasure-seeking infant is not yet "tamed."

At the age of four and five, children's desires are still powerful, but so are their fears. Realizing that their parents have enormous power over them, they imagine violent reprisals for their sexual and aggressive impulses. Striving to be what their parents want them to be is one way of protecting themselves. The *superego*, or conscience, develops in this period. Children begin to internalize their parents' ideas of right and wrong, including their moral ideals. They learn to repress socially unacceptable desires and, ideally, to redirect their energies into approved channels. For a time, during what is called the latency stage, children seem to be asexual. This is not to say, however, that their impulses disappear; the id has simply been forced underground. The desires and fears of childhood, which are stimulated by the reemergence of sexuality in adolescence, remain active in the unconscious, influencing the way the person behaves throughout life.

Freud's view of the process of human development is thus radically different from Cooley's and Mead's. Where they saw socialization as the gradual, complementary merger of individual and society, Freud argued that socialization was forced on small children, very much against their will. Moreover, Freud believed that socialization is never complete. The id continues to press for gratification. The ego's function is to control these lustful, antisocial drives, while at the same time modifying the unrealistic demands of the perfection-seeking superego. Driven one way by biology, the other by society, we are—in Freud's view—eternally discontent (see *Civilization and Its Discontents*, 1930).

Erik H. Erikson: The Eight Ages of Man

In the late 1940s and early 1950s, Erik H. Erikson, one of Freud's greatest students, began to expand both the scope and content of his teacher's theory of human development. One of Erikson's most significant contributions to the study of socialization is his vivid description of the problems of adolescence and young adulthood. It is he who gave us the familiar term *identity crisis*. But this concept is only a small part of Erikson's comprehensive theory of human development, which brings Cooley, Mead, and Freud together, integrating the physiological, psychological, and social elements of the process. Erikson does this by focusing on the ego in its role as mediator between the individual and society.

Erikson's central concern is with the feelings people develop toward themselves and the world around them. He describes socialization as a lifelong process, beginning at birth and continuing into old age. In *Childhood and Society* (1950) Erikson describes eight stages of human development. Each stage constitutes a crisis, brought on by physiological changes and new social environments, to which the growing person must adapt. Erikson describes positive and negative responses to these crises, but emphasizes that elements of both exist in most people. When things go well, the maturing ego works out solutions to these crises that build up to a stable identity.

Trust vs. Mistrust (Infancy) During their first year children are totally dependent on adults, primarily their mothers. Even their own sensations of comfort and discomfort are unfamiliar, unpredictable. Children whose mothers respond warmly and consistently to their needs begin to develop feelings of *basic trust.* Comfort becomes what Erikson calls an inner certainty, and children come to believe that the world is reliable. If mothers are patient when infants bite while nursing or grasp so hard that it hurts, allowing children to develop control at their own pace, they also begin to trust themselves. Infants whose mothers are undependable and rejecting find the world a fearful place; there is no one they can count on to ease their discomforts. If mothers are erratic about caring for them, children may be afraid to let mother out of their sight, fearing that she might never return. The quality of maternal care in this first year shapes infants' basic orientation toward themselves and other people.

Autonomy vs. Shame and Doubt (Early Childhood) For the first two years of life children spend endless hours trying to make their bodies do what they want them to do. By the age of three, their muscles and nerves have developed to the point where they are capable of grasping, reaching, crawling, controlling their bowels, and so on—delightful accomplishments from their point of view. However, while these accomplishments bring new autonomy, they raise doubts as well. A child crawls around the corner to another room, then realizes he is alone and cries out. Besides the doubts of going it alone, there is the shame of losing self-control, as when a toilet-trained toddler wets the neighbor's rug.

Much depends on children's parents. If adults allow the young ones to explore and develop at their own pace, they gain confidence in their ability to govern themselves—what Erikson calls *autonomy.* On the other hand, if children interpret constant supervision as a sign that they cannot take care of themselves, they may begin to overdiscipline themselves to avoid punishment or ridicule and shame (the feeling of being exposed). Neglected children, whose parents allow them to get into situations where they are hurt, may experience similar feelings of self-doubt. Erikson suggests that to develop self-confidence, children should be encouraged to "stand on their own feet," but they must also be protected from experiences of shame and doubt.

Initiative vs. Guilt (The Play Stage) At four or five, children begin to extend their mastery over their own bodies to the world around them (if, that is, they have developed some sense of autonomy). They enjoy attacking and conquering the material world; in their play and fantasies they begin to act out adult roles, transforming (and hence mastering) the world in their imaginations. Most important, in Erikson's view, children begin to *initiate* purposeful activities on their own. Earlier, their play consisted mostly of exploring and imitating others.

Children's feelings of self-worth grow if their parents and others who are important to them respect their efforts. Ridicule and disinterest make children wonder about the values of their actions and goals; they may punish themselves for their failures. There is a danger, then, of children developing more or less permanent *guilt* feelings about any self-initiated activities at this age. Ideally, children begin to turn from their attachments to their parents to the world beyond—without losing the exuberance of early childhood.

Industry vs. Inferiority (School Age) The social setting now shifts from home to school and the larger community. At six, if not earlier, children enter the impersonal world of unrelated children and adults, of rules and organized games. As they begin to acquire the skills and technology of their society, they "learn to win recognition by producing things" (p. 259). Ideally, they come to enjoy the exercise of mental and physical skills, and take pride in *industry*. However, if they are not emotionally prepared for school, if they fail to do well in school, if they find that their race or family background or looks or even the way they dress automatically disqualifies them in other people's eyes, the experience will be negative. Some children develop a deep sense of *inferiority* in this stage, a fear of being required to perform and failing. Some overcommit themselves to the sphere of work, trying to compensate for feelings of inadequacy.

Identity vs. Role Confusion (Adolescence)
With childhood drawing to a close and adulthood looming ahead, adolescents become preoccupied with the question of *identity*. It is not that they don't know who they are before this time, but rather that they have been changing and shaping themselves in many different ways. The time has come to draw together all that has made up their lives, to give a more permanent shape to who they are and where they are going as adults. What Erikson means by *identity* is being able to derive a sense of continuity about one's past, present, and future, coordinating feelings about the self with the image reflected in the social looking-glass. There is also the danger, however, that a person will not be able to integrate his or her various roles into a clear identity. The self, then, remains diffuse.

Intimacy vs. Isolation (Young Adulthood)
Erikson sees young adulthood, like each of the stages before it, as a turning point. Think how many young people fall madly in love at twenty, only to find that after a few months they feel stifled by so much closeness. The other person seems to be taking over their life, swallowing them up. They can't find that comfortable sense of self anymore, someone sees through their acts—and they pull back. This is true in close friendships as well as in love affairs. As Erikson suggests, *intimacy* requires vulnerability; caring deeply for another person always involves some risk—the risk of being hurt, of losing that person. Without a clear sense of identity, without an ability to trust, it may be difficult to take these risks. Young people who are unsure of themselves, who fear commitment, find intimate relationships anxious and stormy—however much they desire love and companionship. Isolation—keeping to oneself or moving from one intense but short-lived relationship to another may feel safer, but it limits personal and social growth.

Generativity vs. Stagnation (Young Adulthood and Middle-Age) In young adulthood, there is still time for exploring and dreaming; the future is still an open book. In middle-age, however, realistic alternatives seem limited; a way of life has been chosen. Erikson identifies the "need to be needed" as the central theme of adulthood. Perhaps nothing satisfies this need so much as an infant, whose helplessness seems to cry out for intimacy and giving. This is one of the points where the needs and desires of one stage mesh with those of another. An infant satisfies an adult's desire to give, while an adult satisfies the infant's needs for warmth and security. This is why Erikson speaks of a *life cycle*.

Generativity is the feeling that one is making a significant contribution, that one is guiding new generations—either directly, as a parent, or indirectly, by working to better society. The better people feel about themselves, the closer they are to other people, the more likely they are to feel productive or industrious, to work creatively, to take on social commitments. For some people, however, middle-age is painful. Childish self-absorption and "early invalidism, physical or psychological" (p. 267) are signs that a person has not found generativity. It is almost as if they were reliving unresolved crises of earlier stages. Yet as with all stages, Erikson points out that elements of both resolutions—generativity and stagnation—are found in even the healthiest person.

Integrity vs. Despair (Old Age) The last stage in Erikson's "Eight Ages of Man" is one of reflection and evaluation. In a very real way, coming to terms with death means coming to terms with life—with where one has been, with what one has done with one's time on earth. By *integrity* Erikson means that a person sees meaning in both the good and bad, the joys and pain of his or her life; that he or she has arrived at a higher level of self-acceptance. The despair that comes from looking back and seeing one's life as a series of missed opportunities and realizing that it is too late to start over is difficult for a younger person to imagine.

In describing the "Eight Ages of Man," Erikson focuses on the potential for negative as well as positive developments in each stage, and how the growing person's adjustment in one stage affects his orientation in the next. Thus, gaining a sense of initiative aids a person in being industrious, though the sequence is not rigid. Erikson believes that the concerns of every stage are present throughout a person's life, though each pair has its time of prominence. This means that a person can overcome an early sense of shame or mistrust by working at it later, or that a person can lose an early strength like initiative through great strain later on. No crisis is completely resolved once and for all; the most the growing person can do is to achieve a positive balance of healthy and pathological tendencies. Moreover, no one can maintain feelings of trust, autonomy, or initiative in isolation. Positive feelings toward the self and the world must be verified and reinforced in each stage.

Erikson pictures the social order as growing out of (and therefore in harmony with) developmental stages. In his view, as a peo-

---

table 5:1   ERIKSON'S EIGHT STAGES OF LIFE

AGE	PSYCHOSOCIAL CRISIS	PREDOMINANT SOCIAL SETTING
Infancy	Basic trust vs. mistrust	Family
Early childhood	Autonomy vs. shame and doubt	Family
Four to five	Initiative vs. guilt	Family
Six to twelve	Industry vs. inferiority	School
Adolescence	Identity vs. role confusion	Peer group
Young adulthood	Intimacy vs. isolation	Couple
Young adulthood and middle age	Generativity vs. stagnation	New family; work
Old age	Integrity vs. despair	Retirement

SOURCE: Adapted from Erik Erikson, *Identity, Youth and Crisis* (New York: Norton, 1968).

ple work out the solutions to developmental problems, the solutions become institutionalized in the culture and are thereby available to future generations.

The underlying assumptions ... are (1) that the human personality in principle develops according to steps predetermined in the growing person's readiness to be driven toward, to be aware of, and to interact with, a widening social radius; and (2) that society, in principle, tends to be constituted as to meet and invite this succession of potentialities for interaction and attempts to safeguard and to encourage the proper rate and proper sequence of their unfolding. (p. 270)

This interrelationship between personal crises in growth and social structure is the most striking part of Erikson's theory, which he has applied to studies of Hitler, Luther, Gandhi, and others.

Jean Piaget: Cognitive Development

Anyone who has spent time with children knows the drama of a child's first words, the frustrations of trying to reason with a three-year-old, the delight on the face of a ten-year-old who has just grasped a new concept. Learning to talk, to think, and to reason are among the basic processes of socialization. For this reason, we turn to the great child psychologist Jean Piaget, whose insights into cognitive development are unsurpassed. Piaget was one of the first to recognize that cognitive development is a social as well as a psychological phenomenon. The stages he outlines complement and reinforce the theories of personality development we have been discussing, adding a new dimension to our picture of socialization.[7]

---

[7] For more detailed discussions of Piaget, see Furth (1969) and Piaget and Inhelder (1969).

Sensorimotor Stage (Infancy–Two Years) In the sensorimotor stage, roughly corresponding to Erikson's first stage, children gradually acquire what Piaget calls *motor intelligence*—that is, a physical understanding of themselves and their world. At first, infants do not realize that shaking a rattle produces the sound they hear; they experience the shaking and the noise that results as separate phenomena. In time, however, they learn to associate the two, and shake a rattle deliberately. The main cognitive development in this stage is the discovery of *object permanence:* infants learn that mother, their toys, and other objects do not dissolve when they leave their range of vision. They also begin to distinguish their own body from the environment. This cognitive development (object permanence) parallels the emotional development of trust. Each involves the growing familiarity of children with the people and objects in their world.

The Intuitive Stage (Early Childhood) The acquisition of language is the single most important development in this period (Erikson's second and third stages). Language enables children to communicate with other people, to think, to represent the external world, the past, and the future. With language, children can carry out mental experiments and evaluate themselves (by assuming the attitudes of others through words). In short, words make it possible for children to conjure up mental images of objects and experiences not present in their immediate environment, thus dramatically widening their horizons.

This is not to say that the two- to seven-year-old thinks and reasons like an adult. Typically, they cannot consider more than one point of view, more than one dimension, at a time. For example, J. L. Phillips (1969) asked a four-year-old boy if he had a brother.

The child answered, yes, he had a brother named Jim. "Does Jim have a brother?" Phillips asked. Pausing a moment, the child answered, "No." In addition to not being able to consider various points of view simultaneously, young children tend to jump to conclusions: they do not try to test and prove their ideas.

With language, children can assert themselves more aggressively than they can with their bodies, which are considerably smaller than those of the authorities in their lives. Language is also the primary medium for self-evaluation. Taking the role of a parent, children begin to chastise themselves—hence the possibility of developing feelings of doubt and guilt in this stage.

Stage of Concrete Operations (School Age)
In Piaget's third stage (Erikson's age of industry vs. inferiority), children's thinking matures markedly. As they learn to manipulate the tools of their culture (what Erikson calls *industry*), they begin to understand the rule of cause and effect; to comprehend the law of conservation (that mass remains consistent, despite changes in form); to classify objects along more than one dimension, and to perform other logical operations. All of this development is a direct result of their experiences with the material world. Children also learn to consider other people's viewpoints, and most important, to coordinate them with their own (Mead's game stage).

In this stage, children are extremely concrete: that is, they think in terms of real objects and situations that they can handle physically. They know the difference between internal events, such as dreams, and real things. This concreteness in part explains children's susceptibility to feelings of inferiority, which Erikson described. Children evaluate themselves in terms of physical size and prowess, and in terms of other objective

achievements, such as the things they can do and make. Less observable qualities or attributes count little in the value systems of young children. Feelings of pride or inferiority develop as children compare their bodies

Piaget argues that intelligence develops in stages. This child, aged seven, is thinking about whether a given quantity of water becomes "more" if it is poured into a taller glass. (The New York Times)

and skills with their peers' and observe their reactions.

Stage of Formal Operations (Adolescence)
The most obvious cognitive change in this stage is that at eleven or twelve, children begin to think in terms of abstract concepts, theories, and general principles. Whereas younger children test their ideas by trying them out, adolescents can formulate hypothetical problems in their heads.

The development of abstract thinking has emotional consequences. Younger children tend to experience their emotions as direct responses to people and events: you love people because they are good to you, hate people because they are mean. The discovery of ambivalence—feeling hate and love for the same person—is a direct outgrowth of the ability to think in abstract terms. The development of abstract or formal thinking also explains adolescents' ability to reflect on their self-image and future hopes. Trying to combine personal desires and social demands, adolescents strive for an identity, as Erikson suggested.

In summary Piaget shows that there are very real differences in the *way* children think at different ages. Is cognitive development "wired into" the growing person? Or do these stages reflect the influence of culture on children and the way they are socialized? Neither of these would be accurate in Piaget's view. "Stages are . . . the products of *interactional* experience between the child and the world, experience which leads to a restructuring of the child's own [cognitive] organization" (Kohlberg and Gilligan, 1971, p. 1059). Is the development of abstract reasoning (and, by extension, an identity crisis) inevitable? Lawrence Kohlberg, who has devoted much of his career to investigating Piaget's theories empirically by testing large numbers of people at different ages and in different cultures, found

that "the adolescent revolution is extremely variable in time, [and] that for many people it never occurs at all" (Kohlberg and Gilligan, 1971, p. 1065). He estimates that perhaps 50 percent of Americans never develop formal reasoning at all. Kohlberg is mainly interested, however, in questions of judgment and the development of moral thinking. Building on Piaget's pioneering work in this field, Kohlberg describes six stages of moral development. Along with psychological and cognitive growth, moral development adds a third dimension to the process of socialization.

Lawrence Kohlberg: Moral Development

Kohlberg's investigative methods are quite simple: he presents children with a moral dilemma. For example, he describes an episode like the following. A man's wife is dying and there is only one drug that can cure her, but the small dose that is needed costs $2,000. Unable to raise the money, the man asks the druggist to let him pay part now, the rest later. The druggist refuses, and in desperation, the man breaks into the drugstore and steals the medicine. Is he right or wrong? After presenting this and similar questions to American, Chinese, Malaysian, Turkish, and Mexican children, Kohlberg concluded that the way people think about moral issues is not simply a reflection of their culture, but, like emotional growth and cognitive skills, something that develops in stages as the child gains experience in the world.

The Preconventional Level[8] Kohlberg uses the term *preconventional* to describe children

---

[8] Kohlberg does not specify age ranges for each stage because he found the rate of moral development varies from person to person, with some individuals remaining at immature levels.

who may behave well, but who have not yet developed any sense of right and wrong. The preconventional level includes two stages. In *stage 1*, children do as they are told solely because they fear punishment; they are simply deferring to superior power. In *stage 2*, they begin to realize that certain actions bring rewards. But "human relations are viewed in terms like those of a market place.... Reciprocity is a matter of 'you scratch my back and I'll scratch yours,' not of loyalty, gratitude, or justice" (Kohlberg and Gilligan, 1971, p. 1067). Malaysian boys at this second

stage, for example, thought that the man in Kohlberg's story "should steal the medicine because he needs his wife to cook for him."

The Conventional Level As children grow they become increasingly concerned about what other people think of them. As a result their behavior becomes largely other-directed. In *stage 3*, children begin to seek their parents' approval by being "nice." Gradually, ideas about right and wrong—whatever they may be in the child's society—take on a meaning of their own. Children have entered

figure 5:1 Cross-cultural patterns of moral development for middle-class urban boys in the United States, Taiwan, and Mexico.

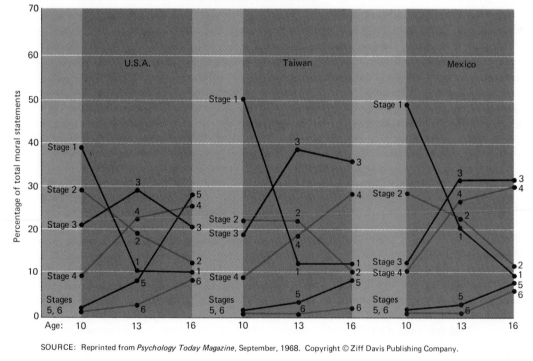

SOURCE: Reprinted from *Psychology Today Magazine*, September, 1968. Copyright © Ziff Davis Publishing Company.

At age ten, in each country, stages are used in order of difficulty, with most responses in *stage 1*. At age thirteen, *stage 3* is used most. At age sixteen, American boys have reversed the order of age ten stages (with the exception of *stage 6*). *Stage 5* thinking is used more by the American boys at sixteen than by the Taiwan or Mexican boys. But it *is* present in these countries, so it is not only an American way of thinking.

stage 4 when they begin thinking in terms of rules. A child in this fourth stage might, for example, say that the man in the story above should not have broken into the drugstore because it is always wrong to steal. Rigidly conventional thinking characterizes this stage.

The Postconventional Level As growing children move out from their homes and begin to associate with people whose ideas may be different from their own, their perspectives widen. In *stage 5*, children recognize moral conflicts and evaluate different points of view in terms of general rules and legal principles. For example, they understand why the man decided to break into the drugstore, but wonder: Suppose everyone decided to steal, what then? Following this line of reasoning they begin to question the morality of charging so much money for drugs. As the conflicts between individual needs and the need for social order, between the norms adults profess and those they practice, become clearer to them, children begin late in the fifth stage to sense strong feelings of good and evil within themselves. At this point the young person is becoming self-directed: he or she behaves one way instead of another to avoid self-condemnation. Gradually, they develop "universal principles of justice, of the reciprocity and equality of human rights, and of respect for the dignity of human beings as individual persons" (Kohlberg and Gilligan, 1971, p. 1068). (This is Kohlberg's *stage 6*.)

It is no coincidence that as children's ability to think about moral issues matures, as their identity and cognitive skills develop, they are meeting many children and adults outside their home. In the next section we will consider the family, schools, and peers as agents of socialization.

AGENTS OF SOCIALIZATION

The concept of childhood did not exist in the Middle Ages, a time when infants were considered "nonpersons." High infant mortality meant that they simply didn't count for society. Those children who did survive were pushed into the adult world as apprentices of one kind or another as soon as possible. People expected a seven- or eight-year-old to work for a living (usually in his father's occupation), just like everybody else (Ariès, 1962, p. 128).

Growing up in the modern world takes sixteen, twenty, and sometimes even more years—primarily because there is so much to learn, both technologically and socially. The separation of work and family, specialization, social mobility, the lack of fixed traditions, proliferating subcultures, and the generation gap all contribute to the complexity of modern life. A person must learn to play many roles, and socialization has become a lifelong process, as Erikson described so well in his "Eight Ages of Man." The family, schools, peers, lovers and spouses, even children (if people have children), all play a part.

The Family

People have children for any number of reasons: to watch a young person grow; to perpetuate their family name; in the hope that a child will fill some vacancy in their own lives, perhaps by realizing their own frustrated dreams; because they assume all *normal* people marry and raise families; to prove their virility or femininity; or perhaps because their method of birth control failed (Stone and Church, 1973, p. 145). Parents' motives—subtly communicated in the way mothers hold their newborn infants, satisfy their needs, respond to their first explorations—make a difference to their children.

Self-Image and Self-Control The self-image that children eventually develop begins to take shape during their struggle to master their own bodies and the world around them. At the same time, children try to reconcile their own desires with the demands placed upon them—as we saw in the discussions of Mead, Cooley, and Erikson. The family is the whole world to children in their first years of life. The people who raise them—both parents, a single parent, a grandmother or older sister, or a governess—are the only looking-glass that matters. Am I lovable? Am I a good person? Am I competent (can I control myself)? Should I trust other people?

Is the world a good, safe place, or is it full of troubles, pain, and deceit? Who am I and who am I not? Directly and indirectly, the people who care for small children answer these questions. Well before children are able to talk and question and examine the facts, they form a picture of themselves and their world, which is based on their family's attitudes and feelings.

Values and Roles Parents teach children what matters in life, and who counts, often without realizing the full impact of their value messages. The desire to achieve and to excel; the need for popularity at all costs; the belief

From an early age, children learn what their families value most. This little girl is getting to know the violin firsthand, from her father, a concert violinist. (Gene Maggio)

that a girl must be pretty, accommodating, and coy instead of bold and direct, and that catching a husband is the only goal worth seeking for a female, are passed from parent to child. Gordon Allport's accounts of kindergarten children trying dutifully to express the "correct" prejudices, although they had no understanding of the concept of race whatever, poignantly illustrate the way attitudes are learned (1954). One little boy told his mother, "No, Mother, I never play with niggers. I only play with white and black children." A little girl, confused but anxious to please, came running home one day in a flurry. "Mother, what is the name of the children I'm supposed to hate?" Allport concluded, "It takes a child well into adolescence to learn the peculiar double-talk appropriate to prejudice in a democracy." (See chapter 9 on prejudice.)

The behavior adults encourage and discourage and the ways in which they discipline children also affect their basic orientation toward the world. But values and child-rearing styles are not uniform from family to family. A study by Melvin Kohn (1963) suggests that they are influenced by social class. The working-class parents he studied value obedience, neatness, cleanliness, and respect. They want their children to conform to traditional standards of behavior; they demand that children do as they are told. Focusing on the immediate consequences of a child's actions, they tend to enforce discipline with physical punishment. Middle-class parents, in contrast, are more concerned about the child's motives and intentions than with actions per se. Usually, they attempt to reason with the child, trying to make him understand why he should or should not do this or that. Why? Because they value curiosity, happiness, and, above all, self-control. They want the child to be self-directed. However, middle-class parents often practice a psychological punishment—the

withdrawal of love and emotional support.

Kohn suggests these different approaches are directly related to the parents' occupations. Whereas most white-collar jobs require some measure of initiative and independence, as well as an ability to get along with people and to manipulate ideas, blue-collar jobs usually consist of carrying out a supervisor's directions. Success in the blue-collar world depends on following rules and orders, and working-class parents train their children to follow orders. Similarly, middle-class parents try to prepare children for the social reality they know. (In the next chapter we will consider the way children learn other social roles—being male or female—and how this affects them throughout life.)

Authoritarian and Permissive Parenting
Discussions of the relative merits of authoritarian parenting (forcing a child to obey) and permissive parenting (giving a child more or less free reign) tend to take on moral overtones. Allport (1954) argues that authoritarian parents give children the impression that "power and authority dominate human relationships—not trust and tolerance." Moreover, children who are taught not to have tantrums, and not to masturbate, learn to mistrust their own impulses—and, by extension, to "fear evil impulses in others."[9] In contrast, "the child who feels secure and loved *whatever he does* . . . develops basic ideas of equality and trust" (italics added). Obviously, Allport is advocating permissiveness. No doubt he would agree with English educator A. S. Neill, founder of Summerhill, who stated categorically, "I believe that to impose anything by authority is wrong" (1960, p. 114).

---

[9] Other critics of a stern upbringing argue that authoritarian parents may provoke antisocial behavior and rebellion with their sterness, or on the other hand, generate passivity and dependence as the child simply gives in (Baumrind, 1966). But as sociologists, we should note that these critical professors are themselves middle class.

Diana Baumrind (1966) disagrees. The permissive school of child-rearing is based on the idea that by not interfering with the child, parents communicate their approval and respect for him. But isn't it possible that the child experiences noninterference as indifference? Baumrind suggests that permissiveness handicaps the child in two ways: first, by depriving the child of the chance to learn the costs of nonconforming behavior; second, by not giving the child opportunities to argue and rebel, thereby formulating his own positions. In Baumrind's view, parents should be authoritative, not authoritarian—enforcing their own rights as well as the child's "in a rational, issue-oriented manner," so that the child learns how to balance responsibility and freedom.

Of course, the best intentions and theories may fall by the wayside in the day-to-day interaction of parent and child. Parents learn to be parents, "the hard way, by practicing on their first-born" (Stone and Church, 1973, p. 146). Research by Hilton and others indicates that new mothers are more anxious, and therefore more attentive and interfering than experienced mothers. Their behavior is more extreme. By the time a second or third child arrives, the mother is more relaxed: she knows what to expect and how to handle most problems that arise. Experienced mothers tend to rely on the child to express his needs and make his way; they do not fuss so much. Thus no two children, not even members of the same family, are socialized in exactly the same way.

The Schools

In modern societies the school is the primary agent for weaning children from home and introducing them into the larger society. Life in school is a drastic change from life at home. In the family, relations are built around emotional ties ("I'm spanking you because I love you"). At school, children are expected to obey—not because they love their teachers or depend on them—but because rules are rules and they exist to be obeyed.

The students walk into the room the teacher has been assigned. The school year has begun. Usually the class sits down before the teacher makes his first remark. Sometimes the class stands up, waiting. Whatever happens, the first move of the year is the teacher's.

He introduces himself, calls the roll of pupils' names (usually in alphabetical order), and then assigns seats. . . .

The first day of class is used to familiarize the students with the routines and rules the teacher intends to impose upon the class throughout the year. . . . The "do's" and "dont's" are paraded out. Don't leave your seat without permission; don't talk out; do raise your hand if you want something; do remain quiet at the beginning of class; don't chew gum. . . . (Kohl, 1969, pp. 22–25)

School thus socializes young people to a uniform set of values and to the organizational life they will experience as adults. Everyone is expected to obey the same rules. Students are rated more for what they do than for who they are, and their ratings become a matter of record. In the words of one high-school student:

"The main thing is not to take it personal, to understand that it's just a system and it treats you the same way it treats everybody else, like an engine or a machine. . . . Our names get fed into it—*we* get fed into it—when we're five years old, and if we catch on and watch our step, it spits us out when we're 17 or 18." (Noyes and McAndrew, in Silberman, 1971, p. 155)

In most schools, every moment of the students' day is planned and scheduled for them. Students do not participate in decisions about rules or curricula or other issues that affect their lives; they don't even have the right to speak up, move around, or go to the bathroom without permission. An extensive study of today's schools concluded:

[T]here is no more firmly rooted tradition than the one that holds that children must sit still at their desks without conversing at all, both during periods of waiting, when they have nothing to do, and during activities that almost demand conversation. Yet even on an assembly line, there is conversation and interaction among workers, and there are coffee breaks and work pauses as well. (Silberman, 1971, p. 128)

The contrast between the traditional classroom and the home is dramatic.

The avowed purpose of school, of course, is to teach young people technical and intellectual skills and cultural values and attitudes, to prepare them for their roles as adults in a subordinate position vis-à-vis a knowledgeable teacher. Whether this system works is debatable, as we will see in chapter 16.

Peer Groups

One of the most important side effects of entering school is that children begin to spend more and more time among peers. Power in the family and the schoolroom is one-sided; parents and teachers can force children to obey rules they neither understand nor like. But peers are relatively equal. By virtue of their age, sex, and rank (as child and as student), peers "stand in the same relation to persons in authority" and therefore "see the world through the same eyes" (Davis, 1948, p. 217). Among equals, children learn the true meaning of exchange and cooperation. Peers share forbidden knowledge including sex lore and ways to evade and manipulate parents and teachers.

The importance of peer groups increases over the years, reaching a climax in adolescence, when popularity becomes all-important for most young people. James Coleman (1961) believes this happens because parents and other adults abdicate, leaving young people largely to their own devices. Adolescents develop a society of their own—with their own jargon, symbols, heroes, values, and "only a few threads of connections to the outside adult society." Most of the young person's time is spent in the clannish and sometimes cruel peer group. Coleman argues that in some ways the adolescent society is subversive—that is, it subverts the goals adults set for young people. For example, hard-working, conscientious students are rarely the most popular; teenagers are not very kind to overachievers. On the other hand, Coleman found that the cliques or in-crowds that form among young people usually reflect the adult world's emphasis on economic background and family status. Having a car (for boys) and nice clothes (for girls) count as much in adolescent society as standing up to authority and other acts of bravery. Coleman suggests that the youth subcultures of the late 1950s were almost a parody of adult society, where, after all, intellectual prowess is not always valued.

In peer groups young people can defend themselves against the ambiguities of adolescence. In most nontechnological societies, children win adult status early by undergoing the traditional rites of passage. When they emerge from such ceremonies, boys are men and girls are women, with all the accompanying rights and responsibilities. In our society, adolescence is a no man's land.

Just when [they are at their] peak sexually, adolescents must remain celibate; just when they have the most strength and energy, they are given no productive, satisfying work to do; just when they are at their intellectual height, and when their need for power is greatest, they are denied the right to participate in society's decision-making. (Boroson, in Newkirk, 1971, p. 86)

During adolescence, peer groups play a strong role in shaping the values, attitudes, and style of young people. (Margot Granitsas/Photo Researchers)

By aligning themselves *with* peers and *against* adults, young people who are still financially dependent on their parents (and who may remain so for years if their parents finance college and graduate education), who are still practicing instead of participating in the work of society, can achieve some sense of autonomy.

In the last decade peer groups have become important agents of socialization during post-adolescence, as growing numbers of people consider "singlehood" as a way of life, not just a temporary condition. (*Newsweek* magazine [July 16, 1973, p. 52] reported that 12.7 million Americans between the ages of twenty and thirty-five are single, an increase of 50 percent over the last ten years.)

Many single men and women live in a subculture of their own, built around clubs and apartment complexes, transitory relationships, and the continuing search for identity (as opposed to the traditional search for a mate). To some degree, the peer group—the people who frequent a club or bar, the group that works or plays together—becomes an extended family.

ADULT SOCIALIZATION

Socialization does not end at age nineteen or twenty. Entering the work force, moving into one's own apartment, marrying, becoming a parent, changing jobs or neighborhoods or spouses, and growing old all require learning new roles. For example, when a couple move in together, they are still the same people they were the week before when they lived separately. Yet there are changes. One may find it difficult to reassure the other that wanting some time alone is not rejection—a problem that may never have come up before. Arguments take on a new significance—they can't go home to cool off for a week anymore. Similarly, when a couple decide to separate, each has to relearn the role of being single. After six or eight years of marriage, dating may feel as awkward as it did in early adolescence.

Adult socialization builds on the norms, values, and habits learned in childhood and adolescence. For an adult, learning new roles is largely learning new ways of expressing existing behaviors or values. For example, if a woman who has spent many years as a wife and mother and working for the PTA and various charities, becomes active in Women's Liberation groups, she is still seeking the pleasures of belonging to an organization, still working for a cause in the hope of making things better. Of course, she may seem quite different to her family and friends and even to herself, but adult socialization is largely a reshaping of existing orientations.

Marriage and Parenthood

Not too long ago, marriage was a step into the unknown—very few couples lived together before their wedding. In many cases one or both were virgins. Today, most couples know a great deal more about one another than their parents did when they got married. This is not to say that learning to be married is easier now than it was then. On the contrary. In the past people got married because they wanted a respectable sexual relationship and a family. Today marriage is not a prerequisite for sex or respectability, and the population explosion makes having children a dubious virtue, so there is now less reason to get married in the first place.

Premarital sex surely makes wedding nights less awkward and embarrassing. On the other hand, contemporary couples may be more self-conscious about their sex lives than their parents were. They expect more. A great many couples think something must be wrong if they do not make love as often as they did when first together, or if they do not experiment as they read others do. In some circles, the husband or wife who resents his or her spouse's extramarital activities finds little support. In addition, the traditional roles of wife-homemaker-mother and husband-breadwinner-father are no longer givens. Although more and more people today accept women's rights to pursue their careers, we have not, as a society, resolved the question of who is going to take care of the children. Finally, with divorce becoming more common and more acceptable, marriage itself is not the final commitment it once was. So to a large extent today, the absence of clear models forces couples to define their roles as husband and wife on their own. For some people this freedom is welcome; for others, however, it is a trying experience.

The process of defining roles begins anew when a child is born and the family of two becomes three. Having worked out a routine for living with one another, the couple now must learn how to deal with the frustrations and interruptions of a young child. In a very

table 5:2 PROPORTIONS OF CREATIVE OUTPUT PRODUCED IN EACH DECADE OF LIFE

FIELD	NUMBER OF MEN	NUMBER OF WORKS	AGE					
			20s	30s	40s	50s	60s	70s
Scholarship								
Historians	46	615	3	19	19	22	*24*	20
Philosophers	42	225	3	17	20	18	*22*	20
Scholars	43	326	6	17	*21*	*21*	16	19
Means			4	18	20	20	*21*	20
Sciences								
Biologists	32	3,456	5	22	*24*	19	17	13
Botanists	49	1,889	4	15	*22*	*22*	*22*	15
Chemists	24	2,120	11	21	*24*	19	12	13
Geologists	40	2,672	3	13	22	*28*	19	14
Inventors	44	646	2	10	17	18	*32*	21
Mathematicians	36	3,104	8	*20*	20	18	19	15
Means			6	17	*22*	21	20	15
Arts								
Architects	44	1,148	7	24	*29*	25	10	4
Chamber musicians	35	109	15	*21*	17	20	18	9
Dramatists	25	803	10	27	*29*	21	9	3
Librettists	38	164	8	21	*30*	22	15	4
Novelists	32	494	5	19	18	*28*	23	7
Opera composers	176	476	8	30	*31*	16	10	5
Poets	46	402	11	21	*25*	16	16	10
Means			9	23	*26*	21	14	6

Note: Maximum values are shown in italics. Total output in each field = 100.

SOURCE: Wayne Dennis, "Creative Productivity between the Ages of 20 and 80 Years," *Journal of Gerontology,* vol. 21 (January 1966): 2. Data gathered by analyzing published biographies of contributors to the fields listed above.

Declining productivity and old age do not necessarily go together. Much of the total contribution to scholarship, science, and art made by men who live to old age comes in their later years. For the men represented in the above table (all of whom lived to age seventy-nine and over) 20 percent of their output in scholarship, 15 percent in the sciences, and 6 percent in the arts was made during their seventies.

real sense, their live is not their own any more (they can no longer just "pick up and go"). Relationships in the family continue to change as children grow up; the couple faces middle-age; the children leave home and Mom and Dad learn to be a couple again; one spouse dies. Each change brings new roles to be learned.

Growing Old

For many people in our society, socialization to old age is socialization to withdrawal (see Riley et al., 1968). Whereas in many traditional societies old people are revered, in ours they are usually shunted aside. The elderly are expected to exchange their au-

---

IN THE NEWS

Growing Old Alone Together

Age-segregated adult communities may not be what either Margaret Mead or Erik Erikson had in mind when they considered older people's needs for institutional support, but such communities are growing throughout the country. At present, 1.5 million retirees live in "adult mobile-home parks," and another 500,000 live in retirement villages. Instead of continuing to participate in the social life of the communities in which they spent most of their adult lives, 10 percent of Americans over sixty-five are now living in communities open only to others of their own age group. Children are allowed by invitation only. Anthropologist Sheila K. Johnson writes:

As recently as fifteen years ago there were no such communities, and in the early 1960s, when they first began to be built, sociologists made dire predictions about them. They argued that it was mentally unhealthy for older people to live apart from young people and children, and that it would deprive society of much valuable experience.

One of the reasons for the growing popularity of such communities may be that our society has not paid enough attention to meeting the needs of older people. Old people do not have the institutionalized social roles that Margaret Mead suggests they should have. Perhaps, in reaction to being ignored by a youth-oriented culture, old people are doing some ignoring of their own.

Sheila K. Johnson suggests that "residents of retirement communities . . . [may be] helping to create a new subculture of aging," which would have a positive effect on the way old people feel about themselves.

It has been said that our youth-oriented society has long treated the elderly much as we treat minority groups, with the strikingly similar result that the elderly have accepted society's derogatory definition of their status. But now, with large numbers of active, not-so-old, retired individuals living together in separate communities, it may become possible for them to forge a new and more positive self-image.

SOURCE: Sheila K. Johnson, "Growing Old Alone Together," *The New York Times Magazine* (November 11, 1973): 40–59.

thority as parents for the pleasantries of grandparenting. Giving advice to their children may be seen as interfering. They are expected to leave their jobs, making room for younger men and women with families to support. Retirement, a "roleless role," is particularly disorienting in a society where a person *is* what he or she *does*. Expectations are reduced; the older person may actually be reprimanded for performing chores that were once performed as a matter of course (for example, mowing the lawn). In addition, old people must learn to cope with their diminished physical capacity.

Anthropologist Margaret Mead suggests that much of the loneliness old people experience stems from their own desire to remain independent, at all cost. Living all their lives in a country that values independence and frowns on dependency, old people become victims of their own socialization:

We have reached the point where we think the only thing we can do for our children is to stay out of their hair, and the only thing we can do for our daughters-in-law is to see as little of them as possible. Old people's homes, even the best, are filled with older people who believe the only thing they can do for their children is to look cheerful when they come to visit. So in the end older people have to devote their energies to "not being a burden." (1971, p. 242)

In peasant communities, where change was slow, old people had valuable knowledge to pass on to younger people. But today, "such memories are no longer useful. We can be dead certain," says Mead, "that when our grandchildren reach [old] age, they will not be living as we live today." But, old people *can* contribute their memories of a changing society to give younger people a broader perspective on current social changes. Older people have lived through wars, riots, economic depressions, and other upheavals. Many of them have witnessed the first automobiles, airplanes, and other modern inventions and can assure young people that change does not mean an end to the world, but merely an end to parts of the world as they knew it.

Mead suggests that old people can reduce their loneliness and despair by utilizing their independence and experience. Society should encourage older men and women to work in day care centers and other community service organizations. In the Soviet Union people who have had experience caring for others are paid to be "grandmothers" in housing projects, where they assist young mothers. This country, too, can find ways to institutionalize meaningful social roles for old people.

summary

Socialization is the process of acquiring the physical, mental, and social skills that a person needs to survive and become both an individual and a member of society. The early twentieth century view of human development was split between the Darwinians, who believed that human nature was biologically determined, and the Pavlovians, who felt that people were simply products of their environment. Today social scientists recognize that the key to individuality is socialization, where biology and culture meet.

The interaction of culture and biology during the socialization process affects a child's development in many ways. Although we know that socialization should begin with mutual trust between parent and child, every society has ideas about the right and wrong ways to satisfy an infant's basic needs. Furthermore, each parent interprets society's child-rearing norms in his or her own way; and the unique genetic make-up of each child influences the way he or she will be treated. Facial features, rate of physical and sexual development, and differences of temperament, size, and strength all can affect the way parents and others respond to an infant. The way in which they respond is influenced by the meaning communities project onto any number of physical characteristics. The responses and expectations of the people in a child's world subtly shape the youngster's self-image.

Many students of social behavior have contributed to our understanding of the process of socialization. Charles Horton Cooley used the image of a looking-glass to explain how others influence the way we see ourselves. The self is a social product, which emerges as the child interacts with other people, and it reflects the feedback he or she receives as a child, a student, a worker—throughout life. George Herbert Mead expanded on Cooley's theory. He argued that by "taking the role of the other" in play, children learn to imitate the *significant others* in their lives. In play they learn to see themselves through other people's eyes. Gradually, children develop a generalized impression of what people expect from them and of where they fit in the overall scheme of things (what Mead called the *generalized other*). Mead believed that the self was composed of two parts: the "I" (the active, spontaneous, idiosyncratic self), and the "me" (the social self).

Whereas Cooley and Mead viewed socialization as the gradual and complementary merger of individual and society, Sigmund Freud argued that socialization is thrust upon the child against his or her will, and that socialization is never complete. For Freud, an essential aspect of socialization is the taming of the *id*, the repository of innate sexual and aggressive urges. The *superego*, or conscience, begins to develop and the child starts to internalize his or her parents' ideas of right and wrong. Socially unacceptable desires are gradually repressed in favor of meeting socially acceptable goals. Gradually, the child develops an *ego*, the conscious part of the self that seeks socially acceptable ways to satisfy biological cravings. Throughout life the ego mediates between the id and the superego. Driven one way by biology, the other by society, we are, in Freud's view, eternally discontent. Erik Erikson, a student of Freud, has described human emotional development in terms of eight stages, ranging from infancy to old age. Erikson's central concern is with the feelings people develop toward themselves and the world around them. In many ways he brings Cooley, Mead, and Freud together, integrating the physiological, psychological, and social elements of socialization.

Jean Piaget adds another dimension to the process of socialization with his analysis of the four stages of *cognitive development*. He showed that there are very real differences in the *way* children think at different ages. Piaget concludes that the stages of cognitive development do not unfold automatically, but are the result of each child's interaction with the world. Lawrence Kohlberg has added much to our knowledge of *moral development*. He has concluded that the way people think about moral issues is not simply a reflection of their culture, but, like emotional growth and cognitive skills, something that develops in stages as the child gains experience in the world.

Socialization is a lifelong process in which family, schools, peers, lovers, and children all play a part. Families inculcate their values in their children—values that, as Melvin Kohn has suggested, are influenced by the parents' social class. School socializes young people to society's values and to the organizational life they will experience as adults. Peer groups also play a large role in socialization. Among friends children can test ideas and share knowledge that may not be easily discussed at home. Peer groups allow young people to defend themselves against the ambiguities of adolescence by aligning themselves *with* each other and *against* adults. To some extent, peer groups at any age become an extended family. Adult socialization builds on the norms, values, and habits learned in childhood and adolescence. Learning new roles through work, marriage, parenthood, and old age is largely a matter of learning new ways of expressing existing behavior or values.

In our society socialization to old age is, for many, socialization to withdrawal. Margaret Mead suggests that old people can remain useful by passing their knowledge on to younger people. They can also reduce their loneliness by using their practical experience in their own communities. Society must, however, institutionalize meaningful social roles for old people.

glossary

autonomy Erikson's term for a child's confidence in his or her ability to govern himself or herself.

cognitive development The gradual maturation of a child's ability to reason and think in abstract terms.

ego Freud's term for the conscious part of the self that finds socially acceptable ways of satisfying the biological cravings of the *id*.

generalized other A child's generalized impression of what other people expect from him or her.

id Freud's term for the innate collection of sexual and aggressive urges, as well as for all bodily pleasure.

identity A sense of continuity about oneself, derived from one's past, present, and future, from what one feels about oneself, and from the image reflected in the social looking-glass. This sense of continuity is formed during what Erikson has termed the *identity crisis*.

life cycle Erikson's term for the stages of life and the ways in which later stages interconnect with earlier ones to make a cycle.

looking-glass self Cooley's term to explain how others influence the way we see ourselves. We gain an image of ourselves by imagining what other people think about the way we look and behave.

significant others When young children play at taking adult roles, they in effect become the people who are important in their social world. Mead called these people *significant others*.

socialization The process of acquiring the physical, mental, and social skills that a person needs to survive and to become both an individual and a member of society.

superego Freud's term for the conscience, the part of personality that internalizes society's views of right and wrong.

references

Gordon W. Allport, *The Nature of Prejudice*, Reading, Mass.: Addison-Wesley, 1954.

Philippe Ariès, *Centuries of Childhood: A Social History of Family Life*, New York: Vintage, 1962.

Diana Baumrind, "Effects of Authoritative Parental Control on Child Behavior," *Child Development*, vol. 37 (1966): 887–907.

Bruno Bettleheim, "The Problem of Generations," in Glen A. Newkirk, ed., *Contemporary Issues*, Glenview, Ill.: Scott, Foresman, 1971.

Warren Boroson, "In Defense of Adolescents," in Glen A. Newkirk, ed., *Contemporary Issues*, Glencoe, Ill.: Scott, Foresman, 1971.

John Bowlby, *Separation: Anxiety and Anger*, New York: Basic Books, 1973.

John A. Clausen, "The Organism and Socialization," *Social Behavior,* vol. 8 (1967): 243–52.

James S. Coleman, *Abnormal Psychology and Modern Life*, Glenview, Ill.: Scott, Foresman, 1972.

———, *The Adolescent Society*, New York: Free Press, 1961.

Charles Horton Cooley, *Human Nature and the Social Order*, New York: Schocken, 1964.

———, *Social Organization: A Study of the Larger Mind*, Glencoe, Ill.: Free Press, 1956.

Stephen J. Cutler, "The Availability of Personal Transportation, Residential Location, and Life Satisfaction Among the Aged," *Journal of Gerontology*, vol. 27 (1972): 383–89.

Kingsley Davis, *Human Society*, New York: Macmillan, 1948.

S. N. Eisenstadt, "Archetypal Patterns of Youth," *Daedalus* (Winter 1962): 28–46.

Erik Erikson, *Childhood and Society*, New York: Norton, 1950.

———, *Young Man Luther*, New York: Norton, 1958.

———, *Identity: Youth and Crisis*, New York: Norton, 1968.

Hans G. Furth, *Piaget and Knowledge*, Englewood Cliffs, N.J.: Prentice-Hall, 1969.

David Gutman, "The Hunger of Old Men," *Transaction* (November–December 1971).

John L. Hampton, "Determinants of Psychosexual Orientation," in Frank A. Beacon, ed., *Sex and Behavior*, New York: Wiley, 1965.

Harry F. Harlow and R. Z. Zimmerman, "Affectional Responses in the Infant Monkey," *Science*, vol. 130 (1959): 421–32.

Jules Henry, *Culture Against Man*, New York: Random House, 1963.

Reuben Hill, *The Family: A Dramatic Interpretation*, New York: Holt, Rinehart Winston, 1938.

Herbert R. Kohl, *The Open Classroom*, New York: Vintage, 1969.

Lawrence Kohlberg, "Moral and Religious Education and the Public Schools: A Developmental View," in T. Sizer, ed., *Religion and Public Education*, Boston: Houghton Mifflin, 1967.

——— and Card Gilligan, "The Adolescent as a Philosopher: The Discovery of the Self in a Postconventional World," *Daedalus* (Fall 1971): 1051–86.

Melvin L. Kohn, "Social Class and Parent-Child Relations: An Interpretation," *American Journal of Sociology*, vol. 68 (1963): 471–80.

George Herbert Mead, *Mind, Self and Society*, Chicago: University of Chicago Press, 1934.

Margaret Mead, *Sex and Temperament in Three Primitive Societies*, New York: Morrow, 1935.

———, "A New Style of Aging," in *Christianity and Crisis* (November 15, 1971): 240–43.

Wilbert E. Moore, "Occupational Socialization," in David A. Goslin, ed., *Handbook of Socialization Theory and Research,* New York: Rand McNally, 1969.

A. S. Neill, *Summerhill*, New York: Hart, 1960.

Noyes and McAndrew, "Is This What Schools Are For?" *Saturday Review* (December 21, 1968), in Silberman, 1971.

Talcott Parsons, "The School Class as a Social System: Some of the Functions in American Society," *Harvard Educational Review*, vol. 29 (Fall 1969): 297–318.

J. L. Phillips, Jr., *The Origins of the Intellect: Piaget's Theory*, San Francisco: Freeman, 1969.

Jean Piaget and Barbara Inhelder, *The Psychology of the Child*, New York: Basic Books, 1969.

Matilda White Riley and Anne Foner et al. *Aging and Society*, vol. 1, "An Inventory of Research Findings," New York: Russell Sage Foundation, 1968.

———, Beth Hess, and Marcia L. Toby, "Socialization for the Middle and Later Years," in David A. Goslin, ed., *Handbook of Socialization Theory and Research,* New York: Rand McNally, 1969.

Maggie Scarf, "He and She: The Sex Hormones and Behavior," *The New York Times Magazine* (May 7, 1972): 30 ff.

Charles E. Silberman, *Crisis in the Classroom*, New York: Random House, 1971.

R. A. Spitz, "The Psychogenic Diseases of Infancy: An Attempt at Their Etiological Classification," *Psychoanalytic Study of the Child*, vol. 6 (1951): 255–75.

L. Joseph Stone and Joseph Church, *Childhood and Adolescence: A Psychology of the Growing Person*, New York: Random House, 1973.

L. P. Ullman and L. Krasner, *A Psychological Approach to Abnormal Behavior*, Englewood Cliffs, N.J.: Prentice-Hall, 1969.

John B. Watson, *Behaviorism* (1924), New York: Norton, 1970.

Lenore J. Weitzman, Deborah Eifler, Elizabeth Hokada, and Catherine Ross, "Sex Role Socialization in Picture Books for Preschool Children," *American Journal of Sociology*, vol. 77 (May 1972): 1125–50.

William H. Whyte, Jr., *The Organization Man*, New York: Anchor, 1957.

for further study

Overview. A comprehensive reference on this subject by sociologists is the *Handbook of Socialization Theory and Research,* edited by David Goslin (Chicago: Rand McNally, 1969). Good essays can also be found in the *International Encyclopedia of the Social Sciences*. A more psychological treatment by an excellent clinician can be found in *The Person: His Development Through the Life Cycle*, by Theodore Lidz (New York: Basic Books, 1968). But beyond such general works, below are some topics you might wish to explore in greater depth for term papers or personal reasons. We omit here references on the family and education, which can be found at the end of the chapters devoted specifically to those subjects.

Brainwashing. Torturing people in order to wash their brains clean of old values and thinking goes on every year in many countries. Sociologists call this *de*socialization, and brainwashing is an extreme form. The most careful studies of techniques and their effects come from the Korean War. They include Edgar Shein, *Coercive Persuasion* (New York: Norton, 1961), and Robert J. Lifton, *Thought Reform and the Psychology of Totalism* (New York: Norton, 1961).

Socialization into the Professions. Many readers will soon enter one of the professions, yet most who do are not aware of what transformations occur. In medicine there are two famous books: *Boys in White*, by Howard S. Becker et al. (Chicago: University of Chicago Press, 1961), and *The Student Physician*, edited by Robert Merton et al. (Cambridge, Mass.: Harvard University Press, 1957). In the latter, see particularly Merton's introduction and the essay by Renée Fox, "Training for Uncertainty." She has also written a fine essay with Harold Lief on training for detached concern, a central quality in professional work. It is found in *The Psychological Basis of Medical Practice*, edited by Lief et al. (New York: Harper & Row, 1963). One of the best short essays on socialization in medicine is by Daniel J. Levinson, "Medical Education and the Theory of Adult Socialization," *Journal of Health and Social Behavior* (December, 1967): 253–65.

Socialization into law is less well studied, but a valuable work is Wagner Thielens, "Some Comparisons of Entrants to Medical and Law School," *Journal of Legal Education*, vol. 11 (1958–59): 153–71. Other interesting articles include, Wagner Thielens, "The Influence of the Law School Experience on the Professional Ethics of Law Students," *Journal of Legal Education,* vol. 29 (1969): 9; Seymour Warkov and Joseph Zelan, *Lawyers in the Making* (Chicago: Aldine, 1965); *The Lawyer in Modern Society*, edited by Vern Countrymen (Boston: Little, Brown, 1966). For good articles by law students, see the journal *Student Lawyer*. The latest full assessment is *New Directions in Legal Education* by Herbert Packer and Thomas Ehrlich (New York: McGraw-Hill, 1972).

Nursing has been carefully studied by sociologists. One of the most interesting books on this profession is *The Silent Dialogue* by Virginia Olesen and Elvi Whittaker (San Francisco: Jossey-Bass, 1968). See also *The Nursing Profession*, edited by Fred Davis (New York: Wiley, 1966).

One of the most fascinating professions in which to study socialization is psychiatry, because the very nature of the work involves the whole person. The most complete self-description is *The Making of a Psychiatrist* (New York: Arbor, 1972), a very readable and sensitive book by David Viscott. Two good accounts by sociologists are Rue Bucher, "The Psychiatric Residency and Professional Socialization," *Journal of Health and Social Behavior,* vol. 6 (1965): 197–206, and the excellent description by A. J. Blum and L. Rosenberg, "Some

Problems Involved in Professionalizing Social Interaction: The Case of Psychotherapeutic Training," *Journal of Health and Social Behavior*, vol. 9 (1968): 72–85.

Old Age. The most authoritative discussions of the social dimensions of aging are the volumes edited by Matilda Riley and Anne Foner, *Aging and Society* (New York: Russell Sage Foundation, 1968). Another good collection of articles is *Middle Age and Aging*, edited by Bernice L. Newgarten (Chicago: University of Chicago Press, 1968). Perhaps the single most brilliant book on aging is Simone de Beauvoir's *The Coming of Age* (New York: Putnam, 1972).

Socialization for the Future. It has been said that society changes so fast that we cannot socialize our children for the future. If that is true (are there not timeless qualities to human relations?), the problem is made worse because we cannot help but be socialized by the past—that is, by the previous generation. The following works provide fascinating ideas and information about the future. Roderick Seidenberg in *Posthistoric Man* (Chapel Hill, N.C.: University of North Carolina Press, 1950) discusses the implications of technology for human values and social life. The same themes are pursued by Lewis Mumford in *The Myth of the Machine* (New York: Harcourt Brace Jovanovich, 1970). Mumford also provides great empirical detail of how human relations have changed. More optimistic is Robert J. Lifton, who wrote the famous essay "Protean Man," which predicts a new, flexible, and open human being. Others who see social freedom as a fruit of technology are Marshall McLuhan, *Understanding Media* (New York: New American Library, 1970) and *Culture Is Our Business* (New York: Ballantine, 1972); Marshall McLuhan and Quentin Fiore, *War and Peace in the Global Village* (New York: Bantam, 1971); and Thomas Hanna, *Bodies in Revolt* (New York: Holt, Rinehart and Winston, 1970).

On February 8, 1964, the eighty-one-year-old chairman of the House
Rules Committee, Howard W. Smith, introduced what he liked to
call "my little amendment" to Title VII of the Civil Rights bill,
which prohibited discrimination in employment because of "race,
color, religion or national origin." Smith proposed including the
word "sex" in this list—and hastened to add, "Now I am serious
about this amendment . . ." The Virginian settled back to listen to
the clerk read through the bill, adding the word sex at appropriate
points.

Emanuel Cellar of New York, who headed the pro-Civil Rights
coalition in the House, took the floor. Would the amendment mean
that women would be subject to the draft, he asked. What about
alimony and child custody? "You know the biological differences
between the sexes. In many States we have laws favorable to
women. Are you going to strike these laws down?" But Cellar could
not resist injecting humor into the occasion. "I can say as a result
of forty-nine years of experience—and I celebrate my fiftieth wedding anniversary next year—that women, indeed, are not the minority in my house. . . . I usually have the last two words, and
those words are, 'Yes, dear.'" Frances P. Bolton of Ohio proposed
transferring the sex issue to Title X, *Miscellaneous*, but Smith
objected. "I think women are entitled to more dignity than that."

SEX ROLES

(More laughter.) Late in the afternoon, the amendment was passed by a vote of 168 to 133.

Women's rights are no longer a joking matter. In the decade since the Civil Rights Act was passed, women have fought for and won equal opportunity in employment and equal pay (at least on paper). They have entered previously all-male professions, as jockeys, for example, and their numbers in male-dominated medical and law schools are increasing. They have gained the right to control their own bodies through legalized abortion. Women's Liberation—and liberated women—are symptoms of widespread change. The development of "the pill" (which became available in 1960), the commercialization of singlehood, frank discussion of open marriage, homosexuals "coming out of the closet," even unisex styles and fashions have challenged traditional assumptions about appropriate roles for women and men—about what it means to be a woman or a man.

This chapter explores male and female biology, the acquisition of sex-typed behavior, attitudes, and interests, and the changing meaning of gender. How different are the sexes and in what respects? Are any of these differences universal? What roles have been set aside for men and women in different societies? in America? How are these roles changing?

HOW DIFFERENT ARE THE SEXES?

For centuries people assumed that the differences between the sexes were inborn or "natural"; that biology decreed varying interests and abilities for women and men. Men were thought to be instinctively aggressive; a woman caring for a child was fulfilling her "maternal instinct." Generations of husbands told their wives not to worry their "pretty little heads" about politics or business, and gallantly protected the "weaker sex" from education. It was not until anthropologists discovered societies where men are passive and vain and women domineering, and societies where there is no difference whatever between the way men and women behave, that people began to seriously question the biological basis of masculinity and femininity. Anatomy was not destiny after all. Feminists especially, but male thinkers as well, began to argue that masculine and feminine behavior differences were learned, not innate. Little girls are given dolls, little boys trucks and guns, and few of us escape the "blue and pink" tyranny (Reuben, 1972). Rather quickly opinion divided into two camps: those who maintained that sex differences were innate and those who argued emphatically and with good evidence that they were not. We are beginning to learn that the truth lies somewhere in between and is more complex than the nature or nurture arguments suggest.

The Biology of Gender

There is no denying the physical differences between males and females. But besides the obvious anatomical distinctions, differences are apparent in the unequal sex ratio at conception (about 106 males are conceived for every 100 females), in the higher rates of prenatal mortality for males (which evens this ratio out), and in chromosomes and hormones. Every human being has twenty-three pairs of chromosomes, all of which are alike except for one pair—the sex chromosomes. There are two kinds of sex chromosomes—X and Y. Females have two X chromosomes, males an X and a Y chromosome. As a result, males produce two kinds of sperms, half with an X chromosome, half with a Y. If an ovum (which is always X) is fertilized by a sperm with an X chromosome, the child will be female (XX). An ovum fertilized by a Y-carrying sperm produces a male (XY). For the first twelve weeks, however, the fetus is sexually undifferentiated. All fetuses have a *rind* that may become an ovary; a *core* that may become testes; both male and female internal duct systems (one of which becomes vestigial); a *genetical tubercle* that will grow into either a clitoris or a penis; and tissue that will fuse to become the scrotum or separate to become the lips of the vagina (Scarf, 1972, p.102). Differentiation depends on hormones that begin working at about three months after fertilization.

Hormones are chemical substances, secreted into the bloodstream by glands, that stimulate or inhibit vital chemical processes. (The term *hormone* comes from the Greek for arouse.) The major sex hormones are estrogen and progesterone (secreted by the ovaries in females) and testosterone and the androgens (secreted by the testes in males). These hormones initiate sexual differentiation in the fetus, and activate the reproductive system and development of secondary sex characteristics in puberty. At some point the male fetus begins to produce testosterone, which inhibits the development of female characteristics.[1] Some months later a recog-

---

[1] Alfred Jost demonstrated this by castrating a male rabbit *in utero*; when born, the animal had female genitalia, despite his chromosome pattern (Jost quoted in Scarf, 1972, p. 102).

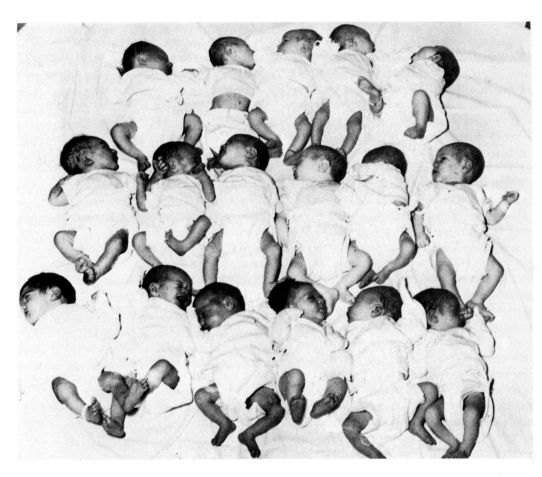

nizable male is born. If testosterone is not produced, a female is born. Interestingly, both males and females produce hormones of the opposite sex. There is abundant evidence that testosterone stimulates libido or sex drive in *both* sexes. The difference seems to lie in the concentration of sex hormones at critical periods. If a female fetus is given testosterone, she will develop male-like genitalia. If a male is castrated before puberty (a brutal form of sterilization, at one time applied to some male singers and harem-keepers), he will not develop secondary sex characteristics (such as a beard) or genital sexuality. But sterilization of an adult male eliminates the production of sperm but has

Whether these babies will grow up behaving as men or women is more than a matter of biology. Almost from birth, society will treat them differently, expecting them to act like boys or girls are "supposed" to act. (UPI)

no effect on sexual appetite or behavior (Gergen, in Vincent, 1968, p. 190). In other words, sex differentiation is multidimensional: genetic sex, fetal and pubertal hormones, internal and external anatomy do not necessarily coincide. There is much variation within the sexes, as well as between them (Money and Ehrhardt, 1972).

Do sex hormones influence behavior? Every so often something goes awry during prenatal development and an infant is incorrectly classified as female or male at birth, creating a "natural experiment." The parents accept the doctor's sex identification and raise the child as a boy or girl—whichever they've been told. The child grows up to be, in his or her own mind, this sex—sometimes despite contrary evidence. John Money and Anke Ehrhardt studied matched pairs of hermaphrodites (children born with the internal organs of both sexes) who were biologically identical, but had been assigned to different sexes. The contrasts between those raised as females and those raised as males were so complete, "the ordinary person meeting them socially or vocationally has no clues as to the remarkable contents of their medical history." Money and Ehrhardt conclude, "nature has ordained a major part of gender-identity differentiation to be accomplished in the post-natal period" (1972, p. 18). Robert Stoller cites the even more remarkable example of a boy who was born without normal male sexual organs, but nevertheless developed a strong and enduring sense of maleness (1968, p. 42). Although exceedingly rare, such cases are instructive because they show that anatomy does not guarantee that a person will grow up thinking he or she is the sex his or her biology indicates. If gender identity were genetically or hormonally determined, misidentification would not be possible. But with these children, upbringing had more impact than biology.

Gender Identity and Socialization

Socialization to gender begins virtually at birth and continues into adolescence, with its biological changes and fumbling discoveries, and adulthood. The groundwork for gender differentiation is laid in infancy.

Infant Care   In large part, infant care is nondiscriminatory. All infants must be fed, bathed, diapered, cuddled, and rested. There is no sex-typing in these basic activities, but there is some evidence that parents respond differently to male and female infants. Sears, Maccoby, and Levin (1957) found that parents tend to handle infant girls more warmly and affectionately than infant boys, and to be more tolerant of assertiveness and physical aggression in infant boys than in infant girls.

Parental preferences for one sex or the other may also influence infant care. Richard Green found that parents who had hoped for a daughter but gotten a son tended to feminize their child. One boy who had what most people would consider female interests told Green:

Well, my problem to begin with is of very long standing. In fact, all my conscious life, I have been aware that I was of the wrong sex, and I can remember quite clearly back as far as my third birthday. I have scattered little memories of this and that, beginning with my parents. They were sort of expecting a girl when I arrived. (1974)

Thus the patterns we suggested above may be reversed: parents who wanted a son may play roughly with an infant girl, encouraging her to display assertive behavior, which most parents suppress in girls. Or, a boy or girl may resist his or her parents' lessons.

Gender Training   When the child reaches the age of two or three, these casual, half-conscious distinctions become explicit lessons. Parents begin to address the child as "Daddy's little girl" or "Mommy's big boy" and to actively discourage (or at least ignore) behavior they consider inappropriate. In some ways the change is greater for boys than for girls. Boys are expected to outgrow dependency and clinging, whereas this kind of behavior is accepted from girls (Bardwick and Douvan, 1971). A mother may begin to ignore a boy's whimpering. If he persists, she may ask him, "Did you ever see your father cry? Do you think Joe Namath or Muhammad Ali cries? Of course not." Gradually boys learn that only girls are supposed to cry. A little girl finds that her parents are genuinely angry when she uses a "nasty" word, but chuckle if her brother does. The message is clear. Sometimes the difference in the ways boys and girls are raised is dramatic. In traditional Puerto Rican families, for example, parents expect boys to fend for themselves and rarely interfere with their wanderings. But a girl's life is closely supervised; daughters are not allowed out of an adult's or brother's sight (Simpson and Yinger, 1972, p. 479). In other families, the differences are subtler, but all children develop concrete notions of girl and non-girl, boy and non-boy even before they understand the facts of life. Girls are supposed to be pretty, clean, neat, sweet, and popular; boys should be clever, strong, and fearless. For most children, striving to live up to these ideals is the path of least resistance.

Of course, parents are not children's only source of information on how they are supposed to act; brothers and sisters, other children, teachers, television, and books provide additional models. Even before children can read, books have a special fascination and magic: they open doors to a world beyond their own experience, and show them what other children do and think, as well as the consequences of such behavior. Lenore J. Weitzman and Deborah Eifler (1972) found that nearly all prize-winning children's books present highly stereotyped and unrealistic images of girls and boys, men and women. Females are decidedly underrepresented in the winners and runners-up for the prestigious Caldecott Medal. Although 51 percent of the population is female, the ratio of male

to female pictures was eleven to one; and one-third of the books involved *males only*. It would be perfectly reasonable for children to conclude that females are not very important, for if they were, more books would be written about them.[2]

When girls did appear in the children's books, they were nearly always indoors, helping, watching, or loving the book's hero. The one exception was a book about a little girl named *Sam* who convinced a boy to act out her mischievous fantasies. But most of the girls were like pretty dolls, concerned only with pleasing others. In contrast, boys were shown rescuing helpless animals and girls, riding turtles into underwater kingdoms, outwitting the gods, and the like. Similarly, men were farmers, housebuilders, kings, fishermen, gods, spiders. They *never* cried. Women were mothers (with the exception of one fairy godmother, who was the only adult woman engaging in any activities that vaguely resembled a career). One set of books, called *Mommies* and *Daddies*, was not very complimentary to mothers: "Daddies," the author wrote, "know you're big enough and brave enough to do lots of things that mommies think are much too hard." Not one of the books mentioned working mothers or showed fathers helping around the house; not one dealt with death or divorce or any of the problems that might trouble children.

Parents, relatives, friends, and books are not the only means by which children learn to be boys or girls. Sex roles are also taught in school. On a typical day at the Educational Alliance Child Care Center in New York City, a visitor can find little girls busily hammering and sawing, and little boys rocking doll

---

[2] According to Robert Stoller, little girls appear to have a "gratifying, unquestioned femininity" by the time they begin to walk, and this positive sense of femaleness may protect them against self-denigration (1968, pp. 62–63).

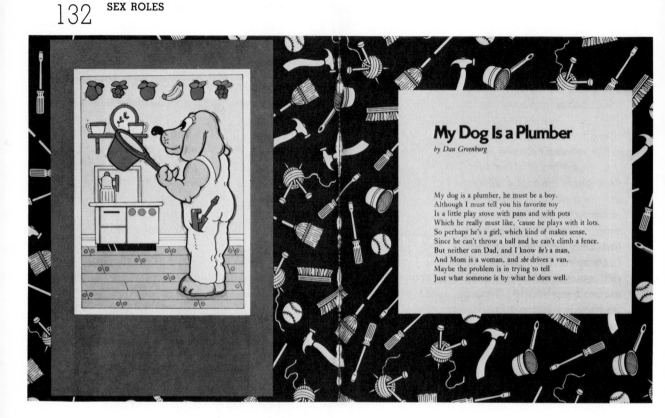

My Dog Is a Plumber

by Dan Greenburg

My dog is a plumber, he must be a boy.
Although I must tell you his favorite toy
Is a little play stove with pans and with pots
Which he really must like, 'cause he plays with it lots.
So perhaps he's a girl, which kind of makes sense,
Since he can't throw a ball and he can't climb a fence.
But neither can Dad, and I know *he's* a man,
And Mom is a woman, and *she* drives a van.
Maybe the problem is in trying to tell
Just what someone is by what he does well.

cradles and setting tables. This daycare center is exceptional. (The very thought of boys playing with dolls would strike terror into the hearts of many parents.) The teachers, who are participating in a demonstration project to combat sex stereotypes, had to make their own books with pictures of women working and fathers cooking, cleaning, and caring for children. Their biggest problem, however, was learning to identify their own, unconscious biases. Even the children, though only four or five years old, resisted innovation. The girls shied away from building blocks—until, that is, they visited a construction site where a woman was working as an engineer (*The New York Times*, April 19, 1974, p. 40).

In most schools, boys and girls are segregated in sports (hardball for boys, softball for girls) and such classes as shop and home economics. In *Sisterhood Is Powerful* (Mor-

This page from a "liberated" children's book encourages boys and girls to think flexibly about sex roles. (Carole Hart et al. *Free To Be You and Me*)

gan, 1970) one young woman describes her experience as the lone female in shop.

The first day I started Shop I was very apprehensive about how boys were going to react to me being in the class. I had two very good friends in that class . . . and they congratulated me on my success. One of the boys is very condescending toward me, always speaking in a patronizing, gentle voice that really makes me angry. "Connie, let me help you," they say. Well! I just want to tell you——(expletives deleted). "Quit it!" I say furiously, but silently. But Shop is fun if the teacher isn't paying attention because you can goof off all you want to. One thing I realized when I walked into the room the first day was that I could *never* cut, because my absence would be too noticeable. (p. 365)

The irony in keeping girls out of shop is that the girls who do become housewives need to know how to use tools as much as or more than their husbands, who may not be home when things break.

In the early 1970s, parents around the country began organizing to combat discrimination in curricula and teaching materials. A group in Kalamazoo, Michigan, for example, is working with the Houghton Mifflin publishing company to create children's readers showing women working and men in the home (*The Wall Street Journal*, October 9, 1973, pp. 1ff). But it is difficult to say whether teaching children of both sexes the same skills in the same classes will alter the personality/attitude dimension of gender training. Harriet Holter (1970) believes that by the time children reach school, such personality dispositions as emotional expressiveness, self-reliance, or competitiveness may be relatively fixed. Studies of the kibbutzim in Israel tend to confirm this view. Despite the conscious attempt to eliminate sex-typing in work and recreation, men and women on a kibbutz are as different from each other as men and women in Ohio or Manhattan. One reason is that although kibbutz pioneers tried to create "occupational unisex," they did not try to alter sex stereotypes—the idea that men are strong, responsible, and rational and that women are soft, nurturant, and decorative. The contradictions between women's occupational and personal roles (woman as strong worker but pliant individual) in part explain the reemergence of the "woman question" on the kibbutz today (Keller, 1973).

We can conclude then, that a child's gender identity—the feeling, "I am a girl" or "I am a boy"—seems to be established before she or he enters school. Gender identity does not develop naturally and inevitably as a by-product of physical maturation, it is acquired gradually through experience (Stoller, 1968; Money and Ehrhardt, 1972). It involves an

Not only boys like woodworking; not only girls like babies. Both these children are learning skills that will make them more flexible men and women. (Top, Gene Maggio. Bottom, Globe Photos)

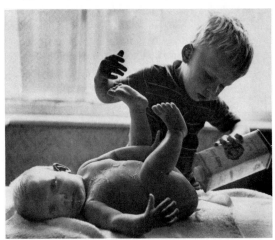

awareness of physical distinctions (anatomy and appearance); a consciousness of sex-specific activities, skills, and modes of self-preservation; and covert feelings of liking or disliking for the interests reserved for one's sex (Kagan, 1964). *Sex* (male or female biology), *sexuality* (erotic response and activities), and *gender* (the psychological characteristics associated with masculinity and femininity) do not necessarily coincide with gender assignment. A person may be anatomically male but feel feminine and be erotically drawn to women, or conversely, be classified as female but feel masculine and be erotically drawn to both sexes.

Gender identity does not depend on an awareness of the facts of life, but sex-role identity does. Gradually the child learns that certain reproductive, erotic, and social activities are appropriate for his or her gender by watching same-sex models and observing how others react to the way he or she dresses, talks, and plays. The role the child is expected to learn depends on the culture and community into which he or she is born.

THE SOCIOLOGY OF GENDER: SEX ROLES AND SOCIETY

Why, generally, do European actresses present multi-dimensioned personalities while our American stars flatten out like uncorrugated cardboard? . . . We caricature screen heroines . . . we categorize . . . overplay . . . overdress. Our women slide into easy character niches. . . .

But European moviemakers don't give us such easy signals . . . in the course of the films their women often reveal themselves as rich, complex human beings. . . . Nothing stagnates, and no one is readable at a glance. (Rosen, 1973, p. 352)

Why do Swedish or French women behave differently from American women, on and off

the screen? As the preceding discussion suggested, we will not find the reason by examining their genes, hormones, or anatomies; they are all biologically female. The reason lies, rather, in culturally patterned expectations about what is appropriate for women or men. This is what we mean by *sex roles*: they are guidelines for gender-appropriate appearance, dress, interests, skills, and self-perceptions; models of what men and women should be like.[3]

Clues to sex-role standards in a society range from laws governing marital relations (and perhaps restricting women's rights) to contests and awards (such as the Miss America pageant) to humor. Why do people laugh at the image of men wearing aprons and doing dishes? Why do so many American organizations issue awards to the Mother of the Year (but not the Father—or even the Parent—of the Year)? How can we explain the emotion-charged responses of a few years ago to young men letting their hair grow long—responses ranging from ridicule to suspension from school? Reactions to deviations from group norms are an index of the strength of those norms, a measure of how far people will go to safeguard gender ideals. Such clues give us a generalized image of how men and women are *supposed* to look and act in this or another society. But perhaps the best way to illuminate sex roles is to contrast our standards with those in other cultures.

Cross-Cultural Variation

When anthropologist Margaret Mead left for New Guinea in 1931, she "shared the general belief in our society that there was a

---

[3] It is important to remember that roles are ideal prescriptions, not descriptions of how people actually are. Obviously, not all women are compassionate and maternal (although most may think they should be), and men can and do cry.

natural sex-temperament which at most could be distorted or diverted from normal expression" (1950, p. xvi). After living with and studying the Arapesh, the Mundugumor, and the Tchambuli, her attitude changed, and she explained why in *Sex and Temperament in Three Primitive Societies* (originally published 1935).

The mountain Arapesh are a very mild-mannered people. They regard competitiveness and aggression as aberrations. An Arapesh may fight to defend a relative, but he would be ashamed to show anger on his or her own behalf. What interested Mead most about this tribe was that they have no idea of any temperamental difference between men and women. They expect all people to be gentle and home-loving; they believe men and women are equally inclined to subordinate their own needs to the needs of those who are younger or weaker, and to derive personal satisfaction from giving of themselves. No Arapesh can bear to hear an infant cry; the nearest man or woman rushes to cuddle and feed an unhappy child. Often, relatives borrow a youngster for the sheer pleasure of participating in his or her upbringing. In short, they are what we would call a maternal tribe. "To the Arapesh, the world is a garden that must be tilled, not for one's self, not in pride and boasting, not for hoarding and usury, but that the yams and the dogs and the pigs and most of all the children may grow" (p. 109).

The neighboring Mundugumor are as fierce as the Arapesh are gentle. The Mundugumor assume a natural hostility between members of the same sex; relations between sexes are only slightly less mistrustful. "The Mundugumor man-child is born into a hostile world, a world in which most of the members of his own sex will be enemies, in which his major equipment for success must be a capacity for violence, for seeing and avenging insults, for holding his own safety very

lightly and the lives of others even more lightly" (pp. 146–47). The birth of a child is an ambiguous event among the Mundugumor. If the child is a boy, the father considers him a rival. Members of this tribe obtain brides by exchanging sisters and daughters, and a father and son have an equal claim on the females that are their daughters and sisters, respectively. If the child is a girl, the mother begins worrying that the father will exchange her for a new, rival bride. Often a couple offers a child for adoption. The children they keep receive only minimal attention and are expected to fend for themselves as soon as they can walk, while their parents plot and scheme ways to satisfy their lust for power, position, and revenge. The aggressive, combative Mundugumor ideal applies to *both* sexes. All Mundugumor exhibit what we might call exaggerated *machismo*.

Members of the third tribe Mead studied did believe the sexes are temperamentally different, but the roles they prescribe for men and women are the exact opposite of ours. Tchambuli women are "solid, preoccupied (with practical matters), powerful, with their shaven unadorned heads." Every dawn they set out for the lagoons to fish and trap, returning at mid-morning to work on the crafts they exchange with other tribes. Tchambuli men drift about the fringes of the women's circle, hoping for an approving word, an invitation, a gift. It is the women who pull the economic strings in Tchambuli society, and the men who devote their lives to self-adornment and the arts of "languishing looks and soft words"; the men who bicker and pout, exhibiting the emotional ups and downs and employing the wiles we call feminine. These roles naturally carry over into mating, where women take the initiative.

A young widow is a tremendous liability to the community. No one expects her to remain quiet until her remarriage has been arranged. . . . This is the comment that is continually made in Tchambuli: Are women passive sexless creatures who can be expected to wait upon the dilly-dallying of formal considerations of bride-price? Men, not so urgently sexed, may be expected to submit themselves to the discipline of a due order and precedence. (p. 193)

Tchambuli sex roles are thus a mirror image of our own. Mead describes Tchambuli women's attitude toward men as "one of kindly toleration and appreciation"; they do not take men terribly seriously.

Commenting on these surprising discoveries, Mead concludes that strange as it may seem "to a civilization that in its sociology, its medicine, its slang, its poetry, and its obscenity accepts the socially defined differences between the sexes as having an innate basis," the characteristics we tend to regard as belonging to one sex or the other are "mere variations of human temperament to which members of either or both sexes may, with more or less success in the case of individuals, be educated to approximate" (p. xvi).

Although published in 1935, *Sex and Temperament* (and other illustrations of different conceptions of proper male and female behavior) received relatively little public attention. In part this was because researchers tended to stress universals and consistencies rather than differences across cultures; in part because ethnocentrism (and androcentrism, or male-centeredness) created unconscious blinders. The data accumulated over the past century, however, leave little doubt that the existence of universal gender prototypes is a figment of our imagination.

Some of the most puzzling cross-cultural variations in attitudes toward sex and sex roles are found in the Trans-Fly region of New Guinea. The Etero prohibit sexual intercourse for 295 days of the year. Their neighbors, the Marind-amin, prefer homosexual to heterosexual relations. Obviously their birth rate is very low; most Marind-amin children have been captured, not born into the tribe. Societies also vary in the degree to which they enforce the roles they prescribe. Many American Indian tribes, for example, institutionalized the *berdache*—a man who dressed and lived like a woman. If a man was not suited to be a fearless male warrior, he had an alternative (Mead, 1935, p. 103).

If men and women *are* born with distinct interests and talents, how do we account for the fact that 76 percent of the physicians in the Soviet Union but only 6 percent of their American counterparts are female (Sullerot, 1971, p. 151)? (See table 6:1.) The recruitment of Soviet women for employment outside the home is unique in the modern world. Marx, Engels, and other communist thinkers equated the subjugation of women with the oppression of the workers: under capitalism, women were chattel. In the early days of the Soviet experiment, women were seen as natural allies, and their role in the Revolution was idealized. In fact, ideology coincided with need in Russia. War had created a shortage of

table 6:1 **A CROSS-CULTURAL COMPARISON OF WOMEN IN THE MEDICAL PROFESSION**

COUNTRY	PERCENT OF FEMALE PHYSICIANS
USSR	76
Great Britain	25
France	22
West Germany	20
Austria	18
Sweden	13
USA	6

SOURCE: Evelyn Sullerot, *Women, Society, and Change* (New York: McGraw-Hill, 1971), p. 151.

WOMAN'S PLACE IN OLD JAPAN

1. A girl should be gentle, obedient, chaste, faithful, kind of heart, and quiet.

2. A girl should observe the distinction between man and woman from childhood, and should not be shown or told of flirtation. She should not associate with anybody without the instruction of her parents.

3. Woman has to regard the home of her husband as her own. No matter how poor or humble her husband's home may be, she must not complain but consider it heaven-sent because of her misfortune.

4. Woman should regard her husband as a master. Her way lies in obedience. She should never be irritable, luxurious or rudely behaved. She should never contradict his orders; she should regard him as heaven. If he leads a dissolute life, she should advise him to the contrary, but never with anger.

5. Woman should get up early in the morning and go to bed late at night. Even though she may have servants, it is in accordance with the manner of woman to do manual work.

6. Woman should not be overclean or conspicuous to attract the attention of others, nor shall she use conspicuous color or dye-stuff for her ornamental apparel. She should communicate with no young men other than her husband on business.

7. Being stupid in nature, woman shall stay at home as much as possible. Seven out of ten women have the following mental defects: disobedience, resentment, slander, jealousy, and a shallow brain. These weaknesses place her beneath man and she must correct them by self-reflection. She should go nowhere without her husband's permission.

8. Woman must ever remember three obediences: to her parents as a child, to her husband as a wife, and to her son in old age. She should never get offended when she is despised or looked down upon, but should show prudence by forbearing criticisms. Then she will live long in congenial happiness with her husband and her home will be peaceful.

In old Japan both males and females were dedicated to their social roles in a way Westerners find hard to conceive. "In the past, a Japanese would feel uncomfortable in thinking of his 'self' as something separable from his role" (De Vos and Wagatsuma, 1970, p. 336). A Japanese woman married to become a member of a family more than to fulfill her own individual psychological needs. Being a correct and proper housewife was indeed a full-time job in traditional Japan, given the complex rituals associated with all relationships and activities. And there were alternatives to the housewife role, notably the profession of geisha. As an entertainer a woman could be dominant, self-assertive. But in the home women deferred, remaining as inconspicuous as possible. Why? "[O]ne might almost equate the Japanese housewife in the traditional family to an efficient secretary in an American business company, where any undue emphasis on the sexual aspects of the secretary as an attractive young woman could become disruptive to the smooth functioning of role relationships within the office" (De Vos and Wagatsuma, 1970, p. 360). A disruptive wife could be sent back to her family in disgrace.

SOURCE: "Woman's Code of Conduct" (originally published 1729), trans. by Kaibara Ekiken; George De Vos and Hiroshi Wagatsuma, "Status and Role Behavior in Changing Japan," in Georgene H. Seward and Robert C. Williamson, eds., *Sex Roles in Changing Society*, New York: Random House, 1970.

manpower; if the country was to modernize, women had to work. Indeed, women were doubly valuable—as workers and as mothers, who in bearing children would contribute needed population.

Today a Russian woman who chooses not to work is stigmatized as a kept woman, a parasite. But conditions for women are far from ideal in the Soviet Union. Russian men consider housework degrading; as a result, Soviet women are housewives as well as workers. And although women have entered many professions (the Soviet Union had the first female astronaut), they are underrepresented in executive and managerial positions in industry and in the Communist party (Field and Flynn, 1970). Nevertheless, the number of female physicians, engineers, and the like in the Soviet Union shows clearly that society, not biology, determines what women can do.

Before Europeans invaded West Africa, most tribes believed men should hunt and women should till the fields. However, when the British and French decided to introduce modern agricultural techniques to Africa, they "naturally" instructed the men. Deprived of their independent economic function, many women became traders and prospered. Today women constitute 80 percent of Ghana's traders, and 50 percent of eastern and western Nigeria's traders. A Yoruba girl does not consider marriage until she is able to earn her own living. Although the Philippine government provides equal opportunity for education to both sexes, many girls drop out at nineteen for fear of not being able to find a husband of equal or better educational status. Thailand, in contrast, has instituted a quota on women medical students to prevent that profession from becoming all-female. In Moslem societies where the sexes are strictly segregated, females are forbidden to study with male teachers or to visit male

THE SWEDISH EXPERIMENT

As early as the 1930s, the Swedish government prohibited employers from discriminating against women for being married or because they might become pregnant. Numerous reforms followed. Unlike their counterparts in the Soviet Union, China, and the Israeli kibbutzim, Swedish reformers did not believe that child-rearing should be taken out of the home. Rather, they argued that fathers should play an active role in child care. "Both men and women have *one* main role, that of a human being. For both sexes, this role would include child care" (Dahlström, 1967, p. 179). The work week was shortened and vacations lengthened to give men more time at home. Women were awarded paid leaves of absence at childbirth, and the government provided part-time child care and part-time jobs for working mothers. The state also assumed some of the financial burden of parenting, out of the belief that home- and child-care should be paid like any other work. But although the legal barriers to equality have been removed, other obstacles remain. In general, men have not given up the desire for full-time wives; girls tend to drop out of school earlier than boys and to enter traditionally female occupations such as nursing; and for young people "the fear of going too far in behavior not typical of one's own sex is very great" (Liljestrom, 1970, p. 208). Surveying the current situation, Dahlström concludes that so long as women retain "a special status from the standpoint of maintenance," they will not shed their image as dependent, supported housekeepers. He adds, "Equality cannot be realized as long as the majority of women are content to bear by themselves the main responsibility for the care of home and children" (1967, p. 178).

SOURCE: Edmund Dahlström, "Analysis of the Debate on Sex Roles," in Edmund Dahlström, ed., *The Changing Roles of Men and Women*, Boston: Beacon Press, 1967.

physicians; these professions are therefore open to women. Over 20 percent of women working in nonagricultural fields in Moslem countries are professionals. This is a higher percentage than in the United States, where only 14 percent are professionals (Leavitt, 1972).

The comparative study of sex roles challenges the implicit equation between women's biological make-up and their worldly achievements. In single-society research, the sociological determinants of sex-based achievements often remain hidden, tempting researchers to attribute sex differences to genetic or hormonal endowment. Cross-cultural data show that this assumption is false. The different rates of women's participation in professional and public life can hardly be attributed to biology, which, as far as we know, does not vary nationally.

Subcultural Variation

Even within a single society, norms about masculinity and femininity vary from one subculture to another. For example, in American society the idea that men should be breadwinners and women homemakers is realized primarily in middle-class settings. Neither image fits the lower class, where both spouses are likely to be working, or the upper class, where neither spouse may have to work. Homebound and child-oriented (at least in principle), middle-class wives do many chores that upper-class women consider unladylike and leave to servants. Not surprisingly, these different milieus present differing definitions of femininity to little girls growing up in them. In one case it means scrubbing floors, washing, ironing, and cooking three meals a day; in the other, it means supervising the people who do such work.

Mirra Komarovsky's *Blue-Collar Marriage* (1967) highlights the differences between working-class and middle-class (college-educated) gender ideals. She found that many working-class husbands and wives got married because they were unhappy living with their parents or because they thought it was time to settle down (marriage being a symbol of adulthood). Middle-class couples, many of whom leave home before they marry, cite a desire for companionship and intimacy as motivations. Although some working-class wives are troubled by the low levels of communication in their marriages, most feel that if a husband is a good provider and a wife a good homemaker neither has any grounds for complaint. They do not expect friendship and understanding from their spouses. After all, they told Komarovsky, men and women are different:

"When I was first married, half of the time I didn't know what she was driving at, what it was all about," confessed a 23 year-old grade school graduate. "Sometimes I'd think I'd got her all figured out and then I don't make her out at all. The women in her bunch understood her pretty well though," he added. "They seemed to understand her better than I did sometimes. They'd tell their husbands about her and the fellows would tell me." His 22 year-old wife remarked, "Men are different. They don't feel the same as us."

"You're supposed to tell your husband everything," said one young wife, "but you don't. Nobody can tell you what you ought to tell him. Sometimes you can tell him just the little old nothings and it is as wrong as it can be. And sometimes you tell him something you think will bring the roof down and he won't even bat an eyelash." (p. 33)

Working-class wives tend to confide in their female relatives and friends, husbands in their men friends; on social occasions, the men and women separate into two groups. Middle-class couples do not make so sharp a distinction between men's and women's worlds. Interestingly, however, working-class mothers were less likely than their middle-class counterparts to feel guilty about taking a job. Working-class mothers who took jobs explained that they needed the money or, simply, that they wanted to get out of the house.

Regional variations in attitudes toward appropriate male and female roles are also apparent. Why, for example, did Wyoming grant women the right to vote fifty years before the country as a whole saw fit to do so? The diversity of state laws on marriage, divorce, alimony, employment, and health standards all attest to the existence of special subcultural and subgroup definitions of masculinity and femininity.

History and mythology reveal changing images of men and women. Women have been variously portrayed as powerful and independent, or as submissive and weak (Neumann, 1963; Lederer, 1968). Some mythologies emphasize traits we consider feminine, such as love, compassion, and fecundity (for example, the earth-mother goddesses); others portray women as awesome, blood-thirsty, cruel, and vengeful (for example, the Indian goddess Kali). Men, too, have taken on a number of antithetical characteristics, appearing here as powerful fathers or suppliant sons, there as bold warriors or effete courtiers. In feudal societies men of privilege, who had serfs or slaves at their command, considered work as a mark of social inferiority. Men earned their reputations through glorious deeds in war and statecraft. But feudal knights also exhibited many traits we now consider feminine. Exempt from gainful employment (like contemporary housewives), they dedicated themselves to service, compassion, and erotic love; they were given to temper tantrums and fits of weeping (Ossowska, 1970, p. 18).

What seems clear is that societies that do differentiate between male and female roles tend to regard their way as the only "natural" or right way, and devote substantial collective energies to enforcing sex-typed behavior. But if differences in feelings and capacities were inborn, their social elaboration, reinforcement, and supervision would not be necessary.

SEX ROLES IN AMERICA

There is no doubt that sex roles are changing in this country. In the past few years television, magazines, and other media have begun presenting alternatives to the man who gets a job, marries, fathers two children, and settles into the comfortable respectability of being a hard worker and a good provider, and the woman who, having realized the wedding of her dreams, devotes her life to her husband, her children, and her home. Indeed, as we suggested earlier, these stereotypes never applied to many lower- and upper-class people. But even though we can discern some important changes in sex roles, it is still possible to identify certain basic beliefs about men and women that have widespread approval and official (legal) support and that affect all Americans to some degree. The core values we will describe are not absolutes. Subtle and flexible, sex roles operate on several different levels and are open to varying interpretations.

What women can do is determined more by society than by biology. (doctor, Bruce Roberts/Rapho Guillumette. architect and executive, Ray Ellis/Rapho Guillumette. carpenter, UPI)

The American Woman

What do Americans believe about the capacities and destinies of women? Popular wisdom holds that all "normal" women want to marry and have children, and that whatever other interests women pursue are secondary. This belief may be expressed in pseudoscientific theories about maternal and nesting instincts, or in humor about women trying to trap husbands, whose instincts are thought to be quite different. Women who don't want to marry or mothers who don't enjoy their children are thought to be irregular—or worse. Until quite recently having children was in itself an honorable occupation, and one of the chief ways for a woman to validate her femininity and fulfill herself as a person. What happened to a woman after her children were grown was not important. (See Bernard, 1971, pp. 80–81.)

A woman's status depends on the men in her life (first her father, then her boyfriends, husband, and sons); she has no independent social standing. Taking her father's name at birth and her husband's name after marriage symbolizes this dependency. We consider it perfectly legitimate for a woman to depend entirely on her husband for support. Indeed, some husbands feel that their wife's taking a job would impugn their masculinity. Other related customs include a man paying for everything on a date.

Homebound and financially dependent, a woman is urged to live vicariously, sharing the triumphs and sorrows of her husband and children, rather than seeking her own goals. Although "the pursuit of self-interest is almost a virtue in the world men inhabit," a woman is expected to sacrifice her own needs for those of her family—and she is supposed to enjoy doing so (Bernard, 1971, p. 26). Open expression of self-assertiveness or aggression are considered unfeminine—unless a woman is defending her home and family, in which case she is allowed to be ferocious. There is a similar ban on a woman taking direct initiative in sexual relations.

A capacity for sympathy, caring, love, and compassion (exemplified in such occupations as nurse and teacher) is central to the female role in America. Women are associated with nurturance and life-preserving activities, such as bearing children and taking care of the helpless and the ailing. *Stroking*—building up another person's ego by downplaying one's own talents—is one of woman's chief functions (Bernard, 1971, pp. 88–94). Whereas men are expected to be achievement-oriented, women are raised to be people-oriented, to place personal loyalty above other considerations. For example, a woman is not condemned for protecting her child, even if he or she is a criminal. Finally, women are encouraged to actively cultivate beauty and sex appeal and to be concerned with personal adornment (traits that not incidentally perform the latent function of stimulating consumption, as well as stimulating men).

Put together, these supposedly feminine characteristics lead Americans to treat women differently than men. "The first step has been taken when feminine gender is ascribed to the female infant. A lifelong train of consequences then ensues. She is thereafter dealt with on the basis of what she is—a woman—rather than on what she does, on her [feminine] qualities rather than on her performance" (Bernard, 1971, p. 26).

To be sure, there have always been exceptions to this role. Intentionally or not, career women, working wives, and working mothers have defied the "rule" that women should be economically dependent on men. Many unmarried women, lesbians, and call girls have rejected being sexually dependent on men. (Call girls, of course, depend on men, but not on one man.) The Women's Movement (which we discuss in chapter 11) has questioned the entire system of female/male relations. But until now, conforming to the conventional ideals of femininity was the path of least resistance for most women.

Costs and Benefits of the Female Role With all the talk about sexism and discrimination against women these days, it is easy to forget that the woman's role includes privileges as well as liabilities (and vice versa for the male role). What are some of these privileges or benefits?

Most obviously, women are not obliged to work forty hours a week all of their lives to provide for others. Furthermore, they have the legal right to claim support from their husbands. In many states, a man is liable for his wife's debts, but she is not responsible for his. Men cannot sue for nonsupport, alimony, or child support (in the rare case where a divorced man is awarded custody of his children), but women can. Of course, women do work; but although employment may be an economic necessity for women, it is not yet a *moral* duty.

Nor do women suffer from the same pressures to achieve that haunt men in our society. Although a woman may strive to reach the top of her profession, there is little shame in failure or in achieving only moderate success. Women do not suffer from the career syndrome. Philip Slater elaborates:

When we say "career" it connotes a demanding, rigorous, preordained life pattern, to whose goals everything else is ruthlessly subordinated— everything pleasurable, human, emotional, bodily, frivolous. . . . Thus when a man asks a woman if she wants a career . . . he is saying, are you willing to suppress half of your being as I am, neglect your family as I do, exploit personal relationships as I do, renounce all sponteneity as I do? Naturally, she shudders a bit. (1970, p. 72)

Women also have more emotional freedom than men, in the sense that they are permitted to express a wider range of emotions and have more outlets for tension and anxiety. The sphere of intimacy and close human contact is more accessible to women; the exercise of nurturance, warmth, and sympathy, which is to some extent denied men in our society, can be its own reward. The fact that women do not very often participate in the "rat race" and are not required to inhibit their emotions may partially explain why women live longer than men and have fewer heart attacks, ulcers, and other health problems associated with tension and stress. Women are treated and institutionalized for mental illness more often than men, however, perhaps because housewives have only one source of gratification whereas men have work and family; because housework is frustrating and demeaning for educated women; because the role of housewife is unstructured and invisible, leaving much time for brooding; and because women's role expectations are unclear and diffuse (Grove and Tudor, 1973; see also Chesler, 1972).

The cult of beauty and erotic love is largely woman's domain. Arousing admiration is an intrinsically satisfying and creative experience for some women. For others, however, being a sex object—or not being one—is dehumanizing. Moreover, the glamour-girl ideology implies that beyond the age of twenty-five everything is downhill for women. Which brings us to the costs of the woman's role.

Women are denied autonomy in most spheres of American life. To channel small girls' talents into domestic/maternal interests, parents subject them to more restrictions and constraints than their brothers. Girls are not supposed to be independent or adventuresome, and the economic dependency they experience as grown women may lead to passivity, timidity, and weakness. (For example, a woman who has no profession or trade and has not worked in ten or fifteen years will think twice before she decides to leave an unhappy marriage.) The taboo on self-development and self-assertion is especially trying for independent, self-propelled women who are not content with the traditional female role.

In her article entitled "Fail: Bright Women" (1969), Matina Horner argued that many women consider success and femininity to be mutually exclusive, and that bright women especially are afraid of success. This conclusion was based on a study of male and female undergraduates. The women were asked to write a four-minute story about Anne, who, at the end of her first term of medical school, was at the top of her class. Over 65 percent wrote stories about Anne losing her friends or feeling guilty and unhappy, and some denied that such a person existed (they suggested that Anne was a code name for a group of students). Only 9 percent of the male subjects wrote negative stories about John (the counterpart of Anne) being at the top of his class. Horner then gave women who showed high "fear of success" two anagram tests, one in which they worked alone, one involving "mixed-sex competition." Thirteen of seventeen women did better working alone.

Not surprisingly this study attracted a great deal of popular and professional attention; the idea that women fear success seemed to click. But Horner's study is far from conclusive. First, it is unscientific to generalize from a sample of less than two hundred undergraduates to the entire female population, as many people have. (*Ms.* magazine, for example, reported: "Psychologists found women's data indicated a hopeless will to fail.") Horner did not study the women whose stories indicated they did *not* fear success; nor did she

study the *men* who feared success. (Other studies have found that as many or more men than women fear success and that a substantial percentage of male students associate high grades with "endless drudgery and premature coronaries" [Prescott, 1971; Robbins and Robbins, 1973].)

David Tresemor, who reviewed the many studies on this topic (1974), found that the percentage of women who wrote stories that suggested a fear of success varied from 11 to 88 percent; the percentage of men, from 14 to 86 percent. His own study of high-school students indicated that students wrote different themes for different stories, mixing positive and negative responses to success stories with little consistency. Tresemor also questions Horner's definition of success. Citing another definition: "He has achieved success who has lived well, laughed often, and loved much," he asks whether the ability to solve anagrams or being first in medical school is truly a measure of success. One question about a woman's being number one in her class at medical school is simply too limited a test. Isn't it possible that Horner's female subjects would have responded differently if they had been told half of Anne's fellow students were female, or that she was in the top ten of her class? Isn't it possible they were expressing fear of failure (that is, fear that she would not remain number one throughout school) rather than fear of success?

In a recent survey of 21,000 college students conducted by the Educational Testing Service (The Graduates, March 1973), researchers found startling differences between the aspirations of college men and women (see table 6:2). As many men with C+ averages planned to attend graduate school as women with B+ and A averages. Although the proportions of female and male students planning graduate study in the arts and

table 6:2 **FUTURE PLANS BY SEX AND UNDERGRADUATE GRADE AVERAGE, 1971 (by percent)**

	WOMEN—GRADES[1]			MEN—GRADES[1]		
	C+ OR LOWER	B	B+ OR A	C+ OR LOWER	B	B+ OR A
Highest Degree Expected						
Bachelor's	30	21	14	29	12	6
Master's	62	65	61	49	46	33
Academic doctorate[2]	4	8	17	8	19	31
Professional doctorate[3]	1	4	6	11	22	28
Other and No answer	3	2	3	3	2	2
Immediate Postcollege Plans[4]						
Full-time work (including military)	85	76	64	80	59	41
Graduate study	11	18	27	11	21	29
Law or medicine	1	3	5	6	14	24
Other professional study	7	8	9	11	16	14

[1]Question: Approximately what overall average grade have you received so far in college?
[2]Includes Ph.D., Ed.D., and D.Arts
[3]Includes M.D., LL.B., J.D., D.D.S., D.V.M., and D.D.
[4]Some respondents indicate more than one activity.
SOURCE: Leonard L. Baird, Mary Jo Clark, and Rodney T. Harnett, *The Graduates,* copyright © 1973 by Educational Testing Service. All rights reserved. Adapted and reproduced by permission.

sciences were about equal, twice as many men as women planned to enter professional schools (for example, in business, law, medicine, and engineering). The authors found that the approval of relatives and friends was the greatest influence on students' career decisions. This suggests that although women may not be *actively discouraged* from entering the professions, they receive less encouragement to do so.

The percentage of women working has risen steadily over the years. In 1972, 49 percent of women between the ages of thirty-five and forty-four were employed (less than 20 percent were in 1940), but women are overrepresented in low-paying jobs and do not earn equal pay for equal work (see figure 6:1 on p. 146). *The Economic Report of the President*, submitted to Congress in February 1974, indicated that women's salaries are about 66 percent of those of men with the same age and education. Perhaps half of this differential can be explained in terms of unequal experience. Often women drop out of the labor force to raise children, returning to an unfamiliar job market in their late thirties or early forties. But this still leaves the remaining difference unexplained. The government report refutes the common notion that women who take jobs are only working for "extras." In reality, three-fourths of working women are either single or are married to a man who earns less than $7,000 a year. Strangely, the tax laws penalize working wives (a working couple pays higher taxes than a one-worker family with the same in-

figure 6:1   Millions of year-round full-time civilian workers and their median income for 1972

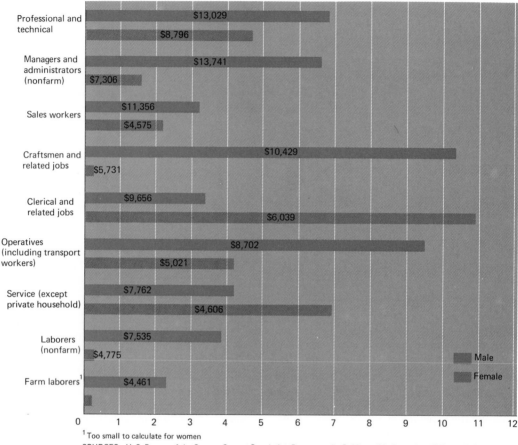

^{1} Too small to calculate for women

SOURCES: U. S. Bureau of the Census, *Current Population Reports*, series P–60, no. 90, December 1973 and U. S. Bureau of Labor Statistics, Employment, and Earnings (monthly, 1972).

come). Similarly, most banks will not count a wife's income toward a loan or mortgage. Their reasoning seems to be that a woman may stop working at any point (after all, they think she is only working for "extras") or become pregnant. Indeed, the biological capacity to bear children is an economic liability for American women. In many states a pregnant woman cannot draw unemployment insurance even if she is laid off for reasons other than pregnancy. And of course,

housewives and mothers are not paid for their work. According to one estimate, if they were, the gross national product would be increased by 38 percent (Bernard, 1971, p. 75). Economic restrictions, such as no pay or low pay without the ability to get a loan, tend to make women permanent minors not only in their own eyes, but in the eyes of society as well.

This is not to say, however, that American women are powerless. Many observers take the formal dependency and subordination of women rather too literally, overlooking the possibilities that women have for exercising power behind the facade of male supremacy. The literature on Jewish, Italian, and black mothers, and the jokes about henpecked husbands attest to the fact that women do dominate in some spheres. Housewives exercise power by running households, dominating kinship networks, arranging a couple's social life, making demands on husbands, supervising their children's lives, and disposing of the family budget. Indeed, housewives may resent intrusions on their territory.

The traditional woman's self-esteem would be seriously threatened if her husband were to play a role equal to her own in the lives and affections of her children or in the creative or managerial aspect of home management. . . . The lesson is surely not lost on her daughter, who learns that at home father does not know best, though outside the home men are bosses over women. (Rossi, 1964, p. 15)

IN THE NEWS

Ending Sex Discrimination: A Few Steps Forward

Since the late 1960s women have begun to challenge the legal and institutional boundaries that have always prevented them from achieving full equality in American society. Within the last few years some progress has been made, although many restrictions still remain.

JOB DISCRIMINATION: On January 18, 1973, American Telephone and Telegraph agreed to pay female and minority employees $15 million in back pay stemming from the company's violation of the Equal Pay Act (*The Wall Street Journal*, April 18, 1974). On September 29, 1973, a federal court ordered the New York Telephone Company to pay seventy women between $450 and $1,000 in compensatory wages (*The New York Times*, September 29, 1973). More than a year later only 48 percent of the money American businesses owed women because of violations of the Equal Pay Act had actually been paid. Not one woman was working as a professional in the Office of Federal Contract Compliance, which is responsible for preventing government contractors from discriminating against women and members of minority groups.

MATERNITY LEAVE: In 1974, by a vote of seven to two, the United States Supreme Court ruled that school boards could not set a mandatory date for pregnant teachers to leave their jobs, but the court did not say that women could decide this matter for themselves.

RELIGION: In 1973 the Committee on Jewish Law and Standards of the Conservative branch of Judaism ruled that women could be counted in the quorum of ten required for a communal service (*The New York Times*, September 11, 1973). A month later, the House of Deputies of the Episcopal Church rejected, for the second time, a proposal that women be admitted to the priesthood (*The New York Times*, September 26, 1973).

THE FAMILY NAME: More and more women are keeping their own name after marriage, adopting a hyphenated name (theirs and their husband's), and in a few cases using their mother's first name as in Sarachild (single or maiden names being, after all, their father's name). Hawaii is the only state that prohibits this. However, many women are running into difficulties: banks refuse to give them and their husbands joint accounts; airlines refuse them family rates (*Time*, May 13, 1974).

"I just want you to know, R. B., how much I admire the way you out-maneuvered Allied on that takeover without losing your femininity." (Drawing by Lorenz; © 1974 The New Yorker Magazine, Inc.)

The difference is that women's influence is often personal, indirect (covert and perhaps manipulative), and emotional (women today cry much as their grandmothers fainted). But the female role does not, as is often claimed, preclude the exercise of power.

Finally, a number of conflicts are built into the female role. Women are supposed to depend on men but to be resourceful in times of crisis, to be domestic and also glamorous, to be faithful to one man but to make themselves irresistible to many. Not surprisingly, a growing number of women are fighting for a relaxation of standards and the eventual elimination of distinct sex roles. But some respond to these conflicts by clinging to the customs and beliefs that make the sexes separate and unequal. So do some men.

The American Man

The male role is as deeply tied to the family as the female's, although the connections are not always so obvious. First and foremost a man is expected to be a good provider for his wife and children. Financial independence is a prerequisite for manhood in our society; respect goes to men who are reliable, hard-working, and achieving. Americans do not think it odd for a man to sacrifice leisure, his time at home, even his health to a career. His accomplishments and property are a measure of his worth. Initiative, ambition, and strength are all part of the "masculine mystique." We say a man is mature if he accepts obligations for dependents, takes necessary risks, makes decisions, and provides security and protection for those in his care.

It is no wonder, then, that so many American fathers encourage their sons to excel in sports (sometimes ignoring that they are not interested in or built for athletics). Sports are not an end in themselves: very few boys will go on to become professional athletes, and few fathers expect them to. But sports teach a boy to be assertive, aggressive, and competitive—all of which are thought to be essential masculine qualities, as Normal Mailer's description of boxer Muhammad Ali suggests: "Ali had shown what we all had hoped was secretly true. He was a man. He could bear moral and physical torture and he could stand" (Mailer, 1971).

Most elementary-school teachers are female and most fathers spend relatively little time at home, so contact with and acceptance by male peers may be especially important to a young boy. To a large degree boys depend on one another for information about the male role. The "locker-room culture" of adults (nights off with the boys, drinking, playing cards, going to a ball game) is reminiscent of youthful team sports. As Joseph Pleck suggests: "It seems hard to get a group of men together for very long without someone suggesting a competitive game" (1972, p. 10). For many American men, realizing that it is too late to become a professional pitcher or linebacker is a sobering reminder that they are growing old.

Sports are one of many object lessons in self-reliance and stoicism. Weakness, doubt, and compromise are signs of failure for men who are raised to conceal or deny such feelings. The taboo on expressing emotions and self-doubt explains the strong silent type in American lore. The 100 percent American he-man is happiest when he is with his buddies or riding the range alone on his horse. Courteous to women, he is also detached and prefers dealing with them on a "man-to-man" basis. (Humphrey Bogart's expression of love to Ingrid Bergman in *Casablanca*, "Here's lookin' at you, kid," would hardly be considered romantic in other countries.) Impervious to pain as well as feelings, he is rugged, resourceful, and enjoys combating overwhelming odds. John Wayne, of course, is the prototype for this "ideal man."

The on-screen John Wayne doesn't feel comfortable around women. He does like them sometimes—God knows he's not *queer*. But at the right time and in the right place—which he chooses. And always his car/horse parked directly outside, in/on which he will ride away to his more important business back in Marlboro country. (Manville, 1969, p. 111)

In recent years the cowboy has been resurrected as the playboy: suave, urbane, shrewd—in a word, cool—who treats women like consumer products, never becoming involved (Balswick and Peek, 1971). Paradoxically, the cowboy and playboy ideals may strengthen the family. "By acting as the cowboy or playboy . . . the married male may effectively rob extramarital relationships of their expressiveness and thus preserve his marital relationship" (Balswick and Peek, 1971, p. 366). Compelled to act unfeeling, a man may "save up" his emotional needs for the woman in his life (Pleck, 1972). Or he may be as cool in his marriage as he is on the outside.

The ban on male emotions does not extend to sexual matters, however. Heterosexual prowess is essential to American manhood. Men are expected to have nearly unlimited appetites for sexual adventure and to enjoy sex for its own sake (unlike women, who are thought to require at least some romantic feelings). Far more stigma is attached to the effeminate boy than to the masculine girl, who can play the role of tomboy. A woman who displays little interest in heterosexual relationships may be labeled prissy or frigid; a man is assumed to be homosexual. And there is no worse insult to an American man—except perhaps the imputation that someone is "trespassing on" his woman.

Costs and Benefits of the Male Role Like the female role, the male role has mixed effects. American men have access to the pinnacles of institutional power; men (white men, that is) not women run the nation's government, churches, corporations, professions, universities, even theaters and art galleries. Men are free to exercise legal and social powers that are denied women and children. With the notable exceptions of the now defunct draft law and alimony statutes, neither law nor custom restricts or discriminates against men solely on the basis of their sex. Men have more opportunities than women to develop their talents and acquire special skills and knowledge to cope with the world. (If a family has only enough income to send one child to college, in all likelihood it will choose their son. Men are overrepresented in all professions.) In general, men earn more than women performing the same work, and are more likely to be promoted to powerful and lucrative executive positions (where they enjoy the ministrations of secretaries, who are nearly always female). The fact that men are encouraged to display initiative and independence from the time they are small must also be counted among the benefits of the male role. Finally, the pervasive myth of male supremacy cannot but buoy the male ego.

It is important to remember, however, that although these potentialities are built into the male role, they are not available to all men.

American men, as shown in this ad and many others, are supposed to be independent and successful, while women are pictured as domestic. (Below, The Wall Street Journal.)

When you see a businessman reading The Wall Street Journal you already know a lot about him

Opportunities for training, economic self-support, and power are clearly more accessible to men at the top of the social pyramid than to those at the bottom. To generalize from the privileged few to the struggling many distorts the actual situation for the vast majority of men, who are not in control of their lives nor anywhere near the seats of economic and political power.

The responsibilities that attach to the male role in America can be a source of great stress and anxiety as well as a source of satisfaction and pride. Being in a position to make decisions is fine if a person knows what he is doing, but it may seem less of a privilege to a man who is uncertain of himself. Complicating this is the fact that men are supposed to maintain the impression of

strength and courage at all times. Fear of inadequacy and failure is the dark side of the pressures on men to prove themselves.

Equally costly is the competitive syndrome that asks men to consider all other men as either inferiors or rivals and requires substantial mobilization of psychic aggression. Famed as male solidarity is, male friendships are not necessarily easy relationships.

When stripped of male sex role "props," such as baseball scores, automobiles, and masculine sex boasting and fantasy, many men find great difficulty in relating to other men. A man in a group said, "You know, I have a pretty good idea of what I can get in a relationship with a woman; but I just don't know what I could get from a man. I just don't know." (Pleck, 1972, pp. 8–9)

In very concrete terms, men do not live as long as women and suffer more heart attacks. It is also very revealing that they have more psychosomatic diseases, such as ulcers, spastic colons, asthma, and migraine headaches. The male suicide rate is triple the female rate, and men are fourteen times as likely to become alcoholics. Moreover, men commit 95 percent of all violent crimes and eight times as many murders as women do. Men also have to fight the wars other men make.

Finally, as with the female role, a number of conflicts are built into the male role. Men are supposed to be single-minded in the pursuit of success but not neglectful of their families; they should be simultaneously interested and disinterested in women; and they must be strong and self-reliant, yet require the care of a nurturant wife.

As a result, masculinity is in many ways a rather vulnerable and precarious status. The male role is demanding and difficult and the rate of "failure" is high in the best of times. In American society, as in other industrial societies, few men can in fact achieve the wealth,

power, and positions of leadership that are held out as ideals for all. *Machismo*, or compulsive masculinity, may be a last resort for men who accept the traditional masculine role but cannot fill it. Machismo has two faces, an overt and a covert one. Overtly it consists of a show of strength and sexual prowess as well as the denigration, exploitation, and often brutalization of women. Covertly, this display masks fears and doubts about self-worth. As an effort to convince other men, women, and above all himself that he is truly all-male, machismo is a front for insecurity, self-doubt, and worldly failure (Aramoni, 1972, pp. 69–72).

Serious doubts and anxieties about masculine identity and purpose are bound to occur as many women forego the need for male protection and successfully compete with men in spheres previously considered off-limits to them. For example, 30 percent of male undergraduates in one study experienced some conflict between the desire for female intellectual companionship and the notion that as men, they should be intellectually superior (Komarovsky, 1973).

Some men have begun to see these changes in the female role as a welcome liberation. Is traditional masculinity worth the price? These men seek a new male ideal, less geared toward competition and dominance. Men will be better off, they argue, if they can learn to acknowledge their human vulnerability and limitations and escape the posturing and pretense of the male role. However, others see change as a dethronement from a previously privileged status. The more they feel they have to lose, the more likely men—and women—are to resist change. The days ahead will not be easy for those who are wedded to traditional gender ideals. There is bound to be anger, conflict, misunderstandings—a tug of war as traditional roles change for both men and women.

CONDITIONS FOR CHANGE

Social necessity has always been a prime agent for change. During both World Wars, for example, American women suddenly became capable of performing work they were thought unsuited for a year earlier: they "manned" the nation's defense plants. In the past, most religions emphasized men's and women's procreative roles. After all, life was precarious, and many children did not survive infancy. Except for priests and other celibates, family and sex roles were interdependent. The moral/religious formula read: female=potential wife and mother; male=potential husband and father. However, the threatening possibility of standing room only on this planet and the easy availability of reliable birth-control devices have diminished the importance and desirability of reproduction. Procreation is no longer an imperative. And while sexual relations are still desirable for conception (artificial insemination can now be used), the reverse is less and less true: conception is no longer the typical outcome of sexual relations.

Other changes are also apparent. The nuclear family has lost many of the functions it once performed, such as education, production, and to a large extent recreation. While important, the functions it retains—the partial socialization of children and the provision of a sense of belonging—have become romanticized and ritualistic. As a result the family-centered female role is less significant and gratifying than nonfamilial roles. Similarly, the emphasis on egalitarian family relations has undercut the dominance of the father-husband; and the pressure for nondiscrimination in employment is eroding the male monopoly in high-paying and prestigious careers. Women are breaking into occupations that used to be labeled "men only," and men are entering female-dominated spheres (such as nursing, and teaching in elementary schools). Opportunities and expectations are changing. New attitudes toward sex and innovative family styles are also chipping away at the traditional roles. Of late we have seen men winning paternity leaves and alimony suits, and numerous changes in adoption, divorce, and the legal rights of spouses. Finally, the "togetherness" ideal in American society desegregates the sexes in play and work, accentuating shared rather than separate experiences.

Thus sex roles are changing because society is changing. Altered occupational, personal, and familial styles reflect the emergence of new priorities and goals, which no longer depend on a hard-and-fast sex-typing of appearance, behavior, and identity. Eventually, when no more than a fraction of the population participates in producing the next generation, the traditional equation between gender and parenthood will seem less obvious. Patterns of marriage and family life may become more flexible, and childless couples, single parents, and new modes of child-rearing will be more common. Already there are fewer and fewer absolute indicators of gender. Should a man help a woman into a car, light her cigarette, open doors for her? Should a woman expect her husband to support her? While the physical distinctions between the sexes remain intact, their social significance has blurred. A nationwide survey suggests that attitudes toward gender are indeed changing. (See pp. 154–155.) Whatever one's view, the momentum of change is bound to create inconsistency and instability. The outcome of efforts to change the gender map will depend on our knowledge and understanding of how sex differences develop and what part they have played in human societies.

THE "NEW VALUES": THE LIBERATED GENERATION?

How has the Women's Liberation movement affected today's youth? A nationwide survey of college and noncollege youth found a majority believe that men and women are born with essentially the same human nature and that any differences between them can be attributed to upbringing. A majority also feel that the idea that women are less logical and more emotional than men is "ridiculous." Women should receive equal pay for equal work, and they should be as free as men to take the initiative in sexual relations. A majority also agree that women's relationships with other women are as important as their relationships with men. Young people are not totally liberated, however. A majority reject the ideas that women can do almost any job as well as men and that women can be happy without men.

Attitudes toward masculinity have also changed. A majority of the young people questioned do not believe that physical strength, keeping emotions under control, or making decisions in the family are essential masculine qualities. Survey results show that 65 percent believe men should be concerned with women's sexual satisfaction, and 59 percent say that a man should satisfy a woman sexually. At the same time, over 70 percent believe a man should be a good provider and hold strong moral views; nearly 60 percent believe men should show women "respect and courtesy"; and 69 percent do not feel it is very important for a man to be willing to help with household chores.

Breaking the data down into four categories (college men, college women, noncollege men, and noncollege women), Yankelovich found college women are the most liberated, noncollege women the least. For example, 64 percent of college women characterize the statement "A woman's place is in the home" as "nonsense," compared to a minority of 47 percent of noncollege women (see the accompanying figures). Yankelovich suggests this is because, for women who lack a college degree, a job is little more than a way to help make ends meet. The idea that wifehood and motherhood alone are not fulfilling roles, a central theme of Women's Liberation, is especially threatening to their self-esteem.

SOURCE: Yankelovich Youth Study © 1973 by the JDR 3rd Fund.

figure 6:2   College and noncollege women's beliefs about sex roles (1973).

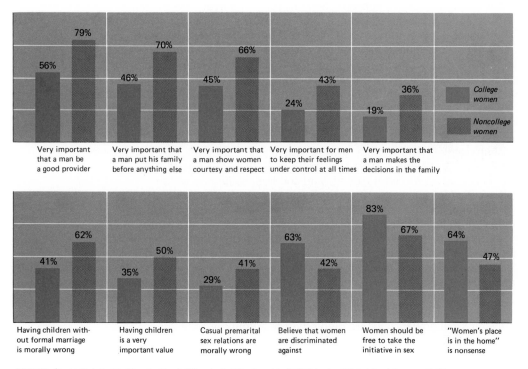

56% / 79%	46% / 70%	45% / 66%	24% / 43%	19% / 36%
Very important that a man be a good provider	Very important that a man put his family before anything else	Very important that a man show women courtesy and respect	Very important for men to keep their feelings under control at all times	Very important that a man makes the decisions in the family

College women / Noncollege women

41% / 62%	35% / 50%	29% / 41%	63% / 42%	83% / 67%	64% / 47%
Having children without formal marriage is morally wrong	Having children is a very important value	Casual premarital sex relations are morally wrong	Believe that women are discriminated against	Women should be free to take the initiative in sex	"Women's place is in the home" is nonsense

SOURCE: Daniel Yankelovich, *Changing Youth Values in the 70's*, Copyright © 1974 by the JDR 3rd Fund, Inc., pp. 34–35.

summary

The traditional assumption that men and women are born with different abilities and temperaments which make them naturally suited for different social roles is a myth. Although genes determine sex, the fetus is sexually undifferentiated until about three months, when hormones begin to act. But *sex* (that is, male or female biology) does not determine either *gender* (the psychological characteristics associated with femininity or masculinity) or *sexuality* (erotic responses and activities). The biological differences between the sexes are not as clear-cut as most people imagine. The discovery that children who have been assigned the wrong sex grow up believing in the assignment substantiates this conclusion.

From the day they are born, children are given both subtle and direct clues as to sex-appropriate behavior and feelings. Children's books, for example, depict boys as bright and adventurous, girls as quiet, helpful, and doll-like; schools have traditionally segregated the sexes for physical education, home economics, and shop.

Cross-cultural studies show beyond any doubt that femininity and masculinity are not inborn qualities, but part of different *sex roles*—that is, social guidelines for sex-appropriate appearance, interests, skills, and self-perceptions. Margaret Mead studied two tribes in New Guinea that did not differentiate between the sexes with regard to temperament: all members of one were encouraged to be what we would call feminine, all members of the other were exaggeratedly masculine. A third tribe reversed our traditional sex roles. Differences in occupational opportunities for women in industrial nations underline the social nature of male and female roles. Even in this country the housewife/mother ideal has never fully applied to lower- and upper-class women.

Nevertheless, traditional masculine and feminine ideals influence most of us. Americans expect women to want marriage and a family, and to put their family first; to depend on their husbands, financially and socially; to live vicariously through their husbands and children; to be passive and self-sacrificing (rather than aggressive and self-assertive), loving and sympathetic, and glamorous. This role exempts women from the moral obligation to support themselves and others and from the pressures of the business world. Women have more emotional freedom than men in this country, but they are not granted equal opportunity and encouragement for self-development, and their participation in the labor market is limited and underpaid. This is not to say, however, that women are totally powerless.

Men, on the other hand, are expected to be good providers, competitive and achieving, self-reliant and unemotional. Men have access to the pinnacles of institutional power; they are granted more autonomy as children and as adults; they are freer in the eyes of the law, earn more than women for equal work, and can bask in the pervasive ideology of male supremacy. But the responsibilities that attach to the male role, the pressures on men to succeed, and the competitive atmosphere in which they live are distinct liabilities; in concrete terms, men do not live as long as women in America. Moreover, only a few men are in a position to exercise self-determination. Recently, some men's groups have begun to argue that traditional masculinity is not worth the costs. These men argue for more flexible sex roles.

Sex roles are changing because society is changing. Given the availability of reliable birth control and the threat of overpopulation, procreation is no longer a moral imperative. Housekeeping and mothering are becoming less gratifying than nonfamilial roles for women. The egalitarianism of modern families has undercut male dominance in the home, and men are losing their monopoly over paid employment. These altered familial, personal, and occupational styles reflect and reinforce the emergence of new priorities and goals which do not depend on a hard-and-fast sex-typing of appearance, behavior, and identity.

glossary

gender The psychological characteristics associated with femininity or masculinity.

hormones Chemical substances, secreted into the bloodstream by the glands, that stimulate or inhibit vital chemical processes.

machismo Compulsive masculinity, evidenced in posturing, boasting, and an exploitative attitude toward women.

sex role Social guidelines for sex-appropriate appearance, interests, skills, and self-perceptions.

references

Aniceto Aramoni, "Machismo," *Psychology Today*, vol. 5, no. 8 (January 1972): 69–72.

Jack O. Balswick and Charles W. Peek, "The Inexpressive Male: A Tragedy of American Society," *The Family Coordinator*, vol. 20 (October 1971): 363–68.

Judith M. Bardwick and Elizabeth Douvan, "Ambivalence: the socialization of women," in Vivian Gornick and Barbara K. Moran, eds., *Women in Sexist Society*, New York: Basic Books, 1971.

Luigi Barzini, *The Italians*, New York: Atheneum, 1964.

Simone de Beauvoir, *The Second Sex*, New York: Knopf, 1953.

Jessie Bernard, *Women and the Public Interest: An Essay on Policy and Protest*, Chicago: Aldine-Atherton, 1971.

Caroline Bird, "The Invisible Bar," in Elsie Adams and May Louise Briscoe, eds., *Up Against the Wall, Mother . . .*, Beverly Hills: Glencoe Press, 1971.

———, with Sara Welles, *Born Female*, New York: McKay, 1968.

Jane E. Brody, "More than 100,000 Persons a Year Are Reported Seeking Sterilization As a Method of Contraception," *The New York Times* (March 22, 1970), p. 22.

Phyllis Chesler, *Women and Madness*, New York: Doubleday, 1972.

Edmund Dahlström, "Analysis of the Debate on Sex Roles," in Edmund Dahlström, ed., *The Changing Roles of Men and Women*, Boston: Beacon Press, 1967.

Marlene Dixon, "Why Women's Liberation?" in Elsie Adams and Mary Louise Briscoe, eds., *Up Against the Wall, Mother . . .*, Beverly Hills: Glencoe Press, 1971.

Carol Ehrlich, "The Male's Socialization Burden: The Place of Women in Marriage and Family Texts," *Journal of Marriage and the Family*, vol. 33, no. 3 (August 1971): 421–30.

Warren Farrell, "Guidelines for Consciousness-Raising," *Ms.* (March 1972): 12–15, 116–17.

Marc Fasteau, "Why aren't we talking?" *Ms.* (July 1972): 163.

Mark G. Field and Karin I. Flynn, "Worker, Mother, Housewife: Soviet Women Today," in Georgene H. Seward and Robert C. Williamson, eds., *Sex Roles in Changing Society*, New York: Random House, 1970.

Betty Friedan, *The Feminine Mystique*, New York: Dell, 1963.

———, "The problem that has no name," in Elsie Adams and Mary Louise Briscoe, eds., *Up Against the Wall, Mother . . .*, Beverly Hills: Glencoe Press, 1971.

John A. Gergen, "Physiological Aspects of Sexual Behavior: Genetics, Hormones, and the Central Nervous System," in Clark E. Vincent, ed., *Human Sexuality in Medical Education and Practice*, Springfield, Ill.: Charles C. Thomas, 1968.

Walter R. Gove and Jeannette F. Tudor, "Adult Sex Roles and Mental Illness," in Huber, 1973.

Richard Green, *Sexual Identity Conflict in Children and Adults*, New York: Basic Books, 1974.

Harry F. Harlow and Margaret Harlow, "The Effect of Rearing Conditions on Behavior," in John Money, ed., *Sex Research, New Developments*, New York: Holt, Rinehart and Winston, 1965.

Ruth Hartley, "A Developmental View of Sex Role Identifications," in Bruce J. Biddle and E. J. Thomas, eds., *Role Theory: Concepts and Research*, New York: Wiley, 1966.

Harriet Holter, *Sex Roles and Social Structure*, Oslo: Universitets Forlaget, 1970.

Matina S. Horner, "Fail: Bright Women," *Psychology Today*, vol. 3, no. 6 (November 1969): 36ff.

———, "Toward an understanding of achievement-related conflicts in women," *Journal of Social Issues*, vol. 28, no. 2 (1972): 157–75.

Joan Huber, ed., *Changing Women in a Changing Society*, Chicago: University of Chicago Press, 1973.

Carol Joffe, "Sex Role Socialization and the Nursery School: As the Twig Is Bent," *Journal of Marriage and the Family*, vol. 33, no. 3 (August 1971): 467–75.

Jerome Kagan, "Acquisition and Significance of Sex Typing and Sex Role Identity," in M. Hoffman and L. W. Hoffman, eds., *Review of Child Development Research*, vol. 1, New York: Russell Sage Foundation, 1964.

Jeff Keith, "My Own Men's Liberation," *Win* (September 1, 1971): 22–26.

Suzanne Keller, "The Family in the Kibbutz: What Lessons for Us?" in Michael Curtis and Mordecai S. Chertoff, eds., *Israel—Social Structure and Change*, New Brunswick, N.J.: Transaction Books, 1973.

Mirra Komarovsky, "Cultural Contradictions and Sex Roles: The Masculine Case," in Huber, 1973.

———, *Blue-Collar Marriage*, New York: Vintage, 1967.

Ruby R. Leavitt, "Women in Other Cultures," in Vivian Gornick and Barbara K. Morgan, eds., *Women in Sexist Society*, New York: New American Library, 1972.

Wolfgang Lederer, *The Fear of Women*, New York: Harcourt Brace Jovanovich, 1968.

Rita Liljestrom, "The Swedish Model," in Georgene H. Seward and Robert C. Williamson, eds., *Sex Roles in Changing Society*, New York: Random House, 1970.

Norman Mailer, "Ego," *Life Magazine*, vol. 70, no. 3 (March 19, 1971): 18–36.

W. H. Manville, "The Locker Room Boys," *Cosmopolitan*, vol. 166 (November, 1969): 110–15.

Margaret Mead, *Male and Female*, New York: New American Library, 1950.

———, *Sex and Temperament in Three Primitive Societies* (1935), New York: Morrow, 1963.

John Money, *Sex Research, New Developments*, New York: Holt, Rinehart and Winston, 1965.

———, and Anke Ehrhardt, *Man and Woman, Boy and Girl*, Baltimore: Johns Hopkins Press, 1972.

Paul Amos Moody, *Genetics of Man*, New York: Norton, 1967.

Robin Morgan, *Sisterhood Is Powerful*, New York: Vintage, 1970.

Erich Neumann, *The Great Mother*, Bollingen Series, XLVII, New York: Pantheon, 1963.

Maria Ossowska, *Social Determinants of Moral Ideas*, Philadelphia: University of Pennsylvania Press, 1970.

Joseph Pleck, "Male Sex Role and Personality: Toward a Research and Clinical Perspective," paper given at Harvard University, February 1972.

D. Prescott, "Efficacy-related imagery, education, and politics," unpublished honor thesis, Harvard University, 1971.

David Reuben, *Any Woman Can*, New York: McKay, 1972.

Lillian and Edwin Robbins, letter, *The New York Times Magazine* (February 4, 1973): 56.

Marjorie Rosen, *Popcorn Venus*, New York: Coward, McCann, and Geoghegan, 1973.

Alice S. Rossi, "Equality Between the Sexes: An Immodest Proposal," *Daedalus*, vol. 93, no. 2 (Spring 1964), 607–52.

Maggie Scarf, "He and She: The Sex Hormones and Behavior," *The New York Times Magazine* (May 7, 1972): 30ff.

Robert R. Sears, Eleanor E. Maccoby, and Harry Levin, *Patterns of Child-Rearing*, Evanston, Ill.: Row, Peterson, 1957.

George Eaton Simpson and J. Milton Yinger, *Racial and Cultural Minorities: An Analysis of Prejudice and Discrimination*, New York: Harper & Row, 1972.

Philip Slater, *The Pursuit of Loneliness*, Boston: Beacon Press, 1970.

Robert Stoller, *Sex and Gender*, New York: Science House, 1968.

Evelyn Sullerot, *Women, Society, and Change*, New York: McGraw-Hill, 1971.

David Tresemor, "Fear of Success: Popular but unproven," *Psychology Today*, vol. 7, no. 10 (March 1974): 82–85.

Lenore J. Weitzman and Deborah Eifler, "Sex Role Socialization in Picture Books for Preschool Children," *American Journal of Sociology*, vol. 77, no. 8 (May 1972): 1125–44.

Mary Wollstonecraft, *A Vindication of the Rights of Women* (1792), New York: Norton, 1967.

for further study

Historical Debate. The social implications of sex differences have been discussed by philosophers, theologians, and novelists. A famous and impassioned book on women's rights, written in 1792, is by Mary Wollstonecraft, *A Vindication of the Rights of Women* (New York: Norton, 1967). Almost a century later, in 1869, another English writer, the philosopher John Stuart Mill, presented the case against the oppression of women in his penetrating book, *The Subjection of Women* (London: Oxford University Press, 1966). In this century Virginia Woolf, in *A Room of One's Own* (New York: Harcourt Brace Jovanovich, 1929), brilliantly argues the costs to women—and men—of women's lack of autonomy and self-reliance. A comparison of these three books, ranging over two centuries, would be fascinating.

Socialization of Sex Differences. One controversy concerns the nature vs. nurture argument regarding sex differences. Proponents of the first argue that sex differences are genetically or hormonally programmed. The second view argues that sex differences in interests, skills, and personality develop through learning, imitation, and selective reinforcement. Some important research has been collected in the following works: Jerome Kagan, "Check One: Male/Female," *Psychology Today*, vol. 3, no. 2, (July 1969): 39–41; Orville G. Brim, Jr.,

"Family and Sex Role Learning by Children: A Further Analysis of Helen Koch's Data," *Sociometry*, vol. 21 (March 1958): 1–16; Herbert Barry III, Margaret K. Bacon, and Irwin L. Child, "A Cross-Cultural Survey of Some Sex Differences in Socialization," in Robert F. Winch and Louis Goodman, eds., *Selected Studies in Marriage and the Family*, 3rd ed. (New York: Holt, Rinehart and Winston, 1948).

Cross-Cultural Studies of Sex Roles and Gender. The most famous book is Margaret Mead's *Sex and Temperament in Three Primitive Societies* (New York: Morrow, 1963). Here the student can learn how differently societies define the roles we assume to be universal. One type of cross-cultural study is historical, for comparisons across the centuries permit us to see contrasting ways of organizing sex differences. A fascinating book drawing on myths, artifacts, and religious rituals is Wolfgang Lederer's *The Fear of Women* (New York: Harcourt Brace Jovanovich, 1968). And finally there is the instructive comparison of other contemporary modern societies. In Lucien M. Hanks, Jr. and Jane Richardson Hanks, "Thailand: Equality Between the Sexes," in Barbara E. Ward, ed., *Women in the New Asia* (Paris: UNESCO, 1963): 424–52, the authors describe contemporary society in which the sexes are hardly differentiated by temperament and skills.

Homosexuality and Departures from Normative Sex Roles. The recent front-page treatment of Gay Liberation has raised many questions about homosexuality and whether it should be considered a perfectly normal human response which is repressed in most people, or a pathological aberration. Some readings to help clarify one's thinking on these issues are: Edward Sagarin, *Odd Man In: Societies of Deviants in America* (Chicago: Quadrangle Books, 1969); Robert Stoller, *Sex and Gender* (New York: Science House, 1968). In *Conundrum* (New York: Harcourt Brace Jovanovich, 1974) Jan Morris describes her change from a celebrated male journalist named James to a woman named Jan.

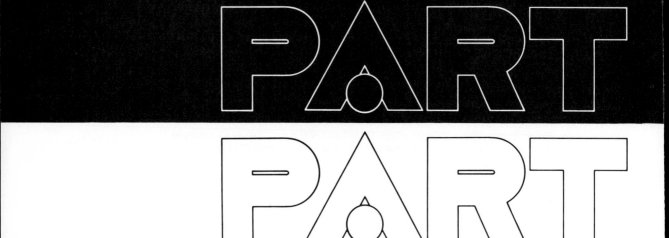

When Stephen Dedalus, the hero of James Joyce's *Portrait of the Artist as a Young Man,* was still a young boy in grammar school, he painstakingly inscribed his own identity on the flyleaf of a geography text:

> Stephen Dedalus
> Class of Elements
> Clongowes Wood College
> Sallins
> County Kildare
> Ireland
> Europe
> The World
> The Universe

Although Stephen was not yet ten, he had already discovered that his own personal identity was closely connected to his many group identities (family, school, town, country, humankind). He understood that to describe himself fully he must also describe the many and various social groups to which he belonged. Like Stephen, all of us are defined and shaped by the groups to which

SOCIAL GROUPS

we belong, whether these groups are chosen by us or assigned to us at birth. If we are at all curious, therefore, about the external forces that mold our experiences, we must pay close attention to the nature of our social groups and to the impact they have on our private lives. Although we like to imagine that we are fully in command of our private behavior, we are, in fact, influenced to a remarkable degree by our group experiences.

Social groups provide the vital link between our private lives and the larger society. They not only offer us security and support, but they shape our values, attitudes, and behavior, because in groups we are directly exposed to the opinions of others, who often matter greatly to us.

Because group life is so essential to human survival and to a sense of well-being, a vast amount of research has been devoted to understanding the varieties of human groups and to exploring how groups influence individual experience. In this chapter we will consider the nature of social groups; the way modern urban society has changed the nature of social relationships; and the search for intimacy and community that persists in modern life.

WHAT ARE SOCIAL GROUPS?

Like many of the terms sociologists borrow from everyday conversation, the word *group* has no single, commonly understood meaning. There are several ways to distinguish among the various meanings of this term. One way is to focus on the patterns of interaction among the members of the group. Thus, we may think of commuters who board the same bus every morning as a minimal group. These travelers see each other every day, know each other's time schedules, and are aware of each other's stops. But beyond this minimal contact, accompanied, perhaps, by a smile or a nod, these passengers have limited amounts of interaction. They comprise a loosely knit group, and their daily contact has little significance for any of them. The group is together by chance, not by choice. They have neither a task to accomplish nor any meaningful bond that unites them. We are all members of many such casual groups but unless something unusual (like an emergency) occurs to change our patterns of interaction in these groups, they have little effect on our daily lives.

When the patterns of interaction become somewhat more involving, however, we begin to assign different meanings to our notion of the group. Think, for instance, of a college classroom. Students usually sit in the same general area for each lecture. They exchange greetings and share information with each other, and they are treated as a group (at least for the semester) by both the lecturer and the college administration. The class has a distinct sense of its "groupness," even though interactions among the students may not carry over into activities outside the classroom. While this kind of group may have

some effect on our personal lives (the classmates, for instance, may be lively or listless, attentive or disruptive, cooperative or competitive), our emotional involvements in the classroom are, nonetheless, usually minimal.

Sometimes we become members of groups without realizing it. When we order a meal in a restaurant, we become part of a team that is organized to accomplish a task. The customer, waiter, headwaiter, busboy, chef, and dishwasher are all cooperating to serve a meal. The restaurant staff, which is together all day as a task group, may not think of itself as a group. The employees may relate to each other only in terms of their assigned work roles and they may not see each other after work, yet, they are decidedly an on-going group with extensive (though not necessarily emotional) patterns of interaction.

Thus, the amount and kinds of interaction among group members can range up and down several scales: the scale of time spent together; the scale of task-oriented interdependence; the scale of multiple shared activities; and the scale of emotional involvement. The higher the score on each of these scales, the more meaningful will the group be for its individual members. It is no wonder, therefore, that groups like combat platoons, which score high in all these dimensions, become so involving that their members will sacrifice their lives in order to preserve the group. Several studies, described in the accompanying box, have found that military heroism really stems from the need for group preservation and not from individual striving for glory.

Group Membership

Given the welter of possible meanings for the deceptively simple word *group,* how can

THE POWER OF SOCIAL GROUPS

Why does a soldier risk his life in a foreign war? Common sense suggests many possible answers: men endure the horrors of combat because they love their country and believe in the cause of the war; men enjoy being soldiers and identify with the symbols and rituals of military life; men are afraid to desert or to show fear because they will be labeled "unmanly"; men assume they will be jailed or even shot if they refuse to obey commands. Studies of German and Allied infantrymen in World War II and of American soldiers in Korea and Vietnam indicate that few of these assumptions are true.

Two sociologists, Edward Shils and Morris Janowitz (1948) shattered the "love-of-country, belief-in-the-cause" theory when they discovered that World War II German infantrymen, far from being Nazi fanatics, were largely apolitical. As one German POW put it: "Nazism begins ten miles behind the front line." The Americans who fought these Germans were hardly any different. Shils (1950) found that only a handful of American soldiers in World War II were motivated by ideological conviction, by hatred of the enemy, or by fear of punishment for desertion.

As for identifying with the rituals of military life, Roger Little concluded, after fifteen months with a rifle company in Korea, that soldiers' attitudes toward the military were ambivalent at best. Soldiers tended to be suspicious of bravery, courage, heroism, and other so-called manly virtues. As one soldier told Little: "You shouldn't stick your neck out unless you have to. . . . If a guy gets a medal for doing his job, it's O.K. But if he's taken a chance or exposed his men, he's no hero because he's made it more risky for everyone" (1970, p. 366).

What matters most to soldiers is staying alive. This primary concern with survival links every soldier to every other soldier with whom he eats, sleeps, and fights. Cut off from civilian life, soldiers begin to think of their platoons as families: buddies speak of one another as brothers. "The men in my squad were my special friends. . . . We bunked together, slept together, fought together, told each other where our money was pinned in our shirts. . . . If one man gets a letter from home, the whole company reads it. Whatever belongs to me belongs to the whole outfit" (Shils, 1950, p. 18). Soldiers obey orders that ask them to risk their lives not for love of country, not for devotion to cause, not for allegiance to the army, but to support and protect the close-knit group that now supports and protects them.

In the Korean War, American POW's learned from their captors about the importance of close human ties. Prisoners were prevented from forming intimate groups. As a result of their social isolation, many of the prisoners broke down physically and mentally and 38 percent of them died in the camps. Once again, the fate of each prisoner depended not so much on the individual's personal characteristics as on his social group experiences.

During the Vietnam War, the crucial human need of group stability and intimacy was not met. One observer of the war (Moskos, 1970) attributed the low morale of American troops to the fact that soldiers served on a rotating basis and never formed intense relationships with comrades. In Vietnam, according to Moskos, it was every man for himself.

Members of a combat platoon generally form a group so tightly knit that men will risk their lives to preserve it. These Vietnam War soldiers are carrying one of their buddies who died during a siege. (UPI)

we possibly produce a single working definition? Many sociologists have tried their hands at definitions, and although there is not universal agreement on the meaning of the word, one noteworthy and frequently accepted definition has been provided by Robert K. Merton. He suggests that a *social group* is a number of people who define themselves as members of a group; who expect certain behavior from members that they do not expect from outsiders; and whom

others (members and nonmembers) define as belonging to a group (Merton, 1968, pp. 339–40). This definition places a heavy emphasis on members' awareness of their groupness. It *excludes* the following collectivities of people, who have the potential for becoming self-conscious groups but have not yet realized that potential:

1. Individuals with common characteristics—old people, smokers, bicycle riders, the poor.
2. Individuals who happen to be at the same place at the same time—theater audiences, pedestrians at a street crossing, shoppers in a supermarket.
3. Individuals who interact regularly but with limited involvement—tenants in an apart-

ment building, Friday pay check depositers, patrons of a bar.

Any one of these nongroups can rapidly become a group—we need only think of senior citizens' clubs, welfare rights organizations, tenants' unions, and theater clubs to realize that the potential for groupness lurks everywhere.

In-Groups and Out-Groups Merton's distinction between members and nonmembers as one criterion for groupness is not an accident of language. Ever since 1906, when William Graham Sumner, an American sociologist, coined the terms in-group and out-group to describe the feelings of "we" and "they" generated by group membership, the notion of an *in-group* as a circle of people in which a person feels at home has been in common usage. In-groups breed a *consciousness of kind*. They are typified by families, friendship cliques, social clubs, and religious and ethnic groups. Consciousness of kind can also emerge among people who have never met. The feminist movement is beginning to create such a consciousness among women; election years generate such a consciousness among political allies; the war on poverty has brought this awareness to the poor.

In-groups usually develop their sense of "we-ness" as a result of sharing common experiences. In one of the most thoroughgoing sociological studies, conducted between 1927 and 1932 in a Western Electric plant, investigators observed in detail the social dynamics of a small group of factory workers whose job it was to prepare banks for telephone switchboards of wires (Homans, 1950). This group of men developed their own rules about how much work each man should produce and, despite the fact that all the men were paid according to the number of units the whole group completed, overproduction ("rate busting") was as much discouraged as underproduction ("chiseling"). The sense of togetherness among the workers was enhanced by an elaborate system of controls, which they designed to keep outsiders from securing information about the group's activities. These factory workers had a strong sense of "we-ness," and they clearly defined nongroup members as outsiders.

An *out-group*, then, is a circle of people to which a person feels he or she does not belong. Out-groups surround us everywhere. If we are drug users, the out-group is the straight world; if we are black, the out-group is the white world; if we are rich, the out-group is the poor; if we are young, the out-group is the old. All these groups of individuals whom we sense differ from us in significant ways comprise our out-groups.

One of the reasons that we are even able to view other people as outsiders (and other groups as out-groups) is that we tend, for convenience, to divide up our world in terms of stereotypes: "all long-hairs are hippies"; "all politicians are corrupt." Carried to its extremes, stereotyping is a dehumanizing process. The Nazis did not see Jews as people; they saw them as contaminating subhumans. This dehumanizing process also occurred in My Lai, Vietnam, the scene of the slaughter of unarmed villagers. The area around My Lai was declared a "free fire zone" in the mid-sixties, after attempts to "pacify" local villagers failed to rid the area of Viet Cong. What this meant was that any Vietnamese was fair game. Seymour Hersh (1970), who uncovered the My Lai incident, suggests that this dehumanizing attitude rested on the GI's ignorance of Vietnamese customs; his inability to distinguish civilians from "the enemy"; and the fact that the body count was the only measure of victory in the war. One GI summed up the essence of dehumanization-by-stereotyping when he asserted: "Anything that's not dead and isn't white is V.C." (Hersh, 1970).

To some extent everyone defines outgroups in terms of stereotypes. The existence of in-groups implies the existence of outgroups; the feeling of "we" implies awareness of "they." Groups are defined as much by a consciousness of the differences between insiders and outsiders as by a consciousness of the likenesses among members (Sumner, 1906).

Reference Groups Sociologically viewed, we may belong to groups we have never encountered. These groups are the ones to which we refer, either consciously or unconsciously, when we try to evaluate our own situations in life.

The groups to which we refer, but to which we do not always strictly belong, are called *reference groups*. Depending on what groups we select to compare ourselves with, we either feel deprived or privileged, satisfied or discontented, fortunate or unfortunate. When a student receives a B on an exam, he or she can either feel terrific in comparison to the C students or inadequate compared to the A students. When a basketball player reaches 6'4", he can either feel tall in comparison with average players or short in comparison with many professionals. When a woman becomes a general practitioner (M.D.), she can either feel accomplished in relation to most women or inferior in relation to neurosurgeons. Our feelings about ourselves are very much determined by what groups we choose as reference groups. Even our thoughts and beliefs can be molded by our real (or imagined) perceptions about the acceptable thoughts and beliefs of our reference groups.

One long-term study of the dramatic effects of reference groups on individual behavior and beliefs was conducted by Theodore Newcomb (1958) at Bennington College, a very liberal women's college in Vermont. Newcomb first studied the students at Bennington between 1935 and 1939. At that time most of the students came from extremely conservative political backgrounds. When the young women arrived at Bennington the liberal political atmosphere (particularly among the faculty) provided them with a new and conflicting set of values and ideas. Newcomb found that in most cases the longer the girls stayed at Bennington (from freshman to senior year) the more politically liberal they became. Those who remained more conservative continued to look to their families for information and approval, even though they were physically separated from home.

The evidence of the Bennington studies is that our values, behavior, and goals are influenced and altered by the people or groups whom we choose for our models. We need not necessarily be members of a group to choose that group as a model. Think, for example, of first-generation immigrants who relinquish the values and customs of their own countries in order to conform to the values of those Americans whom they select as their models—be they bankers or bank robbers. Although we like to think that we create our own standards of goodness and worth, if we look closely we find that our personal standards are strongly influenced by the standards of those to whom we look for approval, acceptance, leadership, or example.

Group Structure

When we talk about in-groups and outgroups or membership and reference groups, we are essentially talking about the *quality* of membership in these groups—about the ways these groups make particular members or nonmembers feel. But it is also possible to think about groups as social forms that are more than the sum of the individuals who compose them. When scientists look at cells, they may not be concerned with any particular molecule in that cell, but with how the cell is put together, what its properties and structures are. Similarly, it is possible to look at groups from the outside to see how they are put together, regardless of the particular characteristics of any specific member of that group. This is a structural way of looking at groups (what they *are*) rather than a functional way (what they *do*).

Group Boundaries and Conflict One of the structural properties of groups is their boundaries. Without boundaries there would be no way of setting groups off, no way of distinguishing members from nonmembers, insiders from outsiders. A fraternity pin is a symbolic but tangible social boundary: those who own one are members, those who do not are nonmembers. When a "brother" (note the symbol of closeness) gives his pin to a woman, he symbolically extends the group boundary to include her. A college decal on a car window is a social boundary; it publicly differentiates insiders from outsiders. Skin color can be a boundary and so can ethnic background. The one-time southern debate over how much African ancestry a person needed to be labeled a Negro was an attempt to define black-white boundaries when visible skin color failed to serve as a boundary clue. Almost anything can be used as a social boundary to distinguish "in" from "out," "us" from "them." A dormitory can be used as a boundary marker and so can a sports car ("we" drive them; "they" don't). Hair, clothing, and music styles surely mark different groups off from each other. Sometimes a colored strip of rag will do the trick. During the college uprisings of the 1960s, students with different political views (rang-

ing from "Burn the place down" to "Restore law and order") were able to show their allegiances and create feelings of "we" and "they" just by wearing different-colored arm bands to signify different political views.

If we recognize that all groups have boundaries, we can begin to ask questions about how these boundaries are created and maintained. One of the most effective ways of creating and maintaining group boundaries is through conflict with outsiders. A common enemy helps draw people together, and through confrontation with out-groups insiders begin to develop a sense of "we-ness."

These demonstrating Japanese students use flags and slogan-bearing helmets as identifiable group boundaries. (Paolo Koch/Rapho Guillumette)

Georg Simmel, an inventive and provocative German sociologist, suggested that: "A state of conflict [with outsiders] pulls the members . . . tightly together. . . . This is the reason why war with the outside is sometimes the last chance for a state ridden with inner antagonisms to overcome these antagonisms" (Simmel, in Coser, 1956, p. 87).

Student activist leaders of the 1960s certainly learned this structural lesson in dramatic and unexpected ways. Because the actual number of activists on American campuses was very small, leaders were forever combating problems of inaction and apathy. However, when college administrators began calling in police and national guardsmen to halt demonstrations, entire student bodies went on strike. Through conflict, boundaries were drawn and students were forced to make choices about which side of the boundary they were on.

The paradox of cohesion through conflict is all around us, but often not recognized. We tend, like news reporters, to see only the drama of conflict and overlook the undercurrents of cohesion. The old union song, "Which side are you on, boys, which are you on," is an attempt to draw sharp boundaries through conflict. It is also an attempt to raise workers' consciousness about where they belong and where their allegiances should rest.

Conflict with out-groups, then, is one way in which social groups create and maintain their own boundaries. The sharper the conflict with outsiders, the tighter the internal cohesion is likely to be (at least until internal conflicts begin). Because conflict is so useful for boundary definition, groups may attract or invent threats where none exist in order to maintain cohesion. Lewis Coser, an American sociologist who elaborated on Georg Simmel's writings about conflict, suggests that white southerners at the turn of the century

stiffened their ranks against the blacks through exaggerated stories of black crimes against whites. The actual numbers of crimes that blacks committed against whites were very small, but stories of rapes, murders, and imminent race wars abounded. As Coser says, "Fear of the Negro, far from deriving from the Negro's actual behavior, is a means of keeping the status system intact, of rallying all members of the white group around its standard" (1956, p. 109).

Of course, no amount of conflict with outside groups can sustain a group that is not a going concern. Unless a group has some basis for cohesion and consensus, it will fall apart and not be able to rally under external pressure. During the depression in America, for example, close families became closer and stronger as they united against their troubles, but weak families disintegrated (Komarovsky, 1971). This is not to say that on-going groups must be conflict-free. Sometimes internal conflict and its eventual resolution help to define and strengthen a group's boundaries. When a group successfully expels its "enemies from within," it publicly reaffirms its boundaries. During the Vietnam War for example, draft resisters presented American society with an acute problem of internal conflict: if individuals were allowed to follow their own consciences and not the edicts of the draft board, how would the nation remain unified in the face of conflict with outside groups? America's solution to this threat of internal dissension was to close its ranks against the dissenters. Draft resisters were either sent to jail or fled the country in self-imposed exile. Both "solutions" maintained the cohesion necessary to continue the war. Through expulsion of the dissenters, America established its boundaries as the type of social group that would not (or could not) tolerate in its midst men who refused to fight when they were called.

IN THE NEWS

Conflict and Cohesion

Greers Ferry, Ark.—"This has been a white fiefdom for a hundred years. They succeeded in keeping blacks out by just such tactics as they are employing now against us. And in the absence of any blacks, *we've become the niggers of Cleburne County*" (italics added).—Dixon Bowles.

Dixon Bowles is the leader of a commune of men and women who call themselves The Group. For two years the commune lived in peace with the rest of the townspeople.

It entered commerce and became the owner or operator of seven thriving businesses. It started the town's first Chamber of Commerce and its first Optimist Club.

Its members became the entire volunteer fire department of the town, which has a population of 389. Other members became leaders of Boy and Girl Scout troops.

The men of the commune wore neatly trimmed short hair and dressed like the other men of the town. Unlike some communes elsewhere, The Group, Inc., as it is called, rigidly prohibited drugs and free love. Several members joined the Baptist and Methodist Churches.

Then they made their mistake. The town held an election last fall, and for the first time since moving to Greers Ferry in 1971 the members of The Group voted. They turned out to be the balance of power between two fiercely contesting factions. The losing faction turned its anger on the commune and on the night of Aug. 23 The Group's home was attacked by a stone-throwing mob.

Votes alone did not cause the people of Greers Ferry to turn so violently against The Group. Even though they were active in the town's economy and lived conservatively, the commune people were perceived to be different. The Group's children attended their own school, which caused some resentment. Townspeople felt that they held themselves aloof, especially intellectually.

But the main cause of the community's uneasiness seems to be its uncertainty over the commune's aims. Some think The Group intends to "take over the community" and turn it into one large commune. That idea is especially prevalent among the hundreds of Northerners, mostly retired people, who have moved here in recent years. The Northerners have stirred up the hill people, some of whom are violently inclined. Mr. Bowles . . . described the method used by a certain retired Northerner to stir antagonism against The Group.

"He goes up to these people who barely got out of the sixth grade and sign their name with an X," Mr. Bowles said, "and he says, 'That's a commune over there. You know what they do in communes? Let me read you this Reader's Digest article. Dah-de-dah, dah-de-dah-dah.' And this guy says, 'Well, son of a bitch,' and before you know it, it's out on the pick-up circuit that we have orgies over here, and dope and it's called commune, therefore it's com-a-nist."

In short, The Group has become the out-group of Greers Ferry, the victim of stereotypes about communes. Fear of differences, it seems, has led the townspeople to create a threat where none really existed. By expelling their newly created out-group, the people of Greers Ferry reaffirmed and strengthened their social boundaries.

Interestingly, once before, The Group had shored up *its* boundaries in a similar way:

Mr. Bowles and 14 other original members, all from Odessa, Tex., have always been "straight" by the standards of many communes. However, during the late nineteen-sixties The Group attracted a number of what Mr. Bowles calls "freaks," and their free-swinging style threatened to change The Group's direction. Mr. Bowles threw them out and The Group returned to its relatively conventional ways.

SOURCE: Roy Reed, "Conformity Backfires for a Commune," *The New York Times*, September 22, 1973, pp. 33; 36.

The expulsion from the Soviet Union of Nobel-Prize-winning writer Alexander Solzhenitsyn was another case of boundary drawing. For some years Solzhenitsyn had openly criticized the Soviet system. Finally, in March 1974, the Soviet leadership decided it was time to reestablish internal unity and to reaffirm the boundaries of acceptable behavior for membership in the Soviet Union. By deporting Solzhenitsyn, Russia was saying it would not tolerate severe criticism from within.

Of course, internal conflict need not always be so threatening to group cohesion that the dissenter must be expelled in order for group unity to be restored. If a group is secure in its own basic cohesion, in its common value system, it can tolerate and adjust to relatively large amounts of dissension. In fact it is this tolerance that often allows members to let off steam before so much pressure builds up that the whole system explodes. It is the rare family that expels its dissenting adolescents, and it is the rare professional organization that excludes its critical or challenging members. On the other hand, though, the more intimate a group the more possibilities there are for conflict since more sides of each person's personality are involved in the group. But a group that is essentially stable can allow conflict within its boundaries because when "we are certain of the irrevocability and unreservedness of our feelings . . . peace at any price is unnecessary" (Simmel, in Coser, 1956, p. 81). Since each group eventually sets its own norms (which are either stated explicitly or implied) about the amount of dissension members may express, these norms help to define the group's boundaries and to reaffirm its sense of uniqueness.

The Influence of Size Although we rarely think of it, the size of a group very much affects our behavior and feelings in that group. We generally tend to attribute our experiences in groups to the personalities of the group's members, but, in fact, the highly impersonal feature of group size often has a great deal to do with these experiences. A person's sense of security, for example, can be greatly altered by the size of a group to which he or she belongs. First children, for example, often resent the birth of a second child; similarly, the addition of a third friend may create uncertainty for the original two.

Comparing *dyads* (two-person groups) and *triads* (three-person groups) provides a dramatic example of the effect that group size can have on group experience. The very existence of a dyad depends upon the participation of both members. If either member withdraws, the group no longer exists. A three-member group, however, can survive the loss of a member. The effects of this purely structural feature—size—on the personal experiences of each group member are very strong. We need only think of the differences in our own responsibility when we are involved in a two-person or three-person conversation. In a dyadic conversation we can never lapse into reverie without jeopardizing or destroying the interaction. But if a third person is present we can pass the responsibility of the conversation on to him or her and indulge in our mental wanderings. The very dependence of a dyad on the continuing participation of both members creates for its members unique intimacy, responsibility, and pressure.

Contributing also to the uniqueness of the dyad is the inability of either member to "pass the buck" to other members. If, for example, two people are living together and one of them finishes off the last piece of cake, both members of the dyad know with complete certainty who did the eating. With three or more people in the house, however, only the cake-eater could know for sure who the culprit was. Groups larger than dyads, then, provide some anonymity and privacy for their members. The dyad participant "is much more frequently confronted with All or Nothing than is the member of the larger group" (Simmel, 1950, p. 135).

Another unique feature of dyads is that they cannot cast one member in the role of mediator. With three or more people, one person can reconcile the other two. Dyads also do not have to deal with problems of intruders or spectators. If two people are interacting directly, they cannot be performing for the benefit of a third party, nor do they have to be sensitive about giving a third party "air time." Also, in dyads there can never be a majority or minority and never a coalition of two against one. All these factors, entirely due to the properties of size, have enormous impact on private experiences.

We tend to attribute power in a group to the strength of individual personalities or talents, but here, too, a structural property—group size—plays a key role. Group size affects the formation of coalitions that may control the balance of power among group members. In his book aptly titled *Two Against One* (1969), sociologist Theodore Caplow describes all the possible outcomes of different coalitions among three people with differing amounts of power. If, for example, A is more powerful than B, and B has the same power as C, then the possibilities for winning coalitions exist between A and B vs. C; B and C vs. A; A and C vs. B. These possibilities for coalition prevent the nondyad group from becoming static. There is always the potential for new alliances. In a two-person group, however, the relationship is less volatile since no new coalitions are possible. Triads are marked by perpetual imbalance: "In most triads members tend to switch coalitions from one disagreement to another simply to maintain

solidarity and avoid permanent exclusion of one member" (Hare, 1962, p. 242).

Adding a fourth member to a triad again changes things drastically. It opens up new possibilities for coalitions (for example, two vs. two; three vs. one). As the size of a group grows, the number of possible relationships increases geometrically. (In a group of three, there are six possible relationships; in a group of four there are twenty-five possible relationships; and in a group of five there are ninety! See table 7:1.)

By increasing group size many features other than pairings also change. In large groups, for instance, it is difficult for any one member to keep all the others in mind when he or she states an opinion or suggests an activity. Thus statements made in large groups sound more like pronouncements than conversation: think of the formal way we discuss ideas in a classroom as compared to the informal way we share the same ideas with a friend. Because we cannot speak directly and uniquely to each member of a large group, our statements become more abstract and general so that they will be relevant to everyone. In large groups, too, individual opinions carry less weight, so to reach con-

table 7:1 INCREASE IN POTENTIAL RELATIONSHIPS WITH AN INCREASE IN GROUP SIZE	
SIZE OF GROUP	NUMBER OF RELATIONSHIPS
2	1
3	6
4	25
5	90
6	301
7	966

SOURCE: A. Paul Hare, *Handbook of Small Group Research* (Glencoe, Ill.: Free Press, 1962), p. 229.

figure 7:1   A sociogram

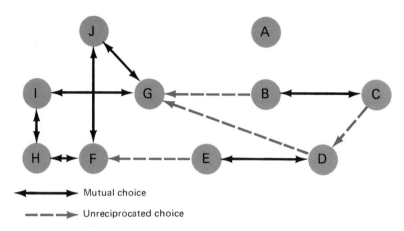

Some years ago, J. L. Moreno devised a technique for describing relationships within a group. The researcher questions each member of the group on his or her personal preferences. For example, he might ask each person: Whom would you like to work with on this project? Whom do you enjoy spending time with after hours? Whom do you consider to be your best friends? These preferences are then transcribed to a diagram. Each circle stands for one person. The solid lines with arrows at each end represent mutual choices; the dotted lines stand for unreciprocated preferences. The resulting *sociogram* enables the researcher to identify popular and influential individuals, cliques, dyads and triads, and isolates—at a glance. For example, in the group of ten pictured here, G is clearly the most popular; four people chose this person. The number of mutual choices in the subgroup to the left (F, H, I, J, G) indicates the presence of a clique. B-C and E-D are dyads. A is an isolate who neither chose other people nor was chosen by them. Sociograms are extremely useful in clarifying communication networks and decision-making patterns in small groups.

sensus, discussion must be limited and the group must resort to more formal means of reaching decisions (like taking a vote). Group size also influences the efforts of individuals to gain control and determines how much pressure there will be to reach a representative decision.

From this very brief discussion we can see how important size is in determining our seemingly personal and unique experiences in different groups. Size, like boundaries, is a structural property of groups, and it influences the behavior of members regardless of their individual psychological make-ups.

Other such important features are (1) the purpose of the group—is it to accomplish something, to make decisions, or to provide pleasure and relaxation; (2) the hierarchial structure of the group—is it rigid and authoritarian or flexible and participatory; (3) the relations of the group with surrounding groups—is it secret or public, accepted or disapproved of, admired or scorned; (4) the history of the group—is it new or old, stable or changing. All these factors strongly influence our group experiences and help to define the nature and types of satisfactions we can derive from group life.

PRIMARY AND SECONDARY RELATIONSHIPS

If we think of the vast differences between life in a tribal village and life in a big city, we can begin to grasp the wide range of possibilities for organizing our social group experiences. In a tribal village, all members may relate to each other daily. They share a common ancestry, as well as goals, values, aspirations, and traditions. Everyone in the tribe is involved with the survival and welfare of the whole. In addition, each member of the tribe has a fixed position in the social order, usually assigned at birth. Geographic mobility is as limited as social mobility; a tribal member lives and dies within very restricted geographic boundaries. Such expressions of individuality as clothing, work aspirations, leisure activities, and friendship circles are all highly circumscribed by the rights and obligations of tribe members. The entire web of each person's relationships is interconnected and predetermined at birth. Since every aspect of an individual's life meshes with every other aspect (family, co-workers, neighbors, and friends are all the same people), a tribal member's entire social identity is involved in each relationship. Personal, social, and economic life are all rolled up together, and the notion of "self" is virtually indistinguishable from the notion of "my tribe."

We need hardly mention the dramatic differences between this type of group life and the kind we are so familiar with in our own urban, industrial society. For the mid-twentieth-century city dweller, social life is much more fragmented. Relatives may live far away, friends may live across town, fellow workers may live in a different town altogether, and neighbors may be anonymous. With no one group, except, perhaps, the immediate nuclear family, do we have regular, continuous, face-to-face interaction. Those who live around us may come from very different backgrounds and have very heterogeneous histories so that we do not necessarily share common goals, values, aspirations, and traditions. The survival and well-being of one group is often antithetical to the survival and well-being of another (think of labor unions and management; cab drivers and bus drivers; industrialists and ecologists). And unlike tribal members who spend their entire lives in one village, we are so mobile that one out of ten Americans moves each year. We also move socially, leaving old friends behind.

Between these extremes lies the whole range of possibilities for human social organization. We have learned to take these two ends of the spectrum for granted, but in earlier times, particularly in the nineteenth and early twentieth centuries, when the world was undergoing breathtaking changes as a result of modernization (industrialization, urbanization, and bureaucratization), the switch from close, intimate villages (typified by rural agrarian communities) to fragmented heterogeneous cities was a source of great dismay, fear, curiosity, and wonder.

From *Gemeinschaft* to *Gesellschaft*

In trying to make sense of the new and sometimes frightening changes in the old and familiar order of things, early sociologists often resorted to extremes of comparison between what was in the past and what would be in the future. The first of these notable commentators was Ferdinand Töennies, a German sociologist, who drew distinctions between what we now call *primary relationships* and *secondary relationships*. Töennies (1887; 1957) elaborated on the contrast between *Gemeinschaft*, or community, and *Gesellschaft*, or society. *Gemeinschaft* is characterized by close, intimate, overlapping, and stable relationships (as in tribal villages). *Gesellschaft* is characterized by the pursuit of self-interest, impersonal attachments, efficiency, and progress.

Emile Durkheim was also concerned with the nature of social relationships within these two contrasting types of societies. He asked questions about the social bonds that hold people together under the two different kinds of social conditions. Although Durkheim intended to describe the distinctions as ideal types, that is, as generalized models, his perceptions about the distinctive nature of these two types parallel those of Töennies and remain powerful to this day.

Durkheim (1893) distinguished between what he called mechanical solidarity and organic solidarity. *Mechanical solidarity* describes the types of relationships that link together members of small, stable communities. These relationships are overlapping and interrelated, and members of the group are interdependent because of the common bonds and habits they all share, not because

they exchange specialized skills both need. The relationships that characterize mechanical solidarity are based on personal, stable, intertwining emotional attachments. Our close friendship groups are based on mechanical solidarity. We turn to our friends for affection, support, help, and advice *because* they are our friends and not because they are necessarily the most efficient supporters, helpers, or advisers in any particular instance.

In contrast, *organic solidarity* is characterized by relationships that are impersonal, transient, fragmented, and rational. In a society marked by organic solidarity, different parts of the society are linked by efficient interdependence, *not* by the bond of homogeneity. Just as the parts of the body differ dramatically from each other in appearance, substance, and function and yet depend completely upon each other for survival, so the

The shift from village life to urban life has changed not just the landscape, but social relationships as well. (Below, J. Allan Cash/Rapho Guillumette. Right, Tim Eagan/Woodfin Camp & Assoc.)

segments of an organically linked society differ drastically from each other, yet depend on each other for survival. In relationships marked by organic solidarity we do not relate to the whole individual, but to those qualities that pertain to the function of the relationship. For example, when we hail a cab on a city street we don't care who the driver is or what his personal characteristics are. All we ask is that he get us where we want to go. He, in turn, doesn't care who we are as long as we can pay the fare. The cab driver and passenger are briefly interacting in terms of a transaction, not in terms of an emotional attachment. The driver is interchangeable with any other driver, and the passenger interchangeable with any other passenger.

The consequences of such a drastic shift in human relations, brought about by the irreversible conditions of modernization, have both fascinated and frightened a large number of social observers, and the total eclipse of human community has been forecast with gloom and doom for at least a century now.

While no one would deny that the shifts from farm to factory, from village to city have brought great changes in human social organization, the initial alarm over these changes has been tempered in recent decades by the discovery that modern relationships are not wholly isolating and alienating and that traditional relationships were not wholly intimate, supportive, and integrating. Even when families are separated by great spaces and different value systems, they still stay in contact and help each other (think of how many college students go home for vacation; receive gifts on holidays; keep their parents informed of their whereabouts). Even in large urban centers people still make friends at work, in the neighborhood, through their children's schools. Even in the most bureaucratic organizations, work groups and friendship cliques form. While these relationships are clearly not as all-consuming as the relationships in a tribal village, they often have their own merits.

Erich Fromm has suggested that modern

society promotes greater independence and self-reliance (1941, p. 124). What he means is that in a society where people have substantial freedom to select their friends, their jobs, and their leisure activities, they are more able to create their *own* identities, rather than being tied to the social roles into which they were born. On the other hand, this type of freedom often leaves us bewildered and confused by the choices at hand: "The structure of modern society affects man in two ways simultaneously; he becomes more independent, self-reliant, and critical, and he becomes more isolated, alone and afraid" (Fromm, 1941, p. 124).

It is likely that the debate over the virtues of *Gemeinschaft* and *Gesellschaft* relationships will continue for some time. People in traditional, small, intimate communities will rail against the narrowness and lack of privacy; and people in large, heterogeneous, anonymous cities will long for some sense of community and safety. As an elderly rural churchman said to a sociologist studying his once close-knit farming village in England: "Newcomers have broken down many of the old community ideas and people have become sentimental about the passing of ways and customs, although many of them were narrow, limiting, and bad. . . . [In the old days] they had sort of a code but all the natural human relations were covered by cruel and ugly taboos which obsessed some of them" (Blythe, 1969, pp. 69–70).

Primary and Secondary Groups

Although the terms *Gemeinschaft* and *Gesellschaft* were originally intended to describe the social organization of entire communities, these concepts have also been adopted for the description of different types of smaller groups. The primary group is analogous to *Gemeinschaft* and the secondary group to *Gesellschaft*.

Primary Groups Several interconnecting features characterize primary groups:

1. continuous face-to-face interaction
2. permanence
3. ties of affection
4. multifaceted relationships
5. non-task-oriented relationships

The nuclear family, at least in theory, is the primary group *par excellence*. Members of the family are frequently in face-to-face interaction; the unit is enduring (even after members move away they are still members of the family); family members are bound together by love and affection; members of the family have many kinds of relationships with each other (ranging from exchange of services, "You set the table, I'll wash the dishes," to emotional support and physical protection); and the family is a unit *because* it is a family, not because it is trying to accomplish something.

These are the structural features of the *ideal* family (or ideal primary group), at least as it is defined in contemporary American society. But between the ideal and the real there is, of course, often much disparity: many families break up and therefore have neither continuous face-to-face interaction nor permanence. Many families spend more time in conflict than in love; many families have severely limited interactions (teenagers, for instance, are often reluctant to share their private lives with their parents); and many families are, in fact, united for the fulfillment of tasks (for example, bearing and raising children, working the farm, dividing up the chores of survival), rather than for the fulfillment of emotional needs.

Although not even the nuclear family, therefore, always fulfills the requirements of the ideal primary group, the list of characteristics helps us to discern how much various groups actually differ from this ideal. These insights can then help us to understand the causes of satisfactions and disappointments in different groups.

Secondary Groups In contrast to primary groups, secondary groups ideally have the following characteristics:

1. limited face-to-face interaction
2. nonpermanence
3. ties of exchange not of affection
4. limited relationships
5. task-oriented relationships

But, just as for primary groups, this theoretical description is an ideal type. Secondary groups do, in fact, produce long, intimate friendships, and despite their initial task orientations, secondary groups can turn into primary groups. A perfect example of this is the highly task-oriented group of office workers that may become a close-knit primary group. Co-workers may develop strong friendships, spending much of their leisure time together.

If you join a secondary group, such as a political club, with the hope of developing enduring friendships, you may be disappointed. This disappointment will result not so much from the personalities of the club's members (or from your own social deficiencies) as from the structure of the group itself. To begin with, the club will meet infrequently and only for a few hours at a time, affording members little opportunity to get to know each other in a variety of situations. The members of the club are together for an explicit, task-oriented purpose and too many diversions from this task will be met with impatience and hostility. Membership in the club is voluntary and temporary, and turnover rates may therefore be high. Although members may hold similar attitudes and values, their basic ties to each other are intellectual and not emotional. For all these reasons friendships may be difficult to form, regardless of the personalities of group members.

We can draw no hard-and-fast distinctions between what constitutes a primary or a secondary group. But we can be sensitive to their varying characteristics, and we can take notice of the impact these characteristics have on our personal experiences.

THE SEARCH FOR INTIMACY AND COMMUNITY

Because the great forces of modernization have led to important changes in the nature of human social organization, there is a longing by many people to return to the intimacy and safety of earlier communities. Attempts to bring people closer together range from two-hour, "human growth" groups to permanent, enduring communes. The most sensational of the short-term experiments have been the variety of self-revelatory and intimacy-promoting gatherings that are loosely labeled *encounter groups.*

Encounter Groups and the "Singles Industry"

The encounter movement, which gained momentum in the 1960s, is an attempt to heighten self-awareness and mutual human trust. Encounter methods vary widely, but a group typically consists of eight to eighteen persons led by a "facilitator."[1] Members of the group are usually urged to express their emotions toward one another both verbally and physically. The by-words of encounter

---

[1] The term "facilitator" is used to describe the person who runs an encounter group in order to de-emphasize the authority and control that "leader" implies.

Being "in touch" with one's body is emphasized by many encounter groups. Here, a bride and groom are encircled and touched by group members. (Paul Fusco/Magnum)

groups are mutual trust, openness, honesty, and naturalness.

Although there are a growing number of techniques for conducting encounter groups, and although more than 6 million Americans have participated in some sort of encounter at some variety of "growth center," there is still a great deal of dissension about the consequences of such instant intimacy. While the effects of encounters on participants are, in the end, the crucial concern of those evaluating this startling new movement, the fact that such an untraditional form of community life has gained such a large following is, in itself, fascinating. We can only marvel at the types of self-exposure that millions of men and women make among total strangers in encounter groups. As one experienced observer has written:

There is no denying the searing shock of what one sees and feels once the mask of everyday polite behavior peels away: the smooth and powerful business executive finally cracking and confessing in wracking sobs that he has never had a friend, never really "talked" to his wife, is a stranger to his children; the "successful" housewife and clubwoman gasping out the tragedy of what she feels is a "wasted life"; the smart junior executive, his tie askew, grimacing in anguish as he confesses aloud for the first time in his life the humiliation and anguish of being a closet homosexual; the beautiful young bride admitting through silent tears that she feels nothing—absolutely nothing—for anyone or anything. (Hoover, 1972)

Carl Rogers, one of the founders of the encounter movement, has tried to explain the popularity of this new approach to human relations.

I believe it is a hunger for something the person does not find in his work environment, in his church, certainly not his school or college, and sadly enough, not even in the modern family. It is a hunger for relationships that are close and real; in which feelings and emotions can be spontaneously expressed without first being carefully censored or bottled up; where deep experiences—disappointments and joys—can be shared; where new ways of behaving can be risked and tried out; where, in a word, [people] approach the state where all is known and all accepted, and thus further growth becomes possible. This seems to be the overpowering hunger which [people] hope to satisfy through the experience of an encounter group. (1970, pp. 11–12)

Encounter groups, then, represent a mating of primary and secondary forms of group life. They are primary in their intimacy, emotional bases, and intensity, but they are secondary in their temporariness and short-term commitments.

Do encounter groups really change behavior? Are they harmful or helpful? Within the last few years, researchers have begun to study the effects of encounter groups. Preliminary results of one study suggest that "encounter groups . . . consistently improve self-satisfaction, self-reliance and comfort with sexuality, and lessen loneliness, alienation and social inhibition" (*The New York Times*, January 13, 1974).[2] The results of another study were more negative. Irvin Yalom and Morton Lieberman (1971) organized eighteen encounter groups at Stanford which were led by people with varied training in group leadership. Out of the 209 undergraduates who participated, 39 dropped out before the experiment ended. Of the 170 who completed the thirty hours of group encounters, 16 suffered "enduring, significant, negative outcomes, which were caused by their participation in the group." The study found that the most vulnerable students were those who had little self-esteem and who

expected great changes from their group experiences.

The growth of the encounter movement, which is aimed at personal fulfillment through group experience, has been paralleled by the growth of the "singles industry." With the break-up of traditional communities, people who have reached adulthood without marrying (or whose marriages have been disrupted) are no longer incorporated into families or village communities. Urban life is not conducive to extended-family living, if only because space is so limited in high-density apartment houses, and the break-up of small communities has robbed people of the protection and sustenance of a community that assumes responsibility for its members. How then, do isolated individuals in a society geared to family units create or locate a community for themselves?

John Goodwin, in his book entitled *The Mating Trade* (1973), explores the many and diverse institutions that have sprung up to service the never-wed, separated, deserted, divorced, and widowed millions in America. Goodwin estimates that there are some 36 million single adults in America, and with the break-up of traditional communities, which often provided meeting places for the unwed, the singles industry has flourished as a means of bringing together unattached adults. There are singles bars, singles clubs, singles magazines, singles parties, singles weekends, singles cruises, and even singles encounter groups.

Once again, this is an example of secondary-group structures being used to foster primary-group relations. The computerized dating services, which Goodwin calls "electronic cupids," are "nothing less than the automation of the hallowed ritual of Boy meets Girl" (1973, p. 79). But that hallowed ritual, particularly for men and women cast adrift in urban settings, is working with de-

---

[2] These findings come from an as-yet unpublished study directed by Dr. James Bebout of the Wright Institute at Berkeley. The study evaluated 1,500 people who participated in 150 groups.

creasing effectiveness, and a modern world is turning to modernized means for filling the gaps that are created by the decline of long-lasting primary communities.

Communes: Old and New

Not all attempts at replacing lost community are based on modern means. The movement toward planned or intentional communities, given so much publicity in the last decade, did not originate with the hippies. The colonies at Jamestown and Plymouth were intentional communities, and the nineteenth century saw the birth of numerous religious communities, including the Shakers, the Hutterites, and the Amana True Inspirationists. John Humphrey Noyes founded Oneida, an experiment in group marriage; industrialist Robert Owen put his ideas about social reform to work in New Harmony; and Fanny Wright set about buying farms for freed-slave communes (Lawson, 1972; Hinds, 1973). Only eleven of the ninety-odd intentional communities founded in the nineteenth century lasted twenty-five years or more. Why?

Curious about this high mortality rate among earlier communes, sociologist Rosabeth Kanter conducted a study of American communes. She discovered that the longevity of earlier planned communities was highly connected to personal sacrifices, including abstinence from alcohol or meat, plain dress, and celibacy, and to irreversible investments, such as turning property and income over to the group. "Sacrifice," writes Kanter, "means that membership becomes more costly and is therefore not lightly regarded or likely to be given up easily" (1972, p. 353). Most successful communes demanded that members renounce all ties with outsiders and in some cases ties with insiders

as well. (Both celibacy and free love helped to prevent the formation of exclusive ties that might undermine group cohesion.) In long-lasting communes, privacy was discouraged or forbidden: common dwelling places, eating and recreational facilities, and group rituals were emphasized. Most strikingly, in those that endured, the community required total submission to authority, and most of these practiced confession, self-criticism, and strict conformity to programmed activities. In all cases, the more the participants invested (emotionally and otherwise) in the community, the greater were the chances of the community surviving.

Modern communes frequently lack these longevity-producing features. Despite the fact that the new wave of communes flourished in the mid-1960s,[3] many of them did not endure. The emphasis in today's communes is on self-expression and autonomy, not submission; on freedom from routine and control, not discipline and communal labor. Exceptions are highly disciplined religious communes and Walden Two, a commune modeled on the older, enduring types (Kinkade, 1973). But for the most part, attempts at re-creation of the traditional community have been short-lived and occasionally chaotic.

To say, however, that modern communes are not long-lasting is not to invalidate their existence. With the loss of permanence in other forms of community life, there is no reason to insist on permanence in communal living. Whatever group satisfactions and rewards can be gained from communal experiences should be appreciated on their own merits without reference to nostalgic standards of longevity and permanence.

---

[3]   One observer of modern commune life, Benjamin Zablocki (1971) estimates that in 1970 there were 1,000 rural and 2,000 urban communes in this country.

summary

Every member of society belongs to certain groups that are either chosen voluntarily or inherited at birth. A *social group* is a number of people who define themselves as members of a group; who expect certain behavior from members that they do not expect from outsiders; who are defined by both members and nonmembers as belonging to a group. Social groups shape people's attitudes, behavior, and values and provide the link between their individual lives and the rest of society. Interaction within groups can range up and down various scales: the amount of time spent together, the degree of task-oriented interdependence, the number of multiple-shared activities, and the degree of emotional involvement. The higher the group rates on each of these scales, the more intense and meaningful the group will be for its members.

Sociologists distinguish several categories of groups. William Graham Sumner first coined the terms in-group and out-group to describe the feelings of "we" and "they" that group members have. An *in-group* is a circle of people in which a person feels at home. It develops from shared experiences that breed a sense of "we-ness." An *out-group* is a circle of people to which a person feels he or she does not belong. Out-groups are by necessity implied by the existence of in-groups and may be largely a result of stereotyping. Another category of groups are *reference groups*: groups to which we refer and compare ourselves but to which we do not necessarily belong. The choice of a reference group strongly affects a person's feelings toward himself or herself.

One way to study groups is to examine their *structural properties*: the ways in which groups are put together, regardless of their purposes. *Group boundaries* are one structural property. There are the ways in which a group defines itself and sets itself apart from outsiders. One effective way to create and maintain group boundaries is through conflict, for it brings the group together in the face of a common enemy. In this way a sense of unity and "we-ness" is attained, as well as a sense of who the outsiders are. Yet if groups are not somewhat unified to begin with, external conflict will harm rather than help them.

Size is another structural property of groups. It can influence power relationships among the members of a group and the power of an individual to gain and hold control. Other structural properties of groups are: the purpose of the group, its hierarchical structure, its relationship to other groups, and its history.

The web of social relationships changed dramatically during the nineteenth and early twentieth centuries with the growth of urbanization and industrialization. Ferdinand Töennies, a nineteenth-century German sociologist, described the contrast between *Gemeinschaft*, a community characterized by close, intimate, overlapping, stable relationships, and *Gesellschaft*, a society characterized by the pursuit of self-interest, impersonal attachments, efficiency, and progress. Emile Durkheim drew upon Töennies' distinctions to examine the social bonds that existed in each type of society. He called the link that binds members of simple societies together *mechanical solidarity*: relationships that are characterized by personal, stable, intertwining, emotional attachments. *Organic solidarity*, which binds people in complex, industrialized societies, is characterized by relationships that are impersonal, transient, fragmented, and rational.

Although the terms *Gemeinschaft* and *Gesellschaft* were originally intended to describe the social organization of entire communities, these concepts have been adopted to describe different types of smaller groups. The primary group is analogous to *Gemeinschaft* and the secondary to *Gesellschaft*. *Primary groups* are characterized by several interconnecting features: continuing face-to-face interaction, permanence, ties of affection, multifaceted relationships, and non-task-oriented relationships. *Secondary groups* have the following characteristics: limited face-to-face interaction, nonpermanence, ties of exchange not of affection, limited relationships, and task-oriented relationships. The nuclear family is an example of a primary group, and a political club is an example of a secondary group.

Modern society, characterized by *Gesellschaft*, has produced yearnings in many people for a return to the more intimate communities of the past. To ease their feelings of loneliness and alienation, people have tried various solutions. The "singles industry," with its aim of bringing unmarried people together for living and entertainment, is one example. Another is the encounter group, which typically consists of eight to eighteen people led by a facilitator, who uses various techniques to engender personal expression. Encounter groups represent a blend of primary and secondary relationships, and though their full impact on individuals is still uncertain, it is significant that over 6 million Americans have participated in some sort of encounter group.

Modern communes represent another attempt to replace lost community. Rosabeth Kanter found that the longevity of earlier planned communities was highly connected to personal sacrifices. In enduring communes the community required total submission to authority, and most of these practiced confession, self-criticism, and strict conformity to programmed activities. Modern communes frequently lack these longevity-producing features. Yet to say that communes are not long-lasting is not to invalidate their existence. Rewards gained from communal experience should be appreciated on their own merits.

glossary

gemeinschaft Ferdinand Töennies's term for small, traditional communities characterized by close, intimate, overlapping, stable relationships.

gesellschaft Ferdinand Töennies's term for societies characterized by rational pursuit of self-interest, impersonal attachments, efficiency, and progress.

in-groups Those groups in which individuals feel at home and with which they identify.

out-groups Those groups in which individuals do not feel they belong, and with which they don't identify.

primary group A small, intimate group, characterized by close, personal relationships and empathy.

primary relationship A close, intimate, and stable relationship that usually involves the whole personality of each individual.

reference group A group or social category that an individual refers to in evaluating himself or herself.

secondary group A group characterized by limited face-to-face interaction, nonpermanence, ties of exchange not of affection, and limited and task-oriented relationships.

secondary relationship A relationship characterized by narrow and specific goals, self-interest, impersonal attachments, efficiency, and progress.

social group A number of people who define themselves as members of a group; who expect certain behavior from members that they do not expect from outsiders; and who others (members and nonmembers) define as belonging to a group.

references

Howard Becker, *The Outsiders*, New York: Free Press, 1963.

Ronald Blythe, *Akenfield: Portrait of an English Village*, New York: Pantheon, 1969.

Theodore Caplow, *Two Against One: Coalition in Triads*, Englewood Cliffs, N.J.: Prentice-Hall, 1969.

Lewis Coser, *The Functions of Social Conflict*, New York: Free Press, 1956.

Emile Durkheim, *The Division of Labor in Society* (1893), trans., George Simpson, Glencoe, Ill.: Free Press, 1947.

Erich Fromm, *Escape from Freedom*, New York: Avon, 1941.

John Goodwin, *The Mating Trade*, New York: Doubleday, 1973.

A. Paul Hare, *Handbook of Small Group Research*, New York: Free Press, 1962.

Seymour Hersh, "My Lai 4," *Harpers*, vol. 240 (1970): 53ff.

William Alfred Hinds, *American Communities*, Secaucus, N.J.: Citadel, 1973.

George Homans, *The Human Group*, New York: Harcourt Brace Jovanovich, 1950.

Eleanor Links Hoover, "The Age of Encounter," *Human Behavior* (January-February 1972): 8–15.

Rosabeth M. Kanter, "Commitment and social organization: A study of commitment mechanisms in utopian communities," *American Sociological Review*, vol. 33, no. 4 (August 1968): 499–517.

———, *Commitments and Community: Communes and Utopias in Sociological Perspective*, Cambridge, Mass.: Harvard University Press, 1972.

Kathleen Kinkade, *A Walden Two Experiment*, New York: Morrow, 1973.

Mirra Komarovsky, *The Unemployed Man and His Family: The Effect of Unemployment upon the Status of the Man in Fifty-nine Families* (1940), New York: Arno Press, 1971.

Donna Lawson, *Brothers and Sisters All over This Land*, New York: Praeger, 1972.

Roger W. Little, "Buddy relations in combat performances," in Oscar Grusky and George A. Miller, eds., *The Sociology of Organizations*, New York: Free Press, 1970.

Robert K. Merton, *Social Theory and Social Structure*, New York: Free Press, 1968.

Charles C. Moskos, Jr., *The American Enlisted Man*, New York: Russell Sage, 1970.

Theodore Newcomb, "Attitude development as a function of reference groups: The Bennington Study," in G. E. Swanson, T. M. Newcomb and E. L. Hartley, eds., *Readings in Social Psychology*, New York: Holt, Rinehart and Winston, 1958.

——— et al., *Persistence and Change: Bennington College and Its Students After 25 Years*, New York: Wiley, 1967.

Carl Rogers, *On Encounter Groups*, New York: Harper & Row, 1970.

Edward A. Shils, "Primary Groups in the American Army," in R. K. Merton and P. F. Lazarsfeld, *Continuities in Social Research*, New York: Free Press, 1950.

——— and Morris Janowitz, "Cohesion and Disintegration in the Wehrmacht in World War II," *Public Opinion Quarterly* (Summer 1948): 280–315.

Georg Simmel, *The Sociology of Georg Simmel*, trans. and ed., Kurt H. Wolff, New York: Free Press, 1950.

William Graham Sumner, *Folkways*, Boston: Ginn, 1906.

Ferdinand Töennies, *Community and Society* (1887), trans. and ed., Charles A. Loomis, East Lansing, Mich.: Michigan State University Press, 1957.

Irvin D. Yalom and Morton A. Lieberman, "A Study of Encounter Group Casualties," *Archives of General Psychiatry*, vol. 25 (July 1971): 16–30.

Benjamin David Zablocki, *The Joyful Community*, Baltimore, Md.: Penguin, 1971.

for further study

Social Psychology. This chapter only scratches the surface of group behavior, which is the topic of an entire discipline, social psychology. Through years of experiments with small groups, social psychology has built up a wealth of insights about how people in groups work together, the ways in which groups influence members' attitudes and even their perceptions of reality, and the structure of group behavior. Two good texts in the field are Paul Secord and Carl Backman, *Social Psychology*, 2nd ed. (New York: McGraw-Hill, 1974), and Edward Sampson, *Social Psychology and Contemporary Society* (New York: Wiley, 1971). In chapter 2 we discussed Philip Zimbardo's experiment with students in a makeshift prison. The impact of assuming the roles of prisoners and guards was devastating and can be read about in "Pathology of Imprisonment," *Society* (April 1, 1972): 4–8.

Rural Life. In this urban age few people know what village life is like. Although it has often been romanticized, here are two field studies of village life that are accurate and well-written: Lawrence Wylie, *Village in the Vaucluse* (Cambridge, Mass.: Harvard University Press, 1964), describes the daily character of a village in southern France; Ronald Blythe, *Akenfield* (New York: Pantheon, 1969) depicts what life is like today in a small English village that the industrial revolution passed by.

Being a Soldier. Few civilians have a clear idea of the soldier's life and the group pressures that affect it. Since the pioneering study by Shils and Janowitz, *Public Opinion Quarterly* (Summer, 1948): 280–315, a number of sociologists have made excellent studies of the modern soldier. A major work about officers is *The Professional Soldier* by Morris Janowitz (New York: Free Press, 1960). Sanford Dornbush, once a West Point cadet, wrote a critical report on that institution, "The Military Academy as an Assimilating Institution," *Social Forces*, vol. 33, no. 4 (May 1955): 316–21. The life of the ordinary American soldier in recent years has been studied by Charles Moskos, *The American Enlisted Man* (New York: Russell Sage Foundation, 1970).

"What is poverty? Poverty is asking for help. . . . I'll tell you how asking for help feels: You find out where the office is, the one from which paupers are supposed to get help. When you find it, you circle the block four or five times trying to get up nerve enough to go in and beg. Finally, the thought of your children's need and suffering pushes you through the door. Everybody is busy and official. After an eternity, a woman comes out to you and you tell her you need help, and you force yourself to look at her.

"She isn't the one you need to see. The first one never is. She sends you to someone else and, after spilling your poverty and shame all over the desk, you find out this isn't the right office. Then you repeat the whole procedure. It doesn't get any easier." (A mother of three, in Ficker and Graves, 1971, pp. 2–5)

* * *

"Welfare!" a brick layer snorts. "Those lazy sluts having kids like it was a factory. . . . You don't work, you don't live, right? . . . I *work* for *my* money," he says. "My job is to work for my family. . . . They don't wanna work, they live for nothing but kicks, nothing but good booze and good sex. . . . What kills me are these people that are on welfare and things like that—or like these colored

SOCIAL STRATIFICATION

people that're always squawkin'. Yet they don't wanna work. I go out, I work sometimes nine, ten days in a row, I got five children." (In Sennett and Cobb, 1972, pp. 135–36)

* * *

By almost any measure, America is the wealthiest nation in the world. The few thousand Americans who live in the Kykuits of this country (the Rockefellers' 4,180-acre estate, outside Tarrytown, New York), vacation at its Hyannisports and Palm Beaches, belong to its Links and Knickerbocker clubs, are rich beyond most people's wildest imagination. Twenty-six million other Americans spend their lives in unrelieved sickness, hunger, and squalor.

These income inequalities are one dimension of social stratification. How do societies distribute desirable resources? How do societies rank their members? What are the consequences of social ranking and inequality? In the first part of the chapter we look at who gets what in America and at the consequences of inequalities. In the second part we ask why. In the final part we look at social mobility and how to relieve the inequalities, taking up the often-debated subject of welfare and some alternatives to it.

THE DIMENSIONS OF STRATIFICATION

The Siriono of Bolivia come as close to being a classless society as any people we know of. Like most hunters and gatherers, the Siriono have very few possessions—at most, a bow and arrow, a crude knife, a bone or stick for digging roots, a bladder for carrying water, a large shell that doubles as a basket and cradle, a pair of sandals, a skin to hold these things. Nomads, the Siriono live from day to day. When the hunt is successful, they gorge themselves (they cannot store meat for more than two or three days); when game elude them and foraging yields little, they go hungry. But feast or famine, food is distributed equally among all members of the band. The Siriono expect those who "have" to share with those who "have not"; they do not tolerate hoarding. As a result, no individual or family has the opportunity to accumulate food and buy the services or deference of another. Economically, all are equals. But the Siriono *do* have a pecking order. Older people, those who exhibit magical talents, and skilled hunters occupy special positions in the band. And the respect and honor they earn through longevity or prowess spill over into political matters, where these individuals carry more than equal weight (Lenski, 1966, pp. 102–12).

On an Israeli kibbutz, social relations are relatively egalitarian. Class differentiations are minimal, and old and young work together. (Wide World Photos)

Social stratification is not simply a question of wealth, even in capitalist societies such as the United States. There are obvious social differences among people who earn $50,000 by drawing salary as a business executive, collecting interest from an estate ("clipping coupons"), selling heroin, winning a Nobel prize, holding public office, or "hitting on the lottery." When we say that people have "class," we mean we admire their style, the way they conduct themselves and spend what they have—not just that they are wealthy. The label "nouveau riche" gives expression to the belief that money, like wine, needs time to mellow. Money may be a prerequisite for status in this country, but it is not a guarantee. The bosses of organized crime, for example, are rich and powerful; they can and do buy politicians. But they cannot buy respect or prestige outside the underworld. On the other hand, ministers and professors enjoy high status in the United States, although their incomes are relatively small. In short, income alone does not determine status. Family name, ethnic and religious background, age, sex, education, occupation, life-style, club membership, neighborhood—even grammar—all influence a person's social ranking.

Sensitive to such differences, Max Weber distinguished between classes, parties, and status groups (in Gerth and Mills, 1946, pp. 180–95). By *class*, Weber meant people who occupy the same rung on the economic ladder; by *party*, people who share interests and seek to further them by gaining access to power. A *status group*, in Weber's scheme, is a group of people whose life-style or pattern of consumption gives them a similar social identity. Weber emphasized that while these three classifications often overlap (it takes money to support an upper-class life-style; poverty usually means powerlessness as well), they do not necessarily coincide. A very rich man, such as Franklin D. Roosevelt, can become a working man's hero and an enemy to his own class, for example. Weber's point was that in complex, modern societies, social stratification is multidimensional. It involves the unequal distribution of power and prestige, as well as wealth. In the pages that follow we will examine these three dimensions of stratification—property, power, and prestige—in the United States.

Income and Wealth

Economic stratification depends on what people earn and what they own. The earnings are income and the "ownings" (property and assets) are wealth. Two people may have similar incomes, but one person's may come entirely from a salary and the other's may come from dividends on vast holdings of securities. The second person is wealthier than the first and ranks higher on the economic scale. Both income and wealth are distributed unevenly, but to different degrees.

Income On April 15 every year, the Internal Revenue Service demands an accounting from all adult Americans of what they earn. The official records do not include all non-cash income (expense accounts and other fringe benefits) or noncash social benefits that raise a person's standard of living (Medicaid, food stamps, school lunches, and the like). And there is undoubtedly a great deal of underreporting, deliberate and accidental (Rose, 1972, p. 162). Nevertheless, government statistics do give a clear picture of the range of incomes and the dimensions of inequality in this country.

In 1972 the median family income was $11,120 per year—double that in 1960 (*Statis-*

table 8:1 **MEDIAN EARNINGS, BY OCCUPATION, SEX, AND RACE, 1971**
(For Year-Round Full-Time Workers)

OCCUPATION[1]	MALE			FEMALE		
	TOTAL (IN DOLLARS)	WHITE	BLACK	TOTAL (IN DOLLARS)	WHITE	BLACK
All workers	9,399	9,659	6,669	5,593	5,641	5,014
Professional and technical workers	12,518	12,629	10,046	8,312	8,294	8,298
Farmers and farm managers	4,308	4,356	(NA)	(NA)	(NA)	(NA)
Managers and administrators, except farm	12,721	12,781	9,867	6,738	6,690	(NA)
Clerical workers	9,124	9,257	7,742	5,696	5,685	5,779
Sales workers	10,650	10,769	(NA)	4,485	4,448	(NA)
Craftsmen, foremen	9,627	9,749	7,556	5,425	5,511	(NA)
Operatives	7,915	8,198	6,188	4,789	4,825	4,448
Private household workers	(NA)	(NA)	(NA)	1,926	1,870	1,895
Service workers, except private household	7,111	7,560	5,566	4,159	4,169	4,039
Farm laborers	3,752	4,134	(NA)	(NA)	(NA)	(NA)
Nonfarm laborers	6,866	7,129	5,990	4,548	4,645	(NA)

(NA) Not available.
[1]Occupation of longest job.
SOURCE: Bureau of the Census, *Current Population Reports*, series P–60, no. 85.

tical Abstract, 1973, p. 328).[1] Approximately 16.6 percent of American families earned $5,000 or less; 27.0 percent between $5,000 and $10,000; 49.1 percent between $10,000 and $25,000; 7.3 percent over $25,000. Breaking the population down into fifths, we find that the poorest 20 percent of Americans earned only 4.5 percent of all personal income—about one-fourth what their share would be if income were distributed equally in the United States. The wealthiest 5 percent of Americans earned over 17.0 percent of all personal income, about three times their "share."

Education and occupational differences explain these gradations in part. While the median income of white family heads who had not gone beyond elementary school was $7,629 in 1972, the median income of high-school graduates was $12,426, and that of college graduates $17,497. For black family heads, the corresponding 1971 figures were $5,407, $8,814, and $14,063, respectively. These figures suggest that education is an excellent investment. In fact, statistics show that every year of college is worth roughly $70,000 in lifetime earnings. This figure is probably exaggerated, however, for many of the people who go to college usually come from middle- and upper-class, achievement-oriented families and would probably earn better than average incomes without ad-

[1] Unless otherwise indicated, all data are from the 1973 edition of *Statistical Abstract of the United States*, or *Current Population Reports*, series P–60, no. 90, December 1973.

vanced education. Still, the more education a person has, the better his or her chances of working in a high-paying occupation. Self-employed professionals receive the highest wages in this country (a $17,169 median income in 1971); nonfarm laborers earn the lowest ($4,847). Table 8:1 shows the percentage of white and black Americans working in different occupations, and the median incomes for males and females in each occupation. Clearly, race and sex influence a person's economic standing in the United States.

Wealth   The rich and superrich derive only a small proportion of their incomes from wages and salaries. Whereas Americans who earned $20,000 or less in 1966 drew 87 percent of their income in wages and salaries, those in the over $100,000-a-year bracket earned 15.2 percent of their income from salaries, 13.3 percent from small businesses they owned, and 66.8 percent from stocks, bonds, real estate, and other capital (Tumin, 1973, p. 55). The government's profile of American "wealthholders" is shown in Table 8:2.

Wealth—especially stocks and bonds—is concentrated even more than income. In principle, any person can "own a piece of America" by buying stocks or bonds. In reality,

---

table 8:2   AMERICAN WEALTHHOLDERS,[1] 1969

NUMBER OF WEALTHHOLDERS

Male	5,643,000 (62.6 percent)
Female	3,370,000 (37.4 percent)
Total	9,013,000

SIZE OF ESTATE	NUMBER	PERCENTAGE
$ 60,000–99,999	3,341,000	37.1%
100,000–499,999	5,214,000	57.9
500,000–999,999	311,000	3.4
1,000,000–9,999,999	143,000	1.6
10,000,000 +	4,000	(less than 0.05)

ASSETS	AMOUNT (IN BILLIONS OF DOLLARS)	PERCENTAGE
Total	1,625.8	
Real estate	428.3	26.3
Bonds	85.4	5.3
Corporate stock	551.5	33.9
Cash	189.9	11.7
Notes and mortgages	59.4	3.7
Insurance equity	31.0	1.9
Other	280.0	17.2
Debts	*203.7*	12.6
Net worth (less deficit)	1,422.2	

[1]People whose tax returns showed gross assets of $60,000 or more.
SOURCE: *Statistical Abstract of the United States,* 1973 (Washington, D.C.: Government Printing Office, 1973), p. 342.

those who "own" the corporations by holding stocks are a small proportion of the population. According to Robert J. Lampman (1962), 1.6 percent of the adult population owns *82.2 percent* of all stocks—plus 88.5 percent of corporate bonds, 100 percent of state and local bonds, and 38.2 percent of federal bonds.

Taxes The federal income tax is supposed to be a progressive tax, that is, the more money a person earns, the higher his or her rate of taxation. In 1973 the income tax rate for an income of $2,000 or less was 14–17 percent; for $20,000–22,000, 38 percent; for $100,000 or more, 70 percent. Progressive taxes are designed to distribute the cost of public goods and services according to people's ability to pay, and to deprive the rich of some luxuries in order to provide the poor with necessities (Fried et al., 1973, p. 45).

But does our tax system actually reduce income inequalities? To some extent, yes. The poor pay proportionately lower federal taxes than do middle- and high-income people, and they benefit more from "transfer payments" (welfare, Medicaid, workmen's compensation, unemployment insurance, and other subsidies that are not drawn from a person's salary, as Social Security is). The federal government allocated $28.3 billion to poverty programs in 1972 alone.

But in many ways the tax laws favor the well-off. Interest earned from state and local bonds is tax exempt; so is 22 percent of income earned from the production of oil, gas, and other minerals, and 50 percent of income earned through capital gains (profits on stocks, real estate, and other property). According to one estimate, if all earnings were taxed at federal income tax rates, the government would have collected an additional $77 billion in 1972 (Fried et al., 1973, p. 51). In addition, many of the taxes Americans pay are regressive; for example, when every-

---

SUBSIDIES TO THE RICH

According to government figures released in the late sixties:

— 381 people with incomes of $100,000 a year or more did not pay one penny in federal income taxes in 1968.

— Over 1,000 people who earned $200,000 or more paid the same proportion of their incomes in taxes as did people earning $15,000–$20,000.

— Most taxpayers in the $500,000–$1,000,000 group paid the same proportion of their incomes in taxes as did people earning $20,000–$50,000.

— The super-rich, with incomes over $5 million, paid the same proportion of their incomes in taxes as people who earned $500,000.

Mr. G., for example, earned $1,284,718, primarily through capital gains, only half of which are taxable. Mr. G. would have paid income tax on $600,000 if he had not taken out a loan for $10 million. Interest payments on the loan came to $588,000, and interest payments are tax deductible. Mr. G. paid exactly $383 in income taxes. Mr. I., whose income was $1,313,000, didn't pay any income tax. Why? He listed $125,000 for "intangible drilling expenses" (a legal deduction), claimed a spectacular loss of $828,000 on his farm, and received a $865,000 deduction under the oil depletion allowance. In effect, the U.S. Treasury underwrites these gentlemen's business ventures.

SOURCE: Philip M. Stern, "How 381 super-rich Americans managed not to pay a cent in taxes last year," in Jerome H. Skolnick and Elliott Currie, eds., *Crisis in American Institutions*, Boston: Little, Brown, 1970.

---

one is taxed at the same rate, regardless of income, the poor actually contribute a higher proportion of their income than middle- and high-income people do. The federal payroll (or Social Security) tax, state and local taxes (including sales tax), and property taxes are all regressive. In 1965 people who earned $2,000 or less paid about 25 percent of their income in state and local taxes; people who earned $15,000 or more, only 7 percent (Miller, 1971, p. 16).

Regressive taxes and tax loopholes shift a substantial part of the tax burden *back* to poor and middle-income families. Benjamin Okner, a Fellow at the Brookings Institution, calculates that federal taxes (income and payroll) reduced income inequality in the United States by only 4 percent in 1966 (Rose, 1972, p. 162). Does this figure represent progress? Has poverty decreased?

The War on Poverty—Victory or Defeat?
The government's definition of poverty is based on the Department of Agriculture's estimate of the minimal cost of living for a family of four.[2] In 1972 a nonfarm family with

an annual income of less than $4,275 was considered officially poor. About 12 percent of Americans fell into this category. Poverty is most prevalent among female-headed households and black Americans. In 1972, 33 percent of black Americans earned less than $4,275 compared to about 9 percent of white Americans; 38 percent of female-headed households were poor, compared to 8 percent of male-headed households. However, almost 75 percent of America's poor are white, and over 55 percent live in male-headed households.

Table 8:3 shows that the number of poor Americans dropped from 40 million in 1960 (before the War on Poverty) to 24 million in 1969. The figure then rose slightly in 1970. As

---

[2] This figure should provide a family of four with a minimum food plan, indoor plumbing, a double bed for every two people, eating utensils, and a few other essentials. However, it is not enough to buy much meat or fresh

fruits and vegetables. There is no allowance for dental care or entertainment, and very little for clothes. The government estimates a family of four would have needed $9,100 to live comfortably (a "moderate income") in 1972.

---

table 8:3 POVERTY IN THE UNITED STATES, 1960–1973

YEAR	NUMBER IN MILLIONS	PERCENTAGE OF POPULATION	POVERTY LINE	PERCENT OF MEDIAN INCOME	NATIONAL MEDIAN INCOME
		The Poor			
1960	39.9	22.2	$3,022	53.8	$ 5,620
1963	36.4	19.5	3,128	50.0	6,249
1966	28.5	14.7	3,317	44.2	7,500
1969	24.1	12.1	3,743	39.7	9,433
1971	25.6	12.5	4,137	40.2	10,285
1972	24.5	12.0	4,275	38.4	11,120
		The Near-Poor[1]			
1960	54.6	30.4	$3,778	67.2	
1963	50.8	27.1	3,910	62.6	
1966	41.3	21.3	4,146	55.3	
1969	34.7	17.4	4,679	49.6	
1971	36.5	17.8	5,171	50.3	
1972	34.7	16.8	5,344	47.9	

[1]People earning less than 125 percent of the poverty-level income.
SOURCE: Adapted from Edward Fried et al., *Setting National Priorities: The 1974 Budget* (Washington, D.C.: Brookings Institution, 1973), p. 42. (Updated from "Characteristics of the Low Income Population: 1972," *Current Population Reports*, series P–60, no. 88, June 1973.)

Edward Fried and his colleagues (1973, p. 45) suggest, more Americans are able to purchase the necessities of life today than was true in the past. But the *gap* between the poor and other Americans has not changed. The number of people earning only half the median income was the same in 1971 as it was in 1963, 36 million. The distribution of income is more equal today than in 1929 during the Great Depression, but has not changed greatly since 1944 (see figure 8:1). But despite this deviation from absolute equality, America is one of the most nearly equal nations in the world. The distribution of income here is

figure 8:1   Measuring income inequality—the Lorenz curve

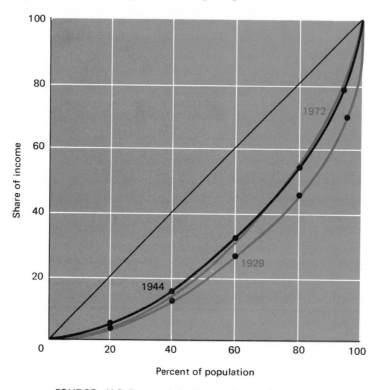

SOURCE: U.S. Bureau of the Census, *Current Population Report*,
P-60, no. 89, table D, p. 3.

The Lorenz curve is a simple method for portraying economic inequality in a graph. The straight diagonal line in the graph represents absolute equality, with each percentage of the population earning exactly that proportion of all income. Thus, the lowest 20% would earn 20% of all income, the lowest 40% would earn 40% and so on. The curve represents the actual distribution of income: at the lowest point, the poorest 20% of the population earned 5% of the income. The second point stands for the bottom 40%; the third point for the lowest 60% and so on. The space between the line and curve shows the degree to which income distribution deviates from absolute equality. The farther away the curve is from the line, the greater the inequality of income. The curves for 1970 and 1944 show similar distributions of income, but the curve for 1929 shows far greater inequality.

similar to that in Great Britain, Canada, and Japan; only Denmark, the Netherlands, and Israel are closer to absolute income equality (Miller, 1971). This degree of equality is small comfort to America's poor, who still acutely feel the differences between their lot and the affluence they see around them.

Power

The presidency of the United States is generally conceded to be the most powerful office in the world. The trappings of the office alone show this: the White House and Camp David, the planes ready to fly the president anywhere at a moment's notice, the access to prime-time television to address the nation whenever he wants. The president never has to pay rent at the White House, wait for a haircut, or be put on "hold" by a secretary. The decisions the president makes are not like other people's either. Few of us think in billions of dollars, in millions of people, of the risk of triggering a nuclear war. The view from the top of the American power structure is very different from the one gained at the bottom.

Basically, *power* is the ability to mobilize collective energies, commitments, and efforts. Personal power is the freedom to choose, to design one's own destiny. Social power is the ability to affect public affairs, even if others oppose you. Social power may be formal or informal. By formal power or *authority*, we mean the prerogatives that legitimately go with an office, such as the presidency of a nation or company. By informal power, we mean *influence*, the know-how and know-who to pull the strings behind the scene. (We will explore the question of political power in greater depth in chapter 14.) The president of this country has a great deal of formal power; Martin Luther King, Jr.,

Power is the ability to mobilize collective energies, commitments, and efforts. Although he never held elective office, Martin Luther King, Jr., wielded great social power by appealing to the nation's political and moral values. (Wide World Photos)

had enormous informal power. But how many others share this power in our society?

Not surprisingly, this is one of the most hotly debated questions in sociology. C. Wright Mills argued that the heads of government, the military, and business in this country constitute a "power elite."

[T]hey are in command of the major hierarchies and organizations of modern society. They rule the big corporations. They run the machinery of state and claim its prerogatives. They direct the military establishment. They occupy the strategic command posts of the social structure, in which are now centered the effective means of the power and the wealth and the celebrity which they enjoy. (1956, p. 4)

These are the men who make the decisions that determine how the rest of us will live. They move back and forth between the private and public sectors, never for a moment forgetting who they are, who their friends are, or where their interests lie. They are accountable only to themselves, and relatively immune to public pressure and the public interest.

David Riesman (1953), among others, disagreed with Mills. Where Mills saw one solitary elite, Riesman saw many competing elites whose varied goals and interests prevent them from pooling their resources. As a result, social power is widely dispersed; no one group commands. While this pluralistic system protects us from any kind of dictatorship, in Riesman's view it also deprives us of effective leadership. Decisions made through bargaining and compromise are not always the best decisions, however democratic their origins.

One point on which Mills and Riesman definitely agree is that the vast majority of Americans—the masses—have little power to speak of, personal or social. In Mills's words:

The powers of ordinary men are circumscribed by the everyday worlds in which they live, yet even in these rounds of job, family and neighborhood, they often seem driven by forces they can neither understand nor govern. "Great changes" are beyond their control, but affect their conduct and outlook nonetheless. The very framework of modern society confines them to projects not their own, but from every side, such changes now press upon the men and women of the mass society, who accordingly feel that they are without purpose in an epoch in which they are without power. (1956, p. 3)

Mills's and Riesman's theories can neither be proved nor disproved unless power can be measured in some way. How do you calculate a person's or group's sway over events? One measure of power is the *offices people hold*. We can reasonably assume that the president of a big corporation or the mayor of a large city has more power than ordinary people. But what about the people who work behind the scenes, who do not appear on official rosters? Another measure of power is *reputation*. We can ask people to identify the influential members of their community and conclude that individuals listed over and over belong to the local elite. But how do we verify the judges' opinions? A third measure of power is *participation in key decisions*. Who attends the crucial meetings? Who speaks for what groups? Who has lunch with whom? Who seems to have the final word? While this may seem the best method, in-depth analyses of key decisions require almost unlimited time and effort, and the combined skills of a psychologist and detective (Dahl, 1963). How many people admit to bribing, blackmailing, strong-arming, or even just pulling strings to get their way? As John Kenneth Galbraith once said, "Power obviously presents awkward problems for a community which abhors its existence, disavows its possession, but values its exercise" (in Domhoff and Ballard, 1968, p. 103).

An equally important question in this context is whether people *feel* they are able to influence the decisions that affect them (regardless of whether they do in fact exercise power). This is what is meant by "political efficacy." Robert Dahl (1963) found that the subjective sense of power rises with income, education, social status, and political participation. The more influential a person feels, the more likely he or she is to vote, to join organizations and attend meetings; and the more a person participates in political and community activities, the more likely he or she is to feel influential. Participation or withdrawal is self-reinforcing. Like wealth and power, political efficacy is cumulative; the more you have, the more you get (Mills, 1956, p. 10). The same can be said of prestige.

Prestige

Consider the following advertisement:

We don't think anyone in this city can rival our assortment of chic wares from the world famous House of Dior, each bearing the inimitable stamp of his renowned good taste.

Christian Dior was a national asset to France and a by-word for taste. In fact, upon his arrival in New York (just after he launched his New Look), he received more publicity than did Winston Churchill on his trip. Ah, fashion!

What intrigues us, of course, is that even though Monsieur Dior is no more, his vitality and zest, his unexpected and highly *civilized* mode of fashion still zips around the world, touching all kinds of fashion. Today, there is no more well-known name anywhere on our planet than Dior.

Here is a random sampling of the exquisite *vendibles* you can find all around our store bearing the Dior label. We'll start with his signature luggage. Delectable. Noticeable at any airport. Woven in a tough, *take-it-on-the-chin* fabric, the pattern suddenly dawns on you. It's a design of C's and D's (Christian Dior, of course). (Trahey Agency)

After all, what good is carrying Dior luggage if nobody knows that it's Dior luggage? Dior luggage, like designer-initialed scarves, shirts, dresses, and underwear, is a status symbol. It shows that the individual has money and, more important, good taste.

Trivial as this example may seem, prestige is obviously one of the important dimensions of social stratification. People rank one another according to how they earn their money (their occupation), how they spend it (their "consumptive class"), who they are (their ancestry), who they know, how successful and well known they are, and how respectable.

For example, being listed in *The Social Register* or in *Who's Who in America* is definitely a status symbol. These publications have long reigned as *the* guides to who counts in this country. *The Social Register* describes itself as a list of "distinguished" people—by which it means people who come from the right families, attend the right schools, belong to the right clubs, and live in the right neighborhoods. Applicants to *The Social Register* are only considered if they bring recommendations from several people already on the list. You cannot pull strings to get into *Who's Who in America*, however—a fact of which its editors are inordinately proud. *Who's Who* lists, in its own words, "the best known men and women" who have achieved "special prominence" by virtue of "reputable achievements" or "official positions" in government or religious and educational establishments. Coincidentally, perhaps, about 80 percent of the people in *Who's Who* are also in their local *Social Register*—most of them bankers, lawyers, engineers, businessmen, architects, doctors, artists, public officials, educators, clergymen, and social workers (Baltzell, 1966). Of course, neither listing is prepared in a scientific way, and both publications exclude (deliberately) the vast majority of Americans, who are only moderately distinguished or definitely undistinguished.

Occupation Ratings Probably the best measure we have of prestige in America is the Hatt-North scale of occupational prestige, which was designed for the National Opinion Research Center (NORC) in the 1940s. Paul Hatt and Cecil North (1947) compiled a list of ninety occupations and asked a cross section of Americans which term expressed their own personal opinion of each occupation's standing: excellent, good, average, somewhat below average, or poor. They then assigned a numerical value to each rating (100 for excellent, 80 for good, and so on), calcu-

---

table 8:4 PRESTIGE RANKING OF OCCUPATIONS IN THE UNITED STATES, 1963

U.S. Supreme Ct. Justice
Physician
Nuclear physicist
Scientist
Government scientist
State governor
Cabinet member in the federal government
College professor
U.S. Representative in Congress
Chemist
Lawyer
Diplomat in the U.S. Foreign Service
Dentist
Architect
County judge
Psychologist
Minister
Member of the board of directors of a large corporation
Mayor of a large city
Priest
Head of a dept. in a state government
Civil engineer
Airline pilot
Banker
Biologist
Sociologist
Instructor in public schools
Captain in the regular army
Accountant for a large business
Public school teacher
Owner of a factory that employs about 100 people

Building contractor
Artist who paints pictures that are exhibited in galleries
Musician in a symphony orchestra
Author of novels
Economist
Official of an international labor union
Railroad engineer
Electrician
County agricultural agent
Owner-operator of a printing shop
Trained machinist
Farm owner and operator
Undertaker
Welfare worker for a city government
Newspaper columnist
Policeman
Reporter on a daily newspaper
Radio announcer
Bookkeeper
Tenant farmer—one who owns livestock and machinery and manages the farm
Insurance agent
Carpenter
Manager of a small store in a city
A local official of a labor union
Mail carrier
Railroad conductor

Traveling salesman for a wholesale concern
Plumber
Automobile repairman
Playground director
Barber
Machine operator in a factory
Owner-operator of a lunch stand
Corporal in the regular army
Garage mechanic
Truck driver
Fisherman who owns his own boat
Clerk in a store
Milk route man
Streetcar motorman
Lumberjack
Restaurant cook
Singer in a nightclub
Filling station attendant
Dockworker
Railroad section hand
Night watchman
Coal miner
Restaurant waiter
Taxi driver
Farm hand
Janitor
Bartender
Clothes presser in a laundry
Soda fountain clerk
Share-cropper—one who owns no livestock or equipment and does not manage farm
Garbage collector
Street sweeper
Shoe shiner

SOURCE: Adapted from Robert W. Hodge et al., "Occupational Prestige in the United States," in Seymour Lipset and Reinhard Bendix, eds., *Class, Status, and Power,* 2nd ed. (New York: Free Press, 1966), pp. 324–25.

lated the average rating for each occupation, and listed them accordingly. The job hierarchy shown in table 8:4 is what one might have expected. Supreme Court justices, doctors, scientists, governors, and cabinet members are at the top; garbage collectors, street sweepers, and shoe shiners at the bottom; school teachers, builders, farmers, and policemen in between. But there are some surprises. Americans are not as anti-intellectual as many intellectuals think: college professors rank eighth (well ahead of bankers). Oddly, movie stars and athletes were awarded no more prestige than welfare workers, farm owners, and undertakers![3]

These occupational rankings have proven to be highly stable. The NORC study was repeated in 1963 and in an expanded form in 1964 and 1965. Although blue-collar occupations gained prestige and three categories of white-collar work (managerial, clerical, and sales) dropped somewhat, there were very few changes over the twenty years. In another study, inspired by the NORC survey, Joseph Gusfield and Michael Schwartz (1963, pp. 265–71) tried to learn why people consider some occupations highly prestigious and others degrading. Is it because they consider some jobs more important than others? more desirable? cleaner? stronger? Is it because some jobs seem more secure, a route to success? because they believe the occupants of certain jobs are honest? because they associate some occupations with rich, white Americans (wasps) and others with foreign-born or black or poor people? The authors found that people use different criteria to rate different occupations,[4] but the overall ranking was very close to that in the

NORC study. Indeed, parallel research in other countries, industrialized and underdeveloped, revealed striking uniformity in job ranking (Hodge, Trieman, and Rossi, 1966). Summarizing these studies, Hodge, Siegel, and Rossi (1966) conclude that people rank occupations according to their importance for society, the power and influence that accompany them, educational requirements, income, the nature of the work and dress (white vs. blue collar), and the characteristics of the people who fill each occupation.

The Hatt-North scale is a limited tool. It does not tell us anything about how family names, connections, life-style, or other intangibles affect a person's social standing. But it does show quite clearly that Americans award prestige unequally, that we are conscious of prestige differences, and that there is some degree of consensus about who counts in this country.

Classes in America

When asked, most Americans identify themselves as middle-class. This is part of our reverse snobbism. American culture glorifies the common man, "the average Joe"; the idea that no one is any better than anyone else is a central part of our national creed. Yet we have seen that there are startling inequalities in this country. Can "aristocracy cohabit with democracy" (Baltzell, 1966, p. 266)? Mrs. Marietta Endicott Peabody Tree's grandmother, a wealthy lady and a member of one of this country's most "distinguished" families, thought not. Mrs. Tree recalled:

[T]he "first and only" time her grandmother ever slapped her was when, as a young girl, Marietta referred to an acquaintance as "very middle class." After the slap came these stern, grandmotherly

---

[3] These occupations appeared on an extended scale, and ranked forty-fourth (Tumin, 1973, p. 66).

[4] Examples of the kinds of criteria the study asked people to use are dirty or clean, useful or useless, honest or dishonest, rural or urban, secure or insecure.

words: "There are no classes in America—upper, lower or middle. You are never to use that term again." (Birmingham, 1968, p. 340)

Only a person of unshakeable position could insist on this view. There are obvious inequalities in the distribution of wealth, power, and prestige in America. To deny this would be foolish. Even a child knows how to distinguish between her "own kind" and families that are above or beneath hers socially.

Still, it is extremely difficult to identify distinct classes or social strata in America. The Lynds (1929, 1937), pioneers in the study of stratification in this country, believed that power and prestige are a function of wealth. W. Lloyd Warner and Paul S. Lunt (1941) believed the Lynds had overemphasized economic differentials. An anthropologist by training, Warner was acutely sensitive to the rituals of class and differences in life-style. "Something more than a large income is

necessary for high social position," he wrote. "Money must be translated into socially approved behavior and possessions, and they in turn must be translated into intimate participation with, and acceptance by; members of a superior class" (Warner et al., 1949).

In the Yankee City studies, Warner and his colleagues used two measures of stratification. First, they asked selected members of the community to explain their own personal view of stratification (how did they measure status?) and to rank individuals and groups (the subjective approach to measuring class). Then Warner devised an objective "Index of Status Characteristics" based on occupation (a measure of level of education and income), source of income,[5] type of home, and neighborhood. Putting the two together, Warner concluded that there were six classes in Yankee City: upper-upper (1.4 percent), lower-upper (1.6 percent), upper-middle (10 percent), lower-middle (28 percent), upper-lower (33 percent), and lower-lower (25 per-

More than money is needed to confer upper-class status—wealth must be spent in socially approved ways. This mansion on Long Island, New York, would certainly qualify. (Photo Researchers)

---

[5] Inherited wealth, earned wealth, profits and fees, salary, wages, private relief, public relief, or nonrespectable income.

cent). But how many people could say whether they themselves belong to the upper-middle or lower-middle or perhaps upper-lower class? Very few.

Over the years since Warner's study, rising wages and salaries for workers have acted as an economic leveler. The unionized worker has steadily improved his or her economic position and now may earn more than many white-collar workers. This, plus the belief that America is the land of opportunity and the feeling that no people are any better than anyone else even if they are better off, tends to retard the development of class consciousness in this country. In addition, racial, ethnic, and religious affiliations cut across economic lines. As a result Americans have multiple social identities that interfere with the development of a coherent class or rank consciousness (see Wrong, 1972).

LIFE CHANCES: THE CONSEQUENCES OF POVERTY

Nelson Rockefeller's secretary cannot afford to eat in the same restaurants as her employer, visit the same doctors, or own several lavish homes. But she can expect to live as long as, or even longer than her boss; she can afford nutritious meals, good medical care, and pleasant housing. The life chances of the working, middle, and upper classes are about the same. But the poor die earlier than other Americans. They are more susceptible to chronic and debilitating illnesses, physical and mental. They inhabit housing long since abandoned by others or "projects," and receive medical care from overcrowded and often substandard clinics. They are victimized by criminals on the one hand, the police and courts on the other. And they pay more than

working-, middle-, and upper-class Americans for what they buy. In short, poverty is not only uncomfortable and degrading, it is a health hazard.

Nutrition

In the late sixties, Senators Joseph S. Clark and Robert Kennedy visited a neighborhood just blocks from the Capital building. Clark reported:

Gloria Palmer, a round-eyed, solemn-faced little girl of ten stood shyly outside her slum home in Washington, D.C., and shifted her six-months-old baby brother from one arm to another, while two other tots leaned against her and stared up at the two United States Senators. . . .

I asked Gloria—one of eleven children of Wilhelmina Palmer—what she had eaten for lunch. "We didn't have any lunch," said Gloria quietly, and added, "But we have blackeyed peas for supper a lot." I asked her little brother, George, age seven, "What did you have for lunch yesterday?" George replied, "Soup." "And what did you have for breakfast?" "Soup," George said. (Clark, 1971, p. 10)

Hard as it is to believe, millions of Americans (mostly children) live on beans, rice, peanut butter, grits, biscuits, corn bread, powdered milk, Kool-Aid, and one can of meat a month. From 30 percent to 50 percent of poor children suffer from protein, iron, and vitamin deficiencies. Malnutrition stunts growth and makes a child more vulnerable to disease, but this is not all. There is a growing body of evidence to suggest that severe protein deficiency in the first twelve to eighteen months of life causes irreparable damage to the brain and nervous system. In addition, undernourished children are apathetic, lethargic, unable to pay attention for more than very brief spells, and often irritable and agitated (Read, 1971). In short, hunger interferes with learning.

Medical Care and Mental Health

"I went there at 9 o'clock like they said," recalled the young New York Negro mother. "About 12:30, I saw the doctor and he said I was in the wrong clinic. I went to the other clinic and waited until 2 o'clock and there were still people in front of me. The kids get out of school at 2:30, so I had to leave. That's just the way it is if you're poor." (*Newsweek*, July 7, 1969)

Clinics in low-income neighborhoods are understaffed and overcrowded. Clients rarely see the same doctor more than once, making it impossible to establish rapport and trust. Doctors, themselves middle class, find it hard to relate to lower-class people and to the conditions that make the poor disease-prone. Often, the poor feel intimidated by the staff, the red tape, and the possibility of costly fees and medicine (only 34 percent of people with incomes under $2,000 have health insurance). As a result, most will try old remedies, over-the-counter drugs and simple stoicism, visiting a clinic only as a last resort and in emergencies (Rainwater, 1968). And even then they may not be able to follow the regimen the doctor prescribes.

E. Pavenstedt (1965) is one of many psychiatrists who associates severe psychiatric disorders with disorganized, calamity-stricken homes. He writes of the "very low-lower class":

Consistency was totally absent. . . . The mother might stay in bed until noon [one day] and get up at 6 A.M. [the next]. . . . As the children outgrew babyhood, the parents differentiated very little between the parent and the child role. The parents' needs were as pressing and as often indulged as were those of the children, with strong competition for the attention of helpful adults. . . . The overwhelming demands of adults [produced] constant crises . . . for every recurring frustration is experienced as crisis. . . . Abandonment and neglect of children is commonplace. (pp. 94–95)

While not all social scientists would agree with this characterization, numerous studies have shown that the incidence of some severe psychiatric disorders increase as one moves down the socioeconomic ladder (Hollingshead and Redlich, 1958). Whereas middle- and upper-class people seek therapy with private doctors, the poor are most often treated with drugs, shock, psychosurgery, and custodial hospitalization—which is no treatment at all in most cases (Coles, 1964).

Housing

The streets of Kenwood-Oakland, a poor section of Chicago, are lined with garbage. The sidewalks are crumbling; many of the buildings are condemned and abandoned. One woman told Senate investigators she was afraid to go to sleep, there had been so many fires because of faulty wiring. Her roof leaked whenever it rained, and the sewage was backed up in her toilet. The winter before, she and her seven children had had no water for two weeks (U.S. Senate Select Committee on Nutrition and Human Needs, November 1969).

Conditions in housing projects are better. But Lee Rainwater (1971) found that 20 percent of the apartments in Pruitt-Igoe, a highrise, low-income project in St. Louis, were vacant, and most tenants (half of them fatherless families, half living on public assistance) wanted to move. They complained of broken glass, dangerous and broken elevators, people urinating in the halls, and outsiders drinking in the stairwells and laundry rooms. Most were afraid of being held up or robbed, which they said were frequent occurrences. Rainwater characterized Pruitt-Igoe as "a world of trouble." Since then officials have written off the project as a disaster, evacuated the tenants, and dynamited the buildings!

The Urban League estimates that there were 6.7 million occupied substandard housing units in this country in the late 1960s, 4 million of them without indoor plumbing. About 6 million homes were overcrowded (more than one person per room). As with many things, the poor pay more (25–35 percent of their income) for less (Ficker and Graves, 1971, pp. 91–102).

Criminal Justice

A redevelopment administrator in New Haven, Connecticut, told a group of people who were protesting the city's failure to enforce housing codes in that city's slums, "there are law violations and there are law violations" (Ryan, 1971, p. 187).

The courts, if not the law, favor white-collar offenders—slumlords who fail to repair housing-code violations, businessmen who use deceit in advertising or fraud, individuals or companies who violate price-fixing codes, embezzlers, and the like. More often than not,

white-collar criminals are fined and given suspended sentences (Lundberg, 1969, pp. 124–28). In contrast, residents of low-income neighborhoods are frequently arrested for drunkenness, gambling, and such ambiguous crimes as vagrancy, which together account for about 60 percent of all arrests. Why? In William Ryan's view (1971), the police see their role as keeping order, not enforcing the law.

Poor people are more likely to be arrested than to receive a summons (as the nonpoor do); less likely to be released on their own recognizance (although they are the least able to afford bail); more likely to be sent to jail following conviction (Cratsley, 1972, p. 192). Many poor people spend months, even years, in jail waiting for trial—if their court-appointed lawyers and the district attorney's office do not convince them to plead guilty to a lesser charge (to save "the people" the expense of a trial). The poor are also more likely to be the victims of crime than affluent Americans (see table 8:5).

table 8:5 VICTIMIZATION BY INCOME (rates per 100,000 population)

OFFENSES	INCOME			
	UNDER $3,000	$3,000–5,999	$6,000–9,999	OVER $10,000
Total	2,369	2,331	1,820	2,237
Rape	76	49	10	17
Robbery	172	121	48	34
Aggravated assault	229	316	144	252
Burglary	1,319	1,020	867	790
Larceny ($50 +)	420	619	549	925
Car theft	153	206	202	219

SOURCE: *The Challenge of Crime in a Free Society* (Washington, D.C.: Government Printing Office, 1967), tables 11 and 12.

The lure of easy credit in many poor neighborhoods can be a financial trap for poor people who cannot qualify for credit cards in large department stores. High interest rates may increase the cost of merchandise significantly. (Joel Gordon)

The Poor Pay More

Merchants who locate in low-income neighborhoods have a captive audience. Most of their customers do not have the cash to pay for television sets, sewing machines, and other appliances America seems to promise its citizens, and they do not qualify for credit at stores in higher-income areas. Ghetto merchants lure potential customers into the store with promises of easy credit, on the "dollar down, dollar a week" model.

Small weekly payments create the illusion of low prices. In reality, a television marked $220 may cost as much as $300 when paid for on an installment plan. Once the customer signs the papers, he has no choice but to pay. Should he default, the merchant can place a lien on the person's salary, repossess the goods, or sell the contract to a credit agency that will take the individual to court. In addition, such merchants often substitute inferior or slightly used goods for the items a customer saw in the ad or selected in the store. Marking goods up 100 percent or even 200–300 percent is common practice. Door-to-door salesmen use the same tactics on a small scale. The following story is typical:

"A salesman came by soon after we moved in. I told him, 'We don't want to buy anything because we moved and still owe a lot of money on the furniture.' The salesman said he would leave whatever we bought for two weeks and we wouldn't have to pay; 'After that, pay me one or two dollars a week,' he said." The couple took a spread and two pairs of curtains; they didn't sign anything. . . . "A month later, the salesman returned with a Marshall and two policemen. The salesman said 'We came to get $52.' I told him I didn't have it. . . . They took a T.V., radio and two-wheeled bike." (Caplovitz, 1963, p. 164)

The poor are frequent victims of business fraud and deceit. They even pay more for groceries.

The unequal distribution of life chances seems less formidable to correct when reduced to simple numbers. In 1972 it would have taken $12 billion to raise every family in America above the poverty level.[6] This is about what Americans spend yearly on cigarettes ($11.7 billion). Why, then, do millions of Americans go hungry and sick?

TWO THEORIES OF SOCIAL STRATIFICATION

Why do societies distribute wealth, power, and prestige unequally? There are essentially two answers to this question. According to one school of thought, stratification is functional and inevitable; without it, people would have no incentive to perform socially necessary work. Another school holds that inequality is neither inevitable nor functional; it is simply a question of people who *have* exploiting people who *have not*. Kingsley Davis and Wilbert E. Moore (1945, 1953) debated this issue with Melvin M. Tumin (1953)

---

[6] *Current Population Reports*, series P–60, no. 500–88, June 1973, table 8.

in the pages of the *American Sociological Review*, a debate which lasted for seven years.

The Functionalist Theory of Stratification

Davis and Moore reasoned as follows: If all the jobs that need to be filled in a society were equally important and equally pleasant, and if all members of society were equally capable of filling these jobs, there would be no need for stratification. But the fact is, they are not. Some tasks are clearly more essential than others, and some require a great deal more talent and training. For example, almost anyone can learn to dig ditches in a matter of hours, but it takes years of schooling to become a physician. Medical school is tedious and demanding. For a year or more, medical students devote themselves full-time to the business of memorizing the facts of human anatomy. As interns they are expected to work long hours, sacrificing their nights and weekends and social life. They earn very little for their efforts; many go into debt to finance their education. And the job of physician itself is not very pleasant. How many people would choose to spend their lives around the sick and dying if they did not know they would be amply rewarded in money and respect?

This is the key to Davis and Moore's argument. Societies must motivate people to seek socially important positions and to fill these positions conscientiously by awarding their occupants *more* of those things that contribute to sustenance and comfort, humor and diversion, self-respect and ego expansion than they would otherwise receive. In other words, societies have to entice people into essential jobs that are difficult to fill by rewarding them unequally.[7] Otherwise, many essential tasks would not get done. Thus social inequality is both necessary and functional. In the long run, the entire society benefits.

One Critique Melvin Tumin (1953) could not disagree more. Tumin argues that stratification does not facilitate but rather limits competition for socially important positions to those who can afford training, eliminating people who may be equally or better qualified for the job. Perhaps a few poor people make their way into satisfying and important careers, but the vast majority do not. Nearly 20 percent of physicians in this country and over 40 percent of all professionals followed in their fathers' footsteps. There is no way to calculate the number of potentially brilliant doctors, statesmen, teachers, and so on who were too poor to attend college. The lower class's talents, energy, and potential are lost in a stratified society. Davis and Moore seem to overlook the role inheritance plays in recruitment to important positions.

These authors do not consider the motivation of "the masses," other than to suggest that most members of society accept the stratification system and believe they get what they deserve. But as the riots of the sixties demonstrated so clearly, marked inequalities create distrust, hostility, and suspicion among different segments of the population—a condition that can hardly be called "functional." People who are struggling to survive in a society that boasts hundreds of millionaires have little motivation to abide by society's norms, to respect the dictates of culture. And how many of the millionaires are

actually performing socially useful work? Tumin drives his point home by criticizing the notion that doctors receive high incomes because their jobs are both important and hard to fill. Doctors are scarce, not because the long years of training discourage people from pursuing a career in medicine, but because medical schools turn down thousands of qualified applicants every year. Physicians, who operate one of the most powerful lobbies in the country—the American Medical Association—protect their incomes by limiting their numbers. Again, society as a whole loses.

Tumin concludes that even if some economic incentive is necessary to motivate people to fill certain essential roles, it is hard to see how extreme inequality such as exists in this country is either functional or inevitable. He suggests that the functionalist theory of stratification is little more than a rationalization of the status quo. Stratification exists because the rich and powerful use their considerable resources to hold onto what they have.

The Conflict Theory of Stratification

According to the second school of thought, then, the rich are rich because they hold a monopoly over society's scarce and valued assets and use their monopoly to dominate the poor. In effect, the poor subsidize the affluent, as Herbert Gans suggests (1973). Poverty creates a pool of laborers who are willing ("or at least unable to be unwilling") to perform menial, dirty jobs for low wages, creating surplus capital that can be used to support the arts and other lofty pursuits. The poor buy the things that other people do not want, for example, day-old bread and secondhand clothes. They remind other people that they are fortunate, and give those who

---

[7] Important jobs that are easy to fill do not require as high rewards. Teachers, for example, may be as important as doctors in technological societies, but more people have the talents, training, and desire to teach than to practice medicine. As a result, teachers receive more modest compensation than doctors.

help them the opportunity to feel righteous and altruistic (Gans, 1973, pp. 105–14). And without poor people the social scientists who study poverty, the journalists who write about it, the welfare and public health officials who run programs to alleviate it would all be out of work—not to mention thousands of numbers runners, heroin dealers, manufacturers of cheap wine, faith healers, pawnbrokers, and radicals. In short, the rich could not be rich (or "cultured" or charitable) if they did not exploit the poor so successfully.

The chief spokesman for this view was, of course, Karl Marx. Although Marx recognized the many dimensions of stratification, he believed that a person's social position ultimately depends on his or her relationship to the means of production (land, factories, and so on). These relationships constitute the objective class structure. Throughout history, the propertied class has exploited the non-propertied masses; the development of capitalism merely accentuated the gap between the powerful and the powerless, the rulers and the ruled. Marx argued that the capitalist class imposed poverty, ignorance, and powerlessness on the workers through a combination of coercion and deception, fostering a false class consciousness among the workers to obscure objective class structure. He saw the nation state as an instrument of oppression, religion as a method of diverting and controlling the masses, the family as a device for keeping wealth and education in the hands of the few. However, in crowding workers into factories and cities, capitalists had planted the seeds of their own destruction. Marx believed it was only a matter of time before the workers would realize that they were being exploited, that they outnumbered the owners, and that they "had only their chains to lose" in attempting to overthrow their oppressors. The result would be revolution and the creation of a classless society.

Marxist theory offers only one set of possible consequences of stratification: economic classes, capitalist dominance, working-class exploitation until the development of class consciousness, class conflict, and ultimately, a classless society. In the United States workers have not remained impoverished as in Marx's day, nor are economic interests always the determining factor in politics. Marx underestimated the power of other social dimensions both in creating special interests and in other cases for promoting social cohesion. The postcapitalist society he envisioned has yet to be achieved even in avowedly communist nations. Marx's contribution, then, has been less in social prediction than in pointing out the importance of social class as a crucial variable in the social sciences.

THE LAND OF OPPORTUNITY: AN EVALUATION

The belief that any person who gets an education, works hard, and takes advantage of opportunities can "get ahead" is a central theme in the American dream (and one reason why Marxism has never attracted American workers). But is this country truly a land of opportunity? Have we moved any closer to the ideal of equal opportunity in the last decade? Can we?

Social Mobility

The first step toward answering these questions is to determine the degree of social mobility in this country. By *social mobility* we mean the movement of people from one social position to another. The term *vertical mobility* refers to changes in status, upward or downward. A living example of upward mobility is Leonard Stern, whose father came to this country from Germany several decades ago. The elder Stern and a friend decided to import canaries when their textile business got into trouble. They were moderately successful but then the canary business, too, fell into debt. Meanwhile, Leonard had gone to college and acquired an M.B.A. at record speed. He took over the business in 1959. The younger Stern built the family's Hartz Mountain Company into a $150-million-a-year enterprise, and by the time he was thirty-five he had amassed over half a billion dollars (*Fortune*, September 1973, pp. 172–73). There are fewer stories in *Fortune* magazine of people slipping down the socioeconomic ladder (downward mobility), perhaps because readers do not like to be reminded that this is the opposite side of the coin. The term *horizontal mobility* refers to changes in position that do not appreciably alter a person's status, as when an oil company executive becomes the secretary of transportation.

The amount of mobility depends on how rigid and how unequal the strata are. In a classless society, where everyone is equal, there is no mobility. In a society with unequal strata, mobility may or may not be possible.

Open and Closed Systems In a truly *open class system* (if such existed; this is an ideal type), there are inequalities but few impediments to social mobility: positions are awarded on the basis of merit, and status is tied to individual achievement. Family origins, race, creed, color, sex, and other ascribed (or inherited) characteristics do not matter. Anyone with talent and ambition can advance. Class lines are blurred in open systems, and there is little class consciousness (in the sense of political solidarity among

people in similar economic situations). This is not to say that an open society is an equal society; there is a difference between equality of opportunity and equality of situation (when all members of a society have the same standard of living). Open systems provide the opportunity to succeed or fail.

A closed or *caste system* (also an ideal type) is the opposite: status is determined at birth; people are locked into their parents' social position, and their opportunities are limited accordingly. In caste systems, ascribed characteristics outweigh achievements. Caste lines are clearly defined, and legal and religious sanctions are applied to

South Africa's system of social apartheid represents a closed, or caste system of stratification. Blacks, who actually number a majority, are strictly separated from whites and must carry special police passes. (UPI)

IN THE NEWS
Life as an Untouchable

India—Legally, castes no longer exist in India. But a stratification system centuries old does not disappear by mere edict, and the effects of caste linger. At the bottom of the caste system are the harijan, or untouchables. Barriers to their mobility are still strong.

Laxmi Rani is terrified to leave her mud hut in the morning and climb on her bicycle to pedal to school four miles away.

"I will be beaten," the 16-year-old girl said, "I will be abused. I think the people are displeased. I think they do not want anybody of low caste to get an education."

Laxmi, the only untouchable in the mango-shaded village of 3,000 to attend high school—she is in the 12th grade—added: "I am missing my examinations now. What will happen to me?"

This girl has already been beaten by relatives of a high-caste, or Brahman, landlord. Her fears are that the intimidation will continue.

"In this case they were trying to intimidate Laxmi Rani because she is the smartest girl in the village—smarter than the landowner's daughter—and they didn't want a harijan who was smarter than a Brahman. By shaming her, by harassing her, they wanted the girl to stop going to school or leave the village" [said Chedi Lal Sathi, a Congress party official who works with untouchables].

Complaints to the police about the beating were of no avail. When her father tried to report the incident to local police, he, too, was threatened. Traveling to a nearby city, he complained to police there, but they simply asked the local police to investigate and the matter was dropped.

As in numerous cases involving untouchables—at least 200 die each year in caste murders and there are frequent reports that others are burned or maimed—the police were unsympathetic.

"In villages and towns a harijan who wants a higher education is a threat to the landlords and upper castes," said Mr. Sathi. . . . "If harijans learn their rights, if they become literate, then exploitation will have to stop. If they become educated, then who will do the menial jobs, the servants' work? Who will accept the conditions and wages that harijans tolerate?"

The actions of the upper castes are not simply a matter of vanity or the attempt to enforce custom. The stratification system is based on certain realities of economics and power, as well as prestige.

Source: Bernard Weinraub, "Low-Caste Indians Still Know Terror," *The New York Times* (October 1973): 3.

those who attempt to cross them. The South African apartheid system (which is euphemistically described as "separate development") exemplifies a rigid caste system. In South Africa, blacks, Asians, and whites live in separate neighborhoods, attend separate schools, obey separate laws, suffer different punishments. It was in South Africa that Ghandi began his crusade against caste systems, first attacking discrimination against overseas Indians, later his own people's attitudes toward untouchables as well as British colonialism. Although the caste system has been legally abolished in India, attitudes about caste members remain. (See the accompanying box.)

Most societies fall between the two extremes of open and closed stratification systems, including the United States. Forty or fifty years ago, the social structure of the South was more castelike than it is today. Jim Crow laws prevented blacks from crossing racial lines, and many preachers taught that black skin was an emblem of the Hamitic curse. Today the law explicitly forbids racial discrimination, and there are signs that the Civil Rights Act of 1964 has worked to some extent. Surveying the most recent data, Richard Freeman (1973) concludes that black women and young black college graduates are earning as much as their white counterparts today, whereas twenty years ago, they earned substantially less (perhaps 30–40 percent less) than whites with equivalent education. Despite the progress, blacks remain an "outgroup" in American society, if not an "outcaste." (We will discuss black and white relations in greater depth in chapter 9.)

Horatio Alger: Myth or Reality? As a whole, Americans today are better off than their parents and grandparents were. In 1950 the median family income was $5,601; by 1972 it had risen to over $11,000. More than 50 percent of American families had incomes of $11,000 or more in 1971, compared to 14 percent in 1950. This "success story" is partly an illusion: the dollar does not buy nearly as much today as it did in 1950 because of inflation. Still, Americans as a whole are somewhat better off. *Structural mobility*— changes in the number and kind of jobs and in the number of people available to fill them—accounts for some of the rise in incomes.

The labor market has grown dramatically since the turn of the century, with the total number of jobs more than doubling. Perhaps most important, the number of white-collar jobs has skyrocketed (and white-collar workers earn more than blue-collar, service, or farm workers). These changes can be traced to industrialization on the one hand and to massive migration from farms in this country and abroad to American cities on the other. In the short run mechanization eliminates jobs, but in the long run it opens up whole new fields of employment (mechanics to fix the machines, for example). These new jobs require specialized skills, and the demand for educated workers increases. Employers who need highly trained personnel cannot afford to hire brothers and cousins first. As a result, the job market becomes more and more open—that is, more people are hired for *what* they know, not *who* they know.

Technology also contributes to geographic mobility: it becomes easier for people to move to areas where jobs are plentiful. An influx of unskilled and semiskilled laborers, such as occurred here in the late nineteenth and early twentieth centuries, frees experienced workers to move up the occupational ladder. (A man who did all the work in his shop can hire assistants, use his own time to expand operations, don a white collar, and so on.) The fact that white-collar workers tend to have fewer children than workers in other categories further stimulates upward mobility. Quite simply, they do not "produce" enough children to refill their ranks, which gives other groups a chance to move up.[8] Thus, changes in the birth rate, improved technology, the demand for more and more education, and migration have acted to expand and change the American labor market.

Sociologists measure mobility by comparing fathers' jobs to sons' (intergenerational mobility). Using this measure, Peter M. Blau and Otis Dudley Duncan (1967) conclude that Americans as a whole are upwardly mobile,

---

[8] Changes in the death rate may have a similar effect. One reason why Soviet women have achieved more high-level positions than women elsewhere is that so many Soviet men were killed in World War II.

but that most advance only a step or two. (See figure 8:2 in the following section.) Inheritance plays an important role in determining occupational status. As noted earlier, about 40 percent of professionals in this country are the sons and daughters of professionals. This is nearly five times as many as would be expected in a perfectly open society. (If society were perfectly open or mobile, there would be no correlation between fathers' and sons' occupations, ascribed characteristics, and status. See Tumin, 1973, p. 127.)

Even though ours is not a perfectly open society, Americans have always believed the opportunities for advancement are greater here than in any other nation. Is this true? Seymour Lipset and Reinhard Bendix (1959) think not. Comparing the number of people who move across the manual-nonmanual line, they found relatively little difference in mobility rates for the United States, Europe, Scandinavia, and Japan—despite the fact that some cultures encourage mobility and others discourage it. The mobility rate in this country is about 34 percent, compared to 32 percent in Sweden; 31 percent in Great Britain; 29 percent in France; 25 percent in West Germany and Japan (Lenski, 1966, p. 41). Lipset and Bendix conclude that industrialization creates high social mobility rates in a culture, and that there is nothing special or distinctive about America.

S. M. Miller and others have questioned both Lipset and Bendix's data and their interpretation. Is the fact that sons of blue-collar workers become clerks really evidence of great opportunities? Miller argues that statistics on the number of working-class people who rise to the elite are more significant.[9] About 10 percent of working-class people

obtain elite status in this country, compared to 7 percent in Japan, less than 4 percent in France and Sweden, and 1.5 percent in West Germany (Fox and Miller, 1965; Blau and Duncan, 1967, pp. 432–35). By this measure, the United States is considerably more open than other industrialized nations.

Reducing Inequality

The available data on social mobility suggest that most Americans can look back on and forward to slow but more or less steady improvement in their standard of living and occupational status. This improvement leaves the nation's poor farther and farther behind. As indicated earlier, the gap between the median income and the poverty line has doubled in the last ten years (from $2,600 in 1960 to over $6,000 in 1971). Thus, the poor are relatively worse off. What can be done to reduce this inequality?

Education For years most Americans have believed that the principal way to break the cycle of poverty is to close the education gap. In the 1960s the government spent massive amounts on preschool programs and job training, the courts began to attack de facto school segregation, and a number of colleges instituted open enrollment of all high-school graduates. But as Charles Silberman (1971) suggests, these programs were overly optimistic. Americans tend to romanticize the role education plays in social mobility. Politicians, for example, are extremely fond of reminiscing about how they climbed out of poverty on their diplomas. But history suggests otherwise. Many immigrant groups "did not begin to view education as important, either in itself or as a means of mobility, until *after* they had become middle-class" (Silberman, 1971, p. 56).

---

[9] By *elite* Miller means "professional, technical and kindred workers," such as lawyers, engineers, and other highly trained occupations.

This is not to say that education has no effect on mobility. As figure 8:2 shows, 76 percent of those who continue their education beyond college and 70 percent of college graduates are upwardly mobile.[10] And college graduates earn about $6,000 more a year than high-school graduates. Income thus

[10] Interestingly, college dropouts are more likely to be downwardly mobile than people who completed only eight years of school—perhaps because most of the people who enroll in college come from relatively affluent backgrounds.

seems to be directly related to education. However, if we trace these data back one generation, we find that parents' education, occupation, and income have a decisive impact on the amount of education their children obtain. Thus, education may merely reflect family background and its impact on economic success.

Blau and Duncan (1967) devised the diagram shown in figure 8:3 to depict the complexities of occupational inheritance. The dia-

figure 8:2   Education and intergenerational mobility

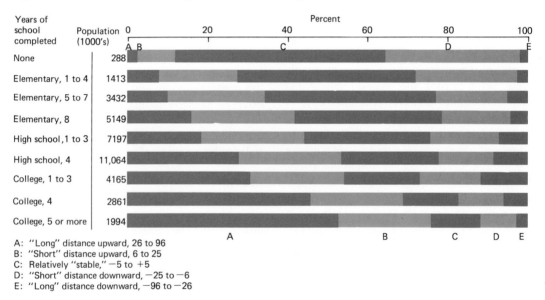

A: "Long" distance upward, 26 to 96
B: "Short" distance upward, 6 to 25
C: Relatively "stable," −5 to +5
D: "Short" distance downward, −25 to −6
E: "Long" distance downward, −96 to −26

SOURCE: Peter M. Blau and Otis Dudley Duncan, *American Occupational Structure* (New York: Wiley, 1967), p. 157, figure 4.5.

Although education helps an individual up the social ladder, most people remain relatively close to their father's status. The chances of a long jump (A) increase with education. Less than a fifth of those who complete elementary school rise far above their father's position, but a half of those who go beyond four years of college do so. The majority of Americans, however, either rise only a few steps (B), remain at the same level (C), or fall only a few steps (D). The lower the education, the greater the relative stability; people with no education are least likely to gain or lose status, presumably because they cannot easily rise without some education, but cannot fall very far because they are already at the bottom. Although rapid ascent and relative stability correlate with differences in education, large drops in status do not, indicating that factors other than education are involved in downward mobility.

gram is based on correlations between fathers' educations and occupations and sons' educations, first jobs, and current occupations. Each arrow represents a direct influence; the wider the arrow, the stronger the influence. The arrows with no source indicate other factors not accounted for by the model. As these arrows show, sons do not inherit their occupational status directly. Rather, their fathers' occupation influences their level of education, and this in turn influences their occupation. Thus, a young person whose parents work in low-income, low-

prestige jobs is the least likely to pursue the education that might enable him or her to escape poverty.

Christopher Jencks (1972) interprets these same data in another way. Looking at the large amount of unexplained variance, he writes: "Anyone who thinks that a man's family background, test scores,[11] and educational credentials are the only things that determine the kind of work he can do in

[11] I.Q. test scores, the prevalent though flawed test of intelligence.

figure 8:3 Education, background, and social mobility

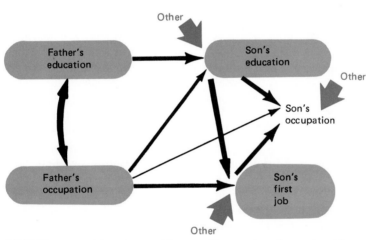

SOURCE: Adapted from Blau and Duncan, *The American Occupational Structure* (New York: Wiley, 1967), p. 170, fig. 5.1.

Both education and social background are used to explain a person's social status, but neither education nor occupational inheritance alone determines a person's occupation. This path diagram was devised by Blau and Duncan to show the influence of background and education on men. The heavier the line, the greater the influence. The son's education strongly affects his first and subsequent jobs. But his education is determined in part by his *father's* education and occupation. This link is stronger than the one between the father's occupation and the son's. Occupational inheritance, then, is indirect and works through the father's influence on his son's education. The chain of causation among the father's and son's educations and occupations is even more complex, but these chains are less important to note than the fact that many of the determinants lie *outside* these paths entirely. The heavy arrows marked "other" designate these unaccounted-for influences.

America (and what he will earn) is fooling himself. At most, these characteristics explain about half the variations in men's occupational statuses" (p. 192). Pointing to the fact that people working in the same occupation do not necessarily earn the same amount of money, Jencks suggests that policymakers and theorists have overlooked some of the crucial variables—namely, how much an individual cares about money and how much he is willing to sacrifice for it; such immeasurable talents as being able to persuade people to buy bigger cars than they want; and luck, the accidents that cause a person to pick one job instead of another (pp. 226–27). Jencks concludes:

Despite much popular rhetoric, there is little evidence that academic competence is critically important to adults in most walks of life. If you ask employers why they won't hire dropouts . . . they seldom complain that dropouts can't read. Instead, they complain that dropouts don't get to work on time, can't be counted on to do a careful job, don't get along with others in the plant or office, can't be trusted to keep their hands out of the till, and so on. (*The New York Times*, August 10, 1969)

In short, Jencks believes that it is unrealistic to expect the schools to work miracles. Isn't it possible that all the attention public officials have given to education—all the ads warning young people about the dire consequences of dropping out of school—have done little more than convince employers not to hire dropouts? Jencks calls attention to the Coleman Report, a government-sponsored study of school desegregation in the South, published in 1966. The authors found, to their surprise, that neither integration nor better schools (better facilities and higher expenditures per pupil) had a significant effect on student achievement. The evidence indicated that students' backgrounds—their family and neighborhoods, what they learned on the streets, from television, and from their

friends—had far more impact on their development than schooling. None of these researchers is suggesting we abandon the educational system. Integrating and improving schools are worthy goals, in and of themselves. But we cannot expect educational reform alone to close the poverty gap. (We will return to the subject of education in chapter 16.)

Income Redistribution   If Americans are serious about reducing inequality, Jencks argues, they will not focus on schools or even individual mobility but on reducing overall inequality through income redistribution. This could be done by closing tax loopholes, providing an income floor below which no one will fall, and keeping the rich from passing on their wealth. America already makes a modest effort with programs that redistribute some money to the poor. The government is spending over $86 billion a year in cash transfers, to rich and poor alike (Fried et al., 1973, p. 69), and this figure does not include various services the government provides to the poor. Where does this money go?

Social Security accounts for $54 billion. Payments are based on the amount of money a person earned before he or she retired (with the poor receiving proportionately more than more affluent people). In 1973 the average payment to an elderly couple was $3,500 a year. Recipients are allowed to earn up to $65 a month without losing benefits; thereafter, the government deducts $1 for every $2 they earn. Another $20 billion goes to the blind and disabled and to retired veterans, government employees, and railroad workers.

Cash transfers to people who are neither disabled nor old account for less than $10 billion a year. The government pays out about $5.2 billion a year in unemployment insurance. To be eligible, a person must have worked for a certain number of weeks before being laid off. He or she must register with an employment office and accept a suitable job. Benefits are paid for a maximum of twenty-six weeks (or thirty-nine weeks if the national unemployment rate is above 4.5 percent for three consecutive months). This income is tax exempt.

By far the most controversial program is Aid For Dependent Children, or welfare, which costs the government $4.3 billion a year. The typical welfare family is a mother with three children. (About 55 percent of welfare recipients are children, 19 percent mothers, only 0.9 percent "able-bodied fathers.") Contrary to popular myths, nearly half the families receiving welfare are white, and most stay on the welfare rolls for less than two years ("Welfare Myths vs. Facts," 1972, pp. 14–16).

Thus, cash transfers are administered through a hodgepodge of uncoordinated programs, developed piecemeal over the years. There is no provision for the working poor—that is, adults who work part or full time but do not earn enough to support their families. In effect the law discourages many from seeking employment. For example, in many states a single mother looses all benefits if she takes a job. By the time she deducts a babysitter from her salary, her earnings may well fall below the welfare payment. Until quite recently a mother could not obtain assistance for herself or her children if their father was living with them, whether or not he had a job—a policy that encouraged families to break up or fake separation. In addition to these problems, welfare payments vary tremendously from state to state. Monthly benefits per person range from $14.41 in Mississippi to $95.01 in Massachusetts. These startling differences encourage migration to such places as New York and California, where payments are relatively high. In 1970 the number of people on welfare in New York exceeded the entire population of Baltimore. Even so, there are perhaps as many as 4 million poor families who receive no assistance whatever.

Corruption compounds these problems. Before an investigation of New York's Human Resources Administration in 1968, a group of city workers who called themselves "the Durham mob" managed to send themselves over $1 million in phony paychecks. One former official attempted to buy a house in Los Angeles with a check intended for the poor; the money withheld from paychecks to Youth Corps workers for Social Security had disappeared (*The New York Times*, January 12, 1969).

Most damaging is the humiliation that accompanies welfare. In Detroit, for example, welfare workers have conducted "special investigations" at 3 A.M.; some threaten clients with loss of payments for "faulty housekeeping" (*Newsweek*, February 8, 1971, p. 103). In the words of Daniel P. Moynihan:

This is the heart of it. The issue of welfare involves a stigmatized class of persons. The recipient knows this. . . . It cannot be stated too often that the issue of welfare is not what it costs those who provide it, but what it costs those who receive it. (1973, p. 18)

What can be done to "clean up the welfare mess"? The central problem is how to provide poor families with an income that would guarantee a minimum standard of living without destroying the incentive to work. Under the current system families lose all financial assistance (and sometimes public housing, Medicaid, and the like as well) if the parents go to work. The negative income tax would change this. All families would be guaranteed a minimum amount, say $1,600 a year, by the federal government (plus whatever allotment states chose to provide). For every $2 earned, the guarantee would be reduced by $1. Thus, a family that earned $1,000 would lose $500 in federal payments, but its total income would be $2,100 ($1,600 − $500 + $1,000 = $2,100). The chief advantages of a negative tax are that it provides work incentive; it sets national standards; it would be less cumbersome and expensive to administer than existing programs; and it would eliminate the humiliations of welfare. President Nixon sent a variant of this proposal containing stiff provisions requiring registration for work or job training to Congress in 1970, but the Family Assistance Plan, as it was called, did not pass the Senate (conservatives balked at the idea of a guaranteed income; liberals thought the income guaranteed was too low). But even if the national allotment were raised, is money enough to break the cycle of poverty?

The Culture of Poverty

Is it possible that the poor themselves may thwart attempts to reduce inequality? that second- and third-generation poverty may make people unsuited for life in the working or middle class?

Oscar Lewis introduced the term *culture of poverty* in *Five Families: Mexican Case Studies in the Culture of Poverty* (1971). An anthropologist, Lewis spent much of his career living with and studying the very poor in Latin America and the United States. After a time he began to notice surprising similarities in the way people in different societies cope with chronic poverty on the one hand, and a culture that stresses individuality and upward mobility on the other.

Lewis found that the very poor generally do not participate in society's major institutions. Often they fear and mistrust government, avoid when possible the public and private agencies that are designed for them, and develop a cynical attitude toward the church. Nor do they create organizations of their own

(with the exception of youth gangs). The families Lewis studied knew little about the world outside. This low level of organization carries over into the family. Most believe in marriage. But for men who are never steadily employed and have almost nothing in the way of property to pass on to their children, marriage makes little sense. Many women, too, opt for living with a man without the legal ties that would bind them to a man who may prove unreliable. As a result, "illegitimacy" rates are high in all slums, and many families are mother-centered. "The absence of childhood as a specially prolonged and protected state in the life cycle" combined with an early initiation into sex make growing up in poverty different from growing up in more affluent and stable homes. Lewis notes particularly the present-time orientation, lack of impulse control, and fatalism that develop among very poor people. He concludes:

By the time slum children are six or seven years old, they usually have absorbed [these] basic values and attitudes of their subculture and are not psychologically geared to take full advantage of changing conditions or increased opportunities which may occur in their lifetime. (1970, p. 69)

If, as Lewis says, the poor have a life-style that prevents success, then simply providing more money or education cannot break the cycle of poverty. Are the failures of the American poverty programs due to the incapabilities of the poor themselves, as Edward Banfield suggests in *The Unheavenly City* (1970)?

Not all of those who recognize the differences in behavior between the poor and the rest of society accept that this difference is cultural and therefore quite difficult to change. To sociologists like Elliot Liebow (1967) the conditions of poverty are sufficient to explain the responses of the poor. No unique culture is involved. The poor are trying to achieve the same goals as the rest of society, but they cannot, and so they try to hide this failure from others and themselves.

Many similarities between the lower-class Negro father and son (or mother and daughter) do not result from "cultural transmission" but from the fact that the son goes out and independently experiences the same failures, in the same areas, and for much the same reasons as his father. What appears as a dynamic, self-sustaining cultural process is, in part at least, a relatively simple piece of social machinery which turns out, in rather mechanical fashion, independently produced look-alikes. (Liebow, 1967, p. 223)

To Liebow, as we noted in chapter 3, the basic problem is that a black man hasn't the skills to obtain a job that pays enough to support a family. From this comes the instability of family life, the contempt for work that the rest of society also scorns, the search for thrills, and other characteristics of the poor. The solution is not to change values but the conditions of neglect, exploitation, and outright racism. Changing the poor means changing the larger society. Lewis himself agrees with the necessity of taking the social structure into account:

There is nothing in the concept [of the culture of poverty] that puts the onus of poverty on the poor. Nor does the concept in any way play down the exploitation and neglect suffered by the poor. Indeed, the subculture of poverty is part of the larger culture of capitalism, whose social and economic system channels wealth into the hands of a relatively small group and thereby makes for the growth of sharp class distinctions. (p. 79)

summary

This chapter examines stratification: the way societies distribute desirable resources and rank their members. Property and wealth are only one dimension of stratification. As Weber pointed out, class (economic rank), party (degree of power), and status group (patterns of prestige) do not always overlap.

The first part of this chapter focuses on these three dimensions of stratification—property, power, and prestige. The distribution of income is unequal in this country: the poorest 20 percent of Americans earn only 4.5 percent of all income, the wealthiest 5 percent account for more than 17 percent. The graduated income tax reduces inequality somewhat, but in many respects the tax laws favor the rich. While the number of poor people has decreased considerably, in 1972 over 24 million Americans were still poor.

Power—the ability to mobilize collective energies, commitments, and efforts by means of authority (the legitimate prerogatives of office) and/or influence (informal, unofficial power)—is also distributed unequally in America. Mills argues that power is concentrated in the hands of a small, cohesive elite; Riesman contends that it is dispersed among many competing elites. But both agree that the majority of Americans are relatively powerless.

Prestige is a function of how people earn their money and how they spend it; who they are and what they know; and how successful, renowned, and respected they are. The best measure we have of prestige is the NORC occupational scale, which has shown that over the years (and even in different countries) people are quite consistent in ranking occupational prestige.

Although most Americans identify themselves as middle class, clearly people in this country are conscious of social or class differences and there is some consensus about who "counts." However, different social scientists emphasize different dimensions and therefore do not agree on the structure and number of social classes in this country. In the second part of the chapter we examine some of the consequences of stratification for the minority of people at the bottom of the social scale.

Functionalists argue that the unequal distribution of desirable resources provides incentive for people to perform necessary work. According to conflict theorists, the poor are poor because the rich exercise a monopoly over society's resources and systematically deny opportunities to the poor.

One reason workers in this country have never adopted the Marxian view of class struggle is the American myth of unlimited opportunity. How open or mobile a society is America? Americans today are generally better off than in previous generations. Much of this increase can be attributed to structural mobility—changes in the number and kind of jobs and the number of people available to fill them. But although most Americans move only a small step above their parents, this nation is considerably more open than other industrialized nations (at least by some measures).

Despite open mobility, America still has millions of poor people. What can be done to reduce inequality? For some time we have assumed education was the key, but Blau and Duncan show that the relationship between education and income is complex. Jencks argues that we cannot expect education to work miracles. Another approach is to redistribute income to the poor. In the United States such programs, developed piecemeal over the years, have proved ineffective and tend to discriminate against the working poor. New programs are being designed in the hope of changing this. Still, the question remains as to whether growing up poor makes people unsuited for life in the working or middle class. Opponents of the culture-of-poverty concept suggest that the behavior of the poor is born of exploitation and neglect, implying we cannot reduce poverty significantly without changing the entire system of stratification.

glossary

authority Formal power; the prerogatives that legitimately go with an office or position; official power.

caste system A rigidly stratified, socially immobile class system in which status is ascribed, not achieved; the opposite of an open system.

class People who occupy the same rung on the economic ladder (Weber).

culture of poverty Oscar Lewis's term for a lifestyle based on accommodation to poverty in an affluent society that stresses individuality and upward mobility.

horizontal mobility A change in position that does not alter socioeconomic status.

influence Informal power based on know-how and know-who.

open class system A class system in which status is acquired, not ascribed; the opposite of a caste system.

party People who share interests and seek to further them by gaining access to power (Weber).

power The ability to mobilize collective energies, commitments, and efforts.

power elite A concentrated group occupying the command posts of society and determining its direction; in such a society power is highly concentrated (Mills).

prestige The status of people according to occupation, ancestry, and social acceptability.

progressive tax A tax that takes a larger share of a rich person's income than a poor person's; the opposite of a regressive tax.

regressive tax A tax that takes a larger share of a poor person's income than a rich person's; the opposite of a progressive tax.

social mobility The movement of people up and down the stratification system.

status group People whose life-style or patterns of consumption give them a distinct identity (Weber).

stratification System for distributing desirable resources and ranking members of a society.

structural mobility Changes in the number and kind of jobs and in the number of people available to fill them. Individual mobility may be increased by such changes.

transfer payments Government allotments for which no goods or services are received in return.

vertical mobility Changes in a person's status, upward or downward.

references

E. Digby Baltzell, "Who's Who in America and the Social Register," in Bendix and Lipset, 1966.

Edward C. Banfield, *The Unheavenly City*, Boston: Little, Brown, 1970.

Reinhard Bendix and Seymour Martin Lipset, eds., *Class, Status and Power*, 2nd ed., New York: Free Press, 1966.

Stephen Birmingham, *The Right People*, Boston: Little, Brown, 1968.

Peter M. Blau and Otis Dudley Duncan, *The American Occupational Structure*, New York: Wiley, 1967.

David Caplovitz, *The Poor Pay More: Consumer Practices of Low-Income Families*, New York: Free Press, 1963.

Joseph S. Clark, "Starvation in the Affluent Society," in Ficker and Graves, 1971.

Robert Coles, "Psychiatrists and the Poor," *Atlantic Monthly* (July 1964): 102–106.

John Cratsley, "The Crime of the Courts," in Bruce Wasserstein and Mark J. Green, eds., *With Justice for Some*, Boston: Beacon, 1972.

Robert Dahl, *Modern Political Analysis*, Englewood Cliffs, N.J.: Prentice-Hall, 1963.

Kingsley Davis and Wilbert E. Moore, "Some Principles of Stratification," *American Sociological Review*, vol. 10 (1945): 242–49.

———, Replies to Tumin, *American Sociological Review*, vol. 18 (1953): 394–96.

G. William Domhoff and Hoyt B. Ballard, eds., *C. Wright Mills and The Power Elite*, Boston: Beacon, 1968.

Robert L. Eichhorn and Edward G. Ludwig, "Poverty and Health," in Meissner, 1966.

Victor B. Ficker and Herbert S. Graves, *Deprivation in America*, Beverly Hills, Calif.: Glencoe Press, 1971.

Thomas Fox and S. M. Miller, "Intra-country Variations: Occupational Stratification and Mobility," *Studies in Comparative International Development*, vol. 1 (1965): 3–10.

Richard Freeman, in Arthur M. Okun and George L. Perry, *Brookings Papers on Economic Activity*, vol. 1, Washington, D.C.: Brookings Institution, 1973.

Edward Fried et al., *Setting National Priorities* Washington, D.C.: Brookings Institution, 1973.

Herbert J. Gans, *More Equality*, New York: Pantheon, 1973.

H. H. Gerth and C. Wright Mills, eds., *From Max Weber: Essays in Sociology*, New York: Oxford University Press, 1946.

Joseph R. Gusfield and Michael Schwartz, "The Meaning of Occupational Prestige: Reconsideration of the NORC Scale," *American Sociological Review*, vol. 28 (1963): 265–71.

Paul K. Hatt and Cecil C. North, "Jobs and Occupations: A Popular Evaluation," *Opinion News* (September 1947): 1–13.

R. J. Herrnstein, *I.Q. in the Meritocracy*, Boston: Little, Brown, 1973.

Robert W. Hodge, Paul M. Siegel, and Peter H. Rossi, "Occupational Prestige in the United States: 1925–1963," in Bendix and Lipset, 1966.

Robert W. Hodge, Donald J. Trieman, and Peter H. Rossi, "A Comparative Study of Occupational Prestige," in Bendix and Lipset, 1966.

August B. Hollingshead and Frederick C. Redlich, *Social Class and Mental Illness: A Community Study*, New York: Wiley, 1958.

Irving Howe, ed., *The World of the Blue Collar Worker*, New York: Quadrangle, 1972.

Christopher Jencks et al., *Inequality: A Reassessment of the Effect of Family and Schooling in America*, New York: Basic Books, 1972.

Robert J. Lampman, *The Share of Top Wealthholders in National Wealth, 1922–1956*, Princeton, N.J.: Princeton University Press, 1962.

Gerhard Lenski, *Power and Privilege: A Theory of Social Stratification*, New York: McGraw-Hill, 1966.

Oscar Lewis, *Anthropological Essays*, New York: Random House, 1970.

———, *Five Families: Mexican Case Studies in the*

Culture of Poverty, New York: New American Library, 1971.

Elliot Liebow, *Tally's Corner*, Boston: Little, Brown, 1967.

Seymour Martin Lipset and Reinhard Bendix, *Social Mobility in Industrial Society*, Berkeley, Calif.: University of California Press, 1959.

Arthur M. Louis, "The Doors of Some Surprisingly Prosaic Businesses Open on a Street of Gold," *Fortune* (September 1973): 170ff.

Ferdinand Lundberg, *The Rich and the Super-Rich,* New York: Bantam, 1969.

Robert S. Lynd and Helen Merrell Lynd, *Middletown*, New York: Harcourt Brace Jovanovich, 1929.

———, *Middletown in Transition*, New York: Harcourt Brace Jovanovich, 1937.

Hanna H. Meissner, *Poverty in the Affluent Society*, New York: Harper & Row, 1966.

Herman D. Miller, *Rich Man, Poor Man*, 2nd ed., New York: Crowell Collier Macmillan, 1971.

C. Wright Mills, *The Power Elite*, New York: Oxford University Press, 1956.

Daniel P. Moynihan, *The Politics of a Guaranteed Income*, New York: Vintage, 1973.

Benjamin Okner, "Transfer Payments," in Kenneth E. Boulding and Martin Pfaff, eds., *Redistributing to the Rich and Poor: The Grants Economics of Income Distribution*, Belmont, Calif.: Wadsworth, 1972.

E. Pavenstedt, "A Comparison of the Child-Rearing Environment of Upper-Lower and Very Low-Lower Class Families," *American Journal of Orthopsychiatry*, vol. 35 (1965): 89–98.

Lee Rainwater, "The Lower Class: Health, Illness and Medical Institutions," in Irwin Deutscher and Elizabeth J. Thompson, *Among the People: Encounter with the Poor*, New York: Basic Books, 1968.

———, "A World of Trouble: The Pruitt-Igoe Housing Project," in Ficker and Graves, 1971.

Merrill S. Read, "Malnutrition and Learning," in Ficker and Graves, 1971.

David Riesman, *The Lonely Crowd*, New York: Doubleday, 1953.

Sanford Rose, "The Truth About Income Inequality in the U.S.," *Fortune* (December 1972): 90ff.

Eva Rosenfeld, "Social Stratification in a 'Classless' Society," *American Sociological Review*, vol. 16 (1951):766–74.

William Ryan, *Blaming the Victim*, New York: Vintage, 1971.

Richard Sennett and Jonathan Cobb, *The Hidden Injuries of Class*, New York: Knopf, 1972.

Charles E. Silberman, *Crisis in the Classroom*, New York: Vintage, 1971.

Philip M. Stern, "How 381 Super-rich Americans Managed Not to Pay a Cent in Taxes Last Year," in Jerome H. Skolnick and Elliott Currie, eds., *Crisis in American Institutions*, Boston: Little, Brown, 1970.

Melvin M. Tumin, "Some Principles of Stratification: A Critical Analysis," *American Sociological Review*, vol. 18 (1953):387–93.

———, *Patterns of Society*, Boston: Little, Brown, 1973.

W. Lloyd Warner and Paul S. Lunt, *The Social Life of a Modern Community*, New Haven: Yale, 1941.

———, Marchia Meeker, and Kenneth Eels, *Social Class in America*, Chicago: Science Research, 1949.

"Welfare Myths vs. Facts," Department of Health, Education, and Welfare (SRS) 71–127, in *Society*, vol. 9, no. 4 (February 1972): 14–16.

Dennis H. Wrong, "How Important Is Social Class?" in Howe, 1972.

Michael Young, *The Rise of the Meritocracy, 1970–2033*, New York: Random House, 1959.

for further study

Life-Styles. Social stratification affects the daily life of people living in different social classes. The following books and articles depict life-styles in different social classes in America, tracing the impact of stratification on how different people spend their days: E. Digby Baltzell, *Philadelphia Gentlemen: The Making of a National Upper Class* (New York: Free Press, 1958); Richard Sennett and Jonathan Cobb, *The Hidden Injuries of Class* (New York: Vintage, 1972); Michael Harrington, *The Other America* (Baltimore, Md.: Penguin, 1962); and Ferdinand Lundberg, *The Rich and the Super-rich* (New York: Bantam, 1969).

Mobility. A great American preoccupation is social mobility, particularly upward mobility. Two sociological classics which focus on several facets of mobility are *Middletown*, by Robert S. Lynd and Helen Merrell Lynd (New York: Harcourt Brace Jovanovich, 1937), and *Caste and Class in a Southern Town*, by

John Dollard (New York: Doubleday, 1957). Philip Slater in *The Pursuit of Loneliness* (Boston: Beacon, 1970) suggests that the pressures and strivings in American society destroy our lives and our social community.

Caste Systems. In this chapter we have focused on American patterns of stratification, but much has also been written about other forms and their consequences. One of the best books on caste is Bryce Ryan's *Caste in Modern Ceylon* (New Brunswick, N.J.: Rutgers University Press, 1953). Kingsley Davis has written an excellent book on the demography of caste, *The Population of India and Pakistan* (Princeton, N.J.: Princeton University Press, 1951). Melvin Tumin has studied social relations in Guatemala, and wrote about them in *Caste in a Peasant Society* (Princeton, N.J.: Princeton University Press, 1952).

Egalitarian Systems. An excellent book which explores how less-rigid and less-steep class differences would affect American society is *Socialism* by Michael Harrington (New York: Bantam, 1973). This might be compared to a description of social relations in a socialist country: *Industrial Democracy*, by Paul Blumberg (New York: Schocken, 1969), and Donald Lane, *The End of Inequality? Stratification Under State Socialism* (Baltimore, Md.: Penguin, 1971). The impact of egalitarian relations on socialization is closely studied by Melford E. Spiro in *Children of the Kibbutz* (New York: Schocken, 1965).

The term *minority* is something of a misnomer, for in many areas the so-called *minority group* actually outnumbers the majority. In South Africa, for example, nonwhites constitute 80 percent of the population, yet they are treated as a minority by whites who have the power of a majority. They have assigned an inferior status to nonwhites, denying them access to social power. Louis Wirth defined a *minority* as "a group of people who, because of their physical or cultural characteristics, are singled out from the others in the society in which they live for differential and unequal treatment, and who therefore regard themselves as objects of collective discrimination. The existence of a minority in a society implies the existence of a corresponding dominant group with higher social status and greater privileges. Minority status carries with it the exclusion from full participation in the life of the society" (1945, p. 347). In many societies, including our own, this definition applies to children (who have virtually no legal rights), the aged, and women

RACIAL
AND ETHNIC
MINORITIES

(who number 51 percent of the American population, but occupy few positions of power). Most societies also contain religious, ethnic, and racial minorities. All of these groups are "singled out . . . for differential and unequal treatment."

In this chapter we focus on racial and ethnic minorities in America. We begin with brief portraits of America's minorities, which describe each group's cultural orientation and relations to society as a whole. In the second part of the chapter we explore the roots of prejudice and discrimination. We discuss the meaning of race and whether there is any basis for the belief that blacks have "natural rhythm," or that Jews have a special talent for finance. The third part of the chapter describes different patterns of discrimination and the way people respond to them. Finally, we evaluate the current state of race relations, giving special attention to institutionalized obstacles to racial and ethnic equality in the United States.

ETHNIC DIVERSITY IN AMERICA

Sunday is still the most important business day on Delancey Street on New York City's largely Jewish Lower East Side (Saturday being the Jewish Sabbath). Next door lies Chinatown, with its own language and customs, temples and grocery stores. Little Italy is just across Canal Street, its streets lined with social clubs and funeral parlors and, on saints' days, with booths selling sausage and pastry from old-country recipes (and perhaps buttons reading "Kiss me, I'm Italian"). These are but three of the many ethnic groups that make up America.

An *ethnic group* is "any group that is defined or set off by race, religion, or national origin, or some combination of these categories." This is not to say that race, religion, and national origin are equivalent. They are not. Race refers to inherited physical characteristics, which have no connection to religion or nationality, both of which are cultural institutions. But these classifications are similar "in that all of them serve to create, through historical circumstances, a sense of peoplehood" (Gordon, 1964, p. 28). In other words, an ethnic group is a group of people whose ancestry and heritage make a difference—to them, and to the society in which they live. Customs, language, religion, family names, social ties, food, dress, and appearance all play a part in defining ethnic groups.

For some Americans ethnic identity is only marginally important—something to march and sing and drink about on special holidays. For others, such as the Amish, maintaining ethnic integrity is a constant struggle against school officials and other intruders. The Amish, of course, choose to isolate themselves from mainstream America. In contrast, blacks, Indians, and others have historically had little choice about their isolation. And then there are the so-called "white ethnics," who seem to have gotten lost in the recent flood of interest in Afro-American, Indian, and Spanish-American cultures.

How do these very different groups relate to one another? Why have they not disappeared into the "melting pot"? In part because established Americans have usually treated newcomers (and Indians, Mexican-Americans, and blacks) as foreigners and avoided them; in part because the groups themselves have an emotional investment in their ethnic communities and identities and have resisted enculturation. Portraits of the largest ethnic communities in this country follow.[1]

Black Americans

The self-transformation of "Negroes" and "colored people" into blacks is one of the most dramatic chapters in recent American history. In the space of twenty years, blacks have successfully challenged the traditional "lily white" version of American history, which portrayed blacks as docile and willing slaves and Indians as blood-thirsty savages, and said nothing about the way Irish, Italian,

---

[1] We use the term *community* advisedly. Not all black- or Jewish- or Indian-Americans identify with their ethnic communities or consider their origins significant.

and Jewish immigrants literally fought for acceptance and success in this country. It is blacks, more than any other group, who are responsible for a reawakening in recent years of ethnic consciousness and pride.

The 25 million Americans who trace their ancestry back through 300 years of poverty, exploitation, and violence to Africa are this country's largest racial minority. As late as World War II, 80 percent of black Americans lived in the South, where they functioned in large part as farm workers. Today, 50 percent live in the North and 52 percent in metropolitan areas. These city dwellers are young. (The average age in the black community is twenty-one to twenty-two years, compared with twenty-eight to twenty-nine years in the population as a whole.) And they are proud.

To understand black pride, white Americans will have to learn black history, its joys as well as its sorrows. The African roots of this history are obscure. (Slave-owners made a concerted effort to separate members of the same tribe and to wipe out African customs.) As a result, little is known about the specific origins of black Americans. We do know that the first African immigrants settled in Virginia as indentured servants in 1619, and that by the end of the century nearly all blacks and their descendants had been relegated to perpetual servitude under the law. Slavery was a barbaric institution, but it was not always insurmountable.[2]

My mother was the smartest black woman in Eden. She was as quick as a flash of lightning, and whatever she did could not be done better. She could do anything. She cooked, washed, ironed, spun, nursed and labored in the field. . . .

My mother certainly had her faults as a slave. . . . She was too high spirited and independent. I tell you, she was a captain.

The one doctrine of my mother's teaching which was branded upon my senses was that I should never let anyone abuse me. "I'll kill you, gal, if you don't stand up for yourself," she would say. "Fight, and if you can't fight, kick; and if you can't kick, bite." Ma was generally willing to work, but if she didn't like doing something, no one could make her do it. At least, the Jennings [the masters] couldn't make, or didn't make her. (in Lerner, 1972, pp. 34–35)

Slavery was abolished in 1865, but white terrorism and discrimination were not. Jim Crow laws, which barred blacks from public facilities, and when these failed, lynchings, kept blacks "in their place." For example, in July 1919 a mob took seventy-two-year-old Berry Washington from jail and lynched him from a tree near his house. Why? He had defended himself against two white men who were threatening a widow and her daughters (Lerner, 1972, pp. 188–89). During Jim Crow, blacks worked in fields, on river boats and trains, as domestics, as "boys." They went to school (sometimes only when it rained) and built schools; they formed their own baseball leagues and vaudeville circuit (whose blues singers began to attract white attention in the twenties). The black church was perhaps the most important institution in the black community throughout this time; it was both a tranquilizer (promising freedom in the next world) and a stimulant (creating solidarity, reinforcing indignation).

As World War I approached, blacks began leaving the South in increasing numbers, some as soldiers in all-black regiments, others in search of work at factories in Chicago, Detroit, and other big cities. Harlem, Roxbury, Chicago's South Side became cities within cities. Many of their residents were as poor as they had been in the South. But in the North, blacks fought back when they were attacked.

---

[2] In *Time on the Cross* (Boston: Little, Brown, 1974), Robert Fogel and Stanley Engerman explode the traditional image of slaves as docile and lazy. On the contrary, slaves were industrious and devoted to their families. In short, they made significant achievements despite their adversity.

The urban riots in the early part of this century were interracial.

However, the decisive battle against segregation began in the South, with boycotts and nonviolent demonstrations. Blacks marched, picketed, and sat-in at "white only" restaurants.

At noon, students from a nearby white high school started pouring into Woolworth's. When they first saw us they were sort of surprised. They didn't know how to react. . . . We just kept our eyes straight forward and did not look at the crowd except for occasional glances to see what was going on. . . .

The mob started smearing us with ketchup, mustard, sugar, pies, and everything on the counter. [We] were joined by John Salter, but the moment he sat down he was hit on the jaw with what appeared to be brass knuckles. Blood gushed from his face and someone threw salt into the open wound. . . .

About ninety policemen were standing outside the store; they had been watching the whole thing through the windows, but had not come in to stop the mob or do anything. . . . After the sit-in, all I could think of was how sick Mississippi whites were. (Anne Moody, in Lerner, 1972, pp. 428–31)

The black migration north continued, and the ghettos grew, largely untouched by civil rights victories in the courts and in Congress. A new generation of leaders, street wise and uncompromising, began to attract attention. Black children started asking: Who is Frederick Douglass? Nat Turner? Sojourner Truth? Touissant L'Overture? The Black Panthers, among others, responded with classes in black history and self-defense and with free breakfast programs. Given the long-standing belief that blacks were "culturally deprived," that the ways of the black community were nothing more than adaptations to discrimination, the fact that blacks stopped asking white America for answers in the late 1960s was nothing short of revolutionary.

Although too brief to do justice to the full history of blacks in America, this account gives some idea of the roots of black culture, which today is a mixture of southern and city tunes, of revolutionary rhetoric and Biblical intonations, of combativeness and cool.

Jews

As the children of immigrants my brothers were aware of the fact that they represented the "undesirables," the "foreigners," as others had been "undesirables" in previous decades. They realized, too, that the only way to rise above undesirability was not merely to become desirable, but to become indispensable. This would require equal amounts of education and sacrifice. They filled every hour not devoted to study with part-time jobs as truant officers, book salesmen, teachers of English to foreigners—wearing out their eyes, their pants and their books, drinking black coffee to stay awake, postponing marriage, sharing clothes, colds, money and dreams. (Sam Levenson, in Freedman and Banks, 1972, pp. 194–97)

Like Sam Levenson, thousands of contemporary American Jews grew up on the streets of New York, under the watchful eyes of parents who believed that, by becoming educated, their children would "get ahead." Today, although only 23 percent of all Americans are college educated, 42 percent of Jews hold college degrees (Gallup, 1972, no. 70).

The first Jews came to America from Brazil in 1654, but it was not until the 1840s that Jews began arriving in the thousands, fleeing pogroms (periodic massacres of Jews) in Europe. Today there are more Jews in America—about 6 million—than in any country in the world (the Soviet Union is second, Israel a close third). Nearly half live in or around New York City. The Jewish community in this country is characterized by high levels of education, above-average income, a tradition of family-owned businesses, and a group-identity stemming from 2,000 years of political insecurity.

It is this sense of peoplehood that sets Jews apart. Jews are not a race; physically, they are indistinguishable from other peoples of European and/or Semitic descent. And their religious beliefs and practices are as varied as those of the different Christian denominations. They come from Germany, Russia, and Poland; from France, England, Spain, Syria, and Morocco. Many are as Americanized as any immigrant group, and many are not religious. What sustains the Jewish community, here and elsewhere, is a strong sense of peoplehood, a deep emotional identification with Jewish history and with one another.

Urbanites and entrepreneurs through much of their past, Jews adapted to America with relative ease. Not that they did not encounter discrimination—time and again they have been accused of disloyalty (because of their association with Israel), of participation in international conspiracies, of unscrupulous business practices. Traditionally, many corporations, major law firms, banks, and private clubs did not admit Jews (some still do not), and until World War II many universities maintained strict quota systems. Jews prospered nonetheless—in part by using old-world skills to start businesses (the garment industry, for example), in part by taking advantage of public education, and in part by continuing to some extent to see themselves as the "chosen people," whatever their circumstances—a doctrine Jews share with Black Muslims. Of course, most Jews are not wealthy, and many are poor, but as a group, Jews have prospered and are highly represented in business and professions: 30 percent of Jews earn $15,000 and over, compared with 14 percent of the total population, and 40 percent are in busi-ness and professions, compared with 22 percent nationally (Gallup, 1972, no. 70).

Chicanos

The third largest minority in this country are the 5 million Catholic, Spanish-speaking Americans of Mexican descent, or Chicanos. The Spanish settled in what is now the American Southwest before New England was colonized, but not until 1848 did they and their land become part of the United States. Soon after, English-speaking settlers were edging them out: if all else failed, they were "sent back" to Mexico. Except in New Mexico, where Hispanos were able to hold their ground, most withdrew to rural towns and mining camps that were soon forgotten. When they went into Anglo areas to work as migrant laborers, they were housed in segregated camps; when they moved to big cities, they lived apart. The English-speakers called them "greasers" and "spics"; they called the English-speakers "anglos," "gringos," "gabachos." Many did not want to send their children to schools where they were slapped for speaking Spanish and often renamed (from Jesus to Jesse, for example).

Hostilities between Chicanos and Anglos reached a peak in Los Angeles in 1943, when police and restless sailors stormed the *barrio* (or neighborhood), beating and then arresting some 600 of their victims in what came to be called the "zoot suit riots." In the fifties, however, an influx of Cold War related industries brought jobs to the Southwest, and by 1960 nearly half the Chicanos owned their own homes. (Still the median income for Chicanos remained about two-thirds that for the nation as a whole.) At about the same time, Chicanos began to exercise their voting power, supporting John Kennedy and later George McGovern. César Chavez, a man appropriately compared to Martin Luther King, Jr., succeeded in organizing grape pickers and other agricultural workers for a struggle that continues today. And a new pride and militancy began to grow among the young: *La Raza Unida* was born. (More on this in chapter 14.)

Puerto Ricans

The United States acquired Puerto Rico in 1898, and in 1917 all Puerto Ricans were declared American citizens. Mainland companies began to open branches on the island, but were met with violent, nationalist resistance. A compromise was reached, granting Puerto Rico aid in modernization and economic development as well as commonwealth status. The majority of Puerto Ricans did not benefit from economic expansion, however, and when the airlines introduced low fares after World War II, increasing numbers left the island to seek their fortune in New York. Today there are about 1.7 million Puerto Ricans on the United States mainland, most in and around New York City.

In city ghettos Puerto Ricans often suffer double discrimination—for their language and for their color (which actually ranges from black to white, but Puerto Ricans are usually labeled nonwhite). What makes the Puerto Rican situation unique is that immigration is a two-way street: the island is close enough for immigrants to return home, and most do, temporarily or permanently. As a result, there is less incentive to learn English and American ways. Moreover, the Puerto Rican community here is divided—between those who practice traditions (the authoritarian father; strict surveillance of daughters) and those who think modern; between those who seek Americanization and those who do not (Simpson and Yinger, 1972, pp. 478–80). A nine-year-old girl told

Oscar Lewis: "I have been here for a long time already so I am forgetting Spanish. English is what comes to my head. In school, I want to say '*ven aca*' and what comes out is 'Come on.' *Mami* says that if I learn to talk English she'll beat me" (1965, pp. 256–57).

American Indians

Indians are the poorest of the poor in America. Their past and present are stories of lies and abuse. The wars against the American Indians reached a peak toward the middle of the nineteenth century, when the eastern United States was becoming crowded, and the transcontinental railroad made travel easier. During this period gold was discovered in the sacred Black Hills of Dakota and in other Indian lands, and adventurers could still make a profit from buffalo hides. Over 500,000 Indians died before the century was over. The 300,000 who survived war, disease, hunger, and bounties ($25 to $100 per scalp in many places) were forced onto inhospitable reservations that were administered by the notoriously corrupt Bureau of Indian Affairs (BIA).

Today, about two-thirds of the 790,000 American Indians live on reservations, under the trusteeship of the BIA. Many of the reservations are more like Third World countries than like part of the richest nation in the world. Only one out of five adults on the 25,000-square-mile Navajo reservation, for example, has a high-school diploma; the median educational level is 5.3 years (compared to 12.1 years nationally). The Navajo nation today numbers 137,000 and over half the adults are either unemployed or work only part time. The per capita income is $1,000 (compared to $4,000 nationally). Outsiders own 80 percent of the general stores on the reservation. Housing, built by outsiders, is substandard. Many Navajo rent one- or two-

The impoverished living conditions of these Indians are typical of many Navajos. Houses on reservations often lack both running water and electricity. (Paolo Koch/Rapho Guillumette)

tion. Indian leaders are advisers at best; the BIA still holds a veto power over all plans. (In the words of anthropologist David Aberle, "The Navajo Government is treated in a style I recognize from having served on the student council of my high school.") Nor does the government recognize the Navajo language and culture. Classes at BIA schools are taught in English only, and Navajo history is an elective or extracurricular activity—if it is taught at all. Forty-nine of sixty schools are boarding schools, designed earlier in this century to forcibly separate Indian children from their family and customs—"for their own good." Alcoholism is a serious problem on reservations, even in grade school, and the suicide rate among Indians is ten times the national average (*The New York Times*, October 29, 1973, p. 69C).

In the early 1970s the rise of ethnic consciousness among other minorities, such as blacks and Chicanos, was beginning to affect Indians as well. In 1973, the newly organized American Indian Movement (AIM) returned to the scene of the 1890 massacre at Wounded Knee and occupied reservation headquarters. This was not simply theater. Once again the government had reneged on extravagant promises; once again it had subverted Indian efforts to achieve self-determination and reform the BIA (Collier, 1973).

Chinese- and Japanese-Americans

The Chinese began immigrating to the West Coast in the middle of the eighteenth century. Laboring on the railroad, washing, and cooking (women were scarce in the Old West), they earned a reputation as hard workers. However, when the railroad was finished and unemployment began to rise, Occidental settlers turned on the Chinese. The Chinese Exclusion Act of 1882 halted further immigra-

room houses, 80 percent of which have no running water or plumbing and 60 percent of which have no electricity.

Although the government no longer pursues a policy of termination (breaking tribal properties into individual holdings and thereby "terminating" the tribe), it maintains a patronizing attitude toward tribal organization, and in most places the Chinese were denied schooling, jobs, and housing. They withdrew to ethnic enclaves in coastal cities, keeping largely to themselves until anti-Chinese feelings subsided. The border was reopened to the Chinese in the early fifties, and today there are about 435,000 people of Chinese ancestry in the country.

The Japanese came somewhat later, spreading out on farms all along the West Coast. But anti-Oriental sentiments ran high, and in 1924 Japanese immigration was halted. Then, in 1942, 110,000 Japanese, including 70,000 who were American citizens, were rounded up and placed in "relocation centers," even though most had become American citizens and supported the Allies. During their internment, Japanese families lost an average of $10,000 each (Simpson and Yinger, 1972, p. 121). Despite this, the Japanese have prospered in America. Like the Jews, they emphasized the value of education and specialized in middle-level professions such as engineering, accounting, and management. They also practiced the middle-class values of hard work, thrift, and self-control.[3] Although the Japanese have kept

---

[3] When a few Japanese teen-agers were caught shoplifting in Sacramento, nearly 500 Japanese parents went to a meeting with a psychiatrist and parole officer to discuss the problem, although police had told them it was nothing to worry about (Peterson, in Kurokawa, 1970).

their language and cuisine alive, the traditional Japanese family has largely disappeared (arranged marriages are a thing of the past, for example), and the 591,000 people of Japanese ancestry in this country today are thoroughly Americanized.

White Ethnics

White ethnics have been called by many names—"the silent majority" (by Richard Nixon), "the little man" (by George Wallace), "the man in the middle" (by sociologist David Riesman). These are the policemen, truck drivers, lathe operators, and office workers who earn between $5,000 and $10,000 a year and own their own homes in areas such as Boston's Charlestown or Cleveland's West Side (Binzen, 1970, p. 5). They are the children and grandchildren of eastern and southern Europeans, who themselves had been free of serfdom for barely a hundred years.

Although they are very fiercely loyal to America, white ethnics have never quite felt at home in this Protestant, Anglo-Saxon dominated country. They do not take to the culture of "quantity, homogeneity, replaceability and mobility" that characterizes America today (Novak, 1971). "This alienation is reflected in distrust of most politicians, in contempt for

---

table 9:1 THE FIVE LARGEST ETHNIC GROUPS IN THE UNITED STATES

ORIGIN	POPULATION (IN MILLIONS)	PERCENT OF TOTAL POPULATION
English, Scottish, or Welsh	29.5	14.4
German	25.5	12.5
Irish	16.4	8.0
Spanish	9.2	4.5
Italian	8.8	4.3

SOURCE: *Current Population Reports*, series P–20, no. 249, 1973, pp. 1 and 19.

white rich and black poor, in a bristling defensiveness and a yearning for the recent past when life was simpler and loyalties less complex, when children were reared by the Bible and the beltstrap, when the schools stuck to the three R's, and when patriotism meant 'My country, right or wrong'" (Binzen, 1970, p. 11). They believe in paying their own way, in respect for authority, in taking care of their own, and in living with their own. They resent the "breaks" they believe blacks and other nonwhite minorities are getting. It isn't so much that they are racists as that they are loyalists, from cultures where anyone not from your village was a foreigner (Binzen, 1970, p. 9).

RACE, PREJUDICE, AND DISCRIMINATION

The presence of varied ethnic and racial groups in the same society creates problems as well as opportunities. Diverse styles, languages, and traditions do enrich a culture, but they may also accentuate in-group/out-group tensions. In America race has always served as a dividing line between "us" and "them."

What Is Race?

Biologically a *race* is a population that through generations of inbreeding has developed several distinctive physical characteristics that are transmitted genetically. In principle it should be relatively simple to divide the human species into distinct categories and assign each individual a racial identity. In reality it is not.

Suppose we begin with the three groups most people identify as races—the white or Caucasian race, the yellow or Mongoloid race, and the black or Negroid race. Few of us have any difficulty telling Africans from Orientals or Europeans. But where do we put the peoples of southern India who have black skin but straight hair and "Caucasian" features? Do we classify the Bushmen of southern Africa, who have yellowish skin and epicanthic folds (which make the eyes appear slanted), Mongoloid?

In an effort to define racial categories, physical anthropologists have long studied physical differences among groups of people, including skin color, hair texture, facial features, head size and shape, body build, and blood types. They have found that some characteristics are adaptive. Dark skin, for example, with its high concentration of the pigment melanin, protects Africans and other equatorial peoples from harmful ultraviolet sun rays. The light skin of people in northern regions is also adaptive. Ultraviolet rays facilitate the body's production of Vitamin D, necessary for bone growth. Too much Vitamin D, however, may be harmful. It seems, then, that dark skin protects people in southern latitudes from producing too much Vitamin D, while light skin maximizes its synthesis (Loomis, in Ember and Ember, 1973, pp. 179–80).

But studies of physical differences have not led to clear and distinct definitions of racial categories. William Boyd, for example, attempted to classify people according to blood types. He found, among other things, that the cDe gene is very common among people who live in sub-Saharan Africa. However, the gene is also found in Europeans, Asians, even Navajo Indians. Moreover, blood types do not correlate with outward appearance. The Papuans of New Guinea look very much like Africans; they could easily disappear into the streets of Nairobi or New York's Harlem. But the "negroid gene," cDe, is exceedingly rare in New Guinea. In short, it is impossible to say where one race stops and another begins.

As Theodosius Dobzhansky suggests, the number of races you find depends on the criteria you use:

Boyd has recognized five, and Coon, Garn, and Birdsell nine or thirty or thirty-two races. Does it follow that some of these classifications are wrong? No, all may be right; it should always be kept in mind that while race differences are objectively ascertainable facts, the number of races we choose to recognize is a matter of convenience. (1962, p. 266)

Dobzhansky himself identifies thirty-four races, including such "emerging races" as North American blacks and Neo-Hawaiians, but he cautions that races are not clear and distinct like breeds of dogs (1973, chapter 2). The human species is the product of over 2 million years and 100,000 generations of adaptation, migration, sexual selection, and cultural conditioning. There is as much variation *within* races as there is among them.

Nevertheless, people perceive and react to racial differences, and this is why sociologists study them—not because skin color, hair texture, or other physical characteristics are intrinsically significant. A sociological definition of *race* is a group of people whom others believe to be genetically distinct, and treat accordingly.

Racial Myths

Numerous myths about racial and ethnic differences circulate in American society—for example, the notion that blacks have natural rhythm, the belief that Jews have a talent for finance. And while there is no biological basis for these stereotypes, there are social explanations. As slaves, blacks were forced to perform the most menial jobs; they were not allowed to form organizations of any kind. But slaves *were* allowed to make music. When slavery ended blacks were still in demand as entertainers. After all, no respectable white family would allow their children to enter the theater. The field was relatively open. Blacks cultivated the talents they had opportunities to use. Similarly, Jews became traders and moneylenders because for centuries they were not allowed to own land anywhere in the world. Like black Americans, they took advantage of the one field open to them, a field respectable Christians shunned.

Still, many people, noting certain differences in achievement by race, conclude that the biology of race is responsible. As a result, there is a long list of writing affirming or denying racial predisposition to cultural achievements, athletic ability, and intelligence. What is the truth about such claims?

Race and I.Q. In 1969 Arthur Jensen, a respected educational psychologist at the University of California at Berkeley, published an article on race, heredity, and intelligence in the *Harvard Educational Review*. The average score for black Americans on I.Q. tests, he reported, is ten to fifteen points lower than the average of whites. Reviewing the literature on this subject, Jensen concluded, "It [is] a not unreasonable hypothesis that genetic factors are strongly implicated in the average Negro-white intelligence difference"(1969).

Not surprisingly, Jensen was immediately labeled a white supremacist. Students at Berkeley invaded his classes and prevented him from teaching; spokesmen for the American Psychological Association issued a press release that characterized his findings as "unwarranted"; the *Harvard Educational Review* hastily collected a series of rebuttals, which were attached to reprints of the article. In Jensen's own words, "Almost overnight I became a *cause célèbre*, at least on college campuses. I had spoken what [columnist] Joseph Alsop called the 'unspeakable.' To many Americans, I had thought the unthinkable" (1973, p. 80). For some years now, any implication that one race is innately superior to another has been socially and academically taboo. Yet the suspicion that this is true lingers on. What are the facts?

Few researchers dispute the fact that there is a ten- to fifteen-point difference in average I.Q. for whites and blacks. The controversey centers rather on the *interpretation* of this finding, and few scientists agree with Jensen. If blacks are innately "slow," how do we account for the fact that about 25 percent have higher than average I.Q.'s (Simpson and Yinger, 1972, p. 56); that blacks living in the North score higher on I.Q. tests than either blacks *or whites* living in the South (Klineberg, 1944)? Numerous studies indicate that schooling, teacher expectations, and the test situation itself influence I.Q. scores. For example, black youngsters do better on intelligence tests when the examiner is black (which is not usually the case) and when they are told that they are being tested for coordination rather than intelligence, coordination being something that blacks feel more confident about (Katz, 1964).

Melvin Tumin (1973, pp. 164–67) attacks Jensen's conclusions on four grounds. First, he argues that racial comparisons would be meaningful only if we were able to assign every individual a clear racial identity, but we can't do this. Approximately 70 percent of black Americans have some white ancestry (and 20 percent of whites have some black ancestry; Hunt and Walker, 1974, p. 12). How can we assume that "black genes" are creating an I.Q. difference? Second, the idea that I.Q. differences reflect *biological* differences is based on the assumption that I.Q. tests measure innate intelligence. This is not the case. The I.Q. test measures performance of certain cultural skills, and while it has proven to be a relatively accurate predictor of school achievement, there is no conclusive evidence that it measures a person's inborn abilities. Third, research indicates that environment

THE POLITICS OF INTELLIGENCE TESTING

Eugenics—the "science" of improving the quality of the human race through selective breeding—first became popular in this country at the turn of the century. Interestingly, the three men who were responsible for translating and importing the first intelligence tests—Lewis Terman, Robert Yerkes, and Henry Goddard—were all active in the eugenics movement. Terman was gravely concerned about the genetic consequences of charity. He wrote, "[O]nly recently have we begun to recognize what a menace [feeble-mindedness] is to the social, economic and moral welfare of the state.... [O]rganized charities ... often contribute to the survival of individuals who would not otherwise be able to live and reproduce.... If we would preserve our state for a class of people worthy to possess it, we must prevent, as far as possible, the propagation of mental degenerates ... the increasing spawn of degeneracy." As chairman of the Committee on Inheritance of Mental Traits of the Eugenics Research Association, Yerkes was responsible for "discovering" that Poles were only slightly more intelligent than blacks. Goddard, who set up a testing center for the United States Public Health Service on Ellis Island, labeled 83 percent of Jewish immigrants, 80 percent of Hungarians, 79 percent of Italians, and 87 percent of Russians as feeble-minded. The overtly racist immigration act of 1924, which established national quotas, was based on these findings. Thus from the very beginning, intelligence tests have been used to rationalize discrimination.

SOURCE: Leon J. Kamin, "Heredity, Intelligence, Politics and Psychology," Princeton University, unpublished paper, 1973.

has a substantial effect on intelligence, perhaps more than heredity. Jensen downplays the differences between black and white schools, neighborhoods, jobs, and experiences. He assumes that blacks and whites from similar socioeconomic backgrounds are alike in all respects but heredity.

Tumin argues that the level of prejudice and discrimination in this country makes it impossible to equate blacks and whites, even if their incomes and educations were alike. If we were able to find people whose experiences were identical, only then could we make valid racial comparisons, concluding that whatever differences we found were innate. But we cannot. Tumin concludes that there is no substantial evidence that the difference in I.Q. averages has anything whatever to do with genetic endowment.

Race and Culture Another racial myth, that whites are culturally superior to other peoples, is based on an ignorance of history. The great civilizations of China, Africa, and South America—the Shang dynasty, the Sonniki Kingdom of Ghana, the Mayan civilization—predate the birth of Western civilization by centuries. Nor is there any evidence that one race is more or less temperamental, healthy, or moral than any other (see Simpson and Yinger, 1972, pp. 56–59).

For example, the relatively high rate of broken homes among black Americans can, in part, be traced to welfare laws. Until the late 1960s, a family could receive assistance for children only if the father were absent. In short, if there are differences between blacks and whites, Jews and Gentiles, they exist largely because these groups have not enjoyed and do not enjoy the same opportunities. The significant differences are social, not biological.

Prejudice and Discrimination

The word *prejudice* comes from the Latin *prejudicum*, a pretrial that determined a defendant's social status in ancient Rome. The results decided how the court would treat the accused. In contemporary usage, prejudice still means a prejudgment. It is an irrational and categorical like or dislike of a group of people because of characteristics associated with their race, religion, ethnic group, sexual orientation, or perhaps occupation. When a person is so convinced that all members of a group are immoral, violent, and backward (or moral, brilliant, and creative), that he or she cannot see them as individuals and ignores evidence that refutes his or her other convictions, he or she is prejudiced. Prejudice justifies the fear and hostility people feel toward out-groups and provides a rationale for maintaining intergroup boundaries. Often, it becomes a self-fulfilling prophecy. If you start by saying that women are not qualified to be anything but secretaries, and then use this as an excuse to exclude them from executive training programs, you prove the original assumption correct by creating and enforcing unpreparedness among women (Simpson and Yinger, 1972, p. 156).

Prejudice is an attitude; *discrimination*, an act. Ordinarily we use this word to describe the act of disqualifying or mistreating people on grounds rationally irrelevant to the situation (Antonovsky, 1960). But granting people privileges on the basis of imagined characteristics that attach to race, religion, or sex is also discrimination. Discrimination is not necessarily an expression of prejudice. For example, a black store owner may decide not to hire Jews, not because he himself is prejudiced against Jews, but because he believes his customers are. A white woman who has many black friends may refrain from dating blacks because she thinks, rightly or wrongly, that this would alienate all of her friends, black and white. However, discrimination tends to create and support prejudice by keeping people apart and limiting opportunities to disprove rumors and stereotypes.

Why are people prejudiced, and why are some people more prejudiced than others? Prejudice exists on three levels. It is a *psychological* phenomenon that seems to fulfill certain needs in people. It is also a *cultural* phenomenon, reflecting the traditions and history of a people. And it is part of the system of *stratification*, reinforcing the way power is distributed in a society.

The Psychology of Prejudice Suppose a man works six or seven days a week in a factory, trying to support his family in the way he thinks they expect, but never seems able to make ends meet and is perennially in debt. If he analyzes his situation rationally, he would probably blame the upper classes generally and his employers specifically for failing to pay him an adequate wage. But these people have the power to cut off his income; to oppose them openly would be self-destructive. He might also blame himself for his financial problems, but this too makes him uncomfortable. Instead, he looks to the Mexican immigrants who have begun working in his factory. He doesn't really know them, but he suspects they are willing to work for low wages and that many other Mexicans are eager to take his job. By a process of twisted logic, he blames the Mexicans for his poverty. Soon he is exchanging rumors about "them" with his cronies and supporting efforts to close the border. Hating Mexicans makes the man and his friends feel a little better. When they forcibly eject a group of Mexicans from the local tavern, they feel at last they've accomplished something. "That'll show 'em."

This psychological portrait of prejudice is based on frustration-aggression theory. According to this view, people are goal-directed creatures who become angry and hostile when their desires are frustrated. If they do not know who or what is blocking their ambi-

tions or believe the obstacle is too threatening and powerful to attack, they displace their hostility to a substitute target or scapegoat who is more accessible and, conveniently, too weak to retaliate.

Once a scapegoat is found people justify their irrational feelings and behavior by "discovering" evidence that the out-group is indeed wicked and inferior. In this way people can maintain some feeling that they are reasonable and kind. The catch is that in verbally or physically attacking Mexicans, Jews, or any other group, prejudiced people avoid confronting the true enemy. Their situation does not change, and frustration and hostility grow.

The stereotypes that develop about minority groups serve a similar psychological function. In the old South, for example, many whites believed blacks were violent by nature, and that black men were "over-sexed" and hence a chronic threat to the purity of white women. In reality, it was the whites who were most violent, and white men who were sexually exploiting black women. But it is easier, psychologically, to condemn unacceptable feelings and behavior in others than to admit to them oneself. That is called *projection:* seeing qualities in others that you do not like in yourself, and condemning them for it. Projection explains the curious combination of guilt and license, aversion and fascination that often characterizes minority/majority relations.

In the aftermath of World War II, T. W. Adorno and co-workers (1950) undertook a study of prejudice in an effort to understand why the German people had condoned brutal atrocities against Jews. They also hoped to establish some way of identifying "potentially fascistic" individuals. Adorno concluded that racism is an expression of a particular psychological make-up that he called the *authoritarian personality.* This is a second theory of the psychology of prejudice. The authoritarian personality is motivated by deep feelings of insecurity. According to Adorno prejudiced people are also rigidly conventional, moralistic (with a tendency to see people as good *or* bad), enamored of pseudoscientific theories (for example, about racial superiority), unrealistic in their goals and expectations (and therefore continually frustrated), and preoccupied with power and status (they are prejudiced *toward* the upper classes). They cannot tolerate ambiguity or weakness. Although Adorno's study has been criticized methodologically, it has proved to be a rich source of new ideas for research into the psychology of prejudice. Is prejudice related to age? education? intelligence? (And if so, why?) Do people who score high in ethnocentrism on psychological tests act in a prejudiced way? These areas are being researched today (Simpson and Yinger, 1972, pp. 77–93).

Prejudice and Culture In many societies prejudice is part of the culture, a social habit handed down from generation to generation. Children learn to value their whiteness or blackness and to avoid or defer to members of different races and ethnic groups, much as they learn their gender identity and sex role. Learning prejudice (including sex prejudice) is part of socialization in some societies; it is not an isolated phenomenon.

As we saw in chapter 5, Allport found many youngsters were confused about whom they were supposed to hate and shun. But despite this initial confusion, children do learn what groups of people to like or dislike and why. They learn from parents, siblings, friends, and of course television, which until recently "taught" young Americans that black people are like Amos and Andy, and Indians are hostile, ignorant savages. Eugene Horowitz (1947) found that children develop antiblack

feelings as early as kindergarten: white four- and five-year-olds showed a distinct preference for white playmates. A Southerner describes his socialization for racial and religious prejudice as follows:

I grew up just 19 miles from Appomattox. The teaching I received both in school and from my parents was hard core South, with no chance of insight into the thinking and ways of other peoples. I was taught to look down upon Negroes, tolerate Jews (because we had to do business with them) and ignore Catholics.

We celebrated Jefferson Davis's birthday, but ignored Lincoln's; the name Robert E. Lee was spoken with reverence and Appomattox was a shrine. The Golden Rule only applied to others who were either Methodist or Baptist, white and without a foreign-sounding name. (Letter to the Editor, *The New York Times*, May 16, 1963)

Cultural stereotypes can and do change. Forty years ago a survey of Princeton students found that most thought blacks were lazy, superstitious, and ignorant—the classic Steppin' Fetchit. Table 9:2 on page 240 shows that attitudes have changed at Princeton (although, interestingly, the percentage who think blacks are musical has increased). Tragically, studies conducted in the 1940s and 1950s suggested that black children had the same derogatory image of blacks as white children had (Clark and Clark, 1947). But this has changed. A poll conducted in 1969 revealed that 74 percent of blacks believe "black is beautiful" (*Newsweek*, June 30, 1969). (We will discuss the attitudes of blacks and whites toward one another in depth later in the chapter.)

Still, Americans are highly conscious of racial and ethnic identities, and stereotypes persist, even if they are couched in humor. One wonders whether the television show *All in the Family* is popular because members of minority groups nearly always come out on top in the show, or because Archie Bunker

table 9:2 **CHARACTERISTICS PRINCETON STUDENTS ASSIGNED TO BLACKS: STEREOTYPES ARE FADING**

	1933 (PERCENT)	1951 (PERCENT)	1967 (PERCENT)
Superstitious	84	41	13
Lazy	75	31	26
Happy-go-lucky	38	17	27
Ignorant	38	24	11
Musical	26	33	47

SOURCE: Marvin Karlins, Thomas Coffman, and Gary Walters, "On the Fading of Social Stereotypes: Studies in Three Generations of College Students," *Journal of Personality and Social Psychology* (September 1969): 4–5.

has made bigotry respectable (Rose, 1974, p. 139.)[4] In fact two researchers who studied viewers of *All in the Family* concluded that "nonprejudiced viewers and minority group viewers may perceive and enjoy [the program] as satire, whereas prejudiced viewers may perceive and enjoy the show as 'telling it like it is.' . . . By making Archie a 'lovable bigot' the program encourages bigots to excuse and rationalize their own prejudices" (Vidmar and Rokeach, 1974).

Prejudice and Stratification Flare-ups of bigotry often can be traced to economic conditions that make it profitable for one group to exclude and stigmatize another. Oliver Cox may have exaggerated when he wrote, "Race prejudice in the United States is . . . a calculated and determined effort of a white ruling class to keep some people or peoples of color and their resources exploitable" (1948, p. 475). But there is some truth in what he says.

In the words of one unusually candid nineteenth-century Southerner, "[H]aving learned to make cotton and sugar [we] find slavery useful and profitable, and think it a most excellent institution. We of the South advocate slavery, no doubt, from just as selfish motives as induce the Yankees and English to oppose it" (in Simpson and Yinger, 1972, p. 114). Antiblack feelings climbed with the price of cotton.

Similarly, in the early 1870s, when the Gold Boom faded and the Central Pacific Railroad began to bring thousands of settlers to California to compete for a declining number of jobs, the once-welcome Chinese (who had helped build the railroad) became villains almost overnight. By 1880 it was nearly as safe politically to oppose Orientals as it was to oppose sin (Simpson and Yinger, 1972, p. 118). Thus economic competition transformed a trickle of Oriental immigrants into "the yellow hordes" by igniting prejudices that laid dormant in the culture.

Prejudice justifies social rank—both low and high, as, for example, when some people argue that members of minorities are poor because they don't want to work or because

---

[4] The same question could be asked about black comedian Redd Foxx's show, *Sanford and Son*, which closely resembled *All in the Family*. (The character Foxx played had no use for Puerto Ricans, for example.)

they aren't capable of learning skilled trades. In conclusion, prejudice stems from a combination of psychological and social predispositions. It is most likely to occur in a culture that supports this kind of thinking and among people who have to defend or justify their social status.

PATTERNS OF ETHNIC RELATIONS

Relationships between racial and ethnic groups in a heterogeneous society range from full integration to the absolute intolerance that motivates extermination. Both of these extremes are rare, however, and intergroup relations are usually more complex than the everyday definitions of such words as *integration* and *segregation* imply. Nevertheless, it is possible to identify certain basic patterns.

Patterns of Acceptance

In a fully integrated society, race, religion, and national origins would not influence a person's access to society's rewards. Being born a Lopez or an O'Reilly or a Goldberg would be neither an asset nor a liability; it simply wouldn't matter. The society would be structured to protect individual rights and to ignore ethnic identity. Perhaps the best way to illustrate this is to call attention to the "armed truce" between people of British and French descent in Canada. In the United States this distinction is insignificant: people of British and French descent are fully integrated.

There are essentially two routes to integration: amalgamation and assimilation. *Amalgamation* occurs when members of different ethnic and racial groups mix indiscriminately: a new hybrid culture emerges (cultural amalgamation), and perhaps a new "race" as well.[5] Ethnic differences disappear. This is what Israel Zangwill had in mind when he described America as a melting pot: "There she lies, the great melting pot—listen! Can't you hear the roaring and bubbling? Ah, what a stirring and seething—Celt and Latin, Slav and Teuton, Greek and Syrian, Black and Yellow—Jew and Gentile" (1909, pp. 198–99).

Assimilation means that immigrants give up their old ways and adopt the language, customs, religion, and dress of the country to which they've moved. For example, the American public school system was specifically designed to teach the waves of immigrants that began coming here in the nineteenth century the English language and English customs, to enforce what Stewart and Mildred Cole (1954, pp. 135–40) call "Anglo-conformity." (Later, public education was extended to blacks, Indians, and Chicanos—for the same purpose.)

Amalgamation and assimilation are most likely to occur if (1) the immigrants' appearance and customs resemble those of the dominant group, (2) they arrive in small numbers, (3) they are too far from their homeland to return for visits, and (4) they possess skills that the dominant group admire and need (Warner and Srole, 1945; Silvers, 1965). Yet the fact that an immigrant group is able to fill some economic need (as the Jews did in Europe and the overseas Indians did in East Africa) does not guarantee their acceptance (Hunt and Walker, 1974, p. 20). To the contrary. If members of a group fill the need for

---

[5] Perhaps the only place in the United States where biological amalgamation has occurred is Hawaii, where Polynesians, Chinese, Japanese, Europeans, and Americans have intermarried more or less freely.

menial and domestic workers, they may be stigmatized; if they are conspicuously successful, they may inspire envy.

Is America the melting pot of Zangwill's dream? No, according to Milton Gordon (1964). Gordon makes the important distinction between behavioral assimilation (immigrants adopting the language and behavioral patterns of the host culture) and structural assimilation (immigrants gaining admission to the host's government, businesses, schools, churches, clubs, and ultimately its families). While most ethnic groups have undergone behavioral assimilation and structural integration into secondary relationships in America, relatively little integration has taken place on the level of primary relationships (see chapter 7). In part this is because Americans of northern European descent integrated only with themselves, in part because later immigrants resisted complete assimilation to Anglo-Saxon, Protestant culture.[6]

When people migrate to a strange country, they usually huddle together for comfort and support, re-creating as many of their old-country institutions as they can. Their children may succumb to the lure of democracy and equality, assuming that if they act American they will be fully accepted as Americans. However, when they see that the doors to private clubs are not open to them and the sons and daughters of established Americans not available to them, they return "to the homelier but dependable comfort" of their ethnic communities. Gordon notes that integration has taken place within religions (German, Russian, and Sephardic Jews have

intermarried, for example), but for the most part not between religions. Of course, the invitation to participate in the American mainstream has never been extended to blacks, Indians, Chicanos, and other racial and quasi-racial groups.

An alternative to integration is *cultural pluralism*, wherein different ethnic groups maintain their cultural identities and distinct ways, but no one group enjoys special privileges or suffers discrimination. Cultural pluralism is based on the belief that ethnic diversity strengthens a society. Horace Kallen (1965, p. 220) compared a pluralistic society to a symphony: each instrument (each ethnic group) contributes distinct themes and melodies, harmonies and dissonances. In Switzerland, for example, Protestants and Catholics of German, French, and Italian descent coexist peacefully and equally. Each group has its own language and customs. This diversity is viable because all consider themselves Swiss as well as German or French, because the religious differences cross-cut national differences (preventing the formation of solid political blocs), and because members of all groups can easily visit their ancestral country.

An analogy might be drawn between the ethnic mix in Switzerland and the sometimes uneasy pluralism of America's large cities, with their Little Italies, Chinatowns, Germantowns, and other ethnic enclaves. Nowhere is this better illustrated than in New York City. But Americans as a whole have never found the heterogeneity of New York very attractive. "The only New York image that has permanently impressed itself on the national mind is that of Wall Street—a street on which nobody lives. Paris may be France, London may be England, but New York, we continue to reassure ourselves, is *not* America" (Glazer and Moynihan, 1970, p. 2). The only area in which we do tolerate and indeed protect pluralism in this country is religion.

---

[6] Indeed, many immigrants never intended to become Americans. The Germans wanted to build a "new Germany" in Texas; the Irish petitioned Congress (unsuccessfully) for a territory of their own; and Scandinavians established colonies in the Northwest, beyond the reach of Americanization (Glazer, 1954).

Patterns of Rejection

In a *segregated* society, contacts between different groups are restricted by law and/or custom. Segregation is based on the premise that ethnic and racial groups are inherently unequal, and that the differences between them are permanent (hence the myths of racial inferiority). An individual's ethnic identity determines his or her social status; members of minorities are denied full participation in social institutions and relegated to activities that benefit the majority (Hunt and Walker, 1974, pp. 6–7). Clearly, segregation is an imposed arrangement, designed and enforced by the majority.

Segregation is a matter of law in South Africa, where blacks (the native Bantu) and to a lesser extent coloreds (people of mixed ancestry and overseas Asians) are not allowed to live in white neighborhoods, use white facilities, or participate in white government. Blacks are required to carry passbooks at all times, and may be arrested and jailed merely for being in a white district without authorization. In many ways, South Africa is unique. Unlike British, French, and Portuguese colonials, 3 million *Afrikaners* have no home to return to should the 15 million blacks demand independence.

The history of racial segregation in the United States goes back hundreds of years. It began when the new Americans started to distinguish between white indentured servants, who were released at the end of their contracts, and black servants, who were not. Gradually slavery was written into law, and black people were reduced to the legal status of two-thirds of a person. The Emancipation Proclamation abolished slavery, but not servitude. Except for the small number who prospered during Reconstruction, blacks became sharecroppers, working white-owned land for very low wages. When Union troops

Until the Civil Rights legislation of the 1960s made segregation illegal, public facilities were rigidly segregated for southern blacks and whites.

withdrew from the South, states, counties, and towns began to pass the legislative programs that came to be known as Jim Crow. Blacks were disenfranchised (through property qualifications, literacy tests, and "grandfather clauses")[7]; public facilities such as restaurants and trains were segregated; interracial marriages outlawed; lynchings ignored.

By World War I, large numbers of blacks were moving north, urged on by industrialists who desperately needed workers. Riots broke out in New York, Chicago, and elsewhere, as blacks competed with European immigrants for space. But racism was still considered a southern problem. Congressional attempts to knock down Jim Crow failed. Then, in 1954,

---

[7] When property qualifications failed to disenfranchise all blacks and as many whites as blacks failed the literacy tests, many southern legislatures decreed that a person could not vote unless his or her grandfather had—and blacks' grandparents hadn't.

the Supreme Court overturned the separate-but-equal doctrine in its decision on *Brown vs. the Board of Education of Topeka*, citing evidence gathered by social scientists that segregated schools affected the "hearts and minds [of black children] in a way unlikely ever to be undone." Soon after, the young Reverend Martin Luther King, Jr., was organizing a boycott in Montgomery, Alabama.

The Civil Rights Movement succeeded dramatically in some respects. Today, the United States is desegregated, in the sense that *legal* barriers to interracial contacts have been removed. As Martin Luther King, Jr., once remarked, "The law may not make a man love me, but it can restrain him from lynching me, and I think that's pretty important" (in Rose, 1974, p. 103). But this is not yet a racially integrated society; there is no "easy and fluid mixture of peoples of diverse racial, religious, and nationality backgrounds in social cliques, families (i.e., intermarriage), private organizations and intimate friendships" (Gordon, 1964, p. 246). Moreover, the white exodus to the suburbs has made most of America's big cities minority enclaves. Indeed *de facto*[8] segregation may be increasing.

Expulsion is another form of minority rejection. In 1972, for example, Uganda's General Amin deported 27,000 Indians, many of whom were second- and third-generation Ugandans, with only a few months' warning, appropriating their homes, businesses, and savings (see Kramer, 1974). This country, too, has expelled minorities. In the 1830s the Cherokee Indians were forced to march from their homelands in Georgia to an arid reservation in Oklahoma. As many as 4,000 died on what came to be known as the Trail of Tears. As we mentioned earlier, during World War II the American government forcibly sent over 100,000 Japanese to "relocation centers" for the duration of the war. Both the Soviet Union and Germany deported millions of minority citizens during that war.

The severest response to minority groups is *extermination*. The Nazis murdered 6 million Jews between 1933 and 1945—as well as countless gypsies, communists, and other ethnic and political minorities. A century before, Americans slaughtered the Indians (a story that has been "whitewashed" for years). American Indians fought the European invaders, but to little avail. About two-thirds of the Indian population was wiped out. Some died in battle, but just as many died from the white man's diseases, from which they had no immunity, and from starvation, after white hunters killed off the buffalo.

Minority Responses

How do minorities respond to discrimination and abuse? How do people cope with a society that defines them as undesirable? *Acceptance* of the majority culture is one response. Some members of a minority will try to "pass"—change their name, their appearance (with hair straighteners or skin bleaches), and their way of life, thus shedding their minority identity. Passing means rejecting one's family and origins, and may leave a person stranded between two worlds, neither of which accepts him or her entirely. And there is always the possibility of "discovery."

For sheer survival, psychological as well as physical, others play the role the majority assigns to them, obeying the etiquette of racism, deferring in most interracial contexts. The classic example of this response to segregation is Uncle Tom, who smiled and shuffled and "Yes Mam'd" his way through Harriet Beecher Stowe's novel. Simpson and

---

[8] Segregation in fact, as opposed to segregation by law (*de jure* segregation).

Yinger tell a revealing story about Uncle Toms:

A Negro drives through a red light in a Mississippi town. The sheriff yells, "Where you think you going?" The Negro thinks fast and answers, "Well, boss, when I see that green light come on an' all them white folks' cars goin' through, I says to myself, 'That's the white folks' light!' So I don' move. Then when that ol' red light comes on, I jus' steps on the gas. I says, 'That mus' be the niggers' light!'" The sheriff replies, "You're a good boy, Sam, but the next time you kin go on the white folks' light." (1972, p. 224)

It's obvious who had the last laugh here. Flattery, deference, and feigned stupidity can be effective forms of passive aggression—as when a slave pretended he was so simple-minded he couldn't understand a job he didn't want to do.

Psychological theory suggests, however, that if people are abused day after day, their anger will build until they find some way to vent it. Sociologists have speculated that the relatively high crime rate in black ghettos is evidence of displaced aggression (see Simpson and Yinger, 1972, pp. 224–25). Hitting back at whites is too dangerous, so blacks take out their hostility on one another—or so the argument goes. It is difficult to prove or disprove this theory, but we should point out that when racial tension runs high, the majority may interpret any effort by minorities to climb the economic and social ladder as aggression. For example, thirty or forty years ago a black person who obtained advanced education or bought fine clothes and cars was labeled "uppity," a trouble-maker. More recently, Black Panthers organized patrols to follow police around black communities with the aim of preventing brutality. They were policing the police. But was this aggression or self-defense?

The alternative to acceptance (real or feigned) and aggression (direct or indirect) is *avoidance*. For example, when anti-Chinese sentiments began to increase in the American West, Chinese families withdrew to cities on the West and East coasts, shutting themselves off from the hostile society around them (Yuan, 1963). Self-segregation not only provides insulation from aggression and slurs; it also enables minorities to maintain close family ties, to assist one another, to practice their own way of life and keep their culture alive. Separatist movements such as the Black Muslim movement have always played an important role in the black community in this country. The Muslims have no plan to go to war with white society; rather, they want as little to do with white society as possible.

The Psychological Consequences of Racism
What does living in a society that preaches black inferiority do to a black person, inside? In *Dark Ghetto* (1965), psychologist Kenneth B. Clark argues that chronic social injustices "corrode and damage the human personality, thereby robbing it of its effectiveness, of its creativity, if not its actual humanity. . . . Human beings who are forced to live under ghetto conditions and whose daily experience tells them that almost nowhere in society are they respected and granted the ordinary dignity and courtesy accorded to others, will, as a matter of course, begin to doubt their self worth" (pp. 63–64). Clark notes that black children often describe black dolls as ugly, dirty, or bad. Similarly, the preoccupation with hair straighteners and skin bleaches among the black bourgeosie in the fifties and early sixties suggests that they accepted the white dislike of black physical traits.

Recent investigations, however, show that blacks have as much self-esteem as anyone else—perhaps more. For example, Morris Rosenberg and Roberta G. Simmons (1971) interviewed black and white children in pre-

table 9:3 CHILDREN'S OPINIONS OF "MOST PEOPLE'S" RANKING OF BLACKS, BY RACE AND AGE

OF FOUR RACIAL-RELIGIOUS GROUPS, "MOST PEOPLE" RANK BLACKS:	8–11 YEARS BLACKS WHITES (PERCENT)		12–14 YEARS BLACKS WHITES (PERCENT)		15+ YEARS BLACKS WHITES (PERCENT)	
First	63	1	32	1	15	—
Second	17	6	26	4	14	1
Third	9	24	20	24	26	17
Last	11	69	23	71	44	81
Difference in percent ranking blacks "Last"	58		48		37	

SOURCE: Morris Rosenberg and Roberta G. Simmons, *Black and White Self-Esteem: The Urban School Child,* Washington, D.C.: American Sociological Association, 1971, p. 34.

table 9:4 WHITE CHILDREN'S OPINIONS OF "MOST PEOPLE'S" RANKING OF RELIGIOUS GROUPS, BY RELIGIOUS AFFILIATION

OF FOUR RELIGIOUS GROUPS, "MOST PEOPLE" RANK PROTESTANTS:	PROTESTANT RESPONDENTS (PERCENT)	NON-PROTESTANT RESPONDENTS (PERCENT)
First	55	32
Second	38	56
Third	6	10
Last	1	2

OF FOUR RELIGIOUS GROUPS, "MOST PEOPLE" RANK CATHOLICS:	CATHOLIC RESPONDENTS (PERCENT)	NON-CATHOLIC RESPONDENTS (PERCENT)
First	80	45
Second	19	48
Third	1	5
Last	—	2

OF FOUR RELIGIOUS GROUPS, "MOST PEOPLE" RANK JEWS:	JEWISH RESPONDENTS (PERCENT)	NON-JEWISH RESPONDENTS (PERCENT)
First	5	2
Second	21	8
Third	72	65
Last	2	25

SOURCE: Morris Rosenberg and Roberta G. Simmons, *Black and White Self-Esteem: The Urban School Child,* Washington, D.C.: American Sociological Association, 1971, p. 34.

dominantly black and racially mixed schools in Baltimore. Many of the children were not conscious of the low status assigned to blacks in society at large, living as they did in nearly all-black worlds. Others more or less accepted the white stereotype of blacks as slow and lazy, but did not feel this image applied to them personally. And some attributed the negative evaluation of blacks to white irrationality. As for their feelings about themselves, Rosenberg and Simmons found black children were *less* likely to consider

---

SELF-ESTEEM AND SOCIAL RANKING

Many sociologists have long taken for granted the idea that children internalize their society's values and standards in the process of growing up. From this it logically follows that black children who see a negative image of their group in the social looking-glass must experience some ambivalence about themselves, perhaps even a degree of "ethnic self-hatred." (The Supreme Court school desegregation decision of 1954 was based on this premise.) Rosenberg and Simmons (1971) found, however, that most black children rank blacks *high* on the social ladder, just as white children, except for Jews, rank their own religion high (see tables 9:3 and 9:4). The authors conclude that children do accept society's evaluations of most groups (their evaluations of other groups mirror those of adults), but pull their *own* group out of order to protect feelings of group pride and self-esteem. By the time they are fifteen or over, however, black youngsters have more social experience, and recognize that most Americans do not rank blacks very high (see table 9:3).

SOURCE: Morris Rosenberg and Roberta G. Simmons, *Black and White Self-Esteem: The Urban School Child,* Washington, D.C.: American Sociological Association, 1971.

---

poor grades or test scores evidence of personal inadequacy than were white youngsters. Thus prejudice may insulate a person from self-criticism. When a black child or adult fails, he or she can blame white society.

Most studies of the consequences of discrimination have focused on the victims rather than on the victimizers. We do not know how to calculate the psychological and social costs of treating a whole group of people as less than human. What research there is in this area suggests that members of the dominant group in a segregated society suffer from insecurity and fear, particularly if that society respects rationality and democratic values. In South Africa, whites fear the possibility of a black revolution. Whites in small towns in the American South often own more than one firearm, and New Yorkers avoid the streets at night, closing themselves in with three and four locks. "Thus a pattern of discrimination is supported only at the cost of much irrationality, moral confusion, arrogance, and fear" (Simpson and Yinger, 1972, p. 242).

PROTEST AND PROGRESS

On August 28, 1963, about 200,000 black and white Americans, gathered jubilantly at the steps of the Lincoln Memorial in Washington, listened raptly as Martin Luther King, Jr., told the nation, "I have a dream. . . ."

The euphoria of that sunny afternoon was short lived.[9] Just a month later a bomb exploded in the basement of a black church in Birmingham, Alabama, killing four small

---

[9] This section is based, in part, on a series of four articles commemorating the tenth anniversary of the March on Washington that appeared in *The New York Times,* beginning August 26, 1973.

girls. Congress began to move. The Public Accommodations Act was passed in 1964, the Voting Rights Act a year later. The legal obstacles to integration had been destroyed, but relations between blacks and whites became increasingly abrasive over the years. The Student Nonviolent Coordinating Committee (SNCC) expelled its white members, and its leaders began talking of Black Power. Roy Innis, a charismatic nationalist, became the director of the Congress on Racial Equality (CORE). Confused by the new militancy in the black community, startled to find Dr. King marching in Chicago, white liberals began to pull back. It was one thing to fight segregation in the South; another to discover discrimination in your own back yard.

Meanwhile the black exodus from the South continued: over a million blacks moved north between 1960 and 1970. But the Civil Rights Movement had barely touched the North. The church-born rhetoric of freedom, dignity, and equality seemed strangely out of tune on the hot, crowded streets of the ghetto. The Watts riot of August 1965 set the pattern for the next three summers. Dr. King's assassination in April 1968 sparked a new round of destruction, a grim memorial to a man who had dedicated his life to nonviolence and brotherhood. The Kerner Commission, appointed to explain the riots to a bewildered and frightened white America, issued an unexpected indictment that same year:

What white Americans have never fully understood—but what the Negro can never forget—is that white society is deeply implicated in the ghetto. White institutions created it, white institutions maintain it, and white society condones it.

The Commission went on to prophesy:

Our nation is moving toward two societies, one black, one white—separate and unequal. . . . To pursue our present course will involve the continuing polarization of the American community and, ultimately, the destruction of basic democratic values.

When the riots stopped, an uneasy quiet settled on the race issue. The leadership of the Civil Rights Movement dispersed to such issues as welfare and prison reform, and to local political and economic campaigns. The gap between those blacks who were able to take advantage of newly opened opportunities and those whose lives are encircled by poverty widened. But despite the erosion of black leadership and unity, despite setbacks and phantom hopes, much has changed since August 28, 1963.

One of the most significant achievements of the Civil Rights effort was the development of black pride. A number of studies have found that feelings of racial pride are "widespread throughout the Negro community. Ninety-six percent of [one] sample agreed that 'Negroes should take more pride in Negro history'" (Campbell and Schuman, 1968). Also, four out of ten of the respondents thought that "Negro school children should study an *African* language" (Caplan, 1970, pp. 66–67).

The awakening of black pride has touched all corners of American society. In a sense, blacks made ethnicity respectable.[10] And they gave hope to other groups—to Chicanos, Indians, peace demonstrators, women, homosexuals, even the "white ethnics" who don't want their children bused to schools in black districts—all of whom adopted the tactics and slogans of the Civil Rights Movement. In short, the spirit of togetherness that motivated the March on Washington has

---

[10]   In 1971 the Ethnic Heritage Studies Act authorized the government to spend $50 million over two years on ethnic studies. The act states: "in a multi-ethnic society a greater understanding of the contributions of one's own heritage and those of one's fellow citizens can contribute to a more harmonious, patriotic, and committed populace."

given way to a new pattern of race and ethnic relations based on ethnic pride.

Where Do We Stand?

The picture of America that emerges in the seventies is uneven and contradictory. Blacks have gained in some areas and fallen behind in others. Ten years ago, half as many blacks as whites completed high school; today a black student is almost as likely to obtain a diploma as a white student. There are twice as many blacks in college today as there were in 1960, and twice as many blacks hold professional, technical, and related white-collar jobs. However, the median income of black male *college* graduates is only $100 more a year than the median income of white male

This ad is advertising more than furniture. It signals a change in the way whites are beginning to think about blacks. (Kroehler)

This ❤ family loves a lot of living.

The more action you put into your life, the more life you can take out of your furniture. So Kroehler builds furniture that can take this constant use.

Our hard wood frames are locked together as a unit with double dowels and reinforcing blocks—not just glue. Fabrics are all Performance Tested for wear. And balanced comfort is engineered into everything we make. Along with honest good looks available in a style to match your taste with hundreds of fabrics, patterns and colors to match your decor.

KROEHLER Citation

Naugahyde vinyl fabric

high-school graduates.[11] A black person's chances of holding a white-collar job are only half as good as a white person's, and the unemployment rate for blacks is twice that for whites. The median income for black families is still substantially lower than the white median income (see table 9:5). Only 34 percent of black families have intermediate or comfortable incomes, compared to 59.2 percent of white families, and over a third of the nation's 25 million blacks live in poverty (25 percent receive some kind of public assistance). The most concrete gains for black Americans over the last ten years have been in politics. In Mississippi, for example, black voter registration leaped from 5.2 percent in

[11] In 1970 the median income for black male college graduates was $8,715; for white male high-school graduates, $8,613 (Bureau of the Census, *Current Population Reports,* series P–23, no. 46, p. 25).

1960 to 59.4 percent in 1970; in Alabama it soared from 13.7 percent to 54.7 percent. As of 1974 there were 16 black Congresspersons (15 Representatives and 1 Senator), 108 black mayors, and a total of 2,991 elected black officials. This is an increase of *152 percent* over the number of blacks in elective offices during just a five-year period. In part the number of black mayors reflects the fact that whites have more or less abandoned inner cities to blacks, who are nearly a majority in most big cities.

Neighborhood racial isolation has not declined since 1960. On the contrary, it may have increased, particularly in the North. Indeed, things have changed more in the South than in the North and West. Twenty years after the Supreme Court ruling on school desegregation, 9 percent of black students in the South attend all-black schools (compared to 98 percent ten years ago) and 54 percent attend schools where blacks are a majority. Desegregation in the North seems to be a greater problem than it is in the South. (See the box on page 251.)

The employment picture is mixed too. Whereas 50 percent of whites hold white-collar jobs, only 29.8 percent of blacks do. And although 10.6 percent of whites are in managerial positions, only 3.7 percent of nonwhites are (Department of Labor Statistics for 1972).[12] Blacks are conspicuously underrepresented in securities, insurance, restaurants and bars, food processing, utilities, and retail stores. And while some of the black middle class has benefited from newly opened opportunities in the last decade, those who do not have white-collar skills have been left behind.

[12] Washington, D.C., has the highest percentage of blacks in managerial positions in the country (undoubtedly because the federal government is less discriminatory than private business), and St. Louis has the highest percentage of black professionals. New York is above average in both fields.

---

table 9:5 A MEASURE OF CHANGE SINCE 1960

PERCENT OF AGE GROUP WHO ARE HIGH SCHOOL GRADUATES 25–29 YEARS	WHITE	BLACK
1960	63.7	38.6
1972	81.5	64.0

PERCENT OF AGE GROUP WHO ARE COLLEGE GRADUATES 25–29 YEARS	WHITE	BLACK
1960	11.8	5.4
1972	19.9	8.3

MEDIAN INCOME OF FAMILIES (IN 1972 CONSTANT DOLLARS)	WHITE	BLACK
1964[1]	6,858	3,724
1972	11,549	6,864

[1]1960 data are not available.

SOURCE: Bureau of the Census, *Current Population Reports,* series P–23, no. 46.

IN THE NEWS

Twenty Years After the Brown vs. Topeka Decision

Once, liberals considered segregation a southern problem and scorned the South for its bigotry. Today, however, the South seems to be pulling ahead of the North, at least in school integration. As of 1972, 70 percent of black students attended predominantly black schools outside the South; compared to 54 percent of black students in the South. New York and Chicago schools are more racially segregated now than ever before. And unless the courts resolve the issue of busing students across city/suburban lines, this trend is likely to continue. Twenty years after the Supreme Court ordered public schools to integrate, a reporter surveys the situation.

According to interviews with education specialists and a survey of a number of large cities, the meager—some say "disastrous"—record of the North in creating biracial classrooms results from antipathy to busing for purposes of integration, the complacency and timidity of school boards and other units of government, protracted litigation, the exodus of whites to the suburbs and segregated housing patterns.

None of these developments is new. . . . What is relatively new, however, is the widespread recognition by ordinary politicians, school officials and lower-court judges that so-called de facto segregation—that is, school segregation caused by housing patterns rather than overt political decisions about the placement of pupils—presents what might well be the *most painful and ambiguous question facing the nation* (italics added).

On one side are millions of black children trapped in schools that remain, for the most part, separate but unequal. On the other are millions of white parents who do not regard themselves as racist but who look with evident dismay on the idea of returning their children to the cities and school systems they fled.

The complexity of the question is illustrated by random comments from those most affected:

A black mother in Philadelphia, Mrs. Shirley Waites: "I'm in favor of busing to achieve integration. Obviously, you can't achieve it any other way." A black mother in Detroit, Mrs. Doris McCrary: "I don't discuss busing. As far as I'm concerned I've always been against busing. I have built my kids where they have self-confidence in themselves. If you take them out to Grosse Pointe where they would be looked down on, that would do something to their self-image." A white mother in Pontiac, Mich.: "I'd go to jail first. We moved here to get good schools."

Dr. [Kenneth] Clark, whose psychological findings were cited in the 1954 Supreme Court decision outlawing school segregation, said that "the major problem now in the desegregation of the schools is clearly the Northern urban problem. There is no question of this."

He asserted that the major stumbling block to effective integration of Northern schools "is the intransigence of the Northern school boards—their *refusal to obey law.*" . . . Spot checks of a number of large cities showed [growing resistance to school busing in June 1973].

SOURCE: Excerpt from William E. Farrell, "School Integration Resisted in Cities of North," *The New York Times*, May 13, 1974, p. 24.

figure 9:1   Infant mortality rates: 1940–1971 (by race)

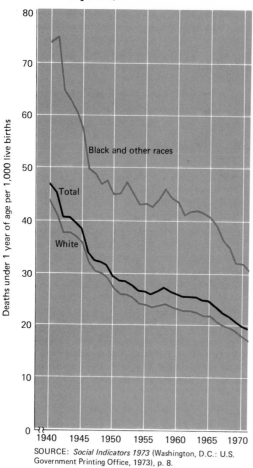

SOURCE: *Social Indicators 1973* (Washington, D.C.: U.S. Government Printing Office, 1973), p. 8.

In 1940, the infant mortality rate for blacks and other nonwhites was about 75 percent higher than it was for whites. By 1971, both rates had dropped dramatically, yet the nonwhite rate was still about 75 percent higher than the white rate.

Attitudes of Whites   In 1963, the year of the March on Washington, the majority of white people still believed blacks had fewer ambitions and looser morals than whites, and over one-third thought blacks were innately inferior to whites (Brink and Harris, 1963, p. 148).

By 1968 white attitudes had changed (table 9:6). Angus Campbell who conducted a survey of white people in fifteen major cities suggests that the most significant changes are that whites attribute the problems of blacks to lack of motivation rather than to innate, biological differences; and that although most whites feel blacks are pushing too fast and that violent rhetoric and acts are not justified, only a few condone violent reprisals against blacks (Campbell, 1971, pp. 4–5).

Campbell also analyzes data collected in 1964 (after the March on Washington but before the riots), 1968 (at the peak of civil disorders), and 1970 (after two years of relative quiet). Over these years more and more white people reported meeting blacks at work, in school, in their neighborhoods, and in public places. Thirty-one percent had black friends in 1970 (compared to 17 percent in 1964). Campbell attributes these changes in large part to the upward mobility of blacks in the last decade, which reduces class differences and thereby weakens the basis for prejudice. He concludes:

It cannot be doubted that since World War II there has been a massive shift in the racial attitudes of white Americans. . . . [But] despite the changes we have noted and the trends we foresee, the white population of this country is far from a general acceptance of this principle and practice of racial equality. . . . We are at present at a point of uneasy confrontation. The black demands for change in the status of black people in this country are insistent and sometimes abusive. Most white people agree that change should occur but they want to move gradually and they are repelled by the violent aspects of black rhetoric and action. Change is taking place but black expectations rise as achievements rise. American society is developing a new pattern of relationships between white and black and the period of change is a time of tension for both races. (pp. 159–62)

table 9:6 ATTITUDES OF WHITES TOWARD BLACKS, 1968

86% —would not mind having a qualified black person as a supervisor

69% —believe orderly protests against racial discrimination are justified

68% —believe landlords and real estate agents discriminate against blacks

67% —favor laws to prevent discrimination in hiring and promotions

49% —would not mind at all if a black family with the same education and income moved in next door

At the same time:

67% —believe blacks are pushing too fast

56% —believe blacks are responsible for their disadvantages in education, jobs, and housing

51% —oppose laws to prevent discrimination in housing

33% —would rather their children had only white friends

24% —would not vote for a qualified black mayoral candidate, even if their party nominated him.

SOURCE: Angus Campbell, *White Attitudes Toward Black People*, Ann Arbor, Mich.: Institute for Social Research, 1971, pp. 4–5.

Attitudes of Blacks How do blacks assess their situation in America? A survey conducted for CBS by the Opinion Research Corporation of Princeton in the spring of 1968, just a month after Martin Luther King, Jr., was assassinated, found both satisfaction and restlessness in the black community (Chandler, 1972, pp. 17–35). The overwhelming majority (78 percent) said black progress was too slow (68 percent of whites in Campbell's survey said black progress was too *fast*), and most believed white America was indifferent to black problems (see table 9:7).

The subject on which blacks strongly disagreed with whites was tactics. Two-thirds of blacks thought peaceful demonstrations were a good way for people "to get what they want," but only one-third of whites favored this tactic. And while a strong majority of blacks favored boycotts and pickets, less than one-third of whites approved of these measures. Less than 10 percent of *both* races, however, favored demonstrations that might lead to violence (Chandler, 1972, p. 27). In most areas, however, there was much agreement between blacks and whites, and both groups were quite moderate despite the turmoil of those months. For example, although 42 percent of blacks blamed racial tension on whites (compared to 9 percent of whites) and 31 percent of whites blamed racial tension on blacks (compared to 1 percent of blacks), 48 percent of blacks and 54 percent of whites thought *both* races were responsible for the problem.

A survey conducted by *Newsweek* in June 1969 suggested that more and more black Americans were becoming disillusioned. Only a small minority (25 percent) thought the federal government was helping blacks in 1969 and most (69 percent) believed white Americans were either hostile or indifferent

table 9:7   ATTITUDES OF BLACKS IN 1968

78%	–blacks are not making enough progress
45%	–blacks have not made more progress because of discrimination
22%	–blacks have not made more progress because they haven't worked hard enough
59%	–whites in America are not sympathetic toward the problems of black people
67%	–whites do not want complete racial equality[1]
80%	–blacks have played an important part in American history
86%	–schools should teach subjects that will enhance black children's pride in their race
59%	–in general, police have been too brutal in their treatment of blacks

[1]54% of whites surveyed agreed.
SOURCE: Robert Chandler, *Public Opinion,* New York: Bowker, 1972, pp. 17–35; © 1968, 1972 by Columbia Broadcasting System, Inc.

MINORITY YOUTH AND THE "NEW VALUES"

In his 1973 survey, Daniel Yankelovich found minority youth disheartened by blatant discrimination, cynical about American society, and doubtful about their futures. The overwhelming impression was one of frustration. Fifty-five percent of minority youth described America as a "sick society" (compared to less than a third of white youth); 76 percent did not consider this a democratic society (compared to 56 percent of young whites); only 56 percent expressed positive feelings about their futures (while 79 percent of whites were optimistic).

More minority than white youth labeled themselves radical (one-third vs. one-fifth), and they were generally more liberal about such issues as amnesty for draft evaders and legalization of marijuana. A majority of nonwhite young people endorsed the "new values." For example, two out of three nonwhites believed in sexual freedom, but only two out of five whites did. At the same time, however, minority youth were more concerned about education, work, and money than other young people, and in some ways more traditional. Fifty-five percent thought a woman's place is in the home (45 percent of whites agreed), and half believed it is important for a man to be strong physically (compared to a quarter of white young people).

SOURCE: Yankelovich Youth Survey © 1974 by the JDR 3rd Fund

toward blacks. (See the accompanying box for a summary of the attitudes of nonwhite [mostly black] youth.) Kenneth Clark describes these changes as an "end of innocence" in the black community, which passionately believed the Civil Rights Movement would succeed in the early sixties. Initial bitterness over the fact that white liberals walked out before the struggle was over has, in Clark's view, given way to a new realism and self-reliance. Increasingly, blacks are shedding the illusions they had about white America helping them. More and more they are working to gain political and economic control of their neighborhoods, their schools, their lives. In the words of Richard Hatcher, the first black mayor of Gary, Indiana, "That's not separatism—That's good old Americanism" (*Newsweek,* June 30, 1969, p. 17).

Obstacles to Full Equality: Institutionalized Racism

In the last decade blacks have made some gains, and in the future, Chicanos, Puerto

Ricans, and Indians may follow the same path. But unless we eliminate *institutionalized racism*, a true pluralism of ethnic groups will remain a dream. This term refers to a social phenomenon: over time, habits of discrimination have become crystallized into the social structure, in institutional patterns of employment, schooling, housing, government, and so on. Once this happens, these institutions need not be "prejudiced" to discriminate—just by continuing to operate the way they always have, they perpetuate lines of discrimination.

As Stokely Carmichael and Charles V. Hamilton wrote in *Black Power* (1967), institutionalized racism "originates in the operation of established and *respected* forces in society" (italics added). For example, if a suburban community zones against low- or even middle-income housing, it automatically excludes most black families, without ever mentioning the word *race*. A banker will refuse loans to black would-be businessmen if he simply applies existing guidelines (credit standards, collateral requirements, and so on), without regard to race. The custom of neighborhood schools, a cherished tradition in this country, is as effective in segregating schools as a law that prohibits "mixed education" (Knowles and Prewitt, 1969, chapter 1). These practices in turn perpetuate the disadvantages of race in the next generation.

summary

A *minority* is a group of people who are singled out for unequal treatment in the society in which they live because they are physically or culturally different from the majority. This chapter focused on the numerous groups in America whose race, national origin, and/or history give them a sense of peoplehood. Included are: 25 million blacks, who trace their history back through 300 years of discrimination to Africa; 6 million Jews, who migrated to America in the mid-nineteenth and early twentieth centuries; 5 million Chicanos, who have lived apart in the Southwest; Puerto Ricans, who became American citizens in 1917; Indians, the poorest of the poor in the United States; approximately a million Americans of Chinese or Japanese descent; and white ethnics from southern and eastern Europe.

Race and misconceptions about race have shaped ethnic relations in this country. Biologically, a *race* is a population that through generations of inbreeding has developed distinctive physical characteristics. Physical anthropologists who study these characteristics have not been able to agree on definite racial categories. Nevertheless, people believe certain groups are genetically distinct and treat them accordingly. For example, some white Americans believe blacks are poor because they are not capable of improving their situation. This myth fuels the argument that blacks are innately less intelligent than whites as shown in average I.Q. differences—an argument that rests on the erroneous belief that an I.Q. test is an objective measure of innate or biological capacity. It is not. Nor is there any evidence that one race is culturally or morally superior to another. The significant differences between groups of people are social, not biological.

Prejudice is an irrational, categorical like or dislike for a group of people because of real or imagined characteristics associated with their race, religion, or national origin. *Discrimination* is granting or denying privileges on grounds rationally irrelevant to the situation. Prejudice and discrimination may or may not go together. Prejudice is a combination of psychological and social predispositions. It seems to satisfy certain psychological "needs" (the need to vent hostility; the need for absolutes which Adorno identified as part of the "authoritarian personality"). Prejudice is most likely to occur in cultures that teach inequality and among people who have to defend their social status.

Race, religion, and ethnic background would not influence a person's opportunities in a fully integrated society that emphasized individual rights and individual differences. One route to integration is *amalgamation* (cultural and/or biological fusion). The second is *assimilation*—replacing minority ways with the language and culture of the majority (behavioral assimilation) and admitting members of minorities into secondary and primary relationships with the majority (structural assimilation). Assimilation into the American mainstream has generally stopped at the level of secondary relationships—in part because the Protestant, Anglo-Saxon majority has not welcomed newcomers, in part because immigrants have resisted Anglo-conformity. The term *cultural pluralism* refers to a pattern whereby ethnic groups maintain their distinctions but coexist peacefully and equally. Switzerland and, to some degree, America's big cities are examples.

Segregation, the restriction by custom and law of contacts between members of different groups (usually ethnic and/or racial), is based on the belief that these groups are inherently unequal. This is the dominant ideology in South Africa, and it still influences the structure of American society. Other forms of minority-rejection are *expulsion* (such as the forced march of the Cherokee Indians) or *extermination* (the slaughter of Indians and Jews).

Minorities cope with discrimination and abuse by trying to pass, by playing the role assigned to them (often a form of "passive aggression"), or by avoiding the majority (as the Chinese did). The psychological consequences of racism are still being studied. Recent research indicates that despite white prejudice and discrimination, black children had high self-esteem. The majority response to racism may be to fear the minority group that it discriminates against.

Racial and ethnic relations in America today are at a crossroads. The Civil Rights Movement succeeded in destroying the legal barriers to equality and stimulated black pride. In the last decade blacks have made significant gains in education and employment, but still encounter discrimination in promotions and salary. And the Civil Rights Movement barely touched the lives of the poor. A survey conducted in 1968 found that although many whites thought blacks were pushing too fast, few condoned violent reprisals against blacks and most attributed black problems to lack of motivation, not biological incapacity. A survey of blacks at about the same time revealed a mixture of satisfaction and restlessness, pride and frustration. Most of the blacks surveyed did not think white America was sympathetic.

What lies in the future? *Institutionalized racism*, habits of discrimination that have become crystallized into the social structure, in patterns of housing, education, and so on, still blocks the way to true ethnic pluralism.

glossary

amalgamation The fusion of culturally and/or racially distinct groups into a new hybrid culture and/or "race."

assimilation Minorities giving up their ancestral customs and adopting the culture of the majority.

assimilation, behavioral Minorities learning the language and culture of the majority (Gordon).

assimilation, structural Minorities gaining entry into the majority's government, business, churches, schools, and, ultimately, primary relationships (Gordon).

authoritarian personality Interrelated personality traits (rigidity, moralism, preoccupation with power and status) that accompany prejudice (Adorno).

cultural pluralism Ethnic groups maintaining their cultural identities and differences but nevertheless coexisting peacefully and equally.

discrimination Granting or denying privileges on grounds rationally irrelevant to the situation.

ethnic group A group of people whose race, religion, or national origins distinguish them from others, and whose history has given them a sense of peoplehood.

expulsion A form of minority-group rejection in which members of a minority are forced to leave their homes and businesses. The group may be forcibly resettled or required to leave the country.

extermination The severest form of minority-group rejection. Members of a particular minority are killed through planned government action.

institutional racism Habits of discrimination that have become crystallized into the social structure, in institutional patterns of housing, schooling, employment, etc. These patterns persist despite an absence of conscious or deliberate discrimination.

integration The elimination of majority/minority distinctions in a society that ranks people according to individual characteristics, not race or ethnic background.

Jim Crow The legal and social barriers constructed in the South in the late nineteenth and early twentieth centuries to prevent blacks from voting, using public facilities, and mixing with whites. (Jim Crow was the name of a blackface minstrel character.)

minority A group of people who are singled out for unequal treatment by the society in which they live, and consider themselves to be victims of collective discrimination.

prejudice An irrational, categorical like or dislike for a group of people.

race A population that through generations of inbreeding has developed more or less distinctive physical characteristics that are transmitted genetically. Sociologically a race is a group of people whom others believe are genetically distinct and treat accordingly.

segregation Laws and/or customs that restrict contact between groups. Segregation may be ethnic or racial, or based on sex or age.

segregation, *de facto* Segregation in fact, which results from such social patterns as "living with your own kind," but is not a matter of official policy.

segregation, *de jure* Segregation by law.

references

T. W. Adorno et al., *The Authoritarian Personality*, New York: Harper and Row, 1950.

Aaron Antonovsky, "The Social Meaning of Discrimination," *Phylon* (Spring 1960): 13–19.

Peter Binzen, *Whitetown USA*, New York: Vintage, 1970.

William Brink and Louis Harris, *The Negro Revolution in America*, New York: Simon & Schuster, 1963.

Angus Campbell, *White Attitudes Toward Black People*, Ann Arbor, Mich.: Institute for Social Research, 1971.

—— and Howard Schuman, "Racial Attitudes in Fifteen American Cities," A report prepared for the National Advisory Committee on Civil Disorders, Ann Arbor, Mich.: University of Michigan Press, 1968.

Nathan Caplan, "The New Ghetto Man: A Review of Recent Empirical Studies," *Journal of Social Issues*, vol. 26, no. 1 (1970): 59–73.

Stokely Carmichael and Charles V. Hamilton, *Black Power*, New York: Vintage, 1967.

Robert Chandler, *Public Opinion*, New York: Bowker, 1972.

Kenneth B. Clark, *Dark Ghetto*, New York: Harper & Row, 1965.

—— and Mamie P. Clark, "Racial Identification and Preference in Negro Children," in T. M.

Newcomb and E. L. Hartley, eds., *Readings in Social Psychology*, New York: Holt, Rinehart and Winston, 1947.

Stewart G. and Mildred Wiese Cole, *Minorities and the American Promise*, New York: Harper & Row, 1954.

Robert Coles, *Children of Crisis*, New York: Dell, 1967.

Peter Collier, "The Red Man's Burden," *Ramparts* (February 1970): 10–16.

———, "Wounded Knee: The New Indian War," *Ramparts* (June 1973): 25–29, 56–59.

Oliver C. Cox, *Caste, Class and Race*, New York: Doubleday, 1948.

Theodosius Dobzhansky, *Mankind Evolving*, New Haven: Yale University Press, 1962.

———, *Genetic Diversity and Human Equality*, New York: Basic Books, 1973.

Morris Freedman and Carolyn Banks, eds., *American Mix*, New York: Lippincott, 1972.

The Gallup Poll: Public Opinion, 1935–1971, New York: Random House, 1972.

Nathan Glazer, "Ethnic Groups in America: From National Culture to Ideology," in Monroe Berger et al., eds., *Freedom and Control in Modern Society*, New York: Van Nostrand, 1954.

——— and D. Patrick Moynihan, *Beyond the Melting Pot*, 2nd ed., Cambridge, Mass.: MIT Press, 1970.

Milton M. Gordon, *Assimilation in American Life*, New York: Oxford University Press, 1964.

Eugene L. Horowitz in Theodore M. Newcomb and E. L. Hartley, eds., *Readings in Social Psychology*, New York: Holt, Rinehart and Winston, 1947.

Chester L. Hunt and Lewis Walker, *Ethnic Diversity*, New York: Dorsey, 1974.

Arthur R. Jensen, "How Much Can We Boost IQ and Scholastic Achievement?" *Harvard Educational Review*, vol. 39 (Winter 1969): 1–12.

———, "The Differences Are Real," *Psychology Today* (December 1973): 80–86.

Horace M. Kallen, "Democracy vs. the Melting Pot," *The Nation*, vol. 100 (February 18, 1965): 190–94.

Irwin Katz, "Review of Evidence Relating to the Effects of Desegregation on the Intellectual Performance of Negroes," *American Psychologist*, vol. 19 (June 1964): 381–99.

Otto Kerner et al., *Report of the National Advisory Commission on Civil Disorders*, New York: Bantam, 1968.

Otto Klineberg, ed., *Characteristics of the American Negro*, New York: Harper & Row, 1944.

Louis Knowles and Kenneth Prewitt, *Institutional Racism in America*, Englewood Cliffs, N.J.: Prentice-Hall, 1969.

Jane Kramer, "The Uganda Asians," *The New Yorker* (April 8, 1974): 47–93.

Minako Kurokawa, ed., *Minority Responses*, New York: Random House, 1970.

Gerda Lerner, ed., *Black Women in White America*, New York: Vintage, 1972.

Oscar Lewis, *La Vida*, New York: Vintage, 1965.

W. Farnsworth Loomis, "Skin-Pigment Regulation of Vitamin-D Biosynthesis in Man," *Science*, vol. 157 (August 9, 1967): 501–506. Also in Carol R. Ember and Melvin Ember, *Anthropology*, New York: Appleton, 1973.

Gary T. Marx, *Protest and Prejudice*, New York: Harper & Row, 1967.

Michael Novak, "White Ethnic," *Harpers* (September 1971): 17–27.

William Petersen, "Success Story—Japanese Style," in Minako Kurokawa, 1970.

Peter I. Rose, *They and We*, 2nd ed., New York: Random House, 1974.

Morris Rosenberg and Roberta G. Simmons, *Black and White Self-Esteem: The Urban School Child*, Washington, D.C.: American Sociological Association, 1971.

R. Rosenthal and L. Jacobson, *Pygmalion in the Classroom*, New York: Holt, Rinehart and Winston, 1968.

Ronald J. Silvers, "Structure and Values in the Explanation of Acculturation Rates," *British Journal of Sociology*, vol. 16 (March 1965): 68–79.

George E. Simpson and J. Milton Yinger, *Racial and Cultural Minorities: An Analysis of Prejudice and Discrimination*, 4th ed., New York: Harper & Row, 1972.

Melvin Tumin, *Patterns of Society*, Boston: Little, Brown, 1973.

Neil Vidmar and Milton Rokeach, "Archie Bunker's Bigotry: A Study in Selective Perception and Exposure," *Journal of Communication*, vol. 24, no. 1 (Winter 1974).

W. Lloyd Warner and Leo Srole, *The Social System of American Ethnic Groups*, New Haven: Yale University Press, 1945.

Louis Wirth, "The Problems of Minority Groups," in Ralph Linton, ed., *The Science of Man in the World Crisis*, New York: Columbia University Press, 1945.

John Womack, Jr., "The Chicanos," *New York Review of Books*, suppl. (August 31, 1972): 20–32.

D. Y. Yuan, "Voluntary Segregation: A Study of New York Chinatown," *Phylon* (Fall 1963): 255–65.

Israel Zangwill, *The Melting Pot*, New York: Jewish Publishing Society of America, 1909.

for further study

The references we have used in each section are among the best and provide an excellent start toward more fully understanding some aspects of ethnic relations. The most authoritative general text is *Racial and Cultural Minorities*, by George Simpson and Milton Yinger (New York: Harper & Row, 4th edition, 1972). A short and very readable account is Peter Rose's *They & We: Racial and Ethnic Relations in the United States*, 2nd edition (New York: Random House, 1974).

Prejudice. Why are people prejudiced? What are the social and personal dimensions of prejudice? In this chapter we have addressed these questions briefly, but they deserve deeper examination. A classic that is still widely read is Gordon Allport's book *The Nature of Prejudice* (Cambridge, Mass.: Addison-Wesley, 1954). Sociologist Herbert M. Blalock, Jr. systematically examines the research on prejudice and discrimination in *Toward a Theory of Minority-Group Relations* (New York: Wiley, 1967). A more personal view can be found in Frantz Fanon's *The Wretched of the Earth* (New York: Grove Press, 1963).

American Indians. An ethnic majority that was reduced to a minority are the American Indians. The National Geographic Society has published a general book about Indians written almost entirely by Indians, *Indians of North America*, 1974. Two excellent books about specific tribes are Earl Shorris, *The Death of the Great Spirit* (New York: New American Library, 1971), and Alfonso Ortiz, *The Tewa World* (Chicago: University of Chicago Press, 1969). Two books that give the Indian perspective on the "American dream" are Dee Brown's *Bury My Heart at Wounded Knee* (New York: Bantam, 1972) and Vine Deloria, Jr., *Custer Died for Your Sins* (New York: Avon, 1970). A classic that compares how Indian tribes responded to and changed from contact with American settlers is *Acculturation in Seven American Indian Tribes*, Ralph Linton, ed. (New York: Appleton, 1940).

Blacks in America. Though we have suggested some books on the subject of the black American, there are many more. E. Franklin Frazier, one of the first black sociologists, has written *The Negro in the United States* (New York: Macmillan, 1957). In *The Black American in Sociological Thought* (New York: Capricorn, 1972), Stanford M. Lyman examines the various ways that sociology has dealt with blacks in America. Malcolm X's *The Autobiography of Malcolm X* (New York: Grove, 1966) takes you through his experiences and changing awareness as he became a spokesman for Black Power. Claude Brown's *Manchild in the Promised Land* (New York: Signet, 1965) is another personal account. A classic study is *An American Dilemma*, by Swedish economist Gunnar Myrdal (New York: Harper & Row, 1962).

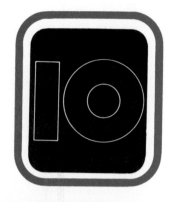

Unsafe at Any Speed, Ralph Nader's exposé of the $100-billion-a-year automobile industry, documents the enormous power that giant corporations wield in our society. The book is a study in "corporate collectivism," focusing on General Motors, the leader of the four companies that together produce 99 percent of American cars. Nader describes monopolistic practices that limit competition and reveals how the auto industry manipulates consumers to accept profit-making goods, even though they may not be needed or safe. Are the 50,000 or more traffic deaths a year in this country inevitable, as most people believe? Nader thinks not. Poor design and engineering are profitable. The American public is losing—losing lives, resources, and fresh air.

Giant organizations that mass-produce everything from automobiles and fashions to entertainment, education, and food are facts of modern life. Four companies produce over half of the steel manufactured in this country. Ninety percent of the electric lights, 80 percent of the cigarettes, even 94 percent of the baby food, and

ORGANIZATIONS AND BUREAUCRACY

74 percent of the zippers we buy are produced by the four largest companies in each area. Keeping pace with industry, the nation's three top unions speak for 15 million of the 18 million union members in America. The growth in government over the last 150 years is staggering. During Andrew Jackson's administration, the total federal budget was $20 million a year; today the figure is nearer $200 billion, with the president alone drawing $200,000 a year in salary. There are more federal bureaucrats (over 3 million) in America than there are farmers (Mott et al., 1973, pp. 143–45).

How did this come about, and what do such diverse organizations as General Motors, a university, and the federal government have in common? This chapter examines organizations, describing the rise of modern bureaucracies, the distribution of power in today's organizations, the ways in which people become (or resist becoming) cogs in the "bureaucratic machine," and trends in worker-management relations that may alter organizations of the future.

FORMAL ORGANIZATIONS

An *organization* is a group that has been consciously designed to seek specific goals. People organize to pursue collective aims for the simple reason that if they did not—if seven, eight, or more individuals each did whatever he or she thought best, without consulting the others—they might end up working at cross-purposes. So they form a committee or a business firm, a union or a religious council. The members decide who will have responsibility and authority over what areas, and establish procedures for communicating with one another. Procedures are also devised for making decisions, coordinating activities, reviewing policy and strategies, resolving conflicts among members and keeping them in line, and filling and refilling the organization's ranks (see Blau and Scott, 1963, pp. 1–2).

Once established, organizations tend to become self-perpetuating—that is, they develop an existence apart from the specific people who founded them. This is one of the primary differences between organizations and other kinds of social groups. Family members are not replaceable; relationships among members are *expressive*, that is, they are centered on the emotional dimension of the relationship. In contrast, relationships in an organization are *instrumental*; they are built around the completion of specific tasks. Members of an organization may come and go, but the offices and procedures and identity of the organization remain more or less stable. The Roman Catholic church is a prime example of an enduring organization. General Motors, A.T.&T., the League of Women Voters, the Scouts, all share these basic features of an organization.

Of course, a business that cannot pay employees will fall apart (unless, like an acting or dance company, it provides other satisfactions). A political party, too, can collapse if its goals and tactics begin to seem unrealistic or dated. Similarly a union whose leadership sides more closely with management than with its members will be weakened. Organizations endure if they continue to provide the goods and services that originally motivated people to join them. By "goods and services" here we mean everything from job satisfaction to salaries (in business organizations), to the assurance of national defense (in armies), to the hope of influencing government (in special interest lobbies). Maintaining internal discipline by rewarding members who contribute to organizational goals and punishing or ostracizing those who do not is also important. Organizations must be able to recruit members who accept and support their goals, or to inspire and perhaps coerce the uncommitted.

In summary, then, the major difference between organizations and other social groups is that organizations are formally established for the express purpose of pursuing a specific goal, whether it is practicing the true religion, making money, electing a candidate, or keeping criminals off the streets[1] (Blau and Scott, 1963, p. 3). A division of labor and authority into clearly defined roles, set channels of communication, explicit rules and procedures, and formal and informal sanctions are all part of the self-perpetuating design of organizations.

Types of Organizations

Although all organizations are alike in some respects, the differences between them can be highly significant. Some organizations

---

[1] Of course, organizations serve other functions as well—they are a place for people to make friends, pass time, perhaps a route to personal advancement and power. But their stated goals are their raison d'être.

are concerned with economic matters (for example, businesses), some with power (political organizations). Still others are designed to resolve intergroup conflicts in a society (the court system) or to teach and maintain social values (churches and schools). (See Parsons, 1960, chapter 1.)

People may or may not join an organization of their own free will, as Amitai Etzioni points out (1961, pp. 55–67). Social clubs, churches, political parties, professional associations, and pressure groups are all *voluntary organizations*. People join them out of personal interest, because they share the organization's goals and norms. They can withdraw at any time. At the opposite extreme are the organizations people are forced to join, such as prisons, the military (when soldiers are drafted), and schools (education being compulsory between the ages of six and sixteen). Etzioni calls these *coercive organizations*: they depend on force. Between these two extremes lie a great number of *utilitarian organizations* that people join for practical reasons. The clearest example of this type is the business firm. Although no one actually forces people to take specific jobs in this country, most adults do have to work, and their choice of careers and employers is limited (more limited for some than for others). People devote time and energy to utilitarian organizations, and abide by their rules and regulations because they expect to benefit personally, not because they are emotionally committed to the organization.

Knowing why people join an organization does not necessarily tell us who benefits from it. Business organizations, for example, are run for the benefit of the owners, whose goal is to maximize efficiency and profit. Peter Blau and W. Richard Scott (1963, pp. 40–58) identify three other types according to who benefits most. Unions and religious sects are specifically designed to further the interests of their members. Blau and Scott call these *mutual benefit organizations*, and suggest that ideally they are characterized by a high degree of member participation. *Client-centered organizations*, such as hospitals, schools, and most social agencies, are designed to serve a particular group of people (patients, students, etc.). The main problem in these service organizations is to maintain a balance between client interests and administrative necessity. Finally, there are *commonweal organizations*, which are operated for the benefit of the public-at-large. Examples are the Internal Revenue Service, the Food and Drug Administration, police departments, and other organizations that the public controls (at least in theory).

The importance of these distinctions becomes clear if you think about whether prisons are service organizations, whose primary responsibility is to rehabilitate inmates, or commonweal organizations, responsible for keeping convicts off the streets. The kinds of facilities we build and the kinds of people we staff them with reflect society's view of what prisons should be. The same kind of analysis can be made of universities. From the student's point of view the university is a student-centered service organization, whose primary purpose is to stimulate and educate people. Faculty tend to see universities as communities of scholars and students, or mutual benefit associations. Adding to this confusion, legislators and other government officials consider universities commonweal organizations that should lend their talents and resources to the solution of community and social problems. Much of the controversy on campuses in the 1960s revolved around the question of whether it was ethical for universities to accept research grants from the Defense Department, or to allow the military and corporations manufacturing war materials to recruit on campus. These questions were not widely raised during the 1940s, when the commonweal nature of the university "in the nation's service" was assumed.

Similar questions can be asked about associations that seem to be voluntary. Do people join social clubs or professional associations because they want to, or because they feel they might lose important friends or a promotion if they did not? The categories suggested here are no more than models or ideal types against which the realities of specific organizations may be measured. Organizations have complex social structures.

IN THE NEWS

Lordstown: Informal Structure on the Assembly Line

It is hard to imagine any work more routine, more nonnegotiable than assembly line work. But men at the General Motors Vega plant in Lordstown, Ohio, have found a way to regain control of their working hours through a system they call "doubling up." Management claims that doubling up seriously lowers the quality of work, and the United Auto Workers' Union refuses to acknowledge the practice. But workers are proud of the system they've improvised and intend to fight for it. The following excerpts are taken from an interview of Lordstown workers.

Q: What's doubling up and how did it start?

McGEE: Now what happens is that the guys who have their operations side by side, they're relating together. . . . In other words, they all worked in the same area. They started saying, "Go ahead, take off." It started like an 'E' break—you asked for emergency bathroom call. The utility man might be tied up.

I'd say, "Go ahead, man, I think I can handle it." I'd run to the front of the car and I'd stick in the ring we used to have, and I'd run to the back then. I mean, I'm not running, really running, but I'm moving. I put the gas in, I go up to the front of the car again . . . go back again. I'm getting it done, and I'm not having any recovery time. I'm going right back again.

Well, the guys started doing this on a larger scale.

McGARVEY: You have to double up and break the boredom to get an immediate feedback from your job, because the only gratification you get is a paycheck once a week, and that's too long to go without any kind of gratification from the job.

Q: So there's a philosophy behind doubling up?

GENERAL: Definitely.

McGEE: Sure, if you're on the damned line here and you've found a way to double up and you've found a way to shuck and jive—all day long, have a good time, help each other and get out the work. I don't have to take these pain pills any more. My ulcer's gone.

Q: Has it—and your doubling up—come from laziness or inventiveness?

DICKERSON: Inventiveness. One way to explain the thing is that anytime there's a human need, there's always an invention, or a way to get around it.

The men feel strongly that, because doubling up gave them added responsibility—for two jobs rather than one—the quality of their work actually improves. By bending the formal rules of the company to fit their own needs, the workers at Lordstown feel they have improved not only their own morale, but the company's product as well.

SOURCE: Bennet Kremen, "Lordstown—Searching for a Better Way of Work," *The New York Times* (September 9, 1973): III, 1–4.

Formal and Informal Structure Whatever their orientation and whoever benefits most from them, all organizations seek to define members' responsibilities and regulate their activities. This is an organization's *formal structure*: explicit rules that define each person's duties; written or unwritten organizational charts (see figure 10:1 on p. 266) that describe relationships among members (who has authority over whom); and a system of rewards and punishments (for example, promotions and demotions). In principle, this formal structure governs all members' activities. However, any time people join forces to accomplish a task, friendships and power relationships develop, and with them come cliques, grapevines, and the like. Some people wield more influence than their job title indicates; others less.

In addition, an organization's rules may not keep pace with problems. For these reasons, members improvise an *informal structure*: procedures that enable people to solve problems not covered by the formal regulations, to eliminate unpleasant or unnecessary work, and to protect their own interests. (See box on p. 264.) All organizations have both an official, formal structure, and an unofficial, informal structure of relationships among members. In the pages that follow we will discuss both the formal and informal structures of a wide variety of organizations.

MODERN BUREAUCRACIES

Giant bureaucratic organizations are not a modern invention. The pyramids of Egypt are monuments to organization; the Roman Empire could never have existed without a vast administrative structure. But never before in history have bureaucracies been so pervasive or so powerful. The "Age of Bureaucracy" was launched in the nineteenth century when Western nations began to industrialize.

"The Mighty Machine"

The Greeks understood the principles of the steam engine and probably could have produced one had they so desired. They didn't, presumably because they had an abundant supply of labor in the form of slaves. The practical application of mechanics to production did not interest them. Rather, they aimed their technical inventiveness at surprises and miracles—temple gates that opened by themselves when a priest lit the fire on an altar, for example. This nonutilitarian attitude toward mechanization persisted for centuries. As late as 1870, the French were talking and writing not about Jacques de Vaucanson's silk factory (probably the first industrial plant in Europe), but about his marvelous mechanical duck, which waddled, swam, wagged its head, quacked, and even pecked, digested, and expelled grain (Giedion, 1948, pp. 31–36).

However, by the end of the nineteenth century this dilettantish fascination with machines had blossomed into a full-fledged love affair. It was the wedding of rationality and this-worldliness to the miraculous, sanctified by the creed of Progress. The cotton gin, the steam engine, and the iron horse all made their appearance. Rather suddenly, Europeans recognized the enormous power of mechanization.

Soon, writers on two continents were heralding the dawn of a new age. With machines, humankind would transform the world. "We remove mountains, and make seas our smooth highway; and nothing can

figure 10:1   A formal organization chart

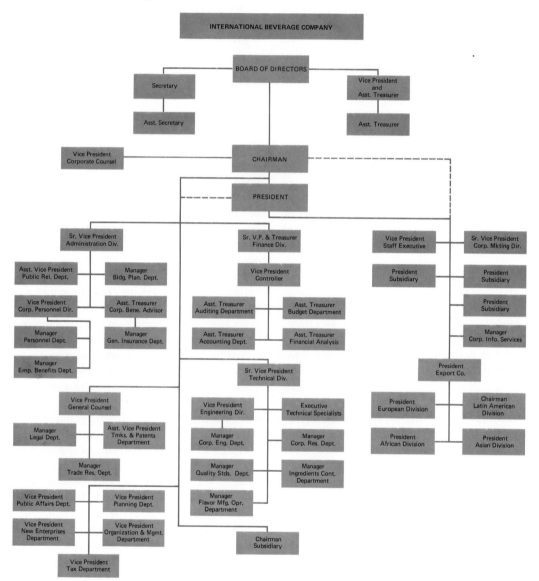

SOURCE: *Corporate Organization Structures* © 1973 The Conference Board, p. 37.

This chart shows the hierarchy of offices in an international beverage company. By following vertical lines to their source, you can see who reports to whom. Generally, the position of an employee's supervisor is an indication of his or her own power in the hierarchy. Note for example, that even though the Vice President of the Tax Department is at the bottom of the chart, he or she reports directly to the Chairman.

resist us," wrote Carlyle. "We make war with rude Nature; and, by our resistless engines, come off always victorious, and loaded with spoils" (Carlyle, in Marx, 1964, p. 171). Machines would wipe drudgery and menial labor off the list of human complaints, freeing people to follow more uplifting pursuits. The forefather of sociology, Saint-Simon, was one of the first, but not the last, to see industrialization as the route to peace and social justice: mechanization would eliminate poverty and want; nationalism and militarism would disappear; no longer would the powerful exploit the weak (Giedion, 1948, p. 30). Machines became a favored metaphor in this period. "What is the heart but a spring, and the nerves so many springs, and the joints but so many wheels, giving motion to the whole body," wrote Hobbes.

Looking back, we can imagine the enthusiasm for mechanization in this earlier time, the sense of unlimited possibilities, the faith people had in reason and progress. By any measure, the standard of living has risen dramatically since the advent of mechanization: we have minimized distances in the jet age; we do have the capacity (if not the will) to feed, clothe, and provide medical care for every person on earth. It is doubtful that these developments would have occurred without the spread of bureaucracy.

Bureaucracy: Ideal and Real[2]

The fully developed bureaucratic mechanism compares with other organizations exactly as does the machine with non-mechanical modes of production. (Weber, in Gerth and Mills, 1946, p. 214)

[2] This section is based on Weber's "Bureaucracy," in Gerth and Mills, 1946; Weber, *The Theory of Social and Economic Organization*, 1947; and Blau and Meyer, 1971, chaps. 2 and 3.

A machine is "an apparatus consisting of interrelated parts with separate functions, used in the performance of some kind of work" (*Random House Dictionary of the English Language*, 1967). If we substitute the word *organization* for *apparatus,* we have a basic definition of *bureaucracy*: an organization consisting of interrelated parts with separate functions. The key terms here are *interrelated* and *separate functions.* Bureaucracy represents the application of mechanics to social organization in the performance of some kind of work.

Weber's Model of Bureaucracy Weber's analysis of bureaucratic structure, written long before red tape became a social problem and the word *bureaucrat* an epithet, remains the classic in the field. Weber traced the development and spread of bureaucracies to large-scale production and advances in technology coupled with the nineteenth-century belief in progress and reason. He believed bureaucracy to be *technically* superior to other forms of social organization, despite its dehumanizing side-effects (which he recognized fully and regretted). "Precision, speed, unambiguity, knowledge of files, continuity, discretion, strict subordination, reduction of friction and of material and personal costs—these are raised to the optimum point in the strictly bureaucratic administration" (Weber, in Gerth and Mills, 1946, p. 214). To dramatize the differences between bureaucracies and other organizations, Weber defined bureaucracy in terms of five characteristics. Together, these characteristics describe an ideal type or model, against which the realities of actual bureaucracies can be measured.

1. **Specialization**: Bureaucratic organization is based on the belief that dividing production into small tasks and having people specialize

in one of these tasks is the most efficient way to perform complex work. If you consider the impossibility of one person learning every step in the production of an airplane or all there is to know today about medicine, the reasoning behind this belief will be obvious. Specialization is more efficient than "generalization." Bureaucracies rely on a complex division of labor, with clearly defined areas of jurisdiction. The men and women in each area are familiar with and responsible for only one step in the production or adminis-

"Grow, industry, grow, grow, grow," sing these employees each morning at a Matsushita television factory in Japan. Identical work-stations signal the regularity of tasks performed in the row at the right. (Fred Ward/Black Star)

tration of the bureaucracy's essential task. This arrangement encourages the development of special competence or expertise in limited areas. But no one person knows the entire process, which can be a terrible handicap if something goes wrong.

2. **A hierarchy of offices**: Once production is broken down into a number of separate activities performed by separate groups of people, the entire operation must be integrated in a workable fashion. If not, experts in one department might design a bolt that is one-eighth-inch larger than the nut designed by another department (Blau and Meyer, 1971, p. 8). In small organizations all the workers can call a meeting to talk about ideas and problems, but in large organizations it is impossible for everyone to meet together. Nor can the boss supervise the activities of

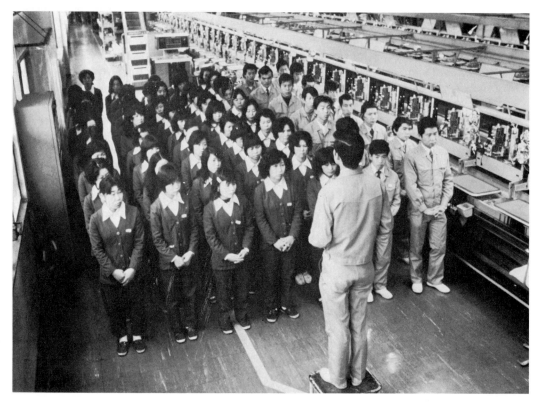

hundreds of employees, even if he or she knows their jobs, which is unlikely. To resolve this problem, workers are organized in a *hierarchy*. Each person is responsible *to* the person directly above him or her in the hierarchy and responsible *for* the actions of those who work under him or her.

Organizational hierarchies are defined in terms of positions or offices. Each office carries with it specific duties, responsibilities, and privileges, as well as a specific salary. Authority rests in the office, not in the person who occupies it. This individual may be promoted or fired, but the office remains the same. An office-holder's power over those beneath him or her in the hierarchy derives from the *position*, not from the individual qualities or "sacred rights" (such as a parent's rights over a child).[3] In addition to being depersonalized, the authority of bureaucratic officials is clearly defined and limited. While they have the power to recommend individuals for promotions or to fire them, supervisors have no authority over subordinates' personal lives, as was true when sons worked for their fathers in family businesses. (Remember, Weber was describing an ideal type. He was not oblivious to the pressures toward conformity in dress, political attitudes, outside activities, and the like in bureaucracies.)

Weber believed hierarchical organization would minimize interpersonal friction. If subordinates accept the hierarchical division of responsibility and authority, and the supervisor's right to regulate their activities, it is no more degrading to accept orders from the boss than it is to obey orders from a policeman (Blau and Meyer, 1971, p. 67). Moreover, when a supervisor makes an unpopular decision, she can avoid subordinates' hostility and maintain good working relationships by blaming the people above her in the hierarchy.

3. **Rules and regulations**: Activities and relationships among officers in a bureaucracy are governed by explicit rules and regulations. In this way, each employee knows (at least in general terms) what is required of him and how his decisions will be carried out. Rules make the workings of even the most complex bureaucracy orderly and predictable. They are the connecting rods in the bureaucratic engine.

4. **Impartiality**: Weber believed that personal emotions impede efficiency and therefore have no place in a bureaucracy. Impartiality toward both co-workers and those who do business with the organization is essential. Ideally this assures that all people will be treated equitably and that personal considerations will be subordinated to organizational goals. If an official promotes a subordinate solely because he or she is a friend, or awards a contract to a company because his or her brother owns it, the organization will suffer.

5. **Technical competence**: Finally, positions in a bureaucracy are awarded on the basis of technical qualifications (as measured by tests or other standardized procedures), and people are paid for their work. However, Weber believed that a salary was not enough to motivate people to work harder, faster, or more efficiently. People must be guaranteed a place, so long as they perform their official duties adequately. Promotions and raises, awarded on the basis of merit and/or seniority, are essential to a bureaucracy's *esprit de corps*. In addition, Weber thought the more complicated and specialized work became, the more bureaucracies would need "personally detached and strictly 'objective' experts."

---

[3] Weber called this *rational-legal authority*, to distinguish it from the kinds of authority one finds in older, more traditional societies. We will return to this distinction in chapter 14.

Does Weber's model of bureaucracy exist in reality? Not entirely. Studies of business firms in 150 societies and an analysis of ten organizations in this country suggest that the five bureaucratic traits don't always appear together (Udy, 1959; Hall, 1963–1964). Wide variations were found in degree of specialization, hierarchical organization, and adherence to rules and regulations, both within and among companies. The fact that an organization relied on specialization did not mean that employees were arranged in a hierarchy or that their relationships were impersonal.

As we suggested earlier, Weber's model is an ideal type which calls attention to significant characteristics by emphasizing, and perhaps overstating, trends. It was not meant to describe reality. "The ideal-type bureaucracy may be used much as a twelve-inch ruler is employed. We would not expect, for example, that all objects measured by the ruler would be exactly twelve inches—some would be more and some would be less" (Gouldner, 1950, pp. 53–54). Other critics have focused not on how accurate Weber's model is, but on how well bureaucracies function.

Ritualism Do rules and regulations facilitate rational decision-making and maximize efficiency, as Weber suggested? Not always. In his classic study of the bureaucratic personality, Robert Merton (1968) suggests that when people become devoted to procedures, as bureaucrats tend to do, they lose sight of why those procedures were created in the first place. Following regulations becomes an end in itself.[4] Rigid adherence to established procedures prevents people from recognizing and adapting to new conditions and problems. They become inflexible. Organizational

goals and efficiency may be lost in the shuffle. The bureaucrat Merton describes feels totally satisfied if he does everything just exactly as he is supposed to, regardless of the consequences. The phenomenon commonly known as "passing the buck" is simply a variation on this theme: unless the official is clear about which rules to follow in a given case, and unless he is certain that it falls within his jurisdiction, he may refuse to take any action at all (Blau and Meyer, 1971, pp. 104–5). Merton argues that bureaucracies encourage overconformity, or ritualism.

Harry Cohen cautions against regarding flexibility as an unqualified asset in bureaucrats (1970). He cites the example of an interviewer who filed the required complaint when an employer refused to hire an applicant because she was black. However, the bureaucrat then visited the employer and advised him to mention insufficient qualifications, not race, when rejecting applicants in the future. From one point of view, this action was highly adaptive: the interviewer avoided antagonizing an employer who could provide jobs for his clients. But, in an indirect way, he broke the law, as well as the rules. Cohen's point is that flexibility as well as excessive rigidity can be harmful to the bureaucracy. Moreover, in many instances a bureaucrat finds he is damned if he does follow the rules (by discriminating employers in this case) and damned if he doesn't (by those who suffer from or disapprove of discrimination).

Protection of the Inept Weber believed that bureaucratic organizations would make the best possible use of available talent. Recent research indicates that bureaucracies tend to protect the inept as well. Given the fact that the boss has the power to promote or fire subordinates, it is in employees' interest to conceal problems and withhold information from supervisors. In William Goode's words,

---

[4] An obvious example of this is grades. Originally intended to be a convenient measure of educational progress, they have become an end in themselves.

"Almost every inquiry into the productivity of workers has shown that the informal work group protects its members by setting a standard which everyone can meet, and they develop techniques for preventing a supervisor from measuring accurately the output of each [person]" (1967, p. 6). Goode also calls attention to the fact that companies are usually reluctant to demote or otherwise discredit incompetent employees. Thus, people who do not meet company standards in one position may be "kicked upstairs" to a less responsible but still prestigious job, or fired but provided with glowing recommendations. Discrimination against blacks, women, Jews, or other minorities and the requirement that workers have at least a high-school diploma to perform work a child could master, also limit competition and thereby protect inept workers who already hold those jobs.

Weber also believed that regular promotions based on merit and/or seniority would contribute to efficiency, but each of these criteria can prove inefficient. If granted solely on the basis of merit, some people will not advance, creating discontent in the lower ranks; if granted on the basis of seniority, inefficient people will be advanced as a matter of course (Goode, 1967).

The Peter Principle Even if promotions are based solely on merit, this method of filling jobs can be disadvantageous. When supervisors need to fill positions, they choose persons who are particularly good at their current jobs. If these people prove capable in the new job, they will very likely be promoted again and again—until they reach their level of *in*competence. For example, an outstanding teacher may be promoted to principal, a very different kind of job which she may perform poorly. However, if she is a good principal, she may be moved up to district superintendent. If she proves to be a poor superintendent, she will not be promoted but will *stay* in the job she cannot quite fill. This is the famous *Peter Principle*: "In a hierarchy every employee tends to rise to his [or her] level of incompetence" (Peter and Hull, 1969, p. 25). Knowing that your knowledge and ability are not quite up to your job can be a frightening experience, leading to poor performance. One way to alleviate the anxiety is to bury yourself in the rules and regulations, ignoring the consequences of your work (Blau and Meyer, 1971, p. 104).

Waste-Making Writing when he did, Weber could not have foreseen all the possible ramifications of ever-increasing size. In principle, people hire assistants when they feel they can no longer handle all of their work alone. In practice, however, people may request additional staff to increase their prestige in the organization. Suppose a bureaucrat hires two assistants (two being safer than one, who might become a competitor). In all likelihood, he will reserve the power to make decisions for himself, thereby adding supervision to his original work load. If all goes well, however, in a year or two his assistants will need assistants, and there will be five or even seven people to do the work of one. But the ritual of shuffling paper back and forth among seven people—by itself—will keep them all *demonstrably* busy. This is the essence of *Parkinson's Law*: "Work expands to fill the time available for its completion" (Parkinson, 1957).

A. Ernest Fitzgerald (1972), who spent several years as an efficiency consultant for the Pentagon, found numerous examples of Parkinson's Law. Investigating the military and civilian firms working for the military, he invariably found overstaffed departments and bureaus—a condition the military thinly disguised under the code words, "maintaining capability." In most cases, when

Fitzgerald recommended cutbacks, the official in charge would challenge the data in order to keep his staff. One manager, however, stood out. Fitzgerald recommended a 56 percent cutback in his area. The manager praised Fitzgerald's methods and data, but claimed it was good to keep so many people employed but unproductive. Laying people off would be wrong.

What if someone were to hire them and put them to work *producing* things, items which would compete in the commercial marketplace? That would never do, our manager said, because competition might set in, driving prices down, and some of the less efficient companies might go broke. This sort of thing could develop into a chain reaction and ruin the whole business climate. (Fitzgerald, 1972, p. 5)

Fitzgerald concludes that the military believes in "The Ape Theory of Engineering." This theory was proposed by a psychologist who calculated that, according to the laws of probability, if enough apes were set down at typewriters, they would eventually write *Hamlet*. Fitzgerald quotes one manager who, in all seriousness, described his approach as follows: "I just assign a thousand or so guys to the problem. One of them is bound to come up with a solution" (p. 7).

MEETING ORGANIZATIONAL GOALS

Corporations, armies, churches, neighborhood associations have one thing in common, as we indicated at the beginning of this chapter: they are conspicuously designed to achieve certain goals. Motivating people to support "the cause," establishing procedures for coordinating activities, making decisions, and dealing with outsiders are essential to any organization. In this section we look at how organizations distribute power and elicit work from their members. We will also consider how workers shape the rules to meet their own needs.

Leadership and the Negotiated Order

Leaders or bosses play many roles in modern organizations. They are decision-makers, administrators who see that decisions are carried out and activities coordinated, and disciplinarians who enforce the rules. They represent the organization to the outside world and to the rank-and-file below them, who do not participate directly in the organization's policy councils.

Alvin W. Gouldner's *Patterns of Industrial Bureaucracy* (1954) is a case study in two different styles of leadership—democratic and authoritarian. The book is based on a three-year study of a gypsum plant located near the Great Lakes, which employed approximately 225 people—75 in the mines, 150 in different "surface" operations—over the course of the study. Gouldner's arrival coincided with a change in management: Vincent Peele, an outsider with his own ideas about how to run a plant, was replacing "Old Doug," as the former boss was known.

In the old days management had been unusually "indulgent" (to use Gouldner's term) toward employees. As long as a worker did his job, his free time while at work was his own. Supervision was minimal and working hours flexible. As a result, employees had considerable control over their working lives. No one was reprimanded for taking time off during the hunting season. In fact, management always gave employees the benefit of the doubt. One mechanic told Gouldner, "Nobody ever gets fired from this plant. Maybe

Bill [a supervisor] fired one guy in all the time I've known him, and *he was given three or four warnings*" (p. 48).[5] As a matter of policy, men injured on *or off* the job were given light work in the sampling room, which became known as "the hospital." In addition, officials allowed workers to borrow company tools and materials for private use. Gouldner found the majority thought this basically democratic company had the "proper attitude" and that they were being treated "humanly."

Peele was a stranger when he took over as manager, and knew little about the way things were done in the plant. Anxious to do

Meeting in the corporate board room, these men are making decisions that will affect employees at lower levels of the company's hierarchy. (Bruce Davidson/Magnum)

his job well, he began to attack what he perceived as laxity. In a very short time, he fired one man for borrowing company-owned material (an acceptable practice in the old days); replaced a popular foreman with a college-educated outsider; formalized warnings with written notices; instituted regular, written work reports; and announced that workers who were absent without a valid excuse would be laid off for an equivalent number of days.

Workers did not take kindly to these changes. Their complaints centered around

---

[5] In part, this generosity existed because employees came from a small, stable community. Most knew each other on the outside, and many brothers, cousins, and friends worked together.

the implication that they had been goldbricking and required close supervision, which they deeply resented. Old Doug's inner circle, his "lieutenants," did not consider Peele a "legitimate heir" and grew pointedly recalcitrant, so that he had difficulty learning exactly what was going on.

Gouldner suggests that Peele became authoritarian almost as a last resort, because he lacked the informal social ties that would have enabled him to manage the employees with a lighter hand.

Like all other solutions Peele adopted to handle the problems of his succession, the development of formal rules also had an anxiety-allaying function. The rules define the new situation into which the successor has entered, allowing him to make decisions with a minimum of uncertainty and personal responsibility. . . . The belief that he was only doing what he must, softened Peele's doubts about his own behavior. As he remarked: "Some of the men probably think I'm a mean cuss, but I've got to follow our Company policy like everyone else. If I don't, someone else will." (Gouldner, 1954, 95–96)

In time Peele was able to establish a bureaucratic system in surface operations, but not in the mines. The hazards of underground work strengthened the miners' feeling that they had a legitimate right to make their own decisions.

Gouldner's study raises an important point about leadership. The power to hire and fire and to impose rules through sanctions is of limited value without the support of an informal organization. Peele discovered very quickly that he could not be all places at all times to see that regulations were being followed. Moreover, his authoritarian style generated a good deal of resentment and apathy. Before the rigid, bureaucratic rules were applied, workers had been largely self-regulating. Afterwards, they used the rules to justify and excuse minimal effort.

"Well, if that's the way he wants it, that's the way he wants it. But I'll be damned if I put in any overtime when things get rough and they'd like us to."

"O.K. I'll punch in just so, and I'll punch out on the nose. But you know you can lead a horse to water and you can lead him away, but it's awful hard to tell just how much water he drinks while he's at it." (Gouldner, 1954, p. 175)

As these quotations suggest, the effectiveness of leadership depends on the kinds of understandings which various people—the men in the mines, the workers on the surface, the office managers—work out among themselves. Anselm Strauss and others have called this the *negotiated order* (1964). Discovered when they studied how psychiatrists, nurses, social workers, psychologists, and attendants work out their relationships when caring for mental patients, this term alerts us to the way in which organizational power becomes shaped and altered. It is not the same as the informal structure of an organization, because the negotiated order will usually involve both informal and formal arrangements. For example, Mr. Peele relied heavily upon formal rules in an effort to renegotiate the organization of the gypsum factory. Central to this process is *legitimacy*—who can persuade others that he or she has the right to a certain organizational power. While Mr. Peele had official power, he lacked legitimacy in the eyes of many employees. One reason he did so goes back to the exchange theory of social life (see chapter 3). The old manager, Doug, had created social debts (by overlooking minor violations of the rules and by protecting subordinates from official sanctions) which the men repaid in extra effort (Blau and Meyer, 1971, pp. 63–68). The negotiated order is an example of social exchange, and Mr. Peele had trouble creating his new order because he did not realize this sociological truth.

Socialization into Organizations

As the preceding discussion suggests (and as we noted in chapter 5), new members of an organization experience a period of initiation, during which they learn the skills and vocabulary of their new position, the formal and informal pecking order of the organization, and its written and unwritten rules. For the organization, socializing new members means "breaking them in." For the boss, it is an opportunity to test neophytes (who might one day become competitors) and to reassert his or her own power. Newcomers learn that pursuing organizational goals is in their own best interests, and that the demands to be made on them are legitimate and meaningful—or at least, unavoidable. For recruits, socialization into an organization means adjusting expectations to reality, learning the "system," establishing new loyalties, and discovering their own strengths and countervailing power.

Anticipatory Socialization Socialization into a new job or position builds on the new member's expectations and desire to convert, to conform, and to do things "the company way." William F. Whyte, Jr., demonstrated this point in *The Organization Man* (1957). The people who interested Whyte "are not the workers, nor are they white-collar people in the usual, clerk sense of the word. These people only work for The Organization. The ones I am talking about *belong* to it as well. They are the ones of our middle class who have left home, spiritually as well as physically, to take the vows of organization life, and it is they who are the mind and soul of our great self-perpetuating institutions" (p. 3).

Raised with visions of split-level houses, two-car garages, a wife and children, and summers at the lake, the executive aspirants of the fifties wanted *to work for somebody else* (unlike their fathers and grandfathers).

Today [1957] it is a very rare young man who will allow himself to talk [of becoming president of a corporation, or building a bridge, or making a million dollars], let alone think that way. . . . The life that he looks ahead to will be a life in which he is the only one of hundreds of similarly able people and in which they will all be moved hither and yon and subject to so many forces outside their control that only a fool would expect to hew to a set course. (Whyte, 1957, p. 144)

Whyte tied the practicality of youth in the fifties to the optimistic belief that the system operated in their best interests, that their goals and the organization's coincided. Far from wanting to change society, they actively sought ways to cooperate with the status quo.

Training and Socialization The demand for college and graduate degrees grew steadily in the fifties, so that by the time Whyte wrote *The Organization Man*, a Bachelor's degree had become a prerequisite for most white-collar jobs. With some exceptions, however, formal schooling did not (and does not) prepare men and women for specific occupational roles. Rather, college offers a general orientation to a wide range of careers—as well as experience with an organization, the university.

Recognizing this, most large corporations conduct formal training programs. "Come graduation," writes Whyte, seniors "do not go outside to a hostile world; they transfer." The locale shifts; the training continues, for at the same time that the colleges have been changing their curriculum to suit the corporation, the corporation has responded by setting up its own campuses and classrooms. By now the two have been so well molded that

Many corporations hold formal training programs to teach new employees "the company way." (Joe Brenneis/IBM)

it's difficult to tell where one leaves off and the other begins (Whyte, 1957, p. 69).[6]

Ostensibly, corporation training programs are designed to teach newcomers the requisite skills of a manager, an accountant, or an engineer. However, all have a hidden agenda, namely, teaching "the company way." Whyte summarizes the corporate litany as follows:

Be loyal to the company and the company will be loyal to you. After all, if you do a good job for the organization, it is only good sense for the organization to be good to you, because that will be best for everybody. There are a bunch of real people around here. Tell them what you think and they will respect you for it. (p. 143)

As training proceeds, recruits realize that they are being evaluated for the way they conduct themselves and get along with others, as well as for their skills. Ideally, when trainees move from the program to a formal position in the organization, they have been sufficiently indoctrinated to fit in smoothly. A recent article on I.B.M. supports Whyte's view of corporate indoctrination.

As [one observer noted] "I.B.M. is a religion, a very successful religion, more so than most. It really indoctrinates people. . . . Those who can't stand the discipline leave. . . . Ultimately, the vast majority of I.B.M.'ers stay put, giving the company a low turnover rate, a high *esprit de corps* and lots of people who will say they're "proud to be a small part of I.B.M." (Shapiro, 1973, p. 35)

---

[6] Whyte found that graduates seek companies with training programs because these programs offer continuity and security (they are comfortable in the role of learner), and also because they reason that a company that invests in their training will want to keep them.

Loss of Idealism and Role Conflict Once managers settle into an organization or professionals into a daily routine, they often find reality more complicated and disappointing than they had expected. Medical students, for example, typically enter school with the idea that all a doctor need do is make an accurate diagnosis, apply the correct treatment, and the problem will be solved—a decidedly Utopian view. In reality, there are many, many questions medical science cannot answer, and no doctor—no matter how conscientious or brilliant—can absorb all there is to know in the field. An important part of the physician's socialization is learning to cope with doubt and uncertainty (Fox, in Merton et al., 1957, pp. 207–41). The neophyte soldier, politician, teacher, or dental technician runs head on into contradictions between the organization's or profession's avowed creed and actual practices. These revelations are particularly disturbing to those who believe in the ideal goals and values, yet find they are routinely expected to engage in "illegitimate" activities (Caplow, 1964, pp. 199–200).

In some cases, conflicts are built into a job or role. Doctors, for example, are supposed to be self-critical but to act decisively when the situation requires it. They should be emotionally detached but never callous; respect their colleagues, but put medical ethics first (Merton et al., 1957, pp. 73–75). A military chaplain is expected to ease soldiers' anxieties about killing even though his religion teaches him to abhor violence.

Added to these problems is the fact that socialization into an organization does not occur in a vacuum. Taking on a new role often requires adjustments in other areas of a person's life. The college graduate who takes a job becomes financially independent of his or her parents, perhaps for the first time. A person who enters a demanding occupation, or is moved up the corporate ladder, or takes a job of questionable respectability, may have to neglect family obligations or give up previous friendships and associations.

TOTAL INSTITUTIONS

At first glance, prisoners, mental patients, monks, and soldiers may seem to have little in common besides their drab uniforms. But Erving Goffman, in *Asylums* (1961), argues that they all live in structurally similar institutions. A monk may take his orders voluntarily; he may wear a cassock instead of army drab or prison gray; he spends his hours in prayer or study, not drills or therapeutic arts and crafts. But the structure of his life in a monastery is much the same as a convict's in a prison, an inmate's in a mental hospital, a draftee's in the army—all of which are total institutions, or asylums in Goffman's terminology. Goffman defines an *asylum* as a place where "a large number of like-situated individuals, cut off from the wider society for an appreciable period of time, together lead an enclosed, formally administered round of life." In asylums, bureaucratic control is carried to its extreme.

Because they are extreme cases, asylums highlight certain features that are less visible in most other bureaucracies. First, the asylum's relation to inmates is *coercive*, even if they volunteered to join. All organizations are coercive to some degree: schools coerce though for fewer hours of the day, and corporations coerce employees to follow company rules. But in total institutions, people lose all control over and all responsibility for their lives.

Once admitted to a total institution, the process that Goffman calls *mortification* begins. Individuals are methodically stripped of the clothes, adornments, and personal possessions people use to define themselves in everyday life. In exchange, they receive standard, nondescript, and often ill-fitting attire—a uniform or hospital robe. They may be disfigured as well, by a military or prison haircut, for example. The spirit is mortified too. The institution designs exercises to break the will: people are forced to perform meaningless acts, to submit to arbitrary and unreasonable commands as well as to personal abuse (verbal or physical). Finally, they are deprived of privacy, both physical (through a debasing physical examination) and social (they must sleep, shower, and eat with a group). They are under constant surveillance,

These prisoners are experiencing "mortification"—the stripping away of personal privacy, possessions, and self that characterizes life in total institutions. (Bruno Barbey/Magnum)

with every moment of every day being planned by others. All of these procedures disabuse people of their feelings of self-worth and train them for deference. Individuals in total institutions are forced into a kind of regression; they are made to feel helpless and therefore dependent on the organization. At this point they are ready to be resocialized to a new role, one the organization designs.

People may react to their confinement in one of three main ways. In hospitals, some actively work to sabotage routines, but their rebellion is generally short-lived because the institution can isolate or drug the rebel. Moreover, the staff can withhold privileges, fail to communicate messages to a doctor, and the like. Second, inmates can simply withdraw, detaching themselves from their surroundings as much as possible. Finally, they can accept their subjugation, as a high

proportion do.[7] For those individuals the asylum becomes a home that they do not want to leave. Indeed, some actively seek out these curtailments of the self, so that mortification is complemented by self-mortification, restrictions by renunciations. Attached to the simple, predictable routines and the security of the asylum, they resist being discharged and, if this fails, many people find ways to be readmitted.[8]

Goffman attributes the extremes of total institutions to the low status accorded inmates, to the fact that inmates greatly outnumber staff, and to the tendency for means to become ends for the staff. Finishing the day's work becomes more important than meeting the institution's goals, which are themselves only poorly defined. "Keeping the lid on" mental hospitals, prisons, and the military occupies hundreds of thousands of bureaucracies.

BEYOND BUREAUCRACY

Cracks in prison walls make headlines. On September 13, 1971, National Guardsmen and state police moved into New York's Attica prison. When the tear gas and smoke cleared, 45 people had been killed (11 of them guards who had been held hostage) and more than 150 were wounded—by "peace officers," not by inmates. So ended one of the most highly publicized prison riots of recent times. But "Attica fever" spread in the following months. Prisoners in Vermont went on strike; a dozen or more were seriously

wounded in a riot at an Illinois penitentiary; convicted soldiers burned down the disciplinary barracks at the army's Fort George in Georgia.

Prison riots are nothing new. What makes these uprisings different is that the prisoners of the seventies are younger, better educated, and more politically aware than prisoners were in the past. Well-versed in unfair bail procedures, interminable delays in court, inadequate legal counsel, arbitrary and ambiguous sentencing, and the impossibility of rehabilitating themselves in a brutal and perverse atmosphere, they see themselves as political prisoners. They rebel against enforced idleness in jails. They demand not only better living conditions and an end to brutality, but the right to due process *in* prison, the right to legal counsel in probation hearings, the right to practice their religion (which is often denied Muslims), and the abolition of mail censorship—all basic constitutional rights (Chaneles, 1973). (We will discuss prison conditions further in chapter 12.)

The prison riots are symptomatic of widespread changes, not only in asylums but in many other bureaucratic organizations. To cite just a few examples: approximately 100,000 employees of 700–1,000 firms are working four days a week instead of five (*U.S. News and World Report*, March 20, 1972, p. 82); the Hewlitt-Packard Company, among others, allows workers to choose their own hours. In the words of one forty-eight-year-old employee, "It makes me feel that the company thinks I'm intelligent enough to keep my own hours. The company is treating us like adults" (*The Wall Street Journal*, July 12, 1973, pp. 1, 25). The new McDonald's headquarters outside of Chicago boasts a soundproof "think tank" with bean bag chairs and adjustable work surfaces that any employee can reserve, and a meditation room

---

[7] A full 40 percent in one hospital, according to Ailon Shiloh (in Wallace, 1971, pp. 8–23).

[8] This phenomenon is widespread enough to warrant a psychiatric term, *institutional transferrence*.

Any McDonald employee can use the company "think tank" simply by reserving it in advance. The tank, because it is open to all, helps to minimize the corporate hierarchy, and provides a relaxing atmosphere for thinking. (Associated Space Designs for McDonald's/Balthazar Korab)

complete with suedelike walls, a hi-fi system, and a waterbed. There are no walls and doors to emphasize hierarchical divisions on the three floors the company occupies (*Time*, February 28, 1972).

Even the military is changing. The "Now Navy" allows well-kept beards, moustaches, and longer hair. In September 1973 West Point published a new manual that stresses *self*-discipline more than rules. The hated practice of confining cadets to their rooms during free hours has been abolished. These innovations reflect changes in both the nature of work and the nature of the work*er*. (In

chapter 19 we will discuss modern work and workers in greater depth.)

The Future of Bureaucracy

Traditional bureaucratic organizations are based on what Douglas McGregor (in Bennis, 1970) called the X Theory of human behavior:

1. The average human being dislikes work and will avoid it if he [or she] can.
2. Therefore, most people must be coerced, controlled, directed, and threatened with punishment if they are to work adequately.
3. The average human being prefers to be directed, wishes to avoid responsibility, has relatively little ambition and wants security above all things. (in Bennis, 1970, p. 30)

Social research has shown, time and time again, that these assumptions are false. Over-control merely exacerbates tensions between management and workers (and between workers and clients), particularly in an "educated society." In some urban areas today, nearly half of all high-school graduates attend college (Bennis, p. 168). The average worker is better educated and more self-directing than his or her parents were, and will not accept X Theory treatment (as the automobile workers at Lordstown and other factories are proving).

In addition, advanced technology is bringing increasing numbers of professionals into businesses and government, professionals whose very expertise places them somewhat beyond the control of their superiors in the hierarchy. "Professionals," writes Warren Bennis, "are notoriously 'disloyal' to organization demands" (1970, p. 177). Professionals tend to see their careers in terms of advancing in their field, not in the organization. Their "most important incentive . . . is to 'make it' professionally," wherever they work. And increasingly, professionals and experts are coming to dominate business and government as well as universities.

Looking to the future, Bennis forecasts major changes in the structure of organizations. Fixed departments and positions or offices will give way to temporary, problem-oriented systems, such as a task force created to attack a specific issue and dissolved when the job is done. Executives will become coordinators and diplomats whose main job will be "producing conditions where people and ideas and resources can be seeded, nurtured, and integrated" (Bennis, p. 184). To supervise professionals and deploy brainpower effectively, executives will have to understand the system and how their own actions affect others. Finally, organizations will become more flexible and humanistic as they begin to recognize workers' desires for involvement, participation, and autonomy on the job (Bennis, p. 12).

Underlying these changes are insights about human behavior which McGregor called the Y Theory. It suggests that:

1. Work is a natural human activity.
2. [People] will work toward goals to which they are committed without coercion, and that commitment follows from the opportunity to realize their own potentialities.
3. Most [people] have a higher level of intellectual capacity than the usual conditions of modern industrial life reveal. (in Bennis, 1970, p. 30)

Many of the largest corporations—I.B.M., Exxon, Xerox, to name a few—are recognizing these qualities and putting them into practice. The result is a different kind of organization, one where executives are trained in several technical areas to gain wider knowledge, where the hierarchy is loose and decisions are made by group discussion, and where employee relations are more personal. These, of course, reverse the characteristics of the classic bureaucratic model we began with, which Max Weber described in the 1920s. Since then, social and economic changes, as well as an increased number of professionals in business and government, have called for revisions in bureaucratic structure to meet the needs both of modern managers and their employees.

summary

An *organization* is a group that has been consciously designed to achieve certain goals. Organizations differ from other groups in their commitment to specific objectives and in their formal structure. Once established, organizations tend to become self-perpetuating; members are replaceable. Organizations can be classified according to their *function* (Parsons); whether they are *voluntary, coercive,* or *utilitarian* (Etzioni); or by *who benefits* from them (Blau and Scott). Whatever their orientation, all organizations have both a formal structure and an informal structure of personal relationships and improvised rules and procedures.

Although bureaucracies are not a modern invention, the "Age of Bureaucracy" began when Western nations started to industrialize in the nineteenth century. Bureaucracy represents the application of mechanical principles to the organization of work. Max Weber identified the distinguishing characteristics of bureaucracy as (1) specialization (the division of production into small tasks); (2) a hierarchy of offices (with each individual being responsible to the person above him or her and for the people below him or her, and authority vested in the office, not in the individual); (3) adherence to explicit rules and regulations; (4) impartiality (because emotions impede efficiency); and (5) technical competence (paying people for their work, and awarding raises and promotions on the basis of achievement and seniority). Weber's description is a model or ideal type; in reality, the completely bureaucratic organization does not exist.

In most organizations the task of motivating people to fill their roles falls to a small number of supervisors or bosses who act as decision-makers, administrators, disciplinarians, and representatives. Gouldner's study of a gypsum plant describes two different styles of leadership, democratic and authoritarian.

The actual operation of an organization is worked out in negotiations between bosses who want to control workers, and workers who do not want to be controlled. The description offered by Strauss of negotiations between various groups in mental hospitals illustrates that rules, even in formal organizations, are human arrangements.

Learning a new job means learning both the written and the unwritten rules. From the boss's point of view, socialization into the job entails asserting power and breaking in recruits; from the recruit's point of view, socialization involves learning the ropes and resisting power. Socialization into an organization builds on the desires and expectations of new members, as Whyte showed in *The Organization Man.* White-collar hopefuls in effect transfer from college to work, where they undergo an initiation into the company way. Loss of idealism and role conflicts are serious problems in some occupations that rely on practices that violate an individual's creeds, present conflicting demands, or force people to neglect other social obligations. Goffman coined the term *total institutions* for jails, mental hospitals, monasteries, and other organizations that socialize people into a total round of life, submerging their private selves and substituting an organizational self.

Prison riots, law suits for civil rights in mental hospitals, the decline in monasteries, and the demand for autonomy in company offices suggest that people are beginning to rebel against bureaucratic control. As the X Theory of human behavior (that people dislike work, will only work if forced to, and prefer being directed) falls into disrepute, some organizations are experimenting with more flexible work arrangements. In part, organizations are changing because the number and importance of professionals in business and government is increasing.

glossary

anticipatory socialization The values and expectations a person develops prior to taking on a new role, through identification and imagination.

bureaucracy An organization consisting of interrelated parts with separate functions, designed to perform some kind of work.

business organizations Organizations designed to maximize profit and efficiency, and run for the benefit of the owners (Blau and Scott).

client-centered organizations Organizations, such as hospitals and schools, designed to serve a particular group of people (Blau and Scott).

coercive organizations Organizations people are forced to join (Etzioni).

commonweal organizations Organizations run for the benefit of the public-at-large and controlled by the public, at least in principle (Blau and Scott).

formal structure In an organization, the elements of formal structure include the explicit rules that define each person's duties, organizational charts describing relationships among members, and a system of rewards and punishments.

informal structure In an organization, the informal structure consists of the procedures that enable people to solve problems not covered by the formal regulations, to eliminate unpleasant or unnecessary work, and to protect their own interests.

mortification The process of stripping a person of his or her civilian identity and physical integrity, in preparation for indoctrination into a new role (Goffman).

mutual benefit organizations Organizations run by and for the members (Blau and Scott).

negotiated order The process by which employees and managers together resolve work-related problems.

organization A group consciously designed to seek specific goals.

Parkinson's Law Parkinson formulated his law to explain why bureaucratic employees often appear busier than they need be: "Work expands to fill the time."

Peter Principle Attempting to account for the incompetence that characterizes many bureaucratic employees, Peter and Hull suggest that, "in a hierarchy, every employee tends to rise to his [or her] level of incompetence."

ritualism Following rules and regulations without regard for the original goals or the consequences of one's actions (Merton).

total institutions Organizations that take nearly complete control of inmates' lives, depriving them of responsibility, privacy, and their civilian identities (Goffman).

utilitarian organizations Organizations people join for practical reasons, because they expect to benefit personally (Etzioni).

voluntary organizations Organizations people join because they support the organization's goals and values (Etzioni).

references

Warren G. Bennis, ed., *American Bureaucracy*, Chicago: Aldine, 1970.

Peter M. Blau, *The Dynamics of Bureaucracy*, Chicago: University of Chicago Press, 1955.

—— and Marshall W. Meyer, *Bureaucracy in Modern Society*, 2nd ed., New York: Random House, 1971.

—— and W. Richard Scott, *Formal Organizations: A Comparative Approach*, London: Routledge & Kegan Paul, 1963.

Theodore Caplow, *Principles of Organizations*, New York: Harcourt Brace Jovanovich, 1964.

Sol Chaneles, *The Open Prison*, New York: Dial, 1973.

Harry Cohen, "Bureaucratic Flexibility: Some Comments on Robert Merton's 'Bureaucratic Structure and Personality,'" *British Journal of Sociology*. vol. 21, no. 4 (December 1970): 390–99.

Amitai Etzioni, *A Comparative Analysis of Complex Organizations*, New York: Free Press, 1961.

A. Ernest Fitzgerald, *The High Priests of Waste*, New York: Norton, 1972.

H. H. Gerth and C. Wright Mills, eds., *From Max Weber: Essays in Sociology*, Oxford: Oxford University Press, 1946.

Siegfried Giedion, *Mechanization Takes Command*, Oxford: Oxford University Press, 1948.

Erving Goffman, *Asylums*, Garden City, N.Y.: Doubleday, 1961.

William J. Goode, "The Protection of the Inept," *American Sociological Review*, vol. 32, no. 1 (February 1967): 5–19.

Alvin Gouldner, *Studies in Leadership*, New York: Harper & Row, 1950.

——, *Patterns of Industrial Bureaucracy: A Case Study of Modern Factory Administration*, Glencoe, Ill.: Free Press, 1954.

Richard H. Hall, "The Concept of Bureaucracy: An Empirical Assessment," *American Journal of Sociology*, vol. 69 (1963–1964): 32–40.

Leo Marx, *The Machine in the Garden*, New York: Oxford University Press, 1964.

Douglas McGregor in Abraham Maslow, "The Superior Person," in Warren Bennis, 1970.

Robert Merton, *Social Theory and Social Structure*, Glencoe, Ill.: Free Press, 1968.

———, George G. Reader, and Patricia L. Kendal, *The Student-Physician*, Cambridge, Mass.: Harvard University Press, 1957.

Robert Michels, *Political Parties*, New York: Hearst, 1915.

Paul E. Mott et al., eds., *From Farm to Factory: The Development of Modern Society*, Columbus, Ohio: Merrill, 1973.

Ralph Nader, *Unsafe at Any Speed: The Designed-In Dangers of the American Automobile*, rev. ed., New York: Grossman, 1972.

C. Northcote Parkinson, *Parkinson's Law*, Boston: Houghton-Mifflin, 1957.

Talcott Parsons, *Structure and Process in Modern Societies*, New York: Free Press, 1960.

Laurence F. Peter and Raymond Hull, *The Peter Principle*, New York: Morrow, 1969.

Harvey D. Shapiro, "I.B.M. and the Dwarfs: Think, Sell, Grow," *The New York Times Magazine* (July 29, 1973): 10ff.

Anselm Strauss et al., *Psychiatric Ideologies and Institutions*, New York: Free Press, 1964.

Stanley H. Udy, Jr., "'Bureaucracy' and 'Rationality' in Weber's Organizational Theory: An Empirical Study," *American Sociological Review*, vol. 24 (December 1959): 791–95.

Samuel E. Wallace, ed., *Total Institutions*, Chicago: Transaction/Aldine, 1971.

Max Weber, *The Theory of Social and Economic Organization*, trans. by Talcott Parsons, Glencoe, Ill.: Free Press, 1947.

William Foote Whyte, *The Organization Man*, Garden City, N.Y.: Doubleday, 1957.

for further study

The study of organizations and their internal structures is one of the most developed areas in all of sociology. A recent and excellent overview of that work is found in Richard H. Hall's book *Organizations: Structure and Process* (Englewood Cliffs, N.J.: Prentice-Hall, 1972). A good overview of work on bureaucracies is Peter M. Blau and Marshall W. Meyer, *Bureaucracy in Modern Society*, 2nd edition (New York: Random House, 1971). As a general reference, see also James G. March, ed., *Handbook of Organizations* (Skokie, Ill.: Rand McNally, 1965).

The Organizational Society.   Have organizations become so pervasive that this is an organizational society? This question is addressed in various ways by Robert Presthus, *The Organizational Society* (New York: Vintage Books, 1962); A. Ernest Fitzgerald, *The High Priests of Waste* (New York: W. W. Norton, 1972); Maurice Zeitlin, ed., *American Society, Inc.* (Chicago: Markham, 1970). Also see the appropriate readings in *Crisis in American Institutions*, 2nd edition, Jerome H. Skolnick and Elliott Currie, eds. (Boston: Little, Brown, 1973). See especially the essay by Heilbroner.

Changing Organizations.   While organizations reach into virtually every aspect of our lives, life within some organizations is loosening up in response to employees' demands that their work be interesting and personally rewarding. The "open" organization is a subject periodically written about in *Fortune, Forbes, The Wall Street Journal,* and the scholarly business reviews of major universities like Harvard, Chicago, and Stanford. See also *The Temporary Society* by Warren G. Bennis and Philip E. Slater (New York: Harper & Row, 1968) and *American Bureaucracy* by Warren G. Bennis, ed. (Chicago: Transaction/Aldine, 1970).

Total Institutions.   The classic statement on how total institutions work and affect both staff and inmates is *Asylums*, by Erving Goffman (New York: Doubleday, 1961). A sampling of work on the subject is found in *Total Institutions*, edited by Samuel E. Wallace (Chicago: Transaction/Aldine, 1971).

On the other hand, inmates may "work the system," something discussed by Goffman but more fully examined by B. M. Braginsky et al. in *Methods of Madness: The Mental Hospital as a Last Resort* (New York: Holt, Rinehart & Winston, 1969). The authors have persuasive evidence that at least in one case the inmates worked the asylums more than the asylum oppressed the inmates.

St. Vitus Dance, one of the most fascinating episodes of medieval history, apparently started in Germany in 1374 (when the Black Death had begun to subside) and spread from there to France, Belgium, and the Netherlands in a matter of months. The "symptoms" were much the same from one place to the next. A strange twitching would seize victims, compelling one after another to dance in wild and delirious ways. Foaming at the mouth, they would hurl their bodies two, even three feet into the air. Some became self-destructive, crashing their heads against walls and plummeting into rivers; some became violent toward others. Some removed their clothes and performed a variety of obscene gestures. Often the fits would last for hours, until the afflicted individual collapsed into what appeared to be a coma. After being revived they told of rivers of blood, the heavens opening, and other strange visions. The dancing mania disappeared as mysteriously as it began, although similar epidemics were reported shortly thereafter in Abyssinia and in Italy, where the malady was attributed to the bite of a tarantula (Hecker, 1844).

One needn't go so far back in history to find other episodes of mass hysteria. On May 11, 1973, seventy children in Berry, Alabama were hospitalized for vomiting, burning eyes and throats, numbness, chest pains, and general weakness. Twenty of them were unconscious when they reached the hospital. After days of testing and observation, a team of specialists concluded there was

COLLECTIVE
BEHAVIOR

nothing physically wrong with the children (*The Wall Street Journal*, November 16, 1973, pp. 1, 31).

Mass hysteria is not the only form of seemingly inexplicable collective behavior. Why do ordinarily law-abiding citizens participate in lynchings, join the burning and looting of riots, lose all semblance of self-control at revival meetings and rock concerts? In short, why do people behave differently in crowds than they do in small numbers? How can we explain the rise, fall, and subsequent resurrection of feminism in this country? Why did Richard Nixon's standing with the American public change so drastically during his second term in office?

Both psychologists and sociologists have long pondered the riddle of mass hysteria, fads, rumors, mobs, the rise of social movements, and the fluctuations of public opinion. While psychologists have focused on the question of why individuals become caught up in the mood of the crowd, sociologists have concentrated on the social conditions that seem to precipitate collective behavior and on the social consequences of such behavior. Neither discipline has entirely solved this mystery, but we have come a long way from the Italians who believed that spider bites caused St. Vitus Dance.

In this chapter we will look at various forms of crowd behavior (including mass hysteria, panics, and riots), social movements (and the Women's Movement in particular), and public opinion as related forms of collective behavior.

COLLECTIVE BEHAVIOR: AN OVERVIEW

Collective behavior refers to the actions of relatively temporary, unstructured groups of people who are focused on and reacting to the same event, information, person, group, or custom. This definition includes a wide range of collective activities: crowds, riots, panics, fashions, crazes, social movements, and public opinion. What do these varied phenomena have in common? They develop more or less spontaneously and spread as if by contagion. Recall, for example, how "impeachment fever" broke out in early 1974 and how each new poll showed that more and more Americans had been "infected" with doubt regarding President Nixon. It is this susceptibility to behavioral contagion that makes rock audiences different from history classes, protest movements different from established political parties.

Preconditions of Collective Behavior

Collective behavior seems to defy explanations. Panics, such as the run on the banks that drove many to bankruptcy and precipitated the Great Depression in 1929, appear totally illogical and unpredictable. Fads, such as gold-fish swallowing in the 1920s or streaking in the 1970s, crop up spontaneously and spread of their own momentum. Or do they? Sociologists think not. Despite the impression of formlessness, there are patterns to collective behavior. It does not simply erupt, any time, any place.

Some forms of collective behavior develop around culturally significant symbols (such as wealth in a capitalist society, where money is a primary measure of self-worth, or the church and clergy in religious societies) and only under certain conditions. If a society encourages people to value things that may suddenly slip out of their hands, changes in the availability of those things is conducive to collective behavior. A run on the banks, for example, will only happen in societies where money is highly valued. Obstacles to desired goals and to expressions of significant values may also generate collective behavior. The 1960s riots in Watts and Detroit, for example, were in part expressions of frustration by blacks who were denied access to the "good life" in America. Unanticipated events, such as a terrorist attack or fire, may have the same effect. Although they do not always generate collective behavior, one or more of these preconditions is always present when collective behavior does occur. Below we will consider three preconditions for collective behavior in greater depth.

Structural Conduciveness The theory of structural conduciveness suggests that preconditions for collective behavior are built into a society's social structure. For example, the possibility of financial panics is inherent in open, fluid money economies, where people are able to speculate and to acquire or dispose of assets on short notice, and where wealth is considered personally and socially important. Such panics cannot occur in traditional societies, where property is acquired only through inheritance and marriage. Thus money economies are conducive to financial panics; traditional societies are not (Smelser, 1962, p. 15). Similarly, the concentration of minorities in urban ghettos, where unemployment is high and housing substandard so that people spend much of their time outdoors, is conducive to other forms of collective behavior: social movements as well as "civic disorders." But the potential for collective behavior alone does not explain its occurrence.

The Unanticipated Event Sudden, unexpected events may create a state of *normlessness*: people do not know what they can or should do, and there are no cultural guidelines to direct them. For example, when a tornado struck Judsonia, Arkansas and surrounding towns in 1952, people had only a minute's warning. One moment the town was standing and people were heading home for dinner. The next moment 600 buildings had been leveled and 800 severely damaged; 46 people had been killed and more than 600 injured; electricity, telephone, and gas lines had been wiped out; and the nearest radio tower stopped broadcasting. The worst problem for police in the hours that followed was traffic: hundreds of cars poured into the area with people seeking relatives, offering help, or perhaps just "sightseeing," mindless of the fact that they were blocking roads needed for emergency vehicles (Barton, 1969, pp. 3–10).

When people are unexpectedly deprived of the world they take for granted, when catastrophic events such as a tornado throw their ability to cope into doubt, *doing* becomes more important than thinking and planning. There is a need to define the situation, to restructure the social world, to reaffirm one's sense of mastery—in action (Turner and Killian, 1972, pp. 72–73).

Unanticipated, unsettling incidents may precipitate mobs, riots, panics, and social movements. The Free Speech Movement at Berkeley, forerunner of a decade of student activism, began when university officials suddenly announced that the strip of land outside the gates that students had traditionally used to raise funds and recruit members for political activities belonged to the university and was subject to its rules (Milgram and Toch, 1969, pp. 556–57). As often as not, however, the precipitating incident—the point of confrontation—is only the tip of the iceberg.

Frustrated Social Concerns The Free Speech Movement of 1964—a semester of sit-ins, strikes, and rallies, some attracting as many as 7,000, during which time students occupied the central administration building and 200 police were moved onto the campus—clearly illustrates the role frustrated social concerns play in collective behavior. Many of the Berkeley activists had participated in the Civil Rights Movement during the previous summer, working for the rights of black Americans in the deep South, only to return to a campus where they themselves were denied such basic rights as peaceful assembly and free speech. Students were not represented in the policy-making councils of the university, so they could not register complaints there. Nor could they appeal to a higher authority, such as the law: a campus is private property, and the trustees had the legal right to say how the land could or could not be used. In short, there were no established, institutionalized channels through which students could express political concerns.

Frustrated social concerns, unanticipated events, and built-in sources of instability (structural conduciveness) do not automatically give rise to collective behavior. Rather they create a sense of disorientation. Existing channels seem inadequate; consciously and unconsciously people seek to define their unrest, to determine what is happening, who or what is responsible, how they should act. This urge to act, in the absence of clear cultural guidelines, sets the stage for collective behavior.

CROWDS

Crowds are temporary collections of people, gathered around a person or event, who are conscious of and influenced by one another's presence. The primary difference between crowds and other social groups is that crowds are ephemeral; they lack a past and future, and are relatively unstructured. For example, the people who collect around an accident will stop interacting as soon as they leave. In his classic essay "Collective Behavior," first published in 1939, sociologist Herbert Blumer labeled such spontaneous congregations *casual crowds*, whose "members come and go, giving but temporary attention to the object which has awakened the interest of the crowd, and entering into only feeble association with one another" (p. 178). Blumer also identified three other types of crowds: conventional, expressive, and acting crowds. Passengers on a plane, shoppers in a store, the audience at a concert are usually *conventional crowds*. These people are gathered for a specific purpose and behave according to established norms. For example, cheering and booing are expected at a football game, but would be considered extremely bad form at a concert of classical music or at a funeral. People shout "bravo" at appropriate moments at the opera; they applaud (but do not cheer) at tennis matches. There is relatively little interaction in a conventional crowd, where members individually pursue a common goal, a destination, a bargain, entertainment.

In expressive crowds, such as the one that gathered at the Woodstock rock festival, the focus is on individual, subjective experience. Interestingly, part of the reason for the peaceful behavior of the Woodstock crowd was that conventional norms were sometimes suspended. (Jason Laure/Rapho Guillumette)

The people at rock festivals, revival meetings, and carnivals (such as those held in New Orleans and in South American cities) are *expressive crowds*: members may behave in ways they would not consider in other settings. The focus is on individual subjective experience, on people letting go. The crowd gives license to loss of self-control, but chaos need not result. The legendary Woodstock Music and Art Fair, held in New York's Catskill Mountains in August 1969, is an example of this type of crowd. An impressive array of rock stars drew over 300,000 young people to the farm where the festival was held. Mechanically, everything went wrong: traffic was stalled for miles; food and water were scarce; sanitation facilities were inadequate. There were "bad trips" on LSD, and hardly anyone got close enough to the stage to hear the music they had come for. Woodstock became a legend because of the peaceful, cooperative way the crowd behaved under these adverse circumstances. For most, being part of the "Woodstock nation" was an exhilarating communal experience. As one young woman told a reporter, "I just had the feeling that, wow, there are so many of us, we really have power. I'd always felt like such a minority. But I thought, wow, we're a majority—it felt like that. I felt, here's the answer to anyone who calls us deviates" (in Turner and Killian, 1972, p. 148). Woodstock would not have been the same if conventional norms had been strictly observed. It would not have been so peaceful if the promoters had attempted to bar people who had not bought tickets (the majority), or if police had made arrests for drugs, which were being hawked openly like hot dogs and beer at a ball game.

An *acting crowd* is an excited, volatile collection of people who are focused on a controversial event that provokes their indignation, anger, and desire to act—for example, a rape or an incident of police brutality, real or imagined. The difference between an expressive crowd and an acting crowd is that the latter is angry and purposeful. The difference between an acting crowd and a conventional crowd is that the members of an acting crowd are aroused to the point where established norms carry little weight.

[The acting crowd] has no heritage or accumulation of tradition to guide its activity; it has no conventions, established expectations, or rules. It lacks other important marks of society such as an established social organization, an established division of labor, a structure of established roles, a recognized leadership, a set of norms, a set of moral regulations, an awareness of its own identity, or a recognized "we-consciousness." Instead of acting, then, on the basis of established rule, it acts on the basis of aroused impulse. (Blumer, in Lee, 1951, p. 180)

PANIC

On November 28, 1942, almost 500 people died in a fire that swept through a Boston night club—largely because the crowd panicked and jammed the revolving front door, which was one of only three exits for the audience of 1,000 or more. Panics occur when people believe that the only way to deal with an imminent threat (physical or psychological) is to flee, and when communication breaks down so that people in the rear of the crowd do not see (or do not believe) that escape routes are blocked, and press forward. Thus panic results from fear, entrapment, and disorganization: people become preoccupied with their own personal safety and behave in an individualistic way that actually endangers themselves and others.

SOURCE: Ralph H. Turner and Lewis M. Killian, *Collective Behavior*, 2nd ed. (Englewood Cliffs, N. J.: Prentice-Hall, 1972), pp. 121–22.

In many ways, these three types overlap. For example, expressive behavior (jumping, shouting) is conventional at sporting events, and fans may throw things at the referees, becoming what Blumer would call an acting crowd. Nevertheless, as ideal types, Blumer's categories are useful in highlighting some of the characteristics of crowds that distinguish them from other social groups.

Mobs

A *mob* is a crowd whose members are emotionally aroused and are engaged in or are ready to engage in violence (Hoult, 1969, p. 206). In short, an acting crowd is a mob. For centuries people in power have had night-mares about the masses rising up in a destructive orgy. Mob action was common in eighteenth- and nineteenth- century Europe: in towns and country, throngs of armed men and women took over markets and ware-houses, demanding rollbacks in prices and sometimes appropriating goods. In England angry bands of craftsmen burned factories and destroyed the machines that threatened their livelihood. On July 14, 1789, Parisians stormed the ancient Bastille in the most famous confrontation of the French Revolution. Violent, unruly crowds have also figured importantly in American history. The nineteenth century was marked by farmers' revolts, miners' rebellions, bloody battles between unions and police, lynchings, and urban riots. The Civil War Draft Riot of 1863, which raged

for four days, was probably one of the worst riots in this country's history. Mobs of young New Yorkers roamed the city's streets, burning, looting, sniping, and lynching, while police stood by. Most of the violence was directed against blacks, who came to symbolize a distant war that many urban Northerners did not want to fight. This outbreak became a

Mobs are emotionally aroused crowds, ready to engage in violence. During the Civil War white rioters in New York City battled with the military, protesting against conscription. A little over one-hundred years later, black rioters in Detroit destroyed much of the city's black neighborhood. For many of the participants, violence expressed frustration over discrimination and enduring poverty. (Left, Culver Pictures; Right, Wide World Photos)

prototype for urban riots in the first half of this century, which are best described as interracial wars, whites fighting blacks, as police did little. The civil disorders of the 1960s, however, were different. The following account of the Detroit riot of July 1967 is based on the *Report of the National Advisory Commission on Civil Disorders*, appointed by President Johnson. Although the *Report* falls short of completely explaining the disorders, it does portray the dimensions of the Detroit uprising in concrete terms. For further explanations of the 1960s riots, see the box on page 294.

Riot in Detroit In the summer of 1967, black ghettos in twenty-three cities exploded. Many white Americans who saw Detroit burn on

URBAN RIOTS OF THE 1960s: WHAT RESEARCHERS FOUND

By the time the urban riots of the 1960s were over "the ghettos were in shambles and white society was in shock" (Fogelson, 1970, p. 4). How and why did it happen? In the aftermath of the riots, several sociologists sought answers to this question.

Surely there is nothing new about ghetto resentment against police insensitivity. It has been expressed openly for decades (Yablonsky, 1962). Nor is there anything new about outbreaks of public disorder (Waskow, 1966). But there was something new about the riots of the 1960s: when looting took place during this decade, it was the looting of durable, material goods—the symbols of economic plenty that have been consistently out of the reach of most ghetto dwellers. When arson took place it was directed against visible, present oppressors (mostly white merchants who sold cheap goods at high prices) and not against symbols of vague, distant oppressors. In fact, as one summary article points out, the riots were far from acausal, they were "a means of achieving desired goals when more legitimate means were unavailable or had met with failure" (Allen, 1970, p. 3). (We will discuss this theory further in chapter 12.)

The aftermath of the riots would certainly support the notion that they were effective means of protest. They brought results that decades of peaceful protest had failed to bring. As one observer put it:"Reporters and cameramen rushed into ghettos elected and appointed officials followed behind; sociologists and other scholars arrived shortly after. The President established a riot commission; so did the governors" (Fogelson, 1970, p. 146).

To explain exactly why each riot occurred exactly when it did is beyond the capabilities of social science. But we do know something about the general features of the 1960s riots. They were not instigated or carried out by criminals; they were generally directed at property, not at people; their aim was to benefit from, not overthrow, the American social system (Allen, 1970). In short, they were "spontaneous protests against unjust social conditions" (Campbell and Schuman, 1968).

In trying to locate the causes and conditions of the 1960s riots, social scientists have taken several approaches. They have looked at the actual interactions between police and rioters to see how the violence escalated (Marx, 1970). They have carefully explored the characteristics of individual rioters (Sears and McConahay, 1969; Caplan, 1970) and for the most part they have found that "rioters did not differ from nonrioters in absolute income; rioters were not the hard-core unemployed; rioters were better integrated than nonrioters into the community, socially and politically; and rioters were not recent immigrants to the city" (Allen, 1970, p. 9). A third set of explorations has been concerned with the social and economic causes for the riots (Lieberson and Silverman, 1965; Fogelson, 1970). These studies have vividly documented the deprivation, hardships, and injustice to which ghetto dwellers are subjected.

their television screens were not only horrified, but baffled. Why were blacks rioting *after* Congress had passed the Civil Rights Acts? "What do they want?" The answer is that Civil Rights legislation had raised hopes but delivered little in the way of concrete improvements. Blacks, particularly in large northern cities, felt they had been cheated and misled. Continuing discrimination in a society that values equality generates rebellion and resentment. Equally important, the Civil Rights and Black Power movements had placed the blame for economic and social inequality squarely on the shoulders of the white institutions that created and maintained the ghetto and on the white society that had silently condoned it for generations.

The National Advisory Commission on Civil Disorders found that 70 percent of the rioters believed they deserved better jobs and blamed their problems on racism, not on lack of training, ability, or ambition. They were proud of their race, believing blacks to be superior to whites in some respects. They mistrusted both white politics and politicians, and they were extremely hostile toward whites in general and toward middle-class blacks who accommodated themselves to white society in particular. They hated the police. But they did not have organizations through which they might realize their ambitions (such as the political machines the Irish had established when they were trying to join the mainstream of American life).

Still, crowds do not become mobs unless they develop a generalized belief about who or what is responsible for their problems (Smelser, 1962). Anger must be focused; the energies and hostility of a crowd must be directed toward a target. In the ghetto, stores that tantalize with the goods America seems to promise, and police, who harrass and sometimes abuse residents but seem unable to protect them, are ever-present reminders of white dominance. Given the high visibility of police, the widespread anger and frustration, and the feeling that there was little to lose, Detroit was a time bomb that July. All that was needed was a spark to set it off. The police provided this spark.

On Saturday night, July 22, the Detroit vice squad conducted raids on five social clubs in the 12th Street area that were suspected of running gambling tables and selling liquor after hours. This mass arrest was the precipitating incident. A month earlier a prostitute on the block had been murdered by a member of the vice squad, or so neighbors believed, but another man was arrested. At about the same time, a gang of white youths shouting "Niggers keep out of Rouge Park"

had killed a twenty-seven-year-old black veteran, in the presence of his pregnant wife. Newspapers had not even reported the slaying. By the time police hauled the last of the party-goers away Sunday morning, July 23, a crowd of 200 had gathered on the street. A bottle hurled from the crowd crashed through the window of the last retreating patrol car. That was the beginning.

By 8 A.M., when police first tried to clear the area, the crowd on 12th Street had grown to 3,000. Outnumbered, police withdrew, trying only to keep the crowd within a six-block-square area. Emboldened by the police retreat, groups of two and three began breaking into liquor, appliance, and grocery stores. Others followed, and for a few hours the street became a carnival. People were laughing, joking, and generally enjoying themselves. When a black congressman tried to speak, he was met by hecklers: "Whose side are you on, man?" At about noon police reinforcements moved quietly into surrounding streets. Soon rumors were spreading: a black man, it was said, had been bayonetted just blocks away.

The crowd's mood shifted from revelry to anger; people began stoning police and setting fire to stores. Finally, at 4:30 Sunday afternoon, exhausted firemen abandoned the area. At this point, Mayor Cavanaugh proclaimed a 9 P.M. to 5 A.M. curfew and summoned the National Guard.

Although 800 state police and 1,200 National Guardsmen had moved into the neighborhood by 2 A.M. Monday morning, July 24, scattered looting and fire bombing continued. At noon President Johnson authorized sending in federal troops. The number of soldiers in Detroit climbed to 5,000 by midnight. Many had traveled over 200 miles and gone without sleep for thirty hours; relatively few had been trained to handle riots. After hasty, on-the-spot instruction in mob control, troops were deployed in small groups.

What they found, however, was dark, empty streets—not mobs.

As the number of fires and lootings declined, reports of snipers increased (reaching a peak of 534 reports on Wednesday, July 26), creating panic and confusion. Indeed, communication was so poor that an army officer's order for all troops to unload their weapons went unnoticed. The following incident was typical.

A radio report of snipers brought several patrols of guardsmen and police to a dark intersection. In the confusion, a soldier accidentally fired his gun. Within seconds everyone rushed for cover. An officer yelled, "What's happening?" "Snipers." Without authorization someone began firing at a building; a nearby tank drove in and sprayed the building with .50-caliber tracer bullets. When police finally searched the building, they found it empty.

By Wednesday police were breaking into homes on the slightest excuse and arresting anyone found to have a weapon. Although it would be exaggerating to say the police rioted in Detroit, they were not acting in a routine manner. There is nothing routine about a riot; both the rioters and the police were caught up in collective behavior.

Before the end of the week, 7,200 people had been arrested. Some were held on buses for thirty hours or more; others spent days in an underground garage without toilets. Forty-three people had been killed, thirty or more by police and soldiers, two by store owners, two or possibly three by rioters. This number included one National Guardsman, one fireman, and one policeman (killed accidentally by a fellow officer). Thirty-three of the victims were black, ten white. Property damage was estimated at $22 million.

Explanations of Crowd Behavior

Why did rioting break out in Detroit? Like many people, President Johnson believed in the "riff-raff theory"—that only criminal types (hoodlums, drifters, bums, drug addicts) would participate in riots. He and others suspected that a hard core of agitators had incited violence in Detroit and other cities, and that the vast majority of ghetto dwellers strongly disapproved. The Kerner Commission disproved this and other myths. The average rioter was better educated, better informed, and more involved in the community than the nonrioter, and he had a job (albeit one he thought beneath him). Nearly 40 percent of ghetto residents in Detroit either participated in the riot or identified themselves as bystanders—hardly a deviant minority. The commission thus confirmed what sociologists have long believed: that the crowd itself generates a collective excitement that influences people's behavior. There are several theories explaining how this comes about.

Emotional and Social Contagion In a now classic work published in 1895 (*The Psychology of Crowds*), French sociologist Gustave Le Bon argued that the transformation of individuals into a crowd "puts them in possession of a collective mind" that makes people think, feel, and act quite differently than they would if they were alone. Crowds give people a sense of invincible power: they "will undertake the accomplishment of certain acts with irresistible impetuosity," wrote Le Bon. The crowd gains control over the individual much as the hypnotist gains control over his subjects: individuals become highly suggestible; they are no longer conscious of their actions. Waves of emotion sweep through the crowd, infecting one person after another as though excitement were actually contagious. The thin veneer of civilization falls away, allowing unconscious motivations and antisocial impulses to rise to the surface. "The age we are about to enter," Le Bon wrote, "will be in truth the *era of crowds*." He meant this as a warning.

Clearly, Le Bon believed an untamed, destructive creature lurked behind the social masks people ordinarily present to one another. Although his distaste for "the masses" is obvious, there is some truth to Le Bon's theory. The anonymity of a crowd does weaken conventional norms, by shifting moral responsibility from the individual to the group. And a large number of excited people in close proximity does create the impression of unanimity and "invincible power." Moreover, emotions and behavior do seem to spread through crowds, as if they were contagious.

In his essay on collective behavior, Herbert Blumer (1951) refined Le Bon's ideas. He traced contagion to an "exciting event" that creates unrest in a crowd. People begin milling about, "as if seeking to find or avoid something, but without knowing what it is they are trying to find or avoid." As people search for clues, excited behavior or rhetoric catches their attention. Instead of interpreting and judging these actions, as they ordinarily would, people respond immediately and directly. Their reactions reinforce the original actors, making them still more excited (what Blumer calls the *circular reaction*). As excitement builds, people become more and more inclined to give immediate expression to their feelings, to act on impulse. This, in Blumer's view, explains "the relatively rapid, unwitting and nonrational dissemination of a mood, impulse or form of conduct" through a crowd. Like Le Bon, then, Blumer emphasizes the irrational nature of collective behavior and implies that people are not quite themselves in crowds.

Norms and Crowd Behavior More recently sociologists have questioned the idea that people behave in an unreflecting, irrational way in crowds (Turner and Killian, 1972). Wasn't looting a rational solution for ghetto residents who felt entitled to goods they could not afford and who saw the police caught momentarily off-guard? Weren't lynch mobs an effective method for keeping blacks in a subordinate position in the deep South? This does not suggest that these methods are desirable, but simply that the people who used them found them effective. Turner and Killian also question the implicit assumption that social pressure fails to operate in a crowd. Isn't it possible that crowd members act in deviant or unusual ways precisely because everyone around them is acting that way, and they feel pressured to join in? Moreover, if crowds influence the way people act, as both Le Bon and Blumer believed, individualistic, psychological explanations of crowd behavior are incomplete at best.

The transformation of a crowd of bystanders (a casual crowd) into a mob (an acting crowd) can be explained by the development of new norms (this is called the *emergent norm theory*). In ambiguous, undefined situations, one or more "innovators" suggest a course of action—either verbally or by taking direct action (for example, throwing a bottle). Others follow. The crowd begins to define the situation, to develop a justification for acts that at first seemed questionable. (Thus a radio announcer's slogan, "Burn, baby, burn" became the rallying cry in the Watts riot.) In this way a new set of norms emerges, and people who do not entirely share the crowd's mood are pressured into conformity, or at least into suppressing contrary impulses.

The important point here is that crowds are neither normless nor totally lacking in organization. In the riots of the 1960s, stores owned by blacks were usually spared, and violence was directed at property, not people. (Nearly all those who died in Detroit were killed by police or in accidents.) Nor are riots, panics, mass hysteria, and other types of collective behavior accidental, unexplainable outbreaks. In Blumer's words, collective behavior occurs when "impulses, desires, dispositions cannot be satisfied by existing forms of living."

SOCIAL MOVEMENTS

A *social movement* is an ongoing, collective effort to promote or resist social change. Social movements are more organized than crowds, and they are focused: goals, justifications, and tactics are more clearly articulated. Like other forms of collective behavior, social movements may also grow out of "structural conduciveness" and/or frustrated social concerns. Although they may include a number of formal organizations, as the Women's Liberation Movement does, for example, they are not as structured as political parties or interest groups. Their membership is shifting and indefinite; their leadership is determined more by popular acclaim than by formal procedures and is more symbolic than actual. (Martin Luther King, Jr., for example, never *controlled* the freedom marchers; rather, he inspired them.) In addition, movements use tactics that place them outside conventional channels of social action—marches and sit-ins, for example (Turner and Killian, 1972, pp. 246–47). The following passage describes the feelings of those who marched in 1965, with Martin Luther King, Jr., from Selma, Alabama, to the state capital:

[T]he scene in Selma had been filmed on television and had been played again and again on the home screen in millions of living rooms. . . . Soon, from all over America, thousands of sympathizers, black and white, were bound for Selma—nuns, newsmen, debutantes, psychiatrists, banjo players, Senators' wives, stock clerks, sculptors, social workers —and for most of a month they lived in Selma's Negro quarter, shared the Negro's food and misery, sang his songs, and scorned his oppressors; helped inspire a new guilt, a new social conscience, a new voting bill in America; helped to instill in many illiterate and uninspired Negroes throughout the land a strange new hope that after Martin Luther King's marchers had crossed the little bridge and completed the fifty-mile journey down the road to the state capital, everything would somehow get better, a kind of miracle would occur; it would be like Lourdes and the faithful might toss away their crutches. (Talese, 1970, p. 175)

In a word, social movements are crusades— crusades that inspire in people a new conception of themselves, of their rights and privileges, of the world they live in, and of a world they envision.

Women's Liberation: A History and an Explanation

Feminism, which gained strength as a social movement in the early 1970s, has a long and often overlooked history. As early as 1792 an English feminist named Mary Wollstonecraft was protesting women's frivolous existence and "slavish obedience" to men. She offered men "rational fellowship" and demanded legal rights and educational opportunities for women. In this country women not only fought for suffrage, but were in the front ranks of the abolitionist, labor, and temperance movements in the late nineteenth and early twentieth centuries (Firestone, 1973). In the 1940s and 1950s, however, women as a group were silent about feminist issues—with the notable exception of Simone de Beauvoir, who explored history, biology, literature, and philosophy to find why women were regarded as the second sex (the title of her book, published in 1953). Then in 1963, Betty Friedan's *The Feminine Mystique* was published, a book that helped to launch a decade of change in America. The private grievances of women whose careers had been thwarted, of isolated suburban matrons, of abandoned mothers with no means of supporting themselves or their children became a public outcry.

Three social forces contributed to the rise

of the Women's Liberation Movement. First, the Civil Rights Movement stimulated protest in a wide variety of groups and provided a model for activism. Second, a growing number of women (including mothers and other married women) had begun participating in the labor force, some but not all out of necessity. Finally, dutiful suburban wives and mothers were finding their nest empty by mid-life.[1] They had nothing substantial or socially useful to do (Dixon, in Adams and Briscoe, 1971, pp. 419–33).

These changes hit educated, economically secure, middle-class women the hardest. Trained from childhood not to be self-reliant, achievement-oriented, or autonomous, and having devoted their lives to serving others, many found themselves dependent, isolated,

and beset by "problems that had no name" (Friedan, 1963, pp. 281–95).

The problem lay unburied, unspoken, for many years in the minds of American women. . . . For over fifteen years there was no word of this yearning in the millions of words written about women, for women, in all the columns, books, and articles by experts telling women their role was to seek fulfillment as wives and mothers. Over and over women heard in voices of tradition and of Freudian sophistication that they could desire no greater destiny than to glory in their own femininity. . . . They were taught to pity the neurotic, unfeminine, unhappy women who wanted to be poets or physicists or presidents. (pp. 281, 284)

Women's Liberation gave a name to the problems that faced conventional women whose children, successful husbands, and

___

[1] In earlier times, when three or more generations lived together and there were fewer devices to simplify housekeeping, women in their fifties and sixties kept busy with grandchildren and household chores.

The Women's Liberation Movement has given a voice to women who have traditionally been barred from full social and economic equality with men. (UPI)

suburban dream houses had not saved them from feeling superfluous.

The movement also appealed to women who were not very happy with full-time domesticity and opted for careers in fields marked "for men only," or tried to combine home and work. Although not systematically discouraged from pursuing an education, women typically ran head on into "an invisible bar" of prejudice and discrimination when they left school.

Girls who go to women's colleges sometimes crash unexpectedly on the Invisible Bar when they look for their first jobs. Men don't have to type and take dictation to earn a chance to begin learning! . . . Big companies give a Princeton senior who has majored in English an aptitude test to see where he might fit, but give a Vassar senior who has majored in English a typing test. (Bird, in Adams and Briscoe, 1971, pp. 361, 379)

Both of these groups fanned the demands for new patterns of earning, marriage and divorce laws, and opportunities for living and learning.

During 1963, commissions to investigate the status of women were organized in fifty states. These commissions not only brought large numbers of politically active women into contact with one another, they created a climate of expectations. Three years later, on June 29, 1966, a small group of women attending the Third National Conference of Commissions on the Status of Women met in Betty Friedan's hotel room to discuss the possibility of founding a civil rights organization for women. They decided to call themselves the National Organization for Women, or NOW. With Friedan as president, NOW began to attract women in the professions, labor, government, and the communications industry. However, it was not until 1969, when several national news stories on Women's Liberation were issued, that NOW's membership reached into the thousands.

From its inception, NOW has concentrated on concrete, short-range goals, such as the Equal Rights Amendment to the Constitution, the repeal of abortion laws, and day care. Despite efforts to attract poor and minority women and career housewives, most of NOW's membership consists of working, upper-middle-class white women.

A second, more radical branch of Women's Liberation began to gather momentum in the same period. By 1966 thousands of young women under thirty were deeply involved in the Student Movement. Like their male counterparts they had "lived in an atmosphere of questioning, confrontation, and change" ever since entering college. The movement had taught them to think of problems of "unfreedom" as political problems. They identified with the radical community and thought of themselves as movement people. More often than not, however, they found they were relegated to such traditional and unrewarding jobs as typing and cooking. They could not, after all, burn their draft cards, and in 1966 and 1967 draft resistance was the major issue in the movement. Many women found they had little to do.

In 1967 and 1968 a few small, independent groups attempted to introduce the subject of women's rights at various political meetings and conventions. They were met with laughter and derision (Firestone, 1973). Most radical feminist groups can be traced to political incidents that enraged a small group of women who were well versed in organizing and then proceeded to apply their skills to their own cause. Rejecting formal structure and leadership of any kind, the radical branch of the Women's Liberation Movement has focused on changing the entire structure of human relations—not just on opening the system to women. The "rap session" was designed to change women's identities as well as their attitudes.

Jo Freeman argues that neither branch of the Women's Liberation Movement would have materialized without the communications networks developed through the commissions on the status of women and the Student Movement. Women's opportunities in this country were as limited in 1945 or 1955 as they were in 1965. "What changed was the organizational situation. It was not until a communications network developed between like-minded people beyond local boundaries that the movement could emerge and develop past the point of occasional, spontaneous uprising" (1973, p. 804).

Equally important was the general ideological climate. The sixties was a period of

THE STUDENT MOVEMENT: FROM THE 1960s TO THE 1970s

From its inception as the Berkeley Free Speech Movement in 1964, the Student Movement grew through the 1960s to embrace a wide range of causes and styles—from demands for student representation on university councils to calls for world revolution, from the politics of confrontation to the "politics of experience" (including "be-ins," drug use, dropping out). But by 1974 campus radicalism had declined to the point where observers were suggesting that 1950s conservatism had returned to the campus. What had happened to the Student Movement?

Daniel Yankelovich attributes the present calm on campuses to the end of both the war in Vietnam and the draft, which had caused widespread disillusionment among young people with American society as a whole.

By 1974 concern over political morality had replaced anger over the war in Vietnam (Gallup, January, March 1974)—a concern students shared with other generations. Although rarely used, institutionalized procedures for unseating corrupt public officials do exist, and by 1973–1974 it was clear that the machinery for impeachment proceedings would be set into motion. As we have suggested, collective behavior occurs when channels for expressing concern either do not exist or are blocked. This was not the case in 1974.

In some areas Yankelovich found moderate reversals in student attitudes. In 1973, 40 percent of the college students polled thought most Americans shared their values, compared to 30 percent in 1971; 60 percent "anticipated no great difficulty in accepting the kind of life society had to offer," compared to 49 percent just two years earlier; 66 percent believed violence is morally wrong, even for a good cause, which was an increase of 10 percent; and 66 percent were "career-minded." Yankelovich concludes,

> We can now see, in retrospect, that both the generation gap and the campus radicalism of the 1960s were transitory phenomena. The radicalism was closely tied to the Vietnam War. And what seemed to be a generation gap was actually the leading edge of a new morality and quest for new self-fulfilling life styles that have now spilled over from the campus to influence all of American youth—and many of their parents as well.

In short, the Student Movement declined as the gap between its goals and those of the larger society began to narrow. In chapter 19 we will look further at the way in which values and attitudes change in a society, focusing particularly on social change in America.

SOURCE: Yankelovich Youth Study © 1974 by the JDR 3rd Fund.

turmoil and change, with numerous groups organizing and demanding a hearing. The idea of a Women's Movement fit easily into already established patterns of thinking. Had the first groups of women who attempted to ride the Civil Rights bandwagon into legal equality been accommodated, however, the *idea* of a movement might never have been translated into *action*. Finally, the commissions and the Student Movement gave women experience in organizing on a grass roots level. As Freeman indicates, "social movements do not simply occur"; they must be constructed (1973, p. 804).

To summarize, this example illustrates the origins and development of social movements. Structurally, they begin when people find that existing institutions are not answering a need. If enough people don't feel this need, the movement does not take hold. For a movement to become permanent it most continue to play a meaningful role in the lives of its members. Some movements, such as the temperance movement are short lived. Others, such as the Mormon religion and Christianity become institutionalized. Movements that succeed, for example, the Civil Rights Movement, leave a legacy of lasting social change.

COMMUNICATION AND COLLECTIVE BEHAVIOR: RUMORS, PUBLIC OPINION, AND PERSUASION

The invention of mass media must also be counted among the great revolutions of modern times and one that relates to the subject of this chapter. Newspapers (which became available in the nineteenth century), radio, and television have created new forms of collective behavior. When millions of people are frightened or angered by the same broadcast, they act very much like people in a crowd who have been ignited by an incident or speech. Even though each is in his or her own home, they are reacting to a common stimulus. And they carry their excitement to friends, relatives, and neighbors, setting off the circular reaction Blumer observed in crowds.

This was clearly what happened when Orson Welles's Mercury Theater broadcast *War of the Worlds* on October 30, 1938. The play began innocuously enough with a program of music from New York's Park Plaza Hotel. Suddenly the music was interrupted for a bulletin about atmospheric disturbances. The radio station then took listeners to a laboratory in Princeton, New Jersey, for an interview with Professor Pierson, who assured the announcer that these disturbances could not possibly be the early stages of an invasion from Mars. The program returned to the Park Plaza. Bulletins continued to interrupt the music, however, and finally the station arranged for an eyewitness report of a strange meteorite.

[ANNOUNCER ONE:] Just a minute! Something's happening! Ladies and gentlemen, this is terrific! This end of the thing is beginning to flake off! The top is beginning to rotate like a screw! The thing must be hollow!

[Murmuring from the crowd; the clanking sound of falling metal; shouts] Good heavens, something's wriggling out of the shadow like a grey snake. Now it's another one, and another. They look like tentacles to me. There, I can see the thing's body. It's large as a bear and it glistens like wet leather. But that face. It . . . it's indescribable. I can hardly force myself to keep looking at it. The eyes are black and gleam like a serpent. The mouth is V-shaped with saliva dropping from its rimless lips that seem to quiver and pulsate. . . . The crowd falls back. They've seen enough. This is the most extraordinary experience. I can't find words . . . I'm pulling this microphone with me as fast as I talk. . . .

[There is an interruption, cut back to the studio, then the broadcast from the farm continues, accompanied by shrieks and strange humming sounds.] A humped shape is rising out of the pit. I can make out a small beam of light against a mirror. What's that? There's a jet of flame springing from the mirror, and it leaps right at the advancing men. . . . Good Lord, they're turning into flame! Now the whole field's caught fire. . . .

[ANNOUNCER TWO:] Ladies and gentlemen, due to circumstances beyond our control, we are unable to continue the broadcast from Grovers Mill. Evidently there's some difficulty with our field transmission (quoted in Cantril, Gaudet, and Herzog, 1947, pp. 15–18). [The secretary of the interior begins advising listeners to put their faith in God.]

Of the 6 million or more people who listened to this broadcast, an estimated 1 million panicked. Telephone lines were jammed with calls to warn relatives and friends and to bid loved ones farewell. Terrified parents bundled children into blankets and rushed to the streets for help; grown men and women hid in their cellars; excited crowds gathered in bars and other public places. Some people started driving, without much idea of where they were going, but they had to do *something*. Others remained glued to their radios in tears and prayer. After a few hours the confusion died down, but newspapers continued to print stories about the night of panic for a full week (Cantril, Gaudet, and Herzog, 1947, pp. 47–55).

Some of this reaction can be attributed to the skill of the dramatist. All that fall regular radio programs had been interrupted for bulletins concerning growing tensions in Europe. Listeners had begun to rely on their radios for news; they had learned to expect interruptions. *War of the Worlds* played on

this familiar experience. At first both Professor Pierson and Announcer Phillips debunked reports of an invasion from Mars, giving expression to listeners' disbelief, sharing their incredulity and bewilderment. Once this rapport was established, however, the pace of bizarre happenings accelerated. "Ladies and gentlemen, *incredible as it may seem* . . ." The use of "expert testimony"—the scientists, military officers, the secretary of the interior—gave credibility to increasingly terrifying descriptions. And although all of these characters were fictitious, the towns and highways mentioned were well known—particularly to the New Jersey-New York audience. How could so many people believe, however briefly, that slimy, luminous Martians were climbing out of a spaceship on a New Jersey farm? The study of rumors provides important clues.

Rumors

A *rumor* is an unverified story that circulates from person to person, most often by word of mouth, and is accepted as fact, although its sources may be vague or unknown. Rumors proliferate in tense and ambiguous situations, when people are unable to learn the facts or, for one reason or another, when they distrust the information they receive. When the Japanese bombed Pearl Harbor, for example, many Americans believed our entire fleet had been wiped out. There were rumors that the Japanese had occupied Hawaii. President Roosevelt's radio broadcast only partially dispelled these stories. Nearly half of the college students interviewed shortly afterward were convinced the president was covering up the true facts (Allport and Postman, 1947). Similarly, when President Kennedy was shot in Dallas hundreds of unconfirmed stories began to circulate by word of mouth: Vice-President Johnson had had a heart attack; eyewitnesses had seen more than one person in the book depository; Oswald was connected to the FBI, CIA, or a communist plot; Dallas police had paid Jack Ruby to silence Oswald.

A rumor may begin as an accurate report but become distorted and exaggerated in the process of transmission. After studying rumor transmission in the laboratory and in the field, Allport and Postman (1947) discovered a basic pattern. A person hears a story that strikes him as interesting. He repeats the story—that is, what he remembers—to a friend. This person talks to others: "Did you hear . . . ?" Gradually, the original story is reduced to a few essential details that are easy to tell. This is what Allport and Postman mean by *leveling*: "As a rumor travels, it tends to grow shorter, more concise, more easily grasped and told. In successive versions, fewer words are used and fewer details are mentioned" (p. 75).

As a result of leveling, certain details gain in importance, and the rumor is *sharpened*— people remember and pass on only part of the original story. And, as a rumor circulates people tend to "correct" details so that the story seems more plausible and coherent. Thus in a laboratory experiment on rumor transmission, subjects confused by a story of an ambulance carrying explosives changed explosives to medical supplies, which seemed more likely; in another rumor, a razor in a white man's hand moved (in the telling) to a black man's hand. Allport and Postman call this unconscious correcting of details *assimilation*. ". . . [w]e find assimilation in terms of deep-lying emotional needs. The rumor [in the lab] tends to fit into, and support, the occupational interests, class or racial memberships, or personal prejudices of the reporter" (p. 115). For example, during the riot in Detroit, residents believed reports of

police brutality because they had come to *expect* the police to be brutal; police and Guardsmen believed rumors about snipers because they *expected* sniping during a riot. In short, rumors tend to confirm people's assumptions.

Rumors usually arise when people are anxious, when they feel something is wrong but are unable to focus or explain their tension. By exaggerating the destruction at Pearl Harbor, people justified the anxiety they felt, to themselves and others; by linking Lee Harvey Oswald to a communist conspiracy, they temporarily warded off the uncomfortable thought that a single person could penetrate the Secret Service guard and assassinate a president. Rumors "explained" the unthinkable. In confusing times any answer may seem better than no answer, and people are inclined to accept reports that confirm their suspicions. Rumors are a form of collective behavior in that they are set off by precipitating incidents; draw on a readiness for certain ideas and on communications networks; give problems a name and a reason; and draw people together around a common concern, belief, or crisis.

Public Opinion

A *public* is a scattered group of people who share a common interest, concern, or focus of attention. (The Mercury Theater audience, environmentalists, and college students are all publics.) One of the effects of mass media is the creation and maintenance of publics. The formation of publics is greatly aided by the mass media because they can give frequent national exposure to an issue, product, team, or politician. The media also influence the ebb and flow of *public opinion*—that is, the prevailing interests (what people define as an issue), attitudes (predispositions to react positively or negatively toward certain people, groups, or events), and opinions (specific judgments of specific issues) of a public. Obviously, there have always been publics, and publics have always had opinions. But modern polling techniques have made it possible to collect these opinions, to bring the views of scattered individuals together into a new form of collective behavior more powerful than a crowd or protest. For a shouting crowd may not represent general opinion, but a poll does. A simple table reflecting widespread opinion that the president should be impeached speaks louder than a demonstration in Washington. We will examine this phenomenon later in the chapter.

When studying public opinion, the distinction between values, which tend to be stable, and opinions, which change more rapidly, is important. A comparison of the attitudes of Vietnam veterans about war in general and the Vietnam War in particular illustrates this point (Yankelovich, 1974). One out of four Vietnam veterans believes we lost that war, compared to one out of eleven among non-college youth as a whole, and only 7 percent of veterans believe the war ended with honor (compared to 13 percent overall). Yet 68 percent of veterans believe we *should* go to war to counteract aggression (compared to 55 percent overall), 54 percent to contain communism (compared to 48 percent overall), and 59 percent to protect American allies (compared to 45 percent overall). The fact that many veterans have negative opinions about the Vietnam War in particular has not changed their basic values about fighting wars in general.

Public opinion can fluctuate widely over a short time. In the fall of 1938, for example, most Americans did not believe war would break out in Europe. The public was evenly divided on the question of whether to sell war materials to Britain and France, the major issue at that time. Two weeks after war broke out, nearly half the American public favored declaring war on Germany *if* Britain and France were defeated, but most considered this a remote possibility. When France fell in the spring of 1940, public attention shifted to our own defenses. The majority of Americans believed we should stay out of the war, not use our own ships to send food to Britain, and establish friendly relations with Germany if Britain fell. By that fall, however, neutrality was no longer an issue. Britain had shown she could fight back, and most Americans wanted to lend her food, money, and planes. Polls conducted in the spring of 1941 indicated that two-thirds of the American public were committed to defeating Nazi Germany. More than 80 percent believed we would eventually enter the war and that we could defeat both Germany and Japan. By the end of 1941 the question on most people's minds was not *if* we would enter the war, but *when* (Cantril, in Turner and Killian, 1972, pp. 183–92).

One of the most dramatic shifts in public opinion in recent years was the swing from support to distrust of President Nixon by the American public. In January 1973, 68 percent of the adults polled approved of the way Nixon was handling his job as president. By March 1974, after the Watergate revelations, only 25 percent approved of the president's performance. Commenting on this rapid shift in public opinion, George Gallup remarked that Nixon's "approval rating has dropped faster, more precipitous[ly] than any one of the Presidents in [the last four decades]. The approval rating is really a confidence rating, and Nixon's clearly lost the confidence of the American people."[2]

---

[2] *Gallup Opinion Index*, February 1973 (no. 92) and April 1975 (no. 106); Educational Broadcasting Corporation, *Bill Moyers' Journal*, "A Question of Impeachment," 1974, p. 15 (transcript).

The Media and Public Opinion The media not only report news, they *make* news. Not the Civil Rights Movement, the Student Movement, nor the Women's Liberation Movement would have had much impact on American society if journalists had not decided they were worth reporting. "News, if unreported, has no impact. It might as well have not happened at all. Thus the journalist is the important ally of the ambitious, he is a lamplighter for stars. . . . [E]ach day, unhaunted by history, plugged into the *instant*, journalists of every creed, quality, and quirk report the news of the world as they see it, believe it, understand it. Then much of it is relayed through America, millions of words a minute" (Talese, 1970, pp. 1–2). In choosing to report and headline some stories instead of others, newspaper publishers and television news editors affect the flow of information.

In addition, the media carry considerable prestige: people tend to believe what they read in the papers or see on the evening news (Jarrell, 1961). This legitimating power of the media makes it hard to distinguish news from propaganda. For example, during the 1960s films on Vietnam from communist news sources were called "propaganda" by the network newscaster who emphasized how low-angle shots and other filming techniques were used to create a certain impression. However, when the networks used Pentagon-made films with the same techniques and using selected footage, they were treated as factual news, and their source was not given (Cirino, 1971, pp. 180–81).

But how much do the media influence opinion? To the extent that they are the only source of information, their influence is bound to be considerable. When researchers try to *change* people's opinions, however, the picture becomes more complex. Summarizing the research on opinion change, Raymond Bauer states, "The audience selects what it will attend to. Since people generally listen to and read things they are interested in, these usually are topics on which they have a good deal of information and fixed opinion. Hence the very people most likely to attend to a message are those most difficult to change; those who can be converted do not look or listen" (Bauer, in Wells, 1972, p. 235).

Moreover, the media work through the social networks that characterize everyday life. Studies by Elihu Katz and Paul F. Lazarsfeld (1955) indicate that mass media influence people *if* their social background predisposes them to accept a report as fact and a particular course of action as legitimate; *if* one viewpoint or another is associated with groups they consider significant (their reference groups); and *if* individuals whose opinion they respect (that is, opinion leaders) call their attention to the issue. Thus social background, reference groups, and interpersonal influence seem to be the deciding factors in the creation of issues and formation of opinions. The media serve to amplify existing trends.

Polling and Public Opinion In the last two decades public-opinion polling has become an industry in its own right. Political candidates depend on polls; so do business, labor, and a wide variety of lobbies and special interest groups (Roll and Cantril, 1972, p. 13). Gallup and other established pollsters regularly assess the American public's attitudes, political views, and behavior. Hardly a week goes by without a report on public opinion appearing in the press.

We discussed how polls are taken in chapter 2, and these methods apply to measuring public opinion as well as to sociological research in other areas. But opinion polling is especially problematic. Suppose, for example, a pollster asks a person, "Do you trust the president?" and the respondent answers,

"No." This seems straightforward, but what does the answer really mean? Perhaps the person distrusts *all* politicians, not just the current president. Perhaps he or she voted for the president and is particularly bitter about his actions. Or suppose a pollster finds that a respondent thinks that the best way to stop crime is to increase the number of police. But is the respondent willing to pay higher taxes for this? To be valid, a poll should ask several questions to make interpretation more reliable.

Measuring the *strength* of an answer is also crucial in opinion polling since most people will try to answer questions, if only to be polite. Do respondents understand the question? A pollster may find that people answer "yes" when asked whether the president should be impeached, but "no" when asked if they think he should be indicted by the House and tried in the Senate. Finally, opinion pollsters must be wary of conventional responses. Few Americans would say they oppose free speech, but many think Communists, Nazis, black militants, and student radicals should be prevented from expressing their views openly (see p. 82). In short, a "poll is only as good as the question it asks" (Roll and Cantril, 1972, p. 103).

Manipulating Public Opinion

Lincoln once said, "You may fool all of the people some of the time, and some of the people all of the time, but you cannot fool all of the people all of the time." The wisdom of this oft-quoted epigram has not prevented many people from trying. Franklin D. Roosevelt, for example, supported American involvement in the war in Europe as early as 1938. He drew public opinion to his side by surreptitiously using American boats to send supplies to Europe. When these boats were attacked, the public began to get very emo-tional about protecting our men and property, and attitudes toward the war shifted. There are essentially two ways to "fool the people": by restricting the flow of information through censorship, or by presenting information in a way that is calculated to gain uncritical acceptance of a partisan point of view, that is, through propaganda and public relations.

Censorship *Censorship* is the restriction of information from reaching its audience. Censorship is essentially a device for preventing collective behavior that might foster social change. Popular American wisdom implies that censorship is something that foreign (especially communist) governments employ, but not our own. The fact that all governments, including our own, practice censorship is rarely mentioned.

During the early 1970s, however, two instances of government censorship in this country attracted the public's attention. In June 1971 the government went to court to prevent *The New York Times* and *The Washington Post* from publishing the Pentagon Papers, a secret 7,000-page report on the origins of the war in Vietnam, prepared within the Pentagon and leaked by Daniel Ellsberg. On July 1, 1971, the Supreme Court decided in favor of the publishers, but it was not the landmark decision journalists had hoped for. The decision was split (six to three), and three justices rejected the government's suit only because they did not feel it had proved that publication of the Pentagon Papers was a threat to national security. The government's right to censor the press was neither approved nor rejected.[3] Public opinion on this issue was divided (see table 11:1 on p. 308). Forty-one percent of the people

---

[3] In a related decision the Supreme Court ruled that local communities had a right to establish their own standards of decency and to ban films, books, and magazines that violate these standards.

table 11:1   PUBLIC OPINION AND THE PENTAGON PAPERS

More Nearly Right: Newspapers or Government?

	NEWSPAPERS PERCENT	GOVERNMENT PERCENT	NOT SURE PERCENT
Nationwide	*41*	*35*	*24*
East	46	30	24
Midwest	46	34	20
Border States	29	41	30
Deep South	30	37	33
West	43	36	21
8th grade educated	34	31	35
High school	37	36	27
College	52	33	15

A cross section of 1,493 households was asked between July 10 and 16, the week after the Supreme Court decision [allowing newspapers to publish the Pentagon Papers]: "From what you know about the information in the Pentagon Papers published by newspapers and the government's attempt to stop its publication, who would you say was more nearly right—the newspapers which printed the secret documents about the war or the federal government which said printing such materials was harmful to the national interest?"

SOURCE: Harris Poll, August 12, 1971.

Louis Harris polled in August 1971 felt the newspapers had been "more right" than the government in this instance, and they supported the Supreme Court decision by nearly two to one. But although 54 percent felt it was time the American public was told the truth about the war, and 47 percent believed we would not learn the truth if newspapers had to get permission to print inside information, 70 percent agreed that "if there is any doubt about violating the national security in publishing documents such as the Pentagon Papers on Viet Nam, then the documents should not be published" (Harris Poll, August 12, 1971).

A second incident of censorship came to light in July 1973, when an Air Force major told a Senate committee that the government had conducted over 3,000 secret bombing missions into Cambodia and falsified reports to cover this up. At the time the government claimed publicly that it recognized Cambodia's neutrality and that we were "winding down" the war. Security around these missions was so tight that the secretary of the Air Force did not even know about the raids. In this case the government was clearly withholding information in order to maintain its peace-making image in the eyes of the American public and the world community. In other words, the government was manipulating public opinion.

Propaganda and Public Relations Censorship is a way of manipulating collective behavior; *propaganda* and *public relations* are methods for inspiring certain kinds of collective behavior, such as voting for a particular candidate, buying bigger cars, demonstrating for or against a piece of legislation. Propaganda appeals mainly to people's emotions and prejudices, not to their critical abilities. This is the main difference between propaganda and simple persuasion through rational arguments. Name calling, the invocation of authorities ("Doctors recommend . . .") and sacred values, appeals to fear, and shows of strength (the bandwagon effect) are some of the more obvious tools of propaganda (Lee and Lee, 1939).

Adolf Hitler was a genius at mass propaganda. His rhetoric and symbols (the swastika, Nazi uniforms and salute), his storm troopers, who "protected" Nazi rallies and broke up opposition gatherings, all created the impression among followers that they belonged to an irresistible movement. Once in office Hitler created a superagency for "public enlightenment" that controlled the press, the arts, and education (Holborn, 1969, pp. 719; 738–39).

Political propaganda is also used widely in this country.[4] Every election year political candidates are packaged by mass-persuasion experts and sold with posters, buttons, straw hats, television spots, articles planted in popular magazines, and "news items" about the candidate which reporters use because the story has already been written for them. During the 1968 presidential campaign, for example, Fred La Rue used music to advertise Richard Nixon in the South. It was, in his words, "a special ballad-type song in the current 'country and western' music style, by which nationally famous artists will 'sing' the message via the radio and television. The multi-stanza ballad will allow issues to be included or excluded *as the local situation indicates*" (italics added; McGinniss, 1969, pp. 120–21). The Republicans were not alone,

of course, in using public relations techniques. McGovern's people wooed popular country singer Johnny Cash throughout the 1972 campaign and used television spots to project an image of their candidate.

Closely linked to propaganda is public relations, another means of manipulating public opinion. *Public relations* is a form of indirect advertising—including press releases (*The New York Times* receives some *5,000* press releases weekly from the business community); "briefings" for businesspeople, community leaders, and politicians; "junkets" (all-expenses-paid trips); gifts; and entertainment. The main purpose of public relations is to present a favorable image of the client to the public.

In 1974 Americans learned how public relations techniques had been used in the White House. Edited transcripts of eight presidential conversations with high-ranking aides, released in April 1974, include repeated references to public relations maneuvers as the White House staff struggled with a flood of damaging news reports about Watergate, campaign donations, and the like. "I can give a show—we can sell them, just like we were selling Wheaties on our position," White House lawyer John Dean told Richard Nixon. During a discussion of how to handle the Senate Watergate hearings, Dean warned the president against allowing White House staff members to testify. Nixon replied "Oh, no, no, no! I didn't mean to have everyone go up and testify. . . . I mean put the story out, public relations people, here is the story, the true story about Watergate." Indeed, the very act of releasing edited transcripts of the tapes was, in part, a public relations tactic. Hopefully the public would conclude that if the president voluntarily made the transcripts public, he must be innocent. To be safe the White House issued an interpretation hours before it released the actual transcripts and gave newscasters little time to read the 1,300-odd

---

[4] Today the Defense Department spends nearly $3.5 million annually on public relations (Fulbright, 1970, p. 32).

pages before the evening news. (Excerpts from the tapes, comparing public statements with private conversations, appear in the accompanying box.)

IN THE NEWS

Public Relations and Private Conversations: The White House Transcripts

In April 1974 President Nixon made public transcripts of conversations he had had with several of his closest White House aides. The transcripts were edited before Nixon made them public.

One of the most damaging revelations in the transcripts was that the president and his aides seemed to regard the "Watergate mess" as a tactical rather than a moral or substantive problem. The edited transcripts are sprinkled with discussions of how "to cut our losses"; considerations of different "scenarios"; talk of "How will it play in Peoria?" The transcripts exposed President Nixon as having been involved in planning a public relations campaign to "keep the cap on the bottle." In many cases the president's private conversations did not substantiate his public statements. Below, is a portion of the edited White House transcript of a meeting between President Nixon and his lawyer, John Dean. Above the excerpt is what the president told the public the night he released the transcripts.

DID THE PRESIDENT SANCTION THE PAYMENT OF HUSH MONEY AND AN OFFER OF CLEMENCY TO HUNT AND HIS COCONSPIRATORS?

Public Statement

PRESIDENT NIXON: I then said that to pay clemency was wrong. In fact I think I can quote it directly. I said: "It is wrong. That's for sure." . . . Now when individuals read the entire transcript of the 21st meeting, or hear the entire tape where we discussed all these options, they may reach different interpretations. But I know what I meant, and I know also what I did.

Transcript

[From the meeting on March 21, 1973]

PRESIDENT NIXON: How much money do you need?

DEAN: I would say these people are going to cost a million dollars over the next two years.

PRESIDENT NIXON: We could get that. On the money, if you need the money, you could get that. You could get a million dollars. You could get it in cash.

I know where it could be gotten. It is not easy, but it could be done.

[President Nixon returned to this subject several times during the meeting]

PRESIDENT NIXON: Just looking at the immediate problem, don't you think you have to handle Hunt's financial situation damn soon?

DEAN: I am not sure that you'll be able to deliver on the clemency. It may be just too hot.

PRESIDENT NIXON: You can't do it politically until after the '74 elections. That's for sure. Your point is that even then you couldn't do it.

DEAN: That's right. It may further involve you in a way you should not be involved in this.

PRESIDENT NIXON: No. It is wrong. That's for sure.

[That night, $75,000 in cash was delivered to Hunt's lawyer.]

In a nationally televised speech, Richard Nixon released over 1,300 pages of his conversations with White House aides. Although he told the public that the transcripts would prove his innocence in the Watergate scandals, people who actually read the conversations found that the president was not entirely guiltless. (Wally McNamee/Newsweek)

One of the most fascinating public relations and advertising campaigns in recent years began during the oil crisis in 1973. For years the oil companies had done everything possible to sell more gasoline. They and the car manufacturers had made the automobile a symbol of personal freedom and power. By issuing credit cards, the major oil companies made it possible for their customers to cruise across the country without spending a dollar in cash. Statistics showed that people were driving millions of miles more every year. Then, in a sudden reversal, Mobil issued a public relations ad that said "Take the bus." The oil companies began attacking the American habit of driving alone in big, gasoline-guzzling V-8's (the bigger the better). They also attempted to persuade the public that the companies were not responsible for the impending oil crisis.

AMOCO, one of the nation's largest oil companies, outlined its arguments as follows. The crisis was due to unseasonably cold weather (which increased the demand for heating fuel), unexpectedly high demands for gasoline during the summer months, and an unusual number of operating problems. A 40 percent decrease in drilling over the last decade left the industry unprepared for rising demands. ("Investors have found surer, more profitable investments than risking their money by drilling holes in the ground," the company claimed.) Pressure from environmentalists made the shortage even more severe: "Environmental Protection Agency regulations [that] prevent the burning of high-sulfur coal in most large metropolitan areas . . . [are] the largest single cause of the tremendous surge in demand for petroleum in the nation" (AMOCO background memorandum, December 15, 1972).

AMOCO's public relations office then translated these arguments into a campaign. First, they would explain the crisis to employees and outline steps to conserve energy within their plants, so that employees could "intelligently respond to comments by their neighbors, friends, and customers." A few ceremonies, such as dimming the AMOCO Torch and Oval sign, were planned. Advertising mats and tips on handling customers would be

"Hire him. He's got great legs."

If women thought this way about men they would be awfully silly.

When men think this way about women they're silly, too.

Women should be judged for a job by whether or not they can do it.

In a world where women are doctors, lawyers, judges, brokers, economists, scientists, political candidates, professors and company presidents, any other viewpoint is ridiculous.

Think of it this way. When we need all the help we can get, why waste half the brains around?

Womanpower. It's much too good to waste.

For information: NOW Legal Defense and Education Fund Inc., 127 East 59th Street, Dept. K. New York, New York 10022

Public relations tactics are often used by groups seeking social change. This ad, sponsored by the National Organization of Women, aims to change discriminatory hiring practices. (J. Consor/NOW)

sent to the company's retailers. Second, every effort would be made to place spokesmen on television talk shows and to contact journalists and weathermen who might advise the public on the energy crisis. News releases would be issued "to keep before the public the fact that American Oil is working to fuel the nation." Regional vice-presidents would visit governors and local leaders to brief them on the situation. Finally, they would "draft suggested form letters for use by the staffs of Congressmen to reply to constituents who write for information about the energy situation."

The campaign did not work. Market research indicated that four out of five motorists believed the oil companies—not consumers or environmentalists—were responsible for fuel shortages.

In recent years many large corporations have begun to broaden their view of public relations. AMOCO, for example, has sponsored conferences on minority problems, pays the salaries of minority counselors who work with youth in the inner city, and runs a Government Action Program designed to encourage employees to become active in politics—all of which have nothing *directly* to do with selling oil. The idea behind such activities is both to improve AMOCO's image in the communities where its offices and plants are located, and also to improve these communities (which in turn will benefit AMOCO).

Public relations techniques are not used only by politicians and corporations. Many groups advocating social change, such as civil rights organizations and groups fighting discrimination due to sex and religion, have effectively used public relations campaigns to gain public support. The aim of these campaigns is generally to present information that the public would otherwise not be aware of. Persuasion through education is their goal.

summary

Collective behavior refers to the actions of relatively temporary, unstructured aggregates of people who are focused on and reacting to the same stimulus. Although it appears spontaneous, collective behavior does not erupt any time, any place. Social structures that encourage people to value unstable things, obstacles to desired goals or to expression of concern over significant values, and unanticipated events that create a state of normlessness are preconditions for collective behavior.

A *crowd* is a temporary collection of people gathered around an event who are conscious of and influenced by one another's presence. Herbert Blumer distinguished between *conventional crowds* (gathered for a specific purpose and abiding by established norms), *expressive crowds* (which encourage loss of self-control), and *acting crowds* (volatile collections of people who are focused on a controversial event that inspires their desire to act). The riot in Detroit was an example of the latter. The riot started in a neglected part of the inner city, where attitudes toward the police were hostile. It was set off by what residents considered unjustified arrests. A crowd gathered, bottles were thrown, and rumors changed a casual crowd into an acting one. Confusion was soon accompanied by scattered incidents of burning, looting, and violence. Ill-prepared troops were called in and a curfew imposed. In the end, 43 people were killed and over 7,000 arrested.

The Detroit rioters were not "riff-raff," as many people supposed. How then do sociologists explain their behavior? Nineteenth-century theorist Le Bon characterized mobs as hypnotized masses of people acting out unconscious motives under the delusion of invincible power. Blumer, too, believed people behave irrationally in crowds: an exciting event catches their attention, they begin milling about, and respond directly and unreflectively to suggestions (setting off the circular reaction). More recently, sociologists have focused less on the individual amidst the crowds and more on the overall structure of collective behavior. Turner's *emergent norm theory* is based on the idea that in ambiguous situations, innovators suggest a course of action, the crowd begins to develop new norms, and bystanders are pressured into conformity (as they are in other groups).

A *social movement* is an ongoing, collective effort to promote or resist social change. Although social movements usually include organizations, they retain much of the spontaneity of crowds and use tactics that place them outside conventional channels for social action. The Women's Liberation Movement is an example. It gave a name to the isolation, dependency, and prejudice that confront both housewives and career women, transforming private grievances into a public outcry. The 1960s gave women a climate that encouraged change, communications networks, and the stimulation of opposition and ridicule. The Student Movement of the 1960s—which embraced a wide range of new values, politics, and life-styles—is another example. Yankelovich attributes the calm on college campuses during the early 1970s to the diffusion of these values and to the end of the war in Vietnam and the draft.

Mass media have created new forms of collective behavior: daily, millions of people read the same headlines, watch the same television shows, and at times, react like members of a crowd. For example, rumors of an invasion from Mars—sparked by the Mercury Theater—created mass panic. A *rumor* is an unverified report that circulates from person to person and is accepted as fact. In the course of transmission, rumors become leveled and sharpened; people "correct" the details for themselves. Rumors tend to proliferate in unstable times when any answer is better than none. They usually tend to confirm people's suspicions.

Mass media help to create *publics* (scattered groups of people who share a common interest, concern, or focus of attention). Reference groups and opinion leaders influence public opinion, and the media amplify existing trends. As the ability to measure public opinion through polls has grown, so have attempts to manipulate it. *Censorship* is a method for preventing the expression of collective behavior seeking change. *Propaganda* and *public relations* (behind-the-scenes advertising) are ways of inspiring and directing collective behavior. The marketing of political candidates, the Watergate cover-up, and oil companies' campaigns to inform the public about the energy crisis and to manipulate public opinion on this issue, demonstrate this. Groups seeking social change may also use public relations to educate the public.

glossary

acting crowd   An excited, volatile group of people who are focused on a controversial event that provokes their indignation, anger, and desire to act (Blumer).

casual crowd   A spontaneous gathering whose members give temporary attention to the object that attracted them and then go their separate ways.

censorship   Restricting information before it reaches its audience.

collective behavior   The actions of relatively temporary, unstructured groups of people who are focused on and reacting to the same event, rumor, person, group, or custom.

conventional crowd   People gathered for a specific purpose who behave according to established norms (Blumer).

crowd   A temporary collection of people gathered around some event, who are conscious of and influenced by one another's presence.

expressive crowd   A crowd that gives people license to express feelings and behave in ways they would not consider in other settings (Blumer).

mob   A crowd whose members are emotionally aroused and are engaged in, or are ready to engage in, violent action.

normlessness   The effort of a sudden, unexpected event that creates a situation where people do not know what they can or should do.

panic   The action of a crowd whose members feel entrapped and seek escape in highly individualistic and counterproductive ways.

propaganda Information that appeals to people's emotions and prejudices and is used to inspire certain kinds of collective behavior.

public A scattered group of people who share a common interest, concern, or focus of attention.

public opinion The prevailing interests, attitudes, and opinions of a public.

public relations Covert behind-the-scenes advertising via press releases, briefings, junkets, and the like.

riot A violent public disturbance, particularly when a crowd of people collectively engage in destructive behavior; it may be caused by an intolerable gap between what people believe they are entitled to and what they actually have.

rumor An unverified story that circulates from person to person, usually by word of mouth, and is accepted as fact, although its sources may be vague or unknown.

social contagion The rapid diffusion of a mood or pattern of behavior through a crowd.

social movement An ongoing, collective effort with focused goals and articulated tactics to promote or resist social change.

references

Vernon L. Allen, "Toward Understanding Riots: Some Perspectives," *Journal of Social Issues*, vol. 26, no. 1 (Winter 1970): 1–18.

Gordon W. Allport and Leo Postman, *The Psychology of Rumor*, New York: Holt, Rinehart and Winston, 1947.

Roberta Ash, *Social Movements in America*, Chicago: Markham, 1972.

Allen H. Barton, *Communities in Disaster*, New York: Doubleday, 1969.

Raymond Bauer, "The Obstinate Audience," *American Psychologist* (May 1964): 319–28.

Carolyn Bird, "The Invisible Bar," in Elsie Adams and Mary Louise Briscoe, eds., *Up Against the Wall, Mother . . .*, Beverly Hills: Glencoe, 1971.

Herbert Blumer, "Collective Behavior," in Alfred McClung Lee, ed., *New Outline of the Principles of Sociology*, New York: Barnes & Noble, 1951.

A. Campbell and H. Schuman, "Racial Attitudes in Fifteen American Cities," in *Supplementary Studies for the National Advisory Commission on Civil Disorders*, Washington, D.C.: Government Printing Office, 1968.

Hadley Cantril, with Hazel Gaudet and Herta Herzog, *Invasion from Mars*, Princeton, N.J.: Princeton University Press, 1947.

Nathan Caplan, "The New Ghetto Man: A Review of Recent Empirical Studies," *Journal of Social Issues*, vol. 26, no. 1 (1970): 59–73.

Robert Cirino, *Don't Blame the People*, Los Angeles: Diversity Press, 1971.

Jerry Cohen and William S. Murphy, *Burn, Baby, Burn*, New York: Dutton, 1966.

Fred J. Cook, "Madison Avenue in Uniform," *The Warfare State*, New York: Macmillan, 1962.

Marlene Dixon, "Why Women's Liberation?" in Elsie Adams and Mary Louise Briscoe, eds., *Up Against the Wall, Mother . . .*, Beverly Hills: Glencoe, 1971.

Educational Broadcasting Corporation, *Bill Moyers' Journal*, "A Question of Impeachment," 1974.

Shulamith Firestone, "On American Feminism," in Peter I. Rose, ed., *The Study of Society*, 3rd ed., New York: Random House, 1973.

Richard Flacks, "The Liberated Generation: An Exploration of the Roots of Student Protest," *Journal of Social Issues*, vol. 23, no. 3 (July 1967): 52–75.

Robert M. Fogelson, "Violence and Grievances: Reflections on the 1960s Riots," *Journal of Social Issues*, vol. 26, no. 1 (Winter 1970): 141–63.

Jo Freeman, "The Origins of the Women's Liberation Movement," *American Journal of Sociology*, vol. 78, no. 4 (1973): 792–811.

Betty Friedan, *The Feminine Mystique*, New York: Dell, 1963.

J. William Fulbright, *The Pentagon Propaganda Machine*, New York: Liveright, 1970.

J. F. C. Hecker, *The Epidemics of the Middle Ages*, London: Woodfall, 1844.

Hajo Holborn, *A History of Modern Germany, 1850–1945*, New York: Knopf, 1969.

Thomas Ford Hoult, *A Dictionary of Modern Sociology*, Totowa, N.J.: Littlefield, Adams, 1969.

Aldous Huxley, *The Devils of Loudun*, New York: Harper & Row, 1952.

Randall Jarrell, "A Sad Heart at the Supermarket," in Norman Jacobs, ed., *Culture for the Millions*, Princeton, N.J.: Van Nostrand, 1961.

Elihu Katz and Paul Lazarsfeld, *Personal Influence*, New York: Free Press, 1955.

Kenneth Keniston, "The Sources of Student Dissent," *Journal of Social Issues*, vol. 23, no. 3 (July 1967): 108–37.

Gustave Le Bon, *The Crowd: A Study of the Popular Mind* (1895), New York: Viking, 1960.

Alfred M. Lee and Elizabeth Lee, *The Fine Art of Propaganda*, New York: Farrar, Strauss, 1939.

S. Lieberson and A. R. Silverman, "The Precipitants and Underlying Conditions of Race Riots," *American Sociological Review*, vol. 30 (1965): 887–98.

Gary Marx, "Civil Disorder and Agents of Social Control," *Journal of Social Issues*, vol. 26, no. 1 (Winter 1970): 19–57.

J. A. McCone et al., *Violence in the City: An End or a Beginning?* Los Angeles: Governor's Commission on the Los Angeles Riots, 1965.

Joe McGinniss, *The Selling of the President 1968*, New York: Trident, 1969.

Stanley Milgram and Hans Toch, "Collective Behavior: Crowds and Social Movements," in Garner Lindzey and Elliot Aronson, eds., *The Handbook of Social Psychology*, vol. 4, 2nd ed., Reading, Mass.: Addison-Wesley, 1969.

Charles W. Roll, Jr. and Albert H. Cantril, *Polls: Their Use and Misuse in Politics*, New York: Basic Books, 1972.

David O. Sears and John B. McConahay, "Participation in the Los Angeles Riot," *Social Problems*, vol. 17 (Summer 1969): 2–20.

Joseph J. Seldin, "Public Relations vs. Public Interest," *The Progressive*, vol. 28, no. 1 (January 1964): 33–36.

Tamotsu Shibutani, *Improvised News: A Sociological Study of Rumor*, Indianapolis: Bobbs-Merrill, 1966.

Jerome H. Skolnick, *The Politics of Protest: Report to the National Commission on the Causes and Prevention of Violence*, New York: Ballantine, 1969.

Neil J. Smelser, *Theory of Collective Behavior*, New York: Free Press, 1962.

Sherwin D. Smith, "The Great 'Monkey Trial,'" *The New York Times Magazine* (July 4, 1965): 9, 14.

Gay Talese, *The Kingdom and the Power*, New York: Bantam, 1970.

Ralph H. Turner and Lewis M. Killian, *Collective Behavior*, 2nd ed., Englewood Cliffs, N.J.: Prentice-Hall, 1972.

A. I. Waskow, *From Race Riot to Sit-in: 1919 and the 1960s*, Garden City: Doubleday, 1966.

Jack M. Weller and E. L. Quarantelli, "Neglected Characteristics of Collective Behavior," *American Journal of Sociology*, vol. 79, no. 3 (November 1973): 665–85.

Alan Wells, ed., *Mass Media and Society*, Palo Alto: National Press Books, 1972.

Lewis Yablonsky, *The Violent Gang*, New York: Macmillan, 1962.

Daniel Yankelovich, "Changing Youth Values in the 70's: A Study of American Youth," © 1974, the JDR 3rd Fund.

for further study

The most comprehensive book on collective behavior is Ralph Turner and Lewis Killian's *Collective Behavior*, 2nd ed. (Englewood Cliffs, N.J.: Prentice-Hall, 1972).

Riots. Riots are difficult to observe, but they are one of the most important forms of collective behavior to study. To put the urban riots of the 1960s in perspective, start with *Report to the National Commission on the Causes and Prevention of Violence* (New York: Ballantine, 1969), and *Violence in America: Historical and Comparative Perspectives*, by Hugh D. Graham and Ted Gurr (New York: Bantam, 1969). One of the best students of the urban riots is Robert Conot, who wrote about Watts in *Rivers of Blood, Years of Darkness* (New York: Bantam, 1967) and Detroit in *American Odyssey* (New York: Morrow, 1974). Compare his account to the 1965 Governor's Commission on the Watts riot by J. A. McCone et al., *Violence in the City: An End or a Beginning?* Several sociologists report on the riots in *The Journal of Social Issues*, vol. 26, no. 1 (1970).

Social Movements. In contrast to crowds and riots, social movements are interesting to study because they embody a serious, long-term effort by a group of people to change society or to create a new institution. They are treated generally by Roberta Ash in *Social Movements in America* (Chicago: Markham, 1972). An excellent sociological account of one movement is Thomas O'Dea's book *The Mormons* (Chicago: University of Chicago Press, 1957).

Political Propaganda. An important new form of influencing collective behavior in contemporary American society is the use of television and modern
advertising techniques for political propaganda. A number of good books have
been written about the hidden techniques by which politicians and their public
relations experts try to shape our opinions. Joe McGinnis's *The Selling of the
President 1968* (New York: Trident, 1969) is a detailed account of the 1968 Nixon
campaign. The issue of political propaganda is put in larger perspective by
Harold Mendelsohn and Irving Crespi in *Polls, Television and the New Politics*
(San Francisco: Chandler, 1970) and Robert Cirino, *Don't Blame the People* (San
Francisco: Diversity Press, 1971).

PART
PART

SOCIAL CONTINUITY AND CONTROL

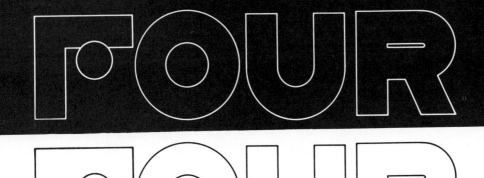

FOUR FOUR

Everyone is familiar with the story of Saint Joan, the fifteenth-century French peasant girl who broke the siege of Orleans and crowned the dauphin at Rheims, only to be captured by the British, tried for heresy, and burned at the stake. In his play *Saint Joan* (1924), George Bernard Shaw suggests that Joan's execution was inevitable. She violated the established order by commanding her social "betters" to follow her, committed "crimes against Nature" by donning men's clothes and becoming a soldier, and defied the church on grounds of individual conviction. For these reasons she had to be destroyed.

In Shaw's play a reluctant chaplain expresses doubts about Joan's culpability just before her trial begins. She seemed to him a simple country girl, hardly a dangerous witch or sorceress. The Inquisitor grows serious:

Brother Martin . . . Heresy begins with people who are to all appearances better than their neighbors. A gentle and pious girl, or a young man who has obeyed the command of our Lord by giving all his riches to the poor, and putting on the garb of poverty, the life of austerity, and the rule of humility and charity, may be the founder of a heresy that will wreck both Church and Empire if not ruthlessly stamped out in time. . . . I have seen this again and again. Mark what I say: the woman who quarrels with her clothes, and puts on the dress of a man, is like the man who

DEVIANCE
AND
SOCIAL CONTROL

throws off his fur gown and dresses like John the Baptist: they are followed, as surely as night follows the day, by bands of wild women and men who refuse to wear any clothes at all. When maids will neither marry nor take regular vows, and men reject marriage and exalt their lusts into divine inspirations, then, as surely as the summer follows spring, they begin with polygamy and end by incest. (pp. 144–45)

We no longer burn people at the stake, but we do execute some, isolate others in prisons and hospitals, and shun others whom we consider deviant. Sociologists are interested in understanding why some forms of nonconformity are so threatening to society, and why societies vary in their reactions to deviance. Why, for example, are people who hear voices, as Joan did, burned in one century, hospitalized in another? Why are people who dress differently or aspire to roles that are traditionally reserved for the opposite sex ridiculed or ostracized?

Throughout this chapter we will attempt to answer these questions. In the first part we define deviance. Then we examine biological, psychological, and sociological explanations of deviance. We will also explore the social consequences for those who are caught breaking social rules and labeled deviant, focusing on who gets labeled and why. The last part of the chapter is concerned with mechanisms of social control. We take a critical look at prisons and suggest directions for prison reform.

WHAT IS DEVIANCE?

A contemporary text on deviance and social control begins, "The subject of this book is knavery, skulduggery, cheating, unfairness, crime, sneakiness, malingering, cutting corners, immorality, dishonesty, betrayal, graft, corruption, wickedness, and sin . . ." (Cohen, 1966, p. 1). This description is only partly true, for, as we have seen, even a saint may be considered deviant. *Deviance* is a blanket term that covers everything from genius and saintliness to crime and insanity, rebellion and eccentricity. Indeed, any behavior that violates social expectations, breaks social norms, strays from the "straight and narrow" path of respectability may be labeled *deviant*.

The sociology of deviance may have begun with Emile Durkheim's observation that behaviors that qualify one person for sainthood may condemn another to prison, a mental asylum, or the stake. (Indeed, the same person may be considered a saint and a sinner, a hero and a heretic in his or her lifetime by different social groups, as Saint Joan was.) Sociologists, Durkheim wrote, "should completely abandon the still too widespread habit of judging an institution, a practice or moral standard as if it were good or bad in and by itself, for all social types indiscriminately" (1964, p. 56). His point, quite simply, was that no act is *inherently* deviant. Deviance is defined by social norms. Even killing another person is considered normal and right if the attacker is wearing a soldier's uniform and fighting for his country. (We never say that a soldier *murdered* one of the enemy.) Thus one person may be honored and another sent to prison for committing the same act.

The changing nature of the social definition of deviance is illustrated by the rise in marijuana smoking. Although possession of the drug is still illegal and subject to severe penalties, as many as 15 million Americans had at least tried marijuana by 1972 (Gallup, April 1972, no. 72). According to Gallup Polls, only 5 percent of college students surveyed in 1967 had tried marijuana, but 55 percent of students surveyed in 1974 had smoked it. Although arrests for possession of marijuana rose 43 percent in 1972 alone (*Uniform Crime Reports*, 1973), public attitudes toward the drug are changing. It will be interesting to see if the penalties against marijuana-smokers are softened, in line with greater public acceptance of the drug.

Deviance varies not only with time and from group to group in one society, but it varies cross-culturally as well. In parts of the Near and Far East, for example, opiates are sold on a cash-and-carry basis in open markets, and people smoke marijuana and hashish publicly. Even in this country attitudes toward drugs in general are highly inconsistent. There is little or no stigma attached to taking tranquilizers, sleeping pills, or pain killers obtained with a doctor's prescription, drinking large quantities of alcohol (at socially appropriate times), or smoking tobacco, all of which pose clear health hazards.

Just as ideas about what is and what is not deviant vary, so do explanations of nonconforming behavior. Once, almost all Americans considered homosexuality an expression of depravity, a sin, a "crime against nature" that showed a person morally unfit for life among decent people. Then homosexuality "became" a mental illness, an unfortunate compulsion that might be cured through psychotherapy. But in 1974 the American Psychiatric Association voted to remove homosexuality from its catalogue of mental illnesses, declaring it to be a "sexual orientation disturbance," not an illness.[1]

---

[1] Interestingly, Sigmund Freud anticipated this shift. In a "Letter to an American Mother" he wrote, "I gather from your letter that your son is a homosexual. . . . Homosexuality is assuredly no advantage, but it is nothing to be ashamed of, no vice, no degradation, it cannot be classified as an illness; we consider it to be a variation of the sexual function" (in Schur, 1965, p. 72).

The definition of deviance varies from country to country, group to group, and time to time. In contemporary America, it is acceptable, in fact desirable, to drink alcohol at socially appropriate times. During prohibition, these people would have been arrested. (Ray Ellis/Rapho Guillumette)

Similarly, behavior that was once considered a sign of possession by the devil and evil spirits, punishable by exorcism or burning, became symptoms of mental illness in the twentieth century, treatable by various kinds of therapies and drugs. Indeed, some contemporary psychologists and psychiatrists even argue that the concept of mental illness is a myth (Szasz, 1970).

Whether an act is stigmatized and the person who commits it labeled evil or sick depends, in part, on his or her social status (see chapters 3 and 8). Many white-collar criminals who violate tax laws, antitrust laws, and the like are fined relatively small proportions of their incomes, but rarely imprisoned (Gibbons, 1968, p. 319). Former vice-president Spiro Agnew walked away from admitted extortion charges a free man. (His penalty was resigning from office, not going to jail.)

And Richard Nixon, after his resignation from the presidency, was fully pardoned for any crimes that he might have committed during his years in the White House. In contrast most car thiefs (71 percent in one study) are sentenced to prison for three years (Mitford, 1973, p. 76). In the final analysis, then, the definition of deviance is at least partly a matter of social power: the people who have the power to enforce their definitions decide what is proper and what is deviant.

EXPLANATIONS OF DEVIANCE

During 1972 police learned of more than 18,000 murders and over 40,000 rapes committed in that year. Close to 375,000 people were robbed and an equal number assaulted. Some 880,000 Americans stole cars. There were 1.8 million cases of larceny (thefts of $50 and over) and 2.3 million burglaries (*Uniform Crime Reports*, 1973). Undoubtedly the true figures are much higher: many crimes are never reported. Data on crimes without victims (gambling, prostitution, drug addiction, and so on) are even less reliable. We know only about those people who come to the attention of authorities. Why do people break the law? As we will show in the pages that follow, the answer to the question of why people deviate isn't obvious at all. Numerous theories have been advanced.

Biological Explanations

In the nineteenth-century world view, people were considered rational. They were supposed to act only in ways advantageous to themselves. "Crime does not pay," so how could someone be rational and yet be a criminal? Cesare Lombroso, an Italian criminologist, suggested an explanation—people could be *born* criminals (Lombroso, 1911). Misinterpreting Darwin's evolutionary theory, he suggested that criminals were throwbacks, more nearly representing our primitive and savage ancestors than modern men and women. This flash hit Lombroso as he examined Villella, an Italian master criminal. He reported excitedly that:

At the sight of that skull, I seemed to see all of a sudden, lighted up as a vast plain under a flaming sky, the problem of the nature of the criminal—an atavistic being who reproduces in his person the ferocious instincts of primitive humanity and the inferior animals. Thus were explained the enormous jaws, high cheekbones, prominent superciliary arches . . . found in criminals, savages, and apes, insensibility to pain, extremely acute sight, tattooing, excessive idleness, love of orgies, and the irresistible craving for evil for its own sake, the desire not only to extinguish life in the victim, but to mutilate the corpse, tear its flesh, and drink its blood. (Lombroso, in Cohen, 1966, p. 50)

Lombroso and his students made dozens of measurements on the heads and bodies of scores of prisoners, and every criminal fit the "animalistic" pattern. But Lombroso made one serious error—he measured only criminals. When a British physician, Charles Goring, measured ordinary citizens, he found that they were no different, at least physically, from criminals (Goring, 1913).

Although Lombroso's theory was abandoned, the search for a biological explanation for deviance lived on. William Sheldon, an American psychologist and doctor, developed another theory linked to physical characteristics (Sheldon, 1949). He grouped people into three body types: soft and round (endomorphs); hard and rectangular (mesomorphs); and lean and fragile (ectomorphs). Endomorphs, Sheldon claimed, are easygoing, friendly, self-indulgent types—the fat, jolly person everyone likes. Mesomorphs, he argued, are energetic, hyperactive, impulsive people who rarely stop to think about what they are doing. Ectomorphs are nervous, sensitive, and withdrawn. To test his classifications, Sheldon examined two hundred boys at a Boston rehabilitation center, studying their biographies and analyzing their physical types. He found that most of the delinquent youngsters were mesomorphs and concluded that their physiology predisposed them to deviance. Mesomorphs, Sheldon argued, are quick to translate impulses into action and lack the sensitivity to consider what they are doing.

Using Sheldon's typology, Sheldon and Eleanor Glueck (1956) compared five hundred delinquent boys to five hundred nondelinquents and found that significantly more of the delinquents were mesomorphs. They concluded that under the right conditions, the "excessive instinctual energy and weak or erratic inhibitory apparatus" of mesomorphs would be expressed in deviant behavior. The Gluecks added that the relatively small numbers of endomorphs and ectomorphs who became delinquent did so to compensate for their less than ideal build. In this way the researchers covered all possibilities. If an ectomorph conformed to the rules, he was doing what they would predict from his body type. If, on the other hand, he became delinquent, he was also doing what they would predict, namely compensating for his body type.

Although biological explanations of deviance have lost popularity, the possibility of physiological *predispositions* for deviance has not been forgotten. The discovery that Richard Speck, who murdered seven nurses in Chicago in 1966, was genetically abnormal stimulated new research in this field. (A normal man has an XY chromosome pattern, a normal woman an XX chromosome pattern; Speck has an XYY pattern.) Although the "XYY" theory of born criminals has been disproved, research in this area continues. Researchers have discovered chemical differences between schizophrenics and other people, and between hyperactive and normally active children. But to date there is no firm proof that genetic or chemical abnormalities *produce* deviant behavior.

Psychological Explanations

Freudian psychologists maintain that all people have deviant impulses, but that in the process of growing up most of us learn to inhibit them most of the time. Freud argued that through identification with their parents, children acquire a superego, or conscience, that forbids certain kinds of behavior, and an ego that enables them to deal realistically with internal drives and social demands (see chapter 5).

Psychoanalytic theory suggests that children who are neglected or mistreated may not relate to their parents or other adults in this important way. As a result they do not learn to take the position of the other—to, for example, see burglary or mugging from the victim's point of view. They develop only weak inner controls, and it is these people who violate social expectations. The technical term for a person who does not feel remorse or guilt for harmful actions and has little sense of right and wrong is *sociopath*. This model is often invoked to explain wanton cruelty and crimes committed without apparent motives.

Other deviants, according to the psychodynamic view, have a weak or erratic superego. Although they know that they are about to do something wrong or cruel, they cannot help themselves and succumb to their impulses. For example, a woman may lead an exemplary life, fulfill her responsibilities toward her family and job, but find the desire to shoplift irresistible. Or a person may conform to social norms among his or her "own kind," but not apply these norms to outsiders. A member of a teen-age gang, for example, may treat fellow gang members as brothers, but may feel no qualms about cheating members of rival gangs. Finally, an *overdeveloped* superego may also lead to deviance. People who are repulsed by their own urges may commit deviant acts to receive the punishment they feel they deserve, for hating their parents or for having sexual fantasies, for example (Cohen, 1966, pp. 56–57).

Other psychologists do not agree that we all have aggressive impulses which must be controlled, but simply argue that we learn from those around us. Albert Bandura and Richard H. Walters, for example, compared groups of delinquent and nondelinquent white adolescent males from financially stable homes (1959). They found that continuously harsh, physical discipline or over-indulgence could lead to delinquency. Boys whose fathers frequently beat them tended to rely on external controls, that is, they based decisions on the chances of being caught, not on inner feelings of right and wrong. Furthermore, they emulated their fathers' violent, retaliatory approach to life. On the other hand, boys who had their parents' uncritical approval grew up believing that anything they wanted to do was good—an assumption the outside world did not always share. Most successful were loving but firm parents.

Sociological Explanations

Although psychological theories of deviance provide insights into individual cases, they do not explain why *rates* of deviance (the number of deviant acts per unit of population) vary from group to group, from neighborhood to neighborhood. Sociological theories address this question. Sociologists have found that social environment influences many kinds of deviance—even something so psychological as psychosis and so personal as suicide (see chapter 2).

Deviance and Anomie   One sociologist who tried to account for varying rates of crime in different social classes was Robert K. Merton (1957). Merton linked high rates of deviance to anomie. As defined by Durkheim, *anomie* is a state of normlessness or confusion that occurs when cultural formulas for living do

not match social realities. For example, the culture may decree that every man must have a job, but the social structure may not provide enough jobs for every man. Merton reasoned that all people internalize, to some degree, the goals that are considered worth striving for in their culture. Everyone, too, internalizes the norms governing proper and legitimate ways of striving for these goals. When opportunities for achieving highly valued goals (as the culture defines them) do not exist, people seek alternatives. Thus "some social structures exert a definite pressure upon certain persons in the society to engage in nonconforming rather than in conforming behavior" (Merton, 1957, p. 132).

Merton defined *conformity* as seeking culturally approved goals by culturally approved means. He outlined four types of deviant behavior that may occur when social realities do not match cultural expectations (see table 12:1). The first type is *innovation*—pursuing culturally validated goals by deviant means. A thief, for example, is pursuing the same objectives as a working person—namely, money, the things it can buy, and the prestige it confers. They are playing the same game, but with different rules. Merton stresses that poverty alone does not boost crime rates. In a rigidly stratified society the poor do not expect to move up the social ladder. "It is only when a system of cultural values extols, virtually above all else, certain *common* goals for *the population at large* while the social structure rigorously restricts or completely closes access to approved modes of reaching these goals *for a considerable part of the same population*, that deviant behavior ensues on a large scale" (p. 146). Innovations may also occur because culturally prescribed goals are unreachable. The fact that success is defined as *more* in American culture helps to explain the high incidence of white-collar crime.

table 12:1 **MERTON'S MODEL OF ADAPTATION TO CULTURAL GOALS**

MODES OF ADAPTATION	CULTURE GOALS	INSTITUTIONALIZED MEANS
1. Conformity	+	+
2. Innovation	+	−
3. Ritualism	−	+
4. Retreatism	−	−
5. Rebellion	±	±

SOURCE: Robert K. Merton, *Social Theory and Social Structure* (New York: The Free Press, 1956), p. 140.

A second way to resolve conflicts between goals and means is *ritualism*, adhering rigidly to norms at the expense of goals. A bureaucrat who follows regulations to the letter regardless of whether he or she gets the job done is the prototype for this type of deviance (see chapter 10). Following the rules becomes a virtue, a goal in itself. Police and firemen, who are prohibited by law from striking, often use ritualism to bring City Hall to the bargaining table. A teacher who maintains order in the classroom and delivers lessons in the prescribed way regardless of whether students learn anything is a ritualist.

Merton notes that ritualists are often not labeled deviant. People may consider bureaucratic rule-sticklers stupid or aggravating, but generally do not put them in the same category as criminals. However, Nazi officials who obeyed inhumane orders were treated as criminals; so was Lieutenant Calley, who was held responsible for the murder of civilians at My Lai.

Merton uses the term *retreatism* to describe giving up. Retreatists are people who have lost the desire to pursue certain cultural goals as well as the belief that following

certain norms is intrinsically worthwhile. Drug addicts, alcoholics, many psychotics, drifters, and bums are examples. These people have withdrawn; they are "*in* the society but not *of* it." In Merton's view retreatism is an escape mechanism, a way in which people protect themselves from confusion and failure.

Cloward and Ohlin (1960) agreed with Merton's description of retreatism. After comparing different types of delinquency, they concluded that youngsters who become involved in the drug subculture are usually "double losers" who lack the opportunity and ability to succeed both in the legitimate world, as conformists, and in the illegitimate world, as innovators.

Retreatism may also explain the high rates of mental illness among poor people in America, where the strain between goals and opportunities is greatest. Hollingshead and Redlich (1958) and Myers and Bean (1968) have found that rates of commitment to mental hospitals vary inversely with social class—that is, the lower the social class, the higher the rate of hospitalization. Data also indicate that outpatient psychiatric care is

In Merton's model of deviance, both gang members and hippies are adapting to conflicts between social goals and means, but in different ways. George, the leader of the Reapers, is an *innovator:* he seeks the culturally approved goals of wealth and status, but by deviant means. People who "drop out," rejecting society's goals (as many hippies did during the 1960s) are *retreatists*. (Top, Steve Salmieri. Bottom, Wayne Miller/Magnum)

figure 12:1 Family income and psychiatric outpatient care, 1969

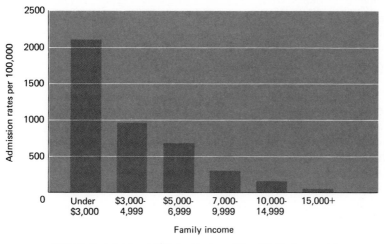

SOURCE: *Statistical Note #47*, National Institute of Mental Health, Survey and Reports Section, Biometry Branch.

Whether these data reflect the incidence of psychological problems or merely rates of treatment in outpatient clinics is debatable. In all likelihood, more middle- and upper-class people have problems than the statistics show, but because they are treated privately, their problems are not a matter of public record.

inversely related to income as well (see figure 12:1).

Finally, people who are alienated from both the goals and standards of their culture may create new ideals and new rules for pursuing them. Merton calls this *rebellion*. The Weathermen, the Panthers, and the Minutemen (right-wing radicals) are examples. Rebellion need not be political, however. Seeking economic self-sufficiency on a rural commune, rejecting conventional marriage and family for freer relationships are also examples of rebellion.

The question still remains as to why rebellious subcultures develop in some corners of society and criminal subcultures in others. Cloward and Ohlin addressed this problem in their study of delinquency (1960). They concluded that the kind of adaptation people who are denied access to legitimate avenues to

legitimate goals make depends on the *opportunity structures* in their environment. Just as some communities offer young people opportunities for education, role-models of people who have achieved success by conventional means, and contacts with people who can advance their careers, so other communities offer opportunities for learning how to hustle and evade authorities, role-models of people who have achieved success as gamblers or pimps, and contacts with the underworld.[2] Ironically, illegitimate opportunity structures thrive in reform schools, prisons,

---

[2] This is not to say that everyone who has the opportunity to enter organized crime does so. Some do and some don't—just as some people with opportunities to succeed by conventional means conform to social expectations and others break away. Sociologists are concerned with *rates* of deviance. Questions of individual choice are psychological questions that require psychological answers.

and other institutions whose putative goals are to rehabilitate deviants. Here, people caught breaking rules are segregated from conforming people and have unlimited time to teach one another deviant skills and attitudes, and to reinforce one another's alienation from society.

By calling attention to opportunity structures, Cloward and Ohlin highlight the often overlooked fact that people must *learn* how to steal, conduct prostitution, shoot heroin, smoke marijuana, find homosexual partners, organize protest marches, or make Molotov cocktails. Deviant behavior is rarely invented on the spot.

Cultural Transmission of Deviance The idea that some people are socialized to what society at large regards as deviance, just as some people are socialized to conformity, was conceived and developed at the University of Chicago in the 1920s and 1930s (Cohen, 1966, p. 94). Clifford Shaw and Henry McKay (1929) found that high crime rates persisted in the same Chicago neighborhoods for over twenty years, even though different ethnic groups had come and gone. Obviously, ethnic traditions could not explain the crime rate. Shaw and McKay concluded that newcomers learned deviant ways from established residents, primarily in play groups and teenage gangs. Eventually they passed these norms and values on to new waves of immigrants. Thus deviance may be learned through the natural process of cultural transmission. In a similar way, people might be socialized to the drug subculture, the homosexual subculture, the radical subculture, and so on.

The effects of norms and values on young people growing up in high-crime neighborhoods was the subject of a study conducted by Walter B. Miller (1958). During a three-year participant-observation study Miller identified the "focal concerns" of lower-class, urban, adolescent males: trouble (with the law and with women); toughness (physical prowess and playing it cool); smartness (being able to outsmart and con others and avoid being conned oneself, as well as a respect for verbal quickness and ingenuity); fate (a sense that many forces are beyond one's control, that success is a matter of luck); and autonomy (a resentment of outside controls—"No one's gonna push me around"). Miller argues that such delinquent acts as drinking or stealing cars are expressions of these important subcultural concerns. Like all adolescents, ghetto youth are eager to demonstrate their adulthood and to gain and maintain status among their peers. Miller argues that delinquency is "a directed attempt . . . to adhere to forms of behavior, and to achieve standards as they are defined in that community" (p. 5).

Of course ghetto youngsters also encounter many role-models who conform to and advocate conventional goals and means. Why do some youths choose deviant over conforming styles? In *Principles of Criminology*, Edwin H. Sutherland (1960) pointed out that *everyone* is exposed to different, often conflicting definitions of right and wrong—to people who value obeying the law and to people who consider the law merely a hindrance and the police as enemies.[3] The standards people adopt as their own depend on the frequency, duration, priority, and intensity of their association with procriminal or anticriminal, radical or conservative, heterosexual or homosexual ideas. Thus if those who matter most to a person devalue conformity, he or she will try to learn techniques for committing deviant acts and will accept rationalizations for committing them.

---

[3] Law-abiding people, for example, may consider income-tax laws obstacles to be overcome with every possible trick.

LABELING AND DEVIANT CAREERS

In the late 1950s some sociologists began wondering if they hadn't been asking the wrong questions about deviance. Virtually everyone breaks rules at one time or another. A survey of nearly seventeen hundred New Yorkers, for example, revealed that 99 percent had violated the penal code at least once. And a random sample revealed that as many as one in five residents of midtown Manhattan is severely disturbed, though none of these is hospitalized (Srole et al., 1962). And Kinsey found that 37 percent of American men reported one or more homosexual experiences. Most of these people do not think of themselves as deviants—nor do other people. Their nonconformity is one, perhaps secret, aspect of an otherwise respectable life. However, others who have performed the very same acts (or been falsely accused of doing so) are branded criminal, psychotic, or queer for the rest of their lives. A key question, then, is why some people get labeled as deviant while others, who commit the same acts, do not.

Labeling

Suppose a man meets a girl in a park; they talk and later go to bed together. The affair lasts a month or two, and then they part. But, suppose the girl is only fourteen, although she looks and pretends to be older. She has become pregnant, and to save face tells her parents she was raped. The man is taken to court and convicted. He loses his job and cannot find another. His future, in that town at least, is ruined. Even if he is acquitted, the accusation and trial would tarnish his re-spectability. Wherever he goes, people stare and whisper: RAPIST. For the girl, refusal to tell anyone who the father of her child is would burden her with the full stigma of unwed motherhood. If she reveals the father, her fate partly depends on how her parents react—on whether they agree to help her support the child, arrange an abortion, or declare her incorrigible and send her to a reform school. In this way she, too, might be labeled deviant.

As Howard S. Becker suggests in *Outsiders* (1963), people perform deviant acts for various reasons. They even may not know they are doing anything wrong, like the man in the story above. Or people may know they are breaking a rule, but calculate that the ends justify the means. Or they may simply have no reputation to maintain, no stake in appearing to be a normal and conventional person. Whatever their reasons for deviating, their fate depends, *not* on the reason, but on whether they are caught and publicly *labeled* deviant.

Deviant labels—queer, lunatic, thief, junk-ie—have an almost magical quality. They tend to wipe out whatever favorable impressions a person may create. One day he is the man next door, a good friend and neighbor. The next day people discover he is not what he was supposed to be, he *is* a homosexual. "The question is raised: 'What kind of person would break such an important rule?' And the answer is given: 'One who is different from the rest of us, who cannot or will not act as a moral human being and therefore might break other important rules'" (Becker, 1963, pp. 33–34). The deviant label becomes a master status, coloring all other aspects of the person's identity (see chapter 3).

Who Gets Labeled? As the statistics at the beginning of this section indicate, only a fraction of the people who break rules are caught and publicly discredited. Sociologists are interested in discovering the kinds of people who *do* get labeled. In the 1960s William J. Chambliss (1973) spent two years as a participant-observer at "Hannibal High School." During this period he became acquainted with the members of two gangs, the Saints and the Roughnecks. The eight members of the Saints came from upper-middle-class families; they were good students and active in school affairs. On weekends and on days when they sneaked out of school (most days, Chambliss found), the Saints amused themselves with various forms of delinquency: heavy drinking, reckless driving, games of "chicken," petty theft, and vandalism. A favorite pastime was removing the wooden barricades and lanterns from street repair sites and watching unsuspecting drivers cruise into the hole. Although their activities were hazardous, townspeople considered them good boys who were sowing a few wild oats. Stealing small items and breaking into empty houses were considered pranks. Not one Saint was arrested in the two years Chambliss spent at "Hannibal High."

In contrast, the six Roughnecks were in constant trouble with the police, and townspeople considered them good-for-nothings. The Roughnecks came from lower-class families and were not particularly good students.

Most weekends they could be found hanging around the local drugstore, drinking from concealed bottles. Almost every month they got into a fight—usually among themselves. Like the Saints, they stole, more for profit than for thrills. Even so, Chambliss estimates that property damage by the Saints cost townspeople *more* than the Roughnecks' thefts. And although the Saints rarely fought, they endangered their own and other people's lives nearly every time they got behind the wheel of a car.

Why did townspeople wink at the Saints but condemn the Roughnecks as delinquents? One reason was that the Saints had cars and left the immediate community for their drinking bouts. The Roughnecks, too poor to own cars, were more visible. In addition, the police knew from experience that the Saints' upper-middle-class parents would cause trouble if their children were arrested, insisting their sons were just having fun and putting police on the defensive. The Roughnecks' parents did not have the power and influence to protect them. Finally, the Saints dressed nicely, drove good cars, and spoke politely to teachers, police, and other authorities. Anyone could see they were "good boys," tomorrow's leaders. The Roughnecks were different: "everyone agreed that the not-so-well-dressed, not-so-well-mannered,

table 12:2 **EFFECT OF FOUR TYPES OF LEGAL FOLDERS ON JOB OPPORTUNITIES (by percent)**

	NO RECORD	ACQUITTED WITH LETTER	ACQUITTED WITHOUT LETTER	CONVICTED	TOTAL
Positive response	36	24	12	4	19
Negative response	64	76	88	96	81
Total	100	100	100	100	100

SOURCE: *The Other Side* (New York: The Free Press, 1963), p. 110.

not-so-rich boys were heading for trouble" (p. 27). In short, the community's social structure protected the Saints but not the Roughnecks (recall the discussion of *Tally's Corner* in chapter 3). Additional studies of social power and labeling are discussed in the accompanying box.

The Consequences of Labeling: Stigma and the Deviant Career Typically, people who are labeled criminals, declared mentally ill, or branded queer are excluded from conventional social life. They may or may not be isolated physically, that is, in a prison or a mental hospital, but nearly always they are isolated socially. A man convicted of a crime describes the experience:

And I always have this feeling with straight people—that whenever they're being nice to me, pleasant to me, all the time really, underneath they're only assessing me as a criminal and nothing else. It's too late for me to be any different now to [sic] what I am, but I still feel this keenly, that that's their only approach, and they're quite incapable of accepting me as anything else. (in Goffman, 1963B, p. 14)

The stigma of deviance may even extend to a person's family, as when a poor family is denied public housing because one child has been arrested or convicted for juvenile delinquency. In the box on page 334, a respected member of the medical profession explains that for years he hid his homosexuality to

---

SOCIAL POWER AND DEVIANT LABELS

A study conducted by Richard Schwartz and Jerome Skolnick offers proof that middle- and upper-class people are often able to "get away" with the kinds of behavior that earn deviant labels for the poor and the powerless. Schwartz and Skolnick sent four different applications to a total of one hundred employers. All four described a thirty-two-year-old, single, male high-school graduate who had held a series of jobs including kitchen helper and handyman. One of the applications stated that the man had been convicted for assault; the second noted that he had been tried for assault and acquitted; the third included a letter from the judge certifying that he had been found not guilty; and the fourth said nothing about a criminal record. The responses (table 12:2) show clearly that employers made little distinction between conviction and acquittal, even when a judge certified the applicant's innocence.

In a second, parellel study, Schwartz and Skolnick interviewed fifty-seven medical doctors who had been accused of malpractice (which is roughly equivalent to being arrested for assault). Thirty-eight had won their cases, fifteen had settled out of court, and four had lost in court. Fifty-two of the doctors reported that the malpractice suit had no effect on their careers, and five indicated that their practices had actually *improved* after the suit. In fact, the doctor who suffered the heaviest loss in court reported the *most* improvement after the case. He reasoned that other doctors felt sorry for him and were sending him more referrals. Thus a doctor who was found guilty escaped labeling, but a high-school graduate who was found innocent was nevertheless stigmatized.

SOURCE: Richard D. Schwartz and Jerome H. Skolnick, "Two Studies of Legal Stigma," in Howard S. Becker, ed., *The Other Side* (New York: Free Press, 1964), pp. 103–117.

IN THE NEWS

The Agony of Secrecy

In December 1973 Dr. Howard J. Brown, professor of the public administration of health at New York University, publicly acknowledged his homosexuality in a statement to a symposium of six hundred physicians.

Dr. Brown revealed how the fear of being discovered had shaped every aspect of his life. Should he be seen in restaurants or theaters with male friends? Could he live with another male? admit that he liked to cook? As a young man, Brown had hoped to become a small town doctor, but moved to New York City's liberal Greenwich Village when he realized the problems for homosexuals in small towns were insurmountable. In 1967 he resigned as New York City's health services commissioner after hearing rumors that a journalist was planning to write a column about homosexuals in city government.

Why did Dr. Brown issue his statement? He told reporters:

You get to a point in your own life where you want to leave a legacy—in a sense this can help free the generation that comes after us from the dreadful agony of secrecy, the constant need to hide.

He added that he knew of many highly respected clergymen, politicians, and doctors who were homosexual, but doubted they would follow him in public disclosure.

They feel such a disclosure would ruin their professional career, destroy their reputation and wreck many friendships. And indeed in my own case, until recently I would have assumed that following my public appearance as a homosexual, that the only proper next step would be suicide.

Interestingly, the Skolnick and Schwartz study we discussed earlier suggests that public disclosure of medical malpractice may carry a lighter stigma than homosexuality. But times are changing. Brown's disclosure led not to ostracism, but to his appointment as chairman of a committee to combat discrimination against homosexuals for the Public Health Association of New York.

SOURCE: Marcia Chambers, *The New York Times* (Oct. 3, 1973): 1, 42.

avoid the severe consequences that revelation would have brought for both himself and his family.

Deviant labels tend to become self-fulfilling prophecies. Chambliss found that with few exceptions, the Saints and Roughnecks lived up (and down) to community expectations. As Goffman has written, "one response to this fate [being labeled deviant] is to embrace it" (1963B, p. 30). This is the final step toward a deviant career. Cut off, the addict begins to associate almost exclusively with other addicts, the prostitute with other prostitutes. (Often these associations are made in prisons and in other institutions aimed at *correcting* deviant inclinations.) Gradually the person develops new understandings and routines. He or she learns techniques for deviating from more experienced offenders. Equally important, career-deviants learn rationalizations for deviant behavior. For example, prostitutes grow to regard their work as a social service and consider those who condemn sex for money as hypocrites. The deviant subculture begins to play an increasingly central role in the person's identity and life-style. As one addict told a researcher, she realized she was addicted when she noticed that all of her friends were junkies (Becker 1963, p. 38). Thus in labeling certain people deviant and shutting them out of conventional life, society virtually *assures* the behavior it is trying to control, an outcome few people consider.

A Critique of Labeling Theory

While this description of the drift into deviant careers is compelling, in several ways it verges on "liberal overkill." Labeling theorists imply that the people who fill the wards of mental hospitals, for example, are there because someone more or less arbitrarily decided to label them sick and subject them to the consequences. They tend to ignore the fact that most of the people in mental hospitals were unable to cope with their lives and their problems outside. Many, too, are dangerous or highly disruptive to themselves and to others. At least one researcher found that both families and authorities consider commitment to a mental hospital a very last resort, and exhaust all other alternatives before launching commitment proceedings (Gove, 1970).

This is not to say that labeling theory is "wrong," but that it only partly explains deviant careers. It does not say why people violate rules in the first place or why some people are able to resist or overcome the stigma of deviance. But labeling theory does help us to focus on the social structure of power behind the rules. What really matters is who makes the rules and who has the power to make the labels stick. This is the underlying theme of social control.

SOCIAL CONTROL

In any community, the purpose of social control is to encourage conformity. The chapter on socialization partly answered the question: Why do most people conform? In different ways each of the theorists discussed in that chapter explained how and why cultural standards become part of the growing child's personality structure. Sociologists use the term *internalization* to describe this process. Internalization means that people have so thoroughly accepted certain norms and values that deviating from them is largely unthinkable. They abide by these rules not because they fear being labeled and punished for nonconforming behavior, but to avoid *self*-condemnation.[4] Deviating from these norms makes most people feel guilty and disoriented. In effect, each person learns to distinguish between "me" and "not me," between behavior that seems consistent with his or her self-image or identity and behavior that does not.

It is easy to forget that internalized norms and values are the basis of social order: people police themselves. But socialization is never "perfect": people may not internalize all of the rules society considers "right." A variety of informal and formal social controls fill this gap.

---

[4] This is Kohlberg's sixth stage of moral development. See pp. 110.

Informal Social Controls

Fear of ostracism pressures people to conform to norms and values they have not fully internalized. A silent stare, the "cold shoulder," gossip, laughter, ridicule, verbal and physical threats, a parent's or spouse's tears and exhortations—as well as smiles and other rewards for conformity—are everyday mechanisms of *informal social control*. Often the mere anticipation of disapproval from family, friends, co-workers, even strangers in a public place stops people from engaging in deviant activities. Indeed, disregard for public opinion—as when people talk to themselves or masturbate in public—is considered a primary symptom of mental illness (Goffman, 1963A).

However, informal controls can work in the opposite direction, pressuring conforming individuals into deviant acts. For example, an adolescent may steal or take drugs to gain prestige among his or her peers, or adults may embezzle to maintain the standard of living people expect of them. In addition, the norms of family and friendship require people to protect deviants who are close to them. The words *tattletale, fink,* and *informer* are not terms of praise. As a result, modern societies depend heavily on institutionalized formal controls.

Formal Social Controls

Formal social controls are all those organizations and roles specifically designed to enforce conformity in a society, including police departments, courts, prisons, juvenile facilities, mental hospitals, drug rehabilitation centers, and settlement houses and other social-work agencies. Police, judges, and prison and hospital guards are the most obvious agents of social control, but psychiatrists, social workers, ministers, teachers, and lawyers are also in positions to enforce conformity. In the pages that follow we will focus on society's efforts to determine how much crime there really is and on efforts to control it.

Measuring Crimes and Corrections Each year the FBI issues the *Uniform Crime Report*, a compilation of national statistics on seven serious crimes: murder, rape, robbery, aggravated assault, burglary, larceny of $50 or more, and auto theft. In 1972 a total of 5,891,900 crimes were committed, including 828,150 crimes of violence and 5,063,800 crimes against property. The FBI also converts the number of crimes into crime rates (crimes per 100,000 population) and measures trends. Crime rates ensure that crimes are related to the appropriate population base. Between 1967 and 1972 the violent-crime rate rose 67 percent; and the rate of crimes against property rose 53 percent (see figures 12:2 and 12:3).

Is the *Uniform Crime Report* an accurate measure of criminal activity in this country? Yes and no. The FBI tabulates only those crimes that come to the attention of police. By all estimates the number of unreported crimes is much higher. For example, in 1965–1966, the National Opinion Research Center (NORC) polled a national sample of ten thousand households, asking whether anyone in the family had been the victim of crime during the preceding year. According to this survey crime rates are about twice as high as FBI statistics indicate.[5] A similar survey conducted in Washington, D.C., revealed an even wider gap (see figure 12:4). When asked why they hadn't reported crimes, most

---

[5] NORC estimates the violent-crime rate per 100,000 to be 358 and the rate of crimes against property as 1,762; the FBI crime rates for the same period were 185 and 793, respectively.

figure 12:2 Crimes of violence 1967–1972

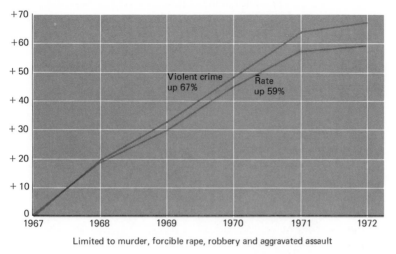

Limited to murder, forcible rape, robbery and aggravated assault

SOURCE: *Uniform Crime Reports* (Washington, D.C.: Government Printing Office, 1972), p. 4.

figure 12:3 Crimes against property 1967–1972

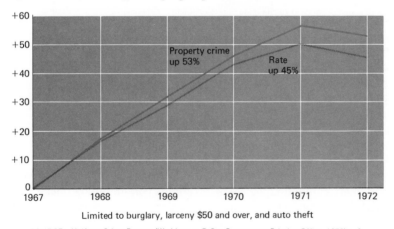

Limited to burglary, larceny $50 and over, and auto theft

SOURCE: *Uniform Crime Reports* (Washington, D.C.: Government Printing Office, 1972) p. 3.

people told NORC interviewers they knew the police couldn't do anything, so why bother? A smaller number said they didn't want to get the offender in trouble. (Eighty-eight percent of murders, 66 percent of rapes, and 75 percent of assaults are committed by family members or acquaintances, [Mitford, 1973, p. 61].) Others said they feared reprisal. Presumably many white-collar crimes go unreported because businesses would rather avoid an investigation of their books, and find it easier to charge consumers an extra 1 or 2 percent than to prosecute embezzlers, shoplifters, and so on.

figure 12:4　**Estimated rates of offense[1]: comparison of police[2] and bureau of social science research survey date, 1967**

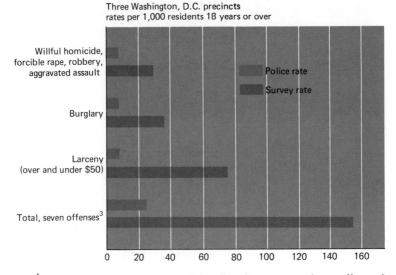

Three Washington, D.C. precincts
rates per 1,000 residents 18 years or over

[1] Incidents involving more than one victim adjusted to count as only one offense. A victimization rate would count the incidence for each individual.

[2] Police statistics adjusted to eliminate nonresident and commercial victims and victims under 18 years of age.

[3] Willful homicide, forcible rape, robbery, aggravated assault, burglary, larceny (over and under $50), and motor vehicle theft.

SOURCE: Albert Biderman, *The Annals*, November, 1967, page 20.

The extent of unreported crime during one year in Washington, D.C., can be seen in the above graphs. The survey rates for various offenses are from three to ten times greater than the reported rates.

Nor does the FBI collect statistics on murder, assault, and theft committed by mine owners, slum landlords, construction companies, car manufacturers, and other corporations that violate health and safety codes (resulting in death and injury) and rob consumers through deceptive advertising and packaging (Mitford, 1973, p. 64). In most cases such violations are not even considered crimes, and charges against companies are settled in civil suits or out of court. (No one goes to jail when workers are killed in a mine that has been repeatedly cited for fire and safety violations.)

The *Uniform Crime Report* also ignores crimes committed by police, who, of course, do not report themselves. In the mid-sixties Albert J. Reiss, Jr. and a team of thirty-six participant-observers accompanied patrolmen in high-crime districts of Boston, Chicago, and Washington, D.C., daily for seven weeks. Although the policemen knew they were being watched, one out of five committed crimes during the course of the study, the most common being stealing from drunks and "deviants," stealing from establishments that had been burglarized, and taking bribes. The Reiss team also observed forty-four police assaults, only seven of which could be characterized as provoked. Given the fact that these officers knew they were being watched and presumably modified their behavior, Reiss concluded that police routinely break more laws than his observations indicated (1971).

The FBI's calculation of rising crime rates is also deceptive. The increase in larceny, for example, reflects higher prices as well as more crimes. The fact that bicycles cost $50 or more today may account for much of the increase in larceny rates. The "crime explosion" also reflects improved, computerized methods of recording crimes. After all, it is to the FBI's advantage to find dramatic increases in the crime rates; the more crimes reported, the more money Congress allocates to the bureau for law enforcement procedures (Mitford, 1973, p. 64).

How do the police and courts handle the 5 million or more crimes that are reported? In 1972 police arrested 22 percent of the close to 5.5 million reported law-breakers—which means that 78 percent went unapprehended. Eighty-three percent of the adults arrested were prosecuted in the courts. Of those, 59 percent were found guilty as charged, and 12 percent were guilty of a lesser charge. About 30 percent of the cases were either acquitted or dismissed.

In 1972, 36 percent of all murder defendants were either acquitted or their cases dismissed at some stage in the prosecution process. Forty-nine percent of those charged with forcible rape were acquitted or had their cases dismissed, and 41 percent of the persons charged with aggravated assault won their freedom through acquittal or dismissal (*Uniform Crime Reports*, 1972, pp. 35, 107). In 1965 less than 3 percent of known, serious crimes actually resulted in prison terms. What these figures show is that the correctional system is highly selective: very few of the people who commit crimes are prose-

cuted to the full extent of the law. And the majority of these are young, male, poor, and in four cases out of ten, nonwhite (Mitford, 1973, p. 133). In other words, prisoners are selected.

The Social Dynamics of Crime Control In theory a policeman's job is to enforce the law. In practice though, police decide *when* and *how* to enforce the law, because arresting all law-breakers would be impossible. In the course of a day police make numerous decisions about what constitutes a crime and what persons should or should not be arrested. In making such decisions, usually in the heat of the moment, police must consider their responsibility to the public and to their superiors for maintaining order. They must also think about maintaining their own authority on the street, if they are to do their job at all (Reiss, 1971). In the end they rely on their own judgment (on "instincts" and experience) in deciding who is a danger to the community and who threatens police authority. In plain language, they arrest people whom they "know" to be potential or actual trouble-makers.

This discretionary application of formal controls was clear in police harassment of the rough-mannered, back-talking Roughnecks and toleration of the smooth, middle-class Saints, mentioned earlier. Jessica Mitford (1973) discovered an even more startling example of police "discretion." Several years ago seniors from a wealthy California high school went on a rampage of vandalism, arson, breaking and entering, car theft, assault, and rape. After a conference with local leaders, police returned the young people to their parents, who promised to discipline them. No formal action was taken. In a nearby ghetto that same week, a nine-year-old boy was arrested for stealing a nickel from a schoolmate and placed in a detention center for six weeks to await a hearing (pp. 55–56).

The ghetto child fit the police image of a criminal type; the wealthy vandals did not. In one experiment at the University of California, twelve sociology students who had clean driving records put Black Panther stickers on their car bumpers. Within seventeen days they had collected thirty citations and used up the $1,000 allotted for the experiment (Mitford, 1973, pp. 53–54).

This screening process continues in the courts. Studies of bail hearings held shortly after a person is arrested indicate that judges tend to trust white middle-class offenders to appear for trial, but demand bail from the poor (white and black), who are least able to afford it (Bell, 1973). Why? The President's Crime Commission (Katzenbach 1967) reasoned:

Most city prosecutors and judges have middle-class backgrounds and a high degree of education. When they are confronted with a poor, uneducated defendant, they may have difficulty judging how he fits into his own society or culture. They can easily mistake a certain manner of dress or speech, alien or repugnant to them but ordinary enough in the defendant's world, as an index of moral worthlessness. They can mistake ignorance or fear of the law as indifference to it. They can mistake the defendant's resentment against the social evils with which he lives as evidence of criminality.

Despite the presumption of innocence in our legal code, a defendant who cannot raise bail is held in jail and in large cities many wait a full year to come to trial.

Ninety percent of people who are arrested and charged agree to plead guilty to a lesser charge. By doing this, they avoid the risk of receiving a verdict of guilty and a more severe penalty. This procedure is known as plea-bargaining or "copping a plea." The Supreme Court declared it legal in 1969, acknowledging that it saves the state the expense of lengthy trials and lessens the already staggering burden on the courts. The Supreme Court only required that the defendants be thoroughly informed of their right to trial and that the "bargains" be officially recorded.

The most notorious example of plea-bargaining in recent years was Spiro T. Agnew's plea of "no contest," whereby he avoided prosecution for extortion and other serious crimes that could have sent him to jail. More often, however, it is the poor who, lacking the money for a good defense, plea-bargain. Statistics indicate that defendants who insist on a trial, if found guilty, receive sentences twice as long as those who plead guilty (Mitford, 1973, p. 76).

Unless a state imposes mandatory penalties for specified crimes, sentencing is left to the judge's discretion. And, as with labeling and arrests, social status and power play a role. Nonwhites typically serve longer terms than whites found guilty of the same crime, but blacks who commit crimes against blacks serve shorter terms than blacks who commit crimes against whites (Bell, 1973). As a rule white businessmen receive very light penalties. "Most judges justify the minimal sentences they give to businessman-criminals—fines, probation, or exceedingly short jail

"You're not guilty, but you're very, very close." (Drawing by Vietor; © 1973 The New Yorker Magazine, Inc.)

terms—on the grounds that when such a man is convicted, he generally loses his job, his standing in the community, and his family's respect" (Lesley Oelsner, in Mitford, 1973, p. 75). Spiro Agnew, for example, was fined $10,000 and given a suspended sentence, but the average car thief goes to jail for three years. (See the discussion of unequal life chances in chapter 8.)

Prisons

Prisons are a relatively modern invention. One-hundred and fifty or two hundred years ago, convicted criminals were killed, maimed, branded (for example, with a scarlet A for adultery), or deported (as often as not, to the New World). The idea of locking people up, which began to take hold in the mid-nineteenth century, was based on the equation of crime with vice and the assumption that isolation and hard work would make the sinner reconsider his or her errant ways and repent. But once prisons were established, they became institutionalized.

What functions do prisons perform? Most obviously, they *punish* criminals for their wrongdoings. Clearly, prisoners do suffer, and most people consider this just. (The desire for retribution may be fading, however. See table 12:3.) Second, prisons are supposed to *protect the public* by taking known deviants off the streets. In addition, they are thought to act as a *deterrent*, discouraging those on the outside from breaking laws and those on the inside from committing crimes after they are released. Finally, there is much talk of prisons *rehabilitating* offenders through training programs and counseling, so that when they are released they approach life with a new, law-abiding frame of mind. These different goals present each prison warden with a difficult and conflicting mandate.

table 12:3 PRESENT AND IDEAL VIEW OF PURPOSE OF PRISON (by percent)		
RESPONSE	PRISONS ARE	PRISONS SHOULD BE
Mainly corrective	57	77
Mainly punitive	19	11
Not sure	24	12
Total	100	100

SOURCE: Harris Poll, *Los Angeles Times*, August 14, 1967.

Somehow he [the prison warden] must resolve the claims that the prison should exact vengeance, erect a specter to terrify the actual or potential deviant, isolate the known offender from the free community, and effect a change in the personality of his captives so that they gladly follow the dictates of law—and in addition maintain order within his society of prisoners and see that they are employed at useful labor. (Sykes, 1958, pp. 44–45)

Prison Life In *The House of the Dead*, Dostoevsky wrote:

Besides the loss of freedom, besides the forced labor, there is another torture in prison life, almost more terrible than any other—that is compulsory life in common.

I could never have imagined, for instance, how terrible and agonizing it would be never once for a single minute to be alone for the ten years of my imprisonment.

Loss of privacy is one of the characteristics of total institutions, as indicated in chapter 10. Under constant surveillance, crowded together with other inmates at all times, required to use open showers and toilets, a person is deprived of the ability to manage the impression he or she makes on others; there is no time off-stage. Public physical examinations (anal and, for women, pelvic) made upon arrival to detect contraband seem designed to strip prisoners of all dignity. Often, new inmates are paraded naked in front of cat-calling residents. As Goffman (1963A) suggests, humiliation and violation of a person's physical integrity are part of the breaking in (or more accurately, breaking down) process. (See the discussion of mortification and total institutions in chapter 10.)

Censorship also represents a violation of privacy. Today many states forbid prison authorities from opening letters to and from a prisoner's lawyers and public officials, but letters to family are read. Prisoners who hope to win parole must say the "right" things, limiting themselves to safe banalities in a way that further weakens family bonds (Schwartz, 1972).

One prisoner told a researcher that the worst part of prison is having nowhere to go when tensions begin to mount. On the outside people can avoid confrontations and consequent "trouble" by leaving the scene; in prison, there is no escaping challenges or insults.

The second biggest problem in this prisoner's view is the absence of heterosexual activity. Homosexuality is more widespread in prisons than most officials would like to admit. Alan J. Davis (1971) estimates there are about a thousand homosexual rapes each year in the Philadelphia prisons alone. Only a handful are reported—because victims fear retribution or being locked in solitary for their own protection. Rape victims also fear that guards will expose them to outsiders. Reasoning that masturbation is a more likely way of coping with heterosexual deprivation, Davis concludes that these attacks are more aggressive than sexual. The aggressor gets his "kicks" from degrading the victim. David A. Ward and Gene G. Kassebaum (1971) found that 50 percent or more of female inmates engage in homosexual activity while in prison. For almost all it is a temporary habit.

The prisoners' third main complaint is the deprivation of meaningful work and of the right to make decisions about how to spend their time. Prisoners do work, but usually at boring, unskilled jobs (such as making license plates) in antiquated, overstaffed shops that bear little resemblance to work on the outside. At one New Jersey prison that houses mostly black offenders who will return to cities, prisoners work in the fields and barns (WNBC, 1974). What use will learning how to milk a cow be to them on the outside?

Do Prisons "Work"?   The cost of locking a person up for a year is between $6,000 and $10,000 (as prison critics note, this is enough to send a person to Harvard with a handsome allowance and a summer vacation in Europe). This amounts to nearly $12 billion annually (WNBC, 1974). What does this money buy?

Clearly, prisons do not protect the public. Only 3 percent of the people known to have committed crimes ever go to jail; 1.5 percent if we include unreported crimes. Moreover, most prison officials estimate that, at most, 15 to 25 percent of inmates are actually dangerous (Mitford, 1973, p. 285).

Nor do most prisons accomplish anything that might be called rehabilitation. Between 67 and 80 percent of inmates return to prison again and again. Indeed prisons may socialize people *to* deviance, as suggested earlier. Many observers consider them "schools for crime," where one-time offenders learn the tricks and rationalizations of deviant careers. In the seventies it might be more accurate to call prisons "schools for radicalism," where the young, alienated prisoners learn to see themselves as victims of oppression. For example, the Symbionese Liberation Army, which kidnapped Patricia Hearst in 1974, apparently originated in California's Vacaville Prison (Sykes, 1974).

And there is little evidence that prisons act as a deterrent to potential law-breakers. In 1961 the penalty for assault with a deadly weapon in California was one to ten years. In 1966 the California legislature raised the sentence for assaulting a police officer with a deadly weapon to five years to life. That year the rate of attacks on police was 15.8 per hundred officers, compared to 8.4 per hundred officers in 1961. In 1961 California raised the sentence for possession of marijuana from an optional one to twelve months to a mandatory one to ten years. Between 1961 and 1966 the number of arrests for possession of marijuana *rose* 500 percent, from 3,500 to 18,000 (Mitford, 1973, pp. 280–81).

Prison Reform   Are there any alternatives to prisons as we know them? Efforts to reform prisons—whether motivated by humanitarian principles or the desire to reduce crime—have focused on three general areas: work programs, conjugal visits, and group therapy (Bloch and Geis, 1970, pp. 469–74). In this country North Carolina led the way with "work furlough" programs, wherein inmates are permitted to leave prison for up to sixty hours a week to work on the outside. Although 16 percent of the inmates have been taken out of the program (most for drinking or visiting friends and family), none of the 1,046 prisoners committed violent crimes. As a result more than thirty states launched similar programs in the 1960s, but usually on a small scale. In the Swedish penal system, widely regarded as the most enlightened in the world, providing prisoners with steady, useful jobs and requiring them to support themselves and their families, while paying restitution to their victims, are central to the rehabilitation effort (Durham, 1973).

Only one prison in this country allows conjugal visits (Parchman State Prison in Mississippi), but many other nations permit spouses to visit prisoners, and some allow prisoners to visit their families for short periods. After six months of good behavior, a Mexican prison (located on a 34,000-acre island) permits prisoners to bring their families to live with them. Sweden sends some convicted criminals on vacations with their families, when the only requirement is that the prisoners attend morning classes. The idea behind conjugal visits is that the people who are most likely to discourage convicts from entering criminal careers are spouses and children. In fact Sweden gives priority to "hard-core" prisoners in assigning a limited number of family apartments. Only about 2 percent of prisoners use family visits as an escape route.

Group therapy programs are difficult to assess. Nearly all forms of psychotherapy depend on uninhibited self-revelation and open expression of feelings. But the psychologists who run such programs in prisons are, after all, prison officials. The inmate is thus put in a double-bind: total openness might well delay his parole, but self-concealment renders the program useless.

Undoubtedly the most radical approach to penal reform is to eliminate prisons altogether. Surprising to most people is the fact that this has been tried in Massachusetts. Dr. Jerome Miller became commissioner of the Department of Youth Services in that state in October 1969. By the fall of 1972 he had reduced the population of juvenile prisons from about 1,350 to 90. Instead of being imprisoned, young law-breakers were returned to their families or placed in foster homes, small unlocked residences, or a few prep schools that ordinarily cater to middle- and upper-class youngsters. Officials helped older boys and girls to find their own homes

Most American prisons require husbands and wives to visit across metal barriers. In newer prisons, such as the Illinois State Penetentiary (above), prisoners live in private rooms equipped with radio, desk, and bed. (Cornell Capa/Magnum; UPI)

and jobs. Only forty or fifty who were considered "dangerous," and an equal number who were "seriously disturbed," were housed in locked facilities. The staff, which included professionals as well as college students acting as "big brothers," had wide discretion in handling youngsters.

The goal of this program was first, to stop the process of labeling youngsters "delinquent," and second, to help them to cope with life on the outside, rather than socializing them to the authoritarianism and brutality of prisons. As of January 1973 there was no evidence of an increase in juvenile delinquency in Massachusetts (and some hint of a drop), and Miller was able to return $2 million of his $10 million 1972 budget to the state treasury (Mitford, 1973, pp. 282–85).

It is doubtful that the American public is ready to tear down its prisons; one experiment with juveniles is hardly conclusive evidence that prisons are useless. In a report on prison reform, sponsored by the Roscoe Pound American Trial Lawyers Foundation, Herman Schwartz (1972) concluded:

[T]he prison problem is beginning to be seen as part of the overall problem of social justice, as a crucial element in the movement to eliminate the racial and other oppression that has stained our history for so many years. . . . On balance, I think we have come a very long way in expanding prisoners' rights in the last few years. But again, the satisfaction must be tempered. Our prison system is so diseased and bankrupt that these achievements represent only the smallest and earliest steps of a very long journey. Whether we can successfully negotiate that journey is indeed problematic.

---

summary

Deviance refers to any behavior that violates social norms and expectations. Whether an act is considered deviant or not depends on who commits it, where, and when. Definitions and explanations of deviance change with the times. They are ultimately a matter of traditions and social power: people who have the power to enforce their definitions decide what is proper and what is deviant.

In the nineteenth century Lombroso argued that criminals were throwbacks to an earlier stage of evolution; in the twentieth century, Sheldon linked delinquency to body types. But although the possibility of biological explanations of deviance remains, to date there is no proof that deviants are "born that way." Some psychologists believe deviants have not learned to inhibit inborn antisocial impulses, while others argue that deviants learn that antisocial behavior is rewarded. But psychological profiles of deviants do not explain why rates of deviance vary from one social group to another. Sociologists focus on this phenomenon.

Robert K. Merton links deviance to *anomie*, a state of normlessness that occurs when people cannot obtain culturally valued goals by socially approved means. He identifies four types of deviant adaptations: *innovation* (pursuing approved goals by deviant means), *ritualism* (adhering to rules at the expense of goals), *retreatism* (abandoning culturally prescribed goals and means), and *rebellion* (substituting new goals and new means for pursuing them). Why do innovative subcultures develop in some groups, rebellious subcultures in others? Cloward and Ohlin believe the answer lies in *opportunity structures*—in the social structure, role-models, and jobs available in a community.

Many forms of deviance must be learned; that is, people can be *socialized* to deviance. Miller suggests that delinquency can be seen as an attempt to conform to such subcultural standards as toughness, smartness, and autonomy.

Virtually everyone violates social norms occasionally, but only some of us are stigmatized as deviant. Some sociologists argue that the stigma results from a person's being caught and publicly *labeled* deviant. Chambliss's comparison of the Saints and Roughnecks suggests that people who come from influential, middle-class families, and who speak politely and dress well are able to resist deviant labeling. People from lower-class families are not: they lack the social power. Deviant labels, as this study showed, tend to function as self-fulfilling prophecies. The "offender" is isolated (socially if not physically), denied opportunities to conform, and thus pushed toward deviant subcultures that offer lessons in breaking rules. These subcultures socialize people for deviant careers.

Most people usually conform because socialization welds social norms to the child's sense of identity: breaking some rules becomes unthinkable. *Informal social controls* (disapproval, ridicule, the threat of exclusion) prevent people from violating norms they have not internalized. But socialization is never perfect, and informal controls may promote as well as prevent deviance, hence the need for *formal social controls*, such as the penal system.

Although incomplete, statistics on crime are the best measure of deviance we have. What happens to known law-breakers? The police and courts exercise considerable discretion in applying the penalties available under the law; only a very small percentage of the people known to have committed crimes are arrested, tried, and sent to prison. The functions of prison include punishing law-breakers, protecting the public, deterring others from breaking the law, and rehabilitating prisoners. High recidivism rates suggest that prisons do punish offenders, but neither rehabilitate convicts nor deter potential criminals.

Prison reform programs center around work furloughs and conjugal visits (the mainstays of the Swedish penal system), group therapy, and the elimination of prisons as we know them (a solution Massachusetts has tried with juvenile offenders). Although true reform may lie in the very distant future, we are beginning to see the prison problem as part of the overall problem of social justice.

glossary

anomie A state of normlessness and confusion that may occur when social realities do not meet culturally induced expectations.

conformity Seeking culturally approved goals by culturally approved means.

deviance Behavior that violates social norms and expectations.

deviant career The adoption of a deviant life-style and identity within a supporting subculture that provides techniques for breaking rules and rationalizations for nonconformity.

formal social controls Roles and institutions consciously designed to enforce conformity.

informal social controls Disapproval, ridicule, the threat of ostracism, and other unofficial pressures to conform.

innovation Pursuing culturally approved goals by deviant means. (Merton)

labeling The assigning of a deviant status to a person which then dominates his of her social identity.

opportunity structure The role-models, instruction, and jobs available in a given community.

plea-bargaining In a criminal trial, a defendant may agree to plead guilty to a lesser charge rather than risk conviction and a more severe penalty.

rebellion Creating new goals and new means for pursuing them. (Merton)

recidivism A return to crime after release from prison.

retreatism Abandoning culturally prescribed goals and means. (Merton)

ritualism Adhering rigidly to norms at the expense of goals. (Merton)

references

Albert Bandura and Richard H. Walters, *Adolescent Aggression*, New York: Ronald, 1959.

Howard S. Becker, *Outsiders*, New York: Free Press, 1963.

———, ed., *The Other Side*, New York: Free Press, 1964.

Derrick A. Bell, Jr., "Racism in American Courts," *California New Law Review*, vol. 61, no. 1 (January 1973): 165–203.

Albert A. Bloch and Gilbert Geis, *Man, Crime and Society*, 2nd ed., New York: Random House, 1970.

Lenny Bruce, *How to Talk Dirty and Influence People*, Chicago: Playboy, 1963.

William J. Chambliss, "The Saints and the Rough-necks," *Society*, vol. 11 (December 11, 1973): 24–31.

Richard A. Cloward and Lloyd E. Ohlin, *Delinquency and Opportunity*, Glencoe, Ill.: Free Press, 1960.

Albert K. Cohen, *Deviance and Control*, Englewood Cliffs, N.J.: Prentice-Hall, 1966.

Alan J. Davis, "Sexual Assaults in the Philadelphia Prison System," in Wallace, 1971.

John Dollard et al., *Frustration and Aggression*, New Haven, Conn.: Yale University Press, 1939.

Michael Durham, "For Swedes a Prison Sentence Can Be Fun," *Smithsonian* (September 1973): 46–52.

Emile Durkheim, *The Rules of the Sociological Method* (1895), trans. by S. A. Solovay and J. H. Mueller, Glencoe, Ill.: Free Press, 1964.

Kai T. Erikson, *Wayward Puritans*, New York: Wiley, 1966.

Donald Gibbons, *Society, Crime, and Criminal Careers*, Englewood Cliffs, N.J.: Prentice-Hall, 1968.

Sheldon and Eleanor Glueck, *Physique and Delinquency*, New York: Harper & Row, 1956.

Erving Goffman, *Behavior in Public Places*, New York: Free Press, 1963A.

———, *Stigma: Notes on the Management of Spoiled Identity*, Englewood Cliffs, N.J.: Prentice-Hall, 1963B.

Charles Goring, *The English Convict*, London: His Majesty's Stationery Office, 1913.

Walter R. Gove, "Societal reaction as an explanation of mental illness: An evaluation," *American Sociological Review*, vol. 55 (October 1970): 873–84.

August B. Hollingshead and Frederich C. Redlich, *Social Class and Mental Illness*, New York: Wiley, 1958.

Nicholas deB. Katzenbach, Chairman, *The Challenge of Crime in a Free Society*, Washington, D.C.: U.S. Government Printing Office, 1967.

John I. Kitsuse, "Societal Reaction to Deviant Behavior: Problems in Theory and Method," in Becker, 1964.

Cesare Lombroso, in G. L. Ferrero, *Criminal Man*, New York: Putnam, 1911.

Robert K. Merton, *Social Theory and Social Structure*, Glencoe, Ill.: Free Press, 1957.

Walter B. Miller, "Lower-class culture as a generating milieu of gang delinquency," *Journal of Sociological Issues*, vol. 14 (1958): 5–19.

Jessica Mitford, *Kind and Usual Punishment*, New York: Knopf, 1973.

Jerome K. Myers and Lee L. Bean, *A Decade Later: A Follow-Up of Social Class and Mental Illness*, New York: Wiley, 1968.

Albert J. Reiss, Jr., *The Police and the Public*, New Haven, Conn.: Yale University Press, 1971.

Edwin M. Schur, *Crimes Without Victims*, Englewood Cliffs, N.J.: Prentice-Hall, 1965.

Barry Schwartz, "Deprivation of privacy as a 'functional prerequisite' in the case of prison," *Journal of Criminal Law, Criminology and Police Science*, vol. 63 (1972): 229–39.

Herman Schwartz, "Prisoners' Rights: Some Hopes and Realities," in *A Program for Prison Reform*, Cambridge, Mass.: The Roscoe Pound-American Trial Lawyers Foundation, 1972.

Richard D. Schwartz and Jerome H. Skolnick, "Two Studies of Legal Stigma," in Becker, 1964.

Clifford R. Shaw and Henry D. McKay, *Delinquency Areas*, Chicago: University of Chicago Press, 1929.

George Bernard Shaw, *Saint Joan* (1924), Baltimore: Penguin, 1951.

William H. Sheldon, with Emil M. Hartl and Eugene McDermott, *Varieties of Delinquent Youth*, New York: Harper & Row, 1949.

Leo Srole et al., *Mental Health in the Metropolis: The Midtown Manhattan Study*, New York: McGraw-Hill, 1962.

Edwin H. Sutherland and Donald R. Cressy, *Principles of Criminology*, 6th ed., Philadelphia: Lippincott, 1960.

Gresham Sykes, *The Society of Captives*, Princeton, N.J.: Princeton University Press, 1958.

———, "Prison Is a Perfect Culture For Growing Conspiracies," *The New York Times* (April 21, 1974): E,5.

——— and David Matza, "Techniques of neutralization: A theory of delinquency," *American Sociology Review*, vol. 22 (December 1957): 644–70.

Thomas S. Szasz, *Ideology and Insanity*, New York: Doubleday, 1970.

Uniform Crime Reports: *Crime in the United States, 1972,* Washington, D.C.: U.S. Government Printing Office, 1973.

Samuel E. Wallace, ed., *Total Institutions*, Chicago: Aldine, 1971.

David A. Ward and Gene G. Kassebaum, "Homosexual Behavior Among Women Prisoners," in Wallace, 1971.

WNBC, "The High Cost of Crime," a special program produced by the editorial services of WNBC, New York, N.Y., written for WNBC, New York, N.Y. by Ann Sternberg, copyright © 1974 National Broadcasting Company, Inc.

for further study

Drugs and Social Control. To the individual, taking marijuana, cocaine, amphetamines, barbiturates, or heroin is a psychological and physiological experience. It is also an experience that involves group pressures and the organization of social control. The best studies of how society turns a drug into a social issue have been done on marijuana. See *The Marihuana Papers*, edited by David Solomon (New York: New American Library, 1968), especially the essay by Alfred Lindesmith. To gain perspective on the American approach to marijuana, see Andrew Skull's essay in *Theoretical Perspectives on Deviance,* edited by Robert A. Scott and Jack D. Douglas (New York: Basic, 1972). At the individual level of becoming a marijuana user, Howard Becker has written two important essays, available in his book *Outsiders* (New York: Free Press, 1963). On addicts, see the essay by Edwin Schur in *The Other Side,* edited by Howard Becker (New York: Free Press, 1964).

Excellent materials have recently appeared on the sociology of drug control. See *The American Connection*, by John Pekkanen (Chicago: Follett, 1973); *Nark!* by the excellent reporter Joe Eszterhas (San Francisco: Straight Arrow Books, 1974); and *The Drugged Nation*, by John Finlator (New York: Simon & Schuster, 1974). Matthew Dumont has written a valuable overview in "The Politics of Drugs," *Social Policy*, Vol. 3 (July 1973), pp. 32–35.

Police. With the references on the social control of drugs, we are already focused on the sociology of police control, both in concrete details and in terms of how the police relate to the larger forces of social control which determine what is illegal and who is dangerous. The most useful way to begin studying the police is to observe them firsthand. Albert J. Reiss has done this in *The Police and the Public,* 2nd ed. (New Haven, Conn.: Yale University Press, 1973). Another important field study of the police is by Aaron Cicourel, *The Social Organization of Juvenile Justice* (New York: Wiley, 1967), especially chapters 4–6. An important study of police corruption is *The Knapp Commission Report on Police Corruption,* Foreword by Michael Armstrong (New York: Braziller, 1973). See also "A Typology of Police Corruption," by Julian Roebuck and Thomas Barker, *Social Problems*, vol. 21, no. 3 (1974), pp. 423–37, and the relevant chapters of *Institutional Racism in America*, edited by Louis Knowles and Kenneth Prewitt (Englewood Cliffs, N.J.: Prentice-Hall, 1969). An important case around which to focus thinking sociologically about police is reported by Roy Wilkins and Ramsey Clark in *Search and Destroy: A Report of the Commission of Inquiry into the Chicago Police Raid on the Black Panther Headquarters, December 4, 1969* (New York: Harper & Row, 1973).

Courts. Although most acts of justice and injustice take place in or near a patrol car, it is the courts that serve as the formal institutions of justice. Two sociological studies of how they work are Robert Emerson, *Judging Delinquents: Context and Process in Juvenile Courts* (Chicago: Aldine, 1969), and David Sudnow, "Normal Crimes," *Social Problems*, vol. 12, no. 3 (Winter 1965), pp. 255–75. For a critical overview, see Isaac Balbus, "Penal Paradox: Efficiency vs. Justice," *Social Policy*, vol. 3, no. 2 (July 1972), pp. 44–49.

If you were born between the end of World War II and 1958, your birth date alone makes you special. Along with others of your generation, you were part of the postwar baby boom. The sudden population jump during those years has affected not just your life, but the life of every American. What is more, it will continue to do so for the rest of your life.

If you were a postwar baby, the makers of Gerber's baby foods and Pamper diapers have you to thank for their success. When you started school few towns could keep pace with the need for more desks and teachers, more labs and gyms and classrooms. Your generation stimulated the rapid expansion of facilities, from hospitals and colleges to municipal parking lots and shopping centers. Year after year of bumper crops of kids created a "youth market" that transformed industries like television, food processing, and tourism. Now, as young adults, they are affecting employment (and unemployment) statistics, buying homes and renting apartments, and beginning to produce babies of their own.

The nation's economy expanded to produce the goods and offer the services the boom generation required. But the baby boom has produced less pleasant side effects as well. The youth market includes not only transistor radios and frisbees but also drugs. Automobile accidents and crime rates have jumped sharply up-

POPULATION
AND
HEALTH

ward—partly because both crime and accident rates have always been higher for people under twenty-five, and there are now so many more people in this age group (Wilson and Dupont, 1973).

Following the postwar baby boom there has been a marked decline in births. Some population experts—called *demographers*—now foresee a future for the United States in which population growth would slow almost to a halt. Once a nation of the young, we could become a nation of the elderly. Like the baby boom, this change in population would transform our way of life.

This chapter deals with *demography*, the study of such changes in population and their effects on society. After discussing the components of population growth, we will describe the world crisis in population and health, addressing the urgent question: How can the population explosion in less developed nations be brought under control? Turning to the United States, we will consider our own problems of excess births and the trends in contraception and abortion. The final section will look at another aspect of demography, the health of the population. Although Americans are one of the healthiest peoples in the world, some segments of the population fare better than others. The poor, in particular, suffer from poorer health—and poorer health care.

STUDYING POPULATION

The study of population centers on just three variables: birth rate, death rate, and net migration (inflow minus outflow). Together, these silent, powerful forces not only produce increases or decreases in population but determine the very shape of society—the size of the labor force, the demands for food and shelter, the proportion of young and old people, the ethnic composition.

Demographers are concerned, then, with the changes in the demographic variables, with the causes of such changes, and with the consequences. They ask: Is the birth rate increasing? Did the baby boom occur because parents wanted larger families or were there simply more families with parents of child-bearing age? As the crop of boom babies grows old, will their predominance turn us into a nation of conservatives? To find answers, demographers need sources of raw information. Two sources they rely upon are government and community records, and the census.

Counting Population

In our highly organized society, key events in one's life—being born, graduating, marrying—quickly become statistics. The recording of such facts by a government or other agency is known as *registration*. Registration has been compared to a motion-picture record of a continuous stream of data on a specific subject.

The periodic head count called the *census*, on the other hand, resembles a still photo, taken with a wide-angle lens and capturing a single moment. The census collects a mass of data about each citizen: sex, age, occupation, and much more.

Census taking dates back about five thousand years. The ancient Sumerians counted heads for the sake of more efficient tax collecting. Other ancient peoples—Chinese, Hebrews, Egyptians—used the census for taxation or to identify men who could serve in the army or as forced laborers. In America, the Comanche Indians counted their people by dividing reeds into five bundles. Each represented a group: warriors, young men, women, children, and dwellings. The colonists also conducted censuses: Virginia in 1624; Connecticut in 1756; and Massachusetts in 1764 (Thomlinson, 1965, p. 41).

According to our Constitution, the government must take the census every ten years to determine congressional representation and taxes. In 1790 the first national census reported upon 3,929,000 individuals in a fifty-six-page pamphlet. The 1970 census counted 204,879,000 people and presented its findings in numerous reports, in varied forms from microfiche to computer tape. The modern census is more than just a head count; it collects many kinds of information about the American people to aid in social prediction and planning.

Even a computer, however, cannot assure total accuracy of a census. For one thing, the Census Bureau admits to underestimating the population. In 1970 about 1.9 million blacks and 3.4 million whites were not counted, for a net undercount rate of 2.5 percent (U.S. Bureau of the Census, *User's Guide*, 1970, p. 5). More recent research estimates the black undercount to be 8 percent (Coale and Rives, 1973, table 5). As a result, these "missing citizens" are underrepresented in government. Because many black people live in cities, the undercount means that federal allotments to cities may be less than they should be, depriving many people of needed services.

If such inaccuracies can be found in the census of a nation with advanced communications technology and a long tradition of census taking, it is mind-boggling to imagine the problems of counting population worldwide. In 1962, for example, Nigeria took its first census since becoming an independent nation. To prepare the citizenry, radio programs made daily announcements in song, and posters were displayed in every town and village. Nevertheless, census takers were beaten and even kidnapped by people who feared they were tax collectors. Some diligent census takers discovered whole new communities, such as a group of fishing villages whose twenty thousand inhabitants had been totally unknown. Too often, however, officials sabotaged the census takers' results. To get more money from the central government for welfare and economic development, they exaggerated the number of people in their districts (Peterson, 1969).

Some countries produce censuses even less accurate than Nigeria's. Consequently, we should allow for significant margins of error in world population statistics. Estimates do indicate that world population was about 3,706,000,000 in 1971. It appears to be increasing at an average annual rate of 2 percent, the highest rate in history (United Nations, 1971).

Whatever its faults, modern societies could not do without the census. As societies become more complex, census data become more varied. So do the uses to which they are put: to plan where and when new schools will be needed, to anticipate tax revenues, to figure out the potential market for a new soft drink. And demographers must rely upon the census for data about population growth or decline.

Population Growth

To determine population growth, demographers study the interaction of birth rates, death rates, and net migration. *Crude birth rate* represents the number of births per thousand people during a given time span. In 1947, during the postwar baby boom, our crude birth rate soared to twenty seven per thousand. At its low points—during the depression and in the early 1970s—it plummeted to eighteen per thousand. Meanwhile our *crude death rate* (deaths per thousand people) has fallen and remains well below the birth rate. In 1900 the death rate was about seventeen per thousand, in contrast to nine per thousand in 1970. Population growth reflects the excess of births over deaths (*Statistical Abstract*, 1973, p. 51).

But population growth also depends upon migration. The United States has traditionally attracted more people than it has lost. In demographic terms, our immigration (or in-migration) has exceeded our emigration (out-migration), resulting in population growth. *Internal migration*, or movement within a country, is also important to measure. The frequency with which a group moves may affect its way of life, for example. And population clusters, such as the concentration of the elderly in Florida, may create distinctive cultures. The rate of population growth or increase is the amount by which the crude birth rate and immigration together exceed the crude death rate and out-migration (see figure 13:1).

Birth Rate From menarche (first menstruation) to menopause (the cessation of fertility) the average woman's fertile period lasts about thirty years. But biological potential for reproduction, or *fecundity*, is only one aspect of a society's birth rate at a given time. No society has ever reached, or even come near, its theoretical biological potential. The *fertility rate* shows the number of children actually produced per thousand women between the ages of fifteen and forty-four.

Clearly, the number of fertile women in the population at any one time will influence the

figure 13:1   The key demographic variables

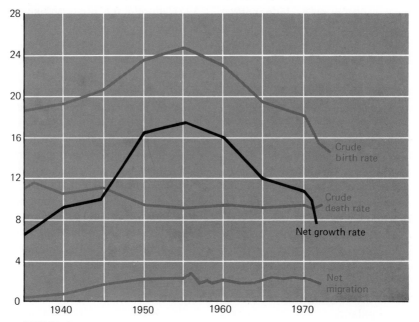

SOURCE: *Statistical Abstract of the United States, 1973.* (Washington, D.C.: Government Printing Office, 1973): table 9, p. 11.

The rate of population growth is the total of the crude birth rate minus the crude death rate plus the net migration rate. In the United States the variations in growth mirror changes in the birth rate rather than the other variables. The death rate is relatively low and stable because many of the forces that carried off large numbers of people—such as influenza or widespread crop failures—have been tamed. Net migration is only a small (though positive) component of growth, since emigration is relatively insignificant and immigration is limited by legal quotas. Earlier in this century immigration played a much larger role in American population growth.

birth rate. However, our postwar baby boom took place at a time when the proportion of potential mothers was not at a peak. Demographers must take into account the number of potential fathers, as well. World War II temporarily lowered the *sex ratio*, or the number of men per hundred women, because so many men were away in the armed services. When the war ended, the sex ratio suddenly increased. Twice during this century, how-

ever, war decimated the population of marriageable males in Germany and Russia. In these countries, birth rates continue to reflect the low sex ratio.

Because most children are born to married parents, the proportion of people getting married can affect the birth rate. For example, many American couples postponed their marriages during World War II. Then, from 1946 to the early 1950s, the proportion of married persons in the population rose significantly, and so did the birth rate. But in Ireland, where about a quarter of the men and women are not married by age forty-five (compared to 6 percent in the United States), the birth rate is far higher than ours. Why? Because the fertility rate is much higher. The couples who do marry have lots of children (Kennedy, 1973, tables 49, 50, 58). The age of marriage can affect the birth rate, too. But again Ireland, which has the highest age of marriage of any other country, does not have the low birth rate to go with this. Of course, the Irish birth rate might be even higher without its customs of late marriage or no marriage at all.

Birth control allows couples to control family size, thus helping to lower the birth rate. Some societies control births by placing a taboo on intercourse—sometimes as long as three years—while a mother is still nursing a child. Other societies may permit abortion, sterilization, or infanticide to limit the birth rate. Most birth control consists of abstinence or contraception.

How did these four factors—fecundity, the sex ratio, the proportion of married couples, and birth control—help to bring about the postwar baby boom? Thomlinson divides the responsibility as follows: the larger number of women, 24 percent; the higher proportion of women who married, 30 percent; the higher percentage of wives who bore children, 34 percent; and the higher rate of births per mother, 12 percent (1965, p. 168).

These figures represent an intelligent guess, not a certainty. Birth rate—its causes and consequences—remains elusive, especially when someone attempts to manipulate it. In 1966, for example, the Romanian government was worried. A few years earlier fertility had dropped below the replacement level. Romanian women were relying upon inexpensive, legal abortions for birth control. To raise the birth rate, therefore, officials suddenly outlawed abortion in November 1966. Unable to get abortions and lured by government incentives to have larger families, Romanian women tripled the birth rate only eleven months after the law went into effect! Two years later, however, previous cultural patterns began to reassert themselves. Women found other means of limiting births, and the birth rate declined once more (Clark, 1973). Clearly, the availability of abortion alone was not responsible for the low birth rate. If our baby boom produced radical changes, imagine the effects of that sudden, brief bulge in Romania's population. For one thing, in 1974 the first three elementary grades were mobbed. Just a few years later, enrollments in those grades will drop suddenly by up to two-thirds!

A more revealing statistic than either crude birth rate or the fertility rate is the *age-specific fertility rate*, or the number of births per thousand women of a given age range. Since women bear children during a limited number of years, it is clearly more significant to know how many children are born, for example, to women twenty to twenty-nine years of age than to all women. The *net reproduction rate* (NRR) is an average of the number of female children born per woman of child-bearing age; that is, the rate at which a woman replaces herself by producing a female child to bear children in the next generation. An NRR of 1.0 would indicate that, on the average, one woman produces one daughter.

Zero population growth (ZPG) occurs when the crude birth rate is equal to the crude death rate. An NRR of 1.0 may eventually bring about ZPG. However, to achieve constant population in the United States once an NRR of 1.0 was reached would take several decades, because of the large number of women of child-bearing age and because of the age composition of the population as a whole.

Death Rate and Life Expectancy *Life span*, the maximum number of years that a human being can possibly live, has not changed substantially over the centuries. But *life expectancy*, the average number of years of life remaining for an individual of a given age, has increased dramatically in the last seventy-five years or so. An infant born in 1920 had a life expectancy of 54.1 years; by 1970

the life expectancy at birth was 70.8 years.[1] This gain looks impressive, but life expectancy at age 60 is only a few years longer now than it was in the past. Only now more people are reaching age 60.

The crude death rate does not fully explain the reasons for the change; age-specific mortality rates are more revealing. The *infant mortality rate*, or deaths per thousand children under one year of age, shows clearly that most of the gain in life expectancy has come because of fewer infant deaths. The 1972 crude death rate of 9.4 per thousand was not much lower than the 1935 figure, 10.9 per thousand. But in 1935 infant deaths stood at 55.7 per thousand, significantly higher than the 18.5 deaths per thousand infants in 1972 (*Statistical Abstract*, 1973, table 65, p. 51).

The chances of dying in the first year of life are still quite high. Age-specific tables show that after the first year the mortality rate drops quite sharply until the later years of life. An infant under one year is now about as likely to die as a person in his early sixties.

A Close Look at Immigration Since the discovery of the New World, one of Europe's big exports has been people; 45 million of them to North America, 20 million to Latin America, 10 million to Australia and South Africa combined. This movement of people from one country to another is called *international migration*.

Why do people migrate? Demographers use the term *push* to describe their reasons for leaving or being forced out, and the term *pull* for the attractions of the new place. In Israel, peopled primarily by immigrants from other nations, both forces were at work in its

---

table 13:1   LIFE EXPECTANCY AND AGE-SPECIFIC MORTALITY RATES, 1969

AGE	LIFE EXPECTANCY[1]	MORTALITY RATE
Under 1	70.4	21.08
5	67.2	0.63
10	62.3	0.26
15	57.8	0.85
20	52.8	1.41
25	48.1	1.45
30	43.5	1.56
35	38.8	2.15
40	34.3	2.24
45	29.9	4.88
50	25.7	7.44
55	21.8	11.42
60	18.1	17.26
65	14.8	25.60
69	12.4	35.53

[1]Note that the longer a person survives, the greater the total number of years he or she can expect to live. Thus, if a person lives to sixty, he or she can look forward to living to seventy-eight, whereas an infant can expect to live only seventy years.

SOURCE: *Statistical Abstract of the United States, 1973* (Washington, D.C.: Government Printing Office, 1973), table 80, p. 58.

---

[1]   Figures broken down by sex show the difference in life expectancy by sex. A male born in 1960 could expect to live to 66.6; a female, to 73.1 (*Statistical Abstract*, 1973, table 78, p. 57).

IN THE NEWS

Long Life—A Regional Specialty?

Franklin, Neb.—Hanna Sanger should have died 7.05 years ago, according to the statistics.

She has always been stubborn and independent-minded, though, so she didn't. And in living a long time here (she's working on her 80th year now)

Mrs. Sanger is carrying on a local longevity tradition.

For Nebraskans, according to the Federal Government, can expect to live longer than the residents of any other state, an average of 71.95 years.

Franklin citizens seem not just longer-lived, but unusually active—bowling, chopping wood, and gardening long after most Americans have retired to their rocking chairs. What makes Nebraskans so hardy? Some say "hard work." Others think it's the extreme climate, or the water, or the air. Dr. Harmon Denham, president of the American Aging Association, believes it's a combination of things.

"Historically, rural residents live longer than urban ones," he said, "and Midwesterners live longer than coastal residents. They have a lower food intake. The pace of life is slower.

"Most importantly, people seem to keep busier in retirement. They don't sit around [and] worry about their health. . . . And there's probably a selective factor: the hardiest residents stay on

while the others move out."
Beaufort, S.C.—Aging, leather-tough Aldridge Glazer has been retired for some years now and he gets a monthly pension check, but it doesn't always stretch over his expenses. . . . Mr. Glazer is an agile, quick 75 years old—a happy state that cannot truly be called rare in this part of the country but that is worth noting.

Why does South Carolina have the lowest life expectancy rate in the United States (66.41) while Nebraska has the highest? There is no one simple explanation, but a network of related causes. For one thing, many South Carolinians are black, and blacks die sooner than whites on the average. Poverty, the coastal climate, poor sanitation, high infant mortality, and few doctors make the picture bleak. So does the high incidence of diseases related to hypertension. Among black males 55 to 64 years of age, 649 in every 1,000 die of such diseases in South Carolina. In Nebraska 42 of every 1,000 white males of the same age die of such diseases.

A reporter asked Thomas C. Barnwell, director of the Beaufort-Jasper Comprehensive Health Care Service, Inc., why the difference between South Carolinians and Nebraskans is so great.

"We really don't know," Mr. Barnwell concedes, "but we'd like to."

"I grew up in Beaufort County," he says, holding up a small box of pills. "I take one of these every morning. They're for hypertension. I have it, too."

SOURCE: Wayne King, "Life in Beaufort, S. C.," and Andrew H. Malcolm "Hearty Longevity at Franklin, Neb.," *The New York Times* (March 17, 1974): 45.

settlement. World War II forced many Jews to leave their European homelands. And Israel exerted pull—the emotional appeal of a traditional homeland; its attraction as an existing independent nation for Jews; and its open immigration policy. Immigration patterns have had an immense impact on Israel, in a number of ways.

From 1948 to 1951, immediately after the establishment of Israel, the new country grew by 24 percent a year. Ninety percent of this growth was due to immigration. For some years after 1952, the growth rate slowed to 3 percent, of which half was still due to im-

migration. By 1970 fewer than half the Jews in Israel were natives, or Sabras (named for a native desert plant); 28 percent were of European and 26 percent of Afro-Asian origin (Friedlander and Sabatello, 1972).

Israel's *population pyramid* shows graphically how immigration patterns have affected the distribution of the population according to age and sex. The pyramid representing native-born Israelis shows that in 1972 some 60.5 percent were under fifteen years and nearly 70 percent under age twenty, while only about 20 percent were between twenty and sixty-five. This profile indicates a country

figure 13:2 Population pyramids for Israel, 1970

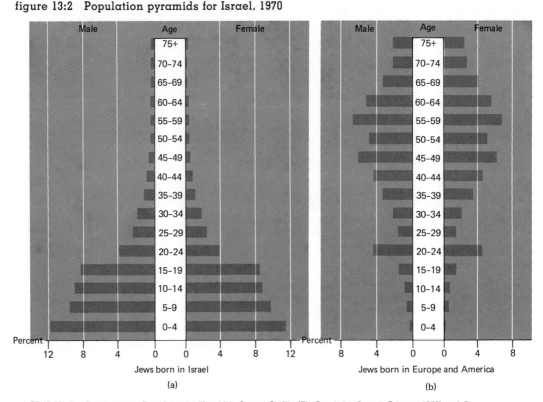

SOURCE: Dov Friedlander and Eitan Sabatello, "Israel," in *Country Profiles* (The Population Council, February 1972) p. 4, 5.

A population pyramid shows the composition of a group by age and sex. The Sabras of Israel are a young group, the children of immigrants by and large, as population pyramid (a) shows. Most Israelis born in Europe and America (b) belong to the older generations.

with few productive workers and an extraordinary number of dependent children. But a pyramid representing Israelis born in Europe and America clearly shows where the missing adults were to be found. This group included few children (only about 3 percent were fifteen or under) but many adults (more than 80 percent) between fifteen and sixty-five.

Consider how such immigration patterns affect the daily lives of Israelis. For one thing, status depends in large part upon immigration. Those who have been in the country the longest—Sabras and pre-Independence immigrants—find themselves at the top of the status ladder. Prestige may be granted to those with more education, but it also depends upon country of origin. Sabras and European immigrants enjoy higher status than other immigrants.

Not surprisingly, the immigrants brought with them a host of problems. The first wave of immigrants, before 1951, came largely from Europe. Many were elderly, and those of

working age had skills appropriate to urban life. They had not farmed, nor did they want to. Later immigrants were mostly Near Eastern and North African. Their families were large, with many children. They had little education, little money, and few skills. Language differences and prejudice weighed against these later arrivals. They required many social services—health, education, welfare, employment and training, and housing—if they were to take their place in Israeli society (Friedlander and Sabatello, 1972).

The United States, too, is a nation of immigrants—including some 10 to 20 million slaves who came against their will. Between 1820, when official statistics were kept for the first time, and 1972, almost 46 million people came to the United States. Nearly 9 million of them came in one decade, between 1901 and 1910 (U.S. Bureau of the Census, *User's Guide*, 1970).

People left the country, too—a comparative trickle in most years, though during the depression the net migration rate showed up on the minus side for the first and only time. Until the 1920s immigration was almost unrestricted; the United States welcomed newcomers to help settle and industrialize the nation. During the 1920s, however, immigration policy began limiting the number of immigrants, especially those from non-European countries. Objections to the discriminatory aspects of this policy led to its modification in the Immigration Act of 1965. Each year nearly 400,000 people enter the United States legally. (Illegal immigration also adds its share; in 1971 officials tracked down 420,000 deportable aliens, most of them Mexican.) We continue to feel the impact of immigration; from 1960 to 1970, immigration accounted for 16 percent of population growth (*Population and the American Future*, 1972, p. 114).

THE POPULATION EXPLOSION

Terms like *population explosion* have become familiar, if frightening, in recent years. One of the first to sound a warning about population growth was a gentleman-scholar, the Reverend Thomas Robert Malthus (1766–1834). First published in 1798, his theories went into a sixth edition in 1826, entitled "An Essay on the Principle of Population, or A View of Its Past and Present Effects on Human Happiness, with An Inquiry into Our Prospects Respecting the Future Remov-

al or Mitigation of the Evils Which It Occasions." Malthus's theory, briefly, was this: People require food, and people will continue to have children. Population, he said, increases in a geometric progression (2, 4, 8, 16) while food supplies increase only arithmetically (2, 3, 4, 5). No population can continue to grow indefinitely, because people will simply run out of food. Increase the standard of living and reduce the number of deaths, and the population will simply increase, thereby wiping out the gains. The standard of living will fall and mortality rise again.

To Malthus, the only answer was to marry late and have fewer children (he did not approve of birth control or abortion). Otherwise, population would inevitably be checked by drastic means: starvation, pestilence, or war.

As Malthus predicted, when the death rate declines and fertility remains high, the population grows very fast. From 1650 to 1850, world population doubled from 500 million people to 1 billion. But it took only eighty years—from 1850 to 1930—for the population to double again. In the 1970s world population is increasing at about 2 percent a year and doubling every thirty-five years (Ehrlich and Ehrlich, 1972, p. 450). Just like interest in a savings account, population increases by compounding.

Is human population reaching the limits of growth predicted by Malthus? Some demographers are haunted by the Malthusian specter of starvation, plague, and war. Others believe that humanity may be able to avert such a disaster. Some evidence suggests that we can achieve a population with low mortality and fertility, or even zero population growth. In fact, industrialized countries have gone through the demographic transition which has brought their rapid rate of population growth down.

The Demographic Transition

The *demographic transition* summarizes in four stages the population dynamics in Europe and America during the last two centuries. Initially, there was a high, steady birth rate and a high death rate, which varied with famines and epidemics. Then gradually in the second phase, the death rate declined. This decline was due less to medicine than to sanitary water and sewage systems, soaps and disinfectants, better transportation for shipping foods, and more productive farming techniques. Because the birth rates remained high, the rapid population growth Malthus observed began. Slowly in the third phase,

the birth rate declined, as people realized they needed to bear fewer children in order for the same number to survive into adulthood. Nevertheless, the widening gap between the two rates meant that population continued to grow faster than at any time in human history. Toward the end of this phase, the death rate leveled out. Today the industrialized nations are in the final phase, with a low, steady death rate and a low but fluctuating birth rate. Population growth in these countries is no longer so explosive.

In the past few decades, the rest of the world has also experienced something like the demographic transition. However, the change has been so rapid and the circum-

figure 13:3   The demographic transition

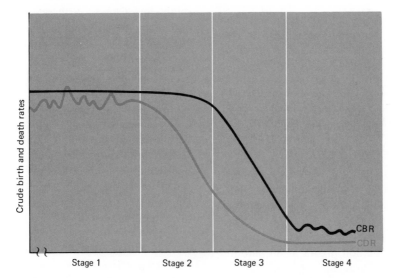

This schematic graph shows the differences in behavior of birth rates and death rates during the demographic transition in the industrialized nations. The gap between births and deaths in stages 2 and 3 produced rapid population growth. Today, the gap has narrowed, although jumps in the birth rate may produce spurts of population growth, as in our postwar baby boom. Even though its population is not growing as fast as that of the developing nations, the industrialized world still must be concerned with population growth because of the heavier demands its people place upon the environment. The United States, for example, has one-sixteenth of the world's population but consumes over one-third of the world's resources.

stances so different that there is serious question whether the developing nations will experience the full transition.

Death rates in developing nations have been dropping more rapidly than they did during the demographic transition in the West. In just five years, from 1945 to 1950, their death rates dropped an average of 24 percent. A more impressionistic view from a Calcutta man reveals the radical change:

"When I was a boy, they took away forty or fifty bodies after a cholera epidemic. It happened every five or ten years. Now they come and vaccinate our children. I have lived here almost seventy years. The biggest change in my time has been health. We've learned how to keep from dying." (Thomlinson, 1965, p. 25)

Philip Hauser tells why:

The same ship that anchors in the harbor of Colombo, Ceylon, can carry in her hold virtually all of the means by which mortality declines were effected in the Western world during the three centuries of the modern era. The ship can carry, in one delivery, fertilizer and tractors for increased productivity; chlorine, insecticides and tooth brushes for improved environmental sanitation and personal hygiene; and the methods of modern medicine, including chemotherapy. (1969, p. 16)

United Nations and government agencies contribute to falling death rates by providing sanitation, public health, and preventive medicine.

With death rates—especially infant mortality—lower, population grows at an astounding rate. Ehrlich provides a graphic description of one teeming city, Delhi:

My wife and daughter and I were returning to our hotel in an ancient taxi. The seats were hopping with fleas. The only functional gear was third. As we crawled through the city, we entered a crowded slum area. The temperature was well over 100, and the air was a haze of dust and smoke. The streets seemed alive with people. People eating, people washing, people sleeping. People visiting, arguing, and screaming. People thrusting their hands through the taxi window, begging. People defecating and urinating. People clinging to buses. People herding animals. People, people, people, people. As we moved slowly through the mob, hand horn squawking, the soot, noise, heat, and choking fires gave the scene a hellish aspect. Would we ever get to our hotel? (1971, p. 15)

This pattern is duplicated on every continent. Rural overpopulation in developing nations is an equally pressing problem as well.

Why Birth Rates Are High Three main variables seem to control fertility in the developing nations: social values governing marriage, number of children, and contraception; the resulting age structure of the population; and the lack of economic development that might make lower birth rates both possible and more advantageous. These combine to produce the Malthusian nightmare of runaway population.

Marriage in developing nations is universal—and early. Take Africa and Asia, for example. Here, the average woman marries before she is twenty. By their late thirties, less than 5 percent are single (Coale, 1973, p. 56). Most women are able, even encouraged to bear children all through their fertile years.

And most of these women want children. One study of rural Moroccan women found out that nearly half wanted more children than they already had. On the average, they wanted 4.6 children. To have four or five children survive, a woman might have to bear eight or nine. Moroccan values clearly favor fertility, not contraception ("Morocco," 1970).

To what degree does ignorance of contraception enter in? Researchers are not sure. Rural Moroccans seemed unfamiliar with birth-control methods. Only a third of the women and about half their husbands admitted knowing anything about how to prevent births. Only 14 percent of married women

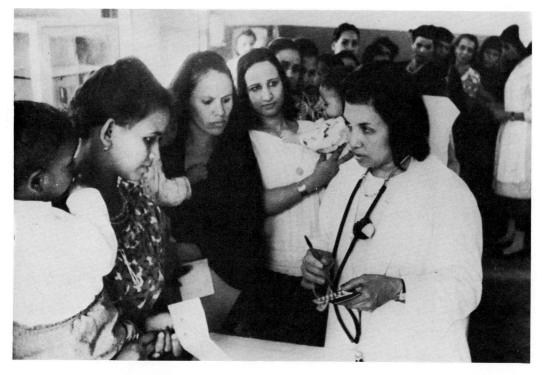

under fifty could name any contraceptive methods. But 60 percent could identify at least one method when researchers read them a list. Thus "ignorance" is hard to distinguish from feeling.

The high birth rates that result from such social values produce a large population of young people. On the island of Mauritius in the Indian Ocean, 44 percent of the people are under fifteen. Older people, born and raised when mortality was higher, are relatively few. Only 3 percent have lived to age sixty-five. The effect of this age distribution is a large *dependency ratio*, or proportion of people of nonproductive age (under fifteen or over sixty-five) in the total population. In Mauritius, 47 percent of the people are in the dependent age group; therefore the dependency ratio is forty-seven. Developed countries have very different ratios. Japan's, for example, is only thirty-nine.

This large young population means a continuing cycle of high fertility, as these young people have their own babies. We have seen the effects of our postwar baby boom—but imagine what would happen if the boom were continuous!

Lack of economic development also contributes to the high birth rate. Some optimists point out that economic development helped the Western nations to bring down their birth rates by making it advantageous to have fewer children and could do the same for developing nations. No longer would parents need a huge brood to ensure enough surviving offspring to support them in their old age, for example. Ironically, however, one of the greatest obstacles to economic development is overpopulation itself.

Overpopulation and Economic Development
Increased population is quite likely to eat up

any economic gains a nation makes. If total national income goes up by 2 percent, for example, and the population grows by the same amount, *per capita income* (or the income available to each citizen if the total of the country were divided evenly) remains the same and people are no better off than be-

figure 13:4 The geography of hunger

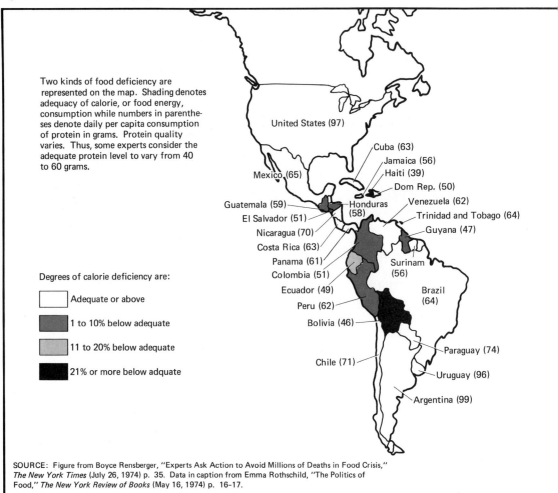

Two kinds of food deficiency are represented on the map. Shading denotes adequacy of calorie, or food energy, consumption while numbers in parentheses denote daily per capita consumption of protein in grams. Protein quality varies. Thus, some experts consider the adequate protein level to vary from 40 to 60 grams.

United States (97)

Cuba (63)
Jamaica (56)
Haiti (39)
Dom Rep. (50)
Venezuela (62)
Trinidad and Tobago (64)
Guyana (47)

Mexico (65)

Guatemala (59)
El Salvador (51)
Nicaragua (70)
Costa Rica (63)
Panama (61)
Colombia (51)
Ecuador (49)
Peru (62)
Bolivia (46)

Honduras (58)

Surinam (56)

Brazil (64)

Chile (71)

Paraguay (74)

Uruguay (96)

Argentina (99)

Degrees of calorie deficiency are:

☐ Adequate or above

▨ 1 to 10% below adequate

▨ 11 to 20% below adequate

■ 21% or more below adquate

SOURCE: Figure from Boyce Rensberger, "Experts Ask Action to Avoid Millions of Deaths in Food Crisis," *The New York Times* (July 26, 1974) p. 35. Data in caption from Emma Rothschild, "The Politics of Food," *The New York Review of Books* (May 16, 1974) p. 16-17.

Undernourishment and malnutrition are chronic in three areas of the world: southern Asia, Africa, and western South America. Countries in these areas must import food. Developing nations as a whole imported 38 percent of all wheat, 55 percent of soybeans, 50 percent of cottonseed oil, and 74 percent of the rice in the

fore. In some countries where population is growing faster than the economy, per capita income is actually declining!

There are other aspects to the problem. When population grows, the number of jobs must grow, too, or there will be greater unemployment or underemployment. In most developing nations too many people are already farming for efficient use of the land. What happens to the leftover people when they seek employment?

This depends on how much industrial capacity there is and how fast it is growing. Economists estimate that investment in ma-

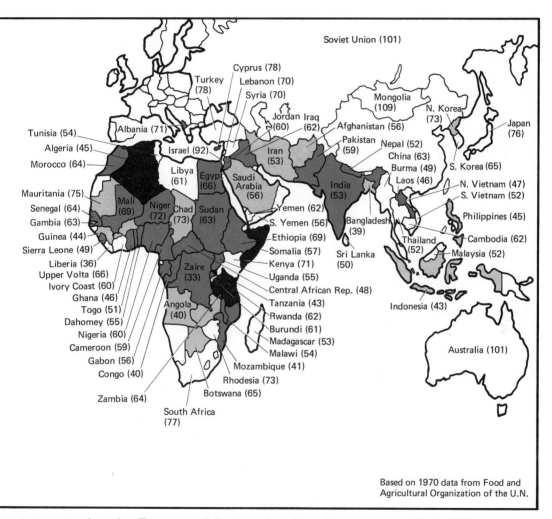

Soviet Union (101)
Cyprus (78)
Turkey (78)
Lebanon (70)
Syria (70)
Mongolia (109)
N. Korea (73)
Japan (76)
Jordan (60)
Iraq (62)
Afghanistan (56)
Tunisia (54)
Albania (71)
Pakistan (59)
Nepal (52)
Algeria (45)
Israel (92)
Iran (53)
China (63)
S. Korea (65)
Morocco (64)
Libya (61)
Egypt (66)
Saudi Arabia (56)
Burma (49)
Laos (46)
N. Vietnam (47)
Mauritania (75)
India (53)
S. Vietnam (52)
Mali (69)
Niger (72)
Chad (73)
Sudan (63)
Yemen (62)
Philippines (45)
Senegal (64)
Bangladesh (39)
Gambia (63)
S. Yemen (56)
Cambodia (62)
Guinea (44)
Ethiopia (69)
Thailand (52)
Malaysia (52)
Sierra Leone (49)
Somalia (57)
Sri Lanka (50)
Liberia (36)
Kenya (71)
Upper Volta (66)
Zaire (33)
Uganda (55)
Ivory Coast (60)
Central African Rep. (48)
Ghana (46)
Tanzania (43)
Indonesia (43)
Togo (51)
Angola (40)
Rwanda (62)
Dahomey (55)
Burundi (61)
Nigeria (60)
Madagascar (53)
Cameroon (59)
Malawi (54)
Gabon (56)
Australia (101)
Congo (40)
Mozambique (41)
Rhodesia (73)
Zambia (64)
Botswana (65)
South Africa (77)

Based on 1970 data from Food and Agricultural Organization of the U.N.

international market. The prices of these products have been rising rapidly. In 1973, for example, the prices of food exports from the United States rose by 55 percent! The result was that American export earnings on food to developing nations alone increased by $3.4 billion.

chinery, factories, and so forth must increase annually at a rate two or three times greater than the increase in the labor force, if per capita income is not to fall. A working population increasing at a rate of 3 percent annually would thus require an increase in capital investment of from 6 percent (Freedman, 1964, p. 161) to 9 percent (DeFleur et al., 1973, p. 251) just to maintain productivity. To increase productivity and thereby raise per capita income, capital investment would have to be substantial—a 12 percent increase in investment per year is considered the rate necessary for a developing country (Keyfitz, in Freedman, 1964, p. 161). Furthermore, a labor force needs training and education, and providing this requires another large investment. Where can this much capital come from in those countries just emerging from a subsistence economy? The land base and income levels are so low that taxing the citizens would accomplish little. Thus, overpopulation and slow economic growth form a vicious cycle, with each worsening the other.

Overpopulation and Hunger These abstract figures on economic development can be translated into something more elemental: the lack of enough food to provide sufficient calories (undernourishment) or sufficient nutrients (malnutrition). In 1967 the president's Science Advisory Committee Panel on the World Food Supply estimated that 20 percent of the people in developing nations were undernourished and 60 percent were malnourished. At the least this means a total of one and a half billion people. Another half billion are either chronically hungry or starving. And this estimate did not include the large number of hungry and malnourished people in developed countries. In the United States, a Public Health survey uncovered 10 to 15 million chronically hungry Americans, a large proportion of them children. Another 10 to 15 million had such low incomes that

malnutrition was inevitable (Ehrlich and Ehrlich, 1972, p. 94). In other words, from 20 to 30 million Americans are suffering from nutritional problems like those of people living in developing countries.

Why should malnutrition and undernourishment be so widespread? Famines have always existed; they are disastrous, of course, but temporary and limited in extent. Famine, however, is not a primary cause of the world's food problems. If food could be distributed to all who need it, enough is now being produced to feed them. Worldwide food supplies are just about keeping pace with population growth. Total food production increased at about 2.8 percent per year through the 1950s and 1960s (Cochrane, 1969, p. 66), just slightly ahead of population growth.

But distribution is unequal. Much of the food the developing nations produce, they sell to developed countries for cash. High-quality protein in the form of soybean and fishmeal products, for example, is exported to the United States for livestock feed. Agricultural productivity is also much lower in the developing countries.

Moreover, feeding people will become harder and harder as population continues to grow. Some estimate that to feed the anticipated population of 1985, the world will need to increase its food production by 43–52 percent. This is a low estimate, one assuming reduced fertility and improved food distribution (Ehrlich and Ehrlich, 1972, p. 85). Gains may be harder to come by since the most productive land is already in use. Furthermore, the high-technology farming that is necessary to increase productivity is threatened by the shortages in fertilizer and oil.

People in the developing nations are not just hungry for food. Even in the remotest village, modern communications are awakening poor people everywhere to one important fact: other people live better. Other people have cars, hospitals, bicycles, plenty of food. Aware of such things, the poor have learned to want and even to expect them. Cochrane sees 1948 as the turning point in a "revolution of expectations" (1969, p. 3). Armed with new wants, the have-nots may create social unrest as they struggle to catch up with their more affluent neighbors. The question remains: What is to be done?

Bringing the Birth Rate Down

To attack the problem directly many countries attempt to use family planning programs as a means of persuading citizens to limit their families. The experiences of Costa Rica and Japan reveal just how complicated it can be to stem the tide of births.

Costa Rica and Birth Control This Central American nation was a classic example of population gone wild. Before 1950 the birth rate was forty-five per thousand and the death rate slightly over fifteen per thousand. This meant a net increase in population of 3 percent annually, or a doubling every twenty-three years. The 1950s brought economic and social development, including better health standards. These helped reduce the death rate to ten but also to increase the birth rate to fifty, a net rate of growth of 4 percent, or a doubling of population every seventeen years! (To determine the time it takes for populations—or your bank account—to double, divide the percent into sixty-nine.)

Then cultural values and family practices started to change and the birth rate began to decline. In 1967 Costa Rica started a family planning program. The program worked, but in large part because it began *after* values favoring small families had taken hold. The birth rate declined 28 percent in the 1960s.

Nevertheless, Costa Rica's problems continue. The economy faces the task of absorbing young adults born during the period of high fertility. As these young people have families of their own—even if they limit births—the recent decline in birth rates will be less rapid in the next decade. A work force of 534,000 in 1970 will expand to nearly twice that by 1985. It will be a long time before zero population growth comes to Costa Rica (Sanders, 1973).

The Remarkable Transition of Japan In Japan, on the other hand, both fertility and mortality began to decline as early as the 1920s. Except for a post-World War II baby boom, these declines accelerated until the rate of natural increase (crude birth rate minus crude death rate) reached 1 percent a year in 1956.

Improvement in the standard of living and in sanitation helped to bring about the early reduction in mortality. Traditionally, literacy and knowledge of personal hygiene have been high in Japan. These conditions laid the groundwork for public health improvements (especially the introduction of DDT and antibiotics) that kept mortality on its downward path after the war. From 1920 to the mid-1960s, mortality dropped from 25.4 to about 7 per thousand (Muramatsu, 1971, pp. 11–13). Note that this death rate is 30 percent lower than ours, though our per capita GNP is four times that of Japan.

In fertility Japan presents a contrast with other developing nations. In the twenty years before the war, the birth rate dropped from 36.2 to 29.4. After a rise to 34.3 in 1947, the rate again declined very dramatically, reaching a low of 16.9 in 1961 and moving slightly upward to 18.5 in 1965 (Muramatsu, 1971, pp. 16–19). The slight prewar fertility decline, credited to postponement of marriage and the modest beginnings of family planning, prepared the Japanese for more intensive fertility control after the war. Abortion became legal in 1948 and 1949: a few years later, national family planning began to furnish all Japanese with contraceptive information and services. Designed to promote maternal health and allow the individual greater choice, these policies encouraged lower birth rates as well. Their effect is clear: population growth declined much more rapidly after they went into effect.

A population growth rate of only 1.0 since 1956 helped Japan achieve its postwar economic "miracle." A stable population allowed substantial capital to be reinvested in industry, while living standards remained high. Now some Japanese worry about a labor shortage!

Government policy helped the lower birth rates along, but we should not lose sight of the ways in which Japanese society itself fostered population limits. Literate and free from taboos on frank discussions of sexual matters, Japanese could read about family planning in their equivalents of the *Ladies' Home Journal* and the *Reader's Digest* (Freedman 1964, p. 171). The media spread the word quickly: small families are desirable. As living standards rose, the benefits of having fewer mouths to feed became even clearer, and the low-birth-rate cycle continued.

Modernization or Birth Control? As we have seen from these examples, the key to lowered fertility is motivation, shaped by social values. A striking example of the link between values and fertility was recently uncovered in a study of Spain (Coale, 1973, p. 63). A demographer drew a map showing the birth rates in Spain's forty-nine provinces and showed it to a language specialist. The areas of similar birth rates almost exactly matched the areas of different Spanish dialects. In other words, fertility patterns corresponded with cultural and linguistic variations. Only regional differences in culture could account for the differences in fertility.

If fertility is to decline, three conditions must be found together. First, the community must accept smaller families. So must the individual. And once men and women have decided that fewer children mean economic and social advantages, they must be able to find effective means of birth control. Birth control, then, must be *acceptable, advantageous,* and *available* (Coale, 1973, p. 65).

As we have seen, some nations enjoy all three conditions. There, fertility starts declining even before industrial modernization begins. In some countries birth rates stay high because all the preconditions are absent. Most nations fall somewhere in between. High mortality may not be a hindrance to modernization, but high fertility certainly is. Lower fertility is still essential to modernization, but modernization need not take place for the three basic fertility-lowering conditions to exist.

POPULATION GROWTH IN AMERICA

The developing nations may outstrip us in population growth, but we will still have about 300 million Americans by the year 2,000, about 100 million more than in 1970 (*Statistical Abstract*, 1973, table 3, p. 6). More people demand more food, more energy, more resources—and create more pollution. If we want to keep up our comfortable way of life, then some feel we had best halt population growth.

If contraception that allowed women to have the number of children they wanted at the time they wanted them were available to all, would this be the answer? Many demog-

table 13:2 **UNWANTED FERTILITY IN THE UNITED STATES, 1970**

RACE AND EDUCATION	MOST LIKELY NUMBER OF BIRTHS PER WOMAN	PERCENT OF BIRTHS 1966–1970 UNWANTED	PERCENT OF BIRTHS 1966–1970 UNPLANNED[1]	THEORETICAL BIRTHS PER WOMAN WITHOUT UNWANTED BIRTHS
All Women	3.0	15	44	2.7
College 4+	2.5	7	32	2.4
College 1–3	2.8	11	39	2.6
High School 4	2.8	14	44	2.6
High School 1–3	3.4	20	48	2.9
Less	3.9	31	56	3.0
White Women	2.9	13	42	2.6
College 4+	2.5	7	32	2.4
College 1–3	2.8	10	39	2.6
High School 4	2.8	13	42	2.6
High School 1–3	3.2	18	44	2.8
Less	3.5	25	53	2.9
Black Women	3.7	27	61	2.9
College 4+	2.3	3	21	2.2
College 1–3	2.6	21	46	2.3
High School 4	3.3	19	62	2.8
High School 1–3	4.2	31	66	3.2
Less	5.2	55	68	3.1

[1]Unplanned births include unwanted births.

SOURCE: *Population and the American Future,* The Report of the Commission on Population Growth and the American Future (Washington, D.C.: Government Printing Office, 1972), table 11.1, p. 97.

raphers say no, pointing to the fact that people want more than the replacement level of 2.25 children per family. In 1965, for example, married women aged thirty-five to forty-four were asked how many children they would like to have. Their answer—an average of 3.4 children per family—would lead to an awesome rate of growth. Other investigators approached this question differently. In subtle ways they determined how many unwanted babies a representative group of women had had, then subtracted this number from the total number of children these women had borne. By this measure, the average ideal family turned out to have 2.5 children, far closer to the replacement rate (Bumpass and Westoff, 1970). A 1970 National Fertility Study concluded that of all births to married women from 1966 to 1970, 15 percent were unwanted. Another 44 percent were wanted but would have taken place later. A total of about 2.65 million babies were unplanned. Clearly, if contraception had been acceptable, advantageous, and available to all Americans, the problem of population growth would have been greatly alleviated.

Contraception

Americans now use more effective contraceptive devices than ever before. About four-fifths of couples using contraception in 1970 favored the most effective methods—the pill, the IUD, and sterilization (Westoff, 1972). Use of these methods increased from 37.2 percent in 1965 to 57.9 percent in 1970. Young couples, especially, chose the pill or the IUD more often than ever before. Older couples, on the other hand, were using sterilization more than before. By 1970 about a third of the couples using contraception chose the pill. Charles Westoff sees the rapidity with which American women have accepted the pill since it first came on the market in 1960, despite its potential side effects, as "an indication of the wide market for effective contraception" (1972, p. 11).

Catholic Americans and Birth Limitation Despite religious prohibitions, Catholics are using birth control much the way their compatriots are. In 1968 Pope Paul VI issued an encyclical, *Humanae Vitae*, reaffirming the traditional Roman Catholic prohibition of any birth-control method except rhythm (abstinence during fertile periods). All the same, American Catholics increased their use of other methods. A series of studies in 1955, 1960, 1965, and 1970 bear out this generalization. In 1955 only 30 percent of Catholic women used methods other than rhythm. By 1970 the proportion had gone up dramatically—to 68 percent (Westoff and Ryder, 1970).

This trend has been even more marked among younger Catholic women; 78 percent of those aged twenty to twenty-four used methods other than rhythm in 1970 (Westoff and Bumpass, 1973, p. 41). Even in 1965, when the rhythm method was still the most popular form of birth control for Catholic women (used by 36 percent of all who practiced contraception), the pill took second place (18 percent). The trend toward less dependence on the rhythm method and greater use of the pill held true for Protestant women as well (Westoff and Ryder, 1967, pp. 4–5).

One survey questioned Catholic women on their reactions to the papal encyclical. Typical of those who acted in opposition to church doctrine was this woman: "I don't think the Church has any right to dictate how many children you should have. I don't think any Church has a right to pry into anyone's private life. The Church doesn't help raise the children nor provide for them. It's just not the business of the Church" (Westoff and Ryder, 1970). Many priests now support women in their decision to use artificial birth-control methods. To sum up, Catholic women seem to be following the American trend toward use of more effective contraception.

Abortion

Until recently abortion was illegal in the United States. Therefore, it was hard to tell just how important it was as a means of birth control in America. In 1973 a Supreme Court ruling (*Roe* v. *Wade*) reflected a changing climate of opinion about abortion. *Roe* v. *Wade* held that abortion during the first twenty-four weeks of pregnancy was a private matter between a woman and her physician; state statutes could not interfere with it.

The following comments from citizens hint at the bitter struggle over abortion in recent years. One population expert expressed support for legalized abortion, calling its illegality "ludicrous." Why? Because, she pointed out, "from what I see of present population problems in the United States, in ten to twenty years women will be prohibited from doing what they are now forced to do and forced to

While most people agree that birth control is necessary to control population and family size, the bitter struggle over abortion continues. (Left, UPI. Right, Leif Skoogfors/Woodfin Camp)

do what they are prohibited from doing now" (Schulder and Kennedy, 1971, p. 127). But a Black Panther spoke out against abortion: "Abortion hides behind the guise of helping women, when in reality it will attempt to destroy our people" (Schulder and Kennedy 1971, p. 156). And a New York doctor, a Catholic, refused even to provide contraception, on the grounds that women have no right to decide whether or not to bear a child (Schulder and Kennedy 1971, p. 172).

More generally, approval of abortion has increased markedly from 1965 to the present. A substantial majority of women now approve of abortion if a mother's health is in danger, if she has been raped, or if her child is likely to be born deformed. A small but significant minority (16.5 percent) approve of abortion for any reason. In general, education goes hand in hand with approval of abortion. College graduates are most likely to approve of abortion under various circumstances (34.6 percent). Working women and non-Catholics approve more often than housewives and Catholics. But surprisingly, young women are *less* likely to approve of abortion than are somewhat older women of childbearing age (Jones and Westoff, 1972).

Legally available abortion immediately reduces the birth rate. In the two years after

New York State passed its liberalized abortion law, New York City experienced dramatic declines in the number of live births. However, legal abortion accounted for only half the decline. The rest was due to new attitudes, which reduced births not only in New York but nationwide. Furthermore, many women who had legal abortions during this period would undoubtedly have had illegal ones otherwise. But making them legal has improved maternal health, especially for the poor, by replacing hasty, often dangerous back room procedures with sanitary, medically supervised ones. Legal abortions are cheaper, and thus available to nearly everyone. When fertility counseling accompanies abortion, the practice often reinforces and expands regular contraceptive practice (Tietze, 1973).

The Birth Dearth: Will It Last?

After running its course, the postwar baby boom was followed by a baby bust. After the boom peaked in 1957, the crude birth rate fell steadily through the 1960s and into the 1970s (see table 13:3). Our birth rate reached a low of fifteen per thousand in 1973. If the decline continues, we can achieve zero population growth much faster than people even five years ago had hoped.

But population growth may not be over yet. As the boom generation moves into its own child-bearing years, an echo boom is expected to take place. To some extent the recent decline occurred because the women bearing children were part of the unusually small group of depression babies. In 1965 there were just a few more women of prime

---

table 13:3 THE BABY BOOM AND THE BIRTH DEARTH

	1945	1950	1955	1960	1965	1970	1973
Live births (millions)	2,858	3,623	4,104	4,258	3,760	3,718	3,141
Crude birth rate (per 1,000 population)	20.4	24.1	25.0	23.7	19.4	17.8	15.0
Fertility rate (births per 1,000 women 15–44 years)	85.9	106.2	118.5	118.0	96.6	87.6	69.3
Children per family	2.5	3.2	3.6	3.6	3.0	2.4	1.9
NRR (female children per female adult)	1.42	1.55	1.73	1.62	1.38	1.24	1.00

SOURCE: *Statistical Abstract of the United States, 1973* (Washington, D.C.: Government Printing Office, 1973), tables 66 and 68, p. 52. Figures for 1973 are from Harold M. Schmeck, Jr., "Birth, Fertility Rates at a New Low in U.S.," *The New York Times* (March 16, 1974): 14, based on data from the National Center for Health Statistics, U.S. Census Bureau. NRR rates by five-year averages, with 1973 estimated from *Population Index,* vol. 39 (April 1973), p. 286.

Although by 1965 the crude birth rate had dropped below the 1945 rate, the *number* of births remained higher in 1965 until 1970 because of the increasingly larger number of women of child-bearing age. Moreover, women were having more babies than in 1945, as shown by the higher fertility rate (96.6 and 87.6 versus 85.9). In this case the fertility rate is a much more accurate reflection of trends than the crude birth rate. Notice the dramatic fall in the Net Reproduction Rate from 1.73 in 1955 to about 1.00 today, foreshadowing eventual zero population growth if this rate continues for a number of years.

TEENAGE MOTHERS

Imagine a television ad for baby food. The mother is in her twenties or thirties. In soft focus she cuddles her smiling, cooing baby. Her home is sunlit and middle class, and you can be sure she is wearing a wedding ring. The hard facts don't quite resemble this dreamy picture.

One-sixth of all babies are born to mothers in their teens. And of these, two-fifths are born out of wedlock. Teenage motherhood is shared by over a quarter of the girls born in 1950. One out of four of these teenage mothers had at least two children before age twenty. Believe it or not, these figures represent a decline in teenage mothers from 33.9 percent in 1939.

Unwed motherhood is largely teenage motherhood. The younger the mother, the less likely she is to be married when her child is born. Half the illegitimate births each year are to teenage mothers. Of births to mothers aged fifteen to seventeen, 40 percent are illegitimate; slightly older mothers (eighteen or nineteen) are twice as likely to be married. We must not overlook the babies made legitimate only by hasty marriage. Nearly six out of ten first babies of girls aged fifteen to nineteen were conceived before marriage (Menken, 1972, p. 46).

While illegitimacy rates have declined for other age groups, they have been increasing for teens. In 1968 single girls fifteen to nineteen years old gave birth at a rate of 19.8 per thousand, up from 16.0 in 1961.

Having a baby out of wedlock has drastic consequences for a teenage girl. As Arthur Campbell put it, "The girl who has an illegitimate child at the age of sixteen suddenly has 90 percent of her life's script written for her. She will probably drop out of school, even if someone else in her family helps to take care of the baby; she will probably not be able to find a steady job that pays enough to provide for herself and her child; she may feel impelled to marry someone she might not otherwise have chosen. Her life choices are few, and most of them are bad" (Campbell, in Menken, 1972, pp. 45–46).

Health complications plague the teenage mothers as well. More babies born to teenage mothers die before age one, especially when the mother has borne other children. Fetal mortality, too, is higher than for the babies of mothers in their twenties. Girls in their teens tend to have babies closer together than other mothers do. Shorter intervals between babies go hand in hand with stillbirth, prematurity, and infant mortality (Menken, 1972, p. 49). Teenage mothers have more complicated pregnancies and they bear more premature infants. Prematurity has been associated with increased mortality and the development of a variety of congenital illnesses and birth defects, such as cerebral palsy, epilepsy, mental retardation, and blindness (Menken, 1972, p. 50).

Why do so many teenagers bear children? Probably because so many fail to use contraceptives. A national survey of never-married fifteen- to nineteen-year-olds showed that nearly half of those with sexual experience had not used any method of contraception at last intercourse. Fewer than a fifth had always used contraception. Those who took no precautions rationalized that they could not get pregnant because they were too young, it was the wrong time of the month, or they had sex too seldom. About one-fourth believed oral contraceptives to be unsafe. Clearly, some misinformation contributes to the high birth rate among these girls.

Perfect contraception is "a model in which couples can avoid having more children than they want and do not have children before they want them" (Bumpass and Westoff, 1970, p. 1177). If teenagers practiced perfect contraception, the results would be startling. Here are some sample projections: if no females under eighteen had babies, the total birth rate among teenagers fifteen to nineteen years old would be reduced by 30 percent. At this rate, in fifty years the population would be 5 percent smaller than it would if the 1968 teenage birth rate continued unchanged. If 75 percent of births to teenagers were postponed till the girls were twenty to twenty-four, and the rest to ages twenty-five to twenty-nine, the population in fifty years would be 6.6 percent smaller. And if there were no teenage births at all, the population would be 15.1 percent smaller. This drop alone would reduce the NRR to just over 1.0—almost a stationary population.

SOURCES: Larry Bumpass and Charles F. Westoff, "The 'Perfect Contraceptive' Population," *Science*, vol. 169 (September 18, 1970): 1177–1182; Jane Menken, "The Health and Social Consequences of Teenage Childbearing," *Family Planning Perspectives*, vol. 4, no. 3 (July 1972): 45–53.

child-bearing years than there were in 1935 (11.1 million as compared to 11 million), although the total population had grown by over 50 million people during those years. But this age group has been growing steadily, to 16 million in 1972. In 1980 there will be about 20.1 million, nearly twice as many as in 1960 (*Population Bulletin*, 1966, p. 65).

Thus, the current low *rate* of births may still result in large crops of babies because there are so many more mothers. Will twice as many mothers mean twice as many children? Probably not, according to most indicators. Young women today are having their children later. Furthermore, they are planning to

have smaller families. Women now in their late thirties have, on the average, three children; but in 1971 married women aged eighteen to twenty-four expected to have an average of 2.4 children per family (Ehrlich and Ehrlich, 1972, p. 36). However, experience shows that families usually end up larger than people expect them to be.

In late 1972 births fell below replacement level for the first time. Optimists hailed this as zero population growth. One called the day of the announcement "a milestone . . . a day as historic as the Fourth of July, the birth date of any President, or the termination date of any war" (Kahn, 1974). But had we really achieved a constant population? On the contrary. Even if we hold to replacement-level fertility—a big "if"—it will still take from sixty-five to seventy-five years for population growth to end, because of the age structure of the population. From replacement level in 1974 to ZPG in about 2040, our population would increase by 81 million (Ehrlich and Ehrlich 1972, pp. 38–39)!

figure 13:5 **United States growth with two-or three-child families**

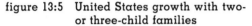
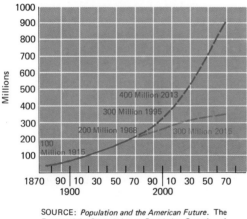

SOURCE: *Population and the American Future.* The Report of the Commission on Population Growth and the American Future (Washington, D.C.: Government Printing Office, 1972) figure 2.3, p. 23.

The difference between having two children and three seems small enough until examined for a whole population. Had American families continued to have three children apiece, the population would double by 2,013 (from 200 million in 1968 to 400 million 55 years later). Recent trends, however, make the two-child family more typical. Even so, there will be another 100 million Americans by the year 2,015.

HEALTH IN AMERICA

While many Americans worry about the population crush, others wonder about the fate of those who are born. Will they lead long, healthy lives? Will they be able to pay for the health care they need? Population policy concerns more than just birth rates and death rates. Though the death rate in the United States is relatively low, it could be even lower. It is raised by the high death rates of certain groups in the population.

Excess Death

From birth to death males have higher death rates than females. At birth there are 106 males for every 100 females, but by age sixty-five the sex ratio has dropped to 72. A difference of this magnitude raises some provocative questions. Is there a genetic cause for the difference? Some say yes, since even males one to eight have higher death rates. But do men experience greater stress and greater pressure to achieve than women? Is the higher male death rate partly a penalty for success as the world sees it? As liberated women put themselves under similar pressures, their death rate may rise to match that of the men. Some optimists look for a different outcome. Suppose men took a hint from the Women's Liberation Movement and began to get off the treadmill. Would their death rate start to decline?

Besides an excess of male over female deaths, avoidable deaths result from smoking (Brody, 1974, p. 8). In the ten years since 1964, when the surgeon general of the Public Health Service officially reported on the hazards of cigarette smoking, about 29 million people stopped smoking. Still, there were 52 million smokers, including a large number of young people (3,000 teenagers begin smoking every day). Americans are smoking new types of cigarettes, with less tar and nicotine—the substances considered harmful. Nevertheless, the Public Health Service estimates that 300,000 people die annually as a direct result of complications from smoking, such as lung cancer and heart disease. Smokers miss 40 percent more working days than nonsmokers do, visit doctors more often, spend more time in hospitals, and require surgery more often (Brody, 1974).

The American people have the highest incomes in the world, and they spend more than anyone else on health care, nearly 7 percent of the GNP. Nevertheless, the United States has a higher crude death rate and a higher infant mortality rate than a number of other nations. More than fifteen other nations have lower rates of infant mortality, for

example. Many underdeveloped countries, such as Mexico and Iran, have far lower crude death rates than the United States. However, the discrepancy is only apparent. Because these countries have high birth rates, and correspondingly high proportions of young people in their overall population, they have fewer people in the years of high mortality. It is more informative and accurate to compare the crude death rates for the United States with those for other developed nations. Even here, however, several countries such as Sweden have lower mortality rates, an indication that they deliver health care more effectively than we do. Likewise, the United Nations found that the life expectancy for males born in 1972 in the United States was lower than life expectancies for males in at least sixteen other nations (United Nations, 1973, tables 13, 15, 18). Once again evidence indicates we could improve our health care.

Socioeconomic factors help to determine mortality rates. As one demographer puts it, "the relatively high mortality of the United States compared with other advanced nations is undoubtedly in large measure a reflection of the high mortality of the disadvantaged in the nation—the lower socioeconomic groups of whites and the even more disadvantaged minority groups" (Kitagawa, 1972, p. 106). Kitagawa's studies show, for example, that those with the lowest incomes have higher overall mortality rates, higher infant mortality, and a higher incidence of infectious and chronic diseases. Education, as well as income, corresponds with lower mortality. Racial differences are particularly marked. From 1959 to 1961, for example, all nonwhite females had a death rate 34 percent higher than that of white females. The rate for all nonwhite males was 20 percent higher than that for white males at all ages. The difference was even greater with

table 13:4 EXCESS MORTALITY IN THE UNITED STATES, 1960 (by percent)

SEX, COLOR, AGE, AND YEARS OF SCHOOL COMPLETED	25 AND OVER	25–64 YEARS	65 AND OVER
Total population	19	26	15
Males	11	25	1
Females	30	29	30
Whites	17	21	15
Nonwhites	36	52	18
White males	10	21	2
0–4 years of school	9	30	3
5–7 years of school	12	29	2
8 years of school	10	25	1
High school, 1–3 years	11	24	0.1
High school, 4 years		16	
College, 1 year or more	0	0	0
Nonwhite males	25	45	0.5
0–4 years of school	25	51	5
5–8 years of school	23	43	−8
High school or college	28	39	−3
White females	27	21	30
0–4 years of school	42	53	40
5–7 years of school	33	36	32
8 years of school	31	30	31
High school, 1–3 years	18	12	26
High school, 4 years		4	
College, 1 year or more	0	0	0
Nonwhite females	49	60	39
0–4 years of school	51	70	41
5–8 years of school	50	63	34
High school or college	44	42	41

SOURCE: Evelyn M. Kitagawa and Philip M. Hauser, *Differential Mortality in the United States: A Study in Socioeconomic Epidemiology* (Cambridge, Mass.: Harvard University Press, 1973), table 8.1.

the young, especially infants (Kitagawa, 1972).

These statistics led Kitagawa to ask: How many people die unnecessarily in the United States today? To find out, she devised an Index of Excess Mortality, which in simple terms measures the deaths that would not have occurred if every subgroup had the same, relatively low, death rate as whites aged twenty-five years and over with at least one year of college. In 1960 this figure was 292,000, or 19 percent of all deaths, 17 percent of deaths among whites, and 36 percent of deaths among nonwhites (Kitagawa, 1972). These deaths must be considered preventable.

Health Care and the Poor

Could we improve mortality rates by improving education for all, thus preparing people for better jobs, more income, and thus better health care? Or can we approach the problem differently, making health care equally available to all? At present the system of health care in the United States falls short in several respects. In proportion to population, there are simply fewer medical facilities in poor areas, both rural and urban. In 1970 the fifteen counties with highest per capita incomes had seven times as many hospital beds per person than did the fifteen counties with the lowest per capita income (Schultze, 1972, p. 222).

Poor people visit doctors less frequently, especially for preventive care. This pattern is particularly striking for children. On the average, poor children under sixteen visited the doctor only .17 times a year, while wealthy children the same age averaged 5.7 visits. Only 10 percent of low-income children have ever visited a pediatrician, compared with 30 percent of upper-income children. School examinations turned up some children with defective vision. Of those from the lowest income group, 31.1 percent received no treatment for the condition; only 13.5 percent of children in the upper-income bracket went without treatment (Hurley, 1970, pp. 91–93). Of children from families with incomes of $3,000 or less, 20.9 percent have not received

American blacks at all income levels visit doctors less often than whites. One quarter of all blacks receive medical care in hospital clinics or emergency rooms. (Dennis Stock/ Magnum)

vaccinations against smallpox and 18.9 percent have not received diphtheria-tetanus vaccinations. For children from families with incomes of $9,000 or more, the figures are 3.9 percent and 1.7 percent, respectively (Hurley, 1970).

The inequities show up in many other areas. The poor of all ages have less private health insurance, especially for children. In 1968, 90 percent of families with incomes over $10,000 had some private medical insurance, while only a third of those earning less than $3,000 did. Of children covered by insurance plans, less than a quarter of those at the lowest economic level were covered for hospitalization expenses. Nine-tenths of those at the upper level had such protection.

Medicaid and Medicare have attempted to improve health coverage for the poor and the elderly, respectively. But these programs do not provide for preventive care, and what they offer varies widely from state to state. The states also administer and regulate their own programs. Thus one state, for example, limits payments to only fifteen days of hospital care. Only a few states include payments for drugs, the services of dentists and optometrists, and private nursing.

Until we solve some of these problems in delivery of health care, some Americans will continue at a disadvantage. In a civilized society population control means maintaining the citizens' good health, not just regulating their numbers.

---

summary

Demography, the study of population, concerns the patterns of birth, death, and migration that determine the size and composition of a society's people. The *census*, which counts people and collects data about them, gives demographers their major source of data.

Population growth depends on the relationship between the three demographic variables: births, deaths, and net migration. The rate of population growth is the extent to which births and immigration exceed deaths and emigration.

The basic model of population change in the West is known as the *demographic transition*. In stage one, before 1750, a high, steady birth rate and an equally high death rate, which peaked during epidemics and famines, kept the rate of population growth low. In the second phase, the death rate began to decline as improved hygiene, public sanitation, and better food supplies took effect. Populations grew rapidly. Next, the birth rate began to decline, and the death rate continued to drop. Finally, in the industrialized nations of today, the death rate is low and steady while the birth rate is low but fluctuating with social trends.

The Reverend Thomas Malthus was the first scholar to analyze population growth and to worry about its consequences for mankind. Increases in food supply could never keep pace with population. The only way to halt population growth would be voluntary abstinence from sexual relations; otherwise, population would be checked drastically by war, pestilence, or starvation.

Malthusian growth still haunts the less developed parts of the world. There, the demographic transition has taken a different form because advanced medicine, hygiene, and increased agricultural productivity have greatly reduced the death rate within just a few years. The birth rates in these countries remain high, as does population growth. Hunger, unemployment, and social unrest result as population growth strains available resources. Birth-control programs help only if they reinforce cultural trends toward smaller families, whether economic development is taking place or not.

Even in the United States, population growth may eventually threaten our way of life. Although birth rates have fallen from the heights of the baby boom—reinforced by legalized abortion and widely available contraceptives—zero population growth is many decades away. Even if women continue to bear children at the new low rates, the enormous numbers of women in the baby boom generation will produce an echo boom.

Quality of life is as important as quantity. In the United States death rates differ according to sex, habits (for example, smoking), race, and class. Across the board, health for the poor is—poor. Better distribution of health care would improve life for all Americans.

glossary

age-specific fertility rate The number of births per thousand women of a given age range in a given time span.

age-specific mortality rate The number of deaths per thousand people of a given age bracket in a specific time span.

census A periodic counting of the population, which also records facts on age, sex, occupation, etc. In the United States the census is taken every tenth year and provides a wealth of statistical data for both demographers and social planners.

crude birth rate The number of births per thousand people in a given time span.

crude death rate The number of deaths per thousand people in a given time span.

demographic transition The period in which population shifts from the "old balance" of high fertility and high mortality to the "new balance" of low fertility and low mortality. During the demographic transition mortality declines or has declined rapidly, while fertility (usually) declines more slowly, causing a period of rapid population growth.

demographic variables Births, deaths, and net migration.

dependency ratio The proportion of people under fifteen and over sixty-five to the total population.

fecundity The biological potential for reproduction.

fertility rate The number of births per thousand women between the ages of fifteen and forty-four.

infant mortality rate The number of deaths per thousand children one year of age or less in a given time span.

internal migration The movement of people from one place to another within the same country.

international migration The movement of people from one country to another.

life expectancy The average number of years of life remaining to a person of a given age.

life span The maximum number of years of a human life.

net migration The difference between immigration and emigration.

net reproduction rate (NRR) An average of the number of female children born per woman of child-bearing age.

new balance A relatively stable population based on low mortality coupled with low fertility.

old balance A relatively stable population based on high fertility coupled with high mortality.

per capita income Income available to each citizen if the total income of the country were divided equally.

population pyramid A graph showing the distribution of a population by age and sex.

registration Recording the key events—birth, graduation, marriage, death, etc.—of a person's life by a government or other agency.

replacement level The point at which a population replaces itself with new people but does not grow.

sex ratio The number of men per hundred women in a population.

zero population growth (ZPG) A population that is stable, neither increasing nor decreasing, because the crude birth rate is equal to the crude death rate.

references

Jane E. Brody, "Decade's Warnings Fail to Cut Smoking," *The New York Times* (January 11, 1974): 1, 8.

Larry Bumpass and Charles F. Westoff, "The 'Perfect Contraceptive' Population," *Science*, vol. 169 (September 18, 1970): 1177–1182.

Leon E. Clark, "Baby Boom by Fiat: The Effects of Population Policy on Fertility in Romania; An Inquiry Teaching Module," *Teaching Notes on Population*, vol. 3 (Spring/Summer 1973): 24–28.

A. J. Coale, "The Demographic Transition Reconsidered," in *International Population Conference*, Liège, 1973.

A. J. Coale and N. W. Rives, Jr., "A Statistical Reconstruction of the Black Population of the United States 1880–1970," *Population Index*, vol. 39, no. 1 (January 1973): 3–36.

Willard W. Cochrane, *The World Food Problem*, New York: Thomas Y. Crowell, 1969.

Melvin L. DeFleur, William V. D'Antonio, and Lois B. DeFleur, *Sociology: Human Society*, Glenview, Ill.: Scott, Foresman, 1973.

Paul Ehrlich, *The Population Bomb*, New York: Ballantine, 1971.

———and Ann H. Ehrlich, *Population Resources Environment*, San Francisco: W. H. Freeman, 1972.

Ronald Freedman, ed., *Population: The Vital Revolution*, Garden City, N.Y.: Doubleday, 1964.

Dov Friedlander and Eitan Sabatello, "Israel," in *Country Profiles*, The Population Council, February 1972.

Philip M. Hauser, ed., *The Population Dilemma*, Englewood Cliffs, N.J.: Prentice-Hall, 1969.

"Higher Education and the Nation's Health," Carnegie Commission on Higher Education, October 1970.

Roger Hurley, "The Health Crisis of the Poor," in Hans Peter Dreitzel, ed., *The Social Organization of Health*, New York: Macmillan, 1970.

Elise F. Jones and Charles F. Westoff, "Attitudes Toward Abortion in the United States in 1970 and the Trend Since 1965," in Charles F. Westoff and Robert Parke, Jr., eds., *Demographic and Social Aspects of Population Growth*, vol. 1, Commission on Population Growth and the American Future, 1972.

E. J. Kahn, *The American People, The Findings of the 1970 Census*, New York: Weybright and Talley, 1974.

John F. Kantner and Melvin Zelnik, "Contraception and Pregnancy Experience of Young Unmarried Women in the United States," *Family Planning Perspectives*, vol. 5, no. 1 (Winter 1973): 21–35.

Robert E. Kennedy, Jr., *The Irish*, Berkeley: University of California Press, 1973.

Evelyn M. Kitagawa, "Socioeconomic Differences in Mortality in the United States and Some Implications for Population Policy," in Charles F. Westoff and Robert Parke, Jr., eds., *Demographic and Social Aspects of Population Growth*, vol. 1, Commission on Population Growth and the American Future, 1972.

Jane Menken, "The Health and Social Consequences of Teenage Childbearing," *Family Planning Perspectives*, vol. 4, no. 3 (July 1972): 45–53.

"Morocco: Family Planning Knowledge, Attitudes, and Practice in the Rural Areas," in *Studies in Family Planning*, The Population Council, October 1970.

Minoru Muramatsu, M.D., "Japan," in *Country Profiles*, The Population Council, March 1971.

———, *Japan's Experience in Family Planning—Past and Present*, Tokyo: Family Planning Federation of Japan, 1967.

William Petersen, *Population*, London: Macmillan, 1969.

Population and the American Future, The Report of the Commission on Population Growth and the American Future, Washington, D.C.: Government Printing Office, 1972.

Population Bulletin, vol. 22, no. 3 (August 1966).

Thomas G. Sanders, "Costa Rica, Population Perceptions and Policy," in Harrison Brown et al., eds., *Population Perspective, 1973*, San Francisco: Freeman, Cooper, 1973.

Harold M. Schmeck, Jr., "Birth, Fertility Rates at a New Low in U.S.," *The New York Times* (April 16, 1974): 1, 14.

Diane Schulder and Florynce Kennedy, *Abortion Rap*, New York: McGraw-Hill, 1971.

Charles Schultze et al., *Setting National Priorities: The 1973 Budget*, Washington, D.C.: Brookings Institution, 1972.

———, *Setting National Priorities: The 1974 Budget*, Washington, D.C.: Brookings Institution, 1973.

Statistical Abstract of the United States, 1973, Washington, D.C.: Government Printing Office, 1973.

Ralph Thomlinson, *Population Dynamics*, New York: Random House, 1965.

Christopher Tietze, "Two Years' Experience with a Liberal Abortion Law: Its Impact on Fertility Trends in New York City," *Family Planning Perspectives*, vol. 5, no. 1 (Winter 1973): 36–41.

United Nations, *Demographic Yearbook*, 1973.

United Nations, *Demographic Yearbook, World Summary*, 1971.

Charles F. Westoff, "The Modernization of U.S. Contraceptive Practice," *Family Planning Perspectives*, vol. 4, no. 3 (July 1972): 9–12.
———and Larry Bumpass, "The Revolution in Birth Control Practices of U.S. Roman Catholics," *Science*, vol. 179 (January 5, 1973): 41–44.
———and Norman B. Ryder, "United States: Methods of Fertility Control, 1955, 1960, and 1965," in *Studies in Family Planning*, The Population Council, February 1967.
———, "United States: The Papal Encyclical and Catholic Practice and Attitudes, 1969," in *Studies in Family Planning*, The Population Council, February 1970.
James Q. Wilson and Robert L. DuPont, "The Sick Sixties, Some Speculations on the Postwar Baby Boom and How It Grew," *Atlantic* (October 1973): 91–98.

for further study

The Census. The United States has one of the most complete and wide-ranging censuses in the world, and thus offers great opportunities to study almost any aspect of this chapter in detail. The United States Commission on Population Growth and the American Future has digested this vast material into a number of outstanding reports. For an overview, see *Population and the American Future* (Washington, D.C.: Government Printing Office, 1972). This lively text reviews findings on population and water supply, pollution, the economy, education, child care, migration, etc.

Birth Control. Some students may wish to know more about birth control including patterns of use, attitudes towards contraceptives, the development of the pill as a new technique, abortion, and related topics. The following books and articles all speak to more than one of these interrelated themes: Norman B. Ryder and Charles F. Westoff, *Reproduction in the United States* (Princeton, N.J.: Princeton University Press, 1971). R. Freedman, P. K. Whelpton, and A. A. Campbell, *Family Planning, Sterility, and Population Growth* (New York: McGraw-Hill, 1959); Charles F. Westoff, ed., *Toward the End of Growth* (Englewood Cliffs, N.J.: Prentice-Hall, 1973); and Judith Blake, "Abortion and Public Opinion," *Science*, vol. 171 (February 12, 1971).

Health Care. The inequities of health care and their relation to life and death are of great concern today. Probably the best and most interesting material, comes from the hearings on health care which Senator Edward Kennedy conducted. Reports of the committee are available in libraries. An authoritative overview of this area is provided by Anne Somers in *Health Care in Transition: Directions for the Future* (Chicago: Hospital Research and Educational Trust, 1971). A good selection of readings in the sociology of health is *The Social Organization of Health*, edited by Hans Peter Dreitzel (New York: Macmillan, 1971). Finally, an important book which goes to the heart of how health insurance should be organized is *Blue Cross, What Went Wrong?* by Sylvia A. Law and the Health Law Project (New Haven, Conn.: Yale University Press, 1974).

Food. Another crucial area for population and health is food—its quantity and nutritional content. The world situation can be assessed in various documents published by the United Nations. See also "The Politics of Food," by Emma Rothschild, *The New York Review* (May 16, 1974), pp. 16–18. A good source for information on food in America is the *Hearings Before the Senate Select Committee on Nutrition and Human Needs*: parts 2–4, March–May 1973. These hearings contain expert testimony about American diets and television advertising of food to children. See also Dr. Michael Jacobson's *Nutrition Scoreboard* (Center for Science in the Public Health, 1974). A recent report on nutritional deficiencies was issued by the National Research Council's Food and Nutrition Board, July 1974.

In the last decade the words *power* and *politics* have been linked to every conceivable kind of human experience. Hippies used the phrase "flower power" to describe the hoped-for effects of openness, innocence, generosity, and nonaggression. Feminist Kate Millet wrote about "sexual politics"; psychiatrist R. D. Laing about "the politics of experience" and "the politics of the family." Both authors emphasize the fact that power—the ability to accomplish things, to overcome opposition, to dominate others—is not limited to government, but exists in all social institutions—even though people may not realize it. Thus any exercise of power in social situations might be labeled politics. A parent has power over a child by virtue of traditions that support unequal family relation-

POWER
AND
POLITICS

ships and his or her superior size, economic status, and perhaps knowledge. Children have power over their parents if their parents value their youngsters' happiness and well-being, want their admiration, and consider being good and loved parents essential to their self-esteem. As a result, homes can and do become political arenas.

In this chapter we are specifically interested in the social structure of political power—the ability to initiate and direct public policy—and in those activities that are directly concerned with the acquisition and use of political power. What is power? How is power channeled in the American political system? Who exercises power in this country today? This chapter addresses these questions.

THE BASIC DIMENSIONS OF POWER AND POLITICS

The foundations for the sociology of power and politics were laid by Max Weber; his essays on the subject are reprinted in *From Max Weber: Essays in Sociology* (1946). There he defines *political power* as the ability of a person or a group of people "to realize their own will in a communal action even against the resistance of others who are participating in the action" (p. 180). How is such power acquired?

Political Power: Its Sources and Uses

The most obvious source of political power is the right to use or to threaten *physical force*. President Kennedy did not have to detonate nuclear weapons to stop the Soviet Union from establishing missile bases in Cuba, for example. Premier Khrushchev believed that as president of the United States, Kennedy had the capacity to inflict serious damage and that he was willing to do so. The risks of "calling his bluff" seemed too high. Often threats and bluffs of force succeed because they are incorrectly estimated or go unchallenged (Bierstedt, in Olsen, 1970).

Other sources of political power include numbers, organization, and such resources as *money, land, prestige*, and *knowledge*. Consider the issue of equal pay for equal work. If only five women in a large company refuse to do their jobs unless they are paid as much as men earn in equivalent positions, their employer may fire them and hire replacements. However, if all or most of the women in the company demand equal pay with men, management will probably be forced to bargain. The principle of majority rule is based on the fact that majorities have the potential to enforce their will. "The power which resides in numbers is clearly seen in elections of all kinds, where the majority is conceded the right to institutionalize its power as authority—a right which is conceded because it can be taken" (Bierstedt, in Olsen, 1970, pp. 17–18).

But numbers alone do not constitute political power. Throughout history small elites have dominated huge majorities because "the masses" lacked organization and resources. Individually, the women in the example above will not be able to change the policy of underpaying female employees. A hundred or even a thousand angry but isolated women will have little effect. Unless they mobilize, establish communications networks, and coordinate their activities, they will accomplish little. They may use their financial resources to buy out the current owners or, more likely, to support themselves while they strike. They might persuade influential public figures to back them or use the media to stimulate public pressure. If they know something about the company that would be damaging to its public image, or if they possess skills the company cannot find elsewhere, they may use these as powerful levers.

Powerful individuals and groups can enforce their will in political decisions in one of several ways. Power can be used to compensate others for complying with one's wishes. The classic example of compensation is political patronage—awarding political appointments to loyal supporters, ambassadorships to campaign contributors, and the like. Paying generous government officials "under the table" to vote a certain way, or awarding a contract to a particular company, or bribing a witness to testify in one's favor are other forms of political compensation. In effect, the briber is paying the other person for the risk he or she takes in lying under oath. Power can also be used to punish people who do not comply with one's wishes, and to withhold expected rewards. This is known as *coercive power* because compliance is involuntary. The National Guard opening fire on protesting students at Kent State or a mayor refusing to issue permits to demonstrators are examples. On a different level, expelling students who are caught cheating, and withholding diplomas from students who have not fulfilled all requirements for graduation are also forms of coercive power. Finally, people can use power to persuade others to comply by manipulating information, emotions, norms, and values. (See the accompanying box and the discussion of propaganda and public relations in chapter 11). As Marvin E. Olsen observed (1970, p. 6), applying punishments or withholding rewards obtains only reluctant compliance, and is therefore less reliable than compensation, from which both parties expect to benefit. To the extent that persuasion succeeds in changing people's minds about an issue or a candidate so that they do not feel they are being coerced or even compromised, it may be the most effective and long-lasting use of power.

Influence Influence is related, but not identical to authority. We say people have *influence* when they are so highly respected, so well liked that they can change people's minds without resorting to compensation, threats, or manipulation. Although enhanced by official position, influence is ultimately a personal quality. Eleanor Roosevelt, for example, never held public office but she did hold much of the public's attention, respect, and admiration. And while she lived in the White House, Jacqueline Kennedy influenced women's fashions, although she never made a single speech on dress design.

POLITICAL PERSUASION

When attempting to persuade the public that the war in Vietnam was an expression of our noblest traditions, the late President Johnson was a master at manipulating information, emotions, norms, and values. His November 1966 speech to an audience of GI's stationed in the Demilitarized Zone was an effective use of the power of persuasion.

The average fellow in the world doesn't ask for much. . . . He wants . . . a roof over his head, a chance for his kids to go to school . . . a little recreation for his family, a movie now and then, or to be able to load them all in the old jalopy and take them to see Grandma on Sunday. But except for you, people couldn't do that. . . . You weren't born into this world . . . to liquidate the freedom and liberty that your grandfathers fought for with bows and arrows or old muskets. You have a heritage, a tradition to carry on.

Johnson added, "My great-great-grandfather died at the Alamo." It reminded newsmen of the times he showed them the little shack where he had been born. According to Johnson's mother, he had definitely not been born in a shack; nor had any of his ancestors been anywhere near the Alamo. But Johnson knew the powerful *symbolic* value of humble origins and frontier heroics.

Lyndon Johnson also used his persuasive talents to convince Congress to pass the Civil Rights legislation of the 1960s and to "sell" the War on Poverty to the American people.

SOURCE: David Wise, *The Politics of Lying* (New York: Vintage, 1973), chap. 2.

Authority and Legitimacy For Weber naked coercive power was only one source of political influence. In all of his writings, Weber stressed the difference between coercive power and authority. *Coercive power* rests on the threat or use of violence; it is the ability to *force* people to comply with one's designs. *Authority* rests on the consent of the governed; it is power exercised in a way that people consider necessary and legitimate. Every year the Internal Revenue Service takes money from all working Americans. Although people grumble about taxes, few question the government's legitimate authority to collect them, and fewer still refuse to pay them. As Weber suggests, all organizations and particularly governments depend on "a certain minimum of voluntary submission; [on] an interest (based on ulterior motives or genuine acceptance) in obedience" (Weber, 1947). Power to which people willingly submit is authority.

Weber identified three types of authority: legal/rational, charismatic, and traditional. *Legal/rational authority* derives from a system of explicit rules or laws that define legitimate uses of power. Authority is vested in offices or positions, not in the people who temporarily occupy those posts. It is limited to "official business." For example, a boss has considerable authority over the way employees spend their working days, but he does not have the authority to tell workers how to spend their weekends. In systems based on legal/rational authority, loyalty to the system largely replaces loyalty to a particular person. Public officials, professionals (doctors, lawyers, teachers, etc.), and to some extent business men and women are expected to put their professions first and to disobey superiors who ask them to break the law or organizational rules. One of the main revelations of the Senate Watergate hearings was how aides in the Nixon administration overlooked this principle. Numerous officials confessed to placing their loyalty to the man above their duty to obey laws and expose criminal acts.

Charismatic authority is the opposite of rational/legal authority. It derives from exceptional personal qualities that people perceive as a "gift of grace." People follow a charismatic leader because they are personally devoted to him or her. But as Weber observed, "The charismatic leader gains and maintains authority solely by proving his strength in life. If he wants to be a prophet, he must perform miracles; if he wants to be a war lord, he must perform heroic deeds" (1946, p. 249). Routine is the antithesis of the spontaneous force of charisma. This is why succession can be problematic. The unique, irreplaceable qualities of a charismatic leader are not likely to appear twice in a row. There are no second Gandhis, Malcolm Xs, or Martin Luther Kings. For this reason charismatic authority is inherently unstable. Nevertheless, such leaders have overcome overwhelming odds. Examples of charismatic leadership in recent history include Gandhi, Martin Luther King, Jr., Malcolm X, and César Chavez.

Traditional authority lies between rational/legal authority and charismatic authority. In traditional societies people tend to regard the way things have always been done as sacred; kings, chiefs, priests, councils of elders, and the like are part of this sacred order. Although traditions may limit a king's or chief's authority, they do have some personal latitude in making decisions. Positions are hereditary and people feel a sense of personal loyalty to the occupants. Thus traditional authority is vested in *both* the office and the officeholder. A familiar example is parents' authority over children.

In practice the three types of authority Weber identified may overlap. John Kennedy, for example, had rational/legal authority by virtue of his election to the presidency, the traditional authority that surrounds the office of the presidency, and charismatic appeal as well.

Whatever system of authority prevails, leaders or people in positions of power invariably try to *legitimize* their acts in terms of

existing values, thereby attempting to establish authority. The legitimacy of an administration or system of government depends on its capacity "to engender and maintain the belief that existing political institutions are the most appropriate ones for the society" (Lipset, 1970, p. 40).

Power and the State

The concept of legitimacy is central to Weber's definition of the state. The *state* differs from other organizations in a society,

In his campaign for the presidency in 1960, John Kennedy drew crowds like a matinée idol even in the South, where his ideas were not always popular. This photograph was taken in Charlotte, North Carolina. (Bruce Roberts / Rapho Guillumette)

Weber wrote, in that it successfully "claims the *monopoly of the legitimate use of physical force* within a given territory" (1946, p. 78). Organized crime may use physical force to coerce people, but ordinarily not with social consent and approval. Only the state is conceded the legitimate right to forcibly arrest, jail, and in some cases kill people.

IN THE NEWS

King of Kings

Every year on the morning of the spring equinox, His Imperial Majesty, Mohammed Reza Pahlevi, King of Kings, Light of the Ayrans, holds court amid the glittering splendor of Teheran's Gulistan Palace to receive the homage of Iran and the world. . . . [I]t is a ceremony of power. . . . At one end of the room, under a massive arch of mosaic mirrorwork that throws back the light of the chandeliers in a million rays of silver, stands the giant divan of jewel-encrusted marble known as the Peacock Throne. At the other end are the tall, white doors through which, every half hour, the monarch and his Empress enter to send a shiver of excitement and apprehension around the room.

He is not very tall, this Shahanshah . . . [but] he carries the authentic, unmistakable scent of power; and as he leaves the room again his subjects smile and release their breath in mingled pride and relief, euphoric in the afterglow of his presence.

Seventy percent of Iranians are illiterate, 60 percent live at a subsistence level, and hundreds of villages in this rich country do not have a doctor. But it seems unlikely that the Shah will be deposed. He not only maintains the legal and political power to dissolve Iran's parliament, he is also a religious leader, the guardian of the Iranian way of life according to the tradition of Shiism (Iran's dominant Moslem sect). He thus combines charismatic, legal/rational, and traditional forms of authority.

SOURCE: David Holden, "Shah of Shahs, Shah of Dreams," *The New York Times Magazine* (May 26, 1974): 9, 37; and *The New York Times* (June 3, 1974): 1, 12.

The way in which political power is organized in a country depends on its history and culture, as Gabriel Almond's classifications indicate (1956). Almond identifies four types of political systems, focusing on their different cultural orientations toward politics. He compares *Anglo-American political systems* to political marketplaces, where different groups bargain for decisions that are favorable to them. Decisions are made through a system of exchange (see chapter 3). In simple terms, Group A wants to build a highway, Group B wants to preserve a park, Group C wants additional funds for school recreation. Group A may promise to vote for school funds if Group C supports the highway, or Group B may offer Group C use of a park if it votes against the highway. Ideology is less important in Anglo-American systems than in the other three types identified by Almond. People see politics as a way of solving problems and pursuing self-interest, not as a "holy cause." Power and responsibility are diffused into a number of autonomous but interdependent government agencies and departments and private organizations. Because the division of political labor is so complex, Anglo-American systems depend on some degree of consensus about the basic values of freedom, mass welfare, and security.

Preindustrial political systems develop when "large groups have fundamentally different 'cognitive maps' of politics and apply different norms to political action." Such systems embrace at least two cultures—the traditional culture, and the Western colonial culture. The two exist in what often appears

to outsiders as an incompatible relationship. For example, political parties may center around powerful families, as tribal governments do. The people may elect a mayor (following Western custom), but see nothing wrong in his awarding all appointed positions and contracts to members of his family. Different ideas of correct and incorrect political behavior make preindustrial systems extremely volatile; the one thing on which people generally agree in such systems is nationalism.

Totalitarian political systems rest on modern methods of communication, organization, and violence, over which the state has absolute control. It alone supervises the media, the schools, the police, and the military. Power is highly centralized in such governments; any and all opposition is sup-

Pomp and ceremony add to the Shah of Iran's mystique. Here, his Imperial Majesty receives tributes from his subjects; a courtier, eyes cast down, holds his hat. (G. Chauvel / Sygma)

pressed. Much of the state's power comes from the fact that any behavior may arbitrarily be defined as treasonous and punished. The arbitrary use of power applies to public officials as well as to private citizens, and prevents an opposition from gathering support. But totalitarian systems do not rest on force alone; as we suggested earlier, this would be impossible. No government can, as yet, oversee every moment of every citizen's life (except in novels such as George Orwell's *1984*). Totalitarian systems depend on relatively high degrees of conformity and apathy among citizens.

Continental-European political systems (those in France, Germany, and Italy) include a number of parties that have conflicting and mutually exclusive designs for politics. Workers demand one kind of government, traditional parties (such as Catholic parties) another, secular, middle-class parties demand still another. Each seeks to convert the opposition, to transform the political system. Whereas political affiliation in Anglo-American systems is based on practical considerations, in Continental-European systems it is an act of faith. Political activities take on religious overtones; ideologies become causes. As a result, the centers of power and authority tend to be in parties and in political subcultures rather than in the formal government.

Power, Politics, and Law

Whatever form politics takes, one of the primary functions of the state is organizing and controlling the use of power. Most modern societies rely on legal systems to confer the authority to use force for social control. Legal systems also limit the authority that people in powerful positions can exercise.

Law and Social Control "The essential talent of the law," wrote Harvard law professor Roger Fisher, "lies not in producing perfect order but in *coping with disorder in an orderly way.* Contract law, negligence law and criminal law 'work' not in the sense of producing a community with no broken contracts, no negligence and no crimes, but by telling us how to respond when things go wrong" (Fisher, 1974, italics added).

The official purposes of law include (1) defining and suppressing deviance (through criminal law); (2) protecting individual and group rights (through civil transactions); (3) preventing powerful organizations from abusing these rights (through financial and corporate law); (4) preventing government from abusing these rights; and (5) settling disputes.

In performing these functions the law gives certain groups the power to say what is acceptable or not as well as the power to enforce their view. For example, in defining marijuana, gambling, prostitution, homosexuality, and other "victimless crimes" as deviant, the law in effect criminalizes these activities. As explained in chapter 12, deviant labels often become self-fulfilling prophecies: stigmatized individuals may be forced into the underworld the law is designed to suppress. Even people who have not broken the law may be stigmatized if police keep arrest as well as conviction records and release them to employers, banks, and others who hold social power. And sometimes vague laws against loitering, vagrancy, creating a public nuisance, or obscenity may give police an excuse to arrest almost anyone they consider a troublemaker.

Similarly, the practice of law may deprive members of certain groups of their guaranteed rights. In this country, every person is presumed innocent until found guilty and every person is entitled to counsel. In reality, the poor often serve time in jail before they are tried because they are unable to raise bail (see chapter 12). Court-appointed lawyers often represent so many clients that they cannot investigate and prepare a case as thoroughly as private lawyers, and often work *with* the district attorney's office.[1]

Finally, the law can be used as an instrument for political repression, even in democracies. For instance, in the late sixties and

---

[1] In 1973 lawyers for the Legal Aid Society in New York went on strike to dramatize their concern about not being able to provide clients with the "lawyering" to which they are entitled (*The New York Times*, December 23, 1973).

early seventies, the United States government used conspiracy laws to punish dissenters. For example, the Chicago 7 were tried for conspiring to cross a state line to incite a riot. The decision against the Chicago 7 was overturned by a higher court, which found that the presiding judge had not conducted a fair trial. Thus even though it lost the case, the government effectively prevented these dissenters from carrying on their normal lives for many months. In summary, the law is not a neutral instrument. It can be manipulated by the powerful to harass groups they consider threatening to the existing power structure, as well as to preserve the common good.

Constraints on Government Power The legal system in this country is an adversary system. The prosecution presents evidence in a way calculated to incriminate the defendant; through an attorney, the defendant presents evidence in a light that demonstrates his or her innocence; the jury or judge decides which argument is true. Similarly, our political system is based on a structure of checks and balances among the three branches of government. Both systems assume that, given the chance, people will use the power they have to further their own interests, and that the best way to prevent the abuse of power is to pit self-interest against self-interest. Competing branches of government, the minority party, elections, the press, and public opinion all act as checks on government power. As a last resort, the Constitution provides for the impeachment of "civil officers," up to and including the president.

The authors of the Constitution met to consider presidential accountability on July 20, 1787. Should the Chief Executive be subject to impeachment and removal from office? George Mason of Virginia thought he should. "Shall any man be above the law?"

he asked. "Above all, shall that man be above it, who can commit the most extensive injustice?" North Carolina's Charles Pinckney had reservations: "Mightn't Congress use impeachment as a rod over the President's head, destroying his independence? Elbridge Gerry of Massachusetts returned, "A good magistrate will not fear impeachments; a bad one ought to be kept in fear of them." When a vote was taken, the "ayes" had it: *The president, vice-president and all civil officers of the United States, shall be removed from office on impeachment for, and conviction of, treason, bribery, or other high crimes and misdemeanors* (Article II, Sect. IV of the Constitution).

Only twice since 1787 has Congress considered removing a president from office. The first impeachment move began in 1867, after Andrew Johnson refused to implement Reconstruction programs Congress had passed over his veto. Johnson was eventually impeached for breaking a law the Supreme Court later declared unconstitutional, but he was cleared in a Senate trial. In July 1974, the House Judiciary Committee approved three articles of impeachment against Richard Nixon. On August 5 of that year, the White House released tapes that indicated the President had indeed been guilty of "obstruction of justice." When it became clear that Mr. Nixon would be impeached and found guilty in the Senate, he resigned, turning the presidency over to Gerald Ford on August 9.

The rise and fall of Richard Nixon, and of Lyndon Johnson before him, show the extent to which political leaders depend on public trust in democracies. In politics, trust is like a blank check. It means that authorities can make decisions and claim the loyalty of individuals and groups without specifying in advance what their cooperation will entail. People are more likely to tolerate delays and sacrifice if they trust the leaders who demand

The Weather
Today—Rain, high in the low to mid 80s, low in the mid to upper 60s. Chance of rain is 60 per cent today, 40 per cent tonight. Saturday— Cloudy, high around 80. Yesterday's temp. range, 77-68. Details, Page D19.

The Washington Post

FINAL
112 Pages — 4 Sections

Amusement	D 1	Metro	D13
Classified	C14	Obituaries	D19
Comics	D20	Outdoors	C 8
Editorials	A30	Sports	C 1
Fed. Diary	D21	Style	D 1
Financial	C 9	TV-Radio	D 8

97th Year ···· No. 247   © 1974 The Washington Post Co.   FRIDAY, AUGUST 9, 1974   Phone (202) 223-6000   Classified 223-6200   20c Second Washington, Circulation 223-6100 Maryland and Virginia   15c

Nixon Resigns

His support in Congress eroded by tapes that proved he had participated in the Watergate cover-up (a clear abuse of power), Richard Nixon resigned rather than face impeachment. (The Washington Post)

them. When politicians lose public trust they must "waste" some of their resources trying to restore their credibility (by visiting foreign leaders, for example) and perhaps enforcing decisions that might be accepted willingly if they were trusted (Gamson, 1968, pp. 42–51).

In 1964, President Johnson was reelected by a landslide; by 1968, however, he had begun to lose legitimacy with the American public, and decided not to seek a second term. Similarly, in 1972, President Nixon was reelected by an overwhelming margin, but as the Watergate cover-up began to unravel, his popularity declined. By the summer of 1974, when Nixon resigned, a majority of Americans had indicated they disapproved of his conduct in office. An equal number gave Congress a poor rating (Gallup Polls, April 28;

figure 14:1   Youth and the power-holders

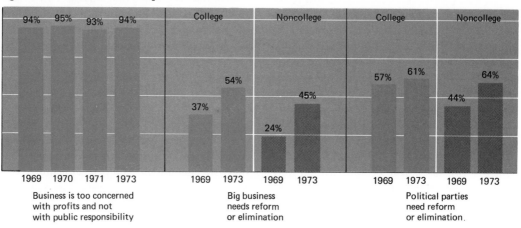

				College	Noncollege		College	Noncollege
94%	95%	93%	94%	37% → 54%	24% → 45%		57% → 61%	44% → 64%
1969	1970	1971	1973	1969 1973	1969 1973		1969 1973	1969 1973

Business is too concerned with profits and not with public responsibility

Big business needs reform or elimination

Political parties need reform or elimination.

SOURCE: Daniel Yankelovich, *Changing Youth Values in the 70's: A Study of American Youth* (New York: JDR 3rd Fund), 1974, p. 37.

May 19, 1974). But despite widespread disillusionment with politicians, most Americans apparently had not lost faith in the political system of the nation. Seven out of ten respondents in one poll expressed confidence in America's future (Gallup Poll, May 19, 1974). (See the accompanying box for students' political attitudes in the 1970s.) Two sociologists have found that many adult Americans retain a blanket admiration for and loyalty to the political system (if not to specific administrations), while a smaller percentage commit themselves to specific policies and candidates (Easton and Dennis, 1969). French adults, in contrast, tend to be highly cynical about politics or to ignore

---

YOUTH IN THE SEVENTIES: POLITICAL SKEPTICS

If the nationwide survey conducted by the Daniel Yankelovich research organization in 1973 is accurate, attitudes toward power and politics are changing. According to this survey, a majority of young Americans—in and out of college—are satisfied with their lives, optimistic about their futures, and feel our society is basically healthy. At the same time, however, six out of ten believe that "special interests" (big business and self-interested politicians) run the government, and that American society is democratic in name only. A majority (54 percent) believe corporations are the real centers of power in this country, and nine out of ten think big business puts profits too far ahead of social responsibility (see figure 14:1). Only one in five young people thinks the war in Vietnam ended with honor. Critical of American foreign policy, four out of five believe "new Vietnams" are inevitable. The percentage of college youth who feel our political parties need fundamental reforms grew from 57 percent in 1969 to 61 percent in 1973; the percentage of noncollege youth who agreed grew even more dramatically, from 44 percent to 64 percent.

Almost half of those surveyed identified themselves as Democrats (45 percent of college youth, 49 percent of noncollege youth). Noncollege respondents were more conservative than college respondents (53 percent of whom said they were radical or liberal). More favor the death penalty for some crimes (52 to 44 percent), life sentences for drug pushers (45 to 30 percent), and a crackdown on pornography (44 to 26 percent). Fewer (14 to 35 percent) describe themselves as active in politics. Both groups, however, seem to be developing a "broad new agenda of social rights." Many young people feel *entitled* to things their parents only hoped for, including the best medical care, whether or not they can afford it (54 percent), the right to participate in decisions affecting one's job (53 percent), a college education for one's children (48 percent), and secure retirement (37 percent).

Yankelovich concludes that one of the most important political questions today is whether our system will prove responsive to the new values and expectations of the noncollege majority. While not as politicized as young workers in Europe and South America, this group is beginning to evidence resentment. "If [our] institutions prove rigid and unresponsive and our political leadership shows insensitivity to the changing needs and values of our youth, then the underlying potential for discontent will become all too real and we will face a period of instability and demagoguery."

SOURCE: Daniel Yankelovich, *Changing Youth Values in the 70's: A Study of American Youth*, New York: JDR 3rd Fund, 1974.

politics whenever possible (Dowse and Hughes, 1972, p. 188). How are these attitudes acquired? Like attitudes toward sex, money, and other things, it is during the process of socialization.

Political Socialization

Studies of children's attitudes toward government indicate that political socialization "begins early, if unsystematically," in the family, where youngsters develop assumptions about "human nature," attitudes toward authority, concepts of legitimacy, group loyalties, and so on. Many of these lessons are implied, not explicit. By the time children reach school, most have definite feelings about such political symbols as the president, even though they know little about the political system (Dowse and Hughes, 1972, chap. 6). Attitudes toward politics, then, seem to predate understanding.

In the early sixties, David Easton, Jack Dennis, and colleagues questioned a national sample of schoolchildren on their ideas about and attitudes toward government. They found that most young children identified government with the father of the country, George Washington, and with President John Kennedy. When asked who made the laws in America, 76 percent of second graders said the president. This personalized image of government begins to change in the fourth and fifth grades, with more and more young people defining government in terms of Congress and voting (see table 14:1). Fifty-seven percent of fifth graders and 85 percent of eighth graders knew that Congress makes the laws in America. The authors attribute this change to a growing awareness that government is a collective enterprise (not the actions of single person) and a deepening understanding of the representative nature of democracy. Young children viewed government in terms of personalized, charismatic authority; older children grasped the concept of legal/rational authority. Virtually all of the children pictured the government in glowing terms, as "something" that protects people, helps them, and cares for them in times of need. The government is not only helpful, in children's view, it exercises leadership ("makes important decisions"), knows more than most people, has power over almost everyone ("can punish"), and practically never makes mistakes. French children, in contrast, see their president as someone who

table 14:1 CHILDREN'S DEVELOPING AWARENESS OF WHO MAKES THE LAWS

GRADE	CONGRESS	PRESIDENT	SUPREME COURT	I DON'T KNOW	TOTAL	N RESPONDING	N NOT RESPONDING
Grade 2	5%	76%	11%	8%	100%	1627	28
Grade 3	11	66	17	6	100	1648	30
Grade 4	28	44	21	7	100	1723	26
Grade 5	57	19	20	3	99	1793	10
Grade 6	65	13	18	3	99	1743	6
Grade 7	72	9	16	3	100	1712	11
Grade 8	85	5	8	1	99	1690	5

SOURCE: David Easton and Jack Dennis, *Children in the Political System*, New York: McGraw-Hill, 1969.

commands others and sees that his orders are obeyed; rarely do these children mention that he is "good" or "helpful" (Greenstein, 1973).

Anthony Orum and Roberta Cohen's recent comparison of black and white schoolchildren indicates that not all American children idealize our government (1973). Black children, like black adults, are more cynical about politics than their white counterparts, and they are less likely to regard the government as benevolent or to idealize the president. Black young people generally know more about the political system than do whites from similar socioeconomic backgrounds, participate in more political discussions and activities, perceive greater differences between parties, and are more likely to take sides. These differences appear as early as fourth grade and remain relatively constant through high school. The authors conclude that political attitudes do indeed develop very early, and that children adopt the political norms and values of their community.

Studies such as these suggest that income, education, religion, and other factors that correlate with party choice and voting have only an *indirect* effect on the formation of political attitudes. Parents, peers, teachers, and neighbors orient children to politics, and insofar as these people's political opinions reflect their incomes and so on, income can be said to influence the development of political attitudes.

THEORIES OF POLITICAL POWER

Throughout history philosophers and statesmen have debated the questions—who exercises social power, why, and what are the consequences? Contemporary theories of po-litical power are largely an elaboration of and reaction against Karl Marx.

Marx: An Economic Theory of Power

Before Marx, political philosophers more or less assumed that social power resided in the state and related organizations, such as the military. Any discussion of politics centered on government. Breaking with tradition, Marx argued that power is rooted in economics. The people who own the "means of production" (the factories, raw materials, and so on) control society; the state is little more than their servant (Olsen, 1970, p. 70).

Marx went on to elaborate a philosophy of history. With the rise of capitalism, society had begun to split into two hostile camps, two diametrically opposed classes—the bourgeoisie (the owners) and the proletariat (the workers or masses). The owners' very existence depends on their ability to exploit the workers. They create "a class of labourers, who live only so long as they find work, and who find work only so long as their labour increases capital. These labourers, who must sell themselves piecemeal, are a commodity, like every other article of commerce, and are consequently exposed to all the vicissitudes of competition, to all the fluctuations of the market" (Marx and Engels, [1847], 1967). And herein lie the seeds of the bourgeoisie's destruction. Workers, Marx argued, will become increasingly insecure and alienated. The traditional and emotional ties that bound lord and serf do not exist between owner and worker in capitalist economies. Work ceases to be a moral duty and source of satisfaction. (There is little craft in performing an assembly line job—workers become appendages to machines—and the products of that work do not belong to them.) "At this stage," Marx and Engels wrote, "the labourers still form an incoherent mass scattered over the whole country, and broken up by their mutual competition." But it is only a matter of time before they realize they are being exploited (develop class consciousness) and rise up against the industrialists, pitting the power of numbers against the power of wealth. In Marx's view, class revolution is inevitable. Beyond revolution he envisioned a temporary "dictatorship of the proletariat" that would restore ownership of the means of production to the workers, laying the groundwork for a classless and just society. Eventually the state would "wither away."

Pareto and Mosca: The Elitist View

Many of Marx's contemporaries disagreed sharply with his reasoning and his predictions, among them Vilfredo Pareto and Gaetano Mosca. Neither of these sociologists thought a classless society was possible, much less desirable. Pareto began with the simple observation that some lawyers are sharper, some royal mistresses more influential, some thieves more successful than others, so that in all human activities there are elites. "I am not interested here in what is desirable," Pareto noted. "I am making a simple study of what is. In a broad sense I mean by the *elite* in a society people who possess in marked degree qualities of intelligence, character, skill, capacity, of whatever kind" (Pareto, in Olsen, 1970, p. 115). And politics is not exempt from this general rule. Throughout history, small governing elites, distinguished by their talents and organization, have ruled the masses by virtue of their superiority. As Mosca put this:

In all societies—from societies that are very meagerly developed and have barely attained the dawnings of civilization, down to the most advanced and powerful societies—two classes of people always appear—a class that rules and a class that is ruled. The first class, always the less numerous, performs all political functions, monopolizes power and enjoys the advantages that power brings, whereas the second, the more numerous class, is directed and controlled by the first, in a manner that is now more or less legal, now more or less arbitrary and violent, and supplies the first, in appearance at least, with material means of subsistence and with the instrumentalities that are essential to the vitality of the political organism. (Mosca, in Olsen, 1970, p. 123)

By elite or ruling class, neither Pareto nor Mosca meant a strictly hereditary class. To the contrary. Both believed that hereditary ruling classes, like strings of horses that have been inbred for too long, degenerate. Once this occurs the capacity of the elite to govern is lost. As Pareto wrote, "History is a graveyard of aristocracies. . . . They decay not in numbers only. They decay also in quality, in the sense that they lose their vigour." But rarely does a closed aristocracy stay in power to the point of incapacity. "The governing class is restored . . . by families rising from the lower classes and bringing with them the vigour and the proportions of residues necessary for keeping themselves in power. . . . In virtue of class circulation, the governing *elite* is always in a state of slow and continuous transformation" (Pareto, in Olsen, 1970, pp. 117–18). This new blood is drawn from sub- or nongoverning elites who are situated between the rulers and the ruled and have the talent and ambition to govern.

Thus Pareto - and Mosca agreed with Michels' "iron rule of oligarchy" (see the accompanying box), but added the qualifier that the make-up of governing elites is constantly changing. (This is what Pareto meant by "circulating elites.") Naïvely perhaps, both

MICHELS' "IRON RULE OF OLIGARCHY"

Writing in 1915, German political scientist Robert Michels attempted to explain why power tends to fall into the hands of a small group of leaders in *all* organizations, whatever their goals and ideology. After studying the labor and socialist movements of his time, Michels concluded that as organizations grow in size and complexity, the need for leadership becomes more and more pressing. Informal decision-making in which all members participate becomes impractical: there are too many issues to resolve; the organization must present a united front to the outside. Leaders, chosen for their special talents in administration and public relations, gradually take command. In time these leaders develop a vested interest in maintaining their position. A combination of admiration and apathy in the rank-and-file accelerates this concentration of power in the hands of a few. Within the ruling clique, maintaining the organization becomes an end in itself. Leaders tend to become conservative, to seek compromises with enemies, to avoid risks, and to modify extreme and unpopular goals—to protect their positions. Nowhere is this process more obvious than in successful, radical political movements; revolutions, Michels argues, are little more than the replacement of one elite by another. In Michels's view, "Who says organizations says oligarchy."

SOURCE: Robert Michels, *Political Parties* (Glencoe, Ill.: Free Press, 1949).

Since the turn of the century political theorists have been divided into two camps: Marx's heirs, who argue that power is held by economic elites and stress the coercive and exploitative uses of power, and Pareto and Mosca's heirs, who believe there are many diverse and competing elites.

C. Wright Mills: The Power Elite

I should contend that "men are free to make history," but that some men are indeed much freer than others. (Mills, in Olsen, 1970, p. 254)

Among American sociologists, C. Wright Mills took the lead in documenting the existence of an American power elite, above and beyond the official political system. (Marx assumed the existence of an elite, but never actually said who they were.) Mills began with the fact that many people who occupy high positions in government have also held high positions in corporations or the military and seem to move back and forth among these centers of power. America's governing elite, wrote Mills, is "a coalition of generals in the roles of corporation executives, of politicians masquerading as admirals, of corporation executives acting like politicians" (1959, p. 278). Tracing their personal histories, Mills found that, by and large, these people come from similar white, Anglo-Saxon, Protestant, old American backgrounds, attend the same Ivy League schools, belong to the same exclusive clubs, visit the same resorts, and so on. Thus if the president of an oil company doesn't know the federal "energy czar" personally, he surely knows someone who knows him (and can place a confidential call, if necessary). Through their psychological and social affinity, the power elite's coinciding interests are reinforced.

believed that ruling classes are more or less open to people with "intelligence and character," and that in the long run, governing elites "represent" the interests of the ruled. Underlying this, of course, is the assumption that the masses are neither desirous nor capable of governing themselves.

Mills argued that the different branches of the elite are interlocking. Congress approves billions of dollars in military appropriations every year, dollars that go more or less directly into corporate pockets. Why? In part for national defense; in part because military contracts create jobs for their constituents, and because business leaders are important campaign contributors. Thus politicians tend to support big business, and business leaders often support politicians. (Ceilings on campaign contributions may lessen the influence business has with government.) All three sectors—economic, political, and military—have a vested interest in what Mills calls "military capitalism."

Mills argued that democratic procedures have become empty rituals. Neither elections nor congressional debate restrain the power elite. Over a decade before Americans learned about the concentration of power among a small group of aides in the Nixon White House, Mills wrote, "the executive bureaucracy becomes . . . the arena within which major conflicts of power are resolved or denied resolution. 'Administration' replaces electoral politics; the maneuvering of cliques . . . replaces the open clash of parties" (in Olsen, 1970, p. 259). Important decisions are made behind closed doors. The middle-level society, which works for the elite, and the lower level have little or no effect on these decisions.

Mills believed the trend toward centralization of power would continue unabated. "The top of modern American society is increasingly unified, and often seems willfully coordinated: at the top there has emerged an elite whose power probably exceeds that of any small group of men in world history" (in Olsen, 1970, p. 261).

The Pluralist View

But where is the evidence that America's political, military, and corporate chieftains are all of one mind or that they cooperate with one another? Isn't the reverse more likely, that is, that they see one another as rivals? This is the question pluralists ask. They agree with Mills that some people are freer to make history than others and that unorganized individuals (the masses) are powerless. But they do not see a ruling clique, a power elite at the top of the power structure in this country (see figure 14:2). Rather, pluralists argue that social power is *dispersed* among a variety of competing interest groups—the oil industry and the coal

figure 14:2 **Elitist and pluralist views of the American power structure**

SOURCE: Adapted from William Kornhauser, " 'Power Elite' or 'Veto groups'?" in Seymour Martin Lipset and Leo Lowenthal, eds., *Culture and Social Character* (Glencoe: Free Press, 1961), pp. 525–67.

The primary difference between elitists and pluralists is that the former see a unified elite at the top of the power structure and the latter do not.

industry, car manufacturers and ecologists, unions and business associations, hunters' lobbies and wildlife funds, and so on. All of these groups influence the political process at different times and with varying degrees of success, but no one group commands. In most cases, they can do little more than veto programs that threaten their interests. In David Riesman's words, "Today we have substituted for [centralized, mercantile-aristocratic] leadership a series of groups, each of which has struggled for and finally attained a power to stop things conceivably inimical to its interests and, within far narrower limits, to start things" (1951, p. 242). (See also Dahl, 1961; Kornhauser, 1961; Keller, 1968.)

Mills, as indicated, believes that coinciding interests, reinforced by social similarity, bind America's executives together in a single, cohesive power elite. Riesman maintains that diverse, often conflicting interests preclude united policy or action. Mills argues that the power elite settle important questions among themselves, behind closed doors; "fundamental issues never come to any point or decision before Congress, much less before the electorate" (1958). Riesman disagrees, arguing that fundamental issues are decided through bargaining among interested parties, and the parties who exercise power vary with the issue. (The American Rifle Association, for example, is not interested in farm subsidies or the National Endowment for the Arts.) Mills laments the erosion of democracy, the loss of responsible and accountable centers of power, the alienation of the powerless many. Riesman laments the erosion of leadership and the lack of direction in American politics.

In *The Power Structure* (1967), Arnold Rose concludes that both sides of this argument are true of America. Rose concedes that foreign affairs seem to be dominated by a small group of people who resemble Mills's power elite, but he suggests that the growth of the federal government and the emergence of new pressure groups (such as Civil Rights organizations) have undercut big business[2] and no such elite dominates domestic affairs. In his view there are many power structures in America, not one, and nationwide decisions are made through a process of bargaining among them (the pluralist view). However, the power structures themselves (political parties, government agencies, legislatures, businesses, and so on) tend to be dominated by oligarchies (the elitist view). Rose also notes that senators, approximately one in five of whom are millionaires (what Mills calls social similarity), tend to vote according to their own, presumably upper-class convictions. In short, Rose sees the American power structure as a complex plurality of elites.

THE ORGANIZATION OF POWER IN AMERICA

The one point on which theorists of all persuasions agree is that single, isolated individuals have little impact on the political process.[3] This section will examine the different types of political organizations that fill the considerable gap between the high levels of government and "the people."

Political Parties

Drawing on Weber, Robert Michels defined a political party as a "society of propaganda and of agitation seeking to acquire pow-

---

[2]   Rose was writing in 1967, *pre*-Watergate.
[3]   Of course, there are exceptions—Ralph Nader, for example, and Madelyn Murray, who waged a one-woman fight to ban prayers in public schools, and won.

er'' (1949, p. 134). Although these are not the words contemporary Americans might choose, this definition is essentially correct. *Political parties* are organizations designed for the explicit purpose of gaining and holding legitimate control of government policies and personnel. Parties perform several crucial functions in large, complex political systems. Ideally, they link the people and the government, transmitting public opinion up the ladder to where decisions are actually made, thereby converting public opinion into legislation. In the other direction, parties mobilize grass roots support for policy decisions. Parties also serve as a link between different branches and levels of government (executive and legislative, federal and state) and between official (governmental) power structures and unofficial (nongovernmental) power structures. On the practical level parties play a dominant role in recruiting personnel for elective office (Dowse and Hughes, 1972, pp. 339–41).

The Two-Party System   Although we are accustomed to thinking in terms of two parties, in some countries there are five or more parties, in others only one (and the struggle for power takes place within the party rather than between or among parties). The two-party system in this country dates back to the early days of the nation, when Republicans (an agrarian, States' Rights party led by Jefferson) vied with Federalists (a mercantile party led by Hamilton that sought to increase the powers of the federal government). Although the Federalist party did not last, a two-party split developed again when Andrew Jackson led the new Democratic party to victory over neo-Republicans Clay and Hamilton (who now called themselves Whigs) and again, in the Civil War, when Lincoln's Republicans enforced federal domination on the South and Southerners fled to the

Democratic party. Gradually, the agrarian-based Democrats aligned themselves with labor, the Republicans with big business, preserving the two-party alignment.

True, there have been third- and fourth-party entrees into the political arena—Theodore Roosevelt aligned himself with the Bull Moose party in 1912; Progressive Henry A. Wallace and States' Rights candidate Strom Thurmond opposed Harry Truman in 1948; George Wallace ran for president on the American Independent party ticket in 1968. In most cases a third party is little more than a distraction, splitting the vote for one of the majority-party candidates. Why is this? Why does the United States consistently generate two parties, while Italy consistently generates several? The answer lies in the structure of the electoral system.

French sociologist Maurice Duverger (1954) argues that two-party systems emerge when there can be only one candidate from each party and the winner of the election takes all. This simple-plurality system discourages third parties because a vote for a minor party is, in effect, a wasted vote. There is almost no chance that the third-party candidate will win. In contrast, in proportional-representative systems, such as Italy has, a party receives the same percentage of seats in the legislature as it receives in the election. In this kind of electoral system a vote for a minority-party candidate is not wasted, for even if the party receives only 10 percent of the votes, the party receives a tenth of the seats in the legislature.

The simple-plurality system not only determines the number of parties in the United States, but also their character. To win state-wide and national elections, American parties must embrace diverse kinds of people and a wide range of interests. Differences of opinion must be settled *before* elections. Critics like Duverger argue that the American system forces parties into bland positions and prevents many groups from being represented. Both the Democratic and Republican parties must lean to the center and create policies that sound attractive to everyone and offend no one. Duverger's analysis suggests that politicians cannot be blamed for political double-talk; the social structure of American parties *forces* them to be that way. However, Duverger points out that the simple-plurality system is more stable than proportional representation, where coalitions must be formed issue by issue in the legislature.

Interest Groups

In a sense, interest groups make up for the amorphous and tentative character of political parties in this country. An *interest group* is an organization created to influence political decisions that directly concern members. They range from business associations (such as the National Association of Manufacturers), to labor unions (most notably the powerful AFL-CIO), agricultural groups (including the National Milk Producers Association), professional associations (the American Medical and Bar Associations), Civil Rights groups (the National Association for the Advancement of Colored People, the American Civil Liberties Union), political groups (Americans for Democratic Action, the John Birch Society), and special interest associations (such as the National Rifle Association). Corporations may form their own lobbies—the most notorious example in recent years being the International Telephone and Telegraph Company's attempt to gain favorable settlement of an antitrust suit by offering to underwrite the 1972 Republican National Convention. In addition, agencies and departments within the government may lobby, using their resources and spokesmen

to influence Congress. For example, members of the Defense Department regularly testify in favor of increased military spending. Foreign governments also place lobbies in Washington to look out for their interests (see Milbrath, 1963).

The activities of the National Rifle Association (NRA) illustrate the way interest groups work. The NRA has an annual budget of over $5 million, most of which is used to publish *The American Rifleman*, circulation 900,000. In 1963, the year President Kennedy was shot,

Common Cause, a citizen's lobby, was active in the court fight to obtain tapes from former President Nixon. (Common Cause)

You are the people.
It is time to give the nation back to its citizens.
Join Common Cause.

Professionals in the nation's capital and over a quarter of a million members active in every state are moving to make government responsive to the public interest.

the House Judiciary Subcommittee on Juvenile Delinquency began to consider legislation that would forbid the mail-order sale of firearms to minors. *The American Rifleman* responded with articles characterizing the bill as irrational and emotional, and urged readers to write congressmen (supplying their names). The committee decided to defer action. In March 1965 President Johnson called for strict gun control in his message on crime to Congress. The NRA sent an urgent letter to members, distorting the administration's bill and warning, "If the battle is lost, it will be your loss, and that of all who follow." This plea was successful, and in December the NRA thanked readers for letters that effectively prevented the passage of gun-control laws. No legislation reached the floor of the House or Senate in 1967, but the NRA continued its attacks, now focusing on individual legislators whom it called "do-gooders" and "fanatics." "All of these people would like to bury your guns. Some of them would like to bury us, also" an editorial read. Not until June 1968, when Robert Kennedy was assassinated, did letters to Congress supporting gun controls outnumber letters opposing it. In October of that year, Congress passed a law limiting interstate shipment of long guns (*Congressional Quarterly,* April–October, 1968).

Interest groups may also negotiate directly with the executive branch (as ITT did), or work through the courts (as the NAACP and ACLU have done). Some support sympathetic candidates with endorsements, campaign funds, and campaign workers. In addition to pressuring law-makers, lobbyists may direct public relations and propaganda campaigns to improve their constituents' image and win popular support for their views.

In most cases lobbyists work for the elite of an organization; they are hired by the leaders of a union, for example, not by the rank-and-file, and are accountable to those leaders.

Still the diversity of interest groups creates numerous cross-currents. Many people are active in (or at least responsive to) different groups at once. For example, a conservative southern Democrat may find herself aligned with outspoken liberals on women's rights; political leaders in the ghetto, fighting for community control, find George Wallace seeking the same goal (but with different motives). Seymour M. Lipset suggests that diverse and conflicting interests, which prevent the formation of solid political blocs, are essential to modern democracies. "Multiple and politically inconsistent affiliations, loyalties and stimuli reduce the emotion and aggressiveness involved in political choice. . . . The available evidence suggests that the chances for stable democracy are enhanced to the extent that groups and individuals have a number of crosscutting, politically relevant affiliations" (1963, p. 77). If interests and affiliations did not overlap, the country might split in half, as America did in the nineteenth century.

Community Power Structures

The organization of political power at the local level has attracted a great many researchers in recent years, if only because it is possible to test theories of power empirically in the microcosms of towns and cities. Sociologists and political scientists have identified several different types of local power structures in this country, but there are no firm explanations as to why these variations occur (Rossi, 1960).

In "Power and Community Structure," Peter H. Rossi (1960) suggests that important variables in the way power is organized at the local level include the degree of professionalization of public officials (whether officials work full time at community work), the number of elected officials (as opposed to appointed officials), the level of partisanship (whether there are clearly defined, competing parties), the political heterogeneity of the electorate, and the extent to which parties represent different ethnic and economic groups. With these factors in mind, Rossi defines four types of community power structures.

In *pyramidal communities* one person or a small clique decides all important issues, and lower-level officials serve mainly to implement their policies. The ruling clique may operate within the official political system, or it may exert pressure from without. An example of the former is Mayor Daley's Chicago machine, a machine so powerful in its day that no Democratic presidential hopeful dared cross the mayor.

Rossi's second type is *caucus rule*, where a larger group of prominent individuals make decisions by "manufacturing consensus" among themselves. An example would be Atlanta, Georgia, of the 1950s, which Floyd Hunter (1953) renamed Regional City in a classic study of community power. Hunter interviewed residents to find out who they thought influential, then tried to learn who had pulled strings on certain decisions. He concluded that a group of forty "influentials," most of whom were businesspeople who operated behind the scenes (and a few of whom had connections in Washington and abroad) dominated local affairs. The mayor, treasurer, and other public officials never made decisions without consulting this group. Caucus rule seems most likely to develop in homogeneous, middle-class suburban communities where "the class basis for countervailing power does not exist," and in cities where the lower classes constitute a majority, prompting businesspeople and professionals to undermine democratic procedures to protect their own interests.

Polylithic communities include a diversity of influential cliques and groups, each with its own sphere of authority. The government is usually run by professional politicians who have relatively solid support; businesspeople and professionals dominate civic organizations. This is what political scientist Robert A. Dahl (1961) found in New Haven, Connecticut. The upper class had largely withdrawn from politics, rather than mingle with "new elements" in the population. In many cases members of the upper class had actually withdrawn from the city itself, moving to the suburbs and enrolling their children in private schools. At the opposite end of the spectrum, the working and lower classes were excluded from decision-making groups. This left the governing of New Haven to a number of different middle-class groups who used their power and influence in different issue-areas (that is, in issues that directly affected their interests). The power structure was "a coalition of public officials and private individuals who reflect the interests and concerns of different segments of the community." As Rossi indicates, power struggles in polylithic communities tend to center around individual and group efforts to expand their spheres of authority.

Rossi's fourth type, *amorphous structures*, would include any community that did not evidence stable patterns of power and influence. (It is a hypothetical type; Rossi could think of no examples.)

In a paper read at an American Sociological Association meeting (1973), John Walton concluded that center cities (particularly in the North and Midwest) are becoming increasingly decentralized or polylithic, while younger cities and suburbs tend to have pyramidal or caucus rule. Among the reasons he cited for the decentralization of power in the cities are the concentration of the poor and nonwhite in cities and the white middle-class exodus to the suburbs; the loss of jobs and declining tax base in inner cities escalating demands for services (such as mass transit, police protection, and day care); and competition for federal funds. Today's cities depend heavily on state and federal programs to provide services for their residents. As a result, local leaders control only part of the resources the city needs. The heads of urban renewal, mass transit, and job-training programs may, for example, report to state and federal officials, not to the mayor, creating numerous centers of power in a city. Looking ahead, Walton suggests that the urban politics of the future will center around group rights (including minority rights and community rights, which often conflict) and the quality of life (environmental problems, crime, and the like).

The Politics of the Powerless

Victory comes to mean achieving a position of power that will enable members of a movement to work out their own destiny. (Killian, 1968, p. 128)

On May 17, 1954, the day the Supreme Court declared the separate-but-equal doctrine unconstitutional, it looked as if the battle against Jim Crow had been won. But within weeks it became clear that white southerners were willing and able to use civil disobedience to maintain their privileges.[4] The NAACP, which had led the Court fight, was an elitist organization, founded at the turn of the century by radical black intellectuals such as W. E. B. DuBois, who rejected Booker T. Washington's philosophy of accommodation. NAACP leaders had done many things *for*

Campaigns to register black voters in the South, directed by Civil Rights leaders such as John Louis, have been a dramatic success. (United Press International)

black people, but they had not done things *with* black people (Killian, 1968, p. 55).

At this early stage, the black population lacked both a strategy and a prophet. Martin Luther King, Jr., supplied both, at least for a time. He was, as Louis Lomax observed, "the first Negro minister I have ever heard who can reduce the Negro problem to a spiritual matter and yet inspire the people to seek a solution on this side of the Jordan, not in the life beyond death" (Lomax, in Killian, 1968, pp. 55–56). King preached that integration was right and segregation evil. He encouraged thousands with the belief that "right makes might." Inspired by the religious/political father of modern India, Mahatma Gandhi, King taught the nonviolent tactics of civil disobedience and nonviolent protest.

What many white liberals overlooked at the time, however, was that Gandhi and his followers did not stop at reforming the Brit-

---

[4] The fact that whites were the first to threaten and use civil disobedience in the South in the 1950s is often overlooked. If blacks were revolutionaries in that period, whites were counterrevolutionaries.

ish—they forced them out of India (and precipitated the collapse of the British empire). Like Gandhi in India, King appealed to America's conscience; and like Gandhi, he forced America to listen. King and other black leaders at that time had no rewards to offer white Southerners in exchange for admitting blacks to white schools, restaurants, and so on; they could not promise to build new factories, raise farm subsidies, or win elections. They had no resources, no positive inducements. But they could create a state of emergency with sit-ins and adverse publicity, and *then* offer racial peace—a restoration of order—if the other side gave in. Thus King spoke of peace, brotherhood, and reconciliation while engaging in a display of naked power. In fact, he condemned violence not only because it was "wrong" but also because it would be ineffective (the other side had more guns): "There is more power in socially organized masses on the march than

there is in guns in the hands of a few desperate men. . . . Our powerful weapons are the voices, the feet, and the bodies of dedicated, united people moving without rest toward a just goal" (King, in Killian, 1968, p. 75).

The latent power King mobilized in the black community in the late fifties and early sixties has since become a staple in American politics, a weapon for the powerless. César Chavez's National Farm Workers Association, for example, had $85 in its treasury when members voted to join the Filipinos' strike against the multi-million-dollar California grape industry in September 1965. A few years earlier, a massive strike would not have been possible. A federal law had allowed

César Chavez addressing farm workers in California. Chavez rose to national prominence in the late 1960s, when the grape boycott became a national *cause célèbre*. (Gerhard E. Gscheidle)

growers to import millions of Mexicans who were not citizens, had no legal rights, and could be deported instantly if suspected of "starting trouble." In 1965, however, Congress had repealed this law—in large part because Chicanos had begun to exercise the power of the ballot in the Southwest (giving massive support to President Kennedy in 1960).

As the grape strike gathered momentum, Chavez emerged as the spiritual leader of his people, much as King had. Under Chavez's leadership an economic issue (wages and benefits) became a moral crusade, under the rallying cries of *La Huelga* (the strike) and *Venceremos* (we will win). Chavez used Gandhi's and King's tactics: mass demonstrations, marches, and fasts. He drew on the sentiment for minority rights which blacks had generated, appealing to Civil Rights leaders, student political organizations, the Catholic church, the AFL-CIO (which gave strikers $5,000 a month), and such national figures as California's Governor Pat Brown and Robert Kennedy. Although the army continued to buy California grapes, the national boycott succeeded in bringing growers to the negotiating table[5] (see McWilliams, 1968; Steiner, 1970; Meier and Rivera, 1972).

Inadvertently, perhaps, the government itself inspired another "revolution of the powerless" when it hired thousands of social workers, lawyers, and VISTA volunteers to bring about the "Great Society" in the midsixties. In a short time, poverty workers—often Office of Economic Opportunity staff members—were organizing clients in local welfare centers around the country. The National Welfare Rights Organization (NWRO)

was founded in 1966 by George A. Wiley, a veteran of the Civil Rights struggle, to coordinate these different groups. Since its inception, the NWRO has concentrated on informing welfare recipients of their rights and, when necessary, staging mass demonstrations to force agencies to give them what they are entitled to under the law. This is more revolutionary than it sounds. If all the people in Los Angeles or Chicago who were legally entitled to welfare received their full benefits, the amount of funding required would probably break the city's budget.

In *Regulating the Poor* (1971), Frances Fox Piven and Richard A. Cloward argue that one of the primary functions of public relief is to "mute civil disorder." When the poor are threatening to disrupt the social structure, as they did in the 1930s and again in the 1960s, the government responds by handing out more and more money—until calm is restored. When the poor are acquiescent, benefits are withdrawn. In the absence of true economic reform, full employment, or a guaranteed income, Piven and Cloward see rising demands as the only source of reform. In their words, "a placid poor get nothing, but a turbulent poor sometimes get something" (1971, p. 338).

The groups we have been discussing are but a few examples of people who, though lacking money, position, and other conventional resources, are making themselves heard. The Civil Rights Movement inspired the powerless in this country (see chapter 11). As a consequence, both Humphrey and Nixon advocated ending the war in Vietnam in the 1968 election, the Democratic party reformed rules for selecting delegates to its national conventions, many men are supporting women's rights, many "straights" are backing Gay Liberation. And although the political scene is quieter today than it was in the late sixties, the attitudes of American youth have changed (see the box on p. 393).

---

[5] By 1974, however, membership in the United Farm Workers of America had dropped from 50,000 to 10,000. The Teamsters had launched an aggressive and sometimes violent campaign to oust the UFWA. Growers had become impatient with the nationalist rhetoric of UFWA spokesmen, workers were disillusioned, and the public, which supported Chavez the first time, seemed to have grown tired of *causas* (*Time*, April 22, 1974).

summary

Max Weber defined *political power* as the ability to "realize [one's] own will even against the resistance of others who are participating in the action." Political power derives from the right to threaten or to use collective force, numbers, organization, such resources as money, land, prestige, and knowledge, or a combination of these. It may be used to compensate people for compliance; to punish those who do not comply and to withhold expected rewards; or to manipulate information and emotions.

Authority is power exercised in a way people consider right and legitimate. Weber identified three types: (1) *legal/rational authority*, which derives from a system of explicit rules and is vested in offices, not specific individuals; (2) *charismatic authority*, which derives from exceptional personal qualities; and (3) *traditional authority*, which derives from sacred traditions of loyalty to a king or chief. Influence derives from respect and affection and enables a person to affect decisions without resorting to threats or manipulation, or offering compensation.

Weber described the *state* as the one organization in a society that successfully claims authority to use physical force. State power may be organized in many ways. Almond distinguished among *Anglo-American political systems*, which resemble marketplaces; *preindustrial political* systems, which combine disparate political norms; *totalitarian political systems*, which rest on a monopoly of organizations, communications, and violence, and on induced apathy among citizens; and *Continental-European political systems*, which are ideologically fragmented and highly partisan.

Whatever form politics takes, most states rely on *legal systems* to confer authority. The official purposes of law are to define and suppress deviance, protect individual and group rights (from individuals, organizations, and government), and to settle disputes. In practice, the law may also give certain groups a degree of arbitrary power, deprive members of some groups of rights guaranteed all people, and serve as a weapon of political harassment. Constraints on state power in America include institutionalized checks and balances, the provision for impeachment, and public opinion.

Although people's opinions about specific politicians change, basic political attitudes, acquired through socialization, are relatively stable. American children have a personalized image of government by the age of seven or eight and gradually expand their understanding to Congress, voting, and the principle of representation. Virtually all of the children in one survey idealized the government. However, a recent study indicated black children are more cynical. Thus socioeconomic factors influence political attitudes indirectly, through parents' and community attitudes.

Who exercises power in a society and why? What are the consequences? Breaking with tradition, Marx linked political power to economics, described capitalist societies as dividing into two hostile camps (the powerful owners and powerless workers), and predicted that revolution was inevitable. Pareto and Mosca disagreed, arguing that governing elites are and always will be a fact of history. They believed that elites, which are constant, renew themselves by recruiting people with new blood and novel talents. Michels emphasized the tendencies of elites to develop into closed groups with strong vested interests in their positions.

Carrying on this debate, C. Wright Mills argued that America is governed by a *power elite*—people from prestigious families and schools who move back and forth among government, the military, and business, deciding important issues among themselves behind closed doors. Agreeing that some Americans are more free and equal than others, Riesman countered that power in America is dispersed among numerous competing elites, which function as veto groups, protecting their own interests (the *pluralist view*). Mills lamented the erosion of democracy; Riesman, the lack of leadership and direction. Rose suggested that while a power elite dominates American foreign policy, numerous competing elites have a say in domestic issues.

To a degree, parties, interest groups, community political structures, and social movements fill the gap between the top and bottom levels of the American power structure. A political party is an organization designed for the explicit purpose of gaining and maintaining legitimate control of government policies and personnel. Duverger showed that the two-party system is linked to electoral systems in which each party can nominate only one candidate, and the winner of the election takes all. Because American parties must attract people with many different views, they must take pointedly unoffensive, bland views.

Interest groups (organizations created to influence political decisions that concern members) compensate for the tentative nature of American political parties. The NRA, for example, has successfully blocked gun-control legislation for years. Lipset believes interest groups create cross-currents that prevent permanent splits in American society.

Rossi characterizes community power structures in terms of the number and professionalization of public officials, the political composition of the electorate, and the socioeconomic composition of political parties. In *pyramidal communities*, one person or a small clique (in or out of government) dominates; in *caucus systems*, a larger group of influentials rule. *Polylithic systems* include diverse influential and powerful cliques, each with its own sphere of authority. *Amorphous systems* have no stable patterns. Walton believes that the dependence of cities on state and federal funds has contributed to their becoming polylithic.

The powerless may also influence politics, as the Civil Rights Movement demonstrated. Dr. King condemned violence not only because it was wrong, but because it would have been ineffective. Promising to end disorder was the black man's best weapon. In many ways, César Chavez modeled himself after King, perhaps with less success. Recently, even welfare recipients have begun to organize and create disorder, their only choice in Piven and Cloward's view. And although the political scene is quieter today than a decade ago, the powerless have made themselves heard.

glossary

amorphous community structure The absence of stable patterns of power and authority in local government; a hypothetical type (Rossi).

authority Power exercised in a way people consider right and legitimate.

caucus community structure Local rule by a relatively large group of influential and powerful individuals (Rossi).

charismatic authority Authority that derives from exceptional personal qualities (Weber).

coercive power Power that rests on the threat or use of violence.

influence The ability to affect collective decisions without resorting to compensation, manipulation, or threats.

interest group An organization created to influence political decisions that directly concern its members.

legal/rational authority Authority that derives from a system of explicit rules defining the legitimate uses of power. It is vested in positions, not in specific individuals (Weber).

pluralism The view that the political power structure is composed of a variety of competing elites and interest groups.

political party An organization designed for the explicit purpose of gaining and holding legitimate control of government policies and personnel.

political power The ability to realize one's will in a communal action, even against the resistance of others who are participating in the action (Weber).

polylithic community structure Local rule by a diversity of cliques and groups, each with its own sphere of authority (Rossi).

power The ability to accomplish things, to overcome opposition, and to dominate others.

power elite A coalition of military, government, and business executives, united by common interests and social affinity. In C. Wright Mills's view, this coalition rules America.

pyramidal community structure Local rule by one person or by a small clique, within or outside the official government (Rossi).

state The one organization in a society that has the authority to employ physical force (Weber).

traditional authority Authority that derives from sacred traditions of loyalty to king, chiefs, and priests (Weber).

references

Gabriel Almond, "Comparative Political Systems," *Journal of Politics*, vol. 18 (1956): 391–409.

Robert Bierstedt, "An Analysis of Social Power," *American Sociological Review*, vol. 15 (December 1950): 730–38; also in Olsen, 1970.

Robert A. Dahl, *Who Governs?* New Haven: Yale University Press, 1961.

Robert E. Dowse and John A. Hughes, *Political Science*, New York: Wiley, 1972.

Maurice Duverger, *Political Parties*, trans. by Barbara and Robert North, New York: Wiley, 1954.

David Easton and Jack Dennis, *Children in the Political System*, New York: McGraw-Hill, 1969.

Roger Fisher, "Preventing Kidnapping," *The New York Times* (March 13, 1974): 35.

William A. Gamson, *Power and Discontent*, Homewood, Ill.: Dorsey, 1968.

Fred I. Greenstein, "Children's Images of Political Leaders in Three Democracies: The Benevolent Leader Revisited," a paper delivered at the Annual Meeting of the American Political Science Association, 1973.

Floyd Hunter, *Community Power Structure*, Chapel Hill: University of North Carolina Press, 1953.

Suzanne Keller, *Beyond the Ruling Class: Strategic Elites in Modern Society*, New York: Random House, 1963.

Lewis M. Killian, *The Impossible Revolution?* New York: Random House, 1968.

William Kornhauser, " 'Power Elite' or 'Veto Groups'?" in Seymour Martin Lipset and Leo Lowenthal, eds., *Culture and Social Character*, Glencoe, Ill.: Free Press, 1961.

Seymour Martin Lipset, *Political Man*, New York: Anchor, 1963.

———, "Social Conflict, Legitimacy and Democracy," in Olsen, 1970.

Karl Marx and Friedrich Engels, *Communist Manifesto* [1847], New York: Pantheon, 1967.

Carey McWilliams, *North from Mexico*, New York: Greenwood, 1968.

Matt S. Meier and Feliciano Rivera, *The Chicanos: A History of Mexican-Americans*, New York: Hill & Wang, 1972.

Robert Michels, *First Lectures in Political Science*, trans. by Alfred de Grazia, Minneapolis: University of Minnesota Press, 1949.

Lester W. Milbraith, *The Washington Lobbyists*, Chicago: Rand McNally, 1963.

C. Wright Mills, "The Structure of Power in American Society," *British Journal of Sociology*, vol. 9 (March 1958): 29–41; also in Olsen, 1970.

———, *The Power Elite,* New York: Oxford University Press, 1959.

Gaetano Mosca, *The Ruling Class*, New York: McGraw-Hill, 1939; also in Olsen, 1970.

Marvin E. Olsen, ed., *Power in Societies*, New York: Macmillan, 1970.

Anthony M. Orum and Roberta S. Cohen, "The Development of Political Orientations Among Black and White Children," *American Sociological Review*, vol. 38 (February 1973): 62–74.

Vilfredo Pareto, *The Mind and Society*, trans. by A. Bongiorno and A. Livingston, New York: Harcourt Brace Jovanovich, 1935; also in Olsen, 1970.

Frances Fox Piven and Richard A. Cloward, *Regulating the Poor*, New York: Vintage, 1971.

David Riesman, with Nathan Glazer and Reuel Denney, *The Lonely Crowd*, New Haven: Yale University Press, 1951.

Arnold M. Rose, *The Power Structure*, New York: Oxford University Press, 1967.

Peter H. Rossi, "Power and Community Structure," *Midwest Journal of Political Science*, vol. 14 (November 1960): 390–401.

Stan Steiner, *La Raza: The Mexican Americans*, New York: Harper & Row, 1970.

I. F. Stone, "Impeachment," *New York Review of Books*, vol. 20, no. 2 (June 28, 1973).

John Walton, "The Structural Bases of Political Change in Urban Communities," Paper presented to the American Sociological Association, August 28, 1973.

Max Weber, *From Max Weber: Essays in Sociology*, trans. by Hans H. Gerth and C. Wright Mills, New York: Oxford University Press, 1946.

———, *The Theory of Social and Economic Organization*, trans. by Talcott Parsons, Glencoe, Ill.: Free Press, 1947.

David Wise, *The Politics of Lying*, New York: Vintage, 1973.

for further study

Economics. Students of society often forget that economics is a branch of politics. A lively and interesting author who has explored the structural relations between economics and politics is John Kenneth Galbraith. *The Affluent Society* (New York: Houghton Mifflin, 1971) relates postwar America's private comforts and public squalor to the distribution of power in this country. In *The New Industrial State* (New York: Houghton Mifflin, 1972), Galbraith explains the imbalances in terms of the immense power that public and private bureaucracies have accumulated; he shows that corporations are more responsive to elite groups of the politically powerful than to the social needs of the people. Galbraith sees a new distribution of political power as the only solution to these modern developments. Most recently, *Economics and the Public Purpose* (New York: Houghton Mifflin, 1974) examines the myths that keep us from seeing, and therefore thinking clearly about, the ways in which corporate power silently shapes the larger politics of society.

Surveillance and Censorship. An important intersection between power, politics, and the individual is the area of surveillance and censorship. These go hand in hand, emanating from a view that those in power should know about you and make their own decisions about what you know about them. One of the most detailed analyses of how the CIA works is *The CIA and the Cult of Intelligence*, by Victor Marchetti and John D. Marks (New York: Knopf, 1974). This book was censored by the CIA. An interesting study of how large credit agencies, like Bank Americard, and national systems, like the driver-licensing system and National Insurance in Great Britain, use computers to gather vast amounts of confidential information about private individuals is James B. Rule, *Private Lives and Public Surveillance: Social Control in the Computer Age* (New York: Schocken, 1974). *State Secrets* (New York: Holt, Rinehart and Winston, 1974), by Paul Cowan and others, contains essays on just what the FBI collects in its files. The whole issue of state secrecy gets careful attention in *None of Your Business: Government Secrecy in America*, edited by Norman Dorsen and Stephen Gillers (New York: Viking, 1974). Of course, the many articles and books on Watergate are a treasure-trove of material on this subject. And, finally, the essays on superordination and subordination and the sociology of secrecy in *The Sociology of Georg Simmel*, translated by Kurt H. Wolff (New York: Free Press, 1964), are classics in the field.

The Grand Jury. A specific use of political power which raises important questions on the balance between justice and oppression is the grand jury trial. In recent years the government has abused this institution by tying up the money and energies of protest groups in grand jury trials convened on very thin evidence. Vivid and thoughtful accounts have been written of some of these trials. Some are: Peter Schrag, *Test of Loyalty: Daniel Ellsberg and the Rituals of Secret Government* (New York: Simon and Schuster, 1974); John C. Raines, ed., *Conspiracy: The Implications of the Harrisburg Trial for the Democratic Tradition* (New York: Harper and Row, 1974); and Murray Kempton, *The Briar Patch* (New York: Dutton, 1973).

"Happy families are all alike; every unhappy family is unhappy in its own way." This is the sentence with which Leo Tolstoy began his novel *Anna Karenina*. But Tolstoy was wrong. Happy families are not all alike, not if we look at them from the sociological perspective. Throughout the world, both happy and unhappy families assume many different forms and shapes and fulfill many different functions. In Samoa, for example, a newly married couple does not move into its own home, but becomes part of an already existing family. In *Coming of Age in Samoa* (1953), Margaret Mead wrote that "the young couple live in the main household, simply receiving a bamboo pillow, a mosquito net and a pile of mats for their bed. . . . The wife works with all the women of the household and waits on all the men. The husband shares the enterprises of the other men and boys." Among the Trobriand Islanders of New Guinea children are the complete responsibility of their mother's brother. In fact, among the Trobrianders children are not even considered to be the biological offspring of their own natural fathers (Malinowski, 1929).

And even within one society happy families are not all alike. In America, for example, the ideal happy family, celebrated in movies and television, consists of a devoted house-bound mother, a work-bound father, and two or more delightful children. (The "ideal" number of children per family varies with the times. Right now it is two; in the past it has been three, four, or more.) Although many American families (happy and unhappy) may in fact fit this ideal, many and perhaps a majority do not. In millions of American families one or more of the ideal elements is missing: there are childless families and families with a dozen children; there are

THE FAMILY

extended families (where grandparents or other kin live under the same roof) and families that are disrupted through death, divorce, separation, or desertion; there are families with working mothers and families with unemployed fathers; and, with increasing frequency, there are new family forms altogether (like communes, group marriages, and unmarried parents).

Because the forms of family life vary enormously throughout the world, it helps to forget the familiar mother-father-child unit and to think of the "family" sociologically. Free of our narrow experience and stereotypes we can think of the family as whatever arrangements people make for creating and raising children. It may not be the biological parents' children, as in societies where uncles or grandparents do the raising, or it may be a commune which serves as a public family (Kanter, 1974). The growing importance of day care centers, schools, and other institutions forces us to think about them as socially part of the family. Whether we like it or not, they care for and socialize children.

In the first part of this chapter, we discuss the ways social scientists have defined the family, focusing on its three main functions. Next, we consider the family cross-culturally, paying particular attention to the Nayar, the Dani, and the Israeli kibbutzim. In that section, we discuss explanations for the variety of family forms found throughout the world. The next part of the chapter focuses on the American family—the meaning and reasons for the nuclear family, and the way social class affects both family-form and child-rearing. We also discuss both romantic love and divorce in America. Finally we examine the changing American family and consider contemporary alternatives to traditional marriage.

DEFINING THE FAMILY

If it is true that different human groups devise different means for nurturing and training their young, how are we to come up with a single, all-encompassing definition of *family?* The most famous attempt at such a definition was made by anthropologist George Peter Murdock after he had surveyed the family forms of 250 different societies. Murdock suggested that: "The Family is a social group characterized by common residence, economic cooperation, and reproduction; it includes adults of both sexes, at least two of whom maintain a socially approved sexual relationship, and one or more children, own or adopted, of the sexually cohabiting pair" (Murdock, 1949, pp. 2–3). But Murdock's definition does not include the Nayar of southern India, for instance, whose families contain neither sexually cohabiting adults nor adults who reside or work together. (For details on the Nayar, see our discussion later in this chapter.) Kathleen Gough (1974), an anthropologist who studied this group, suggested that Murdock's definition must be revised. For Gough a family is a group characterized by the union of a man and a woman in which the children born to the woman are recognized as legitimate offspring of both parents. While Gough's definition would allow the Nayar families to be called families, her definition would exclude such tribes as the Nuer of East Africa. There, an older, wealthy, childless woman may marry a younger woman and claim her children as her legitimate heirs (Lévi-Strauss, 1956).

However the family is defined (and the issue has never been happily resolved) there seem to be three crucial *social functions* that are carried out by families throughout the world:

1. reproduction of new members of the society;
2. child care;
3. socialization of children to the values, traditions, and norms of the society.

Thus, in all societies there is one constant feature: a reliable arrangement for producing, sustaining, and socializing succeeding generations. We call this institution the family.

The Family as a Biological and Social Unit

While it is clear that family arrangements involve important biological elements like heterosexual intercourse, conception and gestation, birth, and infant care, it would be a mistake to think of the family as merely a biological unit. The social contexts, the traditions and sentiments that surround and shape these biological givens, determine the form a particular family system will take. While the biological givens are unchanging, the social forces that channel and direct them are extremely variable. *Social forces,* not personal desires, dictate the types of people who will have intercourse leading to pregnancy. For example, American culture has strong norms against pairs of lovers consisting of old women and young men, old men and teen-age girls, or partners who are already married to others; and in nearly every society, incest is forbidden. The biological acts of intercourse don't vary in any of these cases, but their social meanings vary dramatically. (Recall our discussions of the influence of social structure and of social norms in chapters 3 and 4.)

The distinction between biological and social determinants of family life becomes even clearer if you consider the meaning of "illegitimacy." A so-called illegitimate child surely has two biological parents and is therefore perfectly legitimate from a biological point of view. But a child (at least in America) who is conceived out of wedlock and whom no male acknowledges as his child and whom no male assumes responsibility for, is illegitimate from a *social* point of view. A child will be socially legitimate only if *some* male, even if he is not the actual, biological father (or *genitor* as social scientists call him), assumes public paternity and responsibility. Thus, at least with paternity, the biological and social bases of family life may be separate.

In the case of maternity the separation is a little more complicated since the biological connection between mother and child is so unmistakable: no woman could ever wonder whether or not she had carried and delivered a particular child. Nonetheless, even with this strong biological connection there are cases where physical and social maternity do not coincide. Consider, for example, the cases of children offered up for adoption by their natural mothers, who later want them back. The adoptive mothers, who have cared for the children from an early age and have formed great bonds of mutual attachment with the children, are surely these children's psychological mothers. In such cases the biological and social bases of motherhood are clearly separable. And, in fact, in recent years the courts have begun to recognize the legitimacy of social motherhood, sometimes allowing adopted children to remain with their adoptive parents.

Once we recognize the distinction between social and biological parenthood we can also begin to appreciate how closely the two are intertwined. In no society in the world is biological parenthood uncontrolled. As the British anthropologist Malinowski once observed: "The relation of mother to child, clearly dictated by natural inclinations, is yet not entirely left to them." Thus, everywhere, "biological facts are transformed into social forces" (Malinowski, 1964, pp. 6, 8). By this Malinowski means that all phases of procreation—conception, gestation, and infant maintenance—are everywhere governed by some social rules. The biological sex drive is always harnessed in some way. Thus, in our own society for instance, we have many rules that limit the random expression of sexual desires, particularly if that expression is likely to lead to conception. We have rules about incest, rules about marriage between kin, rules about child marriages, rules about bigamous marriages, and even in some places still, rules about interracial marriages.

It is clear, then, that while family units are based on biological processes, these biological features are universally channeled by social rules and traditions. Having a baby may be a biological fact, but creating a family is clearly a social one.

CROSS-CULTURAL PERSPECTIVES

Once we have acknowledged the social nature of family life, it is intriguing to compare the different social forms of the family that have emerged at different times in different places. By comparing family patterns we not only broaden our cultural perspectives, but we also become aware, through contrast, of the precise nature of our own family patterns. Numerous forms of the family have been recorded by anthropologists and sociologists, and although many of them are very different from our own, none are more or less valid or correct than ours.

The Nayar, the Dani, and the Israeli Kibbutzim

One of the more fascinating forms of family life was found among the Nayar of Kerala, India (Gough, 1974). During adolescence a Nayar girl was encouraged to have several lovers. If she became pregnant, one or more of these lovers was obliged to acknowledge

Among the Bedouins of the Middle East, women live together in huts, apart from their husbands. (Eve Arnold/Magnum)

paternity and to pay the delivery expenses, but beyond this none of the lovers had any further obligations to the girl or to her child. The mother's kin were completely responsible for both the child's care and for the mother's support. The Nayar did have a form of marriage, but it was a ritual marriage that marked a girl's passage to adulthood; it was not a ceremony that heralded the beginnings of a family as we know it. During the ritual marriage, the woman's tribe chose a man to be her husband for three days. After these three days, husband and wife might never see each other again. Their only further obligations arose when the husband died and the wife had to observe his funeral rites.

Once a Nayar woman was ritually married, her sexual relations with other men came under no social control whatsoever. If she gave birth to a child, some man of her own rank was assigned the status of biological father (whether or not he actually was the father). But this assigned father had no rights or obligations concerning the child. Thus, among the Nayar, social fatherhood (that is, acknowledge paternity) was totally unrelated to biological fatherhood. And yet, the business of re-creating the Nayar culture went on just as smoothly as it did elsewhere; children were conceived, born, and socialized in an orderly, socially determined way, and the expectations and rules concerning family life were regular and predictable.

The Dani, of West Irian, Indonesia, have a family system that is equally unfamiliar to us. For the Dani the family is not a very meaningful unit and, in fact, the Dani language does not even have a word for "family" (Heider, 1972, p. 13). Social life is organized not around private, family households, but around compounds which continually shift (sometimes as frequently as every three days). While the Dani do have a ritual marriage (and one man may ritually marry several women), husbands and wives do not necessarily live in the same compounds, and they rarely get together as a unit. There is some cooperation between spouses in regard to house-building and cooking, but family life is at best short-lived. Children, especially boys, spend much of their time away from their parents, and by the time they are ten years old, they generally move in with distant relatives.

The most striking feature of Dani life, for those of us raised in Western cultures, is the seeming indifference to sex. Men and women in Dani compounds generally sleep in separate quarters: the men sleep in the men's houses and women in the women's houses. Dani also practice long periods of ritual sexual abstinence, particularly after the birth of a child. Husbands and wives may abstain from sexual relations for as long as four to five years after a baby is born, and there is no feeling among the Dani that this abstinence creates special hardship. "Thus . . . both men and women remain celibate for long periods of time without discomfort . . . and this is accomplished without rigorous, overt mechanisms of social control" (Heider, 1972, p. 15). Despite its strangeness to us, however, the Dani family system produces healthy, socialized children, just as families do everywhere.

The collective communes in Israel, called *kibbutzim*, provide yet another example of an unfamiliar family life-style. On the kibbutz many of the activities we have come to associate with family life are transferred to the community as a whole. Men are not responsible for the economic support of their wives, but instead both men and women work for the community and are supported by it. Women are not exclusively responsible for the care of their children; instead, child care is the responsibility of the community as a whole (Talmon-Garber, 1962). While the biological mother is responsible for nursing her own children during the first six weeks of life, after this time children are cared for by communal nurses in separate children's houses. Since the children's houses are organized into homogeneous age groups, each child spends his or her childhood with the same group of peers. This group plays an enormously important role in each child's life.

On the kibbutz such household activities as food preparation, laundry, and recreation are all communally organized. The experience of the kibbutz has exploded a number of cherished myths about the indispensability of the small, intimate family and about the tight connection between biological and social parenthood. Psychological and sociological studies of kibbutz life have revealed that communal child-rearing has many virtues and does, in fact, provide a viable alternative to the traditional, isolated nuclear family as we know it (Rabin, 1965; Bettleheim, 1971). An *isolated nuclear family* is defined by social scientists as a husband and wife and their dependent children living apart from other relatives. It is the family form idealized in our own society.

Origins of Different Family Forms

Once we recognize that different societies throughout the world promote different family forms, we must face the complicated question of why. Why do particular societies come to practice their specific forms of family life? Why do the Dani men have several wives simultaneously? Why do some Israelis raise their children communally? Why do the Trobriand Islanders base family heritage on the female's line? While it is true that attributing causes after the fact is always risky, because we cannot study the beginnings of a process that is already completed, nonetheless social scientists have suggested some convincing explanations for the origins of different family forms.

Some Theories of Family Formation   In the nineteenth century Frederic LePlay, a French scientist, suggested that different family arrangements resulted from different combinations of geographic environment and types of human work. Thus, for example, among the ancient Hebrews work was organized around shepherding activities and, because of the harsh terrain, tribes were forced to move continuously to find more fertile fields. This nomadic existence and the precariousness of the environment led to the development of a rigidly organized social life centered around the leadership, knowledge, and experience of the elders (typically the oldest males). Without printed agricultural manuals, knowledge about the location of fertile lands and methods for food production were stored in the memories of the elders. LePlay argued that these men were granted power and authority because they held the clues to survival (1877–1879). The Hebrews' patriarchial family and community structure was therefore an adaptive response to the environment and to the forms of work the Hebrews performed to survive.

By contrast, the fishermen of northern Europe developed a more democratic and egalitarian form of family life. Because the men were so frequently away at sea, the women became extremely self-reliant and enterprising, assuming a great deal of responsibility for family life in and outside of the home.

A third type of family form developed among hunting tribes, where family members were encouraged to be independent and individualistic. As many social scientists now agree, family forms emerge from the subsistence needs of the society. In agricultural and herding societies, where compliance and co-operation are crucial, the family structure is tightly organized and hierarchical. Individual members of such societies might endanger the limited food supply if they did not adhere to established customs and rules for raising food. By contrast, among hunting tribes innovative techniques might produce *more* food rather than less. Therefore, family life is more flexible, more egalitarian, and less tightly organized (Barry, Bacon, and Child, 1957).

In a study of family life in 549 different societies, two researchers discovered a close connection between family organization and patterns of subsistence (Nimkoff and Middleton, 1960). In societies based on agriculture and fishing, family networks are large and cooperative, thereby assuring the survival of all through the cooperative labor of all. In hunting and gathering societies, where subsistence is based on individual enterprise and extensive mobility, family networks are small and cohesive in order to facilitate the groups' continual movement and to ensure the constant availability of a limited food supply.

Modern industrial societies, where families are highly mobile, are more like hunting tribes than like agricultural settlements, and the small nuclear family, stressing independence and individualism, tends to predominate. In a careful analysis of the connection between the modern nuclear family and modern forms of industrialization, sociologist William Goode (1963) suggested several reasons for the fit between the two.

Among hunter-gatherers, like the Kung Bushmen of the Kalahari Desert, frequent mobility necessitates small families. Similarly, in modern industrial societies where people are often on the move, the nuclear family is highly adaptive. (Bushmen, Irven DeVore; Americans, Elliott Erwitt/Magnum)

Goode points out that the geographic mobility demanded by modern industrial societies (that is, the demand that people move to areas where work is available) requires a small family unit that can, in fact, be moved readily. When a member of a family must move to increase economic or social opportunities, it is far simpler to take along a small nuclear family than to consult and accommodate a large number of kin. In addition small nuclear families cannot build up the power and independence that large family dynasties can, and therefore small families are subject to the whims of the marketplace rather than being able to control or oppose industry. For these and other reasons (for example, the lack of space in urban areas to house large family homesteads) the small nuclear family is the one that is idealized in contemporary American society.

THE AMERICAN FAMILY

If we recognize that family forms more or less conform to social requirements (and particularly economic and survival requirements), we can begin to explore the *consequences* of different family forms for the members of particular societies. What, for instance, are the consequences for Americans of the small, isolated nuclear family? (It is isolated in the sense that each new couple set up a household that is independent of either of their parents' homes.) In the first place, married couples become extremely dependent upon each other both emotionally and physically. In the absence of large numbers of kin living under the same roof, the couple must be all things to each other. They must protect and comfort each other; they must provide for each other in times of stress; they must be self-supporting; and they must accomplish all household chores (including child care) on their own. This kind of mutual dependence leads to society's institutionalizing love as the social glue which replaces the structural supports that traditionally bind the family to society. The nuclear family floats relatively free of social bonds. As a result, feelings of love receive much more emphasis in modern society as a basis for marriage. Paradoxically, the prevalence of love as a bond in marriage correlates with high divorce rates.

Another important consequence of the isolated nuclear family is that the division of labor between a married couple must allow one member to always be at home during the child-rearing years. In societies where grandparents, cousins, aunts, and uncles all live together, there is always some adult around to care for children. But when the family structure consists of an isolated nuclear family, the child-rearing tasks as well as the bread-winning tasks must be divided between only two adults. Until recently the American ideal has been for the husband to earn the money and the wife to keep the home fires burning (again, we must remember that between this ideal type and the actual reality there has always been much disparity). Of late the traditional model is beginning to change, but however the chores are divided up, whoever earns the money or tends the house, the labor must be divided between two people rather than being spread about among a group of competent adults.

The great dependence of couples on each other also makes the American family extremely fragile. When one member of an isolated nuclear family is absent (through death, separation, or divorce), the family disruption can be enormous, whereas in large

table 15:1 **HOW FAMILY MEMBERS HELP EACH OTHER**

MAJOR FORMS OF HELP AND SERVICE	DIRECTION OF SERVICE NETWORK				
	BETWEEN RESPONDENT'S FAMILY AND RELATED KIN	FROM RESPONDENTS TO PARENTS	FROM RESPONDENTS TO SIBLINGS	FROM PARENTS TO RESPONDENTS[1]	FROM SIBLINGS TO RESPONDENTS
Any form of help	93.3	56.3	47.6	79.6	44.8
Help during illness	76.0	47.0	42.0	46.4	39.0
Financial aid	53.0	14.6	10.3	46.8	6.4
Care of children	46.8	4.0	29.5	20.5	10.8
Advice (personal and business)	31.0	2.0	3.0	26.5	4.5
Valuable gifts	22.0	3.4	2.3	17.6	3.4

[1]Totals do not add up to 100 percent because many families received more than one form of help or service.
SOURCE: Marvin B. Sussman, "The Isolated Nuclear Family: Fact or Fiction," *Social Problems* 6 (Spring 1959), p. 338.

extended families, the death or departure of one member can be absorbed and relieved by the several remaining members.

The form of the isolated nuclear family also severely limits the life span of any particular family. Since children are encouraged to strike out on their own as soon as they reach maturity, married couples are often left with empty households after their children become adults. This pattern, colloquially labeled "the empty nest syndrome," often causes much loneliness and anxiety for parents who are used to feeling useful, needed, and protective. In addition, when the parents grow old and less capable of attending to their own needs, the ideal of the isolated nuclear family inhibits them from moving in with their grown children. They must either manage on their own or be turned over to institutions specifically designed to care for the aged. Thus, while the isolated nuclear family may, in fact, snugly fit the economic system, it also causes many problems for individuals in societies where it prevails.

Variations of the American Family

One of the great American myths is that most families consist of a loving husband and wife and their well-adjusted, happy children. Generations of schoolchildren learned to read from books describing such a family and their dog, Spot, living in their own home behind a white picket fence. Minority groups with somewhat different life-styles and family structures simply did not exist.

Sociologists, too, have perpetuated the myth of the singular family type in America. The people who study and write about family life most frequently describe young, white, native-born, middle-class families with children (Heiskanen, 1971). And since these types of families most closely approximate the American ideal, it is not surprising that the myth marches on. If we look closely, however, we can find considerable variation in American family life.

Social Class Differences Of all the factors that tend to influence the nature of family life, social class is one of the most important. No matter how social class is defined (by income, education, occupation, or family background), it invariably affects the organization of family life. Of course, on the superficial level, this statement is self-evident. A family's resources clearly influence the quality of the food it consumes, the amount and kind of leisure activities it has, the amount of space it has to live in, and the schools its children will attend (see chapter 8). But beyond these obvious options that money will buy, there are other class differences in family life.

Some of the most important differences among classes are demographic. That is, the number of children born to each family, as well as death rates, tends to vary with social class. Families lower in the social hierarchy are more likely to have (and desire) more children than families in the higher strata. More children mean more expenses, more crowded living quarters, more emotional and physical strain for the parents. Mortality, like fertility, is also related to social class. The death rate is substantially higher among lower-class families, which means that people in the lower social strata are likely to die younger than people in higher strata. The death rate is, of course, related to other class variables as well, such as health care, nutritional variety, living conditions, and occupational hazards. In addition, lower-class families are more likely to be disrupted by illness, early death, desertion, and divorce.

Families from different classes also appear to raise their children in somewhat different ways. Since people who live at different levels in the social hierarchy will have different life experiences, they will also tend to see the world from different perspectives. Thus, a college professor might value educational achievement, intellectual agility, and innovative approaches to problems (all of which are necessary for academic success), whereas a construction worker might value trade expertise, physical prowess, and the ability to carry out orders (all of which are necessary to the competent performance of construction work). With different sets of values about what is good and important in the world, it is only reasonable to expect that men and women from different classes will approach child-rearing in distinctly different ways, particularly since an important part of child-rearing is, precisely, the transmission of parental values.

Sociologist Melvin Kohn (1959), who has studied the relationship between social class and child-rearing, argues that in order to understand why different classes raise their children differently, we must know what the parents value and want for their children. Kohn suggests that one of the most significant value differences between middle- and working-class parents concerns obedience to authority versus inner controls. "Working-class parents want the child to conform to externally imposed standards, while middle-class parents are far more attentive to . . . internal dynamics" (Kohn, 1974, p. 283). Kohn found that working-class parents:

value obedience, neatness and cleanliness more highly than do middle-class parents and that middle-class parents in turn value curiosity, happiness, consideration and—most importantly—self-control more highly than do working-class parents. . . . To working-class parents it is the overt act that matters: the child should not transgress externally imposed rules; to middle-class parents, it is the child's motives and feelings that matter: the child should govern himself. (1974, p. 283)

Kohn suggests that these differences in values stem, in large part, from differences in occupational conditions. Working-class parents anticipate that as adults their children will have to follow the orders of a foreman.

Conformity and obedience, then, become highly valued traits. Middle-class parents tend to envision their children in professional careers, where initiative and self-discipline bring success. But values also stem from education and from experiences in the economic marketplace. If we think about it for a moment it seems quite logical that individuals whose economic and occupational situations are reasonably secure will be more willing to take social and political risks, more willing to be nonconforming than will people whose positions are insecure, because the price of nonconformity will not be nearly so great among those who are economically safe.

What differences do these values make in terms of actual family behavior and child-rearing practices? Apparently, a considerable amount. One of the pioneering studies of child-rearing techniques concludes that, "In matters of discipline, working class parents are consistently more likely to employ physical punishment, while middle-class families rely more on reasoning, isolation, appeals to guilt and other methods involving the threat of loss of love" (Bronfenbrenner, 1958). This finding is certainly consistent with class value differences. Working-class parents, who are more concerned about overt acts of disobedience, will attempt to stop it directly and immediately. The difference between the two classes in punishment behavior seems to hinge on different conceptions of what constitutes punishable behavior. For working-class parents acts with negative *consequences* are punishable (for instance, marking up the furniture with crayons), whereas for middle-class parents acts with negative *intentions* are punishable (for instance, deliberately knocking down a sibling's pile of blocks). Often, of course, the two negatives coincide in a universally punishable activity (for example, stealing candy from the neigh-

borhood drugstore), but when there *are* class differences in punishable activities, they often stem from different conceptions of what is wrong or naughty.

Discipline, of course, is not the only arena in which class differences in values are reflected in class differences in behavior. Since lower-strata families are more concerned with apparent behavior than with some vague notion of inner development, it makes sense that among lower-strata families in general the emphasis would be on maintaining order and exacting obedience rather than on promoting individuality and developing equality within the family. These differences show up not only in behavior toward children but also in the kinds of relationships that parents have with their children. Middle-class fathers are expected to be supportive and considerate of their children. Since this is also expected of middle-class mothers, the differences in the roles that middle-class mothers and fathers play is not so vast (see the box on the next page). Both concentrate their energies and efforts on the inner development of the child.

In working-class families, however, where constraint and obedience are the keynote of upbringing, the mother is more likely to be the supportive parent and the father, if he is meaningfully involved with child-rearing at all, will be the constrainer. When the lower-class father is not involved extensively with the children's upbringing (as is the case in many lower-strata families), then the mother will play both the roles of supporter and constrainer, and the father will bring home the bacon. This sharp division of labor is likely to become blurred as the forces of social change (for example, Women's Liberation and increased occupational opportunities for women) begin to influence young working-class people. But for the time being, the values and practices of each class will

IN THE NEWS

The Future of Fatherhood

Whatever happened to Father—to the father who ruled *his* household with unquestioned authority? Teachers, policemen, social workers, therapists, and mothers have usurped his role in the family, according to psychiatrist and family therapist C. Christian Beels:

The children, no longer dependent for education, protection, patronage or the right to marry, have staged a fairly successful revolt. Most recently, Mother, no longer dependent for income and protection, has declared her independence. . . . [T]he father as we once knew him has become irrelevant.

After analyzing the middle-class father's three traditional roles—as authority figure, disciplinarian, and model for male children—Beels finds that all three have been weakened. Consider authority: fathers do not have time to meet with teachers and other authorities, and important decisions about child-rearing go to mothers by default. When crises arise, families consult professionals who are experts in family problems. Does working and supporting the family give a father authority in the home?

No—the job is something that makes him tired, that takes up his time, that alienates him from his family. He works hard, and [feels he is] entitled to things that will compensate him and make him feel better, rather than positively entitled to dictate policy because of his authority as the breadwinner.

His role as disciplinarian has also faded. Child-rearing has become a psychological science in America (in a sense, we are all Dr. Spock's children), and psychologists generally do not approve of fathers being called in to administer punishment.

Often the father is the nice man who is home in the evenings and on weekends, whose time with the children is so precious that he should spend it developing his relationship with them and not hounding them to [clean] up their rooms. . . . The ultimate father in our society is an agency: family court or the policeman.

Fathers ceased to be full-time role-models when they first began to work away from the home, and then moved their families miles from work to suburbia. Until recently, American men maintained a private world of sports, cars, home repair, and hobbies, into which they could initiate their sons when they came of age.

They were the separate arenas where father and sons could find both the language and the subject matter with which to communicate about the values, problems, and solutions inherent in being a man.

But, with sex roles becoming more flexible, mothers and daughters have entered these areas. Beele concludes: ''[Today's] father is overworked at work, played out and unable to give himself to full-time fathering when he gets home. His wife is also fed up with full-time mothering. Both seem to want part-time work and part-time parenting. Perhaps we should redefine fatherhood altogether. It should not be the full-time job of one parent but the part-time function of both parents in accord with their ability and knowledge.''

SOURCE: C. Christian Beels, ''Whatever Happened to Father?'' *The New York Times Magazine* (August 25, 1974): p. 10ff.

continue to perpetuate themselves, if only because people tend to raise their children much as they themselves were raised.

Love and Marriage

In any society, when two people marry their union binds many other people together as well. Nowhere in the world is marriage a simple, unguided act of commitment involving only two people in love. Just think of the numbers of people immediately involved in any one marriage ceremony. The groom's family, for instance, includes:

1. Groom's mother
   a. her mother (and her mother's family)
   b. her father (and her father's family)
   c. her siblings (and their spouses, their children, and their spouses' families)
2. Groom's father
   a. his mother (and his mother's family)
   b. his father (and his father's family)
   c. his siblings (and their spouses, their children, and their spouses' families)
3. Siblings
   a. siblings' spouses (and their families)
   b. siblings' children

When this limited list is duplicated for the bride's side, we find literally dozens of individuals *immediately* linked to each other as a result of two simple "I do's."

Given the numbers of people who are potentially affected (for better or worse) by two lovers' decisions to "tie the knot," it is no wonder that every society has patterned means for guiding its young people toward "appropriate" marriages. With so many people involved in the outcome, it is risky to leave such an important decision to the discretion of the impractical young.

In some societies, like our own, the guidance is subtly concealed. In others it is codified into systems of arranged marriages. But whatever the strategy there are always some forces at work in every society that channel and influence the romantic impulses of the unpredictable young.

Although systems of arranged marriages seem cruel and unusual to those of us raised with values of individualism and free choice, it is easy to understand why such systems develop and flourish. Think for instance of societies in which newlyweds move into the husband's family's household (patrilocal residence). The husband's family will, in this case, have an important stake in the type of woman the son brings home. They will be concerned, at least, about the following characteristics of the woman:

1. Tribal (or class) background. Does she come from a similar background so that:
   a. she will share the family's value system about what is good and worthwhile;
   b. she will already know the behavioral codes and expectations;
   c. she will have been brought up to expect and understand her role as a junior member of the household.
2. Personality characteristics. Is she submissive and flexible so that:
   a. she will readily adjust to the family's unique patterns of behavior;
   b. she will submit to the authority of the husband's parents;
   c. she will work hard in order to pull her weight in the household.
3. Physical characteristics. Is she physically sound so that:
   a. she can be a hard-working member of the family;
   b. she will bear healthy children for the family.

If a new wife is to live in her husband's household forever, it is reasonable for the members of that household to have some say about their new addition.

But over and above these positive reasons for arranging marriages, there are also cogent reasons for actively discouraging romantic love as a basis for marriage between young people in societies where the newlyweds live with either the bride's or the groom's family. Romantic love, in such situations, would have an enormous potential for disruption. A young person might fall in love with an "inappropriate" mate who would be unacceptable to the existing household. But even if the mate were acceptable, the bond of love between the two lovers might create jealousy and competition for attention among other household members. In addition, if the husband were strongly devoted to his wife, he might join her in a coalition against other household members and thereby threaten their authority over her. For these reasons, at least, traditional societies don't leave affairs of the heart to the discretion of the young, but rather attempt to control them through arranged marriages.

Our own society has a different set of requirements that affects the nature of our love-channeling activities. Since newlyweds in the United States typically set up their own households (neolocal residence), the acceptability requirements of new spouses are not so stringent. But neither are they totally absent. While the new couple may not be *geographically* integrated into a preexisting household, they are, to be sure, *socially* integrated into preexisting families and therefore are subject to certain familial requirements. Since an "inappropriate" marriage may "scandalize the family," whereas an "appropriate" one might bring glory and pride, parents and the rest of society subtly shape children's marriage aspirations from a very early age. (Recall Peter Berger's passage about love in chapter 3.)

Such parental decisions as those concerning residential neighborhoods and school districts influence the kinds of peers that children will find first as playmates and later as spouses. Such intangibles of family life as the development of a sense of "we" and "they," of "our kind" and "their kind," influence young people's values concerning "attractive" others. Such family patterns as the choice of recreational activities, the selection of vacation spots, and the style of celebrating holidays and special occasions all influence the kinds of potential mates that young people will meet or eventually seek on their own.

These kinds of subsurface controls effectively direct a young person's love interests toward an appropriate pool of eligible mates. And, in fact, the effectiveness of these subtle processes shows up in the marriage statistics. Intermarriages in the United States between different races, religions, and nationalities are relatively rare, particularly among the higher strata of the society (Udry, 1971). Homogamous marriages (that is, those between social equals) are still the order of the day in America. Despite our doctrines of equality and classlessness, we continue to promote marriages between socially equal partners. Once the general screening process has taken place, however, and young people have learned what other sorts of people swim in their pool of eligibles, then the impulses and emotions of romantic love are encouraged to take over.

Romantic love is idealized and exalted in American society. We need only think of our clucking responses to someone who marries for money (or power or prestige) to realize how firmly we uphold the virtues of love. From an extremely early age we are taught about the glories of romance. In fairy tales, the prince and princess fall madly in love, and, after some travail, live happily ever after. In comics and magazines, in movies and songs, on radio and television, men and women are forever falling in love. From the very beginnings of our lives we learn that all "normal" people eventually fall in love and marry. Our parents did it and so did their parents. Our teachers, leaders, heroes, and friends all do it, and so, eventually, will we.

Much of our youthful energies and emotions is devoted to the quest for love, and many a psychiatrist's couch groans under the burden of those who have failed in this culturally exalted quest. There are good reasons why romantic love has become an important basis for marriage in our society (just as there are good reasons why arranged marriages have developed in more traditional societies). When a couple in the United States marry and sets up a new household (as approximately 2 million American couples did in 1972), the new family unit is relatively independent (at least geographically) of other kin. As a result the partners are free to love one another without creating tensions, jealousies, and competition among other household members. Also, since the new couple will depend on each other for a wide range of emotional and physical supports, they will be better able to meet each other's needs if they are guided by love rather than by strictly defined rights and obligations. Romantic love also helps young people to lessen the strong emotional ties that bind them to their own families and allows them to move more comfortably out of the familial nest into their own, independent worlds.

But romance as the basis of marriage has its limitations. In some ways, romance is completely antithetical to the daily demands of married life. As it is promoted in songs, fables, and movies, romance thrives on mystery, distance, and uncertainty—"Some enchanted evening/ You will see a stranger/ . . . Across a crowded room." Since married life is anything but mysterious, distant, and uncertain, what happens to romance in the

Although romance has been the basis for many a successful movie, marriages based on romantic illusions often fail. ("Casablanca"/Culver Pictures)

process? As the popular 1940s song put it: "Love was grand when love was new/ Birds were singing, skies were blue/ . . . The thrill is gone." When romance fades, after all those years of myth and search, all too often the marriage fades with it. Thus, by tooting the horn of romance so loudly we may be simultaneously undermining the very relationships we hope to promote: stable, enduring, child-producing marriages.

Since marriage is a business partnership as well as a romantic fairy tale (it involves, among other things, compromises, division of labor, specialization, communication systems—all the trappings of a bureaucracy), to bill it as a flower-strewn paradise is to risk its eventual demise.

Divorce

That American society has been successful in promoting marriage as a way of life is clear from marriage statistics. Nine out of ten people in America get married at least once in their lives (*Population and the American Future*, 1972, p. 67). And, what is more, they do it early in life. The median age for marriage among women is slightly over twenty years and for men between twenty-two and twenty-three. But what happens to all of those marriages that start out with so much love and high hope? Unfortunately, it is very difficult to know for certain what *does* happen.

In the first place, it is almost impossible to come up with a satisfactory definition of what constitutes a happy or an unhappy marriage. One couple's happy compromise may be another's insurmountable stumbling block. If we cannot define "good" and "bad" marriages, we can hardly expect to come up with figures about how many of each kind occur. But even if we rely on information that does seem to be measurable, for instance the number of marriages that end in divorce, we soon discover how complicated the task is.

Measuring Divorce   If we were to compare the number of divorces in any one year to the number of marriages in that year, we would come up with a boggling divorce rate, for example, 36 percent for 1972. (In that year there were 2,269,000 marriages and 839,000 divorces [*Statistical Abstracts,* 1973, p. 51].) But let us look for a moment at the origin of that astronomical rate.

The number of marriages recorded in any one year is a reasonably straightforward statistic. But remember that the population that is eligible or likely to marry in any one year is relatively small. For the most part this population includes people eighteen to twenty-

eight years old who are not already married. The number of divorces in any one year is also a straightforward statistic, derived from court records of divorce proceedings during that year. But when it comes to *comparing* the yearly number of divorces to the yearly number of marriages in order to arrive at a *divorce rate*, the statisticians run into trouble. The population eligible for divorce is many times greater than the population eligible or likely to get married. *Everyone* who is married is a member of the divorce-eligible population. That population includes people married one, five, ten, fifteen, or twenty-five years. Thus, comparing *yearly* marriage data with *yearly* divorce data drastically inflates the rate of divorce because the population from which divorces might come is so much larger than the population from which marriages might come.

Another problem with comparing yearly marriage and divorce data is that those figures reveal nothing about current trends or about changes in divorce patterns. That is, since the same people do not marry and divorce in one year, we cannot know whether marriages today are more or less enduring than those in the past because the increases in divorce proceedings may come from an *older* population married for ten, fifteen, or twenty years; they therefore cannot be included in the population that marries today.

The great difficulty researchers have in calculating divorce rates comes in determining whose divorces should be compared to whose marriages. This dilemma is still unsolved, although attempts are continually made to circumvent the problem. One recent study, for instance, surveyed households throughout the country in an attempt to discover national marriage and divorce patterns. The researchers found that among the population that had been married for the first time twenty or more years before the survey, 80 percent had been married only once; 17.7 percent had been married twice, and 2.2 percent had been married three or more times (Glick and Norton, 1971). In the same study the researchers also found that the highest incidence of divorce occurred among those who married young (below twenty-two for men, below twenty for women) and that young black people have almost twice as many divorces as young white people (46 percent of black people who had married young had been divorced at least once, compared to 25 percent of young white people).

Explaining Divorce Rates Since it is so difficult to calculate current divorce rates, it is also extremely difficult to compare divorce rates over time. But it seems likely that the popular sense of an increase in marital dissolution probably is, in fact, taking place. There would certainly be ample social explanation for such increases in divorces. In the first place, perhaps because of its frequency, divorce is decreasingly stigmatized so that people are more willing to risk the consequences of ending a marriage. In addition, increasing career opportunities for women allow them to consider alternatives to hanging on forever to a failing marriage. What is more, the old saw of staying together for the children is losing its validity as psychologists discover that a divided household is better for children than a household awash with tension (Udry, 1971, p. 458).

Whether the percentage of marriages that end in divorce will increase, decrease, or remain constant is, of course, a matter of speculation. But whatever else divorce does, it doesn't seem to sour people on the institution of marriage. One-fourth of the people who get divorced are remarried within the year, and within nine years of divorce a full 75 percent are married again. Thus, while marriage may be difficult to sustain, it is certainly

Divorce has become more common as couples learn that "staying together for the children's sake" is not always wise. (Ray Ellis/Rapho Guillumette)

not going out of style. Almost everybody does it (and redoes it when necessary).

THE CHANGING AMERICAN FAMILY

The relative ease with which present-day marriages may be dissolved is only one of the recent changes in American family life. Another involves the amount of time a couple spends in married life and the number of years they devote to raising children. As late as 1920 the average American lived fifty-four to fifty-five years. Today the average man lives to be sixty-seven and the average woman to be seventy-four. Thus, couples who marry young and stay married can now expect almost fifty years of togetherness—a long stretch of time encompassing many different life-cycle changes. The most crucial of these changes are, perhaps, the ones that revolve around children.

When the first child is born to a couple, drastic life-style changes occur. The couple are no longer free to come and go as they please, but must make arrangements for every outing, excursion, or supermarket trip. The mother, if she has been working, must either quit her job or make complicated arrangements for child care. Usually the couple must move to larger quarters and perhaps a neighborhood where there are likely to be other young children. In addition, the love, attention, and leisure time that were formerly shared between two people must now be spread out among three or more individuals. These changes can be very trying, and with the birth of a first child a couple is launched into a whole new social framework.

Drastic changes also occur at the far end of child-rearing. As grown children leave home, the couple are once again thrown back on their own resources, and after all those years of activity, commotion, demands, and scheduling, the new regime may be as unsettling to the couple's equanimity as was the birth of the first child twenty years or so earlier.

While this sequence of events concerning the child-rearing aspects of marriage has not changed much over the decades, the amount of time the sequence takes has. In fact, it has changed markedly. For a variety of reasons the child-oriented years of marriage have been compressed into a shorter time span. One of the reasons for this is that couples now have children earlier in their marriages

than they used to. At the turn of the century the average American woman married at twenty-two, had her first child at twenty-three and her last at thirty-two. Today, the average woman marries at twenty, has her first child at twenty-two and her last at twenty-six. This means, of course, that in addition to starting their families earlier, couples also space their children closer together. Thus, as sociologist Arthur Norton has said:

[There is now] a trend among families toward beginning their childbearing sooner, spacing their children closer, and completing childbearing earlier. These factors, coupled with an increase in the length of time couples survive jointly, show that more "child free" years are or will be spent by couples during middle or old age than ever before. (in Winch and Spanier, 1974, p. 168)

When the foreshortened child-oriented years of marriage are linked with the greater longevity for both sexes and the increasingly earlier retirement ages, we can see that one of the crucial changes in married life is the amount of time the couple will spend alone together at the end of their lives (and due to the disparity in mortality rates for men and women, it also increases the amount of time that a woman is likely to be a widow). As sociologist Robert Winch notes, "In 1890 the average marriage was broken by death before the marriage of the last child, whereas the average couple now survives about 15 years after the marriage of the last child" (in Winch and Spanier, 1974, p. 481).

These changes in family life-cycle schedules have, of course, provided women with substantially more free time, particularly in their middle years. As the labor market statistics show, women are using this time to enter (or reenter) the occupational world. In 1971, for instance, over 45 percent of the work force between the ages of thirty-five and forty-four was comprised of women (*Statistical Abstracts*, 1971, table 333).

The more that women work (particularly in satisfying and responsible occupations) the more pressure they will bring to bear on the traditional roles in family life. They will balk at traditional divisions of labor and at traditional patterns of authority. As political scientist Andrew Hacker said recently:

Put very simply, the major change in the family in recent years, and the problems of the future, are both summed up in one word: women. In the past and until very recently, wives were simply supplementary to their husbands, and not expected to be full human beings. Today, women are involved in much greater expectations and frustrations. . . . The trouble comes from the fact that the institution we call marriage can't hold two full human beings —it was only designed for one and a half. (1970, pp. 34–39)

As Hacker's second "half" becomes more of a social and psychological whole, there are likely to be a series of profound reorganizations in that much beleaguered institution called the isolated nuclear family.

Alternative Forms of Marriage

One of the reorganizations, already in its formative stage, may be the attempt to rewrite the marriage script. Instead of expecting a man and woman to be legally linked in a male-oriented, monogamous, isolated household, a new set of expectations and arrangements may arise (as they have already begun to do). Rapid changes have already occurred regarding monogamy and nonmarital sex. With the development of an easy, efficient, accessible, inexpensive contraceptive, these changes are likely to become even more dramatic. As Robert Winch has pointed out:

The rational basis for a society's prohibition of heterosexual intercourse outside marriage has to do with the consequences of such intercourse because many societies—probably most societies—do not have suitable provisions for raising children born out of wedlock. As unwanted pregnancies . . . become rare to non-existent, the society would lose the basis of its interest in trying to control such behavior. Then—with some cultural lag—the strength of legal and moral sanctions against extramarital intercourse would weaken. . . . The first consequence of the development of an efficient contraceptive and widespread access to it, then, would seem to be a disappearance of moral and legal sanctions against extramarital sex. (in Winch and Spanier, 1974, p. 485)

If, in fact, extramarital sex becomes solely a matter of private conscience and not public taboo, and if sexual relations come to occupy two separate spheres—recreational and procreational—then it is likely that some of the powerful motives for undertaking traditional marriages will lose their force. Clearly, attitudes toward the recreational aspects of sexual relations are changing, as every study on the subject indicates. One such study, which surveyed the readership of *Better Homes and Gardens*, showed that fully 91 percent of the respondents felt that children should be planned through the use of birth-control procedures; 79 percent approved of sex education in American schools; and 75 percent favored making birth-control information available to everyone—including unmarried teen-agers. This is a far cry from the national attitudes that showed up in a Gallup Poll in 1936. In that study 70 percent of the American people opposed the legalization of distribution of birth-control information, even to married people (Wattenberg, 1973). (See chapter 6 for Yankelovich's findings regarding the attitudes of young people toward sex and marriage.)

The effects of such changing attitudes (and of rapidly changing sexual behavior) may be far reaching. Couples will feel increasingly free to live with each other before marriage, or after a marriage has terminated. As women come increasingly to determine their

table 15:2 A PILOT STUDY OF THE PROBLEMS OF UNMARRIED STUDENTS WHO LIVE TOGETHER[1]

PROBLEM AREA	NUMBER INDICATING		AVERAGE RATING GIVEN BY THOSE INDICATING SOME PROBLEM
	NO PROBLEM	SOME PROBLEM	
Emotion Problems			
Overinvolvement (loss of identity, lack of opportunity to participate in other activities or with friends, overdependency)	14	21	2.7
Jealousy of partner's involvement in other activities or relationships	14	15	3.1
Feeling of being trapped	18	15	2.9
Feeling of being used	19	13	2.6
Guilt about living together			
—at beginning of relationship	20	9	3.7
—during relationship	25	5	3.8
—at end of relationship	15	2	4.0
Lack of feeling of "belonging" or of being "at home"	22	9	3.4
Sexual Problems			
Differing degrees or periods of sexual interest	10	23	3.4
Lack of orgasm	11	21	3.6
Fear of pregnancy	15	15	3.1
Impotence of partner	23	6	3.0
Problems Related to Living Situation			
Lack of privacy	15	17	3.4
Lack of adequate space	19	13	3.0
Did not get along with apartment or housemates	20	6	2.2
Lack of sufficient money	26	6	3.3
Disagreement over use of money, sharing of money, etc.	27	4	3.5

[1]This table is based on interviews with junior and senior women at Cornell University. Respondents were asked to rate each problem from 1 to 5, with 1: great deal of problem, 5: no problem (no other points defined). The last category (5: no problem) has been separated because it may be qualitatively different from the other rating categories. Average ratings are therefore based on ratings from 1 to 4; thus, the lower the average rating the greater the problem for those experiencing it.

SOURCE: Adapted from Eleanor D. Macklin, "Heterosexual Cohabitation among Unmarried University Students," *Family Coordinator*, vol. 21 (October 1972), p. 42.

own child-bearing histories, they will, in all likelihood, make greater demands on their mates for more equal unions, for greater work opportunities, and they will determine for themselves the number of children they wish to raise.

There are already in this country several types of innovative marriages, which are being pursued by substantial numbers of couples. With increasing frequency, for instance, Americans are undertaking *two-career marriages* in which the work requirements of both the male and the female are given serious consideration before such family decisions as geographic location, vacation schedules, and child-births are made.

Another type of innovative marriage that is attracting an increasing number of couples is the *contract marriage* in which the couple design their own marriage contract, specifying rights and obligations of each spouse concerning domestic and economic activities, division of labor in the household, and the number and timing of children (Edmiston, 1972, pp. 66–74). Arguing in favor of such marriages, feminist writer Susan Edmiston claims:

First we thought marriage was when Prince Charming came and took you away with him. Then marriage was orange blossoms and silver. But most of us never even suspected the truth. Nobody ever so much as mentioned that what marriage is, at its very heart and essence, is a contract. . . . When you say "I do" you are subscribing to a whole system of rights, obligations and responsibilities many of which may be antithetical to your most cherished beliefs. (1972, p. 2)

In the 1960s Margaret Mead began to rekindle interest in an idea first suggested in the 1920s. Marriage would be contracted in two steps. First would be a trial marriage in which young people would live together as long as it suited them but without any permanent commitment. The second step, undertaken once a baby was on the way, would be a legal agreement binding the couple together until the child (or children) reached adulthood. Mead calls the first step *individual marriage* and the second *parental marriage* (Mead, 1966).

While Mead's seemingly revolutionary suggestion is not likely to gain immediate or widespread acceptance, another marriage-model has gained considerable attention (at least if media coverage is any measure of public interest). This schema is known as the *open marriage*. In a best-selling book about the virtues of open marriage, a husband-wife team of anthropologists contrasted their flexible marriage arrangement with the more traditional, or closed marriage. In conventional marriages, claim Nena and George O'Neill (1972), couples feel that they possess each other and conform to rigid marital roles, which include, among other things, absolute fidelity. Open marriage, by contrast, stresses more flexible roles and more consideration of each partner's needs, talents, and desires, and a considerable amount of autonomy and independence for husband and wife.

While the open marriage does not depart drastically in structure from the nuclear marriage as we know it, other, more radical departures have been attempted. There are, for instance, a variety of plural mating arrangements in which several individuals or couples share the responsibilities of house, child-rearing, financial income, and bed. These arrangements meet with varying degrees of success depending on the personalities of the individuals involved and the attitudes of the surrounding community (Constantine, 1970).

The prevailing force behind most experimental forms of marriage is to maximize security and intimacy while at the same time minimizing constraint and imposed obligation. Whether a man and a woman can satisfy the need for variety and safety within the framework of one ongoing relationship is really difficult to predict. As sociologist Jessie Bernard notes:

Human beings want incompatible things. They want excitement and adventure. They also want safety and security. These are difficult to combine in one relationship. Without a commitment, one has freedom but not security; with a commitment, one has security but little freedom. (in Cornish, 1972, p. 3)

The great stumbling block for most experimental forms of marriage seems to center around the issue of fidelity. For individuals raised in a society where sexual possession and exclusiveness are the legal and moral rights of married partners, it is extremely difficult to reformulate the rules so that each partner may go his or her own way while maintaining one central commitment to a spouse. One of the solutions to this enduring dilemma may be to gradually redefine the anticipations concerning the exclusivity of the marriage relationship so that a breach of monogamy will not be interpreted as a breach of love or commitment.

All of these explorations into innovative forms of marriage are earnest attempts to retain commitment and permanence while maximizing individual freedom and growth. No one can predict how these experiments will succeed in the long run; what is certain is that traditional marriage is under fire and is likely to display a different profile as future generations arrive at new solutions to the age-old tension between freedom and responsibility.

summary

There are a variety of ways to define the family, but social scientists generally agree that families everywhere fulfill three crucial *social functions*: (1) reproduction of new members; (2) child care; and (3) socialization of children to the values, traditions, and norms of the society. The family is not just a biological unit, since *social forces*, not personal desires strongly influence both the choice of marriage partners and the form that the family will assume.

The isolated nuclear family that predominates in most Western countries is only one of many possible family forms. Cross-cultural research has revealed numerous other patterns. Many social scientists suggest that family form is determined by other aspects of the society's social structure. Family arrangements are determined by both the geography of a society and by the kinds of work people perform in it. In modern industrial societies, where families are highly mobile due to frequent job-changes, the small nuclear family, stressing independence and individualism, predominates.

The American family—typically, small and living apart from spouses' parents' homes—has several consequences for its members. Married couples become very dependent on each other both emotionally and physically. Further, one member must always be at home during the child-rearing years. The great dependence of couples on each other also makes the American family very fragile, and since children leave home early, the nuclear family is a short-lived unit.

There isn't just one family type in America; social scientists have discovered several variations, influenced primarily by social class. A couple's social class affects the number of children they will decide to have and the likelihood of family disruption by illness, death, desertion, or divorce. Social class also influences the way families raise their children, particularly regarding the values that parents transmit to their children.

In many societies marriages are arranged, particularly if the couple will live with one spouse's parents. By selecting the mate in advance, the family can avoid the problem of gaining an unacceptable member. In America, marriages are not arranged, but from an early age, children learn about the kinds of people who will be acceptable marriage partners. Americans idealize romantic love, but as a basis for marriage, romance has its limitations. The familiarity that comes with marriage often brings an end to romantic illusions.

Although most people are aware that divorce rates are rising, calculating the current rate, as well as monitoring changes in such rates, is very difficult. Social reasons for the growing number of divorces include (1) decreasing stigmatization; (2) increasing career opportunities for women; and (3) the awareness that a divided family is better for children than a conflict-laden one.

The American family has been changing in a number of ways over the past few decades, particularly in ways that concern children. Many women give birth to their last child by the time they reach twenty-six. Since children leave home at about eighteen, married couples have many years ahead, alone together. Role changes are also occurring as more women find satisfying careers outside the home.

Changes in the family have sparked a number of suggestions for alternative forms of marriage. These include the *open marriage*, where roles are looser and couples feel freer to fulfill their own needs outside of the marriage. Some couples form *two-career marriages* and others plan a *marriage contract* before "tying the knot."

glossary

contract marriage A marriage in which the couple designs their own marriage contract, specifying rights and obligations of each spouse concerning domestic and economic activities, division of labor, and the number and timing of children.

family The social institution, found in every society, that provides a reliable arrangement for producing, sustaining, and socializing succeeding generations.

nuclear family A married couple and their unmarried children generally living by themselves with no other relatives.

open marriage A marriage that stresses flexible roles, consideration of each partner's needs, talents, and desires, and a considerable amount of autonomy and independence for husband and wife.

trial marriage An arrangement where a man and woman live together as long as it suits them, without any permanent commitment to remain together.

two-career marriage A marriage in which the work requirements of both the male and the female are given serious consideration before such family decisions as geographic location, vacation schedules, and having children are made.

references

H. Barry, Margaret K. Bacon, and I. L. Child, "A Cross-Cultural Survey of Some Sex Differences in Socialization," *Journal of Abnormal Psychology*, vol. 55 (1957): 327–32.

Bruno Bettelheim, *Children of the Dream*, New York: Avon, 1971.

Urie Bronfenbrenner, "Socialization and Social Class Through Time and Space," in Eleanor Maccoby, Theodore Newcomb, and Eugene L. Hartley, eds., *Readings in Social Psychology*, New York: Holt, Rinehart and Winston, 1958: 400–25.

Larry L. and Joan M. Constantine, "Where Is Marriage Going?" *The Futurist* (April 1970): 44–46.

Sally Woodhull Cornish, "Marriage Has Many Futures," *The Futurist* (June 1972): 103.

Susan Edmiston, "How to Write Your Own Marriage Contract," *Ms.* (Spring 1972): 66–74.

Paul C. Glick and Arthur J. Norton, "Frequency, Duration and Probability of Marriage and Divorce," *Journal of Marriage and the Family*, vol. 33, no. 2 (May 1971): 307–17.

William J. Goode, "The Role of the Family in Industrialization," in *Social Problems of Development*, vol. 7, The United States Papers Prepared for the United Nations Conference on the Application of Science and Technology for the Benefit of the Less Developed Areas, Washington, D.C.: Government Printing Office, 1963.

E. Kathleen Gough, "Nayar: Central Kerala," in David Schneider and E. Kathleen Gough, eds., *Matrilineal Kinship*, Berkeley: University of California Press, 1974.

Andrew Hacker, "The American Family: Future Uncertain," *Time* (December 28, 1970): 34–39.

Karl G. Heider, *The Dani of West Irian*, Andover, Md.: Warner Modular Publications, 1972.

Veronica Stolte Heiskanen, "The Myth of the Middle-Class Family in American Family Sociology," *The American Sociologist*, vol. 6 (February 1971): 14–18.

Rosabeth Moss Kanter, "Parenting and the Presence of Others: Urban Communes as Public Families." Paper read at the Society for the Study of Social Problems, August 1974, Montreal, Canada.

Melvin L. Kohn, "Social Class and Parental Values," *American Journal of Sociology*, vol. 64 (1959): 337–51.

———, "Social Class and Parent-Child Relationships: An Interpretation," in Winch and Spanier, 1974.

Frederic LePlay, *Les Ouvriers Europeens*, 2nd ed., 6 vols., Tours: Mame, 1877–1879.

Claude Lévi-Strauss, "The Family," in Harry L. Shapiro, ed., *Man, Culture, and Society*, New York: Oxford University Press, 1956.

Bronislaw Malinowski, "The Principle of Legitimacy: Parenthood, the Basis of Social Structure," in Rose Laub Coser, ed., *The Family: Its Structure and Functions*, New York: St. Martin's, 1964.

———, *The Sexual Life of Savages in North-Western Melanesia*, New York: Halcyon House, 1929.

Margaret Mead, "Marriage in Two Steps," *Redbook* (July 1966): 48–49, 84–85.

———, *Coming of Age in Samoa*, New York: Modern Library, 1953.

George Peter Murdock, *Social Structure*, New York: Macmillan, 1949.

M. F. Nimkoff and Russell Middleton, "Types of Family and Types of Economy," *American Journal of Sociology*, vol. 66, no. 3 (November 1960): 215–25.

Nena and George O'Neill, *Open Marriage*, New York: Evans, 1972.

Population and the American Future, Washington, D.C.: Government Printing Office, 1972.

Albert I. Rabin, *Growing Up in the Kibbutz*, New York: Springer, 1965.

Y. Talmon-Garber, "Social Change and Family Structure," *International Social Science Journal*, vol. 14, no. 3 (1962).

Athena Theodore, ed., *The Professional Woman*, Cambridge, Mass.: Schenkman, 1971.

J. Richard Udry, *The Social Context of Marriage*, Philadelphia: Lippincott, 1971.

Ben J. Wattenberg, "A Family Survey: Is the Family Really in Trouble?" *Better Homes and Gardens* (March 1973): 2, 30, 31, 33.

Robert F. Winch and Graham B. Spanier, eds., *Selected Studies in Marriage and the Family*, New York: Holt, Rinehart and Winston, 1974.

for further study

Experiments in Marriage. Given the changes described in the chapter, many people are trying out new patterns of getting and staying together—they often find that the old problems of compatibility and possessiveness do not simply disappear as a result of new life-styles. Satisfying human relationships demand sustained attention to what people bring to their marriages, whether conventional or communal. In *The Mirages of Marriage*, William J. Lederer and Dr. Don D. Jackson (New York: W. W. Norton & Co., 1968) explore the false assumptions people have about marriage, and suggest ways to reach more realistic expectations. In *Open Marriage*, Nena and George O'Neill explore ways to bring modern marriage up to date with a view to allowing each partner a sense of autonomy as well as of sharing.

The Black Family. The black family has, until recently, been discussed largely by white social scientists who tended to judge it by white, middle-class standards. This has recently been corrected by a number of black social scientists who point out that there is no single model of the black family. Indeed, social class must be taken into account here as well as among whites, and the typical family is adapted to the social class of members. A good collection of readings representing various points of view is by Charles V. Willie (ed.), *The Family Life of Black People* (Columbus, Ohio: Merrill, 1970). See especially the articles by Elizabeth Herzog, "Is There a 'Breakdown' of the Negro Family," pp. 331–41; Robert Coles, "The Negro Family: Dilemmas and Struggles of the Middle Class," pp. 310–15; Camille Jeffers, "Mothers and Children in Public Housing," pp. 216–30; and David A. Schulz, "The Role of the Boyfriend in Lower-Class Negro Life," pp. 231–43. Another popular and moving book, not directly on the family, but vividly conveying the attitudes and feelings of street corner black men about family, children, and sex, is Elliot Liebow's *Tally's Corner* (Boston: Little, Brown, 1967), which we discussed in chapter 3.

Divorce. Another timely issue concerns the growing rate of divorce and its implications for children. In the past, it was thought that divorce necessarily was harmful to the children of the separated couple, but there is some evidence that this may not be so. Some articles dealing with this aspect are: F. Ivan Nye, "Child Adjustment in Broken and in Unhappy Unbroken Homes," *Marriage and Family Living*, vol. 19 (1957): 356–61; Joseph B. Perry, Jr. and Erdwin H. Pfuhl, Jr., "Adjustment of Children in 'Solo' and 'Remarriage' Homes," *Marriage and Family Living*, vol. 25 (May 1963): 221–23; and Ivan L. Russell, "Behavior Problems of Children from Broken and Intact Homes," *Journal of Educational Sociology*, vol. 31 (1957): 124–29.

The Rights of Children. Childhood, it has been said, is a rather recent invention. Its special status implies both privileges and constraints. Setting children up as a special group with special needs exempts them from some of the obligations of adulthood but also deprives them of adult rights. The demand for some of these rights is the thrust of the recent movement for "children's liberation," which aims to win autonomy for children, and freedom from subjection to parents, school, and community. Two volumes dealing with different aspects of this issue are: David Gottlieb (ed.), *Children's Liberation* (Englewood Cliffs, N.J.: Prentice-Hall, 1973), and Paul Adams et al., *Children's Rights* (New York: Praeger, 1971).

Americans tend to regard education as a panacea. When the Russians launched Sputnik in 1957, how did we respond? By pouring millions of dollars into science education. How can we end prejudice and discrimination against blacks and other minorities? By integrating schools. What can we do to eliminate chronic poverty? Design special programs to educate the poor. (Nearly every night television stations broadcast such messages as, "Drop out now, pay later"; "Learn more to earn more.") How can we fight sexism? Again, one answer is education: revise textbooks to show women doing something other than housework and childcare.

In 1972, 61 million Americans (31 percent of the population) were enrolled in schools. Nearly 80 percent of Americans between the ages of twenty-five and twenty-nine are high-school graduates, and

EDUCATION

19 percent are college graduates. As the number of Americans attending school has increased, so has the number of years Americans spend in school. In 1972, 42 percent of Americans between the ages of three and five were in daycare programs (*Statistical Abstracts*, 1973). At the opposite end of the age spectrum, 180,000 Americans aged fifty and older were attending school (*Current Population Reports*, no. 260, February 1974, p. 20).

Is our faith in education justified? In the first and second sections of this chapter we examine the functions of education and ask whether American schools are performing them. We then look at the social structure of schools and how it affects both students and teachers. In the last part of the chapter we explore new directions in educational reform.

THE SOCIAL FUNCTIONS OF EDUCATION: IDEALS AND QUESTIONS

In small, nontechnological societies children learn everything they need to know by observing and imitating adults. There is little or no formal schooling. Eskimos, for example, do not hold classes in hunting. Rather, when they kill a bear, they give small children spears and encourage them to stab at the animal as they have seen adults do. By the time children are old and strong enough to hunt, they have thoroughly rehearsed this skill and know, from watching and listening, the legends and magic that surround the hunt (Pettitt, 1946). In modern technological societies, informal education is not enough. There are simply too many things to learn, too many skills to master. In the last fifty years schools have become a vital link between the individual and society.

One of the primary functions of formal education is *cultural and political socialization*: teaching students what it means to be American, or English, or Russian, or Chinese. In fact, mass education in this country was specifically designed to Americanize the waves of non-English-speaking peoples who emigrated to the United States during the nineteenth century. Cultural and political socialization is both direct (classes in civics and history, and student government) and indirect. Classes are conducted and students are evaluated in ways that are designed to socialize them to their culture. In the Soviet Union students are divided into "links" or groups, and graded according to how well the group performs, not for individual effort. An exceptionally bright student is only rewarded if he or she helps others in the group who are not as quick (Bronfenbrenner, 1970).

The American grading system, in contrast, stresses individuality. Several students helping one another to solve a math problem during an exam are punished for cheating.

In China government personnel retire to the country for six-week "refresher" courses in communism. The courses include studying the works of communist theorists, farming (to learn "the true feelings of the laboring masses"), and group criticism (to learn "to distinguish right from wrong"). At these schools the individual is under constant group pressure to conform. In the American educational system, teachers are responsible for enforcing conformity. Peers often encourage nonconformity in school—students who let others know they work hard may be labeled "grinds."

The goal of political and cultural socialization directly conflicts with ethnic identity and pride in America. In the effort to achieve cultural integration, our schools have traditionally focused on white history and middle-class culture. Leonard Covello, the first Italian-American principal in the New York City school system, recalls his own school days:

Throughout my whole elementary school career, I do not recall one mention of Italy or the Italian language or what famous Italians had done in the world, with the possible exception of Columbus. . . . We soon got the idea that "Italian" meant something inferior, and a barrier was erected between children of Italian origin and their parents. . . . We were becoming Americans by learning how to be ashamed of our parents. (1958, pp. 57–58)

The demands for classes in black history, and bilingual education for Spanish-speaking children reflect a growing resistance to forced Americanization (see chapter 9).

A second function of formal education is *instruction*: teaching young people the skills and knowledge they will need as adults, and training them to do necessary work.

THE GOALS OF EDUCATION: THE PUBLIC'S VIEWS

A Gallup Poll conducted in 1972 found that most Americans are extremely pragmatic about education. When asked why parents want their children to get an education, respondents answered as follows:

1.	To get better jobs	44%
2.	To get along better with people at all levels of society	43%
3.	To make more money—achieve financial success	38%
4.	To attain self-satisfaction	21%
5.	To stimulate their minds	15%
6.	Miscellaneous reasons	11%

These results show that the majority of Americans emphasize material goals—not intellectual development. [The percentages do not total 100 because respondents were allowed to give more than one answer.]

Gallup also found that the public is concerned about discipline. When asked what things schools should pay more attention to, respondents ranked the choices as follows:

1. Teaching students to respect law and authority.
2. Teaching students to solve problems and think for themselves.
3. Teaching vocational skills.
4. Teaching students to get along with others.

Respondents considered discipline the number one problem in public schools (followed by lack of money, integration-segregation problems, and the difficulty of getting good teachers). Forty-one percent thought students had too many rights and privileges.

SOURCE: Gallup Opinion Index, September 1972, Report No. 87.

(According to a 1972 Gallup Poll, parents consider job-preparation the primary function of education. See the accompanying box.) The need for skilled workers in America has grown dramatically over the last fifty years. White-collar workers already outnumber blue-collar workers, and professionals and technicians now make up the second largest occupational category, after semiskilled laborers (Bell, 1973, p. 17). However, at present our best schools emphasize intellectual development and theoretical knowledge over practical skills. How "practical," for example, is geometry? How "relevant" is French literature? Does a B.A. in English prepare a student for a career as a writer, editor, or teacher? Not really. Career-minded English majors find they need courses in education to teach, a degree in journalism or on-the-job training for minimal pay to write or edit. On the other hand, this country's vocational high schools are usually considered dumping grounds for students who perform poorly in academic programs. Often the skills they teach are obsolete. In 1973 the President's Science Advisory Committee recommended heavy investments in job training—if necessary at the expense of liberal arts (Reinhold, 1973). The battle between those who believe education should be practical and those who feel education is "learning to think" will be heated.

Selecting and developing talent is a third function of education. In small, nontechnological societies boys nearly always enter their fathers' occupations, and girls learn the household roles of their mothers. But modern, technological societies cannot afford to rely on sons and daughters pursuing their parents' occupations. The need for skilled personnel is too great. For this reason an open school system that allows any child with talent and ambition to become a doctor, a lawyer, or the president is not only just, it is necessary. Schools bear primary responsibility for selecting talented children and developing their abilities. At the same time, however, the schools are expected to educate *every* child, whatever his or her talents are. Americans regard a high-school education (and, increasingly, a college education) as a basic right.

Finally, schools are called upon to *innovate* for the rest of society—to conduct medical research and to offer solutions for social problems. For example, we expect grade and high schools to accomplish integration and to break the cycle of poverty. These functions, solving technical and social problems, involve schools in political controversies. Should universities accept defense contracts or take a moral position against war? Should children be bused to strange and perhaps hostile neighborhoods, white or black, because adults decide they must integrate? Are we using children as political pawns, at the expense of their education?

We raise these questions to show that the social functions of education are not simple or clear-cut. To think of schools simply as organizations that dispense knowledge and skills is unrealistic. The conflicts between cultural integration and ethnic pride, intellectual development and job training, mass and quality education, and the schools' responsibilities to society and to children point to the relationship between schools and the political and economic needs of society.

THE AMERICAN EDUCATIONAL SYSTEM: AN EVALUATION

How well do our schools perform the functions we have outlined? How are conflicts in educational goals resolved?

Schools as Agents of Socialization

All available evidence suggests that the school system is an effective agent of socialization. The more education a person has, the more likely he or she is to vote, to participate actively in politics, and to feel he or she has an impact on the political system (see the discussion of political efficacy in chapter 14). In addition, education seems to mute intergroup suspicion and hostility: college-educated people are more tolerant of group differences than high-school graduates or drop-outs.

Whether our schools succeed in creating cultural integration is debatable. Observation of schools in black and Chicano communities and on Indian reservations reveals a policy of forcing Americanization on minority students. For example, approximately one-third of all Indian youngsters attend boarding schools run by the white-dominated Bureau of Indian Affairs. These schools were first instituted in the nineteenth century—for the express purpose of separating children from their "savage" parents so they might learn to be "Americans." Visits to and from parents are discouraged. As many as sixteen thousand Indian children do not go to school at all because their parents refuse to send them away, and every year hundreds run away from school. The Sherman Institute—named for General William Tecumseh Sherman, whose Indian policy was summed up in the quote, "Give them whisky; it kills them off like flies"—is typical of these schools. In 1969 Sherman had an operating budget of $350 per pupil (75 percent of which was used to provide three meals a day). Eight of the school's buildings had been condemned, so dormitories doubled as classrooms. There were no recreational facilities (no gyms) and no laboratories. The shop was equipped by the Navy with tools donated after they had become obsolete. Sherman did not offer classes in Indian culture or languages, even as electives; only three staff members were Indian. Although the Supreme Court has declared prayers in school unconstitutional, students at Sherman were forced to attend church (Brightman, 1971).

Indians are not the only Americans whose heritage is ignored or denigrated in school. Until the late 1960s Texas law forbade teaching in any language but English. In one school students from extremely poor Mexican-American families were fined a penny any time they used Spanish words; in another they were forced to kneel and beg forgiveness for the same "offense" (Silberman, 1971, p. 94). Most textbooks give only brief attention to Indian, Chicano, and black history—if they mention these peoples at all. The following statement is typical.

Following both World War I and World War II, millions of Negroes moved to Northern cities. As voters and officeholders there, they were able to wield great political influence. Many Negroes joined organizations whose main purpose was to obtain for Negroes "equal protection of the laws" in all respects. As more and more Negroes got a better education and improved their economic status in both North and South, they demanded an end to all discrimination. Many whites, many of them influential, supported their cause. (quoted in Knowles and Prewitt, 1969, p. 50)

The reality of crowded ghettos, racial inequalities and tensions is thus "whitewashed" for white and black students alike. Imagine how unrealistic this description must seem to a young person who lives and attends school in a black ghetto. But the assumption in our schools has always been that minorities must be assimilated—for their own good—and that they will not become "Americanized" unless they abandon their different ways. Until recently books on black history simply did not exist.

Busing Cultural integration is one of the issues in the school busing controversy. As indicated in chapter 9, the 1954 Supreme Court decision on school desegregation had more impact in the South than in the North. By 1972, 70 percent of black students in northern and border states attended nearly all-black schools, compared to 54 percent of black students in the South (Farrell, 1974). School segregation in the North reflects segregated housing patterns, not deliberate policy. To overcome this, the Supreme Court ordered the schools of Charlotte, North Carolina, to bus students out of their neighborhoods to achieve racial balance in 1971—a decision that would have applied throughout the country.

This decision touched off a furor among parents and educators. Both former President Nixon and Alabama Governor George Wallace, who was campaigning for the presidency, opposed "forced busing," and parents began to resist. Busing, they argued, violated the time-honored custom of neighborhood schools under local control. It would be too expensive; it would be physically hazardous (what if a child became sick far from home?); it would be "socially dangerous" (what if a white girl decided to date a black student?). Underlying these public objections was the fear that minority youngsters would lower standards and perhaps disrupt white, middle-class schools.

Some black parents also voiced objections to busing. With complete integration whites might control *all* the schools instead of some of them (Knowles and Prewitt, 1969). Would integrated schools teach black studies? Would they be responsive to the needs of black and other minority children? Although black parents, like all parents, want a better education for their children, some blacks are not anxious to be assimilated. Complicating this debate, there is little concrete evidence that integration would really help black students. Irwin Katz found that although black children did well in genuinely integrated schools, they did very poorly where racial tensions ran high (in Hodgson, 1973, p. 40). David Armor insisted that "busing is *not* an effective policy instrument for raising the achievement of blacks or for increasing interracial harmony" (1972, p. 93). Whether Katz and Armor were correct or not (schools have not been integrated long enough to say for sure), the Supreme Court reversed itself in 1974. By a majority of five to four, the Court declared that unless it could be proved that school district lines had been deliberately drawn to maintain school segregation, the courts did not have the authority to order busing across district lines to achieve integration. The suburbs, Chief Justice Burger reasoned, cannot be held responsible for the *de facto* segregation that has created black majorities in the inner city. Justice Thurgood Marshall, who as an NAACP lawyer had argued the *Brown v. Board of Education of Topeka* case before the Supreme Court twenty years earlier, was among the dissenters. Describing the decision as "a giant step backward," Marshall wrote, "unless our children begin to learn together, there is little hope that our people will ever learn to live together." At this point in history, how schools will be integrated, and indeed whether they will be integrated, are open questions.

One suggested remedy for educational inequality is the voucher system. Instead of giving money directly to schools, communities would divide available funds among parents of school-age children. Using tuition vouchers, parents could send their children to any school, public or private, that met standards of quality and nondiscrimination. Vouchers would provide an escape for children once confined within their own (often poverty-stricken) school districts. Vouchers could also help keep financially troubled parochial schools in operation. And because schools would have to compete for students (and money), they might be forced to improve (Cohen, 1971, pp. 198, 200).

Schools and Learning

Peter W. Doe is suing the San Francisco Unified School District for $1 million. Why? Although he was promoted regularly year after year and received his high-school diploma, he cannot read (*The New York Times*, September 16, 1973, p. 75). Peter Doe is not alone. In 1974 the Department of Health, Education, and Welfare released the results of a survey showing that one in twenty Americans between the ages of twelve and seventeen (about 1 million people) could not read at a fourth-grade level. In these days of written employment applications, complicated government forms, four- and five-page credit contracts, and the like, a fourth-grade reading level amounts to illiteracy. (Indeed, 34 percent of the people Harris polled in 1974 could not complete a Medicaid form.) Reading levels are lowest in inner cities and rural areas. Nationwide, 20.5 percent of black males, 9.6 percent of black females, 4.7 percent of white males, and 1.7 percent of white females are functionally illiterate (Reinhold, 1974).[1]

The obvious conclusion is that blacks attend "bad" schools and learn less. (Christopher Jencks estimates that America spends 15 to 20 percent more to educate white children than to educate black children [1972, pp. 23–29].) This is what James Coleman and his colleagues assumed when they undertook a

---

[1] The differences between races do not reflect innate differences; see chapter 9 for a discussion of the IQ controversy.

"Congratulations, keep moving please. Congratulations, keep moving, please. Congratulations . . ." (Drawing by B. Tobey; © 1974 The New Yorker Magazine, Inc.)

massive survey of 645,000 students attending four thousand selected schools (1966). Halfway through the research Coleman told an interviewer, "The study will show the difference in quality of schools that the average Negro child and the average white child are exposed to. You know yourself that the difference is going to be striking" (in Hodgson, 1973, p. 37).

The results were not at all what Coleman expected. He found relatively little difference between predominantly black and predominantly white schools in expenditure per pupil, building age, library facilities, number of textbooks, teacher characteristics, and class size. For example, 98 percent of the white schools and 94 percent of the black schools had chemistry laboratories. Even more surprising, Coleman found that modern buildings, up-to-date texts and curricula, and higher expenditures per pupil had *no* discernible effect on achievement-test scores. Neither did the quality of teachers. The government and most educators have always assumed a cause-and-effect relationship between school resources and student performance: the more money you spend on pupils, the better their education. Finally, Coleman found that blacks who attended integrated schools for an extended period did only slightly better on achievement tests than blacks who attended segregated schools. But the difference was negligible.

A study of nearly seven hundred students at selected four-year colleges led to similar conclusions. Alexander W. Astin (1968) found that, after controlling for background characteristics, the quality of a college (measured in terms of average intellectual level of the student body, the level of academic competitiveness, and financial resources) had little effect on student achievement (measured in terms of scores on Graduate Record Examinations and entry into Ph.D. programs). High-school performance, major, career aspirations, and sex[2] were the best predicters of college achievement.

---

[2] Men did better in the natural and social sciences; women, in the humanities.

What, then, explains group differences in achievement? Coleman concludes that socioeconomic background is the crucial factor. (See the accompanying box for cross-cultural support for this conclusion.)

Taking all these results together, one implication stands out above all: that schools bring little influence to bear on a child's achievement that is independent of his [or her] background and social

figure 16:1   Relationships between variation in student achievement and variations in home and social background

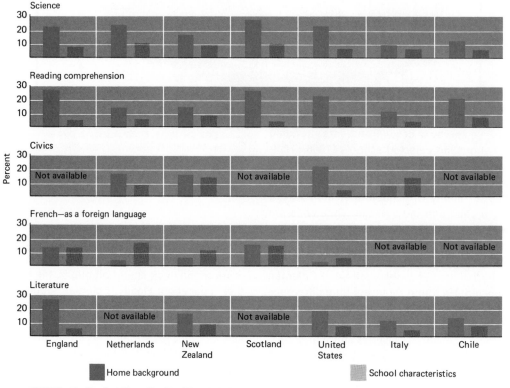

SOURCE: *The New York Times,* May 27, 1973, p. 74C. Based on data from the international Association for the Evaluation of Educational Achievement.

The long-simmering debate over the value of schooling was heightened by the results of a twenty-one country study by the International Association for the Evaluation of Educational Achievement. As some of the results above show, differences in home background were a major factor in explaining variations in reading and science levels.

IN THE NEWS

Home, School, and Achievement

Stockholm—The home is more important than the school to a child's overall achievement. Mass education does not lower academic standards for gifted students, as is widely held. Elitist school systems create and perpetuate inequality.

These conclusions come from a seven-year study of schools in nineteen countries, which was conducted by the International Association for the Evaluation of International Achievement (I.E.A.). Seeking to understand what accounts for differences in achievement, educators measured the performance of 258,000 students in reading comprehension, literature, and science.

In general, the Stockholm report confirmed Coleman's (1966) finding that home background affects academic performance more than the school itself does. Reading comprehension and achievement in science, in particular, seemed to depend upon home background (see figure 16:1). In literature and languages, on the other hand, good teaching and school quality proved more important. Specifically, the data showed:

1. Girls lag behind boys in their interest and performance in science, and the gap grows wider the longer they attend schools for girls only; but the gap narrows significantly in coeducational schools.
2. The number of books and magazines in a student's home has a greater effect on achievement in literature than income and education of the student's family.
3. An analysis of the schools' greater success in teaching science than in teaching reading suggests a serious discrepancy in the schools' relative efforts. "The schools appear to do little to mobilize their resources for the improvement of reading beyond the early years," the report said.

Mass education does not appear to penalize the gifted student. In a separate reading-comprehension study the top 9 percent of American students did better than the top 9 percent in the other fourteen nations in the survey. The same elite group rated seventh out of nineteen countries in science. Moreover, America's mass education system is less class-biased than the more selective systems of countries like West Germany. There, only 1 percent of lower-class children are still in school at age eighteen; in the United States 14 percent are.

But what about educational payoff? Does education have any effect on economic mobility? The study's answer: a tentative yes.

The Stockholm report challenges directly some claims made recently in the study headed by Christopher Jencks at Harvard that the schools fail to reduce social inequality. Although the I.E.A. survey did not examine inequality in income, it concluded that open access to public education is a key factor in allowing lower-class children to rise to the level of the academic elite. This increases their chances of greater economic success.

SOURCE: *The New York Times*, May 27, 1973, p. 57C, based on a survey by the International Association for the Evaluation of Educational Achievement.

context; and that this very lack of an independent effect means that the inequalities imposed on children by their home, neighborhood, and peer environment are carried along to become the inequalities with which they confront adult life at the end of school. (Coleman, in Silberman, 1971, p. 71)

In short, the family, not the school, is the major educational institution—even in modern society. Family differences strongly affect children's chances for equal educational opportunities. Traditionally, equality of opportunity has meant trying to give all children access to the same kinds of educational *inputs*—teachers, facilities, and so on. This is roughly equivalent to giving someone who has never played golf the same set of clubs and balls as an experienced player, and pointing them toward the same green. There is little doubt who will win. Coleman argues that to achieve true equality of opportunity we must treat individuals differently, much as we give a handicap to a beginning golfer. Just as we calculate a fair handicap by counting the average number of strokes it takes a beginner to complete a golf course, so that with his handicap he will come out about the same as the more experienced player, so we should measure educational opportunity by *outcome*. Equal opportunity in education exists when the average scores of graduates from different schools (not per-pupil expenditures, facilities, and the like) are about the same.

The Coleman Report is not the final word on educational differences. Only 59 percent of the schools he and his associates surveyed completed all of the questionnaires. Their calculations reflect school averages, not individual achievement, and may obscure significant individual variations. A number of sociologists have criticized the study and the way data were analyzed. Nevertheless, its conclusions are widely accepted by educational sociologists.

The Screening Function

One way of thinking about educational institutions is as screening systems. At each step up the educational ladder a number of students are excluded or drop out voluntarily. Those who have met the standards advance to the next rung (see figure 16:2). In 1971, 1.15 million Americans received college degrees. Of those, only 2.8 percent earned doctorates, the highest academic degree conferred by American universities (*Statistical Abstracts*, 1973, p. 137). Does that 2.8 percent constitute the "best and the brightest"? Is our educational system open to any child with talent and ambition, as we would like to believe?

The data in table 16:1 suggest that the higher a person's socioeconomic status, the better his or her chances of going to college. In 1965, 90 percent of males and 80 percent of females from upper- and upper-middle class backgrounds were accepted by colleges, compared to 8 percent and 4 percent of lower-working-class males and females, respectively. Does this mean that upper- and upper-middle-class students are more intelligent? Robert J. Havighurst and Bernice Neugarten (1968) analyzed data on students who were all in the top quarter of their classes. They found that 90 percent of the bright upper- and upper-middle-class students enrolled in college and 80 percent graduated, whereas 66 percent of the bright working-class students went to college, and only 29 percent graduated—despite their equal abilities (see table 16:2). Clearly, social class influences a person's chances for finishing high school, getting into college, completing college, and going on to graduate school. This means that a lot of talent in America is screened out and goes undeveloped.

figure 16:2   School retention rates: 1924–1962, from fifth grade to high school graduation

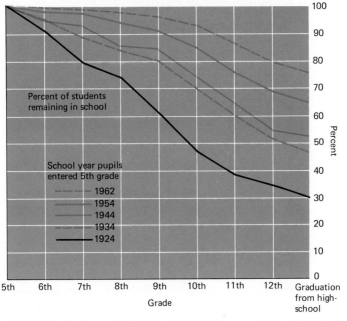

Percent of students remaining in school

School year pupils entered 5th grade
— 1962
— 1954
— 1944
— 1934
— 1924

Percent

100
90
80
70
60
50
40
30
20
10
0

5th   6th   7th   8th   9th   10th   11th   12th   Graduation from high-school

Grade

SOURCE: *Social Indicators, 1973* (Washington D.C.: U.S. Government Printing Office, 1974), p. 78.

At each rung of the educational ladder, a smaller percentage of students remain in school, although the proportion of those completing high school has more than doubled since 1924.

table 16:1   **PERCENT OF A GIVEN CLASS WHO ENTER COLLEGE[1]**

SOCIAL CLASS	1920	1940	1950	1960	1965	
					MALES	FEMALES
Upper and Upper-middle	40	70	75	80	90	80
Upper-middle	8	20	38	50	62	45
Upper-working	2	5	12	25	35+	24
Lower-working[2]	0	0	2	4	8	4

[1]Note that the percentage of working-class students entering college today is nearly as high as the percentage of upper- and upper-middle-class students entering college in 1920.
[2]Since 1920 college has become increasingly accessible to all but the lower-working class.
SOURCE: Robert G. Havighurst and Bernice Neugarten, *Society and Education* (Boston: Allyn & Bacon, 1968).

table 16:2   **LEVEL OF EDUCATION IN RELATION TO SOCIAL CLASS OF YOUTH IN THE UPPER QUARTER OF INTELLECTUAL ABILITY (IQ = 110 +) 1965 (by percent)**

	SOCIAL CLASS			
	UPPER AND UPPER-MIDDLE	LOWER-MIDDLE	WORKING	TOTALS
Do not finish high school	0	2	10	5
High school graduates. Do not enter college	10	10	24	15
Enter college but do not finish	10	26	37	27
Complete a four-year college program	80	62	29	53

SOURCE: Robert J. Havighurst and Bernice Neugarten, *Society and Education* (Boston: Allyn & Bacon, 1968), tables 4.1; 3.5.

Tracking   The screening process begins in elementary school, when children are divided into slow, average, and bright groups on the basis of aptitude and achievement tests and teachers' recommendations. *Tracking,* as ability-grouping is called, is based on the assumption that students will learn more if they do not have to compete with students who are much brighter than they are or wait for students who are slower. It is designed primarily to accelerate above-average children and give below-average children the extra attention they need.

In practice, tracking tends to segregate students along socioeconomic and racial lines—white, middle-class youngsters being assigned to the advanced track, nonwhite, lower-class children to "general" and vocational tracks. According to one study of 467 southern school districts, 60 percent of racial segregation in elementary schools and 35 percent in high schools was justified in terms of tracking ("Testing and Tracking," 1973, p. 15).

In Washington, D.C., where over 90 percent of high-school students are black, tracking perpetuates economic divisions. In 1966, 85 percent of students in neighborhoods where the median income was $3,872 a year found themselves in a basic or general track, even though their schools had college preparatory tracks. Where median income reached $16,374 a year, 82 percent of the students were in college preparatory or honors tracks (Lauter and Howe, 1970, p. 318).

Although tracking does seem to improve the performance of good students, it does not appear to help poor students. In fact, Coleman found ghetto youngsters did best in racially and economically mixed classes. Tracking merely widens the gap between good and poor students, stigmatizing those who are placed in the "dummy" programs. Three researchers (Schaefer, Olexa, and Polk, 1972) discovered a relationship between low track placement and delinquency, lack of involvement in school activities, and drop-out rates, as well as low grades. By lowering the students' self-esteem, they conclude, the system alienates young people from school norms. Thrown back on the peer group, they may turn to antisocial behavior.

Tracking also influences teacher expectations. Low expectations tend to become self-fulfilling prophecies. (See the discussions of labeling and socialization to deviance in chapter 12.)

A fourth-grade math teacher writes a half-dozen problems on the board for the class to do. "I think I can pick at least four children who can't do them," she tells the class, and proceeds to call four youngsters to the board to demonstrate, for all to see, how correct the teacher's judgment is. Needless to say, the children fulfill the prophecy. (Silberman, 1971, p. 139)

Rosenthal and Jacobson (1968) tested this proposition experimentally. They gave elementary-school teachers a list of students, supposedly with very high IQ's, but who were actually selected at random. They told teachers to expect great progress from these students. At the end of the school year the IQ scores of this group had increased significantly more than the scores of students who had not been selected. (The influence of teachers' expectations on students' performance is known as the *pygmalion effect*.) A study by Leacock (1969) confirmed Rosenthal and Jacobson's findings, with an added twist. The author studied four kinds of elementary schools: lower-class white, middle-class white, lower-class black, and middle-class black. In the middle-class schools, teachers treated students better if the children were "supposed" to be bright. But in the lower-class black school, teachers rejected bright children as "smart-alecks" and "wiseguys."

Contest Mobility and "Cooling Out"
Although tracking eliminates some students, a great many complete academic high-school programs every year, with the expectation of going on to college. Ralph H. Turner (1960) compares our school system to a race in which every effort is made to keep as many students in the running for as long as possible. The race is considered fair so long as everyone has equal footing at the start. The outcome depends on individual effort—on "common sense, craft, enterprise, daring and successful risk-taking: as well as on intelligence and hard work." This is why Turner calls our system "contest mobility."

In contrast, the British eliminate all but the brightest students at an early age, before the race begins. Nearly all of the children selected for college preparatory programs do obtain university degrees and the high social and economic status that come with them. Education in Britain, Turner argues, means learning to take one's destined place in the elite, under the sponsorship of those already in power (hence his term "sponsored mobility"). Education in America consists largely of learning to compete (see chapter 4). In Britain children of eight or nine know more or less where they are headed in life.

In America the "finish" is postponed until late adolescence. Less than a third of the 1 million Americans who start college every year graduate. What happens to the others? Some are dismissed outright and suffer the public failure of returning home at the end of their first semester or freshman year. Some quit; but most who do not meet the standards are eased out gradually. Many who enter colleges are assigned to remedial classes or to "terminal programs" in junior colleges; counseled to think about noncollege career alternatives; required to take an Orientation to College course that states the "facts of life" in an impersonal way, enlightening over-ambitious students. If necessary, students are put on probation with two or three semesters' warning—a slow death for those who cannot meet standards. Burton R. Clark (1960) argues that this gentle, slow dismissal is designed to "cool out" young people who have been led to believe that hard work alone will win them the social and economic rewards that come with college degrees. By letting students down slowly, colleges prevent the build-up of potentially disruptive frustration of discovering that the prizes society promises are available only to a very few.

Education and Income

Everyone "knows" that you need a college education to get ahead in America (that is, to earn more money than your parents did). We tend to assume that a B.A. (or, even better, a medical or law degree or a Ph.D.) is a guarantee to gaining the "good life." Indeed, the government has long assumed that the way to reduce income inequality is to educate the poor. Is this assumption correct?

Statistics on education and income suggest it is (see table 16:3). An elementary-school drop-out earns only 64 percent of the average national income; a person with one or more years of graduate school earns 171 percent of the national average. But does this mean that the elementary-school drop-out would be earning nearly three times as much as he does today if he had gone to graduate school? Christopher Jencks (1972) thinks not. Education is not the only difference between the drop-out and the graduate. In all probability they came from very different socioeconomic backgrounds and had very different experiences while growing up. These differences—not education, says Jencks—may account for the income gap between them. Comparing data on people from similar socioeconomic backgrounds who had similar test scores but different educations, Jencks concludes that an extra year of elementary or

---

table 16:3 INCOMES OF FULL-TIME, YEAR-ROUND WORKERS OVER 25 WITH DIFFERENT AMOUNTS OF SCHOOLING, AS A PERCENTAGE OF THE 1968 AVERAGE

AMOUNT OF SCHOOLING	MALES	FEMALES	TOTAL
Didn't Finish Elementary School	70	40	64
Finished Elementary School, No High School	85	47	76
Entered High School, Didn't Finish	96	51	84
Finished High School, No College	111	61	95
Entered College, Didn't Finish	129	71	115
Finished College, No Graduate School	170	84	150
At Least 1 Year of Graduate Work	188	106	171
All Individuals	114	62	100
Grand Mean			$7,995
Number of Individuals in 1,000s	34,432	12,575	47,008

SOURCE: Table 41 in the U.S. Bureau of the Census, "Income in 1968." "Elementary School" includes the first 8 years of schooling. "High School" includes grades 9–12. "Finished College" means a 4-year college. "No High School," "No College," and "No Graduate School" includes individuals who entered these institutions but did not complete the first year.

high school boosts income less than 4 percent; a year of college, 7 percent; a year of graduate school, only about 4 percent (1972, pp. 221–25). (See the discussion of the relationship between class, education, and income in chapter 8.)

In addition as more and more people obtain high-school, college, and graduate degrees, their value in the job market declines. When only 6 percent of Americans entered college, college graduates were an elite minority and could command high salaries. Today, about 40 percent of American students go to college, and a B.A. isn't the badge of distinction it once was. As a result a college degree is now often required for mundane, relatively low-paying jobs.

This is not to say that education is not important, but rather that we cannot expect schools to solve all of our social problems. The way to equalize income, in Jencks's view, is simply to redistribute it through taxation—not to educate the poor. Education is an end in itself, he argues, not a means to individual mobility and social equality. "There is no evidence that building a school playground will affect the students' chances of learning to read, getting into college, or earning $50,000 a year when they are fifty," he writes. "Building a playground may, however, have a considerable effect on the students' chances of having a good time during recess when they are eight" (in Hodgson, 1973, p. 44).

THE SOCIAL STRUCTURE OF SCHOOLS

Beginning at the age of five or six, children spend about a thousand hours a year in school—next only to the amounts of time they spend sleeping and watching television.

In traditional schools they are subjected to a level of regimentation they will not encounter again, unless they enter the military. Where else are people forced to remain silent, to sit still for hours, to line up and march on command, to ask permission to speak or to go to the bathroom? These peculiarities—the amount of time, regimentation, and compulsory attendance—shape the social structure of many schools and the roles of both teacher and student (Jackson, 1968). And as Philip Zimbardo's 1972 study so clearly showed, the social structure of an institution strongly influences the behavior of people in that institution.

Kindergarten is the child's initiation into the student role. On the surface most kindergarten activities seem purposeless.

[T]he teacher asks, "Who wants to be the first one?" One of the noisy girls comes to the center of the room. The voice on the record is giving directions for imitating an ostrich and the girl follows them, walking around the center of the room holding her ankles with her hands. . . . This is apparently a familiar game, for a number of children are calling out, "Can we have the crab?" Edith . . . plays the part of the record with music for imitating crabs by. The children from the first table line up across the room, hands and feet on the floor and faces pointing toward the ceiling. (Gracey, 1972, p. 248)

But the children *are* learning—learning to do what the teacher wants, when she wants it. In kindergarten there is a Story Time, a Nap Time, a Pick-Up Time—in short, an official routine.

The record ends at 2:40. Edith says, "Children, down on your blankets." As the class is lying on blankets now, Edith refuses to answer the various questions individual children put to her because, she tells them, "It's rest time now." (Gracey, 1972, pp. 250–52)

Day after day kindergarten children are shown the rituals of school, including hand-raising and lining-up. They are taught behavior and attitudes teachers believe essential, and drilled in these patterns. Harry L. Gracey compares kindergarten to a boot camp: it is "successful" if youngsters learn to follow routines and obey orders without question, even if the orders are trivial (1972, p. 251).

The Hidden Curriculum

As this analysis of kindergarten suggests, the official curriculum—reading, arithmetic, and other subjects—does not begin to describe the content of education. In a detailed study of elementary schools, Philip Jackson (1968) found that to advance from grade to grade, to survive academically and socially, youngsters must also learn to be quiet, to line up, to wait, to act interested even if they are not, to please teachers without alienating peers, to come to grips with the inevitability of school, and the host of other skills that comprise the *hidden curriculum*.

By the time they enter first grade, most children have learned the three basic facts of school life that will structure their school experience: crowds, praise, and power (Jackson, 1968, p. 6). In school a child's every act is open to public scrutiny, by teachers *and peers*; there is little or no privacy. One of twenty or more in a class, he or she must learn to tolerate delays (waiting to be called on, waiting for the class to line up for recess) and interruptions (children breaking into another's dialogue with a teacher, teachers invading daydreams, bells terminating a struggle with a math problem). For much of the day, however, children are expected to act as though they are alone—even though their friends (and perhaps enemies) are just inches away. School teaches youngsters to be alone in a crowd.

The public nature of school activities is made all the more trying by the fact that the child is constantly being evaluated. In one fourth-grade classroom, for example, pupils recorded their math test scores on large bar graphs in red pencil. After a test the teacher would line them up in the front of the room, score cards in hand, in the order of their grades. That way everyone could see who got the highest and lowest scores. From first grade on, children's victories and failures become a matter of semipublic record: IQ, aptitude and achievement test scores, and grades are all duly recorded. Children also begin to earn a reputation as bright or slow, highly motivated or dawdling, helpful in maintaining classroom order or troublesome. These informal teacher evaluations can be as important as grades. How many teachers will fail a student who has behaved beautifully and tried his or her hardest? "Although it offends our sensibilities to admit it, no doubt that bright-eyed little girl [or boy] who stands trembling before the principal on graduation day arrived there at least in part because she [or he] typed her [or his] weekly themes neatly and handed her [or his] homework in on time" (Jackson, 1968, p. 34).

In addition children evaluate each other, often through teacher encouragement: "Who can tell me if George's answer is correct." Children also decide whether their classmates are teacher's pets or good guys, cheats or good sports. In effect, each child plays to two audiences—teachers and peers—whose standards often conflict. In one second grade, for example, a teacher praised a boy for his "creative dancing," but his classmates teased him for being a sissy (Jackson, 1968, pp. 22–25).

Formal and informal evaluation by teachers and peers may have more impact than we like to admit. Educator John Holt contrasts his seventeen-month-old niece to tense, anxious fifth graders. Every object the baby sees she experiments with. Although she usually fails to make things do what she wants them to, she keeps trying. The older children, in contrast, seem defeated before they begin. Why the difference? Holt reasons, the baby "has not yet been made to feel that failure is shame, disgrace a crime" (1964, pp. 62–63).

Finally, the distribution of power in schools is decidedly unequal. School places children under the absolute and sometimes highly insensitive authority of teachers.

A precocious sixth-grader has become attached to a particular pencil, now down to a small stub. His teacher orders him to use a larger pencil; the youngster politely informs her that so long as his work and penmanship are satisfactory (he is receiving A's on all his work), what pencil he uses is a matter for him to decide. The teacher sends him to see the principal, who summons the boy's parents for a conference to discuss his "disobedience." (Silberman, 1971, p. 88)

Teachers do most of the talking in classrooms (as much as 80 percent according to one study). Students are confined to answering questions and commenting on the teacher's statements. Teachers decide what students will and will not do.

All over the United States, that last week of November, 1963, teachers reported the same complaint: "I can't get the children to concentrate on their work; all they want to do is talk about the assassination." The idea that the children might learn more from discussing President Kennedy's assassination—or that, like most adults, they were simply too obsessed with the horrible events to think about anything else—didn't occur to these teachers. It wasn't in that week's lesson plan. (Silberman, 1970, p. 85)

In effect the teacher is the child's first boss, and learning to do what the boss wants you to do is an essential part of the hidden curriculum. This, in Charles Silberman's view, is the basis for the dichotomy between work and play.

[A] by-product of teacher dominance, one that has profound consequences for children's attitudes towards learning, is the sharp but wholly artificial dichotomy between work and play which schools create and maintain. Young children make no such distinction. They learn through play, and until they have been taught to make the distinction ("Let's stop playing now, children; it's time to start our work"), they regard all activities in the same light. But the dichotomy grows out of the assumption that nothing can happen unless the teacher makes it happen. (Silberman, 1971, p. 90)

Critics of the school system argue that this hidden curriculum stifles initiative and creativity, that the obsession with rules and regulations keeps youngsters in a chronic state of dependency, and that the assumption of distrust regarding students is harmful and unfounded. After conducting a national study of public schools, Charles Silberman concluded that:

The preoccupation with order and control, the slavish adherence to the timetable and lesson plan, the obsession with routine *qua* routine, the absence of noise and movement, the joylessness and repression, the universality of the formal lecture or teacher-dominated "discussion" in which the teacher instructs an entire class as a unit, the emphasis of the verbal and de-emphasis of the concrete, the inability of students to work on their own, the dichotomy between work and play—none of these are necessary; all can be eliminated. (Silberman, 1971)

Others reason that young people must learn to accept orders from a boss, to cope with contradictory evaluations from superiors and peers, and to tolerate frustrations, delays, and being in a crowd—if, for example, they are to function effectively on an assembly line or in a large business organization.

The Teaching Situation

Teachers often start out with high ideals. They like children, remember things they disliked about their own school years, and are determined to do better. All too often, however, the very structure of schools transforms them into the "traffic cop" teachers they vowed never to become. Teachers, unlike other professionals, rarely have offices of their own. Instead they share an open lounge designed primarily for coffee and cigarette breaks. They have little control over curricula, textbooks, and other aspects of teaching that directly concern them. Added to large class enrollments, most teachers must also perform a variety of clerical and menial tasks, such as patrolling the halls and the student-cafeteria. They have little time for either private reflection or consultation with colleagues. Often their principals and city employers distrust teachers as much as teachers distrust students: like clerks and factory workers, most punch time clocks. Their salaries are relatively low, and they generally do not enjoy very much prestige. The National Opinion Research Center found that Americans rank teaching thirty-fifth, between building contractors and railroad engineers.

Added to these factors, teachers are usually evaluated on the relative quiet in their classrooms and on the stillness of their students. Teachers are rarely fired if their students haven't learned anything. When new teachers ask for advice, more often than not they are given tips on discipline. For example, a National Teachers Association manual recommends, "Plan the lesson. Be ready to use the first minute of class time. If you get Johnny right away, he has no time to cook up *interesting ideas* that do not fit into the class situation" (Silberman, 1970, p. 88, italics added). It is no wonder, then, that teachers focus on maintaining order. Indeed, this is what most parents want them to do. A Harris Poll showed that two-thirds of parents (but only 27 percent of teachers) considered discipline more important than learning (Silberman, 1970, pp. 90–92).

With all these problems, some teachers nevertheless manage to do excellent jobs.

Philip W. Jackson tried to discover what the best teachers (as rated by colleagues) had in common. His observations surprised him. The "good" teachers were not the most gifted intellectually. Often they appeared irrational, because they reacted intuitively and did not generalize about their experience. Immersed in the ongoing life of the classroom, all tended to offer simple answers to complex questions: "Why is Fred such a troublemaker? Because he comes from a broken home" (1968, p. 144). Elsewhere, these qualities might be a handicap, but they seemed to work in the classroom. The teacher's close involvement with students can make up for the coldness of school routines. And in a class of thirty students, oversimplifying may be the only way to get any point across.

Student Society

We have talked about the institution's impact on students, but what about the students' responses and values? These form another part of the hidden curriculum.

In the 1960s Patricia Sexton studied freshmen at twenty-three colleges. Only 19 percent said their major interest was the "pursuit of ideas." A whopping 51 percent devoted most of their attention to extracurricular activities such as sports and social life, paralleling Coleman's study of adolescents a decade earlier (1961) (see chapter 4). Only 27 percent in Sexton's study concentrated on their future careers (1967). (See chapter 11 for Yankelovich's findings about the career attitudes of young people in the 1970s.)

Social success seems to be even more prized in high school. Good grades are all right, as long as the student is also athletic (boys) or popular (girls). Tannenbaum (1960) created eight imaginary boys and asked other

students to rate them in order of acceptability. The highest-rated student was the Brilliant Nonstudious Athlete; the lowest, a Brilliant Studious Nonathlete. In other surveys almost no one wanted to date a brilliant girl; brilliant boys were only slightly more acceptable as dates (Coleman, 1961). College plans improve a student's status, but only for students with no overt intellectual interests (Coleman, 1961).

Why the emphasis on athletics and smooth social skills? Partly, perhaps, because schools isolate students, encouraging them to turn to peers and the mass media for their values (Coleman, 1961, p. 9). But aren't these youngsters simply reflecting the values of their elders? Coleman asks: How much do adults value intellectual ability and nonconformity?

Edgar Friedenberg's explanation is more cynical. In a study of student values (1965) he

If schools enforce conformity, teen-agers themselves reenforce it on their own by valuing sameness in both behavior and clothing.

asked students to choose the "ideal" student from a fictitious list. First choice was a neat, helpful, other-directed good student. Last choice was the class nonconformist. Though his description contained no hint of antisocial behavior, the nonconformist was regarded with suspicion. Why do students reject any suggestion of individuality? Perhaps, Friedenberg argues, because schools have taken on the community's task of preparing students for the dull business of living and working in a bureaucratic society. Where nonconformity is feared, people must learn to submit to the judgments of others.

THE FUTURE OF EDUCATION

In the preceding section we focused on problems, but many educators believe there is hope for better schools. In this section we will look at new directions in education: the open classroom, which has captured the imagination of many educators; open admissions to college, which give minority students a second chance; Headstart and "Sesame Street," both designed to close the gap in school readiness; and research into the infant's learning capacity, which is revolutionizing our view of education.

The Open Classroom

To learn is to change. Education is a process that changes the learner. Learning involves interaction between the learner and his [or her] environment, and its effectiveness relates to the frequency, variety and intensity of interaction. Education, at best, is ecstatic. (Leonard, 1968)

[All children], without exception, [have] an innate and unquenchable drive to understand the world in which [they] live and to gain freedom and competence in it. Whatever truly adds to [their] understanding, [their] capacity for growth and pleasure, [their] sense of [their] own freedom, dignity, and worth may be said to be true education. (Holt, 1972)

Abandoning the traditional arrangement of desk-rows and "performances" by individual children, the open classroom strives for flexibility—for students as well as for teachers. (both, Bruce Roberts/Rapho Guillumette)

The *open classroom*, or open education as it is sometimes called, is a direct attack on the distrust and regimentation that underlie traditional education. It is a concerted effort to *de*institutionalize education by letting youngsters learn what they want to learn, when and how they want to learn it. The practice of fighting students' natural inclinations and curiosity and forcing education on them according to an imposed schedule and plan is banished.

In a typical open classroom the uniform rows of desks, all facing front, are eliminated. Instead, seating is flexible, changing as groups come together and move apart for instruction. The room is organized around various interest areas—science, art, reading, and so on. Each area contains a wide variety of appropriate materials, including books, maps, plants, and colorful containers. Instead of doling out materials, teachers make sure everything is accessible. Often students bring in their own things—not for the old-fashioned "show and tell," but to use and learn from.

In the open classroom teachers do not direct from the front but walk around helping students in their projects. Instead of dividing time into rigid blocks, they base their plans on what children need at a given moment. Sometimes classes move outside the school altogether:

Very often things can be learned by experiencing them firsthand. Why read about how a port operates when there is one short bus ride away? Why read a book about how steel is made if there is a steel plant nearby? Does it make sense to study about crime and police protection . . . without ever visiting a real police station? (Wurman, 1972, p. 12)

Outwardly an open classroom may look chaotic: in one corner two children are tend-

ing their soybeans; a girl is working with Cuisenaire rods in another spot, while a group sings a song in the middle of the room. To keep classrooms from degenerating into mere playgrounds, the teacher must plan carefully, maintaining structure and direction. Such a system imposes heavy demands on teachers, but frees them from their usual roles as "timekeeper, traffic cop, and disciplinarian" (Silberman, 1971).

What about discipline? Do open classrooms work only with middle-class children who have been taught from babyhood to be neat and obedient? Apparently not. Open education began with working-class British children, and many open classrooms operate in depressed areas here. Silberman visited some of these classes and found poor children from crime-ridden streets working busily at their projects. In one science area two children were rebuilding a washing machine motor and two others were fixing an old radio. In another class a boy excitedly described all he'd learned dissecting a pig. Equally important, children were enjoying themselves. One child told a visitor, "Last year we had to work all the time. Now we can play all the time." He was "playing" with a difficult mathematical game. Another child's father wrote asking if his son could come to school earlier; he couldn't seem to do everything he wanted during regular hours (Silberman, 1971).

Open education is less common in high schools, where classes are more specialized. However, some schools are taking tentative steps toward giving students greater freedom. Innovations range from doing away with student dress codes to giving credit for work in the community and for individual projects (Silberman, 1973, p. 87). However small, these changes are evidence of a new interest in reducing regimentation in high schools.

Open Admissions

In 1970, under pressure from minority groups, the City University of New York opened its doors to *every* high-school graduate. The program was extremely controversial, for it went right to the heart of the conflict between the ideals of equal opportunity and selectivity. Minority groups argued that they were not responsible for the poor quality of ghetto schools. They demanded another chance for ghetto children to display their talents. Although they agreed in principle, university officials were fearful that teachers would lower standards, depriving better-prepared students of a quality education. Could mass education *and* quality education coexist on a massive scale?

Researchers were waiting when the first New York City open admissions classes graduated in 1974. The results seem mixed, though accurate figures are hard to obtain. What figures there are seem to indicate higher drop-out rates for open admission students, though not too much higher than for regular students. At City College, for example, 55 percent of traditional students who entered in 1970 were still enrolled by the fall of 1973. Of the open admissions students, 43 percent were still in school (Maeroff, March 17, 1974).

Drop-out rates do not tell the whole story, of course. Open admissions have led to overcrowded facilities; remedial programs are frustratingly inadequate. Some believe that standards have dropped, partly as a result of pressure on teachers not to fail too many open admissions students. Once again the educational community must do battle with an old issue: Should college be only for the talented elite or is it the right of everyone, regardless of formerly displayed talent? In June 1974 some proud students—once considered failures—received diplomas because open admissions had given them a second chance. For them, if for no one else, the answer was clear.

Preschool Education

Many educators are attacking the problem of inequality not from the top, but from the bottom. If poor children come to school already behind, why not solve the problem at its source, by changing their preschool environment?

Headstart In 1965 the Office of Economic Opportunity began a preschool program for disadvantaged children. Project Headstart aimed at teaching poor children the word and number skills middle-class children learn at home. Though Headstart teachers concentrated on cognitive skills, the children received medical and nutritional attention as well. By 1969 Headstart was spending about $1,400 per child, compared to the public schools' $700 ("Following Up on Headstart," 1969).

What were the effects? A series of tests in 1969 found no significant difference between Headstart children and others once they entered school. But the Headstart children did show superiority in learning readiness. How can we account for these mixed results? Some felt the tests were inadequate; others believed the schools might be undoing all of Headstart's good work ("How Head a Head Start?" 1969). Still others faulted Headstart programs themselves for being too rigid, too "middle-class" to be useful to minority children (Smith, 1969). No one disputes that Headstart provided the opportunity to treat a lot of neglected health problems, however. And it did generate important research in the area of preschool education—research that is continuing.

"Sesame Street" While the debate on Headstart continued, a new television show, "Sesame Street," began making headlines. The show's creators applied the flashy, fast-paced techniques of advertising to teaching the alphabet, numbers, and other basic skills. With its genial adults and appealing monsters (the voracious Cookie Monster, Oscar the Grouch, who lives in a garbage can, and Big Bird), "Sesame Street" was an immediate hit with its young audience. Parents liked it too. But what about its more serious purpose? Did "Sesame Street" really teach children "recognition of letters, numbers, and simple counting ability"? Did it encourage "reasoning skills, vocabulary and an increased awareness of self and world," as the producers claimed?

In 1970 the Educational Testing Service reported the results of a two-year study of the "Sesame Street" audience. They found that children who watched the show regularly gained significantly over children who

"Sesame Street," a highly popular preschool television program, successfully combines learning and playing. (Charles Rowan/ © 1973 Children's Television Workshop)

watched only occasionally, or not at all (see figure 16:3). Children from poor homes showed the greatest improvement, particu- larly those whose mothers watched and dis- cussed the show with them (Ball and Bogatz, 1970; Malcolm, 1970).

figure 16:3 Sesame Street: First year report card:

Percentage of items answered correctly by all disadvantaged children at pretest and posttest

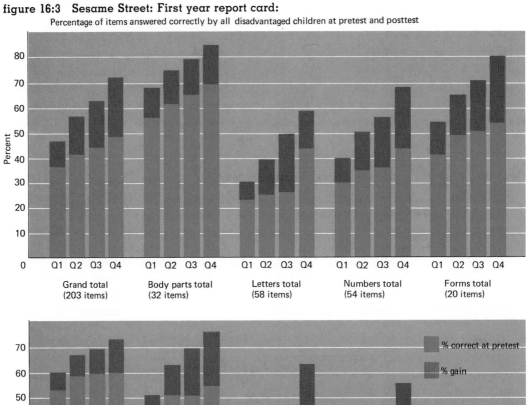

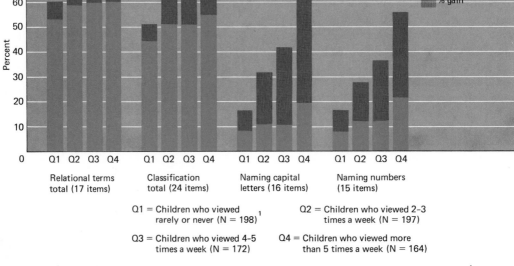

Q1 = Children who viewed rarely or never (N = 198)[1]

Q2 = Children who viewed 2–3 times a week (N = 197)

Q3 = Children who viewed 4–5 times a week (N = 172)

Q4 = Children who viewed more than 5 times a week (N = 164)

SOURCE: Educational Testing Service

[1] Number tested

"Sesame Street" seemed to affect attitudes as well as skills. Second-year research showed regular watchers were readier for school, had better attitudes toward school, and were less racist than nonwatchers (Ball and Bogatz, 1971). One startling finding was that three-year-olds showed the greatest gains in all cognitive areas. Parents used to worry about "pushing" very young children. The study of "Sesame Street" supported the view that very young children learn quickly.

Infant Education Recently the Harvard Pre-school Project rated a group of three- to six-year-olds according to seventeen specific intellectual and social skills (the ability to plan and carry out projects, the ability to attract and hold adults' attention, etc.). Using teachers' reports and their own observations, the researchers divided the children into two groups: an "A" group of very competent children, and a "C" group of those less able to cope. What made the difference?

Researchers turned their attention to toddlers, aged one to three. They found that children with "A skills" had received special attention from their mothers during a critical age period: from ten months to one and one-half years. Not that these mothers hovered over their infants: some, in fact, worked outside the home. Instead, in a very informal way they created a learning environment for their children. They provided plenty of toys and other objects, and gave children considerable physical freedom. An ordinary event, such as a bath, often became an occasion for an informal lesson: "Show me your knee. Now where are your toes?" Later, these mothers answered questions and provided information when asked. None had really tried to teach in any formal way (Pines, 1971).

Studies like this remind us again of an important distinction: education is not the same as schooling. The research on schools by educational sociologists suggests that, *as presently constituted*, schools serve mainly to legitimate inequalities and to prepare students for entering an organizational society. Efforts to change this abound. How much difference they will make remains to be seen.

---

summary

Individually and collectively Americans are deeply concerned about education. Is our faith in formal schooling justified? In the modern world, schools are a vital link between the individual and society. The primary goals of education are *cultural and political socialization, instruction* (teaching young people the knowledge and skills to perform necessary work), *selecting and developing talent*, and *innovation* (directly through research, and indirectly through social involvement in social problems).

How well does the American school system perform these varied and sometimes conflicting functions? Traditionally our schools have acted on the assumption that cultural integration depends on minorities giving up their different ways. Books on Indian and black history did not exist until recently. Today, however, blacks and other minorities are resisting assimilation. This is one of the issues in the busing controversy.

Statistics indicate that our schools do not even teach some children (perhaps a million) how to read. Is it because these children attend substandard ghetto or rural schools? Coleman's massive national study of school districts suggests that socioeconomic background has more effect on performance than school does; Astin's research confirms this on the college level. Coleman argues that truly equal education means teaching all children the same skills, not giving unequally prepared children the same chance to learn as best they can.

Does our school system select the brightest youngsters, regardless of socioeconomic background, for advanced education? Apparently not. Most of the small percentage who graduate from college are middle- and upper-class students. *Tracking* (ability grouping) disqualifies many lower-class youngsters at an early age, subjecting them to self-fulfilling expectations of low achievement. Colleges perform the hidden function of *cooling out* others who unrealistically expect to complete college.

Does an education guarantee that a person will "get ahead"? Although graduates earn considerably more than drop-outs do, education accounts for only part of this gap. In addition, as the number of people who obtain degrees increases, the value of a degree in the job market declines. But education is important in its own right; after all, an average student spends a thousand hours a year in school.

The social structure of school shapes students' and teachers' experiences. Kindergarten is an initiation into the role of student. There children learn to follow routines and obey orders. This is part of the *hidden curriculum*: learning to deal with absolute authority, to live in a crowd (but act as if alone), and to withstand constant evaluation by peers as well although their standards usually do not include academic excellence. (Nor, Coleman points out, do their parents' standards.)

What can be done to improve schools? Open classrooms are a direct attack on the distrust and regimentation of traditional schools. Education is structured around children's natural curiosity, not imposed schedules. Open admissions are an attack on inequality in education, a true second chance for over 40 percent of the minority students who enrolled in college in New York. Headstart was designed to close the gap in school readiness between poor and affluent students *before* they enter school. Although not as effective as hoped, it has solved other problems and provided the base for further research. Studies of "Sesame Street," a television show that seems to improve the basic skills of children who watch regularly, confirm that education can and perhaps should begin earlier than first grade.

glossary

education Both formal and informal lessons in the skills and values of one's culture.

open admissions The policy of some cities and states to admit every high-school graduate to a college or university.

open classroom An educational environment that aims to increase learning by decreasing regimentation. Children are encouraged to develop their own interests, rather than being tied to inflexible routines.

pygmalion effect The effect of teacher expectations on learning and performance, independent of students' aptitudes.

schooling Formal instruction in a classroom setting.

tracking Grouping children according to their scores on aptitude and achievement tests.

references

David Armor, "The Evidence on Busing," *The Public Interest*, no. 28 (Summer 1972): 90–126.

Alexander W. Astin, "Undergraduate Achievement and Institutional 'Excellence,'" *Science*, vol. 161, no. 3842 (August 16, 1968): 661–68.

Samuel Ball and Gerry Ann Bogatz, "A Summary of the Major Findings in 'The First Year of Sesame Street: An Evaluation'." Princeton, N.J.: Educational Testing Service, October 1970.

———, "A Summary of the Major Findings in 'The Second Year of Sesame Street: An Evaluation'." Princeton, N.J.: Educational Testing Service, November 1971.

Daniel Bell, *The Coming of the Post-Industrial Society*, New York: Basic Books, 1973.

Ivar Berg, *Education and Jobs: The Great Training Robbery*. New York: Praeger, 1970.

Lehman L. Brightman, "Mental Genocide," *Inequality in Education*, no. 7 (February 1971): 15–19.

Urie Bronfenbrenner, *Two Worlds of Childhood*. New York: Russell Sage Foundation, 1970.

Burton R. Clark, "The 'Cooling-out' Function in Higher Education," *American Journal of Sociology*, vol. 65 (May 1960): 567–76.

David K. Cohen, "Public Schools: The Next Decade," *Dissent* (April 1971).

James S. Coleman, *The Adolescent Society*. New York: Free Press, 1961.

———, "Equal Schools or Equal Students?" *The Public Interest*, no. 4 (Summer 1966).

Leonard Covello, *The Heart Is the Teacher*. New York: McGraw-Hill, 1958.

Current Population Reports, "Literacy in the United States: November 1969," series P–20, no. 217 (March 10, 1971).

Digest of Educational Statistics, Office of Education, Department of Health, Education, and Welfare. Washington, D.C.: Government Printing Office, 1970.

William E. Farrell, "School Integration Resisted in Cities of North," *The New York Times* (May 13, 1974): 24.

Warren G. Findley and Miriam M. Bryan, *Ability Grouping, 1970: Status, Impact, and Alternatives*. Atlanta: University of Georgia, Center for Educational Improvement, 1970.

"Following Up on Headstart," *The New Republic* (April 12, 1969): 12–13.

Edgar Z. Friedenberg, *Coming of Age in America: Growth and Acquiescence*. New York: Vintage, 1965.

———, "Status and Role in Education," *The Humanist* (September–October 1968).

"Goals of the Headstart Program," Letter to the Editor, *The New York Times* (July 10, 1971).

David A. Goslin, *The School in Contemporary Society*. Chicago: Scott, Foresman, 1965.

Harry L. Gracey, "Learning the Student Role: Kindergarten as Academic Boot Camp," in Dennis H. Wong and Harry L. Gracey, eds., *Readings in Introductory Sociology*, New York: Macmillan, 1972.

W. Lea Hansen and Burton A. Weisbrod, "The Distribution of Costs and Direct Benefits of Public Higher Education: The Case of California," in Harry G. Johnson and Burton A. Weisbrod, eds., *The Daily Economist,* Englewood Cliffs, N.J.: Prentice-Hall, 1969.

Robert J. Havighurst and Bernice Neugarten, *Society and Education*, Boston: Allyn & Bacon, 1968.

Godfrey Hodgson, "Do Schools Make a Difference?" *The Atlantic*, vol. 213 (March 1973): 35–46.

E. Adamson Hoebel, *Anthropology*, 4th ed. New York: McGraw-Hill, 1972.

John Holt, *How Children Fail*. New York: Pitman, 1964.

———, *The Underachieving School*, New York: Dell, 1972.

"How Head a Head Start?" *The New Republic* (April 26, 1969): 8–9.

Ivan Illich, *Deschooling Society*. New York: Harper & Row, 1970.

Philip W. Jackson, *Life in Classrooms*. New York: Holt, Rinehart and Winston, 1968.

Christopher Jencks, *Inequality: A Reassessment of the Effect of Family and Schooling in America*. New York: Basic Books, 1972.

Jerome Kagan, "The Poor Are Educable," *The New York Times Annual Education Review* (January 16, 1974): 57ff.

Stanley Karnow, "China-Journal-IV," *The New Republic* (July 28 and August 4, 1973): 9–21.

Michael B. Katz, *Class, Bureaucracy, and Schools: The Illusion of Educational Change in America*. New York: Praeger, 1971.

Louis L. Knowles and Kenneth Prewitt, eds., *Institutional Racism in America*. Englewood Cliffs, N.J.: Prentice-Hall, 1969.

Herbert R. Kohl, *The Open Clasroom: A Practical Guide to a New Way of Teaching*. New York: Vintage, 1969.

James W. Kuhn, "The Misuse of Education: The Problem of Schooling for Employment," in Berg, 1970.

Paul Lauter and Florence Howe, "How the School System Is Rigged for Failure," in *The Conspiracy of the Young*, New York: World, 1970.

Eleanor Leacock, *Teaching and Learning in City*

Schools. New York: Basic Books, 1969.

George B. Leonard, *Education and Ecstasy*, New York: Delacorte, 1968.

Gene I. Maeroff, "City U. Open Admissions Held a Success," *The New York Times* (March 17, 1974): 1, 52.

———, "Effects of Open Admission Stir New Dispute at City U." *The New York Times* (June 7, 1974): 1, 20.

Andrew H. Malcolm, "'Sesame Street' Rated Excellent," *The New York Times* (November 5, 1970).

New York State Commission on the Quality, Cost, and Financing of Elementary and Secondary Education, *The Fleischmann Report.* New York: Viking, 1973.

Ned O'Gorman, "Headstart: The Torment of ABC's," *The New York Times* (June 8, 1971): 39.

G. A. Pettitt, *Primitive Education in North America.* Berkeley: University of California Press, 1946.

Maya Pines, "A Child's Mind Is Shaped Before Age 2," *Life*, vol. 71 (December 17, 1971): 63–68.

"Poor Reader Sues Coast Educators," *The New York Times* (September 16, 1973).

Robert Reinhold, "Educators Seek Success Factors," *The New York Times* (November 11, 1973): 38.

———, "Johnny Still Can't Read Very Well," *The New York Times* (June 16, 1974): 39.

Donald W. Robinson, "An Interview with Christopher Jencks," *Phi Delta Kappan*, vol. 54, no. 4 (December 1972).

Robert Rosenthal and Lenore Jacobson, *Pygmalion in the Classroom.* New York: Holt, Rinehart and Winston, 1968.

Walter E. Schaefer, Carol Olexa, and Kenneth Polk,

"Programmed for Social Class: Tracking in the High School," in Gary T. Marx, ed., *Muckraking Sociology: Research as Social Criticism,* New York: Transaction Books, 1972.

Patricia Cayo Sexton, *The American School: A Sociological Analysis.* Englewood Cliffs, N.J.: Prentice-Hall, 1967.

Charles E. Silberman, *Crisis in the Classroom: The Remaking of American Education.* New York: Vintage, 1971.

———, "Murder in the Schoolroom: Part I. How the Public Schools Kill Dreams and Mutilate Minds," *The Atlantic*, vol. 225 (June 1970): 82–94.

———, *The Open Classroom Reader,* New York: Vintage, 1973.

Charles Smith, "Poor Head Start and Its Children," *The New Republic* (June 21, 1969): 11–13.

Abraham J. Tannenbaum, "Adolescents' Attitudes Toward Academic Brilliance," Ph.D. dissertation, New York University, 1960.

"Testing and Tracking: Bias in the Classroom," *Inequality in Education*, no. 14 (July 1973).

Martin Trow, "Reflections on the Transition from Mass to Universal Higher Education," *Daedalus* (Winter 1970): 1–42.

Ralph H. Turner, "Sponsored and Contest Mobility and the School System," *American Sociological Review*, vol. 25 (1960): 855–67.

Rush Welter, *Popular Education and Democratic Thought in America.* New York: Columbia University Press, 1962.

"Who's Afraid of Big, Bad TV?" *Time* (November 23, 1970): 60–73.

Richard Saul Wurman, ed., *Yellow Pages of Learning Resources.* Cambridge, Mass.: MIT Press, 1972.

for further study

Becoming a Teacher. Although the teaching profession attracts many college students, they rarely know much about it. The best start is *Crisis in the Classroom*, by Charles E. Silberman (New York: Random House, 1970), which is really a study of teaching. The first parts describe what happens in American classrooms, reforms that have failed, and reforms that work. The last two chapters analyze teaching as a profession and schools of education. More scientific is N. L. Gage, ed., *Handbook of Research on Teaching* (Chicago: Rand, 1963). Although dated, it covers so many aspects of teaching with such intelligence that it is still widely used. More recently, T. Leggatt has analyzed "Teaching as a Profession" in John A. Jackson, ed., *Professions and Professionalization* (London: Cambridge University Press, 1970). Robert J. Havighurst and Daniel U. Levine include good materials on teaching in *Education in Metropolitan Areas* (Boston: Allyn, 1971). This short list does not include many fine books on how to teach well by individual teachers such as Jonathan Kozol, Herbert Kohl, James Herndon, and John Holt.

Community Control. Education has become so much the centerpiece of technological society that teachers claim only they are competent to run it, but parents (particularly minority parents) want local control. This fundamental conflict over the social structure of schools is put in historical perspective by Joseph Cronin in *The Control of Urban Schools* (New York: Free Press, 1973). The battles of the 1960s are well described in Mario Fantini et al., *Community Control and the Urban School* (New York: Praeger, 1970), and Annette Rubinstein, ed., *Schools Against Children* (New York: Monthly Review, 1970). In the eyes of some, teachers' unions have become the enemies of community control. A thought-provoking but biased book is *Teachers and Power*, by Robert Braun (New York: Simon & Schuster, 1972). One system that might bypass problems of community control is vouchers. The best book on this fresh idea is *Education Vouchers*, edited by George LaNoue (New York: Teachers College Press, 1972).

Roots of Schools Today. Many of the institutional arrangements and educational practices today cannot be understood unless one finds out why they started that way decades ago. A group of new historians have given us a bounty of lively books that do just this: Michael B. Katz, *Class, Bureaucracy and Schools* (New York: Praeger, 1971); Carl F. Kaestle, *The Evolution of an Urban School System: New York 1750–1850* (Cambridge, Mass.: Harvard University Press, 1973); Raymond E. Callahan, *Education and the Cult of Efficiency* (Chicago: University of Chicago Press, 1962); and Diane Ravitch, *The Great School Wars: New York City 1805–1972* (New York: Basic, 1974). Even the open classroom is not new, and no student interested in educational reforms should miss Lawrence Cremin's history of the first progressive movement, *Transformation of the School* (New York: Alfred A. Knopf, 1961). Cremin has also written about education *before* what we now know as public schools in *American Education: The Colonial Experience 1607–1783* (New York: Harper & Row, 1972).

"This is the age of the secular city. . . . The world looks less and less to religious rules and rituals for its morality or its meanings. For some, religion provides a hobby, for others a mark of national or ethnic identification, for still others, an esthetic delight. For fewer and fewer does it provide an inclusive and commanding system of personal and cosmic values and explanations" (Cox, 1966, p. 3).

Perhaps it is true that fewer American city dwellers are heeding the chimes from a steeple. But many of them are now hearing the chants and bells of the orange-robed adherents of Hare Krishna. Gods and religions are not disappearing from the American scene; new ones, new movements such as the Jesus People and the charismatics are emerging. And it takes a guru with a persuasive message indeed to pack thousands into the Houston Astrodome as Maharaj Ji did for Millennium '73. Religious behavior in America has not vanished. What is happening is that American religion,

RELIGION

like American society itself, is undergoing complex and unusual changes.

The reaction of a theologian to these changes might be despair or delight. The reaction of a sociologist would be neither to applaud nor decry but to determine what the changes are and what they mean. Sociologists, unlike theologians, are not primarily concerned with the intricacies of religious theory or with the validity of religious practice. Instead, they are concerned with identifying the beliefs individuals hold, with finding out how these beliefs affect both the individual and society, and with discovering how religious beliefs change over time. In this chapter we will investigate what makes up a religion, examine the functions it fulfills for the individual and for society, and explore its role in social change. We will also take a look at the American religious scene not only to assess how religion influences personal life, but to examine the changes occurring today within this scene.

DEFINING RELIGION

The remains of flowers found among the skeletons of a Neanderthal burial site, indicating some kind of burial rite, suggest that human religiosity may extend as far back as 60,000 years. The massive slabs of Stonehenge in England, the temple ruins of Greece from Rhodes to Corfu, the monumental heads carved from volcanic rock on the slopes of Easter Island all attest to the existence of religious behavior among different peoples in different times. What can sociologists say about this pervasive human phenomenon?

Emile Durkheim in *The Elementary Forms of Religious Life* (1912), defined *religion* as a "unified system of beliefs and practices" that pertain to "sacred things" and that unite adherents of the system "into one single moral community" (Durkheim, 1965, p. 47). There are four elements of Durkheim's definition that merit our attention: sacred things, religious beliefs, religious practices, and the moral community.

Sacred Things

All aspects of human experience, according to Durkheim, can be divided into two radically and diametrically opposed categories: the sacred and the profane. The *sacred* is ideal and transcends everyday existence; it is extraordinary, potentially dangerous, awe-inspiring, fear-inducing. The *profane* is mundane and ordinary. Almost anything can be sacred: a grasshopper, a cross, a stone. These are sacred only because some community has marked them as sacred. Once established as sacred, however, they become symbols of religious beliefs, sentiments, and practices.

The sacred may be a supernatural being—god or ghost. Those who believe in one god—the world's 985 million Christians, 14.5 million Jews, and 471 million Muslims—are monotheists. Those who worship more than one god—like yesterday's Greeks and today's Hindus—are polytheists. Some 472 million Hindus, for example, most of them in India, have a pantheon of five great gods—Krishna, Vishnu, Rama, Lakshmi, and Siva—all of whom are subordinate to "the One." Gods are not alone among the sacred. Many worship the sacred ghost or ancestor spirit. Such spirits are also imbued with supernatural qualities, but they are of human rather than divine origin. Shintoism, for instance, with its 60 million disciples, mostly in Japan, is based on reverence toward family ancestors.

A moral or philosophical principle can also be sacred. Three Asian religions—Buddhism, Confucianism, and Taoism—all focus on the achievement of certain ethical and spiritual ideals. Buddhism, with more than 300 million adherents, is less concerned with the God Buddha than with his message of the "four noble truths," the first being that existence is sorrow, and that for anyone to attain *nirvana*, a state of spiritual detachment, he or she must follow a "noble eightfold path." Some of the steps along the way include right thought, right action, right contemplation, and right meditation.

Totems are another example of Durkheim's "sacred things." They are worshiped by primitive people the world over—in North America, Melanesia, and Australia. The totemic object may be a sacred animal, such as the kangaroo or the bear, or even a vegetable, such as corn or grass seed. The *totem* is a symbol, a repository of deep, group-based sentiments and feelings. It is worshiped as a god or an ancestor, or both, and it generally possesses some special quality or significance for the religious community—the capacity, for instance, to provide unique bene-

This stone shrine in the Arizona desert is a sacred place to the Navajo Indians. Symbolic sacrifices are offered today, as they were generations ago, to secure divine favor. (New York Public Library)

fits or to inflict great harm. Totemist religious rituals often include mimicking the behavior of the totem or, on very special occasions, eating it. Symbols of the totem are sometimes tatooed on the skin or carved in solid objects, like the grotesque poles of some American Indians.

On certain islands of Oceania, a warrior successful in battle while using a particular spear will attribute his victory to *mana*—a force that entered his spear. A supernatural force, in other words, is still another example of a sacred thing although it has no shape of its own and inhabits living or inanimate things. Supernatural forces may be good or bad—the good being called *mana*, a word of Melanesian and Polynesian origin. If a farmer high in the Tongan Island mountains should plant a crop next to a large boulder and the crop grows well, he might feel that the boulder has mana. Any good luck charm such as a rabbit's foot is a Western equivalent of

that boulder. Objects or beings with mana are to be associated with or stroked or handled so that their good qualities rub off. Evil supernatural forces, on the other hand, also reside in objects and beings and are *taboo*; they are not to be touched or approached because they cause bad luck or trouble. Typical taboos might include animals, often a totem animal, which are not to be killed, or wooded areas that hunters are forbidden to enter.

Be it a force, a god, a ghost, a moral principle, or a totemic object, all are elements of Durkheim's definition of religion. All are forms of the sacred and all bear witness to the existence of religious behavior.

Religious Beliefs

Religious beliefs explain the sacred and determine and give significance to religious practices. Durkheim defines *religious beliefs* as "the representations which express the nature of sacred things and the relations which they sustain, either with each other or with profane things" (Durkheim, 1965). These beliefs are held not just intellectually but emotionally. The beliefs may appeal to the subconscious as well as the conscious.

Not all who profess a certain religion accept all its beliefs with complete conviction, a point demonstrated by sociologists Charles Glock and Rodney Stark. Gallup Polls have consistently found that about 97 percent of Americans believe in God, a high level of belief compared with Europeans. But how sure people are of this belief is another matter. To ask churchgoers whether they believe in God might seem silly, but Glock and Stark did so by testing the degree of belief held by members in different churches and social groups, and they came up with some not so ridiculous answers. They found that whereas 99 percent of the southern Baptists unequivocally believed in God, only 81 percent of the Catholics and 41 percent of the Congregationalists were quite so certain. Few of those

table 17:1 BELIEF IN GOD (by percent)[1]

WHICH OF THE FOLLOWING STATEMENTS COMES CLOSEST TO WHAT YOU BELIEVE ABOUT GOD?	CONGREGATIONALISTS	EPISCOPALIANS	DISCIPLES OF CHRIST	PRESBYTERIANS	AMERICAN BAPTISTS	SOUTHERN BAPTISTS	SECTS	TOTAL PROTESTANTS	CATHOLICS
"I know God really exists and I have no doubts about it."	41	63	76	75	78	99	96	71	81
"While I have doubts, I feel that I do believe in God."	34	19	20	16	18	1	2	17	13
"I find myself believing in God some of the time, but not at other times."	4	2	0	1	0	0	0	2	1
"I don't believe in a personal God, but I do believe in a higher power of some kind."	16	12	0	7	2	0	1	7	3
"I don't know whether there is a God and I don't believe there is any way to find out."	2	2	0	1	0	0	0	1	1
"I don't believe in God."	1	*	0	0	0	0	0	*	0
No answer	2	1	4	*	2	0	1	1	1
PERCENT =	100	99	100	100	100	100	100	99	100
Number of respondents	(151)	(416)	(50)	(495)	(141)	(79)	(255)	(2326)	(545)

[1]Asterisks indicate fewer than .5 percent.

SOURCE: Charles Y. Glock and Rodney Stark, *Religion and Society in Tension* (Chicago: Rand McNally, 1965), p. 91.

surveyed absolutely denied the existence of God or professed to being agnostics. They merely expressed some degree of doubt or believed not in God but in a "higher power" (Glock and Stark, 1965, pp. 90–91).

Religious Practices

Beliefs are the conceptual aspect of religion; practices and rituals are its visible expression. Practices vary from the simple gesture of removing a hat upon entering a church to the elaborate festivals, ceremonies, and parades of primitive tribes. In a study of primitive religions Anthony Wallace (1966, pp. 53–66) determined that rituals can include anything from the use of drums to the use of drugs. Praying, singing, declaiming, drinking, sacrificing, mimicking, congregating, drugging, feasting, yelling, dancing—all may be ritual activities.

Durkheim defined *rites* as "the rules of conduct which prescribe how a man should comport himself in the presence of sacred objects" (Durkheim, 1965, p. 56). A ritual can recall an aspect of religious belief, honor the sacred, or establish a relationship between the believer and the sacred. Ritual is usually highly symbolic, often condensing elements of belief into a single activity and touching the deepest responsive chords of the participants. Its power transcends theology.

For example, the Lord's Supper or Eucharist has had many theological interpretations over the centuries, and indeed it is a pre-Christian ritual taken over and retheologized. The theology of the Catholics is not the same as that of the Lutherans or the Reformed or the Orthodox, yet the ritual is age-old and has continuing power.

As with beliefs, people who profess a religion do not necessarily subscribe to all its rituals. Not all Protestants who believe in Christ go to church, and not all others who do go to church take part in the Eucharist. A 1961 study of religious practices in Detroit, for example, found that among members of the three major American faiths, Catholics were the most ritualistic, with 70 percent attending church regularly (Lenski, 1961, pp. 33–36). Nationwide in 1973, with 40 percent of the populace attending religious services regularly, Catholics again led, with 55 percent, Protestants came next with 37 percent, and Jews were last with 19 percent (Gallup Poll, 1974, p. 3).

table 17:2 CHURCH ATTENDANCE DURING AN AVERAGE WEEK, 1973 (by percent)

(Projects to 55 million adults)

National	40
Catholic	55
Protestant	37
Jewish	19[1]
Men	35
Women	43
White	40
Nonwhite	41
College	40
High school	38
Grade school	43
18–29 years	28
30–49 years	41
50 and over	46
East	38
Midwest	43
South	44
West	29

[1]Since Jews represent about 3 percent of the U.S. population, the number included in the 1973 audit (179) is necessarily small.

SOURCE: George Gallup, "Churchgoing Decline of Last Decade Result of Sliding Catholic Attendance," *The Gallup Poll*, January 13, 1974, p. 3. Copyright 1974, Field Enterprises, Inc.

The Catholic Mass and Jewish seder are religious rituals. They are similar in form—both are commemorative meals—but the seder is celebrated by families at home, while the Mass is celebrated by a congregation in church. (Left, Ray Ellis/Rapho Guillumette. Right, Hanna Schreiber/Rapho Guillumette)

Attendance at church or synagogue is not, of course, an absolute indicator of personal involvement in religion. Those who do not go to church may stay away from services for nonreligious reasons. One former parishioner put it this way, "There's too much dressing up for church these days; he used to go in his overalls just as good as anybody. But now, it won't do for people to go without being all dressed up and we just haven't got the clothes for that" (Lynd and Lynd, in De-merath, 1965, p. 13). Motivations for church attendance vary tremendously. Is it to pay homage to a supreme being or to pay attention to styles? Is it to hear the word of the prophets or to hear a word about profits? Does it fulfill an inner need or is it merely a habit? "Why, it just never occurred to me to question church going!" said one regular attender. "Most of the time I am just plain bored," said another, "but feel I ought to go" (Lynd and Lynd, in Demerath, 1965, p. 13).

Moreover, not all ritual occurs in church or synagogue. Concentrating on synagogue attendance among Jews, for instance, overlooks the importance of home ritual. More than one-third of American Jews perform rituals at home often enough for their household to be categorized as "traditional" (Goldstein and Goldsheider, 1968, p. 196).

The Moral Community

For Durkheim the foundation of religion was the moral community. "The idea of society is the soul of religion," he wrote (Durkheim, 1965, p. 419). He felt community and religion were inseparable for two reasons—because religion celebrates community and because religion creates community.

Durkheim based his theories about religion and the community on studies of preliterate societies. He observed that in such societies each person is highly dependent on his fellow tribesmen for protection and sustenance. To remain a member of such a society, the individual must abide by its mores, work for its preservation, and sacrifice personal desires for the good of the community. Durkheim speculated that the idea of divinity orig-

inated from the individual's experience of society as a powerful force transcending human desires and life span. He further speculated that the first gods were anthropomorphized versions of primitive man's view of his community. In short, the worship of gods, Durkheim felt, was the celebration and deification of sentiments of community life, and all societies, not simply primitive ones, feel the need for "upholding and reaffirming at regular intervals the collective sentiments and the collective ideas which make its unity and its personality" (Durkheim, 1965, p. 474).

Durkheim also maintained that religion and community are inseparable because religion sustains community. To him, a religion is born when a number of people worship together in a common faith. Close social contact encourages similar sets of values and thus unites persons in a "moral community," which has its own beliefs and rituals. In addition, participation in the moral community can lead to feelings of belonging and the development of friendships. These ties of *communal involvement* are a significant dimension of religious behavior (Lenski, 1961).

The variation in communal involvement can be seen in the 1961 Detroit study. Respondents were asked questions that revealed not only how ritualistic they were, but how many of their friends and relatives were members of their religion. Ninety-six percent of the Jews reported that all or most of their close relatives were Jewish, an extremely high percentage that may be due to discrimination against Jews, which gives them less choice than Catholics and Protestants in their associates, or makes them distrust gentiles. Seventy-nine percent of the Catholics indicated most of their relatives were Catholic, and the corresponding percentage among Protestants was somewhat smaller. "And what about your friends? Are they of your faith?" the Detroiters were asked. Seventy-seven percent of the Jews said yes whereas only 44 percent of the Catholics and a slightly smaller percentage of the Protestants answered affirmatively. Though Jews do not attend services regularly, their religion still shapes their personal life (Lenski, 1961, pp. 33–36).

THE FUNCTIONS OF RELIGION

Sigmund Freud once wrote that religion was created expressly to reduce neurotic anxiety. He felt that man, torn between Oedipal desires for his mother and anger and fear with regard to his father, created and exalted a fearful god in his father's image so that his sexual and aggressive impulses could be checked. Benjamin Franklin once wrote that "all crimes will be punished and virtue rewarded either here or hereafter," a comforting view that God would indeed see to it that social injustices would never go uncorrected.

Whether one endorses these views or not, they do specify two functions of religion: Freud's relates to the individual, Franklin's relates to the community. These are the two categories under which we will examine the functions of religion.

Not all gods, despite Freud, are fearful. Concepts of gods in past and present religions vary. Zeus had his thunderbolts, true, but there have also been comforting gods, gods that increase fertility, gods that protect the hunter and traveler, gods that heal the sick and still the waters. The images of god, along with religious beliefs and practices, seem to fulfill certain individual and social needs, and their variety suggests that religion serves people in myriad ways.

Human Events in the Cosmic Order

Friday at sundown. The Sabbath comes in cold and clear during early spring in Minnesota. In the warm shelter of the Chabad House, the young women greet it with flickering Shabbas candles set on glistening white tablecloths. . . . Barbara is one of them. She is 20 years old, blue-eyed, blond. She is from Los Angeles, the product of a broken home and a half-dozen private schools.

"I had the whole cycle," she explains, matter-of-factly. "Drugs, sex, alienation. I couldn't stand being alone, or not being high. It was existence by escapism. Until a bitter realization that I was still alone—and traveling a horrible road."

Barbara surveys her new surroundings. "I've found peace here," she says, "and purpose." (Spiegel, 1974, p. 48)

Religious art, such as Michelangelo's painting of the Biblical story of the creation, serves two functions for society. It illustrates an explanation for the origin of life and provides people with an aesthetic experience. (Alinari/Scala)

One of the most important functions of religion is to offer answers and rules about life. Religion explains that human life is part of a divine scheme, and like it or not, that is why we are all here spinning through the universe. By following rules laid down by the gods, believers are assured that they will be at least virtuous and at best successful. If life is fraught with sorrow and hardships, religion again supplies answers—that the believer offended an important god or violated a taboo or failed to live according to the rules. If the offender makes amends but the woes still continue, religious teachings may also suggest that sorrow and hardship are really not very important after all because a far better existence awaits the believer in the hereafter.

This comfort in times of distress—particularly in the face of death—is an especially important function of religion. Many religions reassure their adherents that the soul lives on after death: some even provide detailed descriptions of its progress once it leaves the body.

Religion also serves to interpret and consecrate experience in this life. Most religions have some sort of puberty rites that mark the transition from childhood to adulthood. Many have ceremonies celebrating victory in war and the succession of a new ruler to head the state or community. All these ceremonies glorify human life and human achievement, and because they invoke supernatural powers, they offer assurance that the divine is aware of and gives blessing to human affairs.

Religion can also bestow a sense of identity on its followers. Eric Lincoln, a sociologist who has done participant studies of the Black Muslims, has described the spiritual transformation that sometimes occurs when a black person accepts Islam:

The true believer . . . casts off at last his old self and takes on a new identity. He changes his name, his religion, his homeland, his "natural" language, his moral and cultural values, his very purpose in living. He is no longer a Negro, so long despised by the white man that he has come almost to despise himself. Now he is a Black Man—divine, ruler of the universe, different only in degree from Allah Himself. . . . Now he is a Muslim, bearing in himself the power of the Black Nation and its glorious destiny. (Lincoln, 1961, pp. 108–109)

If religion can function to provide a sense of identity, it can also function to provide, in a sense, a loss of identity through dissociation. Anthony F. C. Wallace has pointed out that religion can generate an ecstatic or visionary experience by "crudely and directly manipulating the physiological processes." Such an experience, he says, is often induced by drugs:

Plains Indians, for instance, eat or drink infusions of *peyote*, a cactus containing a number of alkaloids including mescaline, which is a potent hallucinogen. Ancient Greek celebrants of the great god Pan chewed the intoxicating leaves of ivy to induce ecstatic abandon. The Koryak, Chuckchee, and other Siberian peoples chewed the crimson mushroom fly agaric (*Amanita muscaria*) to bring on episodes of euphoria. Scandinavian *berserkers* ate certain kinds of mushrooms to achieve dissociation. Some modern Americans experiment with such "psychedelic" drugs as lysergic acid dyethylamide (LSD) in the hope of spiritual growth. (Wallace, 1966, p. 55)

The reassurances offered by religion have a powerful effect on the human psyche, and many psychologists have felt that religious behavior is so prevalent because it alleviates anxiety. Freud, as we have noted, believed that religion was deliberately established to relieve tensions. In a study of primitive culture on the Trobriand Islands in the Southwest Pacific, Malinowski found that religion lessened the anxiety of fishermen heading out to the high seas. The islanders were excellent fishermen who sought their catch both in lagoon and in the open ocean. The lagoon was calm and protected and, when

fish were plentiful, fishing there was easy. On the open ocean, however, the seas and winds could be dangerous. Malinowski observed that before fishing in the lagoon, the fishermen made no special preparations, but before going to the open sea, the men invoked the help of their gods through a variety of rituals. He concluded that when the Trobriand islanders knew they were entering a dangerous situation they felt the need for religion and divine aid. When they were confident of their skills and their safety, they felt religion was expendable (Malinowski, 1954).

Can Science Replace Religion? Malinowski's example raises the possibility that religion might disappear if mankind found other means of coping with the world. Could scientific knowledge and technological skills ever provide human beings with such confidence in their abilities that the functions of religion would become irrelevant, thus causing religion itself to disappear? Could mankind become so self-sufficient and capable that people would no longer need the protection and guidance of a god?

Science does fulfill a vital role for man by providing answers about the universe, says anthropologist Clifford Geertz, but scientific inquiry cannot deal with all the problems that are part of man's experience. Geertz characterizes science as rational, objective, restrained, a branch of knowledge that uses conscious doubt and systematic inquiry to disclose the natural laws behind everyday reality. He sees religion as requiring acceptance and commitment in dealing with ultimate truths of the cosmic order. Geertz finds three situations in which science must fail: when people are at the limit of their intellectual capacities and remain completely baffled; when they are faced with prolonged and acute suffering; and when they are confronted with overwhelming and senseless evil. In these instances, Geertz feels, science can offer no insight, no reassurance that man is not "adrift in an absurd world." Only the cosmic vision of religion can cope with these situations, and as long as they continue to be part of human existence, religion will have a place (Geertz, 1968).

Religion and the Community

Religion offers both norms of "right behavior" within a community and sanctions against antisocial acts. It can also provide a kind of social cement by offering ways of

---

RIMROCK AND HOMESTEAD

Forty miles apart in the vast stretches of western New Mexico lie the towns of Rimrock and Homestead. Both subsist primarily on farming, though both communities also raise some cattle. Both have similar soil, and both are approximately the same size. In fact, the two towns are very similar in any number of ways except for one crucial difference—the religion of their inhabitants. Life in these two small towns, then, shows the extent and nature of religious influence in the public sphere.

Rimrock was founded in the 1870s by a group of Mormons sent out by their church to settle and preach in the West. They arrived with a strong sense of group purpose and unity, and they built their houses together in the town, with their farmlands fanning out from the center. Their original sense of unity persisted through the years, bolstered by Mormon church beliefs and practices. By contrast, Homestead was first settled in the 1930s by migrants, like the uprooted, uncertain wayfarers described in *The Grapes of Wrath*. Of various religions and independent ways, the Homesteaders built their farms quite far from one another.

In the 1940s and 1950s, two parallel events occurred in the towns that reveal the impact religion can have on the life of a community's residents. After World War II, Rimrock had thirty-two veterans who were faced with the choice of remaining underemployed and poor in Rimrock or leaving the community. The Mormons wanted to keep their group together, so when an opportunity arose to buy a tract of land far too expensive for the veterans, the church welfare agency provided the funds and the land was set up as a cooperative ranch with the veteran-owners holding shares in the operation. In Homestead, a similar opportunity arose to acquire some useful land when the federal government offered to sell a sizable tract for ranching on a cooperative basis. The Homesteaders, however, refused the offer. They could not agree to work cooperatively because each wanted his own private building on the land.

The second incident involved a high-school gymnasium. Rimrock was presented with a plan for a gym and after discussing it in church and school meetings, the townspeople decided to build it with each man agreeing to give either fifty hours of his time or $50 in cash toward its construction. Despite some dissent over the plan, the town members contributed their shares and the gym was completed. The same plan for a gymnasium was put before the Homesteaders. At first, the community voted against it because residents did not want to commit themselves to working on the building. Later, when a little money became available, the town hired builders to do the job. When the money ran out, however, construction stopped and the gym remained half completed. In both instances, the Mormons' religious beliefs favored a political consensus that produced economic and social benefits for the community while the Homesteaders' independence and lack of cooperation bred economic and social weakness. Of course, it must be added that Rimrock and Homestead are isolated, homogeneous communities and that the influence of religion is not always so clear-cut.

SOURCE: Evon Vogt and Thomas F. O'Dea, "A Comparative Study of Values in Social Action in Two Southwestern Communities," in Milton Yinger, ed., *Religion, Society and the Individual: An Introduction to the Sociology of Religion* (New York: Macmillan, 1957), pp. 563–77.

atoning for infractions through prayers, fasting, or penance (see the box on p. 481).

Religious doctrine may do more than affect social behavior; it may also help legitimize—for better or worse—the community's social structure. Where wealth is distributed unevenly or one class is decidedly more privileged than another, religious doctrine may sanction the status quo and thus allay discontent. In fact, in cultures where wealth is privately rather than communally owned, there are many more reports or myths about divine intervention in human affairs. In these visitations, the gods tend to support the propertied groups and disapprove of social disruption, thereby strengthening the social structure when political institutions are incapable of doing so (Swanson, 1969, pp. 153–79). Religion can also encourage social tranquility by assuring that injustices will not go unrectified—as Franklin guarantees in his statement about crime being punished in the hereafter. With such confidence in divine justice, inequities are much easier to accept.

Civil Religion in America Unlike many countries, America does not have an established religion that buttresses and is buttressed by the power of the state. Separation of church and state was established first by practice and then by law in the Bill of Rights. However, sociologist Robert Bellah sees American civil and political life permeated with religious elements so coherent and of such importance for the American people that they constitute a national or "civil" religion (1970, pp. 168–86). To Bellah, a collection of potent beliefs, symbols and rituals, outside the church that pervades and helps legitimize the community is, in effect, a *civil religion*.

At almost every American state or political occasion, says Bellah, God plays an important role. He is mentioned in the pledge of allegiance, in legislative invocations, in all oaths of office, in party conventions, in courtroom procedures, in political speeches, and, inevitably, in presidential inaugural addresses. Even the nation's currency proclaims "In God We Trust." Bellah also points to the traditional feeling in the United States that the nation was established "under God," and that the government derives its legitimacy from its acknowledgment of God-ordained law and from its protection of God-given individual rights.

The God of American civil religion has a number of qualities that make him a unifying figure in a pluralistic society. He is universal rather than sectarian, and he is sufficiently impartial so that no religious group is offended. Also, he is not concerned with personal ends, such as salvation. Instead, the American god devotes his attention to law, justice, order, and other matters of interest to the entire community.

Every religion must have not only its gods but its symbols, its hymns and high priests, its martyrs and rituals. For the American civil religion, the symbols are the flag, the American eagle, and the monuments in Washington, D.C. and in many town squares; the hymns are the "Star-Spangled Banner" and "America, the Beautiful." Among its high priests are George Washington and Thomas Jefferson, and among its martyrs are Abraham Lincoln and John Kennedy. Its rituals commemorating and honoring important events and ideals include the Fourth of July, which, like Christmas, celebrates a significant birth; Memorial Day, which honors the sacrifices of its military men; and Thanksgiving Day, which commemorates the successful voyage across an alien sea and the founding of a new promised land.

Civil religion in America is not merely ceremonial or a matter of myths. A nation of different social, ethnic, religious, and regional groups, America has been bound together largely through a spirit of nationalism and a common dedication to a high political and moral good that its civil religion has inspired. Bellah does not, of course, confuse civil religion with mindless patriotism. He sees the nation's actions judged by a transcendent law: "The concept of civil religion simply points to the fact that some links between [religion, morality, and politics] seem to exist in all societies. At its best, civil religion would be realized in a situation where politics and morality are open to transcendent judgment" (Bellah, 1973, p. 20).

RELIGION AND SOCIAL CHANGE

Religion is created by society, yet it may also help to shape society. One of the issues in churches today is their degree of involvement in social movements and social change. Should the clergy prod the laity on civil rights, on Women's Liberation, on grape and lettuce boycotts? There are those among the laity who grumble that they are not in church to hear about grapes. Conversely, there are those who ask the church to speak out—on birth control, on political corruption, on minimum wages, on imperialistic wars. How religion views the society at large and its role in changing society depends in part upon its institutional form.

Church and Sect

Studies by Ernst Troeltsch (a sociologist of the early twentieth century) demonstrate the problem of institutionalizing religion. To Troeltsch the effectiveness of religion as an ongoing institution is often at odds with its social message. He views religious institutions as being basically either church or sect (Troeltsch, 1957); these, he says, differ from each other in size and in their attitudes toward religiosity and society. (Because church and sect are ideal types, however, any group may not conform to them in every respect.)

Troeltsch describes the *church* as a large, conservative, universalist institution. Most members are born into it, not converted to it. The church promises its members grace, but it makes few demands on them. Because it is large, it tends to acquire a certain amount of social and political power, which it more often than not maintains by becoming associated with government or the ruling classes. Thus the church accommodates itself to the claims of other powerful social-political institutions and tends to support the status quo. The Church of England would come close to fitting this ideal type.

The *sect*, on the other hand, is a small, exclusive, uncompromising fellowship of individuals seeking spiritual perfection. Members are voluntary converts drawn primarily from the lower classes, and their lives are pretty much controlled by the sect. Sects are usually characterized by asceticism, and their attitude toward society tends to be either indifferent or hostile. Most sects are concerned strictly with religious values and withdraw as much as possible from social matters; a few, however, are critical of the social order and have positive ideas about how to improve it.

Marx and Weber

Church or sect, Karl Marx believed that all religious institutions inhibited social change and revolution by legitimizing the status quo. Marx hoped in vain for an uprising among the working classes, and he felt that one reason

table 17:3 CHURCH AND SECT

CHARACTERISTIC	CHURCH	SECT
Size	Large	Small
Relationship with other religious groups	Tolerant	Rejects; feels it has sole truth
Wealth	Extensive	Limited
Religious services	Limited congregational participation; formal; intellectual emphasis	Extensive congregational participation; spontaneous; emotional emphasis
Clergy	Specialized; professional	Unspecialized; little training; part time
Doctrines	Liberal interpretation of scriptures; emphasis upon this world	Literal interpretation of scriptures; emphasis upon other world
Membership	By birth or ritual participation; social institution embracing all socially compatible	By conversion; moral community excluding unworthy
Social class of members	Mainly middle class	Mainly lower class
Relationship with secular world	Endorses prevailing culture and social organization	Renounces or opposes prevailing cultural standards; requires strict adherence to Biblical standards such as tithing, pacificism

SOURCE: Adapted from Glenn M. Vernon, *Sociology of Religion* (New York: McGraw-Hill, 1962), p. 174, supplemented with material from Leonard Broom and Philip Selznick, *Sociology,* 5th ed. (New York: Harper & Row, 1973), p. 411.

they did not revolt was because religion defused rebellion against the social order.

The religion of the lower classes, Marx believed, grows out of their need to understand the reasons for social oppression and their need to cope with it. "Religion is the sign of the oppressed creature," he wrote, "the heart of a heartless world, just as it is the spirit of a spiritless situation. It is the opium of the people" (Marx, in Aptheker, 1968,

p. 33). Although religion ministers to some real needs, it provides false comfort. By promising the working classes a better life in the world to come, it blinds them to the possibilities of creating a better world on earth. In this way it endorses the status quo and supports the dominance of the capitalists.

For Marx capitalism shaped religion, but for Max Weber religion shaped capitalism. Weber thought that religion was capable of inducing social change, and that, specifically, Protestant doctrine created a climate in seventeenth-century Europe that encouraged capitalism to flourish (Weber, 1930).

The influence of religion was not so much through doctrines about economic activity, but more importantly through a set of attitudes about the proper relation between the individual and God (Eisenstadt, 1968). Early Protestantism, and specifically Calvinism, espoused the concept of predestination—the fate of each person was determined at birth. Either the individual was one of the elect or one of the damned. There was no sure way of telling whether one was elected or damned, but the Calvinists believed that anybody who had the good fortune to be successful in his worldly endeavors probably had God's blessing and, consequently, was probably one of the elect. Accordingly, hard work, self-

discipline, and clean living were seen not only as virtues but as signs of salvation. And because a frivolous, expensive life-style was regarded as sinful, profits from hard labor were traditionally plowed back into the business, thereby compounding success. Every Calvinist also believed that the individual was alone before God, and that he had a direct relationship with the deity. Therefore, because every man was essentially for himself, independence and competition were esteemed and encouraged. The values of hard work, individualism, and competition were

Religion can hinder social progress. Despite widespread Indian malnutrition, cattle are never slaughtered because they are held sacred by Hindus. Moreover, cows are allowed to roam the streets freely, creating potential health hazards. (Paolo Koch/Rapho Guillumette)

readily translated, Weber believed, into capitalism—an economic system that has thrived on individualism, the private ownership of goods, the reinvestment of profits, competition, and the independence of decision.

Of course, Protestantism began as a small secessionist movement and thus originally had the qualities of a sect. However, once it was espoused by the rulers and the upper classes of a number of northern European nations, it became a "church" in Troeltsch's sense. Protestantism had its great influence not because it attacked the powerful groups in the social hierarchy, but because it was accepted by them and became a part of the status quo. Only by becoming a church and generating the force of a church did it produce social change.

RELIGION AND THE INDIVIDUAL

Statistically, Americans are a "religious people." Gallup has found that 96 percent of us profess belief in some kind of formal religion (Gallup, 1971, pp. 70–71). But what effect, a sociologist would ask, does religion have on life in the United States? Does religious affiliation have any noticeable impact on our secular activities, our occupations, our family life?

Gerhard Lenski would answer the latter question with a resounding yes. Religion, he maintains, has about the same influence on personal behavior, attitudes, and ideas as social class. Religion, moreover, is a causal factor, not a correlational factor, he adds. It determines behavior directly and independently and is not totally the result of other variables like national origin or education. Lenski developed his ideas after an exhaustive study of religion and the individual

in metropolitan Detroit (Lenski, 1961); we will discuss some of his findings—and those of other sociologists—in this section to see how religion touches various aspects of an American's life.

Politics

Although religion and politics are formally separated in American life, in actual fact the values of one sphere carry over into the other. Take party affiliation, for example. A Gallup Poll in 1971 pointed out that Jews and Catholics are predominantly Democrats. Protestants show a significantly different pattern. While they have about the same percentage of independents (26 percent), the balance is more evenly split between the two major parties: 33 percent are Republicans and 39 percent Democrats. The figures for Protestants are not particularly meaningful, however, because they lump together different regional and economic groups. Figures analyzed by denomination show that other factors besides religion help to determine party affiliation. For example, the Episcopalians and the Presbyterians, the two wealthiest denominations concentrated heavily in the East, have a high proportion of Republicans (44 and 45 percent, respectively), whereas the Baptists, the largest denomination with the poorest members, most of whom live in the rural South, have a high percentage of Democrats (Gallup, 1971, p. 52). Income and region are obviously influential in determining political affiliation, too.

Education

The religious factor can be found in the area of education. A nationwide Gallup Poll in 1971 showed that Protestants and Catholics had similar educational patterns whereas

table 17:4 **PROFILES OF AMERICAN RELIGIONS (by percent)**

CHARACTERISTICS	PROTESTANTS Total	Methodists	Episcopalians	Baptists	CATHOLICS	JEWS
Percentage of population	65	14	3	21	26	3
Education						
College	22	24	47	12	21	42
High school	52	55	42	54	57	42
Grade school	26	21	12	34	23	16
Occupation						
Professional and business	20	22	38	14	22	40
Clerical and sales	12	12	12	10	12	22
Farmers	8	8	1	8	3	1
Manual	40	38	25	49	45	16
Income						
$15,000+	12	13	32	6	15	30
$10,000–$14,999	22	23	25	18	27	26
$7,000–$9,999	20	20	15	20	23	16
$5,000–$6,999	17	17	10	20	5	11
$3,000–$4,999	15	14	7	19	10	9
Under $3,000	13	12	10	16	9	7
Community Size						
1,000,000+	12	10	20	11	31	66
500,000–999,999	10	9	18	9	18	14
50,000–499,999	22	21	25	22	26	14
2,500–49,999	18	19	16	18	10	3
Under 2,500 (rural)	37	41	22	39	14	1
Politics						
Republican	33	35	44	21	19	6
Democrat	39	36	32	52	52	63
Independent	26	26	23	25	27	29

SOURCE: Gallup Opinion Index, *Religion in America, 1971*. Report no. 70, April 1971, p. 57.

Jews attained notably higher levels. Forty-two percent of the Jews had gone to college but only 22 percent of the Protestants and 21 percent of the Catholics had done so (Gallup, 1971, pp. 57–58).

Although, unlike the Gallup Poll, Lenski's Detroit study did not find important differences in the educational level among whites of different religions, Lenski did find differ-ences in the drop-out rate. The rate was determined from the number of people who failed to finish a level of education, be it grade school, high school, or college. Black Protestants had the highest drop-out rate with 67 percent, and Catholics were second at 48 percent. Among white Protestants, the rate was 39 percent and among Jews slightly more than 25 percent. Once started, Jews had the greatest drive to finish their education (Lenski, 1961, pp. 236–40). One of the interesting questions, not well understood, is *how* religion asserts its influence on education and whether it is the primary or subsidiary influence on the motivation to stay in school. Religious affiliation is linked with different economic, political, and ethnic attitudes, and sorting these out is extremely difficult.

Career

Is a particular religion related in any way to career, to whether its adherents wear a blue collar or a white one? In some cases it is. A 1971 Gallup Poll showed that Catholics have become so integrated into American life that their job choices are quite similar to those of Protestants. Jews, however, differ distinctly from both groups. Jews are concentrated in professional, business, sales, and clerical jobs; they are far more likely to wear a white collar than their Christian peers. For example, 20 percent and 22 percent of Protestants and Catholics, respectively, are in the professions and business whereas 40 percent of Jews chose these fields. Twenty-two percent of Jews are in clerical and sales jobs compared with 11 percent of Protestants and 12 percent of Catholics.

That the percentage of Jews in professions and business is so high accounts for their relatively higher incomes. The same 1971 Gallup Poll revealed that 30 percent of the nation's Jews earned more than $15,000 a year compared with 15 percent of the Catholics and 12 percent of the Protestants, black and white. The poll also registered that in the lower-income brackets, those earning less than $5,000 a year were 16 percent Jews, 19 percent Catholics, and 28 percent Protestants. Protestants whose income exceeded $15,000 varied from 32 percent of the Episcopalians to 6 percent of the Baptists.

Lenski found that religion also had an effect, and a very substantial one, on career success. Jews had the greatest success, followed by white Protestants. Lenski's study demonstrated that the success of both these groups contrasted rather sharply with that of the Catholics and black Protestants. Jews and white Protestants also shared certain characteristics that appeared to influence their economic behavior. Both had positive attitudes toward work, believed that ability was more important than family connections, emphasized intellectual autonomy, tended to be self-employed, and had small families. As groups, Catholics and black Protestants either did not share these attitudes or had them to a lesser extent.

Lenski argues that his data support Max Weber's thesis that the Protestant ethic inspires earthly success. Lenski found that persons raised in devout white Protestant families were more likely to be successful than persons raised in less devout white Protestant families. More importantly, he found that economic success correlated with a positive attitude toward work. Highly successful Jews, of course, share this view, and their economic behavior, along with that of white Protestants, may be cited in support of Weber. (For a critique of this view, see Schuman, 1971, pp. 30–48).

Religion and the Family

Studies of religious behavior demonstrate time and again that a salient relationship exists between religious affiliation and the choice of a marriage partner, the decision on divorce, and the planning of a family.

Religion seems to be particularly important to Americans when they choose a mate. Eighty-eight percent of all marriages occur between members of the same religion. According to a 1957 census report, the only source of reliable national data on this matter, Catholics have the highest proportion of members who marry outside their religion (21.6 percent).[1] Only 8.6 percent of the nation's Protestants marry non-Protestants, and only 7.2 percent of its Jews marry non-Jews. Had the census figures distinguished between black and white Protestants, the intermarriage rates for blacks would have been extremely low; for whites they probably would have approached those for Catholics.

Many factors are involved in intermarriage. A study by Heiss (1960) of marriages in New York City suggests that the close proximity of different religious groups increases the rate of intermarriage. He found that in the religiously mixed society of Manhattan, intermarriage rates were 21.4 percent among Catholics, 33.9 percent among Protestants, and 18.4 percent among Jews. The rate for Catholics in New York City was not surprising; it was the same as their nationwide rate. But the rate among New York Jews was twice the national rate, and for Protestants it was four times the national percentage. People who intermarry are also likely to be older and to have been married before (Barron, 1972, p. 44).

Those who intermarry are also more likely to get divorced. Several studies have found that the divorce and separation rates for Catholics and Jews with partners of a different religion were three to six times higher than in marriages between members of the same religion (Barron, 1972, p. 44). For those who do not intermarry, the rates of divorce differ by religion. Lenski in his 1958 survey of Detroit concluded that black Protestants and

white Protestants are far more likely to rescind their marriage vows than are Catholics or Jews. (His figures for Jews may be somewhat misleading because the Jewish sample was very small.) Twenty-two percent of the black Protestants and 16 percent of the white Protestants severed their marriage ties, but only 8 percent of the Catholics and 4 percent of the Jews did so. (Separation rates for Catholics are far higher, of course.) Even more remarkable were the differences in remarriage rates: 86 percent of the black and 75 percent of the divorced white Protestants remarried, but among divorced Catholics, who are expressly forbidden to remarry, only 50 percent again took the vows. Lenski speculated that the low divorce rate among Catholics can be attributed to the pressure exerted by their religion to make their marriage work.

Catholicism also exerts pressure in other ways. Indeed, of the three major religions in the United States, it places the most sanctions upon the lives of its members. The Catholic church is particularly adamant about birth control: all methods are forbidden except rhythm (abstinence from intercourse during fertile periods of the menstrual cycle). Nonetheless, national fertility studies conducted over the last fifteen years reveal considerable erosion of support for church doctrine on birth control as we saw in chapter 13 (Westoff and Bumpass, 1973). In a 1967 article in *Newsweek*, one Pennsylvania housewife argued, "The problem of birth control should be settled by husband and wife—not by the Vatican."

Several trends can be observed in this revolution against the Catholic church. College-educated Catholic women, once the most dutiful followers of birth-control dictates, are now the most rebellious. Among this group, roughly three-quarters use a disapproved method of birth control. "If you take a pill," a Catholic mother has declared, "you are not as conscious of preventing preg-

---

[1] Because of the separation of church and state in the United States, the Census Bureau does not ask about religion. The 1957 survey was taken of religious affiliation, but no questions about religion have appeared in subsequent censuses. In 1968 a National Opinion Research Survey of people who had graduated from college in 1961 and their spouses showed little difference in intermarriage rates from the 1957 census survey (Barron, 1972, p. 43).

figure 17:1 Catholics and contraception, 1955–1970

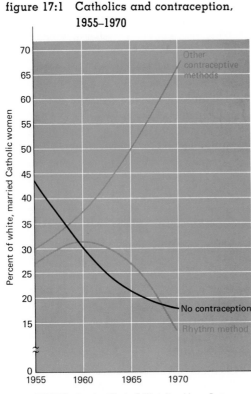

SOURCE: Based on Charles F. Westoff and Larry Bumpass, "The Revolution in Birth Control Practices of U. S. Roman Catholics," *Science* 179, January 5, 1973, table 1, p. 42.

In fifteen years there was a revolution in birth control practices among Catholic women eighteen to thirty-nine. In 1955 over two-thirds of the white, married Catholic women in these fertile years followed church doctrine by using either no contraception whatever or the approved rhythm method; less than one-third were using disapproved methods. By 1970 the proportions were reversed; over two-thirds were resorting to unsanctioned birth control methods (the pill being the favored method by a large margin, particularly among younger married Catholic women). Only 18 percent were using no contraceptive method at all by 1970. Is this falling away from the church simply limited to this area or has the influence of the Catholic church declined more broadly? The last section of the chapter deals with what this trend means.

nancy." The most important fact in this revolution, however, is that the greatest defection from church doctrine has taken place among religious Catholic women.

Although the influence of religious belief on the American family is still strong in every aspect of family life—marriage and children and attitudes about divorce—signs such as these indicate the influence is fading. Whether this also means that religion itself is dying requires a broader look at religion in America.

THE FUTURE OF RELIGION

Times are changing, and some of the most important changes in the religious realm have been of a kind that few would have predicted as recently as the early 1960s. (Lenski, 1971, p. 50)

Secularization

Formal religion in America is on the decline. About that change there is little question. Church attendance has been creeping downward since 1955. Gallup pollsters found that 49 percent of Americans attended religious services once a week in 1955; in 1971 the figure declined to 40 percent, where it remained through 1973 (Gallup, 1974). "Do you think religion is increasing its influence on American life?" they asked. In 1957, 69 percent of the respondents said yes and only 14 percent thought religion was losing its influence. In 1967, the percentages were reversed: 57 percent thought religion was losing ground and only 23 percent felt it was gaining it (Hadden, 1969, p. 25). By 1970, 75 percent agreed that religious influences were declining (Hoge, 1974, p. 167).

Who are the disillusioned? The greatest drop in church attendance has been among Catholics. In 1964, 71 percent of all Catholics attended mass in a given week; by 1973 this figure was down to 55 percent, a drop of over one-fifth. Belief is waning most among Jews and youth. Between 1952 and 1965 the percentage of Jews who expressed belief in God dropped an extraordinary 31 percent—from 70 percent to 39 percent. In 1965 only 17 percent of Jews believed that the Old Testament was the revealed word of God or that there was life after death. Over the same thirteen years, belief in God dropped 15 percent among America's youth—from 87 percent to 71 percent (Marty, Rosenberg, and Greeley, 1968, pp. 60–61). Other studies have demonstrated that the decline in religious belief among students is an even longer-term trend. Between the late 1940s and the late 1960s, a 13 percent to 23 percent drop occurred among students in orthodox beliefs about God and immortality. Similar but lesser declines have been noted among young adults (Hoge, 1974).

Despite the downward trends in religious beliefs, some observers question whether their implications for religion are quite as serious as they appear at first glance. Hoge has noted that American belief in religious orthodoxy has tended to fluctuate—zealous at one time, indifferent the next. Studies of personal belief-commitment systems have indicated that religious orthodoxy is often associated with commitment to family life, to military duty and patriotic wars, to the routing of communism, to dominant social norms. The general acceptance of these values has varied widely during this century—high in the twenties, low in the thirties, high again in the fifties, and low again today. It is a pattern that suggests religious orthodoxy and belief may well increase again in the future (Hoge, 1974).

Trends in the Major Faiths

While disinterest in religion has been spreading among the flock, upheavals have been increasing among the shepherds as well. The voice of the clergy has become increasingly strident over church dogma and church institutional structure. The major faiths are going through a period of critical self-analysis, asking themselves how they can hold onto their membership and make religious practice have greater appeal, meaning, and relevance.

During the 1960s the larger Protestant denominations were exploring ways to resolve theological differences in preparation for merger. Such ecumenical fervor has waned in the seventies. To some Protestant theologians, coming to terms with each other has been less crucial than coming to terms with a world in which "God is dead." This debate revolved around the question of whether the traditional concept of God has any meaning in the modern world. Anglican Bishop J. A. T. Robinson, in his book *Honest to God* (1963), answered no. He argued that the traditional concept of a loving father up in heaven was outmoded and must be replaced. Shortly thereafter, Harvey Cox published *The Secular City* (1966), quoted at the beginning of this chapter, which viewed the world as moving into a secular age in which traditional religion is irrelevant.

Questions about doctrine have been only one part of a wider crisis in Protestantism, according to Jeffrey Hadden (1969, pp. 3–33). The Civil Rights Movement unleashed sources of conflict over the purposes of the church and the authority within it, as well as over beliefs. The main cleavage is between the clergy and the laity. To many church members the purpose of the church is to comfort them; to many in the clergy the purpose is to offer challenges. The question of the social gospel has created great divisions within individual churches and whole denominations and has led to a decline in contributions and in the willingness of church members to assent to policies of church leaders when they attack the status quo. Protestantism is threatened not simply by secularization but by the crises of purpose, belief, and authority.

Catholicism has been undergoing rapid changes. It is reassessing its views toward other churches and wrestling with the burgeoning spirit of individualism and contemporary ferment within its own ranks. In an effort to achieve greater Christian unity, the church has been renegotiating its differences with certain Protestant groups. Catholic and Anglican theologians, for example, have reached agreement on the nature of the priesthood and the ministry; Catholics recognize the legitimacy of the Anglican clergy, and the sharing of communion between the two churches is now possible. Catholics and Lutherans have also reached accord on the issue of papal primacy, a major issue in the Protestant Reformation four centuries ago. A joint study has declared that papal primacy is no longer a "barrier to reconciliation" of the two churches and envisions the day when they will be part of one "larger communion."

All these fraternal moves on the part of the Catholic church are the legacy of Vatican II, the Catholic ecumenical convocation called by Pope John XXIII to reexamine the doctrine and rituals of the Catholic church. The Council, which met from 1962 to 1965, brought sweeping changes within the church, such as the vernacular Mass, but it also led to a crisis of authority. Many among the clergy and the laity are no longer willing to accept the will of the pope. Laymen are more and more asserting their rights to share in decision-making, and priests and nuns are questioning the role of celibacy and their own role in the church.

The Pope is still extremely influential, but internal changes in the power structure are afoot.

In Judaism there is mounting concern over the decline in Jewish religious beliefs and the possible weakening of Jewish communal ties as the children and grandchildren of Jewish immigrants have become Americanized. Much of the blame for the divisions within the family over the issue of Jewishness lies with the parents, says one editor of a Jewish monthly, because they have failed to impress upon their children the importance of the Nazi holocaust and the creation of the state of Israel. "To most American Jews, being a Jew is like being a stamp collector. It's an avocation," says a student supporter of the Radical Jewish Union, who sees Jewishness as a totality. "It encompasses a political ideology, a set of values, a general philosophy, a religion, customs, diet, language—a whole way of life" (*Newsweek*, March 1, 1971, pp. 61–62).

Some Jewish religious leaders are not particularly worried over the decline in orthodox belief because they feel that heterodoxy has always been a part of Jewish tradition. Moreover, though they note a decline in regular synagogue attendance, they are pleased with the stability in synagogue membership. And they have found the increased interest in Jewish education gratifying. Such training through the synagogue and Hebrew schools reinforces the sense of Jewishness that persists in spite of the decrease in formal religious belief.

Is the Secular City at Hand?

The evidence is fairly convincing that traditional Catholic, Protestant, and Jewish religiosity is being challenged in this country. But does this mean that institutionalized religion

IN THE NEWS

Motel Parish

There is a temptation to confuse religion with church. But people may look to religious leaders without wanting the communal involvement of organized religion. One unlikely place they may now find a minister is at a motel. Over 1,300 of the 1,638 Holiday Inns, for example, now have a chaplain on call. Some hold religious services, but their main purpose is to counsel troubled travelers.

"When people are running away from something, they run to a neutral place. A hotel or a motel is a logical choice of a neutral place," [said Rev. Jack Chellew, founder of a motel chaplain program for Holiday Inns of America, Inc. The chaplains] are often aroused in the middle of the night by callers who may be suicidal, lonely, playfully drunk, having a fight with their wives or anxious to borrow money. . . . The average motel chaplain gets about 15 calls a year but some receive many more. [Rev. W. A. Nance, corporate chaplain for Holiday Inns] ascribes the frequency of calls partially to the special loneliness that comes with being isolated in a motel room far from home, where "problems tend to magnify."

Almost 1,000 potential suicides have been prevented by the Holiday Inn chaplains, but the larger problem is the drunk.

"I'll go along with the guy for a while," says one chaplain, "but eventually we'll get at the reason why he felt the need to get drunk that night. A lot of counselling sessions come from those drunk calls."

One advantage of a motel chaplain is that the person will not have to face him in church the next Sunday.

"Three times this year people have called and said they stayed in a Holiday Inn for the single reason that they had heard of the program and wanted to talk to an anonymous chaplain rather than their own clergyman," says [a Toronto minister].

A sociologist who concentrated only on what goes on in churches would miss the motel chaplains and much of the religious activity on the contemporary scene.

Source: Ron Cooper, " 'Room Service? Send 3 Bourbon, 2 Scotch—And One Chaplain,' " *The Wall Street Journal* (May 21, 1974): 1, 40.

is dead or gasping in the United States? Without question, church membership continues to decline. Even so, 79 percent of Americans claim membership in a religious group. Obviously, church membership will have to drop a good deal more before the churches can be described as moribund. Reports of their death, to use Mark Twain's description after reading of his own, are "greatly exaggerated." Religion in America is still big business. Its combined assets in the late 1960s were double those of the top five corporations in the United States (Demerath, 1968, p. 365).

One way of gauging the vigor of an institution is to compare it with another social institution. Swanson (in Greeley, 1969, pp. 32–33) found that religious participation compared quite favorably with political participation. He found, among other things, that roughly 60 percent of the American electorate votes in national elections and that approximately 68 percent of the adult population attends religious services in any given four-week period. In the public's eye, then, religion is no less viable than politics.

The Fundamentalist Revival If formal organized religion is not generating quite the allure it once did, another form of religious experience is again in ascendance in America. The revivalists, the evangelists, the fundamentalists have been back on the religious scene in ever-increasing numbers since the late 1960s. Billy Graham's "old-time religion" continues to rise in popularity, a substantial number of young adults have become Jesus People, and some fundamentalist churches and sects are attracting more and more followers. The Assemblies of God, Pentecostal groups, Evangelicals, Mormons, and Seventh-day Adventists have all had steady increases in membership. The Southern Baptist Convention, a large, relatively conservative denomination, has expanded by more than 2 percent a year since 1957, and the Jehovah's Witnesses have increased annually by 5 percent since 1958, more than doubling their membership (Kelley, 1972, p. 21). Even Catholicism has been reached by Pentecostalism; nearly a quarter million of its members "speak in tongues" and regard themselves as "charismatics," or Pentecostal Catholics.

All these groups are essentially evangelical sects, having all the attributes that Troeltsch described. They tend toward extreme orthodoxy and a fairly literal interpretation of the Bible. Their doctrines emanate from a premil-lennialist tradition in American theology, which holds that the troubles of the world are created by man's sinfulness, and that the human condition cannot be improved until the Second Coming of Jesus. They feel the need for and seek personal salvation in Christ, and they view religious participation as a means of redemption through faith.

Beyond these common doctrines, the groups have other shared characteristics (Kelley, 1972, p. 26). They impose absolute conformity in religious belief on their members through censorship or the threat of expulsion. They believe fervently in the power of faith, with some Protestant Pentecostal groups going so far as to have their followers prove their faith by handling poisonous snakes during services. Jehovah's Witnesses, as another example, refuse to have blood transfusions when there are medically sound reasons requiring them. In short, all fundamentalist groups make strong demands on their members—and all of them turn a fairly cold shoulder toward other religions.

In trying to understand the attraction of these evangelical groups, Kelley has hypothesized that their success rests on the very fact that they make extensive demands on their membership. He believes that everybody has a basic need to find meaning in life, and that people are not satisfied with concepts or theologies. Only when they make personal sacrifices and only when they see others making sacrifices in the name of a belief can they feel they have found something impellingly meaningful. What is free is not worth much. The evangelical movement, therefore, has attracted more and more of a following because it exacts commitment and thereby creates meaning.

The Jesus People are also part of the evangelical revival, though their membership is comprised almost exclusively of middle-class white teenagers, often former drug users.

Sometimes tagged as Jesus Freaks, they seek personal salvation through the teachings of Christ. They attend prayer services and go through baptism rituals. Some live and work together in communes, where the life-style is ascetic and a strict code of morality is observed. Emphasis is placed on the experience of religion, the experience of feeling God's will and performing it. Intellectualism and independent thought are not encouraged.

Religion, then, remains a lively object of study. Commitment to religious behavior has not disappeared; it exists side-by-side with secularization in America. Although the institutions are changing and the beliefs are changing, leading some to think that religion is dying, the functions of religion endure.

Sociologists are divided on whether the Jesus movement is a desirable way for teenagers to deal with their problems. Some say that religion only prevents adolescents from confronting their anxieties about life and sex, while others say that it presents a viable alternative to the drug culture. (Hiroji Kubota)

They endure because mankind's basic questions about existence, about the ultimate, about the meaning of life, and about morality persist. "The basic human religious needs and the basic religious functions have not changed very notably since the late Ice Age," says sociologist and priest Andrew Greeley (1972, p. 1). "What changes have occurred make religious questions more critical rather than less critical in the contemporary world."

summary

A *religion* unites into a moral community those who adhere to a unified system of beliefs and practices that define and relate its members to sacred things. According to Emile Durkheim, the first sociologist of religion, religion both promotes social solidarity, and celebrates the common sentiments of a society. According to Durkheim, nothing is inherently sacred; it becomes sacred when a community designates it so. Gods, ghosts, spirits, moral principles, totems, and natural forces are examples of "things" worshipped by different societies. Just as the forms of the sacred vary, so do the degree of belief in them and the level of ritual or communal involvement. Because of the number of dimensions and the variety of their expression, measuring religiousness is quite complex, and not all sociologists mean the same thing when they talk about religious behavior.

Religion serves a variety of functions for the individual and for the society. People turn to religion to cope with death and to make personal hardships and tragedies easier to bear. They look for the meaning of life and for guides to regulate its conduct. Religion can glorify and celebrate human events and provide transcendent or visionary experiences. To individuals it offers a powerful means of relieving anxiety, but it is not the only force to do so. Over the course of human history scientific mastery has replaced metaphysical explanations with physical ones, raising the problem of whether religion might one day become irrelevant. For society, religion creates and reinforces a sense of community and consensus. It discourages antisocial behavior and offers a means for reintegrating transgressors. It serves to legitimize secular authority.

This legitimizing function may produce a civil religion, according to Robert Bellah. He believes that the United States has developed a *civil religion* with its own symbols, hymns, high priests, and martyrs, which binds together our pluralistic society. American civil religion is not simply patriotism, however, since the political acts are judged by a transcendent law.

Ernst Troeltsch identified two polar forms of religious organization—church and sect—whose relation to society are quite different. *Church* is universal and often allied with the status quo. Most people are born into it and few demands are placed on them. The *sect* is small, exclusive, primarily composed of converts. The sect is either indifferent or hostile to society, but in the process of being transformed into a church may introduce (or retard) social change.

The relation of religion to the society at large has been a source of controversy in sociology. To Marx religion was an essentially conservative institution that provided comfort for the suffering but no impetus to relieve the causes of that suffering. To Weber religion was a primary shaper of capitalism and the social changes it induced. Not only Protestant (particularly Calvinist) doctrines about economic activity, but the values of hard work, individualism, and competition were readily translated into capitalism.

The influence of religion upon the individual is another area of sociological concern. Gerhard Lenski maintains that religion ranks in significance with social class as a sociological variable. His study of the "religious factor" in Detroit, along with the work of other investigators, has turned up marked differences among religious groups in political affiliation and attitudes, education, career choice, income, choice of a marriage partner, likelihood of divorce, and the use of birth control.

Religion in the United States is now undergoing changes, as the influence of churches on American life declines. Belief in traditional Jewish and Christian religious doctrines has dropped dramatically among youth (although among the general population four out of every ten Americans attend church in a given week). The religious ferment is not confined to any one of the major faiths in America. For Jews, the problem of secularization is particularly acute, as the children and grandchildren of immigrants become Americanized and lose their orthodoxy. Among Protestants and Catholics, the ecumenical movement is one trend that is reducing doctrinal differences. However, among other Protestants and Catholics, there has been a new strength in fundamentalism, in which strict adherence to doctrine and practice are demanded.

glossary

church A large, conservative, universalist religious institution, which makes few demands on its members and is accommodated to the culture of a society.

civil religion A collection of religious beliefs, symbols, and rituals outside the church that pervades and helps legitimize a community (Bellah).

communal involvement Bonds of attachment that bind together members of a religious moral community.

mana A benign supernatural force that has no shape of its own but inhabits living or inanimate things.

monotheism Worship of a single god.

moral community A group of people who share common beliefs and practices.

polytheism Worship of more than one god.

profane The opposite of sacred; the everyday and mundane.

religion A unified system of beliefs and practices that pertain to sacred things, and that unite adherents into a moral community (Durkheim).

religious beliefs Representations that express the nature of sacred things and the relations that they sustain, either with each other or with profane things.

ritual The rules of conduct that prescribe how people should behave in the presence of sacred objects.

sacred Pertaining to the object of worship that transcends everyday existence and is extraordinary, potentially dangerous, awe-inspiring, fear-inducing.

sect A small, exclusive, uncompromising fellowship that makes heavy demands on its members and sets them apart from the larger society.

secularization The decline in religious faith and practice or the accommodation of religious beliefs and practices to other social customs.

taboo An object or being that contains a supernatural force that brings bad luck or trouble.

totem A sacred animal or vegetable that serves as a focus of certain primitive religions; a symbol and repository of deep, group-based sentiments and feelings.

references

Milton Barron, ed., *The Blending American*, Chicago: Quadrangle, 1972.

Robert N. Bellah, *Beyond Belief*, New York: Harper & Row, 1970.

———, "American Civil Religion in the 1970s," unpublished paper given at Drew University, March 1973.

Harvey Cox, *The Secular City*, rev. ed., New York: Macmillan, 1966.

N. G. Demerath, III, *Social Class in American Protestantism*, Chicago: Rand McNally, 1965.

———, "Trends and Anti-Trends in Religious Change," in Eleanor B. Sheldon and Wilbert E. Moore, eds., *Indicators of Social Change*, New York: Russell Sage, 1968.

Emile Durkheim, *The Elementary Forms of Religious Life* (1912), trans. by Joseph Ward Swain, New York: Free Press, 1965.

S. N. Eisenstadt, ed., *The Protestant Ethic and Modernization*, New York: Basic Books, 1968.

George Gallup, "Churchgoing Decline of Last Decade Result of Sliding Catholic Attendance," *The Gallup Poll*, January 13, 1974.

Gallop Opinion Index, *Religion in America, 1971*, report no. 70 (April 1971).

Clifford Geertz, "Religion as a Cultural System," in Donald Cutler, ed., *The Religious Situation, 1968*, Boston: Beacon Press, 1968.

Charles Y. Glock and Rodney Stark, *Religion and Society in Tension*, Chicago: Rand McNally, 1965.

Sidney Goldstein and Calvin Goldsheider, *Jewish Americans: Three Generations in a Jewish Community*, Englewood Cliffs, N.J.: Prentice-Hall, 1968.

Andrew Greeley, *Religion in the Year 2000*, New York: Ward & Sheed, 1969.

——, *Unsecular Man*, New York: Schocken Books, 1972.

Jeffrey Hadden, *The Gathering Storm in the Churches: The Widening Gap Between Clergy and Laymen*, New York: Doubleday, 1969.

Jerold Heiss, "Premarital Characteristics of the Religiously Intermarried in an Urban Area," *American Sociological Review*, vol. 25 (February 1960): 47–55.

Dean R. Hoge, *Commitment on Campus: Changes in Religion and Values over Five Decades*, Philadelphia: Westminster Press, 1974.

Dean M. Kelley, *Why the Conservative Churches Are Growing: A Study in the Sociology of Religion*, New York: Harper & Row, 1972.

Gerhard Lenski, *The Religious Factor: A Sociological Study of Religion's Impact on Politics, Economics, and Family Life*, Garden City, N.Y.: Doubleday, 1961.

——, "The Religious Factor in Detroit: Revisited," *American Sociological Review,* vol. 36 (February 1971): 48–50.

Eric C. Lincoln, *The Black Muslim in America*, Boston: Beacon Press, 1961.

Robert and Helen Lynd, *Middletown*, New York: Harcourt, Brace, Jovanovich, 1929.

Bronislaw Malinowski, *Science, Magic and Religion,* Garden City, N.Y.: Anchor Books, 1954.

Martin Marty, Stuart E. Rosenberg, and Andrew Greeley, *What Do We Believe?* New York: Meredith Press, 1968.

Karl Marx, "Contribution to the Critique of Hegel's Philosophy of Right" (1844), in Herbert Aptheker, ed., *Marxism and Christianity*, New York: Humanities Press, 1968.

John A.T. Robinson, *Honest to God*, Philadelphia: Westminster, 1963.

Howard Schuman, "The Religious Factor in Detroit: Review, Replication and Reanalysis," *American Sociological Review*, vol. 36 (February 1971): 30–48.

Irving Spiegel, "Where Women Go to Find Judaism—and Themselves," *The New York Times* (April 17, 1974): 48.

Guy E. Swanson, *The Birth of the Gods*, Ann Arbor: University of Michigan Press, 1969. Also in Greeley, 1969.

Ernst Troeltsch, "Church and Sect," in Milton J. Yinger, ed., *Religion, Society, and the Individual: An Introduction to the Sociology of Religion*, New York: Macmillan, 1957.

U.S. Bureau of the Census, "Religion Reported by the Civilian Population of the United States: March 1957," *Current Population Reports: Population Characteristics,* series p–20, no. 79 (February 2, 1958).

Anthony F. C. Wallace, *Religion: An Anthropological View*, New York: Random House, 1966.

Max Weber, *The Protestant Ethic and the Spirit of Capitalism*, London: Allen & Unwin, 1930.

Charles F. Westoff and Larry Bumpass, "The Revolution in Birth Control Practices of U.S. Roman Catholics," *Science*, vol. 179 (January 5, 1973): 41–44.

Milton J. Yinger, *Sociology Looks at Religion*, New York: Macmillan, 1963.

for further study

The Priesthood. One specific way to explore the changes taking place in religion in America is to examine what is happening to the priesthood. What is the social role of the priest today? What is his relation to the church, to the laity, to society? Some books that explore these questions are Andrew Greeley, *Uncertain Trumpet: The Priest in Modern America* (New York: Sheed, 1968); Charles E. Rice, *Authority and Rebellion* (Garden City, N.Y.: Doubleday, 1971); and David J. O'Brian, *The Renewal of American Catholicism* (New York: Oxford University Press, 1972).

Fundamentalist Sects. The revival of fundamentalist sects in an era of science and self-indulgence has puzzled many sociologists. Dean Kelley looks at this phenomenon in *Why Conservative Churches Are Growing* (New York: Harper & Row, 1972). See also the vivid portrait of *The Preachers*, by James Morris (New York: St. Martin's Press, 1973). Some fundamentalists "speak in tongues" and feel they communicate directly with God. For exploration of these groups, see William W. Wood, *Culture and Personality Aspects of the Pentacostal Holiness Religion* (New York: Humanities Press, 1965); and I. M. Lewis, *Ecstatic Religion* (Baltimore, Md.: Penguin, 1971).

Death. In recent years there has been a renewed interest in death, particularly in finding what people in the Middle Ages called "the good death," that is, when a person prepares for his or her end, bringing together family and friends and perhaps enemies, putting in order as much as possible before dying. Although not heavily laced with theology, this is certainly a religious movement of large proportions. To understand the meaning of death in American life, see the following books: Jessica Mitford, *The American Way of Death* (New York: Fawcett, 1969); Robert J. Lifton and Eric Olson, *And a Time to Die* (New York: Praeger, 1974); Marya Mannes, *Last Rights* (New York: Morrow, 1974); and the classic in the field, Elizabeth Kubler-Ross, *On Death and Dying* (New York: Macmillan, 1970). Two sociological studies of how hospitals and their staffs "handle" terminal patients are David Sudnow, *Passing On* (Englewood Cliffs, N. J.: Prentice-Hall, 1967), and Barney Glaser and Anselm L. Strauss, *Awareness of Dying* (Chicago: Aldine, 1967).

TECHNOLOGY AND SOCIAL CHANGE

Today's landscape is being changed by two forces: urbanization and technology. The development of machine technology has within a century and a half loosened the ancient link between man and his crops and has produced what Philip Hauser terms a *population implosion*—the progressive movement of the world's peoples off the fertile lands into increasingly dense urban areas. In 1800 only 2.4 percent of the world's population lived in settlements larger than 100,000. By 1960, 27.1 percent were located in settlements larger than 20,000 persons, and 19.9 percent resided in places larger than 100,000. Projections of world population growth indicate that by the end of the century about 42 percent of the world's peoples will live in places having more than 100,000 inhabitants (Hauser, 1969, pp. 1–19). This rapid movement from the land to the cities has been accompanied by a massive disruption of relatively stable social

URBAN LIFE
AND
TECHNOLOGY

and cultural patterns. For this reason rapid urbanization contributes to many of the ills that are bemoaned daily in the newspapers and analyzed in the textbooks: street crime, poverty, the energy and ecological crises, among others.

Whereas the mechanization of farm and factory production created an urban, industrialized society, continuing technological advance has produced such widespread change that some sociologists proclaim that we are now moving into a postindustrial society. Whether or not this society will say with the sorcerer's apprentice, "The Spirits I summoned I cannot now dismiss!" is a matter of debate. Has technology helped humanity to overcome nature only to reduce the individual to an appendage of the machine, robbing men of all their creativity and possibly even of their homes on this planet? The following pages will address these questions.

THE URBAN TRANSFORMATION

The date when humans first appeared as a distinct species is still unclear (it was at least a hundred thousand years ago), but it is certain that they have known cities for a much shorter time. The first permanent settlements were created some eight to ten thousand years ago, and their effect upon social organization was enormous. Stationary residence encouraged the development of written language, the calendar, organized scientific inquiry, complex stratification systems, an organized priesthood, institutionalized religion, and the state, among many other important social institutions. Indeed, civilization as we know it is very much a product of urban society; the word *civilization* itself comes from the Latin, meaning "culture of cities."

The Birth of the City

For at least the first three-quarters of human history, human beings were nomadic creatures who traveled about in small families or bands, hunting, fishing, and foraging for food. Because the bounty of nature in most parts of the world was not plentiful enough to support more than a few persons in any one spot, humans were constantly on the move. Without adequate means of storing supplies, these people were unable to accumulate a surplus and therefore lived a rather precarious existence (Childe, 1952).

The Neolithic Revolution At the dawn of the neolithic period, some ten thousand years ago, people began to develop techniques of cultivating plants and domesticating animals. Simple tools were invented for gardening

and pots were made for storage; these technological innovations were a way of multiplying nature's bounty sufficiently to forego nomadic wandering for a rooted residence. The earliest villages were small by today's standards, housing only two hundred to four hundred residents. Because neolithic farming methods were inefficient and because transportation technologies were undeveloped, a village was limited in the amount of adjacent land that it could profitably bring under cultivation. This placed a limit on the expansion of these villages. Instead of the village expanding as its families grew, colonies were established at a distance to accommodate these growing numbers. This was the prevailing pattern of village organization for the next four to five thousand years (Childe, 1952).

The First True Cities In about 6000 to 5000 B.C. in the alluvial plains of the Nile, Tigris-Euphrates, and Indus River valleys there emerged settlements more than ten times the size of any previous ones. Housing between seven thousand and twenty thousand persons, these first true cities developed largely because innovations in agricultural and transportational technologies enabled these societies to take advantage of the valleys' exceptionally fertile soils. Agricultural output increased with the development of the ox-drawn plow, irrigation, newly domesticated plants, and metallurgy. Grain-storage facilities were improved and enough food was produced to support all farming families and a large population of nonfarmers as well. This relative abundance permitted the emergence of a complex division of labor, which has been characteristic of all human societies since. Then, even though the overwhelming proportion of the residents were engaged in farming, some could become specialists in crafts (potters, weavers, blacksmiths) or services (selling, teaching, fighting, governing, or performing rituals). Traders imported goods that were not locally available. To extend their control over all planning and organizing of the community's affairs, the governing classes invented systems of record-keeping. Writing and numerical notation, two of mankind's momentous inventions, grew out of these needs. And because the community's survival depended on successful planting and harvesting of the crops, the scribes and clerks of the courts and temples had to develop exact, predictive sciences—including arithmetic, geometry, and astronomy. The accuracy with which the early calendars predicted celestial events attests to the intellectual precision achieved by these early city dwellers (Davis, 1970, pp. 121–22).

The first cities reached their zenith about 3000 B.C. and then faded away. The next flowering of urban life occurred in classical Greece and Rome. Roman urban life attained a remarkable degree of sophistication, from magnificent public architecture down to such conveniences as water pipes and stepping stones for crossing muddy streets. But these classical cities declined with the fall of Rome. Urban development did not begin in Europe until the rise of the feudal city during the Middle Ages. Although many of these cities survive today, their preindustrial character was quite different, according to sociologist Gideon Sjoberg (1960).

The Preindustrial Feudal City Feudal technology was such that about a hundred thousand persons could inhabit a city. Agricultural techniques were productive enough to allow about 10 percent of an area's total population to live in an urban setting. However, the technological base limited the growth of cities beyond this. Transportation methods were poorly developed and it was therefore difficult to bring in the bulky goods needed for construction and manufacturing. Without large-scale manufacturing, job opportunities

were limited. Poor communication methods limited the effective governing of a large adjacent hinterland. And sanitation and medical techniques were so primitive that dense urban settlements bred disease and death.

The social order of these cities was rigidly stratified and there was little mobility from one stratum to another. Contrary to today's American pattern, the rich lived in the center of the city and the poor on the outskirts. People of like class, ethnicity, and occupation lived in strictly defined quarters wherein they carried out most of their work, worship, and marketing. The most powerful forces regulating people's behavior in these cities were traditional folkways and mores (rather than formal law) enforced through the dominant institutions of family and guild. Guilds controlled the economy of the feudal city, regulating the price and quality of goods and services, the number of people in each craft, their training, and the length of the working day and week. Each guild disciplined its own members and assisted its families in times of need. Guild membership was likely to be hereditary, which created a rigid occupational system allowing little choice of work (Sjoberg, 1960).

The Industrial Revolution and the Urban Explosion The technological innovations of the Industrial Revolution reduced the constraints on the size and density of the city. The mechanization of agriculture increased food production dramatically. Chemical and biological advances also produced new ways of raising animals, new insecticides, new herbicides, new fertilizers, and new plants, which also stimulated food surpluses. Because of the increased productivity, fewer workers were now needed on the farms. Displaced farmers and their families streamed into the cities in search of jobs, which were increasing as a result of the growing factory production—again the consequence of the revolution in machine technology. Techniques for overcoming the obstacles of space also aided the explosive growth of cities. The spread of the railroads allowed the city to extend its grasp of faraway resources needed for growth. The development of cheap steel and the invention of the elevator made possible skyscrapers, which accommodated the residential and office needs of an increasingly dense urban population. And innovations in medicine and public hygiene facilities cut the health risks that had plagued the earlier, preindustrial cities.

Whole nations relocated themselves from the hinterlands to metropolitan areas within a matter of decades. In 1850 only 15 percent of the population of the United States lived in urban areas; by 1900 the proportion was almost 40 percent. The turning point came around 1920, when more than half of all Americans were urban dwellers. Fifty years later, more than 70 percent of the population was urbanized, by which the Census Bureau means living in towns or cities larger than twenty-five hundred persons (Hauser, 1969). Within a generation America shifted from being a rural-based nation to an urban one. (See figure 18:1.)

This rapid urbanization meant the rise of a new social order. Municipal reformer Frederic C. Howe declared in 1906:

The city has become the central feature of modern civilization and to an ever increasing extent the dominant one. . . . Rural civilization, whose making engaged mankind since the dawn of history, is passing away. The city has erased the landmarks of an earlier society. Man has entered on an urban age. (in Fava, 1968, p. 11)

The traditions of rural society—its customs, habits, and indeed, its very way of life—were strained and often cast aside as the urban society grew more dominant and ultimately penetrated even those remaining rural communities through the institutions of government and the mass media.

The widespread social disorganization accompanying the breakup of the old rural order by the machine and the rise of cities was an important stimulus to the development of modern sociology. As the structure of a crystal is best revealed when it is cracked, the structures of human society, which had long been taken for granted and had thus remained "invisible," became apparent in their breakdown and transformation. Social structures and processes were changing at a perceptible rate. Marx, Durkheim, Weber, Simmel, and Tönnies were among those who developed new intellectual tools for understanding these changes, and these tools have served to construct sociology as we know it today.

Modern Urban Life

Describing the character of the modern city and of its social life has been a persistent challenge to sociologists. Much of the pioneering work was done by sociologists at the University of Chicago in the 1920s and 1930s. One of the early classics in urban sociology is Louis Wirth's "Urbanism as a Way of Life" (1938). Wirth saw the city as the prototype of mass society, in which the traditional bases of social solidarity and control—kinship and the neighborhood—are undermined, leaving the individual atomized, depersonalized, and subject more frequently to mental breakdown, suicide, delinquency, crime, corruption, and disorder. Wirth believed that urbanism fosters sophistication, rationality, and a utilitarian accent in interpersonal relations. This cluster of traits, in turn, leads to reserve, indifference, and a blasé outlook, and to anonymity and depersonalization. Wirth understood that the peculiar kind of social relationship fostered by city living is determined by three factors: the *size*, *density*, and *heterogeneity* of the city population. According to his view, larger populations tend to be more diversified and heterogeneous than small ones. Although a city dweller may have an enormous number of encounters with others, these encounters are likely to be segmented and superficial, impersonal and transitory. In place of sustained and intimate relations with relatives and close neighbors, a person encounters the butcher, the taxi driver, the waitress, the news vendor, yoga teachers, and co-workers on the job. In other words, a person's social relations are secondary rather than primary.

These impersonal and anonymous social relations give people in the city a sense of increased personal freedom. Freedom is not an unmixed blessing, however, for it can mean that a person is free to prey on others. With the waning of traditional social con-

figure 18:1 **American urbanization, 1900–1970**

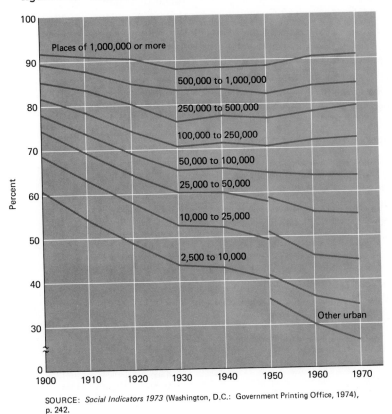

SOURCE: *Social Indicators 1973* (Washington, D.C.: Government Printing Office, 1974), p. 242.

The Census Bureau counts any town of 2500 or more as urban. By this measure, America has become increasingly urbanized. Most of its people still live in smaller cities and towns or in rural areas, however. Only a little over a quarter can be found in places larger than 100,000. (Note: The break in the lines at 1950 reflects a change in the Census Bureau's definition of "urban" to include unincorporated areas over 2500; the inclusion of these other urban areas reduced the percentage of rural population even further.)

straints, the urban society must maintain order through formal mechanisms of control—law and its supporting agencies, the police and the courts. (See figure 18:2.) But because these mechanisms of control are rarely as constraining as tradition and custom, the urban society is more prone to personal and social disorganization, more prone to alienation. In Tönnies's terminology the social relations of an earlier rural age have been replaced in the cities and in urban society with *Gesellschaft*-like relations. (See chapter 7 for the *Gemeinschaft-Gesellschaft* distinction.)

Is the City Alienating?   Does the city necessarily destroy intimate social bonds? Marvin Sussman (1959) found in his study that 70 percent of working-class persons and 45 per-

cent of middle-class persons have relatives in their neighborhoods, and that having a car permitted city dwellers to keep in contact with relatives living further away. He also found that urban relatives commonly help one another by giving sick care, financial aid, child care, and advice.

And what of Asian cities, which often have a preindustrial structure unlike cities in the industrialized countries of the north Atlantic region? Does Wirth's portrait of pervasive social disorganization suit them well? Philip Hauser (in Fava, 1968, p. 93) found that Wirth's description did not apply to Rangoon, Bangkok, Djakarta, or Calcutta. Some segmentation, anonymity, and competition can be found, and there are glaring contrasts between neighborhoods, but these are not the dominant features. And contrary to

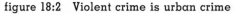

figure 18:2   Violent crime is urban crime

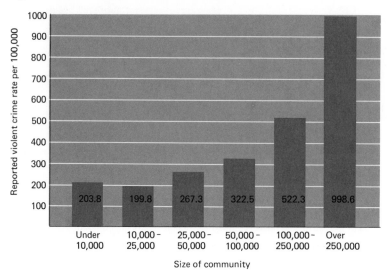

SOURCE: Federal Bureau of Investigation, *Uniform Crime Reports, 1972* (Washington D.C.: Government Printing Office, 1973), p. 4.

The risks of murder, assault, forcible rape, and robbery are far greater in large cities than in medium-size cities, and much greater there than in small towns. The direct relationship between size and violent crime supports Louis Wirth's contention that size is an important variable in explaining the effects of urban life.

Wirth's portrait there appears no increased rationality and sophistication on the part of city dwellers as opposed to the country folk, no breakdown of caste barriers, and no especially pronounced loneliness.

Wirth's emphasis possibly stems from the fact that he drew upon studies that had been done by University of Chicago sociologists, studies that usually focused on the inner city. Metropolitan centers consist not only of an inner city but of an outer city or suburbs as well. To make a general characterization of the entire metropolitan area on the basis of evidence from the inner city is misleading. Herbert Gans, in a well-known paper (in Rose, 1962) argues that the peculiar type of social relations sometimes found in the inner city are not related to large population size, density, and heterogeneity, but rather to residential instability and the economic condition of some inner-city dwellers. Part of the inner-city population is made up of the poor and the "trapped," who live in sections with rapid resident turnover and who therefore suffer most the ill effects of city living. The poor have little alternative but to stay in their deteriorating neighborhoods; the "trapped" cannot afford to follow their friends to the suburbs. The situation is quite different for others, such as the cosmopolites, the unmarried or childless young adults, and those ethnic groups who have recently immigrated to the inner city. The way of life of the ethnic villagers, for example, differs sharply from Wirth's portrait because these people place great importance on kinship ties, have little to do with formal organizations wherein secondary relations prevail, and are suspicious of anything and anyone outside their neighborhood. Gans writes:

While it is true that a not insignificant proportion of the inner city population was, and still is, made up of unattached individuals, Wirth's formulation ignores the fact that this population consists mainly of relatively homogeneous groups, with social and cultural moorings that shield it fairly effectively from the suggested consequences of number, density, and heterogeneity. This applies even more to the residents of the outer city, who constitute a majority of the total city population. (Gans, in Rose, 1962, p. 635)

Because the inner city comprises but a part of the entire modern metropolis, an accurate description of the city must take into account the suburbs.

Life in the Suburbs City life in America is increasingly suburban life. Propelled by the nostalgic belief in the values of intimate, neighborly association, millions have fled the inner city to the surrounding suburbs. The earliest suburbs grew up on the fringes of New York City in the 1850s and were predominantly havens for the rich. In these formerly rural areas the early city planners tried to develop model communities—"garden cities"—that would preserve the idyllic character of country living. At the turn of the century only one-sixth of the population of the United States was living in the suburbs. This pattern changed rapidly with the technological developments of the automobile and mass transport, and with the advent of mass financing for housing construction. During the post-Second World War years suburbs sprouted up almost overnight to house less affluent families. Many of these were "packaged suburbs," having five or six basic types of houses repeating themselves in a gridlike fashion block after block, making a mockery of the garden-city concept. By 1970, 38 percent of the total population of the United States lived in the suburbs, comprising 54 percent of all city dwellers (Commission on the Cities in the '70s, 1972, p. 71).

Many of the portraits of suburban living that are presented to Americans on the silvery screens of television and the movies have been far from attractive. One of the strongest images of the 1950s was James Dean in

Rebel Without a Cause: the inarticulate misfit in a conformist suburb. The 1960s had Dustin Hoffman in *The Graduate* escaping to the bottom of his swimming pool to get away from his parents' hollow and oppressive suburban neighbors. The suburbs were seen to breed mass-produced Americans in mass-produced houses, driven into a desperate round of group activity governed by strict conformity. Incapable of true friendships, they were seen as bored, lonely, alienated, atomized, and depersonalized. Wives were supposed to be domineering, husbands absent, children spoiled, marriages on the rocks of adultery and divorce, and everybody drunk or stoned out of their unhappy minds.

The reality is that the suburbs are far from being all alike; life in them differs largely on the basis of the inhabitants' social class and place in the life cycle (Gans, 1968, pp. 132–40). Most of the postwar suburbs have been settled by the lower-middle class, often with young families, and consequently their way of life has commonly been identified as the suburban one. But sociologists have found that lower-middle-class life-styles are much the same in the suburb as they are in the city. Painted in broad strokes, a generalized picture of the lower-middle-class style shows that social life focuses on friends and neighbors rather than distant relatives. The major recreation is home and child care; indeed, the home is the vital center of life here. These people swell the membership in churches

The suburbs are distinguished not only by class but by place in the life cycle. Young couples may live downtown as long as they are childless. But when a baby or two comes along, the growing family heads for the roomy houses, quiet streets, and convenient play areas of the suburbs. (George Butler/Rapho Guillumette)

and other sorts of voluntary organizations—the Elks, P.T.A., and the like.

Much of the conformity found in the suburbs and derided by the critics is a consequence of the lower-middle class being "on the make." In the fifties, William F. Whyte (in Stein, 1960) studied a Chicago suburb called Park Forest, which was then a home for middle-level "organization men" and their families. The tone of life there was set by the work ethic of the husbands: if you wanted to get ahead, you had to get along, be a company person, and avoid being too different. Houses there were consequently very similar and were furnished in good but modest taste. The accent was on appearances: adults were supposed to look happy and to be friendly with neighbors, and the kids were supposed to get along with one another. Although people were expected to make friends in the community, those friendships were not supposed to interfere with upward mobility.

The image of excessive drinking, widespread adultery and divorce, and intense social competition comes from an exaggerated version of *upper*-middle-class suburban life. One such suburb studied in the fifties by A. C. Spectorsky (in Stein, 1960) was populated by people in the New York City communications industries who commuted to work from a wealthy "exurbia" far outside the city. Reacting to the frantic pace of radio and T.V. work, these men and their families sought a countrified haven from the rat race, and a suburban home seemed to provide such a place. But the wives became bored with the childrens' conversation and hungry for adult companionship. Husbands had to work even more frantically to meet the increased costs of suburban living. Excessive drinking and extramarital affairs offered an escape from the pressures of their life-style. The suburban idyll thus became a part of rather than an antidote to the hectic life.

Other studies have shown upper-middle-class suburbanites to be quite different from the less affluent suburban dwellers (Gans, 1968). Being better educated and more cosmopolitan in their interests, they put less emphasis on home as the center of life. These people tend to be extensively and intensively involved in community activities, social, cultural, and civic. They participate in many shared activities with friends, such as partying, and they are even less likely than lower-middle-class persons to have strong ties with relatives. And again, this life-style is characteristic of the upper-middle class in general, both in the suburb and in the city.

Urban Ecology

The metropolis is divided not only into city and suburb, but into specialized areas of manufacturing, commerce, and housing. Major cities typically have areas that correspond to Wall Street, skid row, the Gold Coast, Watts, and Broadway. But how does this organization develop?

During the 1920s and 1930s a number of sociologists, again at the University of Chicago, felt that urban land specialization could best be explained by analogy to the ecological model in biology. They saw the urban environment as a product of competition and natural selection. The *urban ecologists*, as the group came to be known, hypothesized that established land uses usually resist displacement, and since dissimilar uses are usually incompatible with one another, a single area typically harbors one kind of development (factories *or* low-cost housing *or* entertainment). When competition for the limited urban space becomes particularly intense, however, the land use of the greatest economic significance generally wins out.

Ecological Succession That neighborhoods go through changes is all too obvious, especially to long-time residents. Some neighborhoods physically deteriorate while others are reclaimed and renovated. Industries move to the residential suburbs and provoke zoning battles in the councils of city government. Change is visible enough, but is there a pattern to these changes? The urban ecologists described an *invasion cycle*, which they felt constituted a general pattern (Park, Burgess, McKenzie, 1925). The invasion cycle begins before it is recognized by the area's inhabitants. One brownstone or dilapidated urban mansion in a rundown area is bought and refurbished by an architect, for example. Next, more professionals buy houses nearby, and the inhabitants notice and oppose the invasion. As land values and taxes and rents go up, the older and poorer residents protest that they can no longer afford to live there and have nowhere else to go. If opposition is unsuccessful, a general influx begins. Newcomers flood the area. A "tip point" is

---

IN THE NEWS

The Human Side of Ecological Succession

An area undergoing succession often experiences a good deal of tension, as the views of the new residents clash with those of the old. Take, for example, a Slovak blue-collar neighborhood on Cleveland's East Side, where blacks who had been financially successful enough to move out of downtown ghetto areas were buying homes, and the invasion cycle had reached the general influx stage. The major issue for most of the older residents was the increase in crime. One woman who sold her house at a $4,000 loss spoke of her plans to move to the suburbs.

One of the turning points for me was when I heard people were buying guns. I asked some of the women on the block and found three of them . . . who carry guns in their purses. Imagine, women who have never fired a gun in their lives carry one to go to the Pick 'n Pay.

What do the blacks say?

Everything we have, we worked for. Scraping together $1,500 for a down payment was the toughest thing we've ever done. So maybe blacks are the cause of crime in this area. But it isn't me out there bopping old ladies over the head. Talk about law and order— yes, sir, I'm for law and order. You can put me down as in love with the police. All I wanted was a place I could live and let live. Down at East 100th where we lived, we were robbed three times. We bought the dog and started looking for a house. Originally, I came from a farm in Louisiana; no electricity, no indoor plumbing. So this house, this neighborhood . . . well, I love it, I just love it.

Part of the problem is a difference in perspective. While whites thought the crime rate was skyrocketing, blacks thought it was going down. The whites remembered the area when there was virtually no crime, while the blacks, newly arrived from the crime-ridden inner city, felt far safer than they had before.

SOURCE: Paul Wilkes, "As the Blacks Move In, the Ethnics Move Out," *The New York Times Magazine* (January 24, 1971): 9ff.

reached as the old inhabitants are forced out or no longer wish to remain in the area. The invasion reaches the climax stage when the new inhabitants completely occupy the area. This is how a slum becomes a Georgetown, or a Georgetown a slum. The neighborhood may stabilize in climax or it may undergo further succession.

The Shape of Cities The urban ecologists thought that not only could the *dynamics* of city growth and change be generalized, but that similar outcomes in the overall *structure* of the city could also be detected. Certainly St. Louis, New York, Boston, Los Angeles, and Albuquerque are different in many different ways. Each city has its own unique features, to be sure, but a number of observers have seen general similarities.

On the basis of evidence at hand, Ernest W. Burgess proposed in the 1920s that cities are laid out in a series of *concentric circles* (Park, Burgess, McKenzie, 1925, pp. 47–62). At the center is the business district of shops and offices. By day this section is crowded with people, but by night it empties of all but a few souls who inhabit scattered transient hotels in the area. Adjacent and outward from the business district is an area of transition characterized by residential instability, high crime rates, and various forms of vice. Residents of this zone are racial and ethnic minority groups and outcasts. Beyond the transitional ring are the various residential zones. The innermost is inhabited by working-class people, the next by the middle class, and the outermost by the upper class. While concentric zone patterning is by no means typical of all or even most urban areas, it can be seen in certain cities like Chicago, which developed very rapidly in the period after the Industrial Revolution and before the development of the automobile. (See figure 18:3.)

In the 1930s Homer Hoyt proposed a theory of urban patterning that emphasized the importance of transportation routes—highways, railroad lines, and waterways—in shaping the growth of cities (1943). According to Hoyt's *sector theory,* a business district occupies the center of the city and beyond that, development occurs in sectors that tend to be distributed along major transportation routes, radiating out from the city center. As land uses expand they tend to remain within their respective sectors, but extend outward toward the edge of urban development. Like the concentric zone theory, the sector theory held that lower-class residential areas were adjacent to business or manufacturing areas, while middle- and upper-class neighborhoods were successively further away.

A third theory of urban ecological development, the *multiple nuclei theory*, was proposed by Chauncy D. Harris and Edward L. Ullman (1945). These men identified four principles that shape urban development. These are: (1) similar or related land uses are mutually complementary and tend to locate near one another; (2) dissimilar land uses are mutually destructive and tend to locate at a distance from one another; (3) real estate values limit certain types of development because high costs are prohibitive to certain land uses; and (4) certain land uses can locate only in areas with specialized facilities. On the basis of these principles, Harris and Ullman proposed that the city develops in a series of nuclei, each with specialized activities. For example, a car manufacturing nucleus might develop in an area on the outskirts of town with lots of space, low rents, and good transportation facilities. Manufacturing interests requiring less space might cluster in a nucleus closer to the center of the city, while residential centers might develop on the other side of town. As the city grows, nuclei proliferate and become specialized.

figure 18:3   Models of urban space

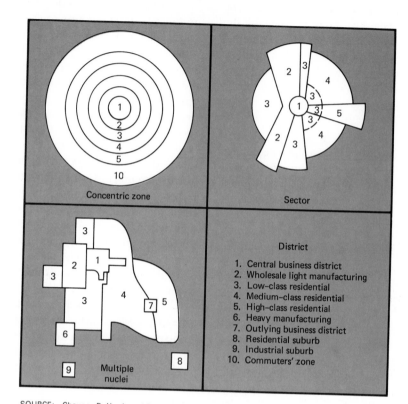

Concentric zone

Sector

Multiple
nuclei

District

1. Central business district
2. Wholesale light manufacturing
3. Low–class residential
4. Medium–class residential
5. High–class residential
6. Heavy manufacturing
7. Outlying business district
8. Residential suburb
9. Industrial suburb
10. Commuters' zone

SOURCE: Chauncy D. Harris and Edward L. Ullman, "The Nature of Cities," in Paul K. Hatt and A.J. Reiss, Jr., eds., *Cities and Society* (Glencoe Free Press, 1957). Courtesy of Professor Harris.

Attempts to describe the structure of cities produced the three alternative models shown here. A newer approach to the analysis of urban structure is called *social area analysis*. Analysts, using the census and other social indicators, attempt to explain residential patterns by correlating broad social categories such as social rank, family structure, and ethnicity. With the advent of the computer, even more factors are being taken into account in models of urban land use and social structure.

During the past decade and a half a number of observers have perceived a new pattern of urban development, one that is regional. A number of American metropolises are growing so large that they are growing together, forming what Jean Gottman has called a *megalopolis*:

As one follows the main highways or railroads between Boston and Washington, D.C., one hardly loses sight of built-up areas, tightly woven residential communities, or powerful concentrations of manufacturing plants. Flying this same route one discovers, on the other hand, that behind the ribbons of densely occupied land along the principal arteries of traffic, and in between the clusters of suburbs around the old urban centers, there still remain large areas covered with woods and brush alternating with some carefully cultivated patches of farmland. These green spaces, however, when inspected at closer range, appear stuffed with a loose but immense scattering of buildings, most of them residential but some of industrial character. That is, many of these sections that look rural actually function largely as suburbs in the orbit of some city's downtown. Even the farms, which occupy the larger tilled patches, are seldom worked by people whose only occupation and income are properly agricultural. And yet these farm areas produce large quantities of farm goods! (1961, p. 5)

The distinction between rural and urban does not apply in this area anymore. Municipalities having more than a hundred people per square mile are stretched along a continuous five-hundred-mile belt from Kittery, Maine, to Quantico, Virginia. Over 40 million people live in this sprawling belt (Tunnard 1967). And there are other emerging megalopolises as well: Pittsburgh–Youngstown–Canton–Akron–Cleveland; Chicago–Milwaukee, and a new strip between Chicago and Detroit; Los Angeles–San Diego; Palm Beach–Miami; Dallas–Fort Worth; and perhaps even Seattle–Takoma. Because this trend seems to be the wave of the future, we must give up the idea that a city is a tightly settled and organized territory in which people, activities, and riches are crowded into a small area distinctly separated from its nonurban surroundings. The unplanned growth that has created these megalopolises—called "urban sprawl" by some—continues unabated. Indeed, this is an essential part of what is often called the crisis of the cities.

The Urban Crisis

Metropolitan Segregation The flight of whites to the suburbs has created a pattern of segregation that is increasingly explosive.

The deteriorating inner city—the core of the metropolis or megalopolis—has been left to the poor and the black, who can least afford to finance its upkeep. Because the buildings are older and the rents lower in the inner cities, the poor and unskilled migrants from the rural areas take up residence there. The movement of blacks off the southern countryside into the northern cities made ghettos of the inner cities. Even though blacks constitute only one-tenth of the total population in America, nineteen of the nation's thirty largest cities are more than 30 percent black. Four are more than 50 percent black. Moreover, four-fifths of all urban blacks live in the inner city, whereas only two-fifths of the urban whites live there. This trend shows no sign of letting up. By the end of the decade it is possible that most of our biggest cities "will be preponderantly black and brown, and totally bankrupt," in the words of the Commission on the Cities in the '70s (1972, pp. 36–37).

The quality of public services and housing in the inner cities is declining because its residents are poor. Cities raise their money for public services—education, mass transportation, hospitals, police, sewers, etc.—through taxes. Poor populations yield smaller taxes. Whereas one in fourteen suburban residents had an income that fell below the poverty line in 1971, one in seven inner-city dwellers was listed as officially poor. And blacks are generally poorer than whites. Nonwhite income for 1973 averaged only three-fifths of white income that year (*Social Indicators, 1973*, 1974, p. 175).

Unemployment rates are also high in the inner-city slums. In 1966, which was a good year for the national economy (3.7 percent unemployment nationwide), some slums had as much as five times the national unemployment rate. But unemployment figures are not the best indicators of work and wage deficiency. In a special study the Department of

Labor determined the "subemployment" rates in several inner-city slums throughout the nation. This figure included all those persons who did not show up in the official unemployment statistics but who made wages inadequate to live on. These subemployment rates were 45 percent in New Orleans's slums, 24 percent in Boston's Roxbury section, 31 percent in New York's Harlem, 47 percent in San Antonio's East and West Sides, and 34 percent in North Philadelphia (Matza, 1971, p. 605). Unemployment seems to hit black teen-agers the hardest. In 1970 teen-age joblessness in America's black urban ghettos soared to 35 percent.

One of the reasons for urban poverty is the decline of job opportunities in the inner cities. Industry and commerce once located in the inner cities are moving to the suburbs. This means that fewer jobs are available to the inner-city resident. New York City alone lost a quarter of a million jobs between 1970 and 1974 (Stern, 1974, p. 1). Job losses were greatest in manufacturing, which is precisely the kind of work that the inner city needs for its increasing population of unskilled minorities.

With modernization, millions of peasants have migrated to cities like Bombay, Calcutta, or Rio de Janeiro, often clustering in vast slums on the outskirts of the city. Because the technological and economic bases cannot support such large concentrations of people, much suffering and squalor have resulted from this "overurbanization." (Paolo Koch/Rapho Guillumette)

Because of the inner cities' deteriorating conditions, there is a strong demand for public services which cannot be supported by the cities' inadequate tax revenues. Widespread unemployment means that more money must be spent on welfare. Because the buildings are older in the inner city, more money must be spent on fire protection. Because crime and poverty are so closely associated, more money must be spent on police services. Health, education, and mass transit get the short end of the budgetary stick. In New York's rich neighborhoods, there is one private doctor for every two hundred persons; in some poor inner-city neighborhoods, there is one per ten thousand persons. Inner-city schools spend two-thirds as much per pupil as some suburban schools do. Rural- or suburban-dominated state legislatures allocate more money to highway construction than to mass transit. Inner-city buildings are falling apart and being abandoned in some cases. Estimates of abandoned buildings in New York City go as high as a hundred thousand (Commission on the Cities in the '70s, 1972, pp. 43–80). And New York City is not alone in its problems; this is the condition of most of America's cities.

City governments cannot reverse this decline because they have no way to make the suburban dweller pay for his use of the city. Suburbanites commute into the city for work and entertainment and thereby use the city's transit, fire, police, and other public services. Increasing toll fees on commuter routes into the cities runs the risk of further losing the commuters' business. Because the suburbanite is getting a good deal, he is not going to put more money into the city's coffers voluntarily. And because the city government seldom encompasses the entire metropolitan region, no unified local government exists that can enforce a more equitable taxation scheme. (The average number of separate governing units for the typical metropolitan area is ninety-one!)

Unslumming the City The causes of urban disorganization and inner-city decline are numerous, and there are numerous proposals for reversing these trends. Some of these concentrate on improving the inner cities, others on coping with sprawling urban growth.

One strategy that has been popular in the past has been to bulldoze slums and build middle-class housing in an attempt to lure the middle class back into the city. This has merely provided the city's already existing middle class with better places to live—with a subsidy. At the same time it has forced the poor into smaller and smaller areas (Gans, 1968, pp. 261–65). The concentration on physical face-lifting has ignored other avenues of renewal.

Another strategy is to upgrade the income of those already in the inner city. Jane Jacobs writes:

The processes that occur in unslumming depend on the fact that the metropolitan economy, if it is working well, is constantly transforming many poor people into middle-class people, many illiterates into skilled (or even educated) people, many greenhorns into competent citizens. (1961, p. 288)

Raising incomes will in turn stimulate the renovation of neighborhoods and reduce population density as these people demand better housing.

Some have championed the idea of building *new towns*, carefully and comprehensively planned communities usually near a larger metropolis, which would take care of urban growth in a systematic fashion. Ebenezer Howard began an English new town, Letchworth, back in 1902, and Britain had over 150,000 people living in such developments by their 1966 census. Columbia, Maryland, and Reston, Virginia, in the United

Although many urban renewal projects are specially planned for those who otherwise would live in substandard housing, the expense of constructing and maintaining these projects puts the rents out of reach of low- and even middle-income people unless there are substantial subsidies from local, state, and federal sources. (James H. Karales/ Urban Development Corp.)

The problems of the cities are so massive that a national policy is needed to help solve the crisis. Tinkering separately with transportation, urban renewal, employment, education, health services, and the rest, does not work. Comprehensive plans for monitoring cities and devising strategies for dealing with their problems are imperative.

States are perhaps the best-known new towns (Schaffer, 1970, pp. 22–25). But this strategy offers only a partial and slow solution to the urban crisis.

Some observers see the need for massive federal aid to the cities. They propose a Marshall Plan for the cities comparable to the outlays that the United States spent on rebuilding western Europe after World War II (Commission on the Cities in the '70s, 1972).

THE TECHNOLOGICAL TRANSFORMATION

Technological developments have changed more aspects of society than simply the kinds of cities we live in. The pace at which we live, the kind of recreation we enjoy, the work we do, even the air we breathe, have sometimes been affected by technology. Technology consists of not only machinery but of ways of organizing resources, including people. For example, a computer is just a piece of equipment, but it demands that a whole social organization of engineers, programmers, and service people support it. Moreover, the group or institution that uses it often changes its way of doing things to accommodate it or to implement its results.

Technology is not limited to economic applications, and these new forms of organizing life reach into every corner of society. Think, for example, of the impact of television upon our culture. Some commentators have seen in the advent of electronic communication, no less than the transformation of how we see—from serial experience to instantaneous perception. This, in turn, implies a nonrational, tribal way of relating to others (McLuhan, 1964, pp. 36–45).

The profound effects of technology are often quite incidental to the original purpose of the invention. The growth of cities was not what the people who invented the reaper or the spinning jenny had in mind. Neither were the destruction of the environment and the changes in work satisfaction and occupational structure, yet technological change has brought these in its wake, too. In the next sections we will look at some of the profound and unanticipated effects of technology upon the environment, work, and the society as a whole.

Technology and Ecology

Man has developed his tools to tame nature and often to tame other men as well. But industrial man has more than tamed nature; he has carved it into his own image. An American Indian woman has said: "When we burn grass for grasshoppers, we don't ruin things. . . . But the White people plow up the ground, pull down the trees, kill everything. . . . How can the spirit of the earth like the White man? Everywhere the White man has touched it, it is sore" (in McLuhan, 1971, p. 1).

Sometimes even benign technology backfires. For example, the advance of the desert in west Africa that has created mass starvation is a product not only of drought but also of technology. Health programs in the area contributed to population explosion among the nomadic herders of this parched area. A U.S. AID program to dig wells encouraged the populace to expand their herds beyond the grazing capacity of the land. The herders' culture places great value on the number of cattle, so thinning the herds was unthinkable—and besides, the extra cattle were needed for the extra population. Lands once able to support the nomads were overgrazed and turned to desert, intensified by prolonged drought. In 1974, 600,000 tons of relief food were pledged to an area that once *exported* grain (Vicker, 1974). Introducing vaccinations and wells has had a deadly effect upon Sahelian Africa. (UPI)

Zen Buddhist D. T. Suzuki believes that the Judeo-Christian tradition has led the West to desecrate nature on a grand scale; for that tradition has preached that man has a rightful dominion over nature. Microbiologist René Dubos (1972) disputes this by showing that abuses of nature have occurred throughout the history of man and throughout the non-Christian world. Others have pointed to capitalism as an aggravating force in this desecration, but socialist countries have serious environmental problems as well. It is undeniable, however, that the profit motive of capitalism has produced a plethora of manufactured commodities that satisfy needs that have been artificially stimulated through mass media advertising campaigns. And workers who receive little or no intrinsic satisfaction in their work seek compensatory gratification in buying a wide range of consumer products. Whatever factors have created an industrialized consumer economy, one thing is clear: industrialized technologies have made a massive assault on the environment and have placed a tremendous drain on the earth's bank of nonrenewable resources.

The scale of this assault has recently been estimated in a study, *The Limits of Growth*, sponsored by the Club of Rome (Meadows et al., 1972). By applying a computerized systems analysis to present trends, this study has explored the earth's capacity to support the human population and economy. The human population has been growing exponentially because the birth rate is increasing and the death rate decreasing. Similarly, the world economy grows exponentially because the means of production increase while their rate of depreciation decreases. The Club of Rome asserts that there are limits in the ability of the planet to support exponential population and economic growth. These limits are the availability of food, raw materials, fossil and nuclear fuels, and the ability of the

earth's ecosystem to absorb wastes and to recycle matter. Two factors that are rapidly pushing the earth's ecosystem toward its upper limits of tolerance are the rapid depletion of nonrenewable resources such as metals and fuels, and the rapid increase in pollution. The effects of pollution are particularly unpredictable. There is almost no knowledge about the upper limits to pollution. Many pollutants are distributed globally and their effects may be felt at a distance from their source. Finally, the Club of Rome study sees a natural delay in an ecosystem's response to stress, a fact that makes it possible that the limits of pollution tolerance could be reached and passed inadvertently.

The study's ominous conclusion is that if present growth trends persist in population, industrialization, food production, resource depletion, and pollution, the earth's upper limits of tolerance will be reached within the next one hundred years. When this occurs, population and industrial capacity will collapse. (See figure 18:4.)

The only possible way to avert world collapse is to halt economic and population growth and establish environmental and economic stability. The authors of the Club of Rome study emphasize that technology alone cannot rescue the world from its predicament. Even if improved technology increased agricultural output, created highly efficient forms of pollution control and of the recycling of natural resources, and offered foolproof methods of population control such that only wanted children would be born, there would still be a world collapse from environmental stress. Eventually, overuse of land would cause erosion and a rapid drop in food production, resources would become depleted, and pollution would start to rise sharply, rapidly accelerating the death rate. Reliance on technological solutions is simply not enough.

figure 18:4 **A model of ecological crisis**

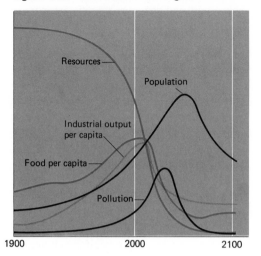

Resources

Population

Industrial output per capita

Food per capita

Pollution

1900   2000   2100

SOURCE: Donella H. Meadows et al. *The Limits to Growth* (New York: Universe, 1972), p. 124.

If present trends continue (based on certain assumptions about the growth of population and industrial capacity), many researchers predict the exhaustion of resources, scarcity of food, and industrial collapse within the next hundred years. Pollution and population will continue to grow for a while after this collapse, but they too will peak. Note that after the collapse, population will still be greater than today but food and industrial capacity will be far lower. Because of this, living standards will drop dramatically.

These conclusions are a matter of debate and not fact, for the Club of Rome study has its critics. Some attack the model, pointing out flaws in its underlying assumptions or its construction ("The Limits of Doomsday Predictions," 1973). Others find that "it is not all that difficult to sketch out a scenario of social catastrophe in a nongrowth society to equal, in its horror, the scenario of ecological catastrophe in a growth society" (Klein, 1974, p. 14). No growth could mean that those in poverty will be trapped there. This, in turn, could increase national and international tensions. Furthermore, the problem of arriving at a no-growth society will place stresses on the political structure. Who will cut back on births and on consumption? How will desirable increases in public services be obtained when every increase in one area of society implies a decrease in resources devoted to another area? Collective decision-making will be imperative; whether this will be harmonious or involve coercion is very much an open question.

This scenario might then suggest that a society which had adopted the values of nongrowth would be introvert rather than extrovert, traditional rather than innovative. Whether it had settled for an egalitarian distribution of wealth or for the perpetuation of inequalities, it would be resistant to change, stressing social control as the inevitable counterpart of social stability. There would be little social mobility, since this tends to be a product of economic growth. There might well evolve a gerontocracy, with power going hand in hand with seniority, since it would no longer be open to the young to secede from existing organizations to start their own. The only frontiers that would be open for exploration would be those of artistic or spiritual activity. The resemblance of the picture to medieval society in Western Europe is not accidental. (Klein, 1974, p. 84)

Technology and Work

Alienation Technology has not only changed the face of the city and natural surroundings but also has affected the organization of work and the satisfaction people derive from their jobs. There exists a long tradition of sociological thinking that sees people alienated from work under the impact of industrialization and the division of labor, which industrialization produced. Karl Marx developed this theme over a century ago, and it has been a cornerstone to social criticism ever since. In the *Communist Manifesto,* he and Friedrich Engels declared:

> Owing to the extensive use of machinery and to division of labor, the work of proletarians has lost all individual character and, consequently, all charm for the workman. He becomes an appendage of the machine, and it is only the simplest, most monotonous, and most easily acquired knack that is required of him. (in Feuer, 1959, p. 14)

The propertyless worker is alienated or separated from his work because the ownership of the tools of production and the product itself has been appropriated by another. The worker is not paid to "express himself"; the boss is only interested in getting the work done. The worker is thus reduced to his mere labor power, which has a market value. His labor power becomes a commodity, a thing to be bought and sold. Man thereby becomes alienated from himself, for his labor power is no longer an inextricable part of his essential self. Work becomes separated from play; work becomes separated from self-expression; work has no intrinsic meaning and is only self-sacrifice undertaken to earn money for leisure-time pursuits. As sociologist C. W. Mills wrote in 1951:

> [Alienation from work] means that the most alert hours of one's life are sacrificed to the making of money with which to "live." Alienation means boredom and the frustration of potentially creative effort, of the productive sides of personality. It means that while men must seek all values that matter to them outside of work, they must be serious during work: they may not laugh or sing or even talk, they must follow the rules and not violate the fetish of "the enterprise." In short, they must be serious and steady about something that does not mean anything to them, and moreover during the best hours of their day, the best hours of their life. . . . Each day men sell little pieces of themselves in order to try to buy them back each night and week end with the coin of "fun." With amusement, with love, with movies, with vicarious intimacy, they pull themselves into some sort of whole again, and now they are different men. (p. 237)

Are Workers Actually Alienated? Determining workers' satisfaction or alienation is a deceptively simple task. Why not just ask them if they are happy with their work? A number of such studies are reported in *Work in America* (1973), a special task force report for the Department of Health, Education, and Welfare. One is a Gallup Poll, which revealed that 80 to 90 percent of those questioned felt that their work was satisfying. In a representative cross section of American workers, about 80 percent indicated that they would continue to work even if they inherited enough money to live without working. Another finding was that as people increased their income and wealth, they did not reduce the amount of time and energy expended in work.

There may be more to this than meets the eye, however. Robert Blauner (1960) cautions that statistics on job satisfaction may be misleading for two reasons. First, job satisfaction is a vague concept, hard to define and therefore hard to assess. Second, "Under normal conditions there is a natural tendency for people to identify with, or at least be somewhat positively oriented toward, those social arrangements in which they are implicated" (p. 336). People might have a difficult time articulating their dissatisfaction and might only appear to be satisfied. *Work in America*, therefore, goes on to probe the true feelings of workers. One man who said he had a "pretty good job" replied when pressed to tell what made the job good: "Don't get me wrong. I didn't say it is a good job. It's an O.K. job—about as good a job as a guy like me might expect. The foreman leaves me alone and it pays well. But I would never call it a good job. It doesn't amount to much, but it's not bad." Is this America's happy worker?

YOUTH AND WORK

Because of the postwar baby boom there are more young people than ever before entering the labor force. Young workers, particularly in the auto industry, have not been reluctant to act out their discontent; absenteeism, tardiness, and arguments with foremen have increased significantly. Other youths have withdrawn into the counterculture. Many older people have concluded that the country is in trouble because of lazy self-indulgent attitudes, but research suggests that the attitudes of youth are more complex.

A 1973 Yankelovich Poll surveyed over three thousand youths both in and out of college to discover their career aspirations and their attitudes toward work. It found that a majority of the young accept the necessity of hard work and are seeking challenging jobs that will provide them with the opportunity for self-fulfillment, self-expression, participation in decision-making, fellowship, and equality. But there exist disparities between college and noncollege youths in their ability to attain intrinsically rewarding jobs.

Among college students there has been a steady increase over the past six years of traditional job aspirations, stressing economic security and the chance to get ahead. College is therefore seen more and more as a training ground for a career. Only about 34 percent of all college students are unconcerned with the extrinsic rewards of work, largely because they take affluence for granted. But a growing number of students, now comprising 32 percent, feel that they can achieve *both* the economic rewards of a career and the intrinsic rewards of self-fulfillment and self-expression. They feel that they can strike a bargain with society, fulfilling themselves while also getting ahead in the world. Quite conveniently, the chances for economic rewards and self-fulfillment appear to be the greatest in the expanding professional, technical, and managerial occupations, which require higher education for entrance. A good "fit" therefore appears possible between what the college students want and what the society has to offer.

Blue-collar youth not in college are increasingly unwilling to accept work that does not offer the possibility of self-fulfillment. In 1969, 79 percent believed that "hard work would always pay off"; in 1973 the proportion of believers had fallen to 56 percent. And the nature of an acceptable "payoff" is changing; more blue-collar youth are emphasizing the need for meaningful and gratifying work. The crucial dilemma, however, is that blue-collar work offers fewer opportunities for gratification. About a third of all questioned blue-collar workers are "just hanging on until something better comes along," whereas only a tenth of all professional and managerial respondents feel this way. But most youths lack the educational certification needed to get these professional and managerial jobs. Only one in four of all youths eighteen to twenty-five years of age finished college. The blue-collar youth without a college education is therefore more likely to be frustrated on his job, unable to fulfill his aspirations.

SOURCE: Yankelovich Youth Study, © 1974 by the JDR 3rd Fund, pp. 17–30.

A better indicator of job satisfaction may be whether or not workers would choose their line of work again if they were given the chance to start over. By this measure job satisfaction appears far lower than the 80 to 90 percent reported by the Gallup Poll. (See

figure 18:5   Job satisfaction

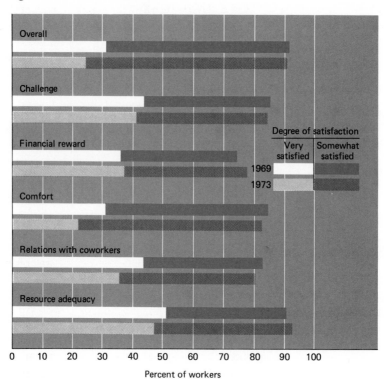

SOURCE: *Social Indicators, 1973* (Washington, D.C.: Government Printing Office, 1974), p. 123.

In 1969 and 1973 the Survey Research Center of the University of Michigan asked a sample of workers to rate twenty-three aspects of their jobs. Analysts then grouped the answers into various dimensions. The overwhelming majority of Americans expressed some degree of satisfaction with their jobs, but the percentage that were very satisfied was significantly lower. Not surprisingly workers seemed most displeased about their compensation. These findings support the conclusion of *Work in America* that American workers are dissatisfied only if the group "somewhat satisfied" is taken to indicate a large pool of people with reservations about their work.

figure 18:5.) One such study reported in *Work in America* finds that 41 percent of skilled steel workers and only 16 percent of unskilled auto workers would choose their jobs again. About twice as many white-collar workers as blue-collar workers are satisfied with their work, but in both groups the percentage satisfied was less than half. Only among professionals was satisfaction really high: 83 percent of the surveyed lawyers, 89 percent of the physicians and biologists, and 97 percent of the urban university professors would choose their profession again (*Work in America*, 1973).

What Makes Work Satisfying? Phil Stallings, a twenty-seven-year-old spot-welder at a Ford assembly plant in Chicago, describes life on the assembly line:

I stand in one spot, about two- or three-feet area, all night. The only time a person stops is when the line stops. We do about thirty-two jobs per car, per unit. Forty-eight units an hour, eight hours a day. Thirty-two times forty-eight times eight. Figure it out. That's how many times I push that button. . . . I don't understand how come more guys don't flip. Because you're nothing more than a machine when you hit this type of thing. They give better care to that machine than they will to you. They'll have more respect, give more attention to that machine. And you *know* this. Somehow you get the feeling that the machine is better than you are. [Laughs]. (in Terkel, 1974, pp. 159–60)

Phil Stallings is clearly alienated from his work. The noise where he stands is tremendous and when he opens his mouth, he is liable to get a mouthful of sparks. Needless to say, he has very little contact with others on the assembly line. "You can work next to a guy for months without even knowing his name." And that assembly line—"It don't stop. It just goes and goes and goes. I bet there's men who have lived and died out there, never seen the end of that line. And they never will, because it is endless. It's like a serpent. It's all body, no tail. It can do things to you." Phil Stallings has to ask the foreman if he can go to the bathroom. "If he doesn't like you, he'll make you hold it, just ignore you." And he certainly does not have pride in his craft. "Whenever we make a mistake, we always say, 'Don't worry about it, some dingaling'll buy it.'"

One important factor in work satisfaction is the degree to which one's task is fractionated and repetitive. Recall Marx and Engels's assertion that the use of machinery and the division of labor robbed work of its individual character and charm. Phil Stallings's product certainly has no individual character and he does not identify with the product of his labors. But listen to a piercer-dragout worker who works in a steel plant with heavy machines: "There's nothing like working here in this mill. Everybody cooperates. Every man works as a member of a team and every man tries to turn out as much steel as they possibly can. We work hard and get satisfaction out of working here" (in Blauner, 1960, p. 346).

Clearly, an important difference between these work experiences is that working on a team affords workers the chance to develop friendships. The formation of friendships and feelings of group responsibility is apparently a major determinant of job satisfaction. This is supported by a study of factory workers that revealed that 65 percent of workers integrated into work groups were pleased with the *intrinsic* and ancillary aspects of their work (that is, the pay, working conditions, and the like), while only 28 percent of isolated workers expressed a similar degree of satisfaction (*Work in America,* 1973).

The degree of control is also important.[1] On the assembly line, the pace is unyielding. But the assembly line employs only 2 percent of America's work force. Today technology often demands greater responsibility from workers and offers greater freedom. In the automated plant the machines do the work without operators, and the men supervise or repair the machines.

[1] *Work in America* identifies several other determinants of job satisfaction. These include *the status of work*, its *prestige* as compared with other jobs; *job content*, the degree to which it is repetitious or challenging; *supervision*, the degree to which the worker is free to make his own decisions and regulate his work; *wages*, high pay and high satisfaction tend to go hand in hand; *mobility*, the availability of opportunities for promotion; *working conditions*, the length and time of day of working hours and the comfort and pleasantness of surroundings; and *job security*, the degree to which the employee is susceptible to layoffs or being fired (1973, p. 94).

The case of continuous process industry, particularly the chemical industry, shows that automation increases the worker's control over his work process and checks the further division of labor and growth of large factories. The result is meaningful work in a more cohesive, integrated industrial climate. (Blauner, 1964, p. 169)

Modern technology then, can actually be arranged in such a way as to *reduce* the division of labor, increase the amount of teamwork, and thereby relieve worker alienation. The Volvo automobile plants in Sweden have successfully experimented with abandoning the assembly line. *All* the auto's parts are conveyed to a work space where a small team of workers assemble the entire car. Working as a team, the group decides who will do what, thus allowing for day-to-day variation. Workers have more contact with each other, have a stronger identification with the product of their labors, and apparently receive direct satisfaction from their work. Absenteeism has decreased dramatically and productivity has remained high.

It is important to note that the Volvo team system not only allows a reduced division of labor but also an increase of the workers' decision-making opportunities. Reorganizing work to extend the control of employees can pay big dividends. For example, Texas Instruments, a manufacturing company, had contracted out its janitorial services. It found that its plant was only 65 percent clean and that among the janitorial personnel there was a 100 percent quarterly turnover rate. To change this situation the company tried an experiment involving 120 maintenance personnel. They divided the personnel into teams of 19 each, involved the teams in planning and goal-setting for the project, trained the teams, and gave them adequate equipment. Scheduling and task assignment were left up to each team, and the teams

were held responsible for their performance. As a result of this effort to increase workers' control over their work, the company found that the plant cleanliness rose from 65 to 85 percent and the quarterly turnover tumbled from 100 to 9.8 percent. In all, the company saved approximately $103,000 per year from the changes. A number of other experiments in work reorganization have been conducted with equally dramatic results. The findings indicate that job satisfaction and productivity can be increased simultaneously if workers are treated like human beings instead of machines (*Work in America*, 1973, pp. 96–100).

Technology and the Occupational Structure
The transformation of the content of work brought about by technological change was accompanied by a transformation in the occupational structure. The advances of the Industrial Revolution turned many a farmer into a machine operator in an urban factory. The statistics show this clearly. In 1820 about 70 percent of the American population worked the farm. This proportion fell to about 40 percent in 1900 and is presently less than 5 percent (Thomlinson, 1965, p. 478).

In time fewer workers were needed for manual labor and more were needed for servicing, distributing, and coordinating. This has meant an enormous rise in paperwork, again reflected in aggregate figures. Whereas clerks constituted only 0.6 percent of the labor force a hundred years ago (Mayer, 1956), they are now the largest occupational group, comprising one out of every five people (*Statistical Abstract*, 1973, table 373, p. 234). Furthermore, with coordination and administration of work becoming more complex, the proportion of nonfarm managers, officials, and proprietors has risen from less than 6 percent of the 1900 labor force to over 10 percent in 1972, an increase of about 80 percent (Thomlinson, 1965, p. 478; *Statistical Abstract*, 1973, table 373, p. 234).

Another significant shift is the increased demands for technical and professional workers. The growth of science and technology during the past few centuries has produced an explosion of knowledge. This in turn has created new occupations that require mastery of a complex body of specialized knowledge and skills. Agricultural societies, with their low level of technological development, needed only a small professional class. Precise figures on the size of this group in preindustrial America are not available, but it must have been small judging from its size in other preindustrial societies. Mexico in the 1940s had only 1 percent of its work force in the professions, and Greece in the 1920s had only 3 percent. In contrast, America had 14 percent of all workers in professional and technical occupations in 1972 (*Statistical Abstract,* 1973, table 373, p. 234).

The point of all these statistics is that Americans are again living in the midst of a radical shift in the occupational structure of our society. Within the past two decades, America has become the first society with a majority of workers engaged in service occupations rather than in the production of foods and goods. A growing service economy also means that there will be a growth in the services of health, education, research, and government. The growth of nonmanual service jobs has meant the increasing expansion of job opportunities for women. Whereas women make up less than a fifth of all production workers, they constitute half of the service sector (Fuchs, 1966, pp. 7–17). The continuing growth of the service sector and the expanding opportunities for women are bound to have an impact on the structure of the family, on women's views of themselves, and on the general definition of sex roles.

The Postindustrial Society

Some sociologists, notably Daniel Bell (1973) of Harvard, see this shift as evidence of a more profound change—the change from an industrial to a *postindustrial* society. This shift will usher in changes as profound as those produced in the change from an agricultural to an industrial society. Bell argues that it will, although it is difficult to define precisely the nature of the changes that loom on the horizon. After all, it is only with the advantage of hindsight that we can begin to comprehend the nature of the extensive changes that industrialization brought in its train.

Bell traces this momentous shift in the technological revolution that we have experienced since the Second World War. Whereas earlier inventions were typically produced by craftsmen or tinkerers unschooled in the principles of theoretical physics and chemistry, new technologies depend upon such specialized knowledge. The development of the machine was the central force in industrial society. In postindustrial society the central force will be the organization of theoretical knowledge. Energy production drove industrial society; information production drives the postindustrial society. Economic growth was the goal of industrial society; advancement of theoretical knowledge is the new goal.

The leadership structure of industrial society will be replaced by new figures of dominance. "If the dominant figures of the past hundred years have been the entrepreneur, the businessman, and the industrial executive, the 'new men' are the scientists, the mathematicians, the economists, and the engineers of the new intellectual technology" (Bell, 1973, p. 343). The class structure of postindustrial society will be based on access

table 18:1 PREINDUSTRIAL, INDUSTRIAL, AND POSTINDUSTRIAL SOCIETY

	PREINDUSTRIAL	INDUSTRIAL	POSTINDUSTRIAL	
Regions:	Asia Africa Latin America	Western Europe Soviet Union Japan	United States	
Economic sector:	Primary Extractive: Agriculture Mining Fishing Timber	Secondary Goods producing: Manufacturing Processing	Tertiary Transportation Utilities Quinary Health Education Research Government Recreation	Quaternary Trade Finance Insurance Real estate
Occupational slope:	Farmer Miner Fisherman Unskilled worker	Semiskilled worker Engineer	Professional and technical Scientists	
Technology:	Raw materials	Energy	Information	
Design:	Game against nature	Game against fabricated nature	Game between persons	
Methodology:	Common sense experience	Empiricism Experimentation	Abstract theory: models, simulation, decision theory, systems analysis	
Time perspective:	Orientation to the past Ad hoc responses	Ad hoc adaptiveness Projections	Future orientation Forecasting	
Axial principle:	Traditionalism: Land/resource limitation	Economic growth: State or private control of investment decisions	Centrality of and codification of theoretical knowledge	

SOURCE: Daniel Bell, *The Coming of the Post-Industrial Society* (New York: Basic Books, 1973), table 1–1, p. 117.

to information and control of decision-making rather than on ownership of property. Thus the lower class will be defined not by their poverty but by their lack of knowledge that would give access to dominant organizations. The primary value of technological society is efficiency, which means greater output for less cost. In order to promote efficiency, Bell argues, human activities are likely to be more bureaucratized. Postindustrial society will not be without its conflicts, Bell contends. The political system will stress the values of equality and popular participation, which contradict the values of hierarchy and subordination found in bureaucratic organizations. These two contradicting forces will generate conflict. There will also be contradictions between postindustrial culture and its social structure. Whereas the modern culture has stressed and will continue to stress the values of self-realization and self-fulfillment—the development of the whole person—the demands of a bureaucratized social structure will pressure people to conform to specialized roles. Thus, it is along these cleavages that postindustrial society will experience strain and conflict.

The Technological Society According to French sociologist Jacques Ellul (1964), technology is like a virus. A virus perpetuates its strain by invading a cell, taking over its chemistry of reproduction, and causing it to stop producing its own kind and begin producing viruses. Similarly, "technique," or technology, takes over society and "dissociates the sociological forms, destroys the moral framework, . . . explodes social and religious taboos, and reduces the body social to a collection of individuals" (p. 126).

This occurs because technology always seeks the most efficient way of performing tasks, no matter if it makes work less satisfying to the individual or fouls the environment or disrupts the social fabric. Trying to curb pollution with new technology (or correct other defects of technological progress) only compounds the problem since the criterion is still efficiency and the new technology has its own imperatives that may lead to equally unfortunate side effects. One of these imperatives is a tendency toward self-perpetuation and immunity from human control, so technology may proliferate if unchecked.

Technology is monolithic, Ellul argues. Although different techniques operate in the spheres of government, economy, and culture, they do not compete with or impede one another because that would be inefficient. When clashes do occur, an efficient solution is worked out. The means of technology become ends. Thus, these spheres form a coordinated whole, dominating society and its mores.

Because of the importance of efficiency in a technological society, Ellul maintains there will be an increasing effort to limit the effects of human error and interference in technological progress. As a result techniques will be developed to manipulate behavior through education, propaganda, and psychology. Ellul suggests that although people will be unhappy about these encroachments on their freedom, they will not revolt, for unhappiness is just another technical problem. Instead, technique will devise one last ignominy, a human technology that will manipulate people into happiness or at least complacency. Thus, technique will become a tyrant, ruling human society with absolute power. "Inside the technical circle, the choice among methods, mechanisms, organizations, and formulas is carried out automatically. Man is stripped of his faculty of choice and is satisfied. He accepts the situation when he sides with technique" (p. 82).

Two main perspectives, then, dominate speculation about the future of industrial society. One, represented by the Club of Rome or Ellul, is pessimistic, predicting increased government control, mechanization, and dehumanization. The other, represented by Bell, is more optimistic, citing the growth of knowledge, the increase of leisure, and greater diversity and individualism. Obviously, each is looking at somewhat different facts or interpreting some of the facts differently. What is clear is that industrial society is moving toward a new phase in which automation and other technological developments will become far more important and will engender significant social change. In the next chapter we will deal with theories explaining social change, including revolution, modernization, and the forces at work in contemporary American society.

summary

Humanity's use of technology is intimately related to the way in which it organizes its settlements. Armed with little more than a club, early humans were forced to wander over the land in small bands in search of food. The discovery of the principles of plant cultivation and animal domestication were major technological advances that provided food surpluses, allowing people to settle in permanent villages and cities. The numerous technological innovations from the fifteenth century onward, culminating in the Industrial Revolution, again stimulated far-reaching changes in settlement patterns. Villages grew into towns, towns into cities, cities into metropolises, and metropolises into megalopolises.

Sociology arose as a discipline to explain the impact of these forces. Much of the pioneering work in the study of the organization of cities—physical and social—was done at the University of Chicago in the 1920s and 1930s. Attempts to explain the physical structure of cities and how land uses changed relied on biological models of competition and natural selection. Since dissimilar uses of land are often incompatible, a single area usually harbors one kind of use. When competition for the limited urban space becomes intense, however, the land use of greatest economic significance usually prevails. Changes occur in predictable succession, described as an *invasion cycle*. The result of these processes has been described by several models of urban structure: *the concentric ring*, *the sector*, and *the multiple nuclei models*.

The Chicago School examined not only the physical structure of the city but the quality of life there as well. The peculiar characteristics of urban life are fostered by the size, density, and heterogeneity of the city's population, according to Louis Wirth. The impersonal and anonymous character of social relations gives people a sense of increased freedom, including freedom from traditional constraints. This is a mixed blessing since it also makes urban society more prone to personal and collective disorganization. These conclusions have subsequently been challenged, most notably by Herbert Gans, who points out that the disorganization in the city is confined to certain types of inhabitants in areas of residential instability and is not produced by size, density, and heterogeneity alone.

To talk about cities today means to discuss the suburbs as well as the downtown areas. The satiric portraits of the suburbs as places where people are turned into conformists of a single stamp is not borne out by sociological research. Suburbs are far from alike, and life in them differs largely on the basis of the inhabitants' social class. Suburbanites bring their values with them.

The flight to the suburbs has created problems of urban growth. In some areas vast megalopolises join once-separate cities. To cope with urban growth, some advocate planned expansion through the use of new towns.

New towns do not solve the major problems of the cities, such as the concentration of the poor and black in the inner cores. Residents of the core require a wide array of public services, but they can least afford to finance these services through taxes. The suburbs isolate themselves from the problems of the inner cities because of the political fragmentation of the metropolitan area. Approaches to solving the urban crisis are quite varied. One has been urban renewal, to attract the middle class back into the city; another has been "unslumming" by raising incomes to create a new middle class within the city.

As technology has changed the kinds of settlements we live in, so too has it changed the kinds of work we do. The transformation to an industrial society raised the specter of the alienated worker, whose life was regulated by the machine. Today, dissatisfaction with work seems to be fairly widespread, even among white-collar workers. However, modern technology may be arranged to reduce repetition, increase autonomy and interpersonal contacts, and relieve worker alienation.

Modern technology is changing the occupational structure and with it the nature of the society in which we live. Daniel Bell views the rise of the service sector and the increase in professional and technical workers as symptoms of the coming of a postindustrial society, where knowledge, not money, will bring power. Efficiency will be paramount, bringing in its wake greater bureaucratization. This development may clash with the political stress on equality and popular participation and with the cultural stress on self-realization and fulfillment.

The arrival of postindustrial society depends on whether ecological disaster can be averted. The Club of Rome predicts that reliance solely on technology without cutbacks to a no-growth society will fail. Jacques Ellul says that even if society survives, it will be dominated by a technology that shapes everything—the economy, the polity, and the culture—to the ends of efficiency. Whether or not we agree with these predictions, we can expect rapid social change in the next few decades, induced by the kinds of forces that these various sociologists have observed.

glossary

alienation According to Marx this condition results from machine-age technology that requires only simple, repetitive tasks of workers, whose labor is purchased like any other commodity.

city A relatively large, dense, and permanent settlement of socially heterogeneous individuals. (Wirth)

concentric ring model A model of urban structure proposed by E. W. Burgess that sees cities laid out with the business district at the core, surrounded by a transitional ring of residential instability and high crime rates, beyond which are the various residential zones.

invasion cycle A general pattern of change in urban land use that begins imperceptibly. Once change is recognized, opposition begins until a "tip point" is reached, when the new users succeed in starting to drive out earlier users. Once the new use is established, the cycle has reached its climax phase.

megalopolis An urban form in which once-distinct cities grow together, forming a functional unit.

multiple nuclei model This model sees the city as composed of many nuclei that specialize and proliferate as a city grows. (Harris and Ullman)

new town A comprehensively planned city, usually near a larger metropolis, built to absorb urban growth in a systematic fashion.

postindustrial society A society in which the social structure has changed from a goods-producing to a service economy, professionals and technicians dominate the occupational structure, and theoretical knowledge shapes social changes. (Bell)

sector model A model describing cities as composed of sectors around a central business district, distributed along major transportation routes radiating outward from the center (Hoyt)

social area analysis Explaining residential segregation in terms of such broad social categories as social rank, commitment to family, and ethnicity.

technological society A society in which technology determines all forms of social life and social values. (Ellul)

urban ecology The study of urban patterns and their changes based on a biological model of competition and natural selection.

urbanization   The increase in the percentage of a population that lives in urban settlements and the consequent extension of influence of urban ways over the populace.

references

Daniel Bell, *The Coming of the Post-Industrial Society*, New York: Basic Books, 1973.

Robert Blauner, *Alienation and Freedom: The Factory Worker and His Industry*, Chicago: University of Chicago Press, 1964.

———, "Work Satisfaction and Industrial Trends in Modern Society," in Walter Galenson and Seymour M. Lipset, eds., *Labor and Trade Unionism*, New York: Wiley, 1960.

V. Gordon Childe, *Man Makes Himself*, New York: New American Library, 1952.

Commission on the Cities in the '70s, *State of the Cities*, New York: Praeger, 1972.

Kingsley Davis, "The Origin and Growth of Urbanization in the World," in Gutman and Popenoe, 1970:120–30.

René Dubos, *A God Within*, New York: Scribner, 1972.

H. Wentworth Eldredge, *Taming Megalopolis*, vol. 1, New York: Praeger, 1967.

Jacques Ellul, *The Technological Society*, New York: Knopf, 1964.

Sylvia Fleis Fava, ed., *Urbanism in World Perspective: A Reader*, New York: Crowell, 1968.

Joe E. Feagin, ed., *The Urban Scene: Myths and Realities*, New York: Random House, 1973.

Lewis Feuer, ed., *Basic Writings of Politics and Philosophy*, New York: Anchor, 1959.

Victor Fuchs, "The First Service Economy," *The Public Interest*, vol. 2 (Winter 1966): 7–17.

Herbert Gans, *Levittowners: Ways of Life and Politics in a New Suburban Community*, New York: Random House, 1967.

———, "Urbanism and Suburbanism as Ways of Life," in Arnold Rose, ed., *Human Behavior and Social Processes*, Boston: Houghton-Mifflin, 1962: 625–48.

———, *People and Plans*, New York: Basic Books, 1968.

Jean Gottman, *Megalopolis: The Urbanized Northeastern Seaboard of the United States*, Cambridge, Mass.: MIT Press, 1961.

Robert Gutman and David Popenoe, eds., *Neighborhood, City and Metropolis: An Integrated Reader in Urban Sociology*, New York: Random House, 1970.

Chauncy D. Harris and Edward L. Ullman, "The Nature of Cities," *Annals of the American Academy of Political and Social Science*, vol. 242 (November 1945): 12.

Philip Hauser, "The Chaotic Society," *American Sociological Review*, vol. 34 (February 1969): 1–19.

Paul B. Horton and Chester L. Hunt, *Sociology*, New York: McGraw-Hill, 1972.

Homer Hoyt, "The Structure of American Cities in the Post-War Era," *American Journal of Sociology*, vol. 48 (January 1943): 475–92.

Jane Jacobs, *The Death and Life of Great American Cities*, New York: Random House, 1961.

Rudolph Klein, "The Trouble with a Zero Growth World," *The New York Times Magazine* (June 2, 1974): 14, 81–84.

"The Limits of Doomsday Predictions," *Science News* (October 20, 1973): 245.

Marshall McLuhan, *Understanding Media: The Extension of Man*, New York: Signet, 1964.

T. C. McLuhan, *Touch the Earth, A Self-Portrait of Indian Existence*, New York: Outerbridge and Dienstfrey, 1971.

Karl Marx and Friedrich Engels, "The Communist Manifesto," in Feuer, 1959.

David Matza, "Poverty and Disrepute," in Merton and Nisbet, 1971.

Kurt Mayer, "Recent Changes in the Class Structure of the United States," in *Transactions of the Third World Congress of Sociology*, London: International Sociological Association, 1956.

Donella Meadows, Dennis L. Meadows, Jorgen Randers, and William Behrens, III, *The Limits to Growth: A Report for the Club of Rome's Projection on the Predicament of Mankind*, New York: Universe Books, 1972.

Robert K. Merton and Robert A. Nisbet, *Contemporary Social Problems*, 3rd. ed., New York: Harcourt, Brace, Jovanovich, 1971.

C. W. Mills, *White Collar: The American Middle Classes*, New York: Oxford University Press, 1951.

Robert E. Park, Ernest W. Burgess, and Roderick D. McKenzie, eds., *The City*, Chicago: University of Chicago Press, 1925.

Frank Schaffer, *The New Town Story*, London: MacGibbon & McKee, 1970.

Gideon Sjoberg, *The Preindustrial City*, New York: Free Press, 1960.

Social Indicators, 1973, Washington, D.C.: Government Printing Office, 1974.

Maurice R. Stein, *The Eclipse of Community: An Interpretation of American Studies*, Princeton, N.J.: Princeton University Press, 1960.

Michael Stern, "Continued Job Declines Threaten City Economy," *The New York Times* (July 21, 1974): 1, 40.

Marvin Sussman, "The Isolated Nuclear Family: Fact or Fiction?" *Social Problems*, vol. 6, no. 4 (1959): 333–40.

Studs Terkel, *Working*, New York: Pantheon, 1974.

Ralph Thomlinson, *Population Dynamics*, New York: Random House, 1965.

Christopher Tunnard, "America's Super Cities," in Eldredge, 1967.

Ray Vicker, "Ancient Enemy: Many People and Cattle Exacerbate the Effects of Drought in Africa," *The Wall Street Journal* (May 24, 1974): 1, 15.

Louis Wirth, "Urbanism as a Way of Life," *American Journal of Sociology*, vol. 44 (July 1938): 1–24.

Work in America: Report of a Special Task Force to the Secretary of Health, Education, and Welfare, Cambridge, Mass.: MIT Press, 1973.

Daniel Yankelovich, Yankelovich Youth Study, © 1974 by the JDR 3rd Fund.

for further study

The City. Many good books have been written about cities, some by sociologists. One of the best is Leonard Reissman's *The Urban Process* (New York: Free Press, 1964). Other good ones are *Cities,* a book by the editors of *Scientific American* (New York: Knopf, 1965); *Cities and Society* (an ecological approach), by Paul K. Hatt and Albert J. Reiss, Jr. (New York: Free Press, 1957); and *The Emerging City*, by Scott A. Greer (New York: Free Press, 1962). The best collection of essays is *Neighborhood, City, and Metropolis*, edited by Robert Gutman and David Popenoe (New York: Random House, 1970). Urban life in other times is portrayed by Henri Pirenne in *Medieval Cities* (Garden City, N.Y.: Doubleday, 1956), and by Stephan Thernstrom and Richard Sennett, *Nineteenth-Century Cities* (New Haven, Conn.: Yale University Press, 1969).

Urban Renewal and the Future of the Cities. Since most Americans now live in urban areas, they face the problems of keeping cities strong and vital. This requires a thorough knowledge of how they are structured and how they are changing as social institutions. See Scott Greer et al., eds., *The New Urbanization* (New York: St. Martin, 1968); Raymond Vernon, *Metropolis, 1985* (Cambridge, Mass.: Harvard University Press, 1960); Robert K. Yin, *The City in the Seventies* (Itasca, Ill.: Peacock, 1972); Jane Jacobs, *The Death and Life of Great American Cities* (New York: Random House, 1961); and the provocative book by Anthony Downs, *Opening Up the Suburbs* (New Haven, Conn.: Yale University Press, 1974).

Technological Society. The sociology of our technological society is powerfully analyzed by Jacques Ellul in *The Technological Society* (New York: Knopf, 1964). Similar ideas can be found in *Posthistoric Man*, by Roderick Seidenberg (Chapel Hill: University of North Carolina Press, 1950). He answers his critics (and some questions you may have, too) in *Anatomy of the Future* (Chapel Hill: University of North Carolina Press, 1961). Another major figure studying technology is Lewis Mumford, who has written many books on the subject, among them *The Myth of the Machine*, 3 vols. (New York: Harcourt Brace Jovanovich, Inc., 1970). Alvin Toffler conveys the impact of technology at the personal level in *Future Shock* (New York: Bantam, 1971). Finally, a fresh and original essay on making machines humane is *Tools for Conviviality*, by Ivan Illich (New York: Harper & Row, 1974).

The Ecological Crisis. The ecological crisis created by our technological, urban society first received widespread attention with Rachel Carson's *The Silent Spring* (Boston: Houghton–Mifflin, 1962). It remains an extraordinary book. In a more recent and more academic book, Barry Commoner warns of coming dangers in *The Closing Circle* (New York: Bantam, 1972). A student who wishes to explore ecological problems and their social dimensions should look at issues of *Nature, Audubon Magazine, Sierra Club Bulletin, Conservationist, Environmental Pollution, Ecology, Ecological Monographs, Ecology Action, Environment, Environmental Action*, the *Journal of Environmental Health,* and *Pollution* for reports of problems and reviews of important books.

During World War II the United States Air Force established numerous resupply bases on several islands in the South Pacific. Many of these islands were inhabited by peoples barely out of the Stone Age; what were they to make of these huge silvery birds dropping from the sky into their midst? White-skinned men wearing bizarre clothes moved about in their strange vehicles, coaxing open the gut of the enormous birds, taking out fantastic things. One day these white-skinned men suddenly left and the gift-bearing birds flying overhead never came down again. On the island of Tana in the New Hebrides, a cult has sprung up among the natives that cherishes the old G.I. jacket of John Frumm, about which nothing is known except that he was one who had powers over the cargo planes. For decades now the devotees of this cult have waited for the return of these silvery birds. Like many of the cargo cults that appeared throughout the South Pacific, the John Frumm cult has constructed a primitive landing strip in the highlands, complete with bamboo control towers, grass-thatched cargo sheds, torch-lit markers on the edges of the strip, and even tin-can microphones and earphones to coax the birds to the ground again. The arrival of the Americans deeply affected the ancient society of Tana, creating a new religion that integrated many of the disturbing new elements by reinterpreting them as signs of redemptive hope for the islanders (Harris, 1971, p. 566).

Societies change their ways of doing, thinking, and believing not only by the intrusion of novelties from the outside but also by

SOCIAL CHANGE

changes from within. Change is increasingly planned change. Many of the developing nations of the Third World are undertaking rapid social transformation in order to catch up with the already industrialized ones.

Sociologists do not focus on every single change that occurs, but only on *social* change. Looking over the past eighteen chapters of this text, it should be obvious that sociologists are predominantly concerned with the patterned ways by which human groups organize the lives of their members. *Social change* is, therefore, an *alteration of the patterns of social organization over time*. The socialization of a child certainly represents a profound change in this child's life, but it does not change the basic organization of the family. Creating communal childcare centers to house, feed, and teach the young (as in the Israeli kibbutz), on the other hand, represents a social change. The way in which a child is socialized differs and the organization of the family is affected.

What are the different kinds of social changes that a society can experience and why do they occur? This chapter will focus on some of the more ambitious attempts to understand and explain social change. After a discussion of some general theories, we will look at revolutionary change by analyzing America's own revolution. We will then turn to modernization—attempts to transform agricultural societies into industrial ones. Finally, we will take a glimpse at what tomorrow's America might be like.

WAYS OF THINKING ABOUT CHANGE

In order to explain social change we first need to describe it. The English language provides a number of different words to use in talking about change: development, progress, evolution, revolution, reaction, disintegration. Underlying these terms are certain dimensions that help us think about different kinds of social change.

1. *Scale.* Changes differ in the magnitude or scope of their impact. A town mayor might order the desegregation of the town's public places, but certainly this is on a very small scale compared to a Supreme Court ruling on desegregation.

2. *Duration.* Change, by definition, occurs over a period of time. Some changes occur within a short time; others take centuries to be completed.

3. *Continuity.* Some changes represent a continuation in the basic pattern of activity; others are discontinuous, sharply breaking away from old patterns and establishing new ones. Instituting martial law and suspending electoral politics would mark a discontinuous break from our political traditions, whereas shortening the campaign period or limiting the amount of campaign funds would not.

4. *Direction.* Sometimes what seems like rapid change turns out to be a repeating set of activities that form a cyclical pattern. Many of these correspond to the biological and astronomical rhythms of nature—the cycles of night and day, of the moon, and of the seasons. Thus, farmers sow in the spring, reap in the fall, and rest in the winter—each season bringing its own pressures and rituals in predictable succession year after year.

Other changes show a linear, or straight-line, progression from one stage to the next.

Many trend changes are of this type. For example, cities have grown in number, size, and influence over the past several thousand years. Still other changes appear to be random because the direction of change is not always easy to discern. This difficulty is especially pronounced when the changes are long term and on a large scale. Thus, some observers assert that Western civilization has been on a decline for the past several centuries; others assert that there has been continuous progress; and still others see history repeating itself in cycles.

THEORIES OF SOCIAL CHANGE

Explaining particular events by identifying particular causes or isolating particular features is helpful, but social scientists have tried to develop general theories to explain social change and social stability. We need to understand the forces that produce regularity and persistence in patterns of social behavior before we can fully understand the dynamic aspects. The past eighteen chapters have shown that sociologists have not yet been able to formulate their understanding of social stability into an organized set of abstract principles. It is therefore impossible to present a single unified theory of social change (Appelbaum, 1970; see Moore, 1963, and Etzioni-Halevy and Etzioni, 1973, for a review of the theories).

Evolutionary Theories

Prior to the eighteenth century, Europeans tended to understand change in religious terms: man is born into his station and occupies it by divine providence. Radical changes come about only by exceptional withdrawals and bestowals of divine grace. With the Industrial Revolution change rather than fixity became the outstanding feature of social life (Lewontin, 1968). The discovery of simpler and seemingly more primitive societies in other parts of the world also challenged people to account for the vast differences in human societies. The earliest popular explanation held that the primitives represented an earlier, evolutionary stage and that the more complex societies of eighteenth- and nineteenth-century Europe were in more advanced stages of development. A natural fact of social life, change had a direction: from simple societies to more complex and differentiated ones. And as wealth multiplied it was clear that change must mean progress. Change was seen as good. Much of the earliest social philosophy carried this strong moralistic undercurrent.

In the nineteenth century, social thinking became less philosophical and more empirical. Much of the debate focused on what caused evolutionary change—some arguing for new ideas, inventions, discoveries; others for class struggles or conflict (Service, 1968).

Emile Durkheim identified the cause of societal evolution as a society's increasing "moral density" (Durkheim, 1964). Simple societies have a relatively undifferentiated social structure, with minimal division of labor among members of the same society. People share a common set of values, and these values provide the chief source of solidarity among members. Durkheim called this kind of moral cohesion "mechanical solidarity," as we learned in chapter 7.

As the population grows, resources become scarcer and division of labor increases in order to exploit these scarce resources efficiently. The society becomes differentiated into increasingly specialized units, which are more dependent upon each other—"organic solidarity." Social differentiation multiplies, common values decrease, the fragmented social order then requires more formal means to hold it together. Civil law and a central government are among the institutions that help societies cohere in the face of growing change and diversity. In sum, Durkheim viewed societies as changing in the direction of greater differentiation, interdependence, and formal control under the pressure of an increasing moral density. Durkheim, of course, is but one of a number of evolutionary theorists; E. B. Tylor, L. H. Morgan, Herbert Spencer, Saint-Simon, A. Compte, and Karl Marx offered different explanations for the evolutionary impulse in societies.

Cyclical Theories

With the onslaught of World War I many thinkers were much less sure that societies were in fact advancing. It was perhaps more accurate to view societies and civilizations as passing through inevitable cycles of development and decay. This theme was announced with immediate impact in 1926 by Oswald Spengler in *The Decline of the West*. Cultures are destined, in his view, to follow a course of growth and decline in much the same way that individual men's lives do. But Spengler's explanation was more poetic than scientific. His appeal was to cosmic destiny rather than finite causes.

Arnold Toynbee's massive, multivolume *A Study of History* (1946) is, on the other hand, a detailed and concrete comparative history of civilizations. While fault has been found with his analyses on many points, Toynbee's significant contribution is his method, which applies key specific questions to each of the twenty-one major civilizations of past and present that he chose for study.

Toynbee's volumes ask four main questions, each with numerous subquestions. The first concerns the genesis of civilization: What are the conditions which allow or stimulate the rise of civilizations— the conversion of what had been preliterate, simple, more or less lethargic peoples into the kinds of civilization of which the classical, the Indian, the Chinese, and the Mayan are notable types? Second, what are the factors involved in the expansion and development, in what Toynbee calls the "growths" of these civilizations? Third, what accounts for the breakdowns of civilizations, that is, the conversion of what had been for centuries a highly dynamic, innovative, intrepid, and enterprising people into one characterized by mere routinization and repetition of the old? Fourth, what leads to the disintegration of historical civilizations, the passing into nothingness or atavistic primitivism of civilizations? (Nisbet, 1970, p. 353)

In answering these questions for individual cultures, Toynbee developed several partial theories. One key explanation for social change was his concept of challenge and response: a civilization's accomplishments are its particular responses to the specific physical and social challenges posed by its environment. When a civilization can no longer respond to challenges, it rigidifies and atrophies.

Pitirim Sorokin's work (1941) has had a more lasting impact on sociological thinking. Rather than viewing civilizations in terms of development and decline, this exiled Russian scholar proposed that they alternate between two extreme configurations, the sensate and the ideational. In the *sensate* phase, everything points to that which can be experienced directly. The emphasis in art is on the representational; in philosophy the emphasis is on rationalism and objectivism. What matters above all for this world view is direct senses. By contrast, *ideational cultures* are typified by the opposite values; truth lies beyond the reach of the senses, inaccessible to human reason. Religion stresses the reality of the other world, as a superrational God, Brahman, Atman, or Tao. Art is abstract and philosophy is oriented to issues of faith and belief. As the culture of a society develops toward one pure type, it is countered by the opposing cultural force. Cultural development is then reversed, moving toward the opposite type of culture. Societies contain both impulses in varying degree, and the tension between them creates long-term instability.

Equilibrium Theories

In the middle decades of the twentieth century many American sociologists shifted their curiosity away from trying to understand social change and focused on how to explain social stability. One of Sorokin's students at Harvard, Talcott Parsons, took over Sorokin's interest in cultural development and stressed the central importance of cultural patterns in controlling the *stability* of a society (1951, 1966). In Parsons's view society has the ability to absorb disruptive forces while maintaining overall stability because it is a dynamic system straining for equilibrium.

The idea of society as a system in equilibrium derives from an analogy made between societies and biological organisms. Each of the specialized parts of an organism is continually active, but all the different changes within the parts are coordinated and integrated so that the total organism is relatively the same from one day to the next. The counterpart of these organs are the specialized structures of society, or its subsystems.

Parsons asserts that each of the subsystems in a society performs a different function. The economic structures adapt a society to its physical environment. Changes in the environment therefore produce changes in the economic structures. Political structures

IN THE NEWS

Cultural Lag Then and Now

Cars. The material basis of the free-and-easy, go-where-you-want character of latterday American culture. Agents of the ordinary citizen's liberation from the strictures of geography. Life for most Americans rests as much today on the internal-combustion revolution of the twentieth century as on the political revolution of the eighteenth.

Yet when cars were first introduced, the cry was, "get a horse," as people passed the driver of a horseless carriage cranking up his new-fangled machine. The mayor of a major American city officially stated that no woman was physically able to undertake the complicated and strenuous operation of driving an automobile. Such reactions are an example of *cultural lag*, a term coined by William F. Ogburn to describe the problem that arises when one part of a culture changes before the other parts have a chance to adapt. Material culture (inventions, artifacts) are much more apt to change rapidly than nonmaterial culture (beliefs, values, laws), creating a period of disequilibrium. Before we dismiss the quaint ideas of our grandparents and great-grandparents about the auto, we might look at some of our own ideas for symptoms of a new instance of cultural lag. Today the old cry rings again.

"Fight pollution, ride a horse," read a sign noticed by a visitor at a shopping center.... The sign was affixed to the bumper of a car spewing out hydrocarbons, carbon monoxide, and nitrogen oxides.... Like virtually all technological developments, the automobile has its bad side.... Destruction and mutilation, measured in the familiar statistics of highway deaths. Choking, frustrating traffic jams. Automobile graveyards, the ugly debris of affluence. Freeway spaghetti that disfigures cities. And air pollution.

Now for the first time since Henry Ford began mass-producing Model T's in 1908, the automobile-based way of life is being directly challenged. With the express aim of reducing air pollution, the Federal Government has proposed to restrict automobile traffic in some 30 metropolitan areas across the country.

The reaction to such proposals as banning autos one day a week or reducing the number of parking spaces employers provide has been predictably vehement.

When a Boston City Councilman heard of the proposed ban on driving, he vowed that no one was going to tell him where or when to drive his car.... "Without a car you're nowhere," they say in Phoenix.

The American love affair with the auto is probably the largest obstacle to the solution of air pollution today—a clear case of cultural lag. Trying to solve environmental problems by removing the center of a highly integrated cultural complex is bound to create disequilibrium and tension.

SOURCE: William K. Stevens, "Nation Dependent on Cars Is Resentful of Curbs Planned as Pollution Check," *The New York Times* (July 15, 1973): 1, 54.

Inventions serve to stimulate change in social life. America has been transformed time after time by inventions such as the airplane, which draws the continent together and hastens communication; electricity, which extends the daylight artificially and drives our industries and our cities; the Xerox machine, which has contributed to the information explosion. (Culver Pictures)

Diffusion is the most powerful force for social change. It occurs when one culture adopts cultural elements from another society. The elements may be technological, like a motor bike, or norms and values. Today American technology and the American lifestyle are being exported and form an important influence on cultures throughout the world. (Georg Gerster/Rapho Guillumette)

are the means of setting and attaining the society's goals. The family instills the prevailing cultural patterns into the new members of society. The church and state are the cultural subsystems and ensure the society's integration and coordination. Because cultural patterns (or basic values) change very slowly, the cultural subsystem is the crucial force for ensuring the continuity of society. Changes in the economic or political systems tend to be slowed down as they come up against the more steadfast cultural system. Because cultural systems tend toward stability rather than continual development (as in Sorokin's model), change in the social system must come from forces outside the system—perhaps from its environment. Overall change in the social system must therefore involve cultural change, and this kind of major change is, in Parsons's view, infrequent.

Conflict Theories

Whereas the equilibrium theories emphasize the integrative and stabilizing processes at work in social systems, the so-called conflict theories highlight the forces producing instability, struggle, and social disorganiza-

Discoveries stimulate change. Columbus's discovery of the New World paved the way for the utter destruction of the native Indian societies while enriching Europe with silver and gold. This enormous influx of bullion lined the pockets of the European trading classes, ultimately increasing their political power over the land-based aristocracies, and supporting the emergence of capitalist factory production. Meanwhile, European cultures were being modified to form new national cultures in the Americas. (Culver Pictures)

tion. Ralf Dahrendorf, a German sociologist who has become a leading figure in his country's political life, pinpoints the differences between these two broad types of theories of social change (Dahrendorf, 1973, p. 103). According to his view the equilibrium theories assume that:

1. every society is a relatively persisting configuration of elements;
2. every society is a well-integrated configuration of elements;
3. every element in a society contributes to its functioning;
4. every society rests on the consensus of its members.

Conflict theories, on the other hand, assume that:

1. every society is subjected at every moment to change; social change is ubiquitous;
2. every society experiences at every moment social conflict; social conflict is ubiquitous;
3. every element in a society contributes to its change;
4. every society rests on constraint of some of its members by others.

Dahrendorf sees the unequal distribution of power and authority as the fundamental source of conflict in a society. Those persons or groups with power want to preserve the status quo. This puts them in conflict with the subordinate groups, whose interest is to change the status quo. Organized interest groups emerge in each of the two broad classes, and these interest groups struggle over numerous issues. This conflict can lead to various changes in the society's structure if dominance relations are changed. The nature, speed, and depth of the conflict and the resulting change depend on numerous variable conditions.

By far the most famous and influential of the conflict theories is that of Karl Marx. In his extensive writings on sociology, politics, economics, history, and philosophy, Marx developed a theory of such complexity and subtlety that it resists summarization. To outline his theory of social change in the broadest of strokes, Marx (1932) saw all societies up to his time as arenas for class struggles. He understood the source of these struggles not to be power but rather the essential foundation of power—the control of a society's resources and productive facilities. Societies have therefore been split into two main camps—owners and nonowners. In ancient societies the split was between master and slave; in feudal societies, between lord and serf; in capitalist societies, between bourgeoisie (industrial owner) and proletariat (industrial worker). Throughout history those groups of families who have maintained control over a society's productive forces have either created or supported whole political systems, laws, religious beliefs, and philosophies to justify and continue their dominance. Representatives of these two opposing classes struggle against each other in ideological, political, and economic battles. In times of economic crisis the struggle becomes more sharply drawn, and the cleavage between classes becomes more apparent. The lower class becomes increasingly impoverished. Activists stimulate their brethren to become aware of their true class interest, of their solidarity with their fellow workers or fellow owners, thereby developing a "class consciousness." Acting in a self-conscious fashion members of the oppressed class muster their forces, develop new ideas about how to organize society, and battle the dominant class in the political or military arena. Marx envisioned that these class divisions would disappear after the final socialist victory (coming after the maturing of capitalist society), when control over the resources and the productive forces is socialized—that is, distributed equally among all of the society's members.

REVOLUTION: THE AMERICAN CASE

Marx understood a revolution to be a casting off of an established political order and the creation of new forms of government, of new patterns of power-holding. Indeed, most people think of a revolution as a large-scale upheaval creating a discontinuity in the politics of a society. Revolutionaries typically intend not to correct a limited number of specific ills but to make broad and idealistically inspired changes. A true revolution involves mass mobilization and mass participation. The *coup d'état* (sometimes called a palace revolution), which occurs throughout the Third World in the present day, is not revolutionary unless it involves the masses and radically restructures the forms of government. Neither are "revolutionary" achievements proclaimed by presidents or premiers when they succeed in some new national venture.

The upheaval of revolution is not an entirely disorganized event. Historian Crane Brinton (1965) studied four revolutions—the English of the seventeenth century, the American and French of the eighteenth, and the Russian of the twentieth—and constructed a hypothetical model for other revolutions. He cautions that this model may not apply to *all* revolutions but only to those mass uprisings in the modern period of Western civilization that have been undertaken in the name of freedom for an oppressed minority, and that have ended in the successful transfer of power.

The revolution begins when the dissatisfied groups press their claims for power and are ineffectively opposed by force. The old regime falls. With the fall of the old regime, moderates rule for a period. Extremists then rise to power and initiate a reign of terror that is coupled with an almost religious fervor and claim to virtue. There then occurs a reaction to extremist rule and a counterrevolution that reinforces the basic principles of the original revolutionaries. This moderating reaction (known as *Thermidor*, from the month of the revolutionary French calendar in which the equivalent reaction stage of that country's revolution was initiated) is typically ushered in by a dictator.

These then are the stages of revolution. We are all familiar with the chronology of the American Revolution, but can Brinton help us understand why it happened there and why it happened then?

The Reluctant Revolution

The American Revolution seemed to start quite by accident. Americans had grown accustomed to the sight of the red-jacketed British troops, even though they didn't like their presence. After all, two regiments had been stationed in Boston Harbor for nearly six years. But when the troops were seen setting out from Boston, it was understood that they were heading toward Concord, where the volunteer army of the Massachusetts colony stored their meager supply of guns and ammunition. Paul Revere rode through the night to notify his comrades, and now the Massachusetts militia was gathered in the town of Lexington on the route from Boston to Concord. After several restless hours, the first British troops came in sight. Captain Parker stationed his seventy lightly armed farmers on the green, where they might be seen and heard by the passing soldiers but would not be engaged. The troops on both sides, however, broke ranks and firing began before the commanders regained control (Morgan, 1956).

While the skirmish was an accident, the times had all the ingredients for an outbreak, confirming Brinton's conditions that characterize a prerevolutionary situation.

1. Revolutionists are not a deprived and oppressed segment of the population; rather, they are relatively well-off, respectable members of society, who recognize the problems and relative deprivations in the situation and have hopes of achieving economic and civil freedoms.

2. The established rulers are, at the same time, disorganized, weak, and divided among themselves. Consequently they are indecisive and contradictory in policy, and lacking in self-confidence. Indecisive policy produces confusion and economic instability, and this creates a noticeable weakness that the revolutionists feel encouraged to take advantage of. Defensive measures taken by the weakened rulers are ineffective, or come too late. And many members of the hitherto ruling class, moreover, recognize their disorganization and the validity in protest.

3. Since the immediate cause of the crisis is a weakened and ineffectual government, the aim of the revolutionists is to change not only the individuals but the forms of government to protect their interests.

4. Intellectuals desert the cause of the old regime, depriving it of its ideological legitimacy.

This was indeed the pattern that led to the skirmish at Lexington. Middle-class Americans, threatened economically with taxes imposed suddenly by the English Parliament, wanted a return to the period of lax colonial administration. In the decade prior to the revolution, England relaxed, then stiffened its demands in order to bring the colonists into line; as these efforts failed, England resorted to even more repressive policies. Each of these measures was received by the Americans as a new imposition, a removal of a freedom they had once enjoyed and were now being deprived of. The colonies, which among themselves had not been able to agree on boundaries or mutual aid during Indian attacks, were able to unite around the principle of "no taxation without representation" in opposition to British policies and government. But centuries of tradition could not be overcome easily, and even after Concord and Lexington leading colonists still hoped to reach an agreement with the king. George III himself forced their hand, declaring the colonies in rebellion. And a recently arrived Englishman, Thomas Paine, in his rapidly circulated pamphlet, *Common Sense*, established the philosophical justification for revolution. He noted that there was no natural reason for any man to be "so exalted above the rest, and distinguished like some new species," as was the king. He further demonstrated that "nothing but misery has come from kings." Americans, well schooled in English history, recalled that English kings had been deposed twice in the preceding century; here was their precedent. They recalled John Locke's assertions that men band together of their own free will in social and governing groups for the specific purpose of protecting themselves and their property. They recognized the corollary that any government that was neither functioning with the consent of the governed nor fulfilling its intended purpose could, and should, be replaced. The basis for continued allegiance to George III was demolished, and the intellectual validation for revolution was established.

Was There a Thermidor?

Although the events leading up to the revolution and even those following the break with England accord well with Brinton's model, scholars still argue about the existence of a period analogous to the French counterrevolution during Thermidor following the excesses of extremist reforms and terror. One school of American historians (called revisionists) see the replacement of the Articles of Confederation by the Constitution as a *coup d'état* by propertied conservatives. Another school, the dominant one, sees the framers of the Constitution not as the betrayers of the revolution but rather as its saviors. This issue largely revolves around the character of the government created by the Articles. Was it an effective government, protecting the rights of individuals against a tyrannical government, or was the government unable to function, threatening the collapse of the Union (Morgan, 1956; Craven, 1973)?

The Critical Period   The Articles of Confederation provided for the unification of the colonies—and then states—under a very weak central government. They protected the power of the states, and did not provide for enforcing any provisions should a state decide not to cooperate.

Following the Revolutionary War the nation was saddled with a war debt, which the Congress successfully reduced through the voluntary contributions of most (though not all) states. The Articles also resolved the problems of disposing of the vast lands to the west, which had previously belonged to the English, by providing that these lands belonged to the national government and not to the individual states they might adjoin, and that new separate states might be created within specific limitations of area, which would have the same rights as other states.

But economic problems abounded, triggered by rampant inflation. In Rhode Island a depreciating paper currency was made legal tender and hordes of happy debtors were paying off their obligations with worthless bills, leaving their creditors bankrupt. As a

postwar depression continued, the problems of businessmen became acute. Due to a lack of centralized authority, however, Congress was powerless to come to their aid. In 1786 Virginia suggested a convention to work for a general interstate agreement to regulate commerce. Delegates from five states met that September, and without waiting for other delegates to arrive, they took a giant step and adopted a resolution calling for a general convention to be held at Philadelphia in May of the following year. The purpose of the convention was expressly stated to be a modification of the federal constitution. All states but Rhode Island were represented at the convention in Philadelphia; and the Constitution of the United States was the result.

Thermidor   The revisionist historians agree that there were problems in the political arrangements designed by the Articles but insist that they were not serious enough to warrant its overthrow and replacement by a strong central government. In his classic study entitled *An Economic Interpretation of the Constitution of the United States* (1949), Charles Beard examined the financial holdings of the framers of the Constitution and found that most had invested in public securities of the United States and therefore stood to gain by strengthening public credit. He also examined the political beliefs of the framers and concluded that many were distrustful of the popular masses and therefore designed a political system in the Constitution that safeguarded their property rights.

No Thermidor   Other historians maintain that the Union was on the verge of collapse and that the inflation and depression of the postwar years threatened the ability of the government to protect private property—certainly one of the central principles of the revolution. Moreover, giving the powers of taxation and legislation to the Congress under the Articles violated another basic principle of the revolution: that of no taxation without representation. The Congress was not chosen by the people but by the state governments. A radical restructuring was therefore necessary to create a representative national government that would be strong enough to deal with the problems of the fledgling nation.

The creation of a stronger federal government under the Constitution is looked upon by the revisionist historians as a counter-revolution (perhaps the equivalent to the Thermidorian stage in Brinton's model). But it is important to note that this stronger central government received no grant of unlimited power; by dividing power among the three branches of government (the executive, the legislative, and the judicial), the framers hoped that the excesses of one branch could be checked by the other two branches.

Was There a Revolution?

How revolutionary were the changes instituted by the rebelling colonialists? Historian Edmund Morgan writes that

[T]he important thing was not to reform society but to keep government subordinate to it. There was no reason, they thought, why a government which had got out of hand might not be replaced by a proper one without destroying the social fabric. . . . One could simply peel off the old government and put on the new. (1956, pp. 88–89)

Precisely for this reason, sociologist Barrington Moore concludes that

Since it did not result in any fundamental changes in the structure of society, there are grounds for asking whether it deserves to be called a revolution at all. At bottom it was a fight between commercial interests in England and America, though certainly more elevated issues played a part as well. The claim that America has had an anticolonial revolution may be good propaganda, but it is bad history and bad sociology. . . . What radical currents there were in the American Revolution were for the most part unable to break through to the surface. Its main effect was to promote unification of the colonies into a single political unit and the separation of this unit from England. (Moore, 1966, pp. 112–13)

Although the American Revolution aimed at national independence and not social reform, it went beyond the original intention and forged a new outlook on human life. The founding fathers recognized that they were taking steps that would alter more than the political and economic lives of their countrymen. In Edmund Morgan's words, "The principles they carried with them to Philadelphia would not all have fitted in their pocketbooks" (1956, p. 132). They established the world's first constitutional republic, whose most distinctive features were consent of the governed by popular vote, limitation of government power over individuals secured by the Bill of Rights, and a commitment to egalitarian principles. The principles enunciated in the Declaration of Independence were repeated in the French Revolution shortly afterwards and have been championed many times since then by other new nations.

The egalitarian principles of the revolution did not extend to the institution of slavery, however. In slavery the principles of equality clashed with the equally powerful principles of the rights of property. When the issue was drawn—and it was, during the drafting of the Constitution and at other times—uneasy compromise resulted, lasting until the Civil War. Although this war ostensibly settled the issue, its legacy remains to the present day, as we have seen in the chapter on minorities. Thus, Americans are still working to reconcile the principles of equality and government by consent with human and political realities.

Barrington Moore (1966) sees the Civil War as closer to a revolution than the Revolutionary War. True, the Civil War was not a mass uprising against an oppressor, but it did result in radical social reform. The southern rural aristocracy had created an antiegalitarian civilization that defended hereditary privilege and hereditary slavery. The notion that all people are created equal was bound to rub the southern planter the wrong way. The northern elites—whose interests were tied to industrial manufacturing—objected to these institutions on moral and practical grounds. After all, slave laborers were not able to buy the commodities produced in their factories. Manufacturers needed a wage-earning labor force in the country in order to develop a strong internal market for their factory goods. Because of the institutional reform wrought by the northern victory, Barrington Moore terms the Civil War the "last capitalist revolution." (Culver Pictures)

Benjamin Rush, a signer of the Declaration and a participant in the constitutional convention, anticipated this in a Fourth of July address in Philadelphia in 1787.

There is nothing more common than to confound the terms American Revolution with those of the late American War. The American War is over, but this is far from being the case with the American Revolution. On the contrary but the first act of the great drama is closed. (in Morris, 1967, pp. 84–85)

MODERNIZATION

People look to the United States for its economic achievements as much as for its political or social ones. In all but the most remote corners of the world, people are hungry for the fruits of an industrial economy and are pushing for a rapid—even revolutionary—transformation of their society. Up until the past few centuries there existed hundreds, and perhaps thousands, of local societies that went about their business pretty much the same way day after day. Most were subsistence economies, living either by nomadic hunting and gathering or by sedentary agriculture. But the societies created by the bourgeois revolutions in North America and western Europe have been expansive. In their search for resources to fuel their economic development, they have penetrated these once-traditional and isolated societies and introduced them to the trappings of modern life. Much of the non-Western world was colonized and brought into this worldwide market system—although the colonies (most ex-colonies now) maintained many of their traditional ways while supplying raw materials to the Western industries. From a distance many of these people saw the riches that industrialism produced. And the native elites in these colonies and former colonies often had a chance to see modern capitalist societies from the inside as they came to London, Paris, or New York for their education. Their appetites whetted for manufactured riches and comforts, different peoples all over the world began trying to transform their nations into modern societies. *Modernization* is usually understood to mean a change toward the type of societies found in the advanced industrial countries. These changes include not only an industrialized economy but a complete transformation of the political, social, and psychological spheres.

1. *Political modernization.* Modernization means the consolidation of policy-making in a centralized state bureaucracy (Black, 1968). The state expands its activities and absorbs functions once carried out by other traditional structures, such as the family and the church. In America and western Europe political centralization and the development of democratic traditions went together. Societies that have more recently embarked on a crash course of industrialization have had a difficult time promoting rapid social transformation within a democratic political structure. But even in those nondemocratic states undergoing modernization, there is a need for the state to seek popular legitimacy rather than relying on more traditional forms of legitimation (such as appealing to the divine right of kings). Popular legitimation is usually sought and created through the organization of mass political parties (Eisenstadt, 1966).

2. *Social modernization.* Modernization also means the following changes in social structure: intensive urbanization; the growth of large-scale and often bureaucratic organizations; leveling of income, education, and opportunity; extension of literacy; extension of communication systems and mass media; improvements in health care; and *social mobilization,* which is the process whereby commitments to traditional economic, political, and social roles are loosened. This makes the individual susceptible to new values, new socialization patterns, and new commitments. In the political sphere this usually means the replacement of local allegiances with an allegiance to the nation as a whole (Deutsch, 1953).

3. *Psychological modernization.* People who live in modern societies are change-

Modernization takes on different meanings depending upon the model the developing nation is following. The United States and Russia are two patterns, based on capitalism and communism respectively. Now a third is available to the Third World, that of China. (Audrey Topping/Rapho Guillumette)

oriented. Less suspicious of novelty, they are more present- and future-oriented rather than backward-looking and bound to tradition. Modern men and women have typically cast off the fatalistic attitudes prevalent in more rigid societies and have acquired a faith that they can dominate their environment. They are, therefore, oriented to planning and organizing. There is also a tendency to hold opinions over a wide range of issues reaching beyond local matters. Of course, this is associated with expanding mass media and a rising educational and literacy level in the population (Inkeles, 1966).

MODERNIZATION AND IBO TRADITIONS

Tradition refers to the customary set of behaviors and symbols of a society. It is not the same as traditionalism, which is a reactionary attitude that involves holding on to some parts of old traditions as a bulwark, or cushion, against new trends. The examples of societies in which traditionalism has hindered change are legion. But it is also possible for a modernizing society to retain strong traditions without this necessarily being traditionalism.

Among the Ibo of Nigeria, for example, tradition *aided* modernization. The Ibo thronged to urban centers and eagerly entered white-collar and mercantile occupations. They embraced education as a means to advancement. They have been especially active politically, to the extent of establishing their own independent nation. When the Biafran war was lost, the Ibo were reabsorbed into the Nigerian economic and political structure with relative speed. Ibo history and customs account for many of these accomplishments.

Traditionally the Ibo have encouraged individual achievement, and virtually everyone could hope to gain prestige by working diligently and using their abilities effectively. The groupings of Ibo society—villages, families, and age and secret societies—competed against each other for wealth and prestige. Following colonization, the Ibo recognized the value of acquiring British skills, and substituted new forms of prestige—owning European possessions, working for the government, and sending children to school—for the old ones. Villages competed in having better markets and in sending their sons to school. Individuals who achieved wealth, position, and education added to the prestige of the groups to which they belonged. Experience in a variety of societies—age grades, secret societies, men's groups, work groups—prepared the Ibo for trade and labor organizations and political societies. A tradition of leadership by a council of elders laid the foundation for those skills that are required for work in legislative councils and other cooperative units of government.

The Ibo had other important features that aided in modernization: high population density and, consequently, mobility. Groups and families moved to new villages, and communities absorbed newcomers—traditions that facilitated not only movement to the cities but also that key requisite for urban existence: the ability to get along with others. For several centuries and perhaps longer, change itself has been a feature of Ibo culture. This, and the many traditions that aided their adoption of European behavior and values, has enabled the Ibo to participate successfully in the modernization of Nigeria.

SOURCE: Ottenberg, 1959, pp. 130–43; Uchendo, 1965.

The changes that occur during the period of modernization can be grouped into certain general categories. *Structural differentiation* is the reorganization of family, economic, religious, and other units into more specialized smaller units or substructures. *Integration* refers to the development of interrelationships among the new substructures that replace the now-obsolete network that existed around the old social units. *Social disturbances* of various sorts result from the unevenness of the differentiation and integration processes (Smelser, 1973).

Strains of Rapid Modernization

The modernization of America and western Europe took place slowly over the course of two centuries. Leaders of developing countries feel they cannot wait that long; they want to accomplish the transformation within a matter of years. After all, didn't Russia manage to build an industrial economy within a few decades following its 1917 revolution? But rapid social transformation involves great dislocation and strains, and it tends to produce widespread feelings of rootlessness, anomie, outbreaks of mass hysteria, and violence (Eisenstadt, 1966).

The sources of imbalanced growth and strain are legion. Populations moving into the cities need jobs; the economy must expand correspondingly. Rapid economic growth requires importing at least some technology from the more advanced countries. The labor force must therefore be trained rapidly to operate this imported technology; universities must churn out skilled people. But the graduates coming out of the universities must find work or they tend to become articulate dissenters and even revolutionaries. A new pace of life and new time schedules must be learned. Long training, regular per-

formance, punctuality, and precision in work are things many people just off the farm are not accustomed to. All want the fruits of modernity *now*, but they must sacrifice for the future because resources must be channeled into building steelworks and highways rather than into manufacturing consumer goods. The expansion of health facilities lowers the death rate, thereby increasing the population size, and this threatens to outstrip any economic gains.

When modernization occurs slowly over a long period of time, new political systems, new value systems, new economic systems, and new personalities have a chance to adjust to one another gradually. These changing patterns reinforce each other, smoothly replacing the traditional ways of life with new and, more importantly, *integrated* patterns of social organization. In contrast, overnight modernization is a powerful solvent tending to produce *social disintegration*. The glue that holds traditional society together looses its adhesive powers. Governmental coordination and control of these large-scale changes become all the more necessary. Because the armed forces of these societies are often the most cohesive institutions capable of planning and organizing large-scale efforts, many modernizing societies experience takeovers by their armies.

Mass Society

Sociologists have characterized this kind of loosely integrated social organization as *mass society*. Masses are huge numbers of people who are not integrated into any broad social groupings or social classes (Kornhauser, 1959, p. 14). The most significant division of the population is between an organized elite and an unorganized, atomized mass. Elites are susceptible to influence by the masses, and the masses are readily available for mobilization by the elites. In the name of an abstract concept the masses can be goaded into action—even violent action—by a charismatic leader. Mass behavior is associated with the separation of symbols from their real meaning and content, and with an increasing reliance on force to resolve social conflicts (Selznick, 1951, p. 329).

A rather unflattering and ominous picture of mass man was painted by José Ortega y Gasset, a Spanish aristocrat saddened by the loss of traditional European culture and society. Writing in the 1930s, at the time when Germany and Italy were experiencing breakdowns in their modernizing efforts (fertilizing the ground for fascism), he noted:

The ordinary man, hitherto guided by others, has resolved to govern the world himself. . . . The psychological structure of this new type of mass-man . . . is as follows: (1) An inborn, root-impression that life is easy, plentiful, without any grave limitations; consequently, each average man finds within himself a sensation of power and triumph which (2) invites him to stand up for himself as he is, to look upon his moral and intellectual endowment as excellent, complete. This contentment with himself leads him to shut himself off from any external court of appeal; not to listen, not to submit his opinions to judgment, not to consider others' existence. His intimate feeling of power urges him always to exercise predominance. He will act then as if he and his like were the only beings existing in the world; and, consequently (3) will intervene in all matters, imposing his own vulgar views without respect or regard for others, without limit or reserve, that is to say, in accordance with a system of "direct action." (1957, p. 97)

An alternative to mass society is the development of a political system that allows for effective participation of the population. One such organization is that found in the more democratic countries—one in which the people participate in mass political parties, form organized interest groups to express their particular goals, and have a national forum to reconcile these different interests. But such a political system requires that all parties agree to play by the rules of the game. This in turn requires that the various political groups have a reasonably large set of common interests. This kind of consensus is difficult to build in societies undergoing rapid transformation, and it is especially difficult when a society is faced with economic stagnation or breakdown. This is why democratic governments are falling by the wayside throughout Latin America, Africa, Southeast Asia, the Middle East, and even southern Europe.

AMERICA TOMORROW

To many of the world's peoples the urban industrial nations are a sort of grand mirror—a mirror in which they can see a reflection of their own future. In this reflection they see darker-skinned people, but the cars, televisions, telephones, flush toilets, and airplanes are essentially the same. But what is the image of America's future? We have no mirrors; nevertheless, we can see forces that are at work shaping our society. In the last chapter, one image for the future, which has been described by Daniel Bell, was a post-industrial society characterized by abundance. There are alternative scenarios as well.

More of the Same?
The Affluent Society

One group of analysts looking into the sociological crystal ball foresees a society of continued affluence. "Post-1984 America" has been described by Lee Rainwater (1972) as being more urbanized, suburban-dwelling, educated, and affluent. The median family income will be at least $16,000 a year, an increase of more than 50 percent over the 1972 median. However, all classes will share in the increased income in about the same proportions, so there will still be the same class distinctions and social problems that see the poorest 20 percent of the population earning less than 5 percent of the money income. The poor and minority group members will still have significantly less of everything.

Increased urbanization and communication will expose "the average citizen to a much wider range of information, and a much wider range of perspectives for interpreting that information [and he or she] . . . is therefore likely to be less insulated from national and worldwide trends in taste, style and innovation than has ever been true." Affluence and cosmopolitanism will combine to permit greater pluralism and a multiplicity of life-styles. This will be particularly true for the upper-middle class, who are more affluent and cosmopolitan than the lower classes, and whose "orientation toward living has always been self-sufficiency and the pursuit of self-gratification . . . [along with a] propensity toward elaborate life style innovations" (Rainwater, 1972, p. 28).

Paradoxically, there will not be more leisure. People become busier the more affluent they are. With time limited and goods and services expensive, people will choose "activities that seem to provide more gratification per time unit." Daily life will become "commodity and service intensive" (Rainwater, 1972, p. 25). The individual's time will become so valuable that it will be more efficient to depend on specialized delivery of services by others. The need for services both on the household level and in the public sector will increase.

Less of the Same?
The Scarcity Society

Affluence depends upon continued economic growth. But as chapter 18 indicates, the resources needed for that growth are not infinite—a fact that casts a more ominous pall upon predictions of the future. During the past few years we have become increasingly conscious that our environment can absorb only so much waste without seriously threatening our own existence. And the raw materials drawn from the nonindustrial nations are no longer as cheap as before. Seeing their nonreplaceable resources sucked into the industrial machines of the advanced economies, many of the developing nations are beginning to demand a larger return for their contribution. Oil-producing countries have joined together in a producers' alliance to cooperate in raising the price of oil to industrial nations. Other producers of raw materials are following this example and are forging cooperative associations to raise their incomes. The leaders of these nations are motivated by the desire to build their countries into more economically independent and affluent societies. International tensions have increased as the domestic economies of industrial nations have felt the pinch. These developments, coupled with several other economic trends, have aggravated inflation and unemployment, both of which threaten political stability in many of the advanced industrial nations. William Ophuls has written:

Virtually all the philosophies, values and institutions typical of modern capitalist society—the legitimacy of self-interest, the primacy of the individual and his inalienable rights, economic laissez-faire, and democracy as we know it—are the luxuriant fruit of an era of apparently endless abundance. They cannot continue to exist in their current form once we return to the more normal conditions of scarcity. (Ophuls, 1974, p. 47)

Political stability in America depends partly on reducing the inequalities of caste and class, which, in turn, depends on economic growth. Even with the economy operating at full employment (that is, with no more than about 4 percent unemployment), it would take about thirty years for the disparity of incomes between white and black families to disappear (Guthrie, in Rainwater, 1972, p. 27). Rising unemployment increases this disparity. Blacks tend to be the last hired and the first fired. When jobs are plentiful, blacks make rapid gains; when jobs decline, as they must in a world of scarcity, black unemployment rises much faster than white joblessness. Scarcity could irritate a potentially explosive condition.

Inflation also generates anxieties that undermine confidence in a country's economic and political systems. Rising consumer prices hit hardest at the poor, who spend a greater percentage of their incomes on food and housing. Inflation devalues the worth of retirement pensions and savings, which people depend on for their security in old age. At a 10 percent annual inflation rate, the value of savings or a pension is halved in a mere seven years. Unable to plan secure futures, people sometimes withdraw support from governments. Referring to the democratic western European societies, Flora Lewis, a *New York Times* reporter wrote in 1974:

The marked trend has been to turn away from recognized leaders and to call out unhappily for other leadership. It is not yet a crisis of democracy, but it is a sagging of confidence that the systems of government that have fostered prosperity can cope with the new economic problems. (p. 7)

The Counterculture: A Force for Change?

A shift away from overconsumption and unbridled industrialism has been part of the program of a small but visible minority that arose during the 1960s in opposition to the war in Southeast Asia, to government, and to many of the established values of the society. Radical politics grew up hand in hand with a change in life-styles. Sexual mores were liberalized, respect declined for organized religion, government, law, conventional patriotism, the police, and the boss on the job.

The sudden growth of the counterculture piqued the interest of a number of social scientists, among them Philip Slater (1970), Theodore Roszak (1969), and Charles Reich (1970). The puzzle was how a society could produce what seemed its very antithesis. Among several complex sources of potential conflict within our culture, two stand out in their analyses: the permissive, child-centered family, and the contradictions between worker-consumer roles.

The youth-centered family ill prepares youngsters for the regimentation they will find in the technocratic world. From a home life centered around satisfying juvenile needs and whims, frequently at the subjugation of parents' needs, these sheltered, pampered young people are thrust into lower-echelon positions in enormous, impersonal corporate structures. In the view of Slater, adults are generous, good-natured, indulgent toward their children but "ruthless toward the non-human environment . . . [and] when the child grows up he discovers the fraud" (1970, p. 47). Reich sees the counterculture, which he calls Consciousness III, as "the product of two interacting forces: The promise of life that is made to young Americans by all of our affluence, technology, liberation and ideals, and the threat to that promise posed by everything from neon ugliness to boring jobs to the Vietnam war and the shadow of nuclear holocaust" (1970, p. 234). It is the conflict between the ideals they grow up on and the ugly realities they must face at the threshold of adulthood that account for the "turning off" of youth and the development of a distinctive youth culture.

Adult roles also contain an inherent contradiction. The same individual is a worker and a consumer, both of which are crucial to the economy. But as Reich analyzes it, "The overpersuaded consumer may no longer be a willing worker. To have consumers for its ever-increasing flow of products, the corporate state must have individuals who live for hedonistic pleasures, constant change, and expanding freedom. To have workers for its system of production, the state must have individuals who are ever more self-denying, self-disciplined, and narrowly confined" (1970, p. 208). For young adults accustomed to life as consumers, the contradiction is heightened. As Reich points out: "When the consumer-worker contradiction . . . hits middle-class youth, it helps to produce a rejection of the whole ethic of the middle class. . . . The end product of the overpampered consumer society may well be a person who reacts against pampering, a rootless and truly liberated individual, one who ultimately threatens the corporate state" (1970, pp. 209, 219).

The Impact of the Counterculture Participants in the counterculture have reacted against society, but was the corporate state ever really threatened? There are some who say the counterculture has already faded away, citing the quiet that now prevails on college campuses and the return to educational commitments. In this view the highly visible and audible youth of a few years past have entered maturity and are tackling the practical problems of adulthood, having learned by experience to accept the majority outlook. But, have they really?

Since the early 1970s the movement's thrust for political change has been blunted (if not completely repressed), but the broader cultural changes have been absorbed by the mainstream of America's youth. A survey by Daniel Yankelovich concluded that:

Radical political values and life styles, values which traveled together since the mid-1960's, have, in 1971, begun to go their separate ways. Changing cultural values—relationships to marriage, authority, religion, work, money, career, sexual morality, and other aspects of the puritan ethic—have become more marked and dramatic each year since these measurements began, including 1971, while political beliefs have moved in the opposite direction away from the 1970 peaks. . . . The vast majority of students—the 89% who do not identify with the New Left—have pressed forward in their search for a cultural revolution while taking a step backwards from political revolution. (1972, p. 7)

The manner by which these counterculture values have been absorbed by the larger society is described in Yankelovich's 1974 study as a "case history of 'cultural diffusion.'"

Social change is often initiated by small extremist groups. The mass of the public reacts initially by rejecting the new ideas, and then begins to consider them with tempered selectivity. The proposals of the extremist groups become, in effect, a vast smorgasbord from which people of more moderate temperament pick and choose those ideas that fit best with their own traditional life styles. (p. 13)

But has this diffusion of counterculture or values produced significant *social* changes? What will be the impact of these values upon the crucial patterns of economic and political organization? If the postindustrial society is at hand, the economic system will remain very much as Charles Reich describes it:

The organizations that make up the corporate state are motivated primarily by the demands of technology and of their own internal structure. . . . The essence of the corporate state is that it has just one

table 19:1 CULTURAL DIFFUSION OF THE NEW VALUES

LATE 1960s	EARLY 1970s
The campus rebellion is in full flower.	The campus rebellion is moribund.
A central theme on campus: the search for self-fulfillment *in place of* a conventional career.	A central theme on campus: how to find self-fulfillment *within* a conventional career.
Growing criticism of America as a "sick society."	Lessening criticism of America as a "sick society."
The Women's Movement has virtually no impact on youth values and attitudes.	Wide and deep penetration of Women's Lib precepts.
Violence on campus is condoned and romanticized; there are many acts of violence.	Violence-free campuses; the use of violence, even to achieve worthwhile objectives, is rejected.
The value of education is severely questioned.	The value of education is strongly endorsed.
A widening "generation gap" appears in values, morals, and outlook, dividing young people (especially college youth) from their parents.	The younger generation and older mainstream America move closer together in values, morals, and outlook.
A sharp split in social and moral values is found within the youth generation, between college students and the noncollege majority. The gap *within* the generation proves to be larger and more severe than the gap *between* the generations.	The gap within the generation narrows. Non-college youth have virtually caught up with college students in adopting the new social and moral norms.
The challenge to the traditional work ethic is confined to the campus.	The work ethic appears strengthened on campus, but is growing weaker among noncollege youth.
A new code of sexual morality, centering on greater acceptance of casual premarital sex, abortions, homosexuality, and extramarital relations is confined to a minority of college students.	The new sexual morality spreads both to mainstream college youth and also to mainstream working-class youth.
Harsh criticisms of major institutions, such as political parties, big business, the military, etc., are almost wholly confined to college students.	Criticism of some major institutions are tempered on campus but are taken up by working-class youth.
The universities and the military are major tragets of criticism.	Criticisms of universities and the military decrease sharply.
The campus is the main locus of youthful discontent; noncollege youth are quiescent.	Campuses are quiescent, but many signs of latent discontent and dissatisfaction appear among working-class youth.
Much youthful energy and idealism is devoted to concern with minorities, and blacks are considered the most oppressed group.	Concern with minorities is lower, and American Indians are considered most oppressed.
The political center of gravity of college youth: left/liberal.	No clear-cut political center of gravity: pressures in both directions, left and right.
The New Left is a force on campus: there are growing numbers of radical students.	The New Left is a negligible factor on campus; the number of radical students declines sharply.
Concepts of law and order are anathema to college students.	College students show greater acceptance of law and order requirements.
The student mood is angry, embittered, and bewildered by public hostility.	There are few signs of anger or bitterness, and little overt concern with public attitudes toward students.

SOURCE: Daniel Yankelovich, *Changing Youth Values in the '70s* (New York: JDR 3rd Fund, 1974), pp. 7–8.

value, the value of technology as represented by organization, efficiency, growth, progress. . . . In short, industrialism placed man under the rule of laws that were inhuman. (1970, p. 94)

Reich believes that countercultural values can tame this monster without resorting to violence by each person refusing to accept the demands of the industrial society. Such optimism is not widely shared. From the analysis of a number of observers it is probable that many of the *cultural* values embodied in the counterculture will continue to flourish but that there will be the continuing tension with the demands of a technological economy that Daniel Bell predicts (1973).

Charting out these trends and projecting them into the future affords us only general predictions—or perhaps better said, hunches. The forces of affluence, of scarcity, and of the new values are all at work on American society, but perhaps some other forces, only dimly perceived today, will emerge in the future. Whatever forces have greatest power, however, it is likely that there will be conscious attempts to guide their impact, for social change is increasingly subject to measurement and planning. This active attitude toward social change may itself represent the most fundamental break with the past and the central theme for social development in the future.

---

summary

Social change may be differentiated from other changes because it alters patterns of social organization over time. Such alterations vary in scale, in duration, in continuity with previous patterns, and in direction. Their causes are many and varied. Three primary forces for change are: contact with and adoption of a feature of another culture (diffusion), discoveries, and inventions.

General theories of social change fall into four main groups. *Evolutionary theories* stress the progressive differentiation and complexity of social structures, although the reasons for this process are in dispute. Durkheim, for example, attributes the changes to increasing "moral density," which takes a society from a simple, homogeneous group cohering because of mechanical solidarity to a highly complex, heterogenous group cohering because of organic solidarity. *Cyclical theories* view societies and civilizations as passing through inevitable stages either of development and decay or, in Sorokin's case, of cultural extremes. The poles in Sorokin's model are the sensate (empirical, realistic, rational) and the ideational (mystical, abstract, transcendent). *Equilibrium theories* stress the adjustments that maintain social stability; social change is generally seen as harmonious. Contrary to this view are the *conflict theories*, stressing the ubiquity of change and conflict. Society, according to these theories, rests on the constraint of one group by another; social change is generally seen as discontinuous as power shifts from group to group.

The most extreme form of discontinuous change is *revolution*, which does not reform the political structure either by modifying it or by replacing those in power but rather calls on mass support to introduce sweeping, programmatic changes. The prerevolutionary situation is characterized by (1) relative deprivation; (2) indecisive action by those in power, revealing the weaknesses of the system even further; (3) the decision to replace the system rather than simply its personnel; and (4) the desertion of the intellectuals, thus depriving the regime of its ideological legitimacy.

After the old regime is overthrown, several typical stages in the course of establishing a new regime can be identified. Brinton describes these as: the rule of the moderates, the takeover by extremists and a reign of terror, and the *Thermidorian reaction*, usually ushered in by a dictator who finishes the work of the original revolution rather than returning to prerevolutionary values. One question in the interpretation of the American Revolution is whether the Constitution, which replaced the decentralized system of the Articles of Confederation with a strong executive, was really a *coup d'état* by the more conservative and wealthier elements of American society. A second question is whether it was simply a war of independence rather than a true revolution.

Today revolutions and political upheavals in general are most likely to occur in countries modernizing rapidly. *Modernization*, the development of an industrialized economy, with attendant changes in the political, social, and psychological spheres, involves differentiation of new structures and their integration; when these processes proceed unevenly, social disturbances result. One analysis of such disturbances sees the problem as masses of people freed from traditional moorings without being integrated into any broad groups or classes. The traditional power of the elites is stripped away as well, and these elites are now vulnerable to the influence of the masses, just as the masses are vulnerable to mobilization around slogans or nationalistic adventures by the elites. Force plays a large role in such mass societies.

Long since modernized, America is facing new challenges. One scenario for the future sees an affluent, suburban, educated, and pluralistic society. Another sees a society beset by the problems of scarcity. One alternative vision, which is being selectively absorbed, is that of the counterculture. Although its political radicalism has been rejected, the cultural elements have been rapidly adopted by a generation of youth. Whether this will produce a disjuncture between the various systems in society is one of the pressing issues of the future.

glossary

continuity The degree to which a change retains in other forms the previous social structure.

cultural diffusion The adaptation of a feature from one culture by another, a basic source of change.

cultural lag The discontinuity that occurs when one part of the culture changes more rapidly than another. Changes in material culture are a frequent source of cultural lag, as nonmaterial culture often changes relatively slowly.

direction The cumulative effect of change, sometimes linear, other times cyclical.

discovery An exploration or investigation that leads to knowledge of something that has already existed; a source of social change.

duration The time span over which a change occurs.

ideational culture A society that perceives reality as abstract, transcendent, and inaccessible to the senses or to reason. The opposite of sensate culture. (Sorokin)

invention A new combination or application of knowledge, particularly in the technological sphere; a basic source of social change.

mass society A society with an organized elite and huge numbers of people not integrated into any broad social groupings or classes. The elites are readily susceptible to influence by the masses and the masses are readily available for mobilization by the elites, creating a volatile political climate.

modernization A form of social transformation resulting from economic development. It is characterized by differentiation, integration, and social conflict.

revolution Extreme discontinuous and large-scale change of the social system, involving rapid replacement of the old forms of government as well as the personnel, mobilization of the masses, and idealized aims for improvement.

scale The magnitude or impact of a social change.

sensate culture A society that stresses the empirical, and that organizes its culture for perception by the senses and reason. The polar opposite of ideational culture. (Sorokin)

social change An alteration of a pattern of social organization over time.

social disintegration The loss of cohesiveness among the institutions of a society undergoing rapid modernization.

social disturbance The result of uneven differentiation and integration in a modernizing society. (Smelser)

social integration The degree to which differentiated substructures of a society work together rather than remain isolated or in conflict.

social mobilization The process whereby commitments to traditional economic, political, and social roles are loosened, making the individual susceptible to new value patterns and new commitments.

structural differentiation The degree to which social structures are organized into more specialized smaller units.

references

Richard P. Applebaum, *Theories of Social Change*, Chicago: Markham, 1970.

Charles Beard, *An Economic Interpretation of the Constitution of the United States*, New York: Free Press, 1949.

Daniel Bell, *The Coming of the Post-Industrial Society*, New York: Basic Books, 1973.

Cyril Black, *Dynamics of Modernization*, New York: Harper & Row, 1968.

Crane Brinton, *The Anatomy of Revolution*, New York: Random House, 1965.

W. Frank Craven, *The American Revolution, A Guide for Independent Study*, Princeton, N.J.: Princeton University Press, 1973.

Ralf Dahrendorf, "Toward a Theory of Social Conflict," in Etzioni-Halevy and Etzioni, 1973.

Karl A. Deutsch, "The Growth of Nations: Some Recurrent Patterns of Political and Social Integration," *World Politics*, vol. 5, no. 2 (January 1953): 168–95.

Emile Durkheim, *The Division of Labor in Society*, New York: Free Press, 1964.

S. N. Eisenstadt, *Modernization: Protest and Change*, Englewood Cliffs, N.J.: Prentice-Hall, 1966.

———, "Post Traditional Societies and the Continuity and Reconstruction of Tradition," *Daedalus* (Winter 1973): 1–27.

E. Etzioni-Halevy and A. Etzioni, eds., *Social Change*, New York: Basic Books, 1973.

Marvin Harris, *Culture, Man, and Nature*, New York: Crowell, 1971.

Alex Inkeles, "The Modernization of Man," in Myron Weiner, ed., *Modernization*, New York: Basic Books, 1966.

William Kornhauser, *The Politics of Mass Society*, New York: Free Press, 1959.

Flora Lewis, "Western Europe Falters," *The New York Times* (March 4, 1974): 1, 7.

R. C. Lewontin, "Evolution—The Concept," *The International Encyclopedia of the Social Sciences*, New York: Macmillan 1968.

Karl Marx and Friedrich Engels, *The Manifesto of the Communist Party*, New York: International Publishers, 1932.

Barrington Moore, *Social Origins of Dictatorship and Democracy*, Boston: Beacon Press, 1966.

Wilbert E. Moore, *Social Change*, Englewood Cliffs, N.J.: Prentice Hall, 1963.

Edmund S. Morgan, *The Birth of the Republic, 1763–89*, Chicago: University of Chicago Press, 1956.

Richard B. Morris, *The American Revolution Reconsidered*, New York: Harper & Row, 1967.

Robert A. Nisbet, *The Social Bond*, New York: Knopf, 1970.

William Ophuls, "The Scarcity Society," *Harper's* (April 1974): 47–52.

José Ortega y Gasset, *The Revolt of the Masses*, New York: Norton, 1957.

Simon Ottenberg, "Ibo Receptivity to Change," in William R. Bascom and Melville J. Herskovitz, *Continuity and Change in African Cultures*, Chicago: University of Chicago Press, 1959.

Talcott Parsons, *The Social System*, New York: Free Press, 1951.

———, *Societies: Evolutionary and Comparative Perspectives*, Englewood Cliffs, N.J.: Prentice-Hall, 1966.

Lee Rainwater, "Post-1984 America," *Society*, vol. 9, no. 4 (February 1972): 18–27.

Charles Reich, *The Greening of America*, New York: Random House, 1970.

Theodore Roszak, *The Making of a Counterculture*, New York: Doubleday, 1969.

Philip Selznick, "Institutional Vulnerability in Mass Society," *The American Journal of Sociology*, vol. 56 (January 1951): 320–31.

Elman R. Service, "Cultural Evolution," *The International Encyclopedia of the Social Sciences*, New York: Macmillan, 1968.

Philip E. Slater, *The Pursuit of Loneliness*, Boston: Beacon Press, 1970.

Neil J. Smelser, "Toward a Theory of Modernization," in Etzioni-Halevy and Etzioni, 1973.

Pitirim Sorokin, *Social and Cultural Dynamics*, New York: American Book, 1941.

Oswald Spengler, *The Decline of the West*, New York: Knopf, 1926.

Arnold Toynbee, *A Study of History*, New York: Oxford University Press, 1946.

Colin M. Turnbull, *The Mountain People*, New York: Simon & Schuster, 1972.

Victor C. Uchendo, *The Ibo of Southeast Nigeria*, Holt, Rinehart & Winston, 1965.

Daniel Yankelovich, *Changing Values on Campus*, New York: Washington Square Press, 1972.

———, *Changing Youth Values in the '70's*, New York: JDR 3rd Fund 1974.

for further study

Revolutions.   The study of revolutions is exciting and rewarding, because the structure of a society becomes more clear when under attack. The most comprehensive and profound book on the subject is *The Natural History of Revolutions*, by Lyford Edwards (Chicago: University of Chicago Press, 1970). Implicitly, it raises an important question: What are the relations between revolution and modernization? While revolutions can be analyzed as social events in their own right, they must also be considered in the larger perspective of social change in the societies where they occur. Consider our neighbor, Mexico, about which we know too little. The following books provide interesting materials for thinking about these questions. Howard F. Cline, *Mexico: From Revolution to Evolution* (New York: Oxford University Press, 1962); Frank R. Brandenburg, *The Making of Modern Mexico* (Englewood Cliffs, N.J.: Prentice-Hall, 1964); Charles C. Cumberland, *The Meaning of the Mexican Revolution* (Boston: Heath, 1967); and Stanley Ross, ed., *Is the Mexican Revolution Dead?* (New York: Knopf, 1966). There are many treatments of the Chinese revolution, one of the most important in world history. Among the best are C. P. Fitzgerald, *The Birth of Communist China* (London: Penguin, 1964), and chapters 18–28 of *East Asia: Tradition and Transformation,* by John K. Fairbank, Edwin O. Reischauer, and Albert M. Craig (Boston: Houghton Mifflin, 1973).

Social Planning.   One of the contributions that sociology has made to intelligent social planning is the development of social indicators. For an overview of social planning and these indicators, see the discussion by Daniel Bell in *The Coming of Post-Industrial Society: A Venture in Social Forecasting* (New York: Basic, 1973) and *Indicators of Social Change*, by Eleanor B. Sheldon and Wilbert E. Moore, eds. (New York: Russell Sage Foundation, 1968). The Office of Management and the Budget recently issued *Social Indicators, 1973* (Washington, D.C.: U.S. Government Printing Office, 1974). An excellent study of social planning is Herbert Gans, *The Levittowners: Ways of Life and Politics in a New Suburban Community* (New York: Random House, 1969). A provocative book about planning in this country is *Who Designs America?* edited by Laurence B. Holland (New York: Doubleday, 1966).

Changing Life- Styles and Values.   During their years in college, many students think more about their life-style and values than at any other time. Reading about alternate perspectives on life not only has personal meaning but also makes one think about the social aspects of work, marriage, aspirations, and anxieties. A rich exploration of American culture is Theodore Roszak's *The Making of the Counter-Culture* (New York: Doubleday, 1969). A disturbing and insightful essay by a sociologist is *The Pursuit of Loneliness,* by Philip Slater (Boston: Beacon, 1971). Warren Bennis and Philip Slater have also written an excellent analysis of American life entitled *The Temporary Society* (New York: Harper & Row, 1969). A suggestive book about alternate life-styles is *Bodies in Revolt*, by Thomas Hanna (New York: Dell, 1972). All considerations of social and personal values must be put in the context of the resources at our disposal. Thus they link back to our discussion of technology's impact on society and the book *Are Our Descendants Doomed?* by Harrison Brown and Edward Hutchings, Jr. (New York: Viking, 1972).

GLOSSARY

The glossary below is an alphabetized list of all the terms and definitions that appear in each chapter. The numbers following each definition identify the chapters where the term is used.

achieved status   A social position a person attains through personal effort. (3)

acting crowd   An excited, volatile group of people who are focused on a controversial event that provokes their indignation, anger, and desire to act (Blumer). (11)

age-specific fertility rate   The number of births per thousand women of a given age range in a given time span. (13)

age-specific mortality rate   The number of deaths per thousand people of a given age bracket in a specific time span. (13)

alienation   According to Marx this condition results from machine-age technology that requires only simple, repetitive tasks of workers, whose labor is purchased like any other commodity. (18)

amalgamation   The fusion of culturally and/or racially distinct groups into a new hybrid culture and/or "race." (9)

amorphous community structure   The absence of stable patterns of power and authority in local government; a hypothetical type (Rossi). (14)

anomie   A state of normlessness and confusion that may occur when social realities do not meet culturally induced expectations. (12)

anticipatory socialization   The values and expectations a person develops through identification and imagination, prior to taking on a new role. (10)

artifacts   The elements of a people's material culture. (4)

ascribed status   A social position that is assigned to a person at birth or at different stages in the life cycle. (3)

assimilation   Minorities giving up their ancestral customs and adopting the culture of the majority. (9)

assimilation, behavioral   Minorities learning the language and culture of the majority (Gordon). (9)

assimilation, structural   Minorities gaining entry into the majority's government, business, churches, schools, and ultimately primary relationships (Gordon). (9)

authoritarian personality   Interrelated personality traits (rigidity, moralism, preoccupation with power and status) that accompany prejudice (Adorno). (9)

authority   Formal power; the prerogatives that legitimately go with an office or position; official power. (8, 14)

autonomy   Erikson's term for a child's confidence in his or her ability to govern himself or herself. (5)

bureaucracy   An organization consisting of interrelated parts with separate functions, designed to perform some kind of work. (10)

business organizations   Organizations designed to maximize profit and efficiency, and run for the benefit of the owners (Blau and Scott). (10)

caste system   A rigidly stratified, socially immobile class system in which status is ascribed, not achieved; the opposite of an open system. (8)

casual crowds   Spontaneous congregations whose members come and go, giving temporary attention to the object that attracted their attention and then going their separate ways. (11)

caucus community structure   Local rule by a relatively large group of influential and powerful individuals (Rossi). (14)

censorship   Restricting information before it reaches its audience. (11)

census   A periodic counting of the population, which also records facts on age, sex, occupation, etc. In the United States the census is taken every tenth year and provides a wealth of statistical data for both demographers and social planners. (13)

charismatic authority Authority that derives from exceptional personal qualities (Weber). (14)

church A large, conservative, universalist religious institution, which makes few demands on its members and is accommodated to the culture of a society. (17)

city A relatively large, dense, and permanent settlement of socially heterogeneous individuals (Wirth). (18)

civil religion A collection of religious beliefs, symbols, and rituals outside the church that pervades and helps legitimize a community (Bellah). (17)

class People who occupy the same rung on the economic ladder (Weber). (8)

client-centered organizations Organizations, such as hospitals and schools, designed to serve a particular group of people (Blau and Scott). (10)

coercive organizations Organizations people are forced to join (Etzioni). (10)

coercive power Power that rests on the threat or use of violence. (14)

cognitive development The gradual maturation of a child's ability to reason and think in abstract terms. (5)

collective behavior The actions of relatively temporary, unstructured groups of people who are focused on and reacting to the same event, rumor, person, group, or custom. (11)

commonweal organizations Organizations run for the benefit of the public-at-large and controlled by the public, at least in principle (Blau and Scott). (10)

communal involvement Bonds of attachment that bind together members of a religious moral community. (17)

competition A social relationship in which two or more parties strive individually for an objective only one can achieve. (3)

concentric ring model A model of urban structure proposed by E. W. Burgess that sees cities laid out with the business district at the core, surrounded by a transitional ring of residential instability and high crime rates, beyond which are the various residential zones. (18)

conflict A social relationship in which two parties conclude that the only way to obtain a contested goal is to thwart, overpower, injure, eliminate, or otherwise neutralize the opposition. (3)

conflict orientation A theoretical perspective that emphasizes conflict, opposition, and change within a society. (1)

conformity Seeking culturally approved goals by culturally approved means. (12)

continuity The degree to which a change retains in other forms the previous social structure. (19)

contract marriage A marriage in which the couple designs their own marriage contract, specifying rights and obligations of each spouse, concerning domestic and economic activities, division of labor, and the number and timing of children. (15)

contractual cooperation A limited preplanned agreement to join forces in specific ways, for a specific period of time to achieve specific goals. (3)

control group In an experiment, the subjects who are not exposed to the independent variable, giving the experimenter a basis for comparison with subjects who are. (2)

conventional crowd People gathered for a specific purpose who behave according to established norms (Blumer). (11)

cooperation A social relationship in which people recognize a common objective and join forces to achieve their goal and share in the rewards. (3)

cross-sectional research A quick way to study long-term changes by studying people in different phases of the change all at the same point in time. This research method can be misleading. (2)

crowd A temporary collection of people gathered around some event, who are conscious of and influenced by one another's presence. (11)

crude birth rate The number of births per thousand people in a given time span. (13)

crude death rate The number of deaths per thousand people in a given time span. (13)

cultural diffusion The adaptation of a feature from one culture by another, a basic source of change. (19)

cultural integration The degree of internal consistency within a culture. (4)

cultural lag The discontinuity that occurs when one part of the culture changes more rapidly than another. Changes in material culture are a frequent source of cultural lag, as nonmaterial culture often changes relatively slowly. (19)

cultural pluralism Ethnic groups maintaining their cultural identities and differences but nevertheless co-existing peacefully and equally. (9)

cultural relativity The doctrine of examining a custom in light of the culture as a whole and of evaluating it in terms of how it works in context, not in terms of right or wrong. (4)

cultural universals The behavior patterns and institutions that have been found in every known culture. (4)

culture All of a people's shared customs, beliefs, values, and artifacts. (4)

culture of poverty Oscar Lewis' term for a lifestyle based on accommodation to poverty in an affluent society that stresses individuality and upward mobility. (8)

demographic transition The period in which population shifts from the "old balance" of high fertility and high mortality to the "new balance" of low fertility and low mortality. During the demographic transition mortality declines or has declined rapidly, while fertility (usually) declines more slowly, causing a period of rapid population growth. (13)

demographic variables Births, deaths, and net migration. (13)

demography The study of population including its changes, and the effects of these changes on society. (13)

dependency ratio The proportion of people under fifteen and over sixty-five to the total population. (13)

dependent variable A quality or factor that the researcher believes is affected by one or more independent variables. (2)

deviance Behavior that violates social norms and expectations. (12)

deviant career The adoption of a deviant lifestyle and identity within a supporting subculture that provides techniques for breaking rules and rationalizations for nonconformity. (12)

directed cooperation The kind of joint activity people in authority enforce on those beneath them. (3)

direction The cumulative effect of change, sometimes linear, other times cyclical. (19)

discovery An exploration or investigation that leads to knowledge of something that has already existed; a source of social change. (19)

discrimination Granting or denying privileges on grounds rationally irrelevant to the situation. (9)

duration The time span over which a change occurs. (19)

education Both formal and informal lessons in the skills and values of one's culture. (16)

ego Freud's term for the conscious part of the self that finds socially acceptable ways of satisfying the biological cravings of the *id*. (5)

ethnic group A group of people whose race, religion or national origins distinguish them from others, and whose history has given them a sense of peoplehood. (9)

ethnocentrism The tendency to see one's own way of life, including behaviors, beliefs, values and norms, as the only "right" way of living. (4)

ethnomethodology The study of the rules that underlie everyday behavior. (3)

exchange A social relationship in which a person or a group assists another for the purpose of obtaining some material or emotional reward. (3)

experimental group In an experiment, the subjects who are exposed to the independent variables and observed for changes in behavior. (2)

ex post facto research A way in which variables that could not be measured at the time of an event can be analyzed after the fact. (2)

expressive crowd A crowd that gives people license to express feelings and behave in ways they would not consider in other settings (Blumer). (11)

expulsion A form of minority group rejection in which members of a minority are forced to leave their homes and businesses. The group may be forcibly resettled, or required to leave the country. (9)

extermination The severest form of minority group rejection, members of a particular minority are killed through planned government action. (9)

family The social institution, found in every society, that provides a reliable arrangement for producing, sustaining, and socializing succeeding generations. (15)

fecundity The biological potential for reproduction. (13)

fertility rate The number of births per thousand women between the ages of fifteen and forty-four. (13)

formal social controls Roles and institutions consciously designed to enforce conformity. (12)

formal structure In an organization, the elements of formal structure include the explicit rules that define each person's duties, organizational charts describing relationships among members, and a system of rewards and punishments. (10)

gemeinschaft Ferdinand Töennies' term for small, traditional communities characterized by close, intimate, overlapping, stable relationships. (7)

gender The psychological characteristics associated with femininity or masculinity. (6)

generalized other A child's generalized impression of what other people expect from him/her, and of where they fit in the overall scheme of things. (5)

gesellschaft Ferdinand Töennies' term for societies characterized by the rational pursuit of self-interest, impersonal attachments, efficiency and progress. (7)

horizontal mobility A change in position that does not alter socio–economic status. (8)

hormones Chemical substances, secreted into the bloodstream by the glands, that stimulate or inhibit vital chemical processes. (6)

hypothesis A proposition about how two or more variables are related to each other. (2)

id Freud's term for the innate collection of sexual and aggressive urges as well as all bodily pleasure. (5)

ideational culture A society that perceives reality as abstract, transcendent, and inaccessible to the senses or to reason. The opposite of sensate culture (Sorokin). (19)

identity A sense of continuity about one's self, derived from one's past, present, and future; from what one feels about oneself, and from the image reflected in the social looking-glass. This sense of continuity is formed during what Erikson called the identity crisis. (5)

independent variable A quality or factor that the researcher believes to affect one or more dependent variables. (2)

infant mortality rate The number of deaths per thousand children one year of age or less in a given time span. (13)

influence Informal power based on the ability to affect collective decisions without resorting to compensation, manipulation, or threats. (8, 14)

informal social controls Disapproval, ridicule, the threat of ostracism, and other unofficial pressures to conform. (12)

informal structure In an organization, the informal structure consists of the procedures that enable people to solve problems not covered by the formal regulations, to eliminate unpleasant or unnecessary work, and to protect their own interests. (10)

in-groups Those groups in which individuals feel at home and with which they identify. (7)

innovation Pursuing culturally approved goals by deviant means (Merton). (12)

institution The relatively stable, widely accepted cluster of norms and values that develop around the basic needs of a society. (3)

institutional racism Habits of discrimination that have become crystallized into the social structure, in institutional patterns of housing, schooling, employment, etc. These patterns persist despite an absence of conscious or deliberate discrimination. (9)

integration The elimination of majority/minority distinctions in a society that ranks people according to individual characteristics, not race or ethnic background. (9)

interest group An organization created to influence political decisions that directly concern members. (14)

internal migration The movement of people from one place to another within the same country. (13)

international migration The movement of people from one country to another. (13)

invasion cycle A general pattern of change in urban land use that begins imperceptibly. Once change is recognized, opposition begins until a "tip point" is reached, when the new users succeed in starting to drive out earlier users. Once the new use is established, the cycle has reached its climax phase. (18)

invention A new combination or application of knowledge, particularly in the technological sphere; a basic source of social change. (19)

jargon The specialized language of a subculture. (4)

jim crow The legal and social barriers constructed in the South in the late nineteenth and early twentieth centuries to prevent blacks from voting, using public facilities, and mixing with whites. ("Jim Crow" was the name of a blackface minstrel character.) (9)

labeling The assigning of a deviant status to a person which then dominates his or her social identity. (12)

legal rational authority Authority that derives from a system of explicit rules defining the legitimate uses of power. It is vested in positions, not in specific individuals. (14)

life cycle Erikson's term for the stages of life and the ways in which later stages interconnect with earlier ones to make a cycle. (5)

life expectancy The average number of years of life remaining to a person of a given age. (13)

life span The maximum number of years of a human life. (13)

longitudinal research Studies designed to measure change over time. (2)

looking-glass self Cooley's term to explain how others influence the way we see ourselves. We gain an image of ourselves by imagining what other people think about the way we look and behave. (5)

machismo Compulsive masculinity, evidenced in posturing, boasting, and an exploitative attitude towards women. (6)

macro-level of social structure The large social patterns that shape an entire society, including the hierarchy of jobs and rewards, patterns of prejudice and discrimination, and the educational system. (3)

mana A benign supernatural force that has no shape of its own but inhabits living or inanimate things. (17)

mass society A society with an organized elite and huge numbers of people not integrated into any broad social groupings or classes. The elites are readily susceptible to influence by the masses and the masses are readily available for mobilization by the elites, creating a volatile political climate. (19)

mean A statistical average calculated by dividing the sum of a series of figures by the number of items in the series. (2)

median The number that falls in the middle of a series of figures. (2)

megalopolis An urban form in which once distinct cities grow together, forming a functional unit. (18)

micro-level of social structure The pattern of personal interactions that defines everyday life. (3)

minority A group of people who are singled out for unequal treatment by the society in which they live, and consider themselves to be victims of collective discrimination. (9)

mob A crowd whose members are emotionally aroused and are engaged in, or are ready to engage in, violent action. (11)

mode The figure that occurs most often in a group of data. (2)

modernization A form of social transformation resulting from economic development. It is characterized by differentiation, integration, and social conflict. (19)

monotheism Worship of a single god. (17)

mores Norms that are held very intensely, such as incest taboos. (3)

moral community A group of people who share common beliefs and practices. (17)

mortification The process of stripping a person of his or her civilian identity and physical integrity, in preparation for indoctrination into a new role (Goffman). (10)

multiple nuclei model This model sees the city as composed of many nuclei that specialize and proliferate as a city grows (Harris and Ullman). (18)

mutual benefit organizations Organizations run by and for the members (Blau and Scott). (10)

net migration The difference between immigration and emigration. (13)

net reproduction rate (NRR) An average of the number of female children born per women of child-bearing age. (13)

new balance A relatively stable population based on low mortality coupled with low fertility. (13)

new town A comprehensively planned city, usually near a larger metropolis, built to absorb urban growth in a systematic fashion. (18)

normlessness When a sudden, unexpected event creates a situation where people do not know what they can or should do. (11)

norms The guidelines that people follow in their relations with one another; shared standards of desirable behavior. (3)

nuclear family A married couple and their unmarried children generally living by themselves with no other relatives. (15)

old balance A relatively stable population based on high fertility coupled with high mortality. (13)

open admissions The policy of some cities and states to admit every high school graduate to a college or university. (16)

open classroom An educational environment that aims to increase learning by decreasing regimentation. Children are encouraged to develop their own interests, rather than being tied to inflexible routines. (16).

open class system A class system in which status is acquired, not ascribed; the opposite of a caste system. (8)

open marriage A marriage that stresses flexible roles, consideration of each partner's needs, talents, and desires, and a considerable amount of autonomy and independence for husband and wife. (15)

opportunity structure The role-models, instruction, and jobs available in a given community (Cloward and Ohlin). (12)

organization A group consciously designed to seek specific goals. (10)

out-groups Those groups in which individuals do not feel they belong, and with which they do not identify. (7)

panic The action of a crowd whose members feel entrapped and seek escape in highly individualistic and counterproductive ways. (11)

Parkinson's law Parkinson formulated his law to explain why bureaucratic employees often appear busier than they need be: "Work expands to fill the time." (10)

participant observation A method in which researchers join and participate in the groups they plan to study in an effort to gain intimate, first-hand knowledge of a way of life. (2)

party People who share interests and seek to further them by gaining access to power (Weber). (8)

per capita income   Income available to each citizen if the total income of the country were divided equally. (13)

Peter Principle   Attempting to account for the incompetence that characterizes many bureaucratic employees, Peter and Hull suggest that "in a hierarchy, every employee tends to rise to his [or her] level of incompetence." (10)

plea-bargaining   In a criminal trial, a defendant may agree to plead guilty to a lesser charge rather than risk conviction and a more severe penalty. (12)

pluralism   The view that the political power structure is composed of a variety of competing elites and interest groups. (14)

political party   An organization designed for the explicit purpose of gaining and holding legitimate control of government policies and personnel. (14)

political power   The ability to realize one's will in a communal action, even against the resistance of others who are participating in the action (Weber). (14)

polylithic community structure   Local rule by a diversity of cliques and groups, each with its own sphere of authority (Rossi). (14)

polytheism   Worship of more than one god. (17)

population   In a research study, all the people an investigator wants to study. (2)

population pyramid   A graph showing the distribution of a population by age and sex. (13)

post industrial society   A society in which the social structure has changed from a goods-producing to a service economy; professionals and technicians dominate the occupational structure; and theoretical knowledge shapes social changes (Bell). (18)

power   The ability to mobilize collective energies, commitments, and efforts. (8, 14)

power elite   A coalition of military, government, and business executives, united by common interests and social affinity. In C. W. Mills' view, this coalition rules America. (8, 14)

prejudice   An irrational, categorical like or dislike for a group of people. (9)

prestige   The status of people according to occupation, ancestry, and social acceptability. (8)

primary group   A small, intimate group, characterized by close, personal relationships and empathy. (7)

primary relationship   A close, intimate, and stable relationship that usually involves the whole personality of each individual. (7)

profane   The opposite of sacred; the everyday and mundane. (17)

progressive tax   A tax that takes a larger share of a rich person's income than a poor person's; the opposite of a regressive tax. (8)

propaganda   Information that appeals to people's emotions and prejudices and is used to inspire certain kinds of collective behavior. (11)

public   A scattered group of people who share a common interest, concern, or focus of attention. (11)

public opinion   The prevailing interests, attitudes, and opinions of a public. (11)

public relations   Covert behind-the-scenes advertising via press releases, briefings, junkets, and the like. (11)

pygmalion effect   The effect of teacher expectations on learning and performance, independent of students' aptitudes (Rosenthal and Jacobson). (16)

pyramidal community structure   Local rule by one person or by a small clique, within or outside the official government (Rossi). (14)

race   A population that through generations of inbreeding has developed more or less distinctive physical characteristics that are transmitted genetically. Sociologically a race is a group of people whom others believe are genetically distinct and treat accordingly. (9)

random sample   A sample which gives every member of the population being studied an equal chance of being selected. In this way, experimenter bias is eliminated. (2)

rebellion   Creating new goals and new means for pursuing them (Merton). (12)

recidivism   A return to crime after release from prison. (12)

reference group   A group or social category that an individual refers to in evaluating himself or herself. (7)

regressive tax   A tax that takes a larger share of a poor person's income than a rich person's; the opposite of a progressive tax. (8)

reliability   The degree to which a study yields the same results when repeated by the original researcher or by other scientists. (2)

religion   A unified system of beliefs and practices that pertain to sacred things, and that unite adherents into a moral community (Durkheim). (17)

religious beliefs   Representations that express the nature of sacred things and the relations that they sustain, either with each other or with profane things. (17)

replacement level   The point at which a population replaces itself with new people but does not grow. (13)

retreatism   A form of deviance characterized by the abandonment of culturally prescribed goals and means (Merton). (12)

revolution   Extreme discontinuous and large-scale change of the social system, involving rapid replacement of the old forms of government as well as the personnel; mobilization of the masses; and idealized aims for improvement. (19)

riot A violent public disturbance, particularly where a crowd of people collectively engage in destructive behavior; it may be caused by an intolerable gap between what people believe they are entitled to and what they actually have. (11)

ritual The rules of conduct that prescribe how people should behave in the presence of sacred objects. (17)

ritualism Following rules and regulations without regard for the original goals or the consequences of one's actions (Merton). (10, 12)

role Expected behavior patterns, obligations and privileges that are attached to a particular status. (3)

role conflict Situations where fulfillment of one role automatically results in the violation of another. (3)

role set The complex of roles that accrues to a single status. (3)

role strain Personal difficulties that result when inconsistencies are built into a role. (3)

rumor An unverified story that circulates from person to person, usually by word of mouth, and is accepted as fact, although its sources may be vague or unknown. (11)

sacred Transcending everyday existence; extraordinary, potentially dangerous, awe-inspiring, fear-inducing. (17)

sample A limited number of people selected from the population being studied. (2)

scale The magnitude or impact of a social change. (19)

schooling Formal instruction in a classroom setting. (16)

secondary group A group characterized by limited face-to-face interaction, non-permanence, ties of exchange not of affection, and limited and task-oriented relationships. (7)

secondary relationship A relationship characterized by narrow and specific goals, self-interest, impersonal attachments, efficiency, and progress. (7)

sect A small exclusive, uncompromising fellowship that makes heavy demands on its members and sets them apart from the larger society. (17)

sector model A model describing cities as composed of sectors around a central business district, distributed along major transportation routes radiating outward from the center (Hoyt). (18)

secularization The decline in religious faith and practice or the accommodation of religious beliefs and practices to other social customs. (17)

segregation Laws and/or customs that restrict contact between groups. Segregation may be ethnic or racial, or based on sex or age. (9)

segregation, de facto Segregation, in fact, which results from such social patterns as "living with your own kind," but is not a matter of official policy. (9)

segregation, de jure Segregation by law. (9)

sensate culture A society that stresses the empirical, and that organizes its culture for perception by the senses and reason. The opposite of ideational culture (Sorokin). (19)

sex ratio The number of men per hundred women in a population. (13)

sex role Social guidelines for sex-appropriate appearance, interests, skills and self-perceptions. (6)

significant others When young children play at taking adult roles, they in effect become the people who are important in their social world. George Herbert Mead called these people "significant others." (5)

social area analysis Explaining residential segregation in terms of such broad social categories as social rank, commitment to family, and ethnicity. (18)

social change An alteration of a pattern of social organization over time. (19)

social contagion The rapid diffusion of a mood or pattern of behavior through a crowd. (11)

social disintegration The loss of cohesiveness among the institutions of a society undergoing rapid modernization. (19)

social disturbance The result of uneven differentiation and integration in a modernizing society (Smelser). (19)

social group A number of people who define themselves as members of a group; who expect certain behavior from members that they do not expect from outsiders; and who others (members and non-members) define as belonging to a group. (7)

social indicators Measures of the quality of life, including such seeming intangibles as aspirations and satisfactions in health, work, friendship, marriage, family, and community. (1, 2)

social integration The degree to which differentiated substructures of a society work together rather than remain isolated or in conflict. (19)

social mobility The movement of people up and down the stratification system. (8)

social mobilization The process whereby commitments to traditional economic, political, and social roles are loosened, making the individual susceptible to new value patterns and new commitments. (19)

social movement An ongoing, collective effort with focused goals and articulated tactics to promote or resist social change. (11)

social structure The pattern of collective rules, roles, and activities in a society. (3)

socialization The process of acquiring the physical, mental, and social skills that a person needs to survive and to become both an individual and member of society. (5)

sociological perspective A way of observing social life that focuses on regular and patterned details, aspects that are not unique to a particular situation or to individuals in that situation. (1)

state The one organization in a society that has the authority to employ physical force (Weber). (14)

status A position in the social structure that determines where a person fits in the community and how he or she is expected to act. (3)

status group People whose lifestyle or patterns of consumption give them a distinct identity (Weber). (8)

stratification The system for distributing desirable resources and ranking members of a society. (8)

stratified random sample A sample that reflects the proportions of different groups in the population being studied. (2)

structural differentiation The degree to which social structures are organized into more specialized smaller units. (19)

structural-functionalism A theoretical perspective which emphasizes the way each part of a society contributes to the functioning of society as a whole. A structural-functionalist tries to discover the social function something serves in society. (1)

structural mobility Changes in the number and kind of jobs and in the number of people available to fill them. Individual mobility may be increased by such changes. (8)

subculture A group whose perspective and life style are significantly different from those of other groups or individuals in their culture, and who define themselves as different. (4)

superego Freud's term for the conscience, the part of personality that internalizes society's views of right and wrong. (5)

survey A set of questions administered to groups of people in order to learn how they think, feel, or act. Good surveys use random samples and pretested questions to insure high reliability and validity. (2)

symbol Anything that represents something other than itself including objects, gestures, colors, designs, or words . (4)

symbolic interactionist orientation A theoretical perspective that focuses on the day-to-day communication that takes place when people interact in face-to-face situations, rather than on the large social structures and institutions. (1)

taboo An object or being that contains a supernatural force that brings bad luck or trouble. (17)

theory A comprehensive explanation of apparent relationships or underlying principles of certain observed phenomena. (2)

total institutions Organizations that take nearly complete control of inmates' lives, depriving them of responsibility, privacy, and their civilian identities (Goffman). (10)

totem A sacred animal or vegetable that serves as a focus of certain primitive religions; a symbol and repository of deep, group-based sentiments and feelings. (17)

tracking Grouping children according to their scores on aptitude and achievement tests. (16)

traditional authority Authority that derives from sacred traditions of loyalty to kings, chiefs, and priests. (14)

transfer payments Government allotments for which no goods or services are received in return. (8)

trial marriage An arrangement where a man and woman live together as long as it suits them, without any permanent commitment to remain together. (15)

two-career marriage A marriage in which the work requirements of both the male and the female are given serious consideration before such family decisions as geographic location, vacation schedules, and having children are made. (15)

urban ecology The study of urban patterns and their changes based on a biological model of competition and natural selection. (18)

urbanization The increase in the percentage of a population that lives in urban settlements and the consequent extension of influence of urban ways over the populace. (18)

utilitarian organizations Organizations people join for practical reasons, because they expect to benefit personally (Etzioni). (10)

validity The degree to which a scientific study measures what it attempts to measure. (2)

values The criteria people use in assessing their daily lives, arranging their priorities, measuring their pleasures and pains, and choosing between alternative courses of action. (4)

variable An attitude, behavior pattern, or condition that is subject to change. (2)

vertical mobility Changes in a person's status, upward or downward. (8)

voluntary organizations Organizations people join because they support the organization's goals and values (Etzioni). (10)

zero population growth (ZPG) A population that is stable, neither increasing nor decreasing, because the crude birth rate is equal to the crude death rate. (13)

NAME INDEX

SUBJECT INDEX

ABOUT THE AUTHORS

Donald Light, Jr. was born in Massachusetts in 1942. After graduating from Stanford University in 1963, he worked in Boston to implement President Kennedy's plan for equal employment opportunities. He did graduate work in sociology at the University of Chicago and at Brandeis University, receiving his Ph.D. in 1970. Since 1969 he has been on the faculty of Princeton University. He has written a number of articles on youth and on the nature of higher education which have appeared in *Daedalus, Sociology of Education* and the *Yearbook of Education, 1974.* Recently, he completed a detailed study of how psychiatrists are trained. Articles on this work have appeared in the *American Journal of Sociology* and in the *International Social Science Journal.* The entire study will soon be published by W. W. Norton as a book. Currently, he is conducting research on the structure of mental health services in several countries.

Suzanne Keller, currently Professor of Sociology at Princeton University was born in Vienna, Austria and came to the United States as a child. After college she spent several years in Europe, mainly in Paris and Munich where she worked as a survey analyst and translator. She received a Ph.D. in sociology from Columbia in 1953. In 1957 she became an Assistant Professor at Brandeis University where she taught courses in social theory, stratification, and the sociology of religion. A Fulbright Lectureship in 1963 at the Athens Center of Ekistics marked the beginning of her interest in architecture and community planning. At the completion of her Fulbright in 1965, Professor Keller joined the Center where she remained until 1967. That year she came to Princeton University as a Visiting Professor, and in 1968 she was the first woman to be appointed to a tenured Professorship there.

Today, Professor Keller is pursuing her interests in teaching, writing, research, public lectures, and world-wide travel. A Federal Grant is currently permitting Professor Keller and an interdisciplinary team to investigate methods for the assessment of a planned environment. She is also active in the Womens' Movement. The author of numerous articles and two books, she has just completed a module on sex roles for General Learning Corporation.

A NOTE ON THE TYPE

This book was set by computer in Univers typeface, a style comparable to the face designed by Adrian Frutiger. Univers was designed to produce an even series of integrated designs from the blackest extended to the lightest condensed. It is probably the most rational large type series ever executed. All versions were planned and executed according to a single original master plan.

This book was composed by Black Dot, Inc., Crystal Lake, Illinois. It was printed and bound by Rand McNally & Co.